HISTORY OF MODERN EUROPE

HISTORY OF MODERN EUROPE

A Survey of the Evolution of European Society
from the National Risings against Napoleon
to the Present Day

BY

CHESTER PENN HIGBY, Ph.D.

PROFESSOR OF HISTORY IN THE UNIVERSITY OF WISCONSIN

THE CENTURY CO.

NEW YORK   LONDON

To
JANE McKINNEY HIGBY

PREFACE

The history of any age must be rewritten from time to time. This is particularly true of the most recent period of modern European history. New evidence constantly comes to light. Fresh works of scholarship present more convincing interpretations of facts. The lapse of the years puts old facts in a new light and changes the perspective of the historian. The written record has to be brought up to date. This is the justification of the author for writing a new volume on an era already well treated in a number of excellent manuals.

The composition of a work surveying the recent history of European society for the use of the student and the general reader is a problem in the selection and organization of material well known to the historical specialist. In carrying out his task the author has tried to be historically minded. He has endeavored to maintain a just proportion between the recent and the more remote in time, and between the near and the more distant in space. He has felt that to emphasize the immediate past at the expense of the earlier years of the nineteenth century, or England, France, and Germany to the neglect of the less known countries of eastern Europe, was to distort the picture and to be unhistorical. He has simply tried to pick out the most significant events, personalities, and movements of the period from the national risings against the Napoleonic régime to the present time, and to arrange them in a way that would portray them as they actually were.

The author is under the deepest obligation to several institutions and to many colleagues for their assistance. While writing his book he has had access to the library of the University of Wisconsin, the Wisconsin Historical Library, the Stanford University Library, and the Hoover War Library. He must often have tried the patience of the staffs of these institutions. He has received many suggestions from and has been saved from many errors by friends who have placed their special stores of knowledge and their critical skill at his disposal. Professor Dana C. Munro of Princeton University, the general editor of the series, and Professor W. E. Lingelbach of the University of Pennsylvania read the whole work. Dr. Henry E. Bourne, editor of the *American Historical Review,* read the first two parts of the book, Professor S. B. Fay of Harvard University the one on "International Relations, 1871–1918," and Professor Ralph Lutz of Stanford University all but one chapter of the section devoted to Europe since the World War. Professor Paul Knaplund of the University of Wisconsin read most of the portions of the work dealing with the British Empire, and Professor George Vernadsky of Yale University nearly all those on Russia. Professor Selig Perlman of the University of Wisconsin looked over the chapter on "The Industrial and Agricultural Revolutions, 1760–1850," Professor Walter Dorn of Ohio State University those on "The Revolutions of 1848" and "The Conquest of the Revolutions of 1848," and Professor Yamato Ichihashi of Stanford University the one on "European Rivalries and Penetration into Asia." These friends have done much to improve the author's book but they are in no way responsible for its form or content.

C. P. H.

Madison, Wisconsin.

CONTENTS

PART IV

INTERNATIONAL RELATIONS, 1871–1918

PART V

RECONSTRUCTION AND EXPERIMENTATION

MAPS

HISTORY OF MODERN EUROPE

HISTORY OF MODERN EUROPE

CHAPTER I

EUROPE AT THE OPENING OF THE NINETEENTH CENTURY

The immediate past bequeathed to the nineteenth-century Europe a confused heritage. From the period prior to 1789 it received the tradition of absolute governments, state churches, privileged social classes, restrictions on labor, industry, and commerce, an organization of society based on agriculture and the great estate, and a belief in conformity and permanence. From the revolutionary period that followed this Ancien Régime it inherited ideas of political, social, economic, and religious freedom and opportunity. This mixed heritage divided the inhabitants of every European state into two hostile parties. The reigning families, the higher clergy, the nobles, all the conservative and unthinking elements of society, looked back on the Ancien Régime as a golden age to be maintained or recovered. The middle classes, and to some extent the peasants, looked forward to a wider and a more permanent realization of the freedom and the opportunity that they had known for a brief moment during the revolutionary years from 1789 to 1814. Some knowledge of the Ancien Régime, the French Revolution, and the Napoleonic period, consequently, is necessary to make intelligible the struggle of conservative Europe during the nineteenth century against liberalism, nationalism, and the Industrial Revolution.

I

THE ECONOMIC FOUNDATION OF THE ANCIEN RÉGIME

From the time of the establishment of civilized ways of living until recent times the social, religious, and political life of Europe rested on an agricultural foundation. Over the greater part of Europe the agricultural unit was the great estate. Originally this had been in the possession of the king, a noble, the Church, or some member of the privileged classes, and had been occupied and cultivated by a more or less dependent population. The relations of the holder of the estate to the land and its tenants had varied greatly. Where medieval conditions still

3

existed the landlord lived in as large and commodious a château or country house as his revenues permitted, while his tenants dwelt in small habitations, often little more than huts, which were usually grouped into villages. Both lord and peasant had rights in the fields, meadows, pastures, and woodland that stretched away from the village in all directions, and lived in the main on the products of the estate. The lord also exercised a great deal of control over the person and the property of his tenants and they owed their lord dues and services of many kinds.

Quite early in the Middle Ages this simple organization of rural life began to break down in different parts of Europe. In England most landlords eventually handed over the responsibility of tilling their estates to farmers, and the former tenants gradually lost their little holdings and became either landless agricultural laborers or workers in the new factories. In the eastern provinces of Prussia the peasants lost their holdings but the so-called Junker landlords continued to supervise the farming of their estates. In France most of the peasant tenants became owners of their plots of ground and the landlords merely retained the right to collect from them certain irksome dues and fees. In other regions of Europe the medieval organization of agriculture tended to survive until far into the nineteenth century.

About the same time the self-sufficiency of the great estates began to break down. Districts commenced to specialize in certain products, the townsmen became more and more artisans and merchants, and lords and peasants devoted themselves more completely to agriculture. The new middle class of artisans and merchants which developed as a result of these changes encountered many obstacles that hindered its growth. Landlords and peasants watched its development with hostility and jealousy. During the Middle Ages robber barons regarded those engaged in trade and industry as lawful prey and extorted heavy tolls from them or shamelessly robbed them at every opportunity. Later, royal and local governments hampered the rise of industry and commerce with taxes, provincial customs lines, and industrial regulations. As a defense against these conditions the townsmen organized craft gilds and struggled to obtain as large a measure of self-government as possible.

A gild included all persons living in a town engaged in a particular craft or trade. Originally it had received its legal authority to regulate a special branch of commerce or industry from the king or some local authority but later the state had assumed full control of the gilds. A member of a gild first served as an apprentice for a number of years. Later, if he succeeded in surmounting the serious obstacles placed in his way, he might become a journeyman and eventually a master. The masters usually controlled the policy of the gild and jealously guarded its particular monopoly. By 1789 the institution of the gild had disappeared in England but still existed everywhere on the continent of Europe.

As a result of these conditions large-scale manufacturing and commercial enterprises were to be found mainly in England, where the Industrial Revolution had got under way. On the Continent the gilds hampered the freedom and development of invention, labor, and capital. Ordinarily a Continental master employed only a few journeymen and apprentices and carried on his business in a little shop in the front part of his dwelling. Peddlers, weekly markets, fairs, and tiny shops provided for the modest demands of peasants, burghers, and landlords. European cities, in consequence, were ordinarily neither large nor numerous, many of them even retaining their moats and walls and other medieval features.

2

SOCIAL ORGANIZATION UNDER THE ANCIEN RÉGIME

The economic organization of the Ancien Régime determined to a large extent its social and political structure. In all European countries the upper class consisted of the higher clergy and the holders of the great estates. In England only the eldest son of a noble inherited the family title, his younger brothers merely belonging to the gentry. On the Continent all the sons of a noble became members of the nobility. Originally the upper class in Europe lived upon the revenues derived from its landed estates. With the development of modern states it began to supplement this source of income by pensions from the royal treasury and by salaries attached to posts in the army, the Church, the administration, and the court. In all countries the members of the upper class enjoyed many privileges, exercised much judicial and administrative authority, and received many marks of deference. They had the virtues and the defects of an aristocracy. At best they lived with dignity, comfort, and a position of prestige in the halls of their ancestors and envisaged life and its problems from the narrow but conscientious point of view of their class. At worst they neglected the responsibilities bequeathed to them, wasted their substance in riotous living, frivolously destroyed their health in coarse or refined amusements, and displayed a reckless contempt for the classes below them in the social scale.

Below the nobles in rank came the middle class, which had developed with the rise of industry and commerce. It included judges, lawyers, government officials, capitalists, doctors, men of letters, masters of gilds, and prosperous farmers. Its members realized their own wealth and enlightenment and resented the privileges and offices enjoyed exclusively by the nobles. In 1789 this class occupied a position of great power and influence in France and England. In most of the other countries of

Europe it was still small at the close of the eighteenth century and hardly dared to express an opinion or demand a more important rôle in the life of society.

Beneath the small, prosperous middle class of the cities a motley throng of artisans, domestics, beggars, and street venders lived a precarious existence. Its members dwelt in a squalid room or two, on narrow streets and alleys, in drab quarters of the towns and cities, subsisted on a coarse, meager fare of bread, vegetables, and wine or beer, and worked for a miserable pittance, under insanitary conditions, from four or five in the morning until eight or nine at night. This proletariat constituted the elements from which hunger and the arts of the demagogue might at any time fashion a brutal, pitiless mob.

In the rural districts the peasants formed the lower class and constituted the mass of the population. In England they had become free, then had gradually lost their holdings, and in the end had been reduced to the position of agricultural laborers or had left the land entirely and had become factory workers. In France most of the peasants had become free tenants by 1789, but they nearly all still paid dues and performed services that dated back to the seigniorial system. In most of central and eastern Europe the peasants still remained serfs and subject to the caprices of their masters. All over Europe they lived hard and bare lives. They ate a scanty and monotonous fare, sheltered themselves in picturesque but comfortless huts and cottages, and suffered from famine, pestilence, ignorance, and superstition. They knew nothing of the past and little of the present beyond the boundaries of their village fields. In the end, worn out by toil and misery, they sank into the grave.

For noble, burgher, and peasant life was more stable and leisurely than it is to-day. The upper classes lived and died in their ancestral seats. From the walls of their country houses the portraits of their forbears looked down upon them. In their fields toiled their hereditary tenants. For generations peasant families lived in the same village, tilled the same patches of ground, and found a last resting-place for their wearied bodies in the same parish churchyards. Château and cottage had little contact with the outside world. No newsboy threw on the doorstep a morning paper filled with news from every continent. No postman brought letters from distant friends and relatives. No messenger-boy delivered startling telegrams from remote points. No shrill telephone bell disturbed the rural calm. The poor and infrequent roads, the clumsy, uncomfortable stage-coaches, the insanitary inns, and the slow-moving sailing-vessels made travel dangerous and wearisome and kept at home all but the most adventurous. Immemorial traditions and the pronouncements of long-recognized authorities ruled the minds and consciences of the majority of men, and few rose above the class into which they had been born.

3

POLITICAL CONDITIONS UNDER THE ANCIEN RÉGIME

In 1789 Europe was divided politically into Great Britain, the national states of France, Spain, and Portugal, the petty city-states and principalities of Italy and Germany, Prussia, the polyglot, heterogeneous collection of semi-feudal provinces known as Austria, the confederation of Swiss cantons, the three Scandinavian kingdoms, the Turkish and Russian empires, and the declining state of Poland. Great Britain, formed by the union of England and Scotland in 1707, dominated Ireland in Europe and a great empire in other parts of the world. France, Spain, Portugal, and Great Britain possessed nearly the same boundaries as they do to-day. Prussia extended farther eastward than now and included far less territory in central and western Germany. Austria ruled an empire now divided between many heirs. The two great powers of Austria and Prussia and some three hundred and sixty-two other German states of small and medium size formed in central Europe a weak confederation known as the Holy Roman Empire. Broken up into an Austrian province and a number of small, independent states, Italy counted for little in the diplomacy of Europe. The Moslems of the Turkish Empire dominated and misgoverned the Christian peoples of the Balkans. The Russian tsars ruled a vast empire in Europe and Asia stretching from the Baltic Sea to the Pacific Ocean and from the Black Sea to the Arctic Ocean. Poland was just on the point of being partitioned by its three rapacious neighbors, Russia, Prussia, and Austria.

In most of these states both rulers and peoples believed in a monarchical form of government. In theory the sovereigns of the last half of the eighteenth century professed to be enlightened despots. In practice their subjects often suffered from arbitrary imprisonment, tyrannical tax-gatherers, shameless exploitation, unfair trials, and the use of torture in judicial procedure. Even in Great Britain, where parliamentary government had been developed, the middle and lower classes had no control over the political machinery.

4

RELIGIOUS CONDITIONS UNDER THE ANCIEN RÉGIME

Under the Ancien Régime the people of Europe were divided by religious and ecclesiastical differences, much as at present. The masters of the Turkish Empire were Moslems. The majority of their European subjects and most of the inhabitants of the Russian Empire were adherents of the Eastern Orthodox Church. The greater part of the people of England and Lowland Scotland, northeastern Ireland, several of the Swiss cantons, and northern and central Europe belonged to one of the various Protestant churches. The rest of Europe gave allegiance to the Roman Catholic Church. In most of the countries of Europe an intolerant state church ruled the minds and consciences of the people and the governing classes still looked upon schism and nonconformity as a sort of treason to the state. Even in England the state had made concessions to the Protestant Nonconformists in a grudging spirit and still discriminated against them. To the Roman Catholics it conceded no legal rights at all. In the hope of attracting settlers, Prussia practised an unusual degree of toleration, but France gave its Protestant subjects no civil rights until 1787. Other states hardly permitted persons not belonging to the state church to remain within their borders.

5

THE FRENCH REVOLUTION

With the lapse of time the Ancien Régime, with its arbitrary absolute governments, its intolerant state churches, its discrimination between classes, and its hampering economic institutions, gradually became a more and more unsatisfactory form of organization for European society. As the middle classes, the peasants, and the city proletariat grew in power and intelligence they resented more and more the conditions and institutions that oppressed them and discriminated against them. Their resentment expressed itself overtly in France through the movement known as the French Revolution.

The inefficiency of the French monarchy precipitated this crisis. Unable to increase its revenues by additional taxes or by further borrowing, the government of France summoned the representatives of the long-ignored French nation to meet at Versailles in May, 1789, for the purpose of extricating the government from its financial difficulties. A majority of the nobles and the upper clergy came to this meeting of the Estates General determined to retain their privileged position in the social order. The middle-class representatives of the unprivileged masses of the nation, the parish priests, and an enlightened minority of the nobles came resolved to have their grievances against the Ancien Régime redressed. With the aid of the people of Paris this party of reform triumphed over the defenders of the Ancien Régime, after a short, sharp struggle that culminated in the fall of the Bastille, and reorganized the Estates General into a National Assembly.

This body then set to work at the task of reforming the institutions of France. Through a series of measures the National Assembly substituted civil equality and political liberty for the absolutism and priv-ileges of the Ancien Régime. The decree of August 11, 1789, the result of the dramatic night session of August 4, abolished serfdom and many privileges of the nobility. The Declaration of the Rights of Man and Citizen, of August, 1789, gave religious toleration to French Protes-tants. A decree of the following December declared them eligible to civil and military offices. Other measures somewhat tardily conferred rights of citizenship on the Jews. The penal code of 1791 abolished judicial torture, the pillory, branding with a hot iron, and public con-fession of guilt (*amende honorable*), made the punishment fit the crime, and established liberty of the press in fact though not in law. A commission for the reform of criminal procedure also introduced trial by jury and oral procedure.

Other measures of the National Assembly greatly modified the eco-nomic institutions of France. A law of March, 1790, abolished without indemnity personal servitude, feudal corvées, seigniorial justice, and the compulsory use of the mill, the oven, and the wine-press of the lord by the tenants of an estate, and made most of the other seigniorial burdens redeemable. A series of decrees confiscated most of the prop-erty of the Church, the crown, and the émigré nobles, and put it into the hands of middle-class speculators. A law of February, 1791, sup-pressed the gilds. Other measures freed internal commerce from tolls and interior customs lines. This legislation removed most of the restric-tions which seriously hampered the middle class and the peasants.

The National Assembly also greatly altered the position of the state church and the relations of Church and State. The confiscation of the lands of the Church in the interest of the finances of the state and the abolition of ecclesiastical tithes led to the suppression of the monastic orders and to a greater dependence of the Church on the support of the state. The Civil Constitution of the Clergy, enacted in July, 1790, changed diocesan and parish boundaries, abolished a number of bish-oprics and archbishoprics, provided a more equitable scale of salaries for the clergy, and practically nullified the power of the Pope over the Church in France. The general result of this legislation was a sub-ordination of the Church to the state.

Another group of laws and decrees transformed central and local governments and the judicial and financial systems in France. The French constitution of 1791 made a unicameral legislative body the controlling organ of the government, replaced the old, irregular, over-lapping administrative districts with a hierarchy of governmental dis-tricts controlled by elected officers and councils, and substituted a uni-form system of civil and criminal courts for the medley of feudal and royal courts of the Ancien Régime. The National Assembly also replaced the burdensome and discriminatory taxes of the absolute monarchy with a rational and fairly just system of taxation. These enactments made France a modern, limited monarchy.

The government established by the constitution of 1791, known as the Legislative Assembly, lasted less than a year. The reforms of the National Assembly injured the interests or shocked the consciences of the King, the royal family, most of the nobles, a majority of the clergy, many pious laymen, and all the other conservative elements of French society, and made them enemies of the revolutionary movement. The flight of the nobles from the country and their plans for overthrowing the new constitutional régime, the refusal of a majority of the clergy to accept the new Civil Constitution of the Clergy, the inept policy pursued by Louis XVI, and the popular distrust aroused by the defeat of the French army in the foreign war gradually created a republican party among the more radical advocates of the French Revolution. With the aid of the populace of Paris this party humiliated and suspended the King and finally in September, 1792, forced the Legislative Assembly to make way for a new constituent assembly known as the Convention.

This body governed France for the next three years and performed some tremendous tasks. Although power shifted from faction to faction and terrible excesses marked its rule, the Convention and its agents sternly put down the risings of the hostile royalists and Girondists, drove back the armies invading France on every border and occupied neighboring provinces long coveted by French statesmen, separated Church and State, legally recognized the transformation of the French peasant into a free proprietor, deprived the Church of its control over marriage, divorce, and the registration of births, marriages, and deaths, and finally drew up the constitution of 1795. Upon the completion of these tasks the Convention made way for the government known as the Directory.

The reforms of the National Assembly, the Legislative Assembly, and the Convention democratized for a brief time French institutions. They substituted for the absolutism of the Ancien Régime, first a limited monarchy and then a republican form of government. They stripped the intolerant state church of its property and privileges, separated Church and State, and gave Jews and Protestants the same rights as other citizens. They substituted for the idea of privileged classes the ideal of social equality. They suppressed the restrictions of the Ancien Régime hampering agriculture, industry, and commerce, made the peasant full proprietor of his land, and opened the way for the middle class to become dominant in the state. The revolutionary leaders, however, introduced their reforms so bruskly that they soon involved republican France in war with monarchical Europe. This struggle finally gave control of the revolutionary movement to the most successful revolutionary general, Napoleon Bonaparte.

6

THE FOREIGN WAR AND THE RISE OF NAPOLEON BONAPARTE

The military struggle of revolutionary France with Conservative Europe began in 1792. Within a year the leaders of the French Revolution found themselves at war with Austria, Prussia, Great Britain, Spain, the United Netherlands, and several smaller German and Italian states. After a few initial defeats the French armies began to win astonishing victories. By the end of 1795 they had expelled from French soil the invading armies, occupied the Austrian and the United Netherlands and the German territories on the left bank of the Rhine River, and forced Spain, Prussia, and the United Netherlands to sign treaties of peace. By 1797 the French armies had defeated the troops of Austria and Sardinia. These unexpected victories extended the boundaries of France to the Alps and the Rhine, and led to the formation on the borders of the latter, of satellite states like the Batavian and Cisalpine republics, which accepted the institutions of revolutionary France and obeyed the orders of its military leaders.

These successes were the direct result of the reforms of the French Revolution. The decrees of the National Assembly and the Convention stirred the new citizens of France to a higher pitch of patriotism than the commands of the absolute monarchy had ever aroused in the hearts of its subjects. The awakened nation felt that it had a vital interest in the outcome of the war and put its moral and physical resources at the disposal of the French Republic. The abolition of privilege gave men of military genius an opportunity to rise to positions of command, and the new national spirit inspired the rank and file of the French armies to heroic deeds. The aged generals and the professional armies of Conservative Europe found themselves unable to contend successfully against the strategy of the new French leaders and the élan of the new national armies.

In time, however, this patriotic fervor waned. Under the government of the Directory (1795–1799) the French nation grew weary of political activity and permitted corrupt and incompetent men to rise to power. In France their rule was marked by financial distress and misgovernment; abroad, by a revival of the foreign war and a succession of military disasters. They maintained themselves in power only by resort to intrigue and the use of force. By their mismanagement of affairs these corrupt politicians of the Directory gave Napoleon Bonaparte an opportunity to seize control of the French government.

This successful general first caught the imagination of the French people by his Italian campaign of 1796. Then his early exploits in Egypt and Palestine increased his personal prestige. Ignorant of his precarious position in the Near East, the French public felt that he could have averted the defeats suffered by France after the renewal of the foreign war in 1799. Learning of the unpopularity of the Directory, Napoleon Bonaparte returned to France late in 1799 and placed himself at the head of a bold conspiracy that seized control of the French government. Once in power, he brought the foreign war to a close by a few brilliant strokes and then turned to the task of completing and consolidating the reforms of the French Revolution.

7

THE BENEFICENT DICTATORSHIP

In the period that followed the signing of the peace treaties of Lunéville (1801) and Amiens (1802), Napoleon Bonaparte, as First Consul of the French Republic, inaugurated a series of beneficent reforms that gave France a new and more efficient administrative system, restored amicable relations between Church and State, and accelerated the speed of the commissions at work at the task of codifying the laws of France. The new administrative system again centralized authority at Paris. It divided France into departments, arrondissements, and communes, placed these administrative districts under the supervision of prefects, subprefects, and mayors, and carefully subordinated them to the authority of the First Consul.

At the time he seized power Napoleon Bonaparte found Church and State separated and in open conflict. In the hope of strengthening his political position by the reëstablishment of peaceful relations between Church and State, he negotiated in 1801 a Concordat with the Pope. This agreement provided that the Roman Catholic Church should be recognized as the church of the majority of the French people, that the bishops and archbishops who had refused to swear an oath of allegiance to the Civil Constitution of the Clergy should resign or be removed from office, that their successors should be appointed by the head of the state and should pledge their fidelity to the republic, that the Church should not disturb the purchasers of confiscated ecclesiastical property, and that the state should pay the clergy suitable stipends and enforce such police regulations as it deemed necessary for the maintenance of public tranquillity. The Organic Articles, promulgated at the same time as the Concordat to regulate the position of French Protestants, placed the members of the Calvinist and Lutheran churches on an equal footing with the communicants of the Roman Catholic Church.

Upon coming into power Napoleon Bonaparte found French law also in a chaotic condition. Successive French sovereigns had imposed a mass of royal ordinances on the old Roman law in use in southern France and upon the bodies of local custom that had grown up in the various districts of northern France. After the outbreak of the French Revolution domestic turmoil and foreign war prevented the earlier governments from fulfilling the expressed wish of the French nation for the reduction of this confused tangle of laws into a few simple, orderly codes. After he had seized control of France Napoleon Bonaparte quickly appointed new commissions to compile civil, criminal, commercial, and rural codes, and a code of civil procedure. Before he fell from power each of these commissions had completed its task. The Civil Code, especially, embodied in French law many of the revolutionary principles. This reëstablishment of autocratic government, the return to a centralized administrative system, the conclusion of a Concordat with the Church, and the codification of the laws of France greatly modified and supplemented the reforms of the revolutionary period.

8

NAPOLEONIC IMPERIALISM

In foreign affairs Napoleon Bonaparte adopted a policy that soon involved France in a series of wars with the other European powers. He sent his political agents into the Near and the Far East, retained control of the Batavian Republic, the Swiss cantons, and northern Italy, reorganized Germany, gained command of the foreign policy of Spain, and made a beginning toward the reëstablishment of France as a colonial power. In 1804 he assumed the title of Emperor. His whole policy seemed to portend the overthrow of the balance of power in Europe. In order to avert this danger Great Britain in 1803 renewed its naval war and two years later Austria, Russia, and Great Britain reopened on the Continent the military struggle against France.

Napoleon, as he was known after his assumption of the imperial title, began the campaign of 1805 with a striking success, at Ulm in southern Germany, over the incompetently led Austrians, and closed it a few weeks later at Austerlitz in Moravia with an overwhelming defeat of the remnants of the forces of Austria and the first army of the slowly advancing Russians. These victories compelled the Austrian government to sign the Treaty of Pressburg, which inflicted on the Hapsburg state serious territorial losses and a heavy indemnity, and made it possible for the French Emperor to aggrandize his new South German allies, dissolve the old Holy Roman Empire, and form the smaller states of southern and western Germany into a Confederation of the Rhine under his own protection.

By his disregard of Prussian neutrality during the campaign of 1805 and his disregard of Prussian interests and ambitions, however, Napoleon brought Prussia into the struggle against France. The campaign of 1806 opened with a crushing defeat of the army of Prussia at Jena, which resulted in the occupation of most of the Prussian provinces by French troops. In the following year the bloody French victories of Eylau and Friedland discouraged the Russian government and opened the way for the negotiation of the Treaty of Tilsit. This agreement deprived Prussia of most of its Polish territory and its provinces west of the Elbe River, burdened it with a heavy indemnity, restricted the size of its army, and humiliated it in other ways.

9

EXTENSION OF FRENCH INFLUENCE IN EUROPE

These campaigns greatly extended French influence in Europe. They pushed the boundaries of France beyond the Alps and the Rhine and incorporated wide stretches of Italian, Dutch, and German territory into France. In Italy France in the end annexed the province of Piedmont, the former Republic of Genoa, the duchies of Parma and Tuscany, and part of the Papal States. In the former Holy Roman Empire it finally acquired the Austrian Netherlands, the provinces on the left bank of the Rhine, and a strip of territory bordering on the North Sea. In 1806 Napoleon also incorporated the Dutch Netherlands into France. From the time of their annexation until the final defeat of the French Emperor in 1814 these territories formed an integral part of France and shared its institutions.

Beyond the boundaries of France Napoleon brought under French influence most of the states from the Illyrian Provinces to the English Channel and from the Strait of Gibraltar to the banks of the Niemen. In Italy he came to control the Kingdom of Naples and the state known successively as the Cisalpine Republic, the Italian Republic, and the Kingdom of Italy. This state finally included the former Austrian province of Lombardy, most of the Italian lands of the former Venetian Republic, the Duchy of Modena, part of the Papal States, and Southern Tyrol. Under the title first of President and later of King, Napoleon ruled it as an autocrat, giving it religious, legal, social, and economic institutions closely patterned after those of France. On the throne of the Kingdom of Naples Napoleon placed in turn his brother Joseph and his brother-in-law Murat. During their periods of rule they abolished in southern Italy fiscal and social inequalities, introduced the Civil Code of Napoleon, established primary schools, and reformed taxation. This penetration of the Italian peninsula by the armies, administrators, and institutions of France roused its people from their lethargy, awakened the dormant national spirit, and for the first time since the days of the Roman Empire gave the peninsula just and efficient government.

In western Germany Napoleon created the dependent states of Berg and Westphalia. He formed the Grand Duchy of Berg from territories ceded by Bavaria in 1805 and Prussia in 1807. He constructed the Kingdom of Westphalia from the former German states of Brunswick and Hesse-Cassel and districts on the left bank of the Elbe River surrendered by Prussia in 1807. To both states he transferred almost bodily the institutions of Napoleonic France.

In southern Germany the three states of Baden, Württemberg, and Bavaria fell under the control of Napoleon. After they came under his influence they introduced many of the French reforms. They suppressed their estates, abolished ecclesiastical tithes, did away with serfdom, reduced seigniorial corvées, removed many toll stations and internal customs lines, and modernized the central and local administrative machinery. In the Catholic states the governments broke for the time being the political power of the Church, secularized much of its property, suppressed many monasteries and convents, and introduced religious toleration for Protestants.

In two other regions of Europe Napoleon created dependent states with French institutions. From the Polish provinces ceded by Prussia in the Treaty of Tilsit he formed the Duchy of Warsaw in 1807. After the defeat of Austria in 1809 he enlarged the duchy by the addition of Austrian territory and transformed it into a grand duchy. He gave the new state a constitution, religious toleration, and the French Civil Code, and abolished serfdom. After 1805 he began to create on the eastern shore of the Adriatic Sea the Illyrian Provinces. In these former Austrian provinces he reorganized the administration and the courts of justice, abolished the manorial courts, serfdom, and seigniorial corvées, suppressed the gilds, and constructed an admirable network of roads. His work in these two regions did much to keep alive Polish nationalism and to awaken the Southern Slavs.

After the disastrous defeat at Jena, the Baron von Stein, the Prince von Hardenberg, and other leaders reorganized the Prussian state to prevent its complete destruction. They abolished serfdom and the old distinctions between noble, burgher, and peasant land, threw occupations open to all, gave the towns a larger measure of self-government, issued decrees intended to give the peasant full control of his holding, and reorganized the army. These reforms prepared Prussia to play a great rôle in the rising of the nations of Europe against the Napoleonic régime.

In southeastern Europe the revolutionary influences emanating from

France combined with other forces to accelerate the disruption of the Turkish Empire and to awaken the latent national feeling of its Christian subjects. In the Rumanian provinces of Moldavia and Walachia the upper classes, brought into contact with the civilization of western Europe through the mediation of Russia, began to cherish the ideals of the French Revolution, to study the Rumanian language, and to establish schools. In 1804 the Serbs around Belgrade rose at the instigation of the Sultan against the tyranny of the rebellious Turkish garrisons stationed in the cities of Serbia. When their master refused to redress their fundamental grievances the victorious Serbian peasants rose in revolt and practically gained their independence. In the Greek provinces of the Turkish Empire the prosperous Greek merchants sent their sons to the schools of western Europe, where they came into contact with the political and literary movements of the period. Upon their return to their native land these Greek students contributed to the awakening of their nation by their studies in the language and literature of the Greeks.

The French Revolution and the Napoleonic period therefore gave a large part of Europe a knowledge of ideas and institutions in marked contrast with those of the Ancien Régime. They introduced into European politics the idea of constitutional government, popularly elected assemblies, and political rights for the individual. They subordinated the Church to the state, secularized large masses of Church property, dissolved hundreds of monasteries and convents, and introduced in many regions the principle of religious toleration. They equalized the burdens imposed by the state and opened every position in the state to the ambitious. They freed many of the peasants from serfdom and made them proprietors of their lands. They liberated commerce and industry from many restrictions. These advantages favored certain elements in European society and created the growth of Liberal parties opposed to a return of the Ancien Régime, and advocates of the new French institutions.

10

DISADVANTAGES OF THE NAPOLEONIC RÉGIME

Certain features of the Napoleonic régime, however, made the Liberals forget for a moment its advantages. They resented the Napoleonic spoliation of their art treasures and the burdensome requisitions for the French armies. They hated the conscription of soldiers by Napoleon and the enormous losses of men entailed by his wars. They groaned at his heavy taxation and heartily disliked his Continental system. These disadvantages of his rule finally gave rise to a great reaction in Europe against the Napoleonic régime.

PART I

THE STRUGGLE OF CONSERVATIVE EUROPE
AGAINST THE NEW FORCES

CHAPTER II

THE REACTION OF EUROPE AGAINST THE FRENCH REVOLUTION AND THE RULE OF NAPOLEON

As a result of the conscription of the youth of Europe, the repeated requisitioning of supplies, the terrible decimation of conscripted troops, the constant shifting of boundary lines and changes in forms of government, the deprivations incident to the Continental system, the frequent acts of tyranny, and the spoliation of art collections, popular resentment against the Napoleonic régime steadily mounted. This feeling of resentment finally gave rise to a series of national and popular revolts. The protest of Europe against the rule of Napoleon began in Spain and spread to Austria, Russia, and Germany.

I

THE NATIONAL UPRISING AGAINST NAPOLEON IN SPAIN

In Spain Napoleon set in motion a national uprising by a series of high-handed measures that wounded the pride and disregarded the prejudices of the Spanish people. Upon learning of the mobilization of the Spanish army in the critical weeks before the battle of Jena, and finding proof in the captured Prussian archives of Spanish plots against France, the French Emperor decided that he could no longer trust the seemingly docile Spanish government. Under the pretext of forcing Portugal to adopt his economic system, directed against Great Britain, he introduced large numbers of French troops into the towns of northern Spain, cajoled the quarreling members of the Spanish royal family into meeting him on French soil at Bayonne, intimidated them into resigning into his hands their rights to the Spanish throne, and then induced a small number of Spanish notables to come and request the appointment of his brother Joseph as King of Spain. After forcing his rule on the Spanish people Napoleon issued a series of decrees that bruskly imposed on them an administrative system patterned after that of Napoleonic France, abolished feudal dues, the Inquisition, and interior customs lines, and reduced the number of monastic institutions. This disregard of their dignity and rights stirred the proud Spanish people to action. On May 2, 1808, the people of Madrid flung themselves on the French garrison and drove it from the city. Within a few weeks 150,000 untrained, ill-armed men had volunteered for the national rising against Napoleonic rule. Although they were unfitted to cope with the veteran armies of France in pitched battles, they took advantage of the broken character of the country to carry on a guerrilla warfare that forced Napoleon to keep large bodies of troops in Spain and seriously strained the resources of the French treasury. Their success encouraged the British government to intervene in the peninsula. Under the leadership of the Duke of Wellington the British regulars, with the aid of the Spanish volunteers, began to drive the French out of both Spain and Portugal. By 1811 they had expelled the French from Portugal. After two more years of fighting they cleared Spain of French troops and forced their way into southern France.

This attempt of Napoleon to gain control of the Iberian peninsula influenced the later history of Europe in many ways. At the approach of the French invaders the Portuguese royal family and many other notables fled to Brazil. This left Portugal practically under the control of the British military authorities. In Spain the leaders of the national rising attempted to force upon the politically unprepared Spanish people the liberal constitution of 1812. In Europe the example of the heroic resistance of the Spanish nation stirred other peoples to similar risings against the rule of Napoleon.

2

THE SEMIPOPULAR MOVEMENT IN AUSTRIA AGAINST THE NAPOLEONIC
RÉGIME

The Spanish national movement first encouraged the Austrian government to action. The governing classes of Austria feared that the Hapsburg dynasty might suffer the same fate as the royal family of Spain, and resented the territorial losses and heavy indemnities imposed on the Austrian state by Napoleon. Their subjects seem to have shared their feeling of resentment and humiliation. The Austrian government, consequently, took advantage of the preoccupation of Napoleon with the rising in Spain to prepare for war. The advisers of the Emperor strengthened the army, secretly incited the former subjects of Austria in the Tyrol to revolt, and even attempted to arouse the patriotism of the Austrian peoples and the latent national spirit of the Germans. In 1809 the war for which they had been preparing broke out. For a moment it looked as though Austria might be victorious. As a result of the excessive caution of the Austrian military leaders, however, Napoleon again triumphed and forced Austria to sign another humiliating peace, involving additional losses of territory and the payment of further indemnities. This disaster brought to power in Austria the cool, suave, clear-sighted diplomat Prince von Metternich, a Conservative with an inbred hatred of the French Revolution and a deep fear of popular movements.

3

THE NATIONAL RISINGS AGAINST NAPOLEON IN RUSSIA AND GERMANY

Three years after the defeat of Austria in the campaign of 1809, the friendly relations established at Tilsit between Napoleon and the Russian Tsar reached a breaking-point. The promised enforcement of the economic system devised by Napoleon to bring Great Britain to its knees deprived the people of Russia of the manufactured and colonial products to which they were accustomed, and closed the British market to Russian wheat, timber, and naval stores. The interests of the two rulers conflicted, furthermore, in Turkey, Poland, and Oldenburg. In 1812 this conflict of interests finally brought the two powers to the point of war.

At first the campaign of 1812 seemed destined to end in the usual Napoleonic victory. The armies under the command of the French Emperor advanced into Russia, defeated the retreating Russians at the battle of Borodino, and finally occupied the city of Moscow. But as soon as his forces entered the old capital of Russia his campaign took an unfortunate turn. Fires that deprived his troops of their expected winter quarters broke out in different parts of the city. For five weeks Napoleon waited in the city in the vain hope that the stubborn Tsar would open negotiations for peace. Finally, too late in the year, the Napoleonic army began to retrace its steps to escape the oncoming Russian winter. The military situation compelled it to retreat by the same route that it had used in advancing into Russia, through a region just denuded of supplies by the passage of two great armies. On the return march, consequently, the soldiers of Napoleon suffered from hunger, from the terrible cold, from the hardships of the forced retreat, and from the incessant attacks of brutal Cossacks and vindictive peasants. As a result of its sufferings the once imposing army of Napoleon reached Poland with its ranks decimated by battle, disease, and desertions, its discipline and organization completely destroyed, and the prestige of its famous commander seriously impaired.

The disastrous campaign of 1812 changed wholly both the military and the diplomatic situation. It destroyed for the French Emperor irreplaceable troops and officers and vast quantities of equipment and supplies. It encouraged General Yorck von Wartenburg, the commander of the Prussian contingent in the Napoleonic army invading Russia, to desert after receiving the assurance of the Tsar that he would not lay down his arms until Prussia had been restored to its former rank as a great power, and stirred the people of Prussia to a patriotic pitch that finally forced the hesitating Frederick William III to join the war against Napoleon. It restored to Austria freedom of action.

As a result of the patriotic rising in Prussia and the independent policy adopted by Austria, Napoleon prepared for the opening of the campaign of 1813 by abandoning Poland and withdrawing his troops to the line of the Elbe. After the renewal of hostilities he found himself unable to follow up two victories because of his lack of cavalry. This encouraged Metternich to terminate the negotiations that he had been carrying on with Napoleon and to throw the gradually mobilized military forces of Austria into the struggle against the French Emperor. The entrance of Austria into the war compelled Napoleon to retreat again and contributed to his defeat at the great battle of Leipzig. This new disaster, in turn, led to the defection of the remaining German allies of Napoleon, and the withdrawal of the rest of his forces behind the Rhine, and destroyed the Kingdom of Westphalia and the Grand Duchy of Berg. Early in the following year the armies of Russia, Prussia, Austria, and the minor states of Europe defeated the forces of Napoleon in France and northern Italy and compelled him to abdicate the French throne and retire to the petty principality of Elba off the western coast of Italy. These national uprisings against the rule of Napoleon, however, put the fate of Europe into the hands of conservative rulers and ministers born during the Ancien Régime and imbued with its ideals.

4

THE RESTORATIONS IN THE WAKE OF THE ALLIED ARMIES

The defeat of Napoleon by the four allied powers—Russia, Prussia, Austria, and Great Britain—destroyed the empire that he had created and put in question the future of the Grand Duchy of Warsaw, the Illyrian Provinces, the Dutch and the Belgian Netherlands, and much of Italy and Germany. After the withdrawal of the forces of the French Emperor behind the Elbe, Russian troops occupied the Grand Duchy of Warsaw. After his defeat at Leipzig, King Jerome fled from the Kingdom of Westphalia, the old ruling families of Brunswick, Hesse-Cassel, Hanover, and Oldenburg returned to their former capitals and attempted to resuscitate their former states, the old aristocratic governments reëstablished themselves in the Hanseatic cities, and the South German states deserted Napoleon and made as favorable terms as they could with Austria. The remaining German territory taken from the French Emperor fell under the control of a temporary government that divided Germany into five administrative districts, each ruled by a military governor subordinate to the allied military authorities and a civil governor subject to the orders of a central council of administration.

In the Netherlands the defeat of Napoleon at Leipzig was followed by a popular revolt against French rule and the setting up of a provisional government that restored political power to the historic House of Orange on condition that it should promulgate a free constitution. In compliance with this stipulation a commission drew up a conservative constitution that vested all executive and much legislative authority in the hands of the sovereign, William I, created a legislative body of fifty-five members, made the judiciary independent, and gave equal rights to all the churches. The new fundamental law abolished the cumbersome machinery which had formerly fostered provincial jealousies and paralyzed the central government of the United Netherlands, but it failed to establish in the new Kingdom of the Netherlands a responsible ministry, trial by jury, or liberty of the press.

The voluntary action of the Dutch people met with the approval of the representatives of the allied powers. At the instigation of Lord Castlereagh, the British representative at the headquarters of the allies, the four allied powers began to discuss the idea of incorporating the Belgian Netherlands into the reëstablished Dutch state in order to create a stronger dike to hold in check revolutionary France. In the first Treaty of Paris (May 30, 1814), consequently, they forced the Dutch to accept the Belgian Netherlands and an indemnity as compensation for the loss of the Dutch colonies seized by Great Britain. In August, 1814, the restored King of the Netherlands took over actual control of the Belgian Netherlands.

In Spain the victories of the Duke of Wellington and his allies opened the way for the return of Ferdinand VII to the throne of his ancestors. The enthusiastic reception accorded him by his subjects as he journeyed from the French border toward Madrid convinced him that the nobles, the clergy, a good many of the generals, and the ignorant and fanatical populace really hated, as much as he did, the liberal constitution imposed on the Spanish people in 1812 by the leaders of the national rising against Napoleon. Because of this conviction Ferdinand VII ventured to annul the constitution of 1812 and to restore the institutions of the Ancien Régime.

The Spanish people paid dearly for their blind fidelity to their old ruling family. They suffered from tyranny and misgovernment. Their restored sovereign reëstablished the old, unwieldy machinery of government, exposed the lives and property of the Spanish Liberals to the fury of the ignorant mob, and banished the Spanish supporters of the Napoleonic régime. A camarilla of ever-changing membership received an unrestricted opportunity to exploit the nation as a reward for amusing the King with risqué stories and accompanying him on his lewd nocturnal adventures. On occasions Ferdinand VII acted like an insane man. Once he ordered the officers who were second in command of the troops stationed in the three principal cities of Spain, to shoot their military superiors and take their places. As a result of the attempt of the King to restore the restrictions of the old colonial system, the Spanish people lost their vast colonial possessions. The American colonists of Spain had refused to recognize the authority of King Joseph, the brother of Napoleon, and had set up provisional governments. The failure of Ferdinand VII to assure them a continuance of their newly found political and commercial freedom finally caused them to declare their complete independence.

In Italy the desertion of Napoleon by Murat, the King of Naples, and the resulting defeat of the Napoleonic forces in the northern part of the peninsula made possible the return of the former rulers. Austria immediately occupied Lombardy, Venetia, and the Illyrian Provinces, and did away with all the institutions introduced by Napoleon except conscription and his system of taxation. The King of Sardinia returned from his island refuge to his former provinces on the mainland and restored as far as was able the Ancien Régime. He replaced the officials appointed by the French with men whose names had been listed in the court almanac of 1798, demoted many of the army officers commissioned by Napoleon, dismissed twelve of the professors at the University of Turin on the ground that they were dangerous radicals, and permitted the monasteries to reopen. He retained, however, the gendarmes and the system of taxation instituted during the French régime, returned to the Church only the unsold lands confiscated from it, and refused to give the nobles their old jurisdiction over the patrimonial courts. The Grand Duke of Tuscany rescinded much of the legislation of the French period, but he remained true to the mild and liberal traditions of his house. In the train of the saintly Pope, Pius VII, there came back to Rome a group of conservative advisers, who inaugurated a period of reaction during the absence of his chief minister, Cardinal Consalvi, at the Congress of Vienna. As a reward for his desertion of Napoleon Murat temporarily saved his tottering Neapolitan throne.

5

THE FIRST RESTORATION IN FRANCE

Upon the entry of their troops into Paris, the representatives of the allied powers found themselves faced with the problem of the future of France. They had to decide on a sovereign, the form of government, the question of boundaries, and how to prevent a new revolutionary outburst by the French people. In solving this problem the famous French politician, Talleyrand, the Prince of Bénévent, played the leading part. Convinced that his defeated country could obtain more lenient terms from the victorious allies if it restored the almost forgotten Bourbons to the French throne, he manipulated the populace of Paris, the members of the imperial senate, and the all-powerful Tsar of Russia in such a way as to bring about the restoration of the Count of Provence, a brother of the Louis XVI guillotined in 1793, as Louis XVIII.

Having set him on the throne, the representatives of the allied powers proceeded to negotiate a treaty of peace with the new sovereign. As Talleyrand expected, they treated France with great consideration. In the Treaty of Paris, signed May 30, 1814, they imposed no indemnity on the state that had harassed Europe for a quarter of a century with requisitions and annexations, and they allowed it to keep the boundaries that it had had on January 1, 1792. These terms gave France a number of enclaved and adjoining districts which she did not possess before the outbreak of the French Revolution. They compelled the French state, on the other hand, to surrender all claims to the countries, districts, and towns beyond these frontiers that had formed a part of France or the French Empire during the Revolutionary and Napoleonic periods.

The representatives of the allied powers, however, saw clearly that the generation which had grown up under the freer conditions and greater opportunities that had prevailed in France after 1789 could not be forced back into the social and political framework of the Ancien Régime. In inviting Louis XVIII to return to the throne of his fathers, the imperial Senate had stipulated that he should accept a hastily drafted constitution which preserved the principal gains of the French Revolution. When he refused to adhere to this document, on the ground that it had been drawn up in too great haste, the representatives of the allied powers compelled him to placate the new French nation that had grown up since 1789 by granting the famous Charter of 1814. This constitution provided for a legislative body consisting of a Chamber of Peers appointed by the King and a Chamber of Deputies elected by an extremely limited suffrage, a definite civil list for the crown, freedom of worship for all creeds, protection for the purchasers of the property confiscated during the revolutionary period, and an independent judiciary. These provisions made France a limited monarchy.

Upon his return to France Louis XVIII found himself in a delicate position. Marshals of Napoleon commanded his armies. Former dignitaries and functionaries of the Napoleonic Empire controlled the administrative machinery of his state. The mass of his subjects desired to retain the political, religious, social, and economic gains of the French Revolution. In his train, however, there entered into France former nobles anxious to regain their confiscated estates and the privileged position that they had once held in the state, and churchmen eager to give the Church its former position in the state. This situation made the problem of reconciling the old and the new France—the returned émigrés and the generation that had grown up since 1789—the chief task confronting Louis XVIII.

The restored Bourbons badly mismanaged this intricate problem. The younger brother of the King, the Count of Artois, placed himself at the head of the extremists among the returned émigrés. These Ultra-royalists insolently inflicted slights on the bearers of some of the greatest names in French history, tried to regain their confiscated estates and to oust the royal advisers from office, opposed the Charter of 1814, and scornfully heaped insults upon the highly prized insignia of the Legion of Honor. Their clerical allies hurled ecclesiastical anathemas at the holders of the Church property confiscated during the French Revolution. The government aggravated the situation by attempting to enforce the English Sunday in France, by maintaining certain unpopular taxes (*droits réunis*), and by retiring many of the Napoleonic officers and replacing these battle-scarred heroes with émigrés of no military experience. The policies followed by the government and the Ultraroyalists created great popular dissatisfaction and encouraged Napoleon to attempt to recover the throne of France.

6

THE SETTLEMENT AT VIENNA

In the first Treaty of Paris the representatives of the allied powers made a beginning toward the settlement of the affairs of Europe. They decided to extend the boundaries of the Kingdom of the Netherlands to the sea, the French frontier, and the Meuse; to reunite the states of Germany by a federative bond; to establish Switzerland as an independent state; to recognize the claim of Great Britain to the island of Malta; to restore to the King of Sardinia his former possessions on the mainland, with the exception of a part of Savoy, and to cede to him the territories of the former Republic of Genoa; and to give control of Lombardy and Venetia to the Emperor of Austria. They left their remaining problems to the decisions of a congress of the European powers to be held at Vienna.

The Liberals of Europe looked forward with high hopes to the assembling of the Congress of Vienna. They confidently expected that it would distribute the Polish, German, and Italian territories reconquered from Napoleon in such a manner as to restore a real and permanent balance of power among the states of Europe. They hoped that it would create an effective international court, abolish the African slave-trade, suppress piracy in the Mediterranean, give the American colonies of Spain their independence, and establish freedom of the seas. Their hopes, however, met with little sympathy from the conservative sovereigns and ministers assembled at Vienna.

Francis I of Austria and his chief minister, Metternich, were typical of the men dominating the congress. The Austrian sovereign shrewdly kept in the background, but his egotism, jealousy, aversion to effort, pettiness, procrastination, and fear of revolution colored all the acts of his government. He found in Metternich a tool well suited to his purpose. Under ordinary conditions his Chancellor would have been a skeptical, aristocratic man of the world, of moderately liberal opinions and with slight sympathy for people outside his own class. His direct contact with the excesses of the French Revolution made him a thoroughgoing Conservative; his ambition caused him to subordinate his own opinions to those of his master; his diplomatic skill enabled him to carry through his policies.

The most liberal of the influential figures at the congress was Alexander I of Russia. The Tsar started out in life endowed with good looks, a pleasing manner, a more than average amount of personal vanity, and a fondness for playing a conspicuous part in affairs. Although born a despot, his early training gave him a veneer of liberalism. The tragic circumstances attending his accession to the throne of Russia caused him to be both morbid and religious. His dramatic defeat of Napoleon made him a mystic. These conflicting characteristics made him an incalculable factor in the politics of Europe; the vast empire at his command made him a force that had to be reckoned with.

The British government sent as its chief representative Lord Castlereagh. Backed by the powerful British navy and the great commercial, industrial, and financial resources of Great Britain, he stood in a position to exert a decisive influence at the congress. He used it in an unostentatious manner to reconcile the conflicting interests of the Continental powers.

The leaders of the four great allied powers—Russia, Prussia, Austria, and Great Britain—intended to arrogate to themselves control of the congress, but they failed to reckon with the diplomatic skill of Talleyrand, the principal French representative at Vienna. Born during the Ancien Régime, he had started life as a member of the French nobility. As he was crippled by an accident, his family had forced him to follow an ecclesiastical career, and he had finally risen to the position of bishop. Upon the outbreak of the French Revolution he had abandoned his clerical office and had thrown himself into the revolutionary movement. He had then served as a member of the National Assembly, as a diplomatic agent of the Legislative Assembly to Great Britain, and as Foreign Minister of the Directory, the Consulate, and the Empire. His long experience and position of influence had made him temporarily indispensable to the restored Bourbons, and Louis XVIII had sent him to represent the interests of France at the congress. He arrived at Vienna the suspected representative of a defeated and discredited state, but he quickly forced the allied powers to take him into their councils.

Besides these representatives of the great powers, there flocked to Vienna agents of every interest that hoped to gain or feared to lose something by the decisions of the congress. Representatives of the states aggrandized by Napoleon came for the purpose of protecting their acquisitions. Dispossessed princes went in order to regain their lost thrones. Cardinal Consalvi carefully watched over the temporal interests of the papacy. Influential members of the Jewish race presented the case of their oppressed fellow-religionists. The great numbers taxed the resources of even the Austrian capital.

The congress never really assembled. The representatives of the four allied powers intended to make the necessary decisions in private conferences. The policy followed by Talleyrand after his arrival at Vienna forced them to include representatives of France and Spain in their secret discussions. Under the leadership of these six powers the representatives of the various states made a long series of agreements that fills many volumes. Then at the close of the congress the representatives of the powers drew up the Final Act of the Congress of Vienna (June 9, 1815), which embodied their principal decisions.

The articles dealing with the disposition of the Grand Duchy of Warsaw and the restoration of Prussia to the position of a great power brought the great states of Europe to the verge of war. Alexander I wished to form from the territory of the former grand duchy a Polish kingdom united to Russia by the tie of a common sovereign. The leaders of Prussia were willing to surrender their claims to the Polish provinces formerly included in the Kingdom of Prussia provided the Prussian state should receive in compensation the whole of Saxony, whose King had hesitated too long in 1813 about deserting Napoleon. The representatives of Austria and Great Britain opposed plans that would thrust Russia farther into central Europe. Seeing in the conflict of opinion an opportunity to reëstablish France as a great power, Talleyrand supported the view of Austria and Great Britain and signed with the two powers a secret treaty of alliance. After coming almost to war over the problem, the powers finally accepted a compromise suggested by Castlereagh. This agreement permitted the Tsar to create a small Kingdom of Poland under his personal rule and compensated Prussia for the loss of its Polish provinces by ceding to her three fifths of the Kingdom of Saxony and a block of territory situated in the Rhine Valley and in Westphalia. This arrangement threw on Prussia a heavy share of the task of defending Europe against a new revolutionary outbreak and divided her lands into two parts, a group of conservative agricultural provinces in eastern Germany and the two newly acquired provinces bordering on France that had shared for a time French institutions and felt the awakening touch of commerce and industry.

The decisions of the Congress of Vienna concerning the organization of Germany greatly disappointed the small party of German Liberals. Austria realized that she could not bring all of her non-German provinces into a German union and had no wish to surrender her absolute control of her German provinces to a confederation with a strong centralized government. Prussia showed no inclination as yet to put herself at the head of a German national movement, and the smaller German states had no desire to give up the independence they had just won during the Napoleonic period. As a result of the pressure of Austria and the particularism of the smaller German states, the negotiators at Vienna organized into a weak German Confederation thirty-eight of the states that survived the Napoleonic consolidations. The new organization had the same boundaries and the same defective political machinery as the old Holy Roman Empire. Austria possessed the presidency instead of the former imperial title. A diet meeting at Frankfort constituted the main organ of government. This body resembled a council of diplomats rather than a legislature. The confederation possessed no official insignia, no army and navy, and no diplomatic representatives. Its loose organization, combined with the hesitant policy of Prussia, enabled Austria to dominate the confederation until Bismarck came into power.

Austria regained her old position as a great power and most of her former provinces. As soon as the Napoleonic Empire began to crumble, the Austrian government forced Bavaria to cede the Tyrol and a number of other territories, and Austrian armies occupied Galicia, the Illyrian Provinces and—as has already been mentioned—the Italian provinces of Lombardy and Venetia. The Treaty of Paris and the Final Act of the Congress of Vienna recognized the right of Austria to occupy these territories.

The deliberations of the powers left Italy, to use the words of Metternich, a geographical expression. Most of the former rulers of Italian states regained their old territories. The representatives of the allied powers handed over the lands of the former republics of Genoa and Venetia to the Kingdom of Sardinia and the Emperor of Austria, cynically justifying their action by remarking that republics were out of style. Marie Louise, the second wife of Napoleon, became ruler of the Duchy of Parma. After Murat attempted to make himself king of all

Italy upon the occasion of the return of Napoleon from the island of Elba, the Bourbons reëstablished themselves at Naples.

The Congress of Vienna attempted to solve many other problems. It tried to regulate the use of the navigable rivers of Europe, added a number of districts to the Swiss Confederation, ratified the agreements already concluded by the Baltic powers, and made a beginning toward the abolition of the slave-trade. Before it finished its deliberations, however, the news reached Vienna of the return of Napoleon to France.

7

THE HUNDRED DAYS

Dissatisfied with his position as the ruler of the petty principality of Elba, and encouraged by reports of the dissatisfaction of the French people with the rule of the restored Bourbons and of the dissensions of the representatives of the powers assembled at Vienna, Napoleon decided to make an attempt to recover the French throne. Setting sail from Elba in March, 1815, with eleven hundred men of his old guard, he landed near Nice and hurried toward Paris. As he marched toward the French capital he met with an astonishing reception. The royal troops refused to seize him; his old soldiers rallied to his standard; the peasants and working-men received him with enthusiasm; and his old ministers and administrators offered him their services again. Without firing a shot or shedding a drop of blood he drove the Bourbons from France and installed himself in his old capital. Even Napoleon, however, realized that he could not resume his former position in France and in Europe. As soon as he arrived at Paris he attempted to conciliate the French people by issuing a liberal constitution, known as the Additional Act, which strictly limited his authority, and he hastened to send assurances of his peaceful intentions to the representatives of the allied powers assembled at Vienna.

These representatives of Russia, Prussia, Austria, and Great Britain promptly decided to treat him as an enemy of Europe. Their decision made a renewal of the European war inevitable. Napoleon, consequently, decided to attack the allied armies in Belgium before reënforcements could reach them. His attempt ended in his decisive defeat at the battle of Waterloo. This disaster caused a second abdication of Napoleon from the French throne, his banishment to the lonely island of St. Helena, a second restoration of the Bourbons in France, the punishment of France for its defection to Napoleon, and the organization of Europe against a new revolutionary outbreak.

8

THE ORGANIZATION OF EUROPE AGAINST REVOLUTION

The reception accorded by the French people to Napoleon on his return from the island of Elba convinced the sovereigns of the allied powers and their leading ministers that they must always be on guard against a new outburst of the revolutionary spirit. With this end in view they formed (November 20, 1815) a Quadruple Alliance, a revival of the union of the four allies concluded at Chaumont in 1814 and renewed later at Vienna. In the new treaty the four powers banded themselves together against the revolutionary principles that had upheld the criminal usurpation of Napoleon, convulsed France, and endangered the peace of other states, and they promised to concert among themselves measures of protection in case of another revolutionary outbreak. To facilitate the execution of the treaty the four contracting powers agreed to renew at fixed periods the meetings of their representatives.

In the minds of many people, however, the Quadruple Alliance became confused with an agreement signed by Russia, Austria, and Prussia on September 26, 1815, known as the Holy Alliance. In this document the mystical, religious Tsar had persuaded his two brother sovereigns to agree to treat each other and their subjects according to the principles of the Christian religion and to regard their peoples as three branches of one family. Ultimately all the European powers except Turkey and Great Britain signed the agreement, out of deference to the Tsar. Although it was, in the words of Metternich, a pious nothing, the Liberals of Europe regarded the Holy Alliance as an instrument of persecution, and the Sultan considered it as the beginning of a new crusade against the Moslems.

9

THE SECOND RESTORATION IN FRANCE

On the morrow of the battle of Waterloo the French leaders had to face a difficult situation. The defection of France from the restored Bourbons had alarmed and angered the allied powers and embittered the relations of the French political parties. The defeat of Napoleon at Waterloo had put France at the mercy of the victorious allies.

As a punishment for disturbing the peace of Europe, the representatives of the four great powers imposed much severer terms on France in 1815 than in 1814. In the second Treaty of Paris (November 20,

1815) they deprived her of additional territory, burdened her with a heavy indemnity, provided for the occupation of her northern provinces by an allied army—commanded by the Duke of Wellington and formed of contingents contributed by the four allies—and compelled the government of Louis XVIII to accept the advice of a council composed of the ambassadors of the allied powers at Paris.

The second Treaty of Paris confronted the government of Louis XVIII with the pressing problem of restoring to France its old independence. The freeing of French soil from foreign troops was largely the achievement of the Duke of Richelieu. In the early days of the French Revolution he had emigrated from France and taken service with the Empress Catherine II of Russia. Her grandson Alexander I conceived a great liking and respect for him and finally appointed him governor of Odessa, in the region which had just been acquired from the Turkish Empire. Under his enlightened administration the town had grown and flourished. When Talleyrand resigned office in 1815, the Tsar recommended the Duke of Richelieu to Louis XVIII for the vacant post of First Minister. When the duke hesitated to accept the office Alexander I induced him to take the position by promising to exert all the authority and influence at his command to obtain better terms of peace for France.

As soon as he had affixed his signature to the second Treaty of Paris, the Duke of Richelieu set to work at the task of freeing the occupied provinces. With this end in view the French government organized a royal army as a guarantee that order would be maintained, and arranged loans from British and Dutch firms to be used in paying off the residue of the war indemnity and other claims outstanding against France. As a result of these measures the duke had little difficulty in persuading the representatives of the allied powers assembled at the Congress of Aix-la-Chapelle in 1818 to agree to withdraw their troops from northern France and to admit the French state as an ally of the powers of the Quadruple Alliance. The progress made by the French government, the singularly elevated character of Richelieu, the fear of the Tsar that his troops might be infected with revolutionary principles, and the judgment of the Duke of Wellington concerning the weakness of the position of the allied army in northern France all contributed toward the decision of the allied powers to free France from foreign troops.

While the Duke of Richelieu was struggling to regain for France its independence, the Ultraroyalist supporters of Louis XVIII were renewing their efforts to reëstablish the Ancien Régime. Upon their return to France after the defeat of Napoleon at the battle of Waterloo, they clamored for the punishment of those responsible for the restoration of Napoleon to power, applauded the execution of Marshal Ney and others responsible for the return of Napoleon from Elba, and did nothing to prevent royalist mobs from instituting a "White Reign of Terror" in the south and west of France. They opposed the Charter of 1814, demanded compensation for the loss of their confiscated estates, and plotted to restore the Church to its old position. In furthering these aims they made use of their influence with the King and the press, their social prestige, and their control of the Chamber of Deputies.

Until 1820 Louis XVIII and his ministers attempted to follow a moderate policy that met with opposition from both the Ultraroyalists, led by the brother of the King, the Count of Artois, and of the motley group of constitutional monarchists, Bonapartists, and Republicans that came to be known as Liberals. The King had learned by experience the necessity of adopting a moderate policy. The Duke of Richelieu, who served as his principal minister until France was freed from foreign troops, had no sympathy with the prejudices and the blind hatred of the Revolution harbored by most of the returned émigrés, and the Duke of Decazes, his colleague and successor, was something of a Liberal and looked for support to the rising middle class.

By 1820, however, a series of unfortunate events made it possible for the Ultraroyalists to compass the political downfall of the powerful Decazes (Richelieu had resigned earlier). Although brought about by their own intrigues, a great increase in 1819 in the representation of the Liberals in the Chamber of Deputies gave the Ultraroyalists a pretext for attacking Decazes. They pretended to hold him responsible for the reëntrance into French political life of Henri Grégoire, a man commonly supposed to have voted for the execution of Louis XVI. In 1819, also, a fanatic made a successful attack on the life of the Duke of Berry, the heir to the French throne, as he emerged from the opera. His opponents, consequently, saddled Decazes with the responsibility of creating political conditions that made possible the tragic event. The Ultraroyalists finally exerted sufficient pressure to induce the King to part with his favorite and to invite Richelieu to take his place.

Richelieu returned to power with the hope of uniting all the friends of the monarchy into one party. In attempting to carry out this policy he failed to enlist the full support of both the King and the Ultraroyalists. The elderly King fell under the influence of a Madame de Cayla, an agent of the reactionary and clerical forces in France, and ceased to give the duke unwavering support. The Count of Artois disregarded his promise of loyalty, made to Richelieu at the time he took office, and allowed his Ultraroyalist followers to denounce the duke in the Chamber of Deputies and to thwart his measures. Disheartened by these attacks, the Duke of Richelieu and his colleagues resigned from office in 1822 and opened the way for the accession to power of an Ultraroyalist ministry, headed by Villèle. Its assumption of office marks the final triumph of the reaction in France against the French Revolution and the rule of Napoleon.

10

THE REACTION IN CENTRAL EUROPE

In central Europe, also, the decisions of the Congress of Vienna did not entirely satisfy the conservative elements in society. The Emperor of Austria and his chief minister, Metternich, had especial reason to fear the principles set free in Europe by the French Revolution and the Napoleonic period. By marriage, diplomacy, and conquest the Austrian Hapsburgs had gradually created in the Danube Valley, a state composed of a heterogeneous group of kingdoms and provinces inhabited by Germans, Czechs, Poles, Ruthenians, Italians, Slovenes, Magyars, Serbs, Croats, Slovaks, and Rumanians. They held this polyglot empire together only by the ties of a common ruler, a loyal army, and a faithful body of administrators. The principles of liberalism and nationalism set in motion by the French Revolution and the Napoleonic period menaced the authority of the dynasty and the integrity of the state. The Austrian government attempted to combat the danger threatening the empire by maintaining an elaborate system of espionage, carefully restricting the entrance of foreigners into the country and the travel of Austrian subjects abroad, rigorous censorship of the press, and strict supervision of the activities of Austrian university professors and their students. This political system was in force in the Austrian Empire until the overthrow of Metternich in 1848.

Inasmuch as the empire included provinces inhabited by Italians and Germans, the Austrian government also watched anxiously for signs of Liberal and nationalist movements in Italy and Germany and took precautionary measures against them. In 1815 it persuaded the rulers of Modena, Parma, and Tuscany to submit to an Austrian protectorate, and concluded an offensive and defensive alliance with the government of the Kingdom of the Two Sicilies, which pledged its timorous, reactionary ruler to follow in the conduct of both domestic and foreign affairs, policies in harmony with those adopted by the Austrian government. These various agreements extended the repressive system in force in Austria to all the states and provinces of the Italian peninsula except the Kingdom of Sardinia and the Papal States, but they could not erase from the minds and hearts of the awakened middle class of Italy the memories of the freedom and opportunity they had enjoyed during the Napoleonic period.

In Germany the Liberals by their excesses finally furnished Metternich the arguments necessary to persuade the sovereigns of the new

German Confederation to adopt the Austrian system of repression. In 1817 a group of exuberant German students celebrated the anniversary of the battle of Leipzig and the posting of the famous theses of Luther by solemnly burning various symbols of the hated Ancien Régime. Two years later a fanatical student, named Karl Sand, assassinated August Kotzebue, who was accused by the Liberals of being an agent of the Tsar. These episodes made it easy for Metternich to convince the Conservative governments of the confederation of a gigantic revolutionary plot against the existing order of society. With the Prussian government, accordingly, he convoked a meeting of representatives of the leading German governments at Carlsbad, for the purpose of devising methods for crushing the Liberal movement in the states of the German Confederation.

Their deliberations resulted in the drawing up of the famous Carlsbad Decrees of 1819. These aimed to establish a close supervision of the professors and students in the German universities, to shackle the German press, and to create a central committee for the investigation of revolutionary plots. With the aid of the states represented at the Carlsbad Conference, Metternich then forced the diet of the German Confederation to adopt the Carlsbad resolutions. The conclusion of the treaties with the various Italian states and the adoption of these decrees seemed to establish on a firm basis in central Europe the Austrian policy of reaction against the principles of the French Revolution.

II

THE REACTION OF GREAT BRITAIN TO THE FRENCH REVOLUTION AND THE NAPOLEONIC RÉGIME

At first many inhabitants of Great Britain sympathized with the revolutionary movement in France. They believed the French people to be on the point of setting up a constitutional system patterned after that of Great Britain, and they hoped that the adoption of British institutions in France would draw the French and British governments closer together. In some English towns the friends of the French Revolution organized clubs for the spread of the revolutionary principles. This agitation among the English lower classes and the excesses of the revolutionary leaders in France, however, soon killed the sympathy the British upper classes may have felt at first for the revolution, and replaced it with a feeling of alarm.

This change of sentiment strengthened the Conservative and reactionary forces in Great Britain. The responsible British political leaders abandoned all thought of political reform and adopted measures to protect Great Britain from the revolutionary infection. At their initiative the British government suspended the Habeas Corpus Act, put down even lawful agitation, passed an Alien Act enabling the government to deport suspected foreigners, imprisoned many leaders of the revolutionary clubs, and made the utterance of words against the authority of the King an act of treason, and the excitement of hatred against the government or the constitution a misdemeanor.

This feeling against the French Revolution explains in part the entrance of Great Britain in 1793 into the struggle of the Continental powers against France. From that date onward Great Britain became the backbone of the opposition to French aggression. Its financial resources subsidized the armies of the states of the Continent. Its fleets exerted a steady pressure on France and its allies. The British military forces contributed materially to the defeat of the Napoleonic armies in Spain and Portugal and at the battle of Waterloo.

The conclusion of peace in 1815 did little to allay the fears of the British governing classes. Impoverished Europe bought as little as possible from British manufacturers and merchants. The resulting economic depression and the reduction of the army and the navy to a peace footing swelled the numbers of the unemployed in the towns and the cities. Bad harvests threw many agricultural laborers out of work. The Corn Laws made wheat high and dear. The rapid introduction of machinery in industry depressed the status of many British artisans. The resulting economic and social distress gave rise to a great popular movement that expressed itself in rioting, in the breaking of the new machines, in great popular meetings, and in a demand for universal suffrage.

The Conservative classes in control of the British government, however, could think of no cure for the troubles of the country except further repression. They saw in every riot the ramifications of a gigantic revolutionary plot. In an effort to protect the existing social order they again suspended the Habeas Corpus Act, restricted the right of assembly, limited the freedom of the press, and made free use of military force to suppress political agitation and social disorder. This policy of repression culminated in the Peterloo Massacre and the Six Acts. Without warning, the military rode into a peaceful assembly at Manchester, killing about half a dozen of its members and wounding some two hundred other persons. In their panic the Prince Regent and his ministers actually approved of the barbarous conduct of the military authorities, and Parliament passed six additional repressive measures. These Six Acts speeded up judicial procedure, prohibited military drill and the bearing of arms, and restricted freedom of the press and of assembly.

The reaction against the conscription, the heavy taxation, the economic policy, and the disregard for the rights of states and peoples incident to the Napoleonic régime swung European society back toward the Ancien Régime. The peoples of Spain, Austria, Russia, and Germany forgot the advantages of the rule of Napoleon and overthrew his empire. In spite of the high hopes of the Liberals of Europe, however, these national and popular risings gave control of Europe again to men born during the Ancien Régime and imbued with its ideals. Although unable to force the institutions and conditions of the eighteenth century upon the generation that had grown up in Europe since 1789, these restored leaders reëstablished a Conservative régime. Their political ideals found expression in the decisions of the Congress of Vienna in 1815, the political program of the Ultraroyalists, who came to power in France in 1822, the system of Metternich in Austria, the treaties concluded in 1815 between Austria and the Italian states, the Carlsbad Decrees of 1819 in the German Confederation, and the Peterloo Massacre and the Six Acts in Great Britain.

CHAPTER III

Events in southern Europe soon confirmed the worst fears of the European Conservatives. In 1820 a series of revolutions, born of the agitation of secret societies and the misgovernment of the restored sovereigns, broke out in that region and engrossed the attention of the conservative rulers of Europe for several years. The revolutionary movement started in Spain and spread to Italy and Portugal.

I

THE SPANISH REVOLUTION OF 1820

In Spain the revolutionary movement began in the army. The despotic, inefficient government of the bigoted, sensual Ferdinand fed all its military forces poorly, sheltered them miserably, and paid them irregularly. The soldiers who were assembled at Cadiz for service against the rebellious colonists of Spain in America had especial reasons for bitterness. They heard fearful tales of hardship and suffering from the returning wounded and invalids and came to feel that they were about to be sent to certain death.

Agents of the revolting American colonies and of the revolutionary society of Cadiz which secretly kept alive the Liberal traditions of 1812 exploited the situation in the expeditionary force. On New Year's Day, 1820, they stirred two military detachments to rise in revolt against the royal government. The rebellious troops proclaimed the Spanish constitution of 1812, replaced the officials of the government with their own appointees, and summoned the inhabitants of the region to join the revolutionary movement.

At first the rising met with little success. The detachment commanded by Colonel Quiroga made an unsuccessful attempt to capture Cadiz. The revolutionary forces lacked cavalry and artillery, the inhabitants of the region surrounding Cadiz failed to respond to the summons of the revolutionary leaders, and their faint-hearted troops began to slink away. In order to rouse the Spanish people from their apathy and to procure food and clothing for his troops, the ambitious Colonel Riego, commander of the second detachment, marched his troops along the coast toward Malaga and then northward in the direction of Cordoba. Failing to obtain the support of either the civilian population or the military garrisons of southern Spain, he finally disbanded his dwindling forces in the mountains between Andalusia and Estremadura. This action seemed to mark the end of the revolution.

In spite of its censorship of the press, however, the Spanish government could not keep the news of the rising in southern Spain from reaching the ears of the upper middle class in northern Spain. The little secret revolutionary societies, the Freemasons, the former deputies of the Cortes that had drafted the Spanish constitution of 1812, the dismissed officials of the Napoleonic régime, the relatives of the victims of the political reaction that set in after 1814, and military conspirators still cherished the ideals of the French Revolution and began to bestir themselves. In February revolutionary elements at Corunna and neighboring cities of Galicia proclaimed the constitution of 1812. In the following month the Liberals at Barcelona and Zaragoza took similar action. In many instances men of moderate opinions put themselves at the head of the revolutionary movements in the interest of the monarchy.

The reports from northern Spain set the populace of Madrid in motion. The inhabitants of the capital began to sing revolutionary songs in the streets, to cheer for the constitution of 1812 under the windows of the royal ministers, and to threaten the royal palace. The troops stationed in the city showed signs of being on the point of mutiny. These developments frightened the King into taking an oath of allegiance to the constitution of 1812 and sharing his power with a provisional committee until the assembling of the promised Cortes. These concessions put the hitherto persecuted Liberals again in control of the government.

Under their leadership the government instituted a series of reforms. The King immediately issued decrees abolishing the seigniorial courts, organizing a national militia for the defense of the revolution, disbanding the expeditionary force assembled at Cadiz, and remedying some of the more pressing complaints of the troops. After it assembled the Cortes voted to confiscate about two thirds of the vast domain in the hands of the Church, in order to relieve the finances, which had been severely impaired by war and misgovernment; closed many of the monasteries; subjected the remainder to the authority of the Spanish bishops; suppressed the Jesuit order in Spain; placed on sale the property of both the Jesuits and the Inquisition; forbade the amassing of ecclesiastical offices in the hands of a single individual; put the clergy under the jurisdiction of the secular courts; abolished interior customs lines, and did away with succession by primogeniture. By these bold measures the revolutionary leaders alienated the nobles and the clergy and their supporters among the lower classes.

2

THE PORTUGUESE REVOLUTION

The success of the Spanish Liberals incited the discontented Portuguese to revolt. During the Napoleonic period the Portuguese royal family fled to Brazil, leaving Portugal largely under British military forces. After the restoration of peace in 1815 a British general, Marshal Beresford, continued to command the Portuguese army and to exercise a sort of dictatorship over the Regency appointed by the absent King. The Regent feared that the maintenance of the large army built up by the British commander would ruin the country, and the Portuguese soldiers complained of the harsh discipline enforced by their British officers, of their poor food, and of the failure of the government to pay them promptly. The growing discontent caused Marshal Beresford to sail to Brazil to explain conditions to the absent King and to ask him for greater powers.

During his absence a revolutionary movement against his rule broke out at Oporto. Its leaders read to the troops drawn up before the statehouse a political program that called for the establishment of a provisional government, the summoning of a Cortes, the drawing up of a constitution, and the maintenance of the authority of the Catholic religion and of the royal family. They thereupon dismissed the British officers and satisfied the other pressing demands of the army. Once under way, the revolutionary movement spread rapidly. Garrison after garrison declared for the revolution and the timid Regent finally promised to summon the Cortes. After the regiments stationed at Lisbon revolted, the Regency surrendered its authority to a provisional committee.

As soon as they were in power the Portuguese Liberals set to work at the task of reforming the country. They adopted a constitution closely modeled after the Spanish constitution of 1812, limited the number of novices that could be accepted by Portuguese monasteries, suppressed ecclesiastical privileges, abolished the Inquisition, threatened to sell the lands of the Church, and did away with seigniorial dues and the hunting rights of the noble landholders. The arrival of the King at Lisbon to take the oath of allegiance to the new constitution seemed to assure the permanence of the new reforms.

3

THE REVOLUTION IN THE KINGDOM OF THE TWO SICILIES

The revolutionary movement likewise spread to the Kingdom of the Two Sicilies. During the Napoleonic period the rigorous rule of Murat caused the growth in Naples of a secret political society known as the Carbonari. After 1815 the despotism and misgovernment of the restored Bourbons kept the organization alive. The society gained adherents among members of the commercial and professional classes, ex-officials of the Napoleonic régime, discontented army officers, and the recently organized militia. Upon hearing of the success of the Spanish Liberals, the leaders of the Carbonari began to plan a similar rising in southern Italy.

In its earlier stages the revolutionary movement in the Kingdom of the Two Sicilies closely resembled the one in Spain. Irritated by the strict discipline maintained by a new commander, a small band of regular troops in the regular army raised the standard of revolt early in July, 1820, marched to the headquarters of General Florestano Pepe, an officer whose pride had been wounded by the King, and asked him to assume the leadership of the revolutionary movement. Upon hearing of the action of this military detachment, the Carbonari of the neighboring districts rose in revolt, other garrisons joined the revolution, General Pepe decided to throw in his lot with the revolutionists, and representatives of the people of the city of Naples appeared at the royal palace and demanded a constitution. The spread of the revolutionary movement and the seemingly universal demand for a constitution finally caused the cowardly, trembling King and his advisers to proclaim the Spanish constitution of 1812, subject to such modifications as an elected parliament should see fit to propose. A few days later General Pepe, at the head of his troops, made a triumphal entry into the city of Naples, and a provisional committee, composed of administrators trained during the Napoleonic period, took control of the government. Under its influence the government freed all persons imprisoned on account of their political opinions, lowered the price of salt, abolished the exceptional military courts, and allowed a large group of newspapers to spring up. In the middle of July the King voluntarily took an oath of allegiance to the constitution.

The inhabitants of the island of Sicily, however, failed to follow the leadership of the Neapolitan Liberals. The Sicilians had long cherished the ideal of independence from the mainland. Consequently when the news of revolution at Naples reached the island, the royal troops and some of the garrison towns declared for the Spanish constitution of 1812, but the majority of the Sicilians, led by the inhabitants of

Palermo, proclaimed the Sicilian constitution of 1812. They owed this constitutional document to the efforts of a few self-sacrificing nobles and William Bentinck, the commander of the British troops stationed in Sicily during the Napoleonic period for the protection of the Neapolitan court. As a result of the action of the Sicilians the Liberals of the Kingdom of the Two Sicilies failed to coöperate in the crisis produced by the intervention of Austria.

4

THE INTERVENTION OF AUSTRIA IN NAPLES

As long as the revolutionary movement had been confined to the Iberian peninsula, Metternich, the Austrian Chancellor, had shown little interest in the suggestions of Tsar Alexander concerning the intervention of the European powers. As soon as the revolutionary movement spread to southern Italy, however, Metternich became alarmed lest it should destroy the Austrian hegemony in the peninsula and possibly jeopardize even the unity of the Austrian Empire. In order to avert the threatening danger, he strengthened the military forces maintained by Austria in Italy and suddenly took up the plan for a conference of the European powers.

As a result of the sudden conversion of the Austrian Chancellor, representatives of the five great powers—Austria, Russia, Prussia, France, and Great Britain—assembled at the little town of Troppau in Austrian Silesia. Completely cured by this time of his earlier Liberalism, Tsar Alexander I came prepared to offer the military resources of the immense Russian Empire for the suppression of the revolutionary movements in both the Iberian and the Italian peninsulas. Metternich wished merely the authorization of the European powers for an Austrian intervention in the Kingdom of the Two Sicilies. On the other hand, the representatives of Great Britain and France, in view of the constitutional and revolutionary traditions of their states, could not consistently approve of the intervention of the European powers in revolutionary movements that avowedly aimed at the establishment of constitutional governments, and they therefore refused to take an active part in the deliberations of the conference. The policy adopted by the two constitutional states forced the three absolute governments—Russia, Austria, and Prussia—to act alone. Their representatives at Troppau formulated the doctrine of their right to intervene in the domestic affairs of other European states in case a revolutionary movement should threaten the peace and order of their own states, and summoned the King of the Two Sicilies to meet them at a congress of the powers to be held at Laibach in southern Austria.

The Congress of Laibach met in January, 1821. At this new meeting of the representatives of the European powers the British government followed the same policy as at the Conference of Troppau. The French government changed its policy. As a result of the increasing influence of the Ultraroyalists in French politics and of a fear that the Italian peninsula would fall completely under the control of Austria, the government of France deserted its former position and instructed its representatives at Laibach to coöperate with the three absolute governments. The agent of the King of the Two Sicilies acted at the congress with characteristic duplicity. Although his master had taken a solemn oath to support the new constitution and had extorted the reluctant consent of the Neapolitan Liberals to the royal departure by the argument that he desired to defend the new constitutional régime in Naples, at the congress the representative of the King eagerly offered to abandon it on the flimsy pretext of sparing his country the horrors of war. Metternich had little difficulty, therefore, in persuading the Congress of Laibach to authorize Austrian intervention in the Kingdom of the Two Sicilies.

The Neapolitan Liberals offered only a slight resistance to the army sent by Austria to suppress the revolution at Naples. The policy followed by the Sicilians during the revolution immobilized a third of the Neapolitan troops. The militia lacked discipline and equipment and finally dissolved completely in the face of the approaching danger. General Pepe consequently found himself compelled to abandon his plans for defense and to allow the Austrian troops to enter the city of Naples.

The entrance of the Austrians into the Neapolitan capital put an end to the constitutional régime in the Kingdom of the Two Sicilies. At a safe distance from his duped subjects the forsworn Neapolitan sovereign nullified the acts of his Liberal ministers, appointed a notorious reactionary as minister of police, and imprisoned or drove into exile all who had played a conspicuous rôle in the revolution. When the leaders of the Liberals were safely out of the way, the King finally ventured back to his capital. For several years, however, he retained a contingent of Austrian troops in his kingdom to prevent a new revolutionary outbreak by his subjects.

5

THE REVOLUTION OF 1821 IN THE KINGDOM OF SARDINIA

Just as the Austrian forces were finishing the task of suppressing the constitutional régime in the Kingdom of the Two Sicilies, a similar revolutionary movement broke out in the province of Piedmont in the

Kingdom of Sardinia. The revolution was the work of a group of Liberals who had won adherents even among the army officers surrounding Charles Albert, a member of the royal family destined to mount the Sardinian throne upon the death of two elderly relatives. The conspirators had national as well as Liberal aims. They set as their goal not only the concession of the Spanish constitution of 1812 but also the expulsion of Austria from the Italian peninsula, an indispensable preliminary step toward the unification of Italy. They failed to take into consideration the lethargy of the Italian middle class, the military strength of their opponents, and the unfavorable European situation.

The conspirators hoped at first to persuade Charles Albert to place himself at the head of the revolutionary movement. For a moment the prince promised to coöperate. Upon reflection, however, he changed his mind, informed the conspirators that they could not count on him, and warned the Minister of War of the plot. Thereupon the revolutionary leaders attempted to call off the proposed rising, but their messengers arrived at Alessandria too late to forestall the seizure of the citadel by a band of military and civilian revolutionists and the unfurling of the tricolor flag of the Kingdom of Italy. At the news of this rising the Liberal leaders at Turin made a belated effort to carry out their original revolutionary plans.

The King of Sardinia proved to be a ruler of far different character from his royal brother at Naples. Upon learning of the rising in his state, he abdicated in favor of his brother and temporarily handed over the administration of the Sardinian government to his nephew, Charles Albert. The new Regent pursued a weak and ambiguous course. He proclaimed the Spanish constitution of 1812, subject to the approval of the new sovereign and a promised parliament, but he refused to abandon the use of the flag of the Kingdom of Sardinia and accorded the envoys of the Liberals of Milan a cool reception. As soon as he heard of the course of events in Piedmont, Charles Felix, the new sovereign, declared null and void all acts of the provisional government that did not receive his approval, and instructed Charles Albert to retire from Turin with the loyal troops.

As soon as the Congress of Laibach heard of this new revolutionary movement, it authorized the Austrian government to intervene with its armed forces in the Kingdom of Sardinia. After the loyal Sardinian troops had made a serious but unsuccessful effort to crush the rising in Piedmont, an Austrian army crossed the border and rapidly suppressed the revolutionary movement. The Sardinian government used the victory won by the Austrian army with the greatest moderation.

6

FRENCH INTERVENTION IN SPAIN

Before the Congress of Laibach broke up, the representatives of the powers decided to meet in 1822 to discuss the affairs of Italy. By the time this proposed Congress of Verona assembled, however, the Spanish question had pushed all other international problems into the background. All the European Conservatives felt that Ferdinand VII of Spain should be freed from the close supervision of the Spanish Liberals and that the revolting colonies of Spain should be brought back under control. The Tsar urged that his troops should be permitted to accord the Spanish Liberals the same treatment that the Italian Liberals had just received, but the other Conservative powers feared to see Russian troops intervene in Spain.

The French Ultraroyalists finally proposed an acceptable solution for the delicate Spanish problem. Hoping by a successful military intervention in Spain to restore the prestige of Louis XVIII and their own party, they offered the services of the French army to the absolute governments of Europe. When the French troops invaded Spain in 1823 the Spanish people failed to repeat the heroic exploits of the Napoleonic period. The peasants, the city rabble, the nobles, and the clergy greeted the French as their saviors from the hated innovations of the Spanish Liberals, and the weak, undisciplined, badly led, and poorly armed Spanish army offered little effective resistance. By the end of the year the Spanish Liberals had surrendered or taken flight and Ferdinand VII and his Conservative supporters had regained control of the country.

The victorious Spanish Conservatives took a drastic revenge upon their Liberal opponents. In many places ignorant mobs wreaked a shameful vengeance on the defeated Liberals. The regency set up at Madrid by the commander of the French troops declared null and void all loans negotiated by the Spanish government after the outbreak of the revolution. Upon his return to his capital, Ferdinand VII annulled all the acts of the revolutionary government and ignored the advice of the moderate French commander-in-chief concerning the granting of an amnesty and the conceding of guarantees for the future.

7

THE EFFECT ON PORTUGAL OF THE SUPPRESSION OF THE SPANISH REVOLT

The reports of the victory of the Spanish Conservatives precipitated a reactionary movement in Portugal. The Liberal government installed in Portugal by the revolutionary movement had failed to repress crime and to restore order in the finances. Its reform measures had alienated the sympathy of the nobles and the clergy. Its imperious decrees had led, in 1822, to a declaration of independence by its colony of Brazil. Its tariff policy had increased the price of bread and had consequently turned the common man against the Liberal movement. Therefore when the revolutionary government attempted to remove some army officers whom it mistrusted, a rising occurred which overthrew the Liberal régime in Portugal.

In 1820 the attempt of the European Conservatives to force a generation that had known the advantages of the French Revolution and the rule of Napoleon to return to many features of the Ancien Régime gave rise to a series of revolutions in southern Europe. The revolutionary movement began in Spain and spread to Portugal, the Kingdom of the Two Sicilies, and the Kingdom of Sardinia. In each state a small band of conspirators, aided by mutinous troops and popular mobs, intimidated the ruler of the state and his Conservative advisers into surrendering control of the government into the hands of the Liberals. In each state the Liberal leaders took the Spanish constitution of 1812 as a rallying-cry and inaugurated sweeping reforms which aroused the opposition of the nobles, the clergy, and the ignorant. Alarmed at the danger to the existing order, the three great absolute governments proclaimed, at the Conference of Troppau in 1820, their right to intervene in the domestic affairs of other states for the preservation of the social order. In 1821, at the Congress of Laibach, they authorized the intervention of Austria in the Kingdom of the Two Sicilies and the Kingdom of Sardinia. The next year, at the Congress of Verona, they accepted the offer of the French Ultraroyalists to suppress the revolutionary movement in Spain. In Portugal the Conservatives finally overthrew the Liberal government without assistance from outside. The first revolutionary protest of the European Liberals therefore ended in apparent failure.

CHAPTER IV

While the Liberals were fighting the Conservatives by conspiracies and sudden uprisings, far more powerful forces were at work modifying the conditions and institutions inherited from the Ancien Régime. Since the beginning of the modern period bold thinkers had been discovering the laws of nature. In the eighteenth century British mechanics and farmers began to make practical applications of the new scientific knowledge. They revolutionized industry by the introduction of machinery, the steam-engine, and new processes of manufacture, and transformed agriculture by new methods of managing the land, the introduction of new crops, and careful attention to the breeding of stock. After the close of the Napoleonic period these discoveries and inventions began to come into general use on the continent of Europe.

I

THE NEW BRITISH INVENTIONS

A number of conditions seem to have promoted the Industrial Revolution in Great Britain in the latter half of the eighteenth century. Religious persecution and devastating wars had driven to British shores thousands of craftsmen endowed with the slowly accumulated skill and ingenuity of the artisans of the continent of Europe. In northern and western England they found themselves free to experiment with new methods and processes of manufacture, unhampered by the restrictions of the gilds. At the same time the commercial expansion that followed the discovery of America and the new route to India created a demand for British goods and fostered the growth of new capital. The skill of British artisans, the freedom to experiment, the new markets for British commodities, and the possession of capital available for profitable investment all favored the development of new methods of manufacture.

The new inventions and processes of manufacture first affected the cotton industry. In 1733 John Kay contrived a fly-shuttle that made it possible for a weaver to dispense with the assistant formerly needed to throw the shuttle back across the warp. As the spinners never had been able to meet the demand for thread, the new device only made the situation of the weavers worse. Their predicament seems to have set a number of men to work on the problem of increasing the supply of thread. About 1766 an English artisan by the name of James Hargreaves invented a spinning-jenny, a machine operated by hand which spun eight threads at a time instead of one. Three years later Richard Arkwright, a shrewd, alert man of humble origin, patented a spinning device known as the water-frame, which really embodied the ideas of other men. Then in 1779 Samuel Crompton designed a spinning-mule which combined the best features of the machines of Hargreaves and Arkwright. These new devices enabled the spinners to produce more cotton thread than the weavers could use. This situation, in turn, set a clergyman of the name of Edmund Cartwright to thinking about the possibility of making a power-loom that would speed up the weaving process. Although he knew nothing about weaving, in 1785, he finally succeeded in inventing a power-loom which he gradually perfected and brought into general use. Before the close of the eighteenth century all stages in the transformation of the growing cotton into the finished cloth had been revolutionized. In 1793, Eli Whitney, an American, invented a cotton-gin that cleaned the picked cotton. Other inventive geniuses perfected carding-machines for straightening and preparing the cotton fibers for spinning, developed cylindrical presses for printing patterns on cotton cloth, and reduced the time required for bleaching cotton goods by applying the chemical discoveries of Karl Wilhelm Scheele and Pierre Berthelot. These new methods of production quickly gave Great Britain supremacy in the manufacture of cotton goods.

During the years that the textile industry was being transformed the methods of manufacturing iron and steel were undergoing a similar revolution. Early in the eighteenth century, possibly by the year 1709, a family of ironmasters by the name of Darby, engaged in the manufacture of pots and other objects made of cast-iron, succeeded in substituting the use of coke for charcoal in the smelting process. They probably owed their success to the use of a larger furnace and a better bellows than rival experimenters employed. As the century progressed the cheaper cast-iron produced by the new process gradually took the place of wood, copper, lead, brass, and in particular malleable iron. The new process of manufacture used a cheaper fuel and saved the highly skilled labor of the forge man. About 1763 John Smeaton completed the transformation of the smelting process by inventing blowing-cylinders that greatly improved the draft of the furnace used in smelting the ore.

About the middle of the eighteenth century Benjamin Huntsman began to experiment with cast-steel in the hope of finding better material for making pendulums and clock springs. About 1740 he hit upon the idea of placing small crucibles of clay filled with scraps of steel in a furnace heated by coke. The intense heat freed the metal of the particles of silicate or slag found in the best quality of iron or steel made by the older process. After the metal had been purified, long tongs removed the crucibles from the furnace and poured their contents into molds. After it had been removed from the molds the metal was forged into bars and slit into rods of a convenient size for the manufacture of cutlery and other objects of steel. In spite of his efforts to keep the new method a secret, the competitors of Huntsman soon learned the process of making cast-steel.

In 1766 two brothers by the name of Cranage took the first step toward revolutionizing the refining process by patenting a reverberatory furnace that heated the iron without bringing it into direct contact with the fuel and its impurities. Although it could not be used for all purposes, the new furnace came into general use during the next twenty years. In 1783 and 1784 Henry Cort completed the process of using coke in the refining of iron by developing methods of first puddling the molten metal and then rolling out the glowing masses of heated iron. His two inventions purified the metal of dross and cinders, saved much time, and greatly increased production.

The story of the transformation of the cotton and of the iron and steel industries illustrates the revolution that ultimately took place in all branches of British industry. The new machines and processes enabled British manufacturers to increase their output enormously and to undersell their competitors on the Continent. Their success gradually convinced British manufacturers in all lines of industry of the necessity of substituting complicated machinery and scientific methods for the human hand and a few simple tools.

The adoption of the new machinery in the textile and the metallurgical industries created a demand for a better motive power. The early cotton-manufacturers ran their spinning-factories with water-power, which did not prove altogether satisfactory. It varied in volume with the seasons and often compelled the manufacturers to locate their textile establishments, smelting-furnaces, and iron-foundries at points where labor was scarce. These defects soon caused them to experiment with the new steam-engine. Early in the eighteenth century Thomas Newcomen had developed a wasteful engine that could be used in pumping water out of mines. In 1762 James Watt, a skilled instrument-maker of Glasgow, began to work at the problem of improving the engine of Newcomen. After several years of experimentation he finally, with the aid of the capital, the skilled artisans, and the generous encouragement of Matthew Boulton, a wealthy manufacturer of Birmingham, developed the modern steam-engine. He added to the engine of Newcomen the separate condenser, the steam-jacket, a cylinder closed at both ends, and lubrication with oil and tallow. About 1775 the engine developed by the two partners began to be used for pumping water from mines, running the textile machinery, and operating the new blowing, forging, rolling, and slitting machines. Two of the earliest users of the new engine of Watt were Richard Arkwright, the founder of the factory system, and John Wilkinson, the greatest of the early ironmasters.

The rapid multiplication of the new machines and engines was made possible by the development of automatic machinery. For twenty years Watt and Boulton specified that the cylinders and other important parts of the engines that they erected should be made by John Wilkinson, who had invented a machine for boring cannon accurately. During the first decades of the nineteenth century inventors developed and brought into general use the planing-machine for producing a smooth, flat surface, the screw-lathe for making a perfect circle, the slide-lathe for automatically cutting a cylinder, and the steam-hammer for shaping glowing masses of hot metal. These delicate instruments of precision enabled the iron and steel masters of England to meet the new demands made upon them.

2

THE RISE OF THE FACTORY SYSTEM

The development of the new machines and of the steam-engine also led to the growth of factories. Before the Industrial Revolution a master usually carried on his petty industry in his own house or cottage, or a tiny establishment. After the introduction of steam-power and machinery the workman no longer owned the equipment with which he worked. The capitalist, who owned the new engines and machines, found it safer and more economical to set them up in a large establishment where he could carefully supervise their operation. This organization of industry affected in many ways the economic and the social life of England.

3

MINING AND TRANSPORTATION

The development of the steam-engine and the new methods of manufacture likewise tended to promote mining. Before the Industrial Revolution Great Britain consumed very little coal and iron. The transformation of industrial methods led to a great expansion of the mining industry. By 1788 the production of iron ore had risen from eighteen thousand to sixty-eight thousand tons. By the end of the century the output of the coal-mines of England had mounted to ten million tons annually.

The Industrial Revolution also created a demand for improved transportation and communication. The self-sufficing estates of the Ancien Régime hardly needed continuous contact with the rest of the world. The master of a craft usually found his raw material and the market for his finished product in his own neighborhood. As a consequence peddlers and messengers, toiling on foot or on horseback along roads well-nigh impassable much of the time, supplied the modest needs of gentleman, burgher, and peasant. The new factories, on the contrary, demanded great quantities of raw material, often drawn from distant markets, and produced far more than the immediate vicinity could consume. This situation gave rise to a remarkable development of canals, roads, and railroads, the application of steam-power on land and water, the modernization of the post-office, and the invention of the telegraph, the oceanic cable, the telephone, the automobile, the airplane, and wireless communication.

Not until 1759 did England begin to build its first canal. In that year the Duke of Bridgewater commissioned James Brindley, an ingenious millwright, to construct an artificial waterway that would connect his coal-mines with the city of Manchester. The opening of the new canal immediately cut in half the price of coal in that market. The mine-owners and manufacturers of central England promptly recognized the advantages of the new waterway in reducing the cost of transporting their products and in broadening their markets, and soon covered central England with a network of navigable canals.

The agitation for improved roads really began before the Industrial Revolution. The growth of London and other English cities, due to the development of commerce, gave rise to a demand for better means of transportation between these urban centers and the agricultural regions from which they drew their food supplies. The rising of 1745 in the Scottish Highlands convinced the British military authorities of the need for better roads. About 1800 the agitation for better highways began to have definite results. The new roads built in Great Britain after that date are inseparably associated with the names of two engineers, Thomas Telford and John McAdam. Both men stressed the importance of thorough drainage, carefully prepared materials, and the sloping of roads from the center toward the sides. Telford gave great attention to the foundation of his roads. McAdam contended that the subsoil would carry any weight if properly drained and covered with an impervious surface. The new roads constructed under the supervision of these men shortened the time and increased the comfort of travel and contributed greatly toward breaking down the isolation of the English villages and country houses.

The development of the stationary steam-engine early suggested the application of steam-power to the propulsion of ships and land vehicles.

Although several of his contemporaries contend with him for the honor of having invented the steamboat, Robert Fulton, an American, certainly first demonstrated the practical value of using steam to drive vessels through the water. In 1807 a steamboat built by him covered the one hundred and fifty miles between New York and Albany in thirty-two hours. After this spectacular voyage the steamboat came into use rapidly in both America and Europe. In 1815 steamers began to ply regularly between London and Glasgow. In 1821 they came into use between Dover and Calais, and two years later between Dublin and Liverpool. In the following year British promoters organized the General Steam Navigation Company to develop trade with the Continent.

In the meantime steam-power began the conquest of the ocean. In 1819 the *Savannah,* a small sailing-packet equipped with both sails and a tiny engine, crossed the Atlantic from the United States to Great Britain using steam-power eighteen of the twenty-three days required for the voyage. In 1833 a vessel driven entirely by steam crossed from Canada to England. In the same decade the cities of London, Bristol, and Liverpool suddenly began to realize the practical value of steam-power, and groups of capitalists in each of the three ports organized steamship companies for promoting steam navigation across the Atlantic Ocean. In 1838, consequently, four steamers reached New York from England, the first arriving after a voyage of seventeen days. Shortly afterwards the Cunard Company inaugurated a regular service with faster ships.

About 1804 Englishmen commenced to experiment with steam-driven land vehicles. In 1825 a railway-line seven miles in length was built from Stockton to Darlington. Upon the advice of George Stephenson, the engineer of the line, the owners experimented with steam-power. The first engine drew a train of thirty-four light cars at a speed of fifteen miles per hour and carried a gross load of ninety tons. From the first passengers insisted on being carried by the new means of transportation, and the company was forced to run a daily coach. Within the next few years several other short lines were constructed.

The steam-railway, however, did not really catch the imagination of the British people until the opening of the line between Manchester and Liverpool. In October, 1829, three locomotives competed over a finished section of the new railroad for a prize of five hundred pounds. Two of the competing engines broke down, but in the presence of a large crowd of people the *Rocket* designed by George and Robert Stephenson fully demonstrated the practicability of the steam-railway. After its completion, the railroad from Manchester to Liverpool succeeded beyond expectation. During the next decade one thousand three hundred and thirty-one miles of railway were constructed, and London was connected with every corner of England. Between 1840 and 1850 Great Britain experienced a veritable railway-building mania that increased the mileage of English railways by over five thousand miles.

The establishment of large-scale industrial enterprises stimulated improvements in communication. In 1840 the British postal service responded to the new demands made upon it by introducing penny postage. By this system it carried mail-matter for a fixed price regardless of the distance to be covered. By the old method the cost of sending communications through the post-office varied with both the weight and the distance.

Almost simultaneously the electric telegraph made its appearance. In 1832 an American artist, Samuel F. B. Morse, who had made studies in chemistry and electricity, conceived the idea of a magnetic telegraph that would convey sound-signals by breaking an electric circuit. In 1838 he demonstrated his device before the President of the United States and his cabinet, and finally he obtained from Congress an appropriation which enabled him to continue his experiments. As a result of the success of an experimental line between Washington and Baltimore a company was organized in 1844 for the construction of a commercial telegraph-line between New York and Washington, and other lines soon began to be constructed in both the United States and Europe.

After speeding up the transmission of messages on land, inventors and promoters began to attack the problem of accelerating communication by sea. In 1851 Calais and Dover were connected by submarine cable. Fifteen years later, after a number of attempts had failed, the Atlantic Ocean was successfully spanned by cable from Ireland to Newfoundland.

4

THE SOCIAL AND POLITICAL EFFECTS OF THE INDUSTRIAL REVOLUTION

The transformation of the economic life of Great Britain brought in its train a host of social and political changes. The center of population soon commenced to shift from the south and east to the north and west of England. The new factories and furnaces developed near the water-power and the deposits of coal and iron, and the workers followed them. The population of the south and east stood still or actually declined, while that of the north and west of England grew by leaps and bounds.

The Industrial Revolution, moreover, caused a concentration as well as a shifting of population. Before the development of the new mechanical inventions and technical processes, a large proportion of the artisans lived in rural regions and supplemented the income derived from their crafts by working a few acres of ground. With the establishment of the new factories the workers began to crowd into hastily constructed factory towns and industrial quarters, where in order to be near their work they lived huddled in flimsy houses on narrow, congested, insanitary streets. This movement of the population caused the growth of factory towns like those of Lancashire and of great industrial cities like Manchester, Birmingham, Sheffield, and Glasgow.

The development of the new industries also created new social classes. The new engines and machinery required a considerable amount of capital and skilful management. The shrewd and the fortunate became owners and managers of the new industrial establishments and swelled the ranks of the rising middle class. Their employees, recruited from the declining yeomen, agricultural laborers, mountaineers from Wales and Scotland, and poverty-stricken peasants from Ireland, became a propertyless, wage-earning proletariat at the mercy of their employers and the governing classes.

At first the upper classes shamefully exploited the new proletariat. They installed the new machinery in old buildings and hastily constructed factories that lacked the simplest devices for the protection of the health and the limbs of the workers. They replaced men with women and children, because these had nimbler fingers and were cheaper and more docile, and often subjected them to brutal taskmasters. When orders pressed, the new employing class worked even children six, seven, and eight years of age as high as sixteen hours a day. They did little at first to improve the sanitary conditions of the new factory towns and industrial quarters.

Both the new members of the middle class and the new proletariat soon began to demand a voice in political affairs. The new industrial regions in the north and west of England felt that they were more deserving of representation in Parliament than towns long buried beneath the waters of the North Sea or deserted villages in somnolent Cornwall. The industrial capitalist desired a place in political life beside the merchant and the landowner. The champions of the new proletariat regarded universal suffrage as a sovereign remedy against exploitation. By 1832 the two classes were strong enough to force the Conservatives of Great Britain to give some heed to their political demands.

5

THE INDUSTRIAL REVOLUTION ON THE CONTINENT

During the French Revolution and the Napoleonic period Great Britain demonstrated to the continent of Europe the importance of the Industrial Revolution. In spite of the enormous financial strain which they had undergone, the British people emerged from the struggle far richer than they had been at the beginning. After the reëstablishment of peace, consequently, the more advanced countries of continental Europe began to renew their experiments with the new industrial methods and to introduce the new engines, machinery, and technical processes that had enabled Great Britain to maintain the struggle against Napoleon and the resources of the Continent.

The Napoleonic struggle had hardly closed when the Belgian provinces of the Kingdom of the Netherlands began to introduce the new British inventions and methods of manufacture. As early as 1813 a steam-engine was built in the Belgian provinces, and during the subsequent decade steam rapidly came into use as a motive power. During the years from 1820 to 1830 the use of coke in smelting, the puddling-furnace, and the rolling-mill crossed the English Channel and modernized the Belgian iron and steel industry. In the next ten years lathes, planing-mills, and slotting-machines followed. As in England, the coming of the new engines and machines into general use caused a great development of coal-mining. By 1835 the Belgian mines employed thirty thousand men. This industrial development undoubtedly accentuated the economic differences between the Dutch and the Belgian provinces of the Kingdom of the Netherlands and constituted one of the causes of their separation in 1830.

The industrialization of the Belgian provinces was also accompanied by improvements in transportation. As soon as peace was signed in 1815, the government resumed work on the Belgian roads and private capitalists promoted a number of new canals. In 1834 the new Belgian government began work on a system of state railways, planned to radiate from Malines as a center toward Ostend, Antwerp, Cologne, and Paris. The new railroads greatly stimulated the movement of population. The first line to be completed ran from Malines to Brussels. Shortly before 1830 the Dutch government estimated that seventy-five thousand persons traveled annually in vehicles between the two points. During the first eight months of its operation the railway carried about half a million passengers between the two cities. By 1850 Belgium had finished its main lines of railway.

In France the spinning-jenny made its appearance before the outbreak of the French Revolution. By the opening of the nineteenth century it had begun to drive out the old-fashioned spinning-wheel. During the Napoleonic wars the blockade maintained by Great Britain fostered the establishment of little spinning-mills in Lille, Alsace, and other districts. In 1820 French cotton-spinners began to use steam-power to operate the new machinery. Not until about 1833, however, could the French spinners successfully compete with British manufacturers. By 1848 the factory system was well established in the cotton industry of France. In other branches of the French textile industry the new machinery came into use very slowly. French inventors, however, contributed toward the revolutionizing of the textile industry by the invention of flax-spinning machinery and the development of the Jacquard loom for weaving complex silk patterns.

France adopted the new methods and machines of the British iron and steel industry very slowly. In 1830 she had only twenty smelting-furnaces that used coke. Sixteen years later she still smelted half of her iron ore with charcoal. The steam-engine also came into general use very tardily. In 1832, at a time when England had over fifteen thousand steam-engines with a total of three hundred and seventy-five thousand horse-power, France had only five hundred and twenty-five steam-engines with a total of nine thousand horse-power. As late as 1847 she had only about ten times this number of steam-engines, with a total of sixty-two thousand horse-power.

After the restoration of peace in 1815, France, like the Belgian provinces, began to improve her transportation facilities. During the fifteen years that the restored Bourbons ruled the state she added one thousand kilometers to her canal system and extended and repaired the fine system of roads that had been built before the outbreak of the French Revolution. Between 1830 and 1848 France doubled the mileage of her roads in good repair. Although a few short lines of railroad were constructed after 1828 for the transportation of commodities by horse-power, the conveyance of passengers by steam-power did not begin in France until 1833. Eight years later, at a time when England had three thousand eight hundred miles of railroad, the total length of the French railways was only eight hundred and eighty-five kilometers. In 1842 the French government finally adopted a comprehensive plan providing for the construction of six state-owned lines of railway radiating from Paris as a center. By the end of 1847 one thousand eight hundred and thirty kilometers of the proposed system had been built and put into operation. By that time passengers could travel from Paris to Brussels or Tours.

The Industrial Revolution hardly affected Germany until after 1840. During the Napoleonic period little spinning-mills sprang up temporarily in the Ruhr region, along the Rhine, and in Bavaria and Saxony. As late as 1840, however, every German peasant family still spun its own flax and wool and often owned or rented a loom. The textile establishments enumerated in the contemporary statistical works hardly deserved to have the term factory applied to them. At that date the cotton-spinning mills of Prussia averaged only one hundred and seven spindles, the three linen-weaving establishments of Berlin employed in all fourteen persons, the three factories for the spinning of wool and the four plants for the manufacture of woolen cloth gave work on an average to only twenty-five persons. As late as 1846 only 14 per cent of the furnaces of Prussia used coke for the smelting of iron ore. The large-scale plants of Silesia and Westphalia for the smelting of iron and the manufacture of iron and steel products were not established until after 1850.

The political organization of Germany long interfered seriously with the development of its railway system. As early as 1803 an official of Electoral Hesse patented a steam-engine designed to propel vehicles on land, but he found no opportunity to demonstrate the value of his model. By 1814 scattered individuals in Germany began to make proposals for the building of railroads. These schemes, however, encountered the almost insuperable hostility of the bureaucracies of the separate German states. As a result a line, covering the short distance between Fürth and Nuremberg, was not actually constructed and put in operation in Germany until 1835. By 1846, however, Berlin, Cologne, and Frankfort had become centers of considerable networks of railroad-lines, and passengers could travel by rail from Berlin to such points as Stettin, Breslau, Leipzig, and Hamburg. Shortly after the middle of the nineteenth century the various German systems began to be connected with each other and with the railway-lines of the surrounding states.

6

THE ENGLISH AGRICULTURAL REVOLUTION

While ingenious British inventors and mechanics were revolutionizing industry by the introduction of the steam-engine, machinery, and new technical processes, British landlords and farmers were transforming the methods employed in English and Scottish agriculture.

After 1700 English gentlemen making the usual grand tour of western Europe commenced to observe the agricultural methods and practices of the Continent. In northern Italy, Provence, Flanders, and parts of the United Netherlands they found the cultivators of the soil utilizing all their land each year, rotating their crops, feeding their cattle scientifically, fertilizing and draining their fields, and growing crops not raised in England. Upon their return to their English estates they tried to introduce on their own lands what they had seen abroad. They began to cultivate their fields with the Dutch plow and the horse-hoe of Languedoc. They no longer left a large portion of their lands lying fallow each year. They introduced the clover of Spain, the grasses of France and Burgundy, and the turnips of Flanders. By the adoption of these new implements, methods, and crops they set in motion a veritable agricultural revolution.

The first pioneer in better methods of tillage was Jethro Tull (1674–1741). After being educated at Oxford and Gray's Inn he followed the fashion of the day for English gentlemen and made the grand tour of the Continent. Even before he went abroad he had shown his interest in agriculture by the invention of a drill for the sowing of seed. This device sowed the seed in regular rows and covered it with earth, doing away with the wasteful custom of broadcasting the seed by hand. The new method of sowing used less seed and produced a larger crop. Upon his return from his tour of the Continent he began to pulverize his arable fields by frequently cultivating them with the horse-hoe. By the adoption of this new method he hoped to avoid the necessity of fertilizing the soil with manure and thus eliminate one of the principal causes of weeds. His ideas, however, delayed planting too long and subjected the growing grain to rusts. His accounts of his efforts exercised considerable influence on later English and French experimenters.

A famous contemporary of Jethro Tull was Charles Townshend (1674–1738). After a distinguished career in British politics he devoted the last eight years of his life to the improvement of his Norfolk estate. He furthered the enclosure movement, practised marling, and planted clover and turnips. Through his warm advocacy of the advantages of planting the vegetable he won for himself the sobriquet of Turnip Townshend. His efforts greatly raised the level of farming practice in one of the poorest counties of England.

The English pioneer in the breeding of improved sheep and cattle was Robert Bakewell (1725–1790). On the farm of four hundred and forty acres which he inherited from his father he applied to sheep and cattle the methods long employed in the breeding of dogs. He chose good stock, kept his animals warm and clean and treated them kindly, bred within the flock and herd, and carefully selected the qualities that he desired to emphasize. By the use of his methods he doubled the weight of his sheep and cattle and improved the quality of their flesh. His Leicestershire sheep and longhorn cattle became famous, but his expenses for breeding, digging ditches, and building stables finally bankrupted him.

Many other members of the British nobility and gentry did notable service in disseminating the new ideas. The Duke of Bedford (1765–1802) paid great attention to animal husbandry and maintained a model farm at Woburn Abbey, where he held under his patronage sheepshearings, plowing contests, and exhibitions of cattle and sheep. Lord Somerville (1765–1819) bred fine merino sheep. Sir John Sinclair (1745–1835) introduced on his Scottish estate improved rotations of crops and better sheep. After two of his tenants had refused leases on ridiculously low terms, Lord Coke of Holkham (1752–1842) decided to try his own hand at farming. As a result of his experiments and observations he did much to transform the appearance and agricultural methods of western Norfolk.

The leader in calling the new methods of agriculture to the attention

of the British public was Arthur Young (1741–1820). In his volumi-
nous writings he sought to substitute for the naked fallows, open fields,
and small estates of the old agricultural régime a system of enclosed
fields, scientific rotation of crops, careful cultivation of the soil, and
selective breeding of cattle. Though he went too far in his denuncia-
tions of commons, open fields, and small holdings, his works found
many readers and aroused an unparalleled interest in agriculture.

This enthusiasm over the new methods of farming expressed itself
in the establishment of professorships in agriculture, the founding of
agricultural societies, and the starting of farm journals and magazines.
The first English magazine for farmers, a monthly, appeared in 1776;
the first weekly journal, in 1808. The first professorship of agriculture
was established at Edinburgh in 1790. The new interest in agriculture
also led to the founding of many local agricultural societies.

This agricultural revolution transformed the English country-side.
The small, scattered, intermingled holdings that characterized the estates
of the old agricultural régime prevented the landlords from introducing
the new methods of farming and stock-raising. In order to have their
holdings and farm animals under their own control they obtained from
Parliament authority to enclose their estates. This enabled the landlord
and his tenants to exchange their scattered arable strips, pieces of
meadow-land, and rights in the stubble fields, common pastures, and
woodlands for compact manageable holdings which they could completely control. They then proceeded to enclose their holdings, drain their
land, carefully fertilize and cultivate its soil, select good seed, rotate
their crops, and breed and care for their cattle and sheep according to
the new methods.

The inclosure movement, however, inflicted hardships on the small
tenant-farmers, the cottagers, and the squatters. The inclosing of the
land demanded a considerable outlay of capital for surveying, hedging,
draining, and fertilizing, and for the purchase of carefully selected seed,
blooded stock, tools, and farm-buildings. The small freehold tenants
proved to be too poor and too conservative to make the necessary expenditures and soon gave up the hopeless struggle between the old
agricultural methods and scientific farming and sold their little holdings.
The abolition of the common pastures left no place in England for the
cow or the goose of the squatter. Consequently the small tenant-farmer,
the cottager, and the squatter became workers in the new factories or
remained in rural England as landless agricultural laborers.

An improvement in farm tools accompanied the adoption of the new
methods of agriculture. At the beginning of the agricultural revolution
the cultivator of the soil had only the hand-hoe, the horse-plow, the
hand-rake, the harrow, the sickle, the scythe, the spade, the fork, and
the flail. Early in the eighteenth century, as we have seen, Jethro Tull

invented the drill and adopted the horse-hoe. About 1786 a Scotchman, Andrew Meikle, contrived a threshing-machine. In 1826 Patrick Bell patented the Bell reaper. These implements made a beginning toward taking some of the drudgery out of farming.

7

THE AGRICULTURAL REVOLUTION ON THE CONTINENT

The English farmer abandoned the medieval agricultural routine much earlier than did the French peasant. With population growing very slowly, internal trade restricted, and exportation often forbidden, the French peasant had very little incentive to change his traditional agricultural methods. He sought merely to produce enough for subsistence and the payment of his rent and taxes. In all parts of France he left from a third to a half of his holding lying fallow each year. Under the two-field system he planted wheat as the main food-crop and used oxen for plowing and hauling. Under the three-field system he employed horses and raised a cereal or a planted crop to feed them.

The defeat of France in the Seven Years' War finally set the French to investigating the causes of British success. This inquiry directed the attention of French thinkers to the English Agricultural Revolution, which was just then at its height. There grew up in France a group of economists, known as the physiocrats, who placed great emphasis on agriculture. They attempted to turn the attention of their contemporaries to the deplorable condition of French farming and to the great importance to society of the cultivator. They considered commerce and manufactures sterile. The master of the new school of economists was François Quesnay (1694–1774), who was born on a farm near Paris and knew the problems of the French peasant quite well by observation. He employed in study the leisure that his position as court physician gave him. At the age of sixty-two he wrote for the famous encyclopedia of Diderot his first article on economics, and he quickly won a considerable following. His adherents made great efforts to diffuse a knowledge of his principles through books, journals, societies, and practical demonstrations and to translate his ideas into administrative measures.

In the later decades of the eighteenth century the propaganda of the physiocrats began to have some effect on French agriculture. In 1767 Béarn inclosed its common pastures. Two years later a royal edict authorized the inclosure of fields everywhere in France and stirred up a considerable agitation for the clearing, draining, and enclosing of waste land. Some of the French nobility experimented with the new crops and the new methods of breeding and caring for farm animals. In some places the horse-hoe of Jethro Tull came into general use. In

1761 a veterinary school was established at Lyons. The chemist Antoine-Auguste Parmentier exposed the falsity of the popular prejudice against the potato and prepared the way for its general adoption as an article of food. The French Revolution swept away the old tenures of land. In spite of these improvements, however, France at the end of the eighteenth century was still a land of fallows, scattered strips of arable land, scrub animals, and clumsy machinery.

In the first half of the nineteenth century French agriculture began to improve slowly. The middle-class purchasers of confiscated property and the returned émigrés gradually awakened to the advantages of the new agricultural methods, and even the conservatism of the French peasant broke down under the impact of the growing demand for farm products resulting from the increase of the population and the growth of commercial and manufacturing centers. The rise of the beet-sugar industry stimulated the growing of sugar-beets, and the development of the woolen industry caused the introduction of merino sheep from Spain. Under the pressure of the new economic forces French agriculture increased its output 60 per cent during the first half of the nineteenth century.

The new agricultural methods made even slower progress in Germany. The close of the Napoleonic period left the German peasant in about the same position that the French peasant held at the outbreak of the French Revolution. The reaction that followed the defeat of Napoleon prevented a rigorous execution of the reform measures of Stein and Hardenberg. The majority of the German peasants did not obtain emancipation from the medieval seigniorial system until after the Revolution of 1848. In Germany, as in France, however, the new economic forces finally began to transform agriculture. The third decade of the nineteenth century witnessed a rapid development of the beet-sugar industry in Germany; the progress of English cloth-manufactures created a demand for improved wool; and the growth of population and the improvements in transportation gradually transformed German agriculture into a business enterprise.

Since the middle of the eighteenth century western Europe has experienced an economic and social revolution. The movement began in England. A series of mechanical inventions and the introduction of the steam-engine of James Watt revolutionized the manufacture of textiles and iron and steel, caused the development of the factory system, stimulated mining and improvements in transportation and communication, concentrated population in factory towns and industrial quarters, and created many new social problems. The introduction of scientific farming and breeding in response to the growth of new markets made agriculture a business and transformed the rural organization of England.

From Great Britain the new industrial and agricultural methods spread to the Continent. After the restoration of peace in 1815 the Belgian provinces of the Kingdom of the Netherlands and France rapidly introduced the new textile machinery, the new methods for the manufacture of iron and steel, and the new motive power. Germany waited until nearly the middle of the nineteenth century before beginning to adopt the new methods of manufacture. Both France and Germany adopted the means of transportation and the methods of farming and breeding with relative slowness. Great Britain, consequently, had a start of several decades over industrial rivals on the Continent.

CHAPTER V

The Conservatives of Europe did not long enjoy in undisturbed peace their victories over the Liberals of southern Europe. In the years after 1823 the new forces of Liberalism and nationalism showed increasing strength. In the next few years a series of episodes and movements indicated that the concert of Europe was breaking up and that the Conservatives were losing control of the political situation.

I

THE BREAK-UP OF THE CONCERT OF EUROPE

As we have seen, during the Napoleonic period the threat of being incorporated in the empire of Napoleon drew Russia, Austria, Prussia, and Great Britain together into a temporary alliance. After the defection of France to Napoleon in 1815, fear of France caused the four allies to form the more permanent union known as the Quadruple Alliance. In 1818, after the restoration of France to good standing, the four powers concluded with France a Quintuple Alliance. The cooperation of first the four and later the five allied states in the cause of peace and the established order created a mutual understanding and an international-mindedness among the rulers and ministers of the European states such as Europe did not see again until after the World War.

The revolutionary movements of 1820 and 1821 broke up this concert of the European powers. Castlereagh, the English Secretary of State for Foreign Affairs, regarded the treaties of 1815 as so many clauses of a civil contract. He fully recognized the value of the cooperation and the recurring conferences of the allied powers, but he insisted on solving diplomatic problems as they arose and avoiding declarations of general principles that might be given an unexpected application. In 1820 and 1821, consequently, he felt that as the representative of a government placed in power by the Revolution of 1688 he could support neither the plans of the Tsar for turning the alliance of the five powers into an engine for the suppression of revolutionary movements in general nor the specific proposals of Metternich for the intervention of Austria in Italy. As the chief minister of an allied power he could not countenance the interference of the European powers in Portugal. On account of both the political traditions and the commercial interests of Great Britain he could not approve of the forcible restoration of the absolutism of Ferdinand VII in Spain in 1823. His successor, George Canning, put still greater emphasis on British interests and abandoned entirely the effort to coöperate with the Continental powers. As a consequence of this situation the British government took no active part in the Conference of Troppau and the congresses of Laibach and Verona. This resumption of an independent policy by Great Britain prepared the way for the defeat of the plans formulated by the Conservative powers of Europe for the revolting colonies of Spain in America.

2

THE DEFEAT OF THE ABSOLUTIST POWERS IN SPANISH AMERICA

As soon as they were in a position to do so the Conservative powers of Europe began to consider the problem of the Spanish colonies in America. The three absolute governments, as a matter of principle, advocated the suppression of the revolutionary movements in the American colonies of Spain and the restoration of these to Spanish control. Spain naturally desired to recover control of its former possessions. the French Ultraroyalists toyed with the idea of carving out kingdoms in South America for a group of Bourbon princes. At the same time the Russian Government issued an imperial ukase that made sweeping claims to a monopoly in the Bering Sea.

The plans of the European Conservatives aroused the opposition of both Great Britain and the United States. The British government desired to retain the new markets thrown open to English merchants by the revolting Spanish colonists, and the United States feared to have the absolute governments of Europe obtain a foothold in America. The government of Great Britain, consequently, took the initiative in opposing the plans of the Conservative powers. In August, 1823, Canning suggested to the American minister at London that their respective governments should take common action for the protection of their interests in America. In October he eliminated the danger of French intervention in America by a blunt warning to the French ambassador at London. In this conversation he warned against French intervention in America, refused an invitation to the proposed European congress, and made clear the intention of the British government to recognize the independence of the Spanish colonies in America if the slightest attempt should be made to restrict British trade with them. Finally, on the last day of the following year the British government recognized the independence of Buenos Aires, Mexico, and Colombia.

In the meantime the suggestion of Canning for common action in Spanish America had stirred the American government to action. The British proposal flattered the vanity of some of the advisers of President Monroe, but John Quincy Adams, his Secretary of State, opposed having his country play the part of a cockboat in the wake of a British man-of-war and advised making an independent declaration. Consequently, in a message sent to Congress on December 2, 1823, President Monroe made his celebrated statement of American policy, known subsequently as the Monroe Doctrine. In this state paper he announced that the United States would not interfere in the affairs of Europe, that Europe in consequence should not intervene in the two American continents, and that henceforth neither North nor South America should be considered a field for European colonization. The simultaneous action of Great Britain and the United States put an effective check on the plans of the Conservative powers of Europe for the former colonies of Spain in America.

3

THE DEFEAT OF THE CONSERVATIVE POWERS IN PORTUGAL

Three years later the European Conservatives suffered a minor reverse in Portugal. After the defeat of the party responsible for the Portuguese revolution of 1820, King John IV returned from Brazil, reëstablished the Liberal constitution, and summoned to power a Prime Minister allied to the English or Constitutionalist party. Upon his death in 1826 his son, Dom Pedro, who had been Emperor of Brazil since it declared its independence in 1822, succeeded him. He remained in office only long enough to modernize the institutions of Portugal. During his short reign he abolished tithes, monopolies, and hereditary privileges, closed monastic institutions and confiscated their property, and granted a constitution modeled after that of Great Britain. When Spain tried to assist a counter-revolution, Canning dispatched five thousand troops to Portugal to protect British interests. The accession to power, shortly afterwards, of the Whigs in Great Britain and the Orleanists in France insured the permanent success of the Constitutional party.

4

THE GREEK REVOLT

Meanwhile a sanguinary revolution had been drenching the Balkan peninsula with blood. The revolt was the work of a secret Greek patriotic society known as the Hetairia Philike, which had been founded in Odessa in 1814. Because of his intimate relations with the impressionable Tsar Alexander I, the organization had selected as its leader for the proposed revolution Alexandros Ypsilanti, a member of a famous Greek family. In drawing up its plans it counted heavily on a general rising of all Christian subjects of the Sultan and on the intervention of the Russian government in behalf of the Greeks. In secret the society received much encouragement from Count Capo d'Istria, a Greek who had risen to be one of the chief advisers of the Tsar.

At the beginning of the revolt the young revolutionary leader made a fatal but understandable blunder. Considering all the Christian inhabitants of the Balkan peninsula under the supervision of the Patriarch of Constantinople as Greeks, Ypsilanti decided to start the proposed revolution in the Rumanian provinces of Moldavia and Walachia, where Russia could easily come to his assistance. The rising, in consequence, started off badly. Fearing the terrible retribution the Turks were sure to wreak on them in case of failure, and hating the Greeks from whose ranks had come many officials responsible for exploiting them in the past, the Rumanian peasants made no response to the proclamations of Ypsilanti and his lieutenants. In a short time his requisitions turned public opinion in the two provinces completely against the revolutionary movement. As a result of the influence of Metternich the Tsar failed to come to the aid of either his favorite or his Christian protégés in the Balkan peninsula. The Turks therefore had no difficulty in defeating the meager forces of Ypsilanti and overrunning the two Rumanian provinces.

The plans of the Greek revolutionists met with more success in the southern part of the Balkan peninsula. Inflamed by national and religious fanaticism, the Greeks of the Morea broke out in revolt and began to exterminate their Moslem neighbors. The excesses of the Greeks equaled the worst atrocities of their Turkish rulers. From the Morea the revolt spread to the rest of the Greek peninsula and to the Turkish fleet, the defection of the Greek-manned navy of the Sultan giving the revolutionists control of most of the islands in the Ægean Sea.

The reports of the sufferings of their coreligionists in the Morea caused the Turks to take a fearful revenge on the Greek inhabitants of Constantinople, Asia Minor, and some of the islands of the Ægean Sea. They hung the Patriarch of Constantinople in his vestments and put to death eighty other high ecclesiastics of the Eastern Orthodox Church. As soon as conditions in other parts of his empire permitted, the Sultan dispatched an army which temporarily overran a large part of the Greek peninsula. Sickness, lack of supplies, and the heroic resistance of the Greeks finally brought the conflict to a standstill and led to the withdrawal of the Turkish army.

In 1824 the Sultan recognized his inability to quell the Greek revolt and turned for help to his nominal vassal, Mehemet Ali of Egypt. In return for the promise of rule over the Morea for his adopted son, Mehemet Ali sent a large expeditionary force and a well-equipped fleet to the Greek peninsula. In spite of the desperate resistance of the Greeks, the Egyptian forces rapidly captured the islands of the Ægean Sea, laid waste the Morea, and captured Athens and Missolonghi.

5

THE INTERVENTION OF EUROPE IN THE GREEK REVOLT

At this point the plight of the Greeks stirred Great Britain, France, and Russia to intervene in the struggle. The revolt of the Greeks had made a peculiar appeal to all peoples in western Europe and America who cherished the glorious traditions of ancient Greece or sympathized with a Christian nation struggling against a Moslem oppressor. The defeated revolutionists of Italy, Portugal, and Poland, romantic enthusiasts like Francis Lieber and Lord Byron, and the embittered and adventurous from many lands volunteered in the Greek cause. Those who stayed at home organized societies, collected funds, and carried on an agitation in the press and in literary works in behalf of the Greeks. The pressure of these Philhellenes, combined with the desire for a restoration of normal commercial conditions in the Near East, finally caused the three powers to intervene.

The Greek revolt put the Russian government in a particularly difficult position. Since the days of Peter the Great the rulers of Russia had emphasized the ties of blood and religion between the Russians and the Christian subjects of the Sultan. After the outbreak of the revolutionary movement among the Greeks, consequently, Russian public opinion brought increasing pressure on the government to intervene.

For six years Metternich fought a losing fight against the danger of Russian intervention in behalf of the Greeks. Conferences of representatives of Russia, Austria, Prussia, and France, held in St. Petersburg in 1824 and 1825, failed to solve the problem and ended in the virtual break-up of the concert of the Conservative powers of Europe. By 1827 the failure of the Russian government to intervene in the Greek revolt threatened to alienate public opinion in Russia and to destroy the influence of the Russian government with the Christian inhabitants of the Balkan peninsula. On both political and commercial grounds Russia felt compelled to intervene in the revolt of the Greeks.

Fear of independent action by the Russian government led France and Great Britain to coöperate with Russia in an effort to put a stop to the civil conflict in the Greek peninsula. Shocked by the merciless massacre of the Greeks and impatient at the interruption of the normal course of trade, the three governments in 1827 finally agreed to demand the conclusion of an armistice between the Greek and the Egyptian forces. The efforts of the navies of the three states to cut off supplies and reënforcements from the Egyptian troops resulted in a naval action that destroyed the fleet of Mehemet Ali and brought his forces in the Morea to a standstill.

This action so infuriated the Sultan that he blindly plunged his inadequately prepared empire into a war with Russia, the power which he held to be chiefly responsible for the destruction of the fleet of his Egyptian vassal. In the first year of the war the Russian troops met with little success in their efforts to invade the Rumanian provinces of Moldavia and Walachia. In 1829, however, the Russian commander boldly cut loose from his military base, pressed through the two Danubian provinces without stopping to take all the Turkish fortresses by siege operations, crossed the Balkan Mountains, and captured Adrianople, the ancient capital of Turkey. This daring maneuver caused the Sultan to sue for peace.

The subsequent negotiations resulted in the conclusion of the Treaty of Adrianople (September 14, 1829). By the terms of this agreement the Turkish government ceded to Russia a considerable area in the transcaucasian region, promised to pay the Russian government a heavy indemnity, consented to an occupation of Moldavia and Walachia and the fortress of Silistria by Russia until the indemnity was paid, and opened the Straits of the Dardanelles and the Bosphorus to states at peace with the Ottoman Empire. In the treaty the Sultan also made certain concessions to his Christian subjects. He granted the two Rumanian provinces of Moldavia and Walachia the right to elect native hospodars, who were to hold office for life, promised to the Serbs around Belgrade the religious liberty and internal autonomy conceded by earlier treaties, and pledged his word to appoint a commission empowered to settle with the envoys of Russia, France, and Great Britain the future status of the Greeks. The treaty left Russia predominant in the Balkan peninsula, severed nearly all the bonds uniting Moldavia and Walachia to the Ottoman Empire, made the Serbs around Belgrade almost completely autonomous, and finally, after a delay of three years, gave the Greeks their independence.

6

THE REVOLUTION OF 1830 IN FRANCE

Peace had hardly been established in the Balkan peninsula when a new revolutionary movement broke out in Europe that for a time pushed the affairs of the Near East into the background. The series of revolutions broke out in France and ultimately spread to the Belgian Netherlands, Germany, Italy, and Poland.

By skilfully working on their fears and suspicions, the Ultraroyalists, who came into power in France late in 1821, induced the French people to accept their first measures without much protest. They carried on a vigorous persecution of Republican and Liberal societies, pushed through the parliament a press law that made the sanction of the government a prerequisite for the publication of a journal, threatened all publications with suspension or complete suppression, transferred press cases from the hands of juries to the jurisdiction of royal magistrates, and exposed to five years' imprisonment and heavy fines persons convicted of publishing writings or illustrations which outraged or turned into ridicule the religion of the state, or excited hatred or contempt of any class. They also inaugurated a policy designed to give the Church control of the schools of the state. Under the influence of the Ultraroyalists the government made a bishop of the Church "grand master" of the schools of the state, dismissed François Guizot and Victor Cousin, two famous professors of the Sorbonne, temporarily shut the doors of the school of medicine of the University of Paris because of the heretical beliefs of two of its lecturers, and closed the École Normale.

These first successes encouraged the Ultraroyalists to push through still bolder measures. In 1823, as we have seen, they sponsored the highly successful intervention of the French government in Spain which restored to Ferdinand VII his freedom of action. In France they abandoned their earlier caution. They insured their control of the machinery of government by appointing Conservatives to the Chamber of Peers and extending the life of the Chamber of Deputies to a term of seven years. They ruined the Liberal press with fines, attempted to restore to the monastic orders something of their former wealth and position, compensated the former émigrés for the loss of their property during the French Revolution, and passed a severe law of sacrilege. In 1824, at the time of the coronation of Charles X as the successor of Louis XVIII, they ostentatiously revived all the religious customs of the Middle Ages. They secretly authorized the return to France of the much-hated Jesuits, proposed a new law of succession that tended to reëstablish inequality, and disbanded the National Guard, a body recruited mainly from the middle classes.

For a time the French people made no protest against the reactionary policies of the Ultraroyalists. The success of the French intervention in Spain flattered their vanity and disproved the dismal forecasts of failure made by the French Liberals. The domestic policy adopted by the government satisfied the clergy, the leaders of society, and the army of administrators. A succession of able ministers managed the finances of the country economically and skilfully. The new methods of manufacturing and farming made France increasingly prosperous. The mass of the people, furthermore, paid little attention to political questions.

The measures of the Ultraroyalists, however, finally created an active opposition. Although the compensation of the former émigrés tended to clear the title of the lands confiscated during the French Revolution and to take the troublesome question out of politics, the holders of the state bonds naturally resented the refunding operation, which greatly reduced the income derived from their investment. The prostration of Charles X at the steps of the altar at the time of his coronation shocked many of his subjects. The magistrates began to refuse to convict Liberal journalists, and the Chamber of Peers defeated a new press law. Extraordinary demonstrations marked the funerals of two noted Liberal deputies. Finally, as a result of the elections of 1827 the Liberals, with the aid of a handful of Ultraroyalist extremists, gained control of the lower house of the French parliament and forced the ministry headed by the Count of Villèle to resign from office.

Thereupon Charles X appointed a ministry headed by Martignac, a reputed Liberal. The new ministry, however, failed in the impossible task of trying to carry on the government with the support of a majority composed of Liberals and Ultraroyalist extremists. Its concessions in regard to the police, schools, elections, and the press failed to satisfy the Liberals and enraged the Ultraroyalists. In 1829, therefore, the two groups combined to overthrow the ministry. This action of the French parliament confronted Charles X with the dilemma of either abandoning the idea of restoring the Ancien Régime in France or pushing through his policy by unconstitutional means.

As a result of his origin and training, the King naturally decided to accept the challenge of the parliament and appointed to office a ministry composed of uncompromising royalists and headed by the Prince of Polignac, a notorious opponent of the Charter of 1814. This appointment precipitated a short, sharp conflict between the adherents of the Ancien Régime and the supporters of the constitution. The Liberals voted an address that respectfully reproached the King for resisting the will of the people. Charles X considered the voting of the address an act of defiance and dissolved the Chamber of Deputies. In the electoral campaign that followed the Liberals greatly increased their majority. The election ended the hopes of the Ultraroyalists for the restoration of the Ancien Régime by constitutional methods.

Faced by this situation, Charles X and his advisers decided to brusk matters and attempt a coup d'état. On July 25, 1830, the King issued three ordinances designed to crush his Liberal opponents. These dissolved the recently elected Chamber of Deputies before it ever assembled, empowered the government to reduce its obstinate opponents to submission or to strike their names from the electoral lists, and put the ministry in a position to crush opposition journals.

The publication of these July Ordinances started a revolution. Headed by Louis Adolphe Thiers, a protégé of the Orleanist family, the endangered printers and journalists summoned the people of Paris to revolt and invited the Chamber of Deputies to defend its rights. The threatened deputies hesitated but the people of Paris acted promptly. Old soldiers of Napoleon and a handful of Republican artisans and students organized an insurrection and commenced to build barricades in the narrow, crooked streets of old Paris. Members of the disbanded National Guard, which had never been disarmed, joined in the revolt. Finally the royal troops began to desert to the side of the Republicans. By July 29 the revolutionists were in control of the city. Their success compelled Charles X to withdraw the fatal ordinances, abdicate in favor of his grandson, and retire to England.

Emboldened by the success of the Republicans, the deputies favoring a monarchical form of government decided to take charge of the revolutionary movement. They appointed a provisional government and intrusted the substance of power to the cousin of the King, Louis Philippe, Duke of Orleans, who for fifteen years had been a potential candidate for the throne. Then they persuaded the Republican leaders, who recognized their weakness, to accept Louis Philippe as a constitutional sovereign. In a dramatic scene on the balcony of the Hôtel de Ville the aged and respected Republican leader the Marquis of Lafayette received the duke. This reception made possible the election of Louis Philippe as King of the French People and the revision of the Charter of 1814 in accordance with the ideas of the victorious Liberals.

The Revolution of 1830 really made only a few changes in the Charter of 1814. It suppressed the clause of the preamble of the constitution which made the exercise of the constitutional rights of the French people appear to be a royal concession and made it impossible for a future sovereign to suspend a law or dispense with its execution. It also eliminated the article which declared the Roman Catholic religion the faith of the state, annulled the titles of nobility created by Charles X, and gave the King full control over the composition of the Chamber of Peers. It also replaced the white flag of the Bourbons with the tricolor standard of the revolutionary period. The election law of 1831 slightly extended the suffrage. The Revolution of 1830 thus defeated the attempt of the aristocracy and clergy of France to restore the Ancien Régime and established in place of the rule of the Bourbons the bourgeois monarchy of Louis Philippe.

7

THE ESTABLISHMENT OF BELGIUM

In the Belgian Netherlands the news of the July revolution in Paris reached a people already on the verge of revolt. The Dutch and Belgian portions of the Kingdom of the Netherlands established in 1814 by the action of the allied powers proved to be entirely unfitted for fusion into a united homogeneous state. The two million inhabitants of the two northern provinces spoke Dutch, adhered for the most part to Protestantism, lived by agriculture and commerce, and considered themselves politically superior to their neighbors in the southern provinces because of the two centuries of vigorous independence they had enjoyed. The nearly three and a half million inhabitants of the southern provinces spoke Flemish or Walloon, looked to France for their culture, belonged to the Roman Catholic faith, and supported themselves mainly by industry. They keenly resented the manner in which Dutch rule had been forced upon them, the placing of Protestantism and Catholicism on an equality by the constitution, the refusal of the Dutch to give the Belgians a representation in the lower chamber of the Estates General proportionate to their relative numbers, the consequent favor shown the Dutch provinces in matters of taxation, the slighting of the Belgians in the distribution of administrative, military, and diplomatic posts, the royal policy concerning the education and appointment of the clergy, the efforts of the King to make Dutch the official language, the saddling of a portion of the Dutch debt on the Belgian provinces, and the disregard of the government for the freedom of the press. By 1830 these conditions had united the Catholic and Liberal parties of the Belgian provinces into a coalition for the redress of their common grievances.

A month after the rising at Paris a serious riot occurred in the streets of Brussels. Owing to the inexplicable supineness of the military forces, the riot soon developed into a revolution. To protect their threatened interests the propertied classes organized a volunteer military force and sent a deputation to present their grievances to the King. While their Dutch sovereign hesitated about making the demanded concessions the revolutionists, their numbers swelled by recruits from neighboring towns, got the upper hand over the mod-

erate elements at Brussels, repelled the efforts of the royal troops to
repress the rising, and set up a provisional government. Most of the
provincial towns followed the example of the Belgian capital. In October, 1830, the provisional government declared the independence of
the southern provinces from the Kingdom of the Netherlands and
shortly afterwards a national congress ratified this declaration.

The success of the revolution really depended on the attitude of
the great powers. Fortunately for the Belgian revolutionary movement,
the question of intervention in the Greek revolt had just broken up
the alliance of the Conservative powers, the British government had
fallen into the hands of the Whigs, and France had come under the
control of Louis Philippe and his Liberal supporters. The two constitutional states, France and Great Britain, consequently agreed to take
joint action in the affair and arranged an armistice between the Dutch
and the Belgian governments. Their intervention insured the establishment of the Belgian provinces as the independent state of Belgium.
The new state adopted a liberal constitution and in 1839 the great
powers of Europe recognized its neutrality.

8

THE REVOLUTION OF 1830 IN GERMANY

In Germany, too, the news of the Revolution of 1830 in France
tended to loosen for a time the grip of the Conservatives. In southern
Germany, where the states of Baden, Bavaria, and Württemberg already had constitutions, the revolutionary movement of 1830 simply
caused a relaxation of the restrictions imposed on parliamentary institutions by the Carlsbad Decrees of 1819 and a strengthening of
the position of the Liberal parties. In Württemberg the government
relaxed the regulations for the press. In Bavaria the King not only
gave the press greater liberty but also he dismissed several of his
reactionary ministers. In Baden the sovereign removed from office
three of his Conservative advisers and the Liberals assumed control
of the diet and abolished tithes and feudal burdens. In all three states
the new freedom found expression in the press and the legislative
debates.

In central Germany the revolutionary movement gave rise to a demand for social, political, and constitutional reforms in Brunswick,
Hesse-Cassel, Saxony, and Hanover. In Brunswick a popular rising
caused a change of rulers, the granting of a constitution which provided for the representation of burghers and peasants in the estates,
the establishment of a civil list for the sovereign, a broadening of the
suffrage, and the enactment of laws relieving the peasants of their

seigniorial dues and conceding the cities a measure of self-government. The course of events in Brunswick illustrates fairly well the history and the results of the revolutionary movement in the other three states of central Germany.

The revolutionary movement of 1830 did not stir the Liberals of Prussia to action. Although Frederick William III failed to grant his subjects the constitution which he had promised them at the time of the national rising against Napoleon, the bureaucracy gave them an efficient government. It established or reorganized several universities, founded a number of secondary schools, improved the elementary schools, and administered the finances of the Prussian state carefully and economically. In 1818 it promulgated a new tariff law that abolished the sixty-seven internal customs lines of the state and established moderate customs duties at the borders. During the next decade it succeeded in forcing into a tariff union (the Zollverein) a number of enclaved and contiguous small states. The new economic policy discouraged smuggling, stimulated commerce and industry, and tended to promote national feeling in Germany. Well governed and growing in prosperity, the inhabitants of the Prussian state paid comparatively little attention to the agitation carried on after 1815 by the German Liberals.

9

THE REVOLUTION OF 1830 IN ITALY

The news of the revolution in France found the inhabitants of central Italy dissatisfied with their situation. Undeterred by the failure, ten years before, of their compatriots in northern and southern Italy, the Liberals of central Italy rose in revolt and drove out the rulers of Parma and Modena and gained control of the greater part of the Papal States. Within a month, however, Austria had suppressed the rising and restored the political system of Metternich in the Italian peninsula.

10

THE REVOLUTION OF 1831 IN POLAND

In 1831 the revolutionary movement finally spread to the Polish Kingdom established by the Congress of Vienna in 1815 to meet the demands of Tsar Alexander I. The Russian sovereign treated the Poles generously. He created for them a state that included about one sixth of the area of the old Kingdom of Poland and possessed a population of about three million two hundred thousand persons. He granted his new Polish subjects a liberal constitution and did much for the improvement of education, the promotion of industry, the development of mining, the building of roads, the navigation of the rivers, the embellishment of Warsaw, and the defense of the new state. He even held out to his new subjects the prospect of a restoration of a part of the territory acquired by Russia as a result of the three partitions of Poland.

The generosity of Alexander I did not prevent the early development of friction between the Poles and their Russian sovereigns. The Poles did not always seem sufficiently grateful to their benefactor and in the Polish diet voiced their demands for further concessions. Both Alexander I and his successor, Nicholas I, made some unfortunate appointments, censored the press, and at times failed to summon the diet every second year. The discontent of the Poles finally gave rise to a military conspiracy.

In 1831 the conspirators rose in revolt. Encouraged by the French Liberals, headed by Lafayette, and alarmed at the proposed use of Polish troops to suppress the revolutionary movements in France and Belgium, they instigated a rather feeble rising. For a time the strange passivity of Constantine, the brother of the Tsar and commander of the Polish army, gave the revolutionists control of the Polish Kingdom. In the end, however, the military forces of Russia had little difficulty in crushing the revolutionary movement in Poland.

The victorious Russian government utilized its victory to repress every manifestation of Polish nationality. It abolished the Polish constitution, filled the principal administrative and educational posts with Russians, incorporated the Polish troops into the Russian army, and made Russian the official language. From 1831 until after the World War the name of Poland did not appear on the map of Europe.

II

THE EFFECTS OF THE REVOLUTION OF 1830 ON THE SWISS CANTONS

In Switzerland the Revolution of 1830 accelerated the movement for the democratization of the loose confederation of aristocratic republics. While the reforms differed from canton to canton, the movement tended to assure to the Swiss freedom of the press, the right of petition, protection against arbitrary arrest, religious toleration, and security of property, and to transfer political power from the patriciates of old families in the agricultural cantons and the merchant aristocracies of the commercial and industrial cantons to the hitherto unrepresented lower classes. The changes eventually affected about two thirds of the cantons.

THE REFORM MOVEMENT IN GREAT BRITAIN

At the same time the Conservatives of Great Britain found themselves confronted by the insistent demands of the growing middle classes. The criminal code shocked humanitarian sentiments, the navigation laws threatened to undermine the loyalty of the colonies and interfere with trade, the obsolete and illogical tariff system hampered the growth of the new industries, the preposterous Corn Laws favored the landed interest at the expense of the manufacturer and the wage-earner, and the intolerance of the state church irritated the Nonconformists and seriously discriminated against Roman Catholics.

Upon his accession to power in 1822, Canning recognized the necessity of making some concessions to the demands of the British middle classes. During the five years that he was in office he and his colleagues in the ministry revised the barbarous criminal code, modified the laws on combination that prevented the wage-earning classes from uniting to better their condition, opened the British colonies to foreign commerce, subject to certain restrictions, abolished many unproductive customs duties, imposed comparatively moderate tariffs on foreign manufactures, and enacted laws admitting raw materials free of duty.

The successor of Canning, the Duke of Wellington, attempted to stem the demand for reform but found himself compelled to repeal the Test and Corporation acts and to put through Parliament a Catholic Emancipation Bill. The Test and Corporation acts were relics of Anglican intolerance inherited from the period of the Restoration. The former excluded from public office all unwilling to deny the doctrine of transubstantiation. The latter made the taking of communion in accordance with the rites of the Established Church prerequisite to holding office in the corporations that governed many British towns and chose their representatives to Parliament. Since 1747 Parliament had regularly passed an indemnity bill that relieved Protestant Nonconformists of the legal penalties imposed by the two intolerant measures. Their repeal in 1828, consequently, merely squared law and practice and removed a technical discrimination that caused considerable irritation.

The Roman Catholics of Great Britain and Ireland suffered much more severely from Anglican intolerance than did the Protestant Nonconformists. In England the laws of Elizabeth compelled every one to attend the services of the Anglican Church, inflicted crushing penalties for the celebration of the mass, and proscribed the whole Roman Catholic priesthood. The victorious Anglicans of the Restoration period passed the Test Act, which made the taking of the communion according to the forms of the Established Church a prerequisite for officeholding. In 1700 the English Parliament adopted a measure that would have driven Roman Catholic landed proprietors entirely out of the country if it had been enforced. In Ireland equally intolerant legislation excluded Irish Roman Catholics from voting, sitting in Parliament, entering the legal or teaching professions, and purchasing, inheriting, or bequeathing land. Although much of this legislation had been relaxed or repealed during the eighteenth century, ambitious Irish Roman Catholics still found themselves excluded from many of the natural rewards of ability. These injustices caused the organization by Daniel O'Connell, an Irish lawyer of great oratorical ability, of an association to obtain redress for the Roman Catholic grievances. Finally, in 1829, the agitation carried on by this society convinced Wellington of the necessity of introducing a bill which opened to Roman Catholics the opportunity for a parliamentary career and most of the civil, corporate, judicial, and political offices.

In the meantime the demand of the middle and lower classes for political reform had been growing stronger. The new industrialists demanded with growing insistence a place beside the landed interest, and the lower classes clamored for parliamentary reform as a panacea for the ills arising from bad harvests and economic changes. As a result of this popular pressure the Whig party finally incorporated parliamentary reform into its political program. When in 1830 they finally came into power, as a result of the strength of the demand for reform and the excitement produced in Great Britain by the revolution on the Continent, the Whig leaders attempted to put through Parliament a bill for the reform of the suffrage.

The Whigs struggled two years to enact their Reform Bill into law. Their first bill met defeat in the committee stage. This made necessary a dissolution of Parliament and a great election campaign. Their second bill passed the lower house of Parliament but failed to get a majority in the House of Lords. Finally, in 1832, as a result of the promise of the King to create enough new lords to insure the adoption of the bill and the fear that its defeat might cause a revolution, the Reform Bill of the Whigs passed both houses of Parliament and became a law.

This legislation only began the work of democratizing Great Britain. It entirely disfranchised fifty small nomination and rotten boroughs, reduced the representation of some thirty others, added to the number of parliamentary representatives of a few of the more populous counties, and gave some of the new industrial cities and towns a voice in Parliament. It abolished all but one of the antiquated English franchises and slightly extended the suffrage. These provisions put the middle classes in power in Great Britain, but left the mass of the British people still unrepresented.

In spite of the apparent triumph of the European Conservatives over the revolutionary spirit in the Iberian and Italian peninsulas in the years between 1820 and 1823, they soon suffered a series of reverses that revealed the growing strength of their Liberal opponents. After 1820 Great Britain adopted a policy of independent action based on British interests and with the aid of the United States forced the Conservative powers of the Continent to give up their plans for re-establishing absolutism in the American colonies of Spain. The Greek revolt of 1821 broke up the alliance of the three great Conservative powers and finally caused an intervention by Russia that resulted in the establishment of an independent Greece and nearly autonomous governments in Serbia, Moldavia, and Walachia. In 1826 Portugal adopted a constitution. In 1830 and 1831 a series of revolutions swept over Europe which put the bourgeoisie in power in France, gave the Belgian provinces of the Kingdom of the Netherlands their independence, increased the power of the German Liberals, and destroyed the last vestiges of freedom in Poland. Simultaneously the British government began to make concessions to the demand for reforms. These initial successes increased the determination of the Conservatives to prevent further innovations and nerved the Liberals to continue their agitation.

CHAPTER VI

After 1830 the tension between the representatives of the old and the new Europe grew stronger. The Conservatives were alarmed at the headway made between 1823 and 1830 by the new social and political forces set in motion by the French Revolution and the Industrial Revolution and made great efforts to check every manifestation of the new forces. The Liberals, encouraged by these successes, increased their activity and new groups, dissatisfied with the middle-class ideals of the Liberals and appealing to the proletariat for support, made their appearance. The years between 1830 and 1848, in consequence, were a period of agitation and repression in most of the countries of Europe.

I

THE POLITICAL SYSTEM OF LOUIS PHILIPPE, 1830–1848

The Revolution of 1830 elevated to the French throne a man whom neither friend nor foe had really fathomed. The origin and the politic conduct of Louis Philippe had created for him a following among the bourgeoisie and made him a potential candidate for the French throne. The French people knew him to be the son of the demagogic Duke of Orleans, a brave soldier in the early days of the French Revolution, an émigré in later years too patriotic to take up arms against his country, and a man who had walked the streets of Paris freely since the restoration of the Bourbons in 1815, sent his children to the schools attended by the sons of the bourgeoisie, and invited the leaders of industry and the professions to his social affairs. They had never divined the son's real political sentiments.

The new French sovereign found himself placed in office by a divided body of supporters and opposed by hostile political groups. The partizans of the overthrown Bourbons refused to recognize him as a legitimist sovereign, but these aristocratic leaders lacked a body of troops to fight their battles. The Republicans, composed of old soldiers, students, and working-men, scrutinized every act of the new government and stood ready to risk their lives in repeated attempts to over-

throw the new political régime. The more conservative adherents of
Louis Philippe regarded the Revolution of 1830 as merely a victory
for the Charter of 1814 and advocated a policy of making no further
concessions to the democratic principle, restoring order at home, and
regaining the confidence of the other governments of Europe. A group
of more radical partizans, headed by the aged and respected Lafayette,
urged the king to make democratic reforms at home and to extend the
assistance of France to the revolutionists in other countries.

Faced by this confused political situation, Louis Philippe acted with
great caution. He made concessions to all the French political factions
and adopted the political programs of none of them. He bestowed rewards on the heroes of the street fighting in the July Revolution and
offered assistance to the wounded, deprived Lafayette of his command
over the revived National Guard, dismissed many of the functionaries
of the Bourbon régime, and excluded the Catholic clergy from the
Council of State, the Chamber of Deputies, and the Council of Public
Instruction, but he granted no domestic reforms, refused to endanger
the safety of his country by quixotic expeditions in behalf of the
revolutionists of Italy, Germany, and Poland, and provided no relief
for the almost desperate workers of France.

This cautious policy aroused great dissatisfaction. In 1831 the workers of Lyons rose in protest against their social and economic misery.
In the following year the Duchess of Berry, the daughter-in-law of
Charles X, left her refuge in England and, consciously imitating the
return of Napoleon from the island of Elba, attempted to rouse the
supporters of the Bourbons to revolt against the Orleanist régime. In
1834, the Republicans, who had reorganized their secret societies and
renewed their propaganda, started insurrections at Lyons and Paris. At
the same time intellectuals like the Count de Saint-Simon and François
Fourier evolved Utopian schemes for the improvement of social conditions that kept society in a ferment.

The new government displayed patience, decision, and firmness in
handling its opponents. It put down the rising of the workers at Lyons,
kept the Duchess of Berry in prison long enough to permit the birth of
a son by a secret marriage to discredit her, and suppressed the Republican risings. The enthusiasm engendered by the socialistic schemes for
ameliorating French society gradually died out. A Liberal Catholic
party broke away from the Bourbons and attempted to reconcile Catholicism and democracy. By 1836, consequently, Louis Philippe could
feel himself firmly established on the throne of France.

During the next four years Louis Philippe struggled for personal
power. Assured of the support of a Catholic party which had developed
as a result of a revival of religious fervor and the alarm felt over the
Republican risings, the King gradually tested the political leaders in

the hope of finding a minister suited to his purpose. Finally in 1840 the crisis over the Near East led to the fall from office of the bellicose Thiers and the accession to power of Guizot. The new Prime Minister proved to be just the agent the King sought.

For the next eight years Louis Philippe and Guizot controlled France by a political system that insured them the support of the middle class brought to power by the Revolution of 1830. In foreign affairs they followed a pacific and opportunist policy. At home they protected French manufacturers from the keen competition of the older English factories by high tariff duties, gave the bankers and capitalists of France a chance to exploit a salt-mine or to build a section of the new railways, and insured themselves a parliamentary majority by distributing offices, concessions, favors, and money to the deputies and their friends. Only a revolution could shake the hold of Guizot and Louis Philippe on the machinery of government in France.

2

THE PROTESTS AGAINST THE POLITICAL SYSTEM OF LOUIS PHILIPPE

The effective political system of the King and his First Minister, however, disregarded the majority of Frenchmen and sought to maintain the existing order of society in defiance of the new ideas at work among the people of France. The politicians out of office raised the cry of parliamentary reform and began an agitation for an extension of the suffrage and the exclusion of office-holders from the parliament. In conscious imitation of the methods found valuable by Richard Cobden in his agitation against the English Corn Laws, the opponents of Guizot organized a series of political banquets. At the seventy or more banquets held by the opposition between 1846 and 1848 inflammatory orators had much to say about the violation of the Charter of 1814, the mistakes of the government, the corruption of elections and of the parliament, and the inglorious foreign policy. As a result of their agitation they hoped to regain office. They had no intention of precipitating a revolution.

Their agitation came at a time of great popular discontent and excitement. The Industrial Revolution had created a growing mass of proletarians conscious of their misery and eagerly searching for a panacea. The poor harvests of 1846 had added much to the popular suffering. The summoning of a United Diet in Prussia, the accession of a liberal Pope, and the victories of the radicals in the Swiss cantons made the King and Guizot seem to be leaders of European Conservatism. The publication of the histories of Thiers, Jules Michelet, and Louis Blanc tended to revive the Republican and Bonapartist traditions in France. The more radical Republicans had come to the conclusion that political reform must be supplemented by a reorganization of society and had forsaken the Republican party and become followers of Louis Blanc and other Socialist leaders.

Louis Blanc belonged to a family that fell into poverty as a result of losing a royal pension through the Revolution of 1830. After this disaster he became a critic of the existing social order. After contributing for several years to other Republican journals, he finally established one of his own. In 1840 he published in his journal a series of articles that later appeared in book form under the title of *The Organization of Labor*. In these articles he maintained that the existing bourgeois society owed its domination to a competition that would eventually destroy both the capitalists and the proletariat. As a remedy for the existing misery and poverty of the lower classes he advocated that the state should put its resources at the disposal of the poor for the establishment of social workshops in each important branch of industry. These organizations would admit all workmen of good character, pay them at an equal rate, and eventually assign them positions by popular vote. The profits of these enterpises would be used for paying the members of the associations for their labor, caring for the aged and infirm, and expanding the system of social workshops. In the end Louis Blanc expected the peaceful absorption of all private concerns by the new organization of labor.

The ideas of Louis Blanc appealed strongly to a proletariat suffering from the effects of the Industrial Revolution. The scanty and somewhat unreliable statistics for the years between the revolutions of 1830 and 1848 indicate that few workers received as much as sixty cents a day. The miners of France seem to have worked for a daily wage of less than forty cents, the engineers of the new railroads for sixty cents, a laborer on the roads, for a little over thirty cents, and a railway switchman, for forty cents. Even at Paris few workers received as much as a dollar a day. The textile workers of France were paid much less. In 1834 the spinners in the cotton-factories of one industrial region worked thirteen hours a day and received only two dollars and eighty cents a week in wages. To the exploited men and women of France, consequently, the ideas of Louis Blanc about the organization of labor seemed to offer a way to a better life.

While Louis Blanc and other French thinkers were pointing out a reorganization of society as the remedy for the evils produced by the Industrial Revolution, Louis Napoleon, a nephew of the famous French Emperor, was attempting to convince the French people that a restoration of the Napoleonic régime would furnish a solution of their difficulties. This claimant for the French throne was a son of the Louis Bonaparte who served as King of Holland from 1806 to 1810. Upon the death of his older brother in central Italy during the Revolution of 1830 and of the son of Napoleon I in 1832, Louis Napoleon had assumed the rôle of pretender to the French throne. Thenceforth he bent all his energies toward attracting the attention of the French people. Twice he presented himself before French garrisons on the frontiers of France in the hope of enlisting their aid in restoring him to the imperial throne. Though they failed, the two attempts gave him considerable publicity. From time to time also he set forth his ideas on public questions. In his *Napoleonic Ideas,* which he published in 1839, he attempted to show that his name stood for a system of government that would realize the beneficent plans of his uncle and that something more than a reckless ambition lay behind his efforts to obtain the throne of France. At all times too he kept the press fully informed of his movements.

In his campaign he received invaluable assistance from the Napoleonic tradition in France. Napoleon had spent his last years in a conscious effort to mold the judgment of history upon his work. From the mists of the lonely island of St. Helena had emerged a new Napoleon, an ever-victorious general, a son of the French Revolution, a lover of the French people. As the events of the Napoleonic period had receded into the past the people of France began to forget the true Napoleon and foster the growth of the Napoleonic tradition. His old soldiers began to cherish his memory. The peasants looked back to him as the protector of their bits of property. The new generation commenced to make unfavorable comparisons between the glorious deeds of the Napoleonic armies and the cautious opportunism of Louis Philippe and his bourgeois adherents.

By 1848 the mounting opposition was on the point of revolt against the political system of Guizot and Louis Philippe. Foisted upon the French people by a group of skilful political intriguers and benefiting mainly the upper bourgeoisie, it ignored the petty bourgeoisie and the proletariat. The slightest incident might precipitate a revolution that would topple the Bourgeois King from his throne.

3

AGITATION AND REPRESSION IN ITALY, 1830–1846

In Italy the Revolution of 1830 left the general situation unchanged. The victory of Austria over the Liberals of Parma, Modena, and the Papal States reëstablished throughout the Italian peninsula the rule of the princes and the domination of Austria. In Venetia and Lombardy the Austrian government continued to exclude Italians from the higher posts in the army and the administration, to exploit the two provinces for the benefit of Austrian producers, and to impose conscription and heavy taxes. In the rest of Italy the princes made no concessions to the demands for reform and with great docility accepted the dictation of Austria.

This situation humiliated important elements among the nobility, the middle classes, and the clergy. Stirred by the same currents of Liberalism and nationalism as the rest of Europe, they dreamed of an Italy freed from foreign domination and the rule of reactionary princes, united into one country, and endowed with the liberal institutions found in England and France. The more moderate elements in Italian society found leadership in the neo-Guelphs, and later in Count Cavour; the young, the enthusiastic, and the more radical, in Giuseppe Mazzini.

Born at Genoa in 1805, Mazzini grew to manhood among a population that vividly remembered the benefits of French rule and actively carried on an agitation for political reform and national independence. After arriving at years of maturity he abandoned his hopes of a literary career and threw himself into the Italian revolutionary movement. He joined the Carbonari and contributed to the journals started from time to time by the Italian Liberals. By 1831 his political activity had caused his arrest and exile by the Sardinian government. After living for a time at Marseilles and Geneva, he spent most of the remaining years of his life in England. During these years of exile he lived upon the money earned by contributing articles to English publications and upon remittances forwarded to him by his mother. From his place of exile Mazzini preached to his fellow-countrymen a lofty ideal. Though he thought Catholicism dead, he bowed in reverence before a supreme unity, God, and preached the duties as well as the rights of man. In order to achieve this goal of humanity the Italian people must be free, united, and republican.

For the achievement of his hopes for Italy Mazzini depended on education and insurrection. Believing the time was ripe for new methods, he sought to enroll the youth and enthusiasm of the younger generation in a secret society known as Young Italy. He met with a success that surpassed his most sanguine hopes. From Genoa and Leghorn the organization spread to many towns of northern and central Italy. At Genoa the party opposed to the incorporation of the city in the Kingdom of Sardinia made common cause with the followers of the great agitator. Elsewhere Mazzini found his recruits mainly among the middle classes, which had tasted for a time during the Napoleonic period the benefits of efficient government and equality of opportunity. He kept in touch with his society through his journal, *Young Italy,* a series of political pamphlets that reached them at irregular intervals through various channels.

This political propaganda nerved the youth of Italy to risk their lives

repeatedly in unsuccessful insurrections. The weakness of this side of
the work of Mazzini is illustrated by two episodes. In the first the
agitator enrolled about eight hundred volunteers, recruited from political exiles from many lands, for a blow against the Kingdom of Sardinia. Foreign governments put pressure on the Swiss authorities to
prevent the expedition from starting; the cosmopolitan adventurer intrusted with the leadership of the little force squandered most of the
funds collected by Mazzini with such infinite difficulty; the expected
risings failed to occur in Genoa and Naples; and the quixotic effort of
Giuseppe Garibaldi to capture the Sardinian navy ended in failure.
After the little band had at last crossed the frontier it marched around
aimlessly for four days and then dispersed having fired hardly a shot.

A later insurrection ended even more tragically. Fired with enthusiasm by the propaganda of Mazzini, two young Venetian nobles,
the sons of Admiral Bandiera of the Austrian navy, deserted their ships
and fled to the Ionian Islands. From this base they organized a small
expedition to assist an imaginary rising in southern Italy. The military
forces of the Neapolitan government had little difficulty in overpower-
ing the revolutionary expedition and executing its leaders. These disasters, however, did not deter Mazzini from calling on the youth of
Italy to volunteer for new insurrections.

But the ideas and methods of Mazzini seemed too radical to many
Italians who earnestly desired unity, independence, and liberal institutions for the peninsula. These more moderate men found a program in
the writings of three famous Italians, whose books appeared in rapid
succession after 1843. They are sometimes referred to as the neo-
Guelphs. In his work entitled *On the Moral and Civil Supremacy of the
Italians* Vincenzo Gioberti, a priest living in exile in Belgium, told his
divided and exploited compatriots that they had already twice held the
primacy of the world through the Roman Empire and the medieval
Church and that they possessed all the elements necessary for a third
and greater supremacy. As a practical means for attaining this goal he
proposed a federation of the Italian princes under the presidency of
the Pope. Although it leaves the modern reader cold, his book stirred
his fellow-countrymen in a manner that made it one of the epoch-
making works of the nineteenth century. In *The Hopes of Italy,* Count
Cesare Balbo, a Piedmontese noble, took up the problem of how the
Austrians were to be expelled from Italy and suggested that Austria
should be persuaded to seek compensation in the slowly disintegrating
Ottoman Empire for the loss of the provinces of Lombardy and Venetia.
In his book *On the Recent Events in Romagna* Massimo d'Azeglio,
a painter of noble rank from the province of Piedmont and one of the
most attractive Italians of the mid-century, told the Italian people that
the time for secret societies and insurrections was past and that the

moment for a public, peaceful, and courageous discussion of Italian problems had come.

Before this last book appeared the inhabitants of Tuscany, weary of the beneficent despotism of the grand duke, had already begun to translate into action the ideas of D'Azeglio. In Pisa, Giuseppe Montanelli, a professor in the university, had started an agitation for reform through public petitions and secretly printed bulletins. In one of the latter the Tuscan agitator summarized the needs of his country as the union of Italy against Austria, and institutions suitable to the time. He enumerated among the necessary institutions the right of petition, municipal reorganization, a reform of the jury system, a National Guard, and a reasonable censorship. Liberals of rank at Siena and Florence soon imitated the methods of the Pisan professor. Enthusiastic young men defied the government by raining pamphlets from the galleries of the theaters, passing them from hand to hand in the streets, leaving them in the palace of the grand duke, and sending them through the mails.

4

REFORMS AND CONSTITUTIONS IN ITALY, 1846–1848

In all the states of the peninsula the Liberals showed their growing strength. In the Papal States the subjects of the Pope were in a chronic state of discontent. In Venetia public opinion, led by Daniele Manin, showed itself ready for a constitutional struggle by forcing the Austrian government to run the proposed line of railway between Venice and Milan by the most direct route. In Sardinia Liberals like Cavour cherished the hope that their own dynasty would place itself at the head of the movement for national independence. In all the states of the peninsula the Liberals carried on a campaign of propaganda for independence and liberal reforms through literary journals, scientific congresses, anonymous pamphlets, university lectures, private conversations, placards, and novels.

For a time the Liberals of Italy thought that the new Pope who was elected quite unexpectedly in 1846, Pius IX, would prove to be the leader whom they sought. He inaugurated his reign by a grant of amnesty to political offenders, the dismissal of his Swiss Guards, and the appointment of a Liberal cardinal as Secretary of State. As a result of these initial measures the new Pope could not leave his palace without being surrounded and acclaimed by his enthusiastic subjects and his name suddenly became the rallying-cry for all the moderate advocates of reform and independence. During the first months of his rule he increased the popular enthusiasm by according the press considerable freedom, creating an advisory Council of State composed of laymen, granting municipal autonomy to Rome, and forming a Civic Guard.

The policy of reform inaugurated by Pius IX compelled the rulers of other Italian states to make concessions to the Liberal movement. In 1847 the Grand Duke of Tuscany surrendered to the demands of his Liberal subjects and conceded freedom of the press, a Civic Guard, and a consultative council. In the Kingdom of Sardinia the demonstrations at Turin in behalf of the papal legate and the agitation of the Liberals of turbulent, democratic Genoa finally convinced Charles Albert of the necessity of imitating the example of the Pope and the Grand Duke of Tuscany.

This breakdown of the system of Metternich in the Papal States, Tuscany, and the Kingdom of Sardinia increased the difficulties of the Austrian government in the provinces of Lombardy and Venetia. The long dormant and neglected Central Congregations, the consultative bodies created in the two provinces at the close of the Napoleonic period, suddenly presented a statement of their grievances and demands. In order to make difficulties for the Austrian treasury the Milanese stopped smoking after January 1, 1848, and even attempted to impose their ban on the use of tobacco upon the Austrian garrison and functionaries. Their efforts led to incidents that cost the lives of many Italians and completed the rupture between the Austrian government and the inhabitants of Lombardy.

In Sicily the agitation set in motion again not only the Liberals but also the advocates of Sicilian independence from the rule of the Neapolitan Bourbons. In January, 1848, the inhabitants of Palermo rose in revolt against the Neapolitan garrison. By the end of the month the Sicilian revolutionists were in possession of the whole island with the exception of the city of Messina, and had defeated a military expedition sent from Naples to relieve the beleaguered garrisons.

Alarmed at the revolt in Sicily and the continuous demonstrations of his subjects at Naples, the King of the Two Sicilies decided to extricate himself from his difficulties and embarrass his fellow-sovereigns by granting his subjects a constitution. The news from Naples and his desire to enlist the support of the Liberals for the war that seemed imminent with Austria as a result of the events at Milan determined Charles Albert, early in February, to grant his Kingdom of Sardinia a constitution. Later in the same month the Grand Duke of Tuscany took similar action. Finally after the news of the February rising in Paris reached Italy the Pope ended the period of concessions by granting his subjects a constitution. The news of the February rising in Paris thus reached a population in Italy in a state of political ferment and ready to take arms for the expulsion of Austria from the peninsula.

5

GREAT BRITAIN, 1832–1854

In Great Britain the elements introduced into British political life by the Reform Bill of 1832 soon made their influence felt by the passage of a series of important legislative measures. In 1833 the reformed Parliament abolished slavery in the colonies and passed an act for the protection of children employed in the textile factories which prohibited the employment of children under nine years of age, restricted the labor of children between the ages of nine and thirteen to nine hours a day and forty-eight hours a week, limited that of young persons between the ages of thirteen and eighteen to twelve hours a day and sixty-nine a week, and provided a system of inspection for the enforcement of the law. In 1834 Parliament enacted a Poor Law that abolished all outdoor relief of the poor with the exception of medical aid, required women to support their illegitimate children, modified the old Law of Settlement of 1662, which hampered the free movement of labor, grouped parishes into unions and compelled the more prosperous parishes to lighten the burden of poor-relief for the poorer parishes, and created a central board to supervise the new system. In 1835 the government guided through both houses of Parliament a Municipal Reform Act which replaced the old, heterogeneous, undemocratic forms of town government by a uniform system that vested authority in each municipality in a mayor, aldermen, and councillors, elected directly or indirectly by the taxpayers. In 1842 Parliament passed an act which prohibited boys under ten years of age and women from working in mines. Two years later it reduced the working day for women employed in factories to twelve hours. In 1850 it cut down to ten hours the hours of labor for women and for young persons between the ages of thirteen and eighteen.

These measures gave expression for the most part to the humanitarian sentiments of the middle classes. They failed to redress the grievances of the classes not yet represented in the British Parliament. For them English thinkers suggested four remedies, the Socialistic schemes of Robert Owen, the organization of trade-unions, the Chartist movement, and the repeal of the Corn Laws.

Robert Owen (1771–1858) illustrates the best type of the men who rose to wealth and power as a result of the Industrial Revolution. He rose rapidly from the position of an apprentice to a clothier to part owner and manager of a large textile factory at New Lanark in Scotland. At this place he began to attract attention as a philanthropist. He found the town inhabited by several hundred pauper children and thirteen or fourteen hundred families, living in one-room houses and prone to theft, drunkenness, and other vices. By the enforcement of strict sanitary rules, the building of decent homes, restrictions on drinking, the basing of promotions on conduct, the establishment of stores where employees could buy articles at cost, and the organization of an educational system Robert Owen made New Lanark a Mecca for contemporary students of social problems. In his search for a remedy for the evils caused by the Industrial Revolution he finally developed theories that stamp him as the pioneer among the Utopian Socialists of the British Isles. As a cure for the unemployment arising from the overproduction of the new machines he advocated the establishment of communistic communities that would provide the unemployed with a variety of occupations and surround them with the proper conditions for the formation of character. He finally sank most of his fortune in unsuccessful attempts to found Socialistic communities. His schemes failed to attract the support of the lower classes and his denunciation of religion as an obstacle to the happiness of mankind alienated the sympathies of the upper and middle classes.

The organizers of the early trade-unions sought to improve the condition of the working classes through raising the scale of wages and limiting the hours of work. They relied on the strike as their chief weapon against the employing class. At this period they met with only ephemeral success. Though for a time the membership of the unions rose to a half-million, they proved to be too weak to withstand the opposition of the employers and the government. The former dismissed the laborers who joined the unions; the latter refused to receive their petitions and condemned their most active leaders to transportation to the colonies.

The Chartists received their name from the Charter published in 1837. This document demanded in the interest of the lower classes of Great Britain manhood suffrage, vote by ballot, abolition of the property qualification for membership in Parliament, payment of the members of the House of Commons, and annual sessions of Parliament. Favored by the prevailing economic distress, the publication of the Charter was followed by a great agitation marked by the formation of societies, the holding of large outdoor meetings, much public speaking, a national convention, an immense petition to Parliament, and a series of small insurrections. In the end the movement fell under the leadership of violent, none too well-balanced men who discredited it. Twice during the following decade the Chartist leaders made unsuccessful efforts to revive the movement and to translate into law the demands of the Charter. Eventually, however, five of the six points of the Charter were embodied in the British constitution.

The leaders of the agitation against the Corn Laws, two rich manufacturers, Richard Cobden and John Bright, advocated a reduction of the price of foodstuffs by a lowering of the high protective tariffs on grain, which benefited the landowners of Great Britain at the expense of British manufacturers and laborers. They carried on their propaganda mainly in the great manufacturing district around Manchester. As in the case of the Chartist movement, the scarcity of work and the lowering of wages gave a great impetus to the agitation. After a protracted struggle against the strongly intrenched landed interest, in 1846 the leaders of the movement finally succeeded, with the aid of Sir Robert Peel, in having the high protective tariff on grain repealed.

The agitation for the repeal of the Corn Laws was a part of the struggle for free trade that had been going on since 1824. In that year William Huskisson had made a beginning toward the abolition of the old system of high tariffs by doing away with a good many bounties and restrictions, providing for the gradual abolition of others, and reducing the customs duties on silk, cotton, woolens, sugar, paper, glass, and other commodities. In the budget of 1842 Sir Robert Peel reduced the tariff on seven hundred and fifty dutiable articles in a list of some twelve hundred. He proposed a duty of 5 per cent on raw materials, 12 per cent on partly manufactured commodities, and 20 per cent on finished products. In the following year he did away entirely with the duty on wool. In 1845 the budget abolished or reduced other duties. Finally, in 1846 Peel introduced a measure that removed all taxes on raw materials and placed a duty of 5 per cent on partly finished commodities, and 10 to 20 per cent on finished manufactures. The success of British industry under the régime of free trade soon took the tariff question out of politics.

Meanwhile the British government made no progress toward a solution of the Irish problem. The poverty-stricken Roman Catholic inhabitants of Ireland waged a fierce Tithe War against contributing toward the support of the established Anglican Church and opposed the introduction of an Irish Poor Law modeled after the English Poor Law of 1834. For a time the discontented Irish found a leader in O'Connell, who attracted large numbers to his movement for the repeal of the union between Great Britain and Ireland and greatly alarmed the British government. However, his failure to translate his eloquence into action eventually destroyed his influence. In 1845 the failure of the potato crop, which had become the staple food of Ireland, made the Irish people almost desperate and started a tide of emigration toward America that finally reduced the Irish population by half.

6

THE BRITISH EMPIRE

The period also witnessed a complete abandonment of the old British colonial system and a revival of interest in the British colonies. The essential feature of the economic system initiated in 1660 had been the regulation of interimperial trade by the British Parliament. This involved a considerable degree of interference with the life of the colonies and had driven thirteen of the British colonies in America to declare their independence. The success of the American colonists and the triumph of the free-trade doctrines of Adam Smith brought the old colonial system into disrepute, and led to the adoption of a free-trade policy in the years from 1842 to 1846 and to the repeal of the Navigation Acts in 1849. Most men, however, drew the inference that colonies were not worth maintaining or acquiring. Disraeli expressed the general view when he characterized the British colonies as "millstones round our necks."

Just at this moment of discouragement, however, a small but enthusiastic group of advanced Liberals, which included Edward Gibbon Wakefield, Lord Durham, Sir William Molesworth, and Charles Buller, began to preach a new colonial doctrine. They saw Great Britain suffering from overpopulation while vast and fertile lands under British control lay idle and empty. They advocated as a remedy for this situation the scientific colonization of the vacant lands, self-government for the new colonies, and the binding of the empire together by ties of sentiment and common institutions. Their agitation exerted a tremendous effect on the empire.

The new colonial policy had a detrimental effect on one section of the empire. The West Indies had been a flourishing region under the old colonial system, but their wealth had been built on slavery and protection. In the nineteenth century they suffered reverse after reverse. The imperial government first abolished the slave-trade and then emancipated the slaves. The government compensated the masters inadequately for the loss of their slaves; the freed negroes refused to work; and the competition of the beet-sugar of Europe proved ruinous. These developments caused the decline both of the British colonies in the West Indies and of the trading-posts on the western coast of Africa.

In South Africa the native problem prevented the British and the Dutch from achieving harmony. The home government adopted the humanitarian views urged by the missionaries, emancipated the slaves in 1833 without adequate compensation for the masters, refused to give the Boers self-government, and adopted a policy that exposed them to native aggression. Irritated by this treatment, many of the Boers set forth in small parties, carrying their families and belongings in tented wagons and driving their cattle before them, into the wild region north of the Orange River and into Natal. The attacks of the Boers on the natives caused the hesitating imperial government to take action again. In 1842 it annexed Natal—an action that caused most of the Boers to abandon the province—and attempted to create a group of protected native states. After considerable vacillation, however, the imperial government recognized the independence of both the Orange Free State (1852) and the Transvaal (1854).

In Canada the leaders of the new colonial policy found an opportunity to put into practice their principles of colonial self-government. In 1830 the six Canadian colonies were ruled by representative legislative bodies having control of legislation and taxation and by governors sent out from Great Britain. The resulting friction finally led to the breaking out of rebellions in both Upper and Lower Canada in 1837. After crushing the revolts the imperial government sent out Lord Durham as Governor and High Commissioner, with large powers. On his return to England he presented a report in which he recommended the union of the two provinces, the construction of railways and canals, and the establishment of a responsible executive. In 1840 the imperial government effected the union of the two provinces but it delayed for six years the establishment of a responsible executive. The new policy fostered the growth of peaceful relations between the British and French inhabitants of Canada and established the precedent for self-government in other parts of the empire.

In Australia the new colonial policy attracted a large number of immigrants of good type. In 1830 Great Britain had three colonies in the Australian continent, peopled largely by convicts. In 1831 the Colonial Office adopted the idea of Wakefield concerning the sale of land in the colonies and the use of the proceeds for the transportation of free men. Under the influence of the new policy the struggling penal settlements became thriving colonies and two new colonies, Victoria (1835) and South Australia (1836), were begun. By 1850 the Australian colonies had reached such a stage of development that the imperial Parliament authorized the legislatures of four of the colonies to draft constitutions for their own government. In 1855 the imperial Parliament ratified the proposed constitutions. By this act the Australian colonies came of age.

The colony of New Zealand owed its development to the same systematic policy of colonization. In 1839 Wakefield and his associates organized a company for the settlement of the islands. Their action forced the British government to annex them in the following year. Quarrels with the native Maoris and the opposition of the missionaries hindered the colonization of New Zealand for a considerable time. By the time the company resigned its charter in 1852, however, the success of the colony was assured.

In India the spirit of Liberalism was reflected in British policy in a number of ways. In 1833 a new India Act forbade the East India Company to engage in trade, recognized the unity of the Indian Empire by creating the office of Governor-General of India, provided for a systematic codification of Indian law that would pay due regard to the rights, feelings, and peculiar usages of the peoples of India, laid down the principle that no Indian might be prevented from holding any place, office, or employment under the company because of his religion, place of birth, descent, or color, and gave free access to all parts of India to all Europeans. Under the influence of this act the British authorities made many reforms in the administrative system, threw many offices open to Indians, subjected the protected native states to a stricter supervision, boldly attacked certain Indian usages which Western morality condemned, such as the self-immolation of widows on the funeral pyres of their husbands, and made increasing grants to schools and colleges for the teaching of Western culture to the peoples of India in the English language.

CHAPTER VII

AGITATION AND REPRESSION IN CENTRAL AND EASTERN EUROPE, 1830–1848

In central and eastern Europe the forces tending to undermine Conservatism did not show the same apparent strength as in Italy, France, and Great Britain in the years between the revolutions of 1830 and 1848. Even in Germany, Austria, Russia, and the Balkan States, however, the Industrial Revolution, nationalism, and Liberalism awakened the spirit of revolt against the political, social, and economic forms inherited from the past.

I

GERMANY, 1830–1848

After 1830 the German Liberals, particularly those living in the South German States, attempted to make use of the new political position which they had acquired as a result of the revolutionary movement of that year. The Liberal majorities in the legislative bodies of the different states took advantage of the changed situation to criticize the policies of their own states and of the German Confederation, to withhold the grants necessary to carry on the state governments in an effort to control governmental policies, and to pass bills of a Liberal tendency; Liberal newspapers sprang up which boldly discussed the political situation; and the Liberals ventured to stage demonstrations that attracted wide attention.

These developments alarmed the German Conservatives. As soon as the enthusiasm engendered by the revolution had somewhat died down, Metternich started to discuss with the governments of Germany the policy that should be adopted in regard to the new constitutions and the increased activity of the Liberals. These discussions finally resulted in the formulation of six articles designed to curb the new legislative assemblies. They asserted that the political powers of a state were vested in its sovereign, that a legislative body must not refuse its ruler the money necessary to carry on the work of the government or pass laws interfering with the obligations of a state to the Confederation, that the separate governments must obligate themselves to prevent attacks on the Confederation, and that the right of interpreting the federal

94

constitution belonged to the federal diet. Fortunately for the plans of the German Conservatives, the Liberals of the Bavarian Palatinate staged a political demonstration just at this time that enabled Metternich to obtain with ease the adoption of his program by the diet of the Confederation. This action inaugurated a new period of reaction. The Conservatives forbade all political societies, made the consent of the police a prerequisite for popular assemblies, revived the former close supervision of the universities, forced Baden to annul a liberal press law, and destroyed the Liberal journals. All but five of the constitutional sovereigns surrendered to the pressure of the Conservative powers and published the six articles. Only the parliament of Württemberg ventured to criticize the reactionary measures.

Having gained this success, Metternich attempted to put through further measures of repression. Utilizing a foolish, unsuccessful rising of the German Radicals at Frankfort as a means of whipping into line the timid and those inclined toward the liberal point of view, he invited the leading ministers of Germany to Vienna in 1834 for the purpose of formulating new ways of repression. Under his leadership they formulated sixty articles directed against the representative system, the journals, and the universities. Though they dared to publish only a few of them, they agreed that all the articles should be as binding as if they had been adopted by the diet of the Confederation.

One ruler of Germany, however, carried reaction too far even for Metternich. Upon the death of William IV in 1837 the crown of Great Britain went by the laws of succession to Queen Victoria, and the rule over the German state of Hanover to the Duke of Cumberland, a son of George III and a leader of the English Tories. In order to sell some of the domains of his new state the new sovereign of Hanover declared null and void the constitution conceded by his predecessor as a result of the Revolution of 1830. His high-handed act called forth a public protest from seven of the most distinguished members of the faculty of the University of Göttingen. As a punishment for their audacity their new ruler dismissed them from their academic positions and exiled three of them from Hanoverian territory. This attack stirred up not alone the opposition of the Liberals but also that of the academic world. Thenceforth the meetings of the learned societies of Germany became forums for the discussion of political questions.

In spite of these reverses suffered by the Liberals, economic forces were silently working for the union of Germany. With the growth of commerce and industry German merchants and manufacturers found intolerable the tariff lines that separated not only state from state but district from district. The finance ministers of the smaller German states, struggling to make their budgets balance without completely crushing the taxpayers, saw with envy the mounting revenues flowing into the Prussian treasury as a result of the new tariff system inaugurated in 1818. The smaller states desired to share in the benefits to be derived from the roads which were being built by the Prussian government to connect its eastern and western provinces. As a result of these forces the German states one after another knocked for admission to the new Prussian Zollverein. In 1828 Hesse-Darmstadt, in contrast with the seven small states that had previously joined, entered the Prussian customs union on the basis of an equal voice with Prussia in determining the policy of the Zollverein, equal fiscal privileges, independent administration of the customs laws and regulations, and apportionment of revenues according to the relative population of the respective states. In the following year Bavaria and Württemberg agreed to suspend all tariffs between their customs union and the Zollverein for a period of twelve years. In 1834 the two South German states, Saxony and Thuringia, found themselves compelled to enter the Prussian customs union. By 1844 nearly all the German states had joined the Zollverein.

In carrying through her economic plans Prussia encountered much opposition. The Liberals suspected a plan promoted by absolute Prussia. The particularists rightly feared that an economic union with the Prussian state foreshadowed the welding of the individual German states into a political union infringing their jealously guarded sovereignty. Wedded as she was to a protective system that prevented her from assuming the leadership of a movement for a German tariff union, Austria watched with great uneasiness the growth of Prussian influence through the Zollverein.

The construction of the new German railways also tended to unify Germany. Travel between the different sections of Germany became more and more common. Business connections between the different German states multiplied. The increased intercourse strengthened the feeling of national unity.

In the meantime the Liberals of Germany still hoped that Prussia would assume leadership of the movement for the unification of Germany. They had long realized that they must have her coöperation in achieving national unity. Though they had long since ceased to expect that Frederick William III would fulfil the promise, which he had made during the uprising against Napoleon, to grant his subjects a constitution, they looked to his successor for the realization of their hopes.

Upon his accession in 1840 Frederick William IV unintentionally gave the Liberals some encouragement. He amnestied the victims of the period of political reaction, restored one of the more famous professors to his position in the University of Bonn, conceded to the provincial estates somewhat larger powers, and relaxed to some extent the censorship of the press. In 1842 he summoned to Berlin for consultation

THE ZOLLVEREIN in 1834

representatives elected by the provincial estates. In 1847 he convened the provincial estates themselves at the Prussian capital.

These slight concessions to the spirit of the times aroused the Liberals of Germany to new activity. Journals sprang up in many localities. Bold pamphlets, like the *Four Questions of an East Prussian,* by the physician Johann Jacoby, appeared. At the opening of the reign the Conservative East Prussian diet ventured to request the new sovereign to grant the constitution promised by his predecessor. In 1845 a member of the diet of Westphalia asked for the extinction of the patrimonial courts, the abolition of the special privileges of the nobles in respect to taxation, reform of the provincial diets, the establishment of a parliament for the Prussian state, and the completion of the Zollverein by the creation of a tariff parliament. After 1839 the Liberal leaders in the South German states began to hold conferences for the discussion of common problems. In 1847 they published a statement of their program, in which they demanded freedom of the press, jury trial and public and oral judicial procedure, abolition of the remaining seignioral burdens, separation of the administrative and judicial branches of the government, self-government for the communes, a reduction of military expenditures, the improvement of the system of taxation, reform of the poor-relief and educational systems, an equalization of the burdens of taxation for the benefit of the middle and laboring classes, and the erection of a tariff parliament for the Zollverein as a first step toward the unification of Germany. The more radical asked for freedom of conscience and assembly, universal suffrage, abolition of the standing army, the organization of a civic militia, a progressive income-tax, jury trial for press and political cases, suppression of all class privileges, poor-relief and education for all, removal of the inequalities between capital and labor, substitution of self-government in place of bureaucratic control, and the convening of a German parliament. The lyric poets took up political themes to a greater extent than in any other period of German history. The United Provincial Diets even made the grant of the money needed for the construction of a new railroad conditional on the concession of their right to hold periodical meetings.

The course of events in other countries increased the agitation in Germany. German Liberals and Conservatives watched with the keenest interest the struggle of the democratic elements in the Swiss cantons, the popular movements in France, and the concessions made to the Italian Liberals after 1846. At the same time the attempts of the King of Denmark to incorporate Schleswig and Holstein into his kingdom aroused the latent national feeling in Germany. By 1848 Liberalism and nationalism were becoming powerful forces in Germany.

The Liberals soon discovered, however, that they could expect no concessions from the new Prussian sovereign. Like his predecessor on the throne, he accepted the ideas of the Ancien Régime. He felt himself to be the servant of God, commissioned to maintain discipline and order on earth and answerable to God alone for the exercise of the power intrusted to him. His constitutional ideal was the old German state of earlier centuries, in which the great landowners, the city magistrates, and the corporations shared power and authority with the king. No power on earth, he told the United Provincial Diets in 1847 in his speech from the throne, should move him to change the natural relationship between prince and people into a conventional, constitutional bond, and neither then nor in the future would he permit a written paper to come between God and his land like a second Providence, to rule him through its paragraphs and to replace the old sacred loyalty. The Prussian government, consequently, unwisely brought the political agitators to trial, arbitrarily dismissed the Liberals from administrative posts, and interfered with the judiciary. This attitude of the vested authorities made the danger of a popular explosion very great.

2

AUSTRIA, 1830-1848

After 1830 the Austrian government attempted to maintain the same condition of political immobility that had long characterized the Austrian state. It supervised and controlled the most insignificant acts of its subjects through a bureaucracy swarming with superfluous officials and immersed in forms and reports. It guaranteed the stability of the state by an army well disciplined but fired to no heroic deeds by national enthusiasm. It maintained a tariff policy that cut Austria off from the rest of Europe by an insurmountable economic barrier. It deliberately fostered national enmities between the peoples in the monarchy, in order to prevent their coöperation in behalf of a reform of the Austrian government. It maintained a censorship of the press, the universities, and the whole spiritual life of its subjects which tended to keep Austria intellectually stagnant. It did nothing to spread education or to improve agriculture. By its political and economic policies it made Austria a sort of European China.

The Austrian government created discontent by its mismanagement of the state as well as by its opposition to innovations. In the twenty-five years of peace following the Congress of Vienna it tripled the Austrian debt and increased the burden of taxation. It pursued a financial system that diverted the available capital from industry and agriculture to speculation in the state debt. It did nothing for the spiritual development of its subjects. It followed a foreign policy that permitted Prussia to assume the economic leadership of Germany and Russia to supplant Austria politically and commercially in the Balkan peninsula. As a result of its mismanagement of affairs the prestige of the Austrian state steadily declined abroad and the domestic discontent with the system of Metternich constantly grew in strength.

While the Austrian government succeeded in keeping the machinery for the enforcement of its repressive policy intact after the Revolution of 1830, it found it impossible to obtain the same coöperation from the officials or to revive the old childlike passivity of its subjects. The higher officials became somnolent. The lower officials often became corrupt or infected with Liberal ideas, or they hesitated to carry out the orders from Vienna for fear of retaliation in case of the ultimate victory of the elements demanding a reform of the state. At the same time the peoples of Austria began to demand political and economic reforms and concessions to the claims of nationality.

In the German-speaking provinces of the Austrian state the breach between the government and its subjects steadily widened. Among the educated classes the government became the butt of the jokes of the theater, the market-place, the counting-rooms, and student circles. In 1841 a picked group of lawyers, professors, judges, manufacturers, and members of the provincial diets organized a Liberal reading society, which became the center of the political opposition. In the same year an Austrian subject established at Brussels a weekly newspaper which reached a large circle of readers among the nobles and burghers of Austria. A few years later an unofficial journal began to be published at Vienna. A group of young writers increased the popular agitation by their discussions of conditions in Austria, and of the necessity for reforms. The diet of Lower Austria voiced the ideas of the more moderate elements of Austrian society by demanding a reform of the schools and the criminal courts, the creation of a fund for the abolition of seigniorial dues and ecclesiastical tithes, the admission of representatives of the cities and market-towns of Austria to seats in the diet, a new press law, and reform of local government. This agitation finally made the discussion of political and social reforms fashionable.

At the same time the new economic forces were creating a proletariat ready for mob violence. The hand-workers suddenly found themselves in competition with the new machines. The employees of the new factories began to suffer because of overproduction and unemployment. The rapid introduction of rail transportation after 1840 swelled the numbers of the lower classes in the cities. In 1847 famine conditions drove the proletariat to desperation. In Vienna the unemployed repeatedly plundered the bakers' shops and the poorer university students went for weeks without any warm nourishing food. The lower administrative officials struggled with the steadily rising price of commodities. The hungry proletariat watched with growing anger the concentration of the attention of the government on the police, the army, and foreign affairs, and public opinion held Metternich responsible for the general misery.

In 1846 the condition of the peasants of Galicia produced an actual uprising. In the whole province the usual gulf separated lord and peasant. In eastern Galicia differences in speech, religion, and nationality aggravated the tension between the Roman Catholic Polish landlords and their Uniate Ruthenian peasant tenants. Rumors circulated that the landlords had concealed from the cultivators of the soil the news of their emancipation by the Emperor. The rotting of the potato crop threatened them with starvation. At the news of the Polish rising of 1846 the Ruthenian peasants formed bands for self-protection and took fearful vengeance on their Polish oppressors. They murdered their landlords, burned their country houses, and devastated many sections of the country-side. Although the Austrian government finally suppressed the Galician rising, the episode brought the problem of the reform of peasant conditions vividly to its attention.

The centralizing policy followed by the Austrian government encountered the strongest opposition in the ancient Kingdom of Hungary. Proud of their time-hallowed institutions and separate history, the Magyars refused to have their country considered as merely a province of the Austrian Empire. They protested with growing vehemence against the conclusion of treaties without the coöperation of a Hungarian parliament, against the sacrifices entailed by the Napoleonic wars, the forced circulation of depreciated money, the arbitrary issuance of ordinances, the separation of Transylvania and other provinces from Hungary, the failure to summon a parliament to redress their grievances, and the censorship of their intellectual life. They voiced these grievances in their county assemblies. In some counties the royal commissioners, in spite of the troops at their disposal, found themselves unable to execute the orders of the Austrian government, and Magyar national feeling began to assume a dangerous form.

In order to calm the popular excitement and prevent an open revolt, the Austrian government commenced in 1825 to convene the Hungarian parliament at irregular intervals. With the revival of parliamentary life two parties quickly made their appearance among the Magyars. The majority of the five hundred great landowners of Hungary formed a Conservative party, which wished to maintain the constitutional rights of the Hungarian kingdom, but they had no desire to see modifications made in the patriarchal organization of Hungarian society which gave them a dominant place in the state. Through their control of the upper house of the parliament, the Table of Magnates, they blocked every proposal for reform. The Liberals, supported by the great majority of the Magyars, demanded, on the contrary, the reforms which would make the institutions of Hungary harmonize with the ideas of the Liberals of Western Europe. In the successive diets convened between 1825 and 1848 they asked in vain for the abolition of spies and censorship of the press, for independence for the courts and finances of Hungary, for the return of Transylvania and other districts to the Hungarian kingdom, the substitution of Magyar for Latin as the official language, a responsible ministry, equal taxation of noble and commoner, protection for the property and the person of the peasant, religious toleration for Protestants, and municipal reform. The principal victory of the Liberals during this period was the surrender of the Austrian government in 1844 to the national demand for the adoption of Magyar as the official language in the Kingdom of Hungary.

Awakening Hungary found leadership in a group of remarkable men. In the parliament of 1825 Count Stephen Széchenyi, scion of one of the most distinguished noble families of Hungary, made himself the leader of the national movement among the Magyars. Abandoning the traditional Latin, he addressed his colleagues in their native tongue. In order to counteract the Germanizing tendencies of the Austrian government, he offered the nation the income of his estates for a year and started a movement that resulted in the founding of the Hungarian Academy of Sciences. In a series of widely read publications he urged his countrymen to imitate the civilization of the progressive states of western Europe, and he took a leading part in such practical enterprises as the development of horse-breeding, the organization of a club to serve as a rallying-point for Magyar nationalism, the establishment of a national theater, making the Danube navigable, organizing a line of steamers for the promotion of inland commerce, and connecting Buda and Pest by a bridge.

By 1840, however, Széchenyi found himself and his ideals pushed into the background by a more brilliant leader, Louis Kossuth. In contrast to Széchenyi, he expressed the ideals for political equality with the great nobles which were cherished by the poorer gentry who found themselves compelled by their poverty to yield leadership to the owners of the great estates and often to earn a living as writers, officials, lawyers, physicians, and teachers. In 1833 he began to attract attention by circulating in manuscript (in order to escape the regulations of the censorship) a day-by-day account of the meetings of the Hungarian parliament. His political activity finally resulted in his trial and condemnation to imprisonment. This action, however, caused a popular agitation that eventually induced the Austrian government to grant Kossuth an amnesty. This incident terminated in favor of the reform party the struggle of the Hungarian parliament for freedom of speech. In 1841 Kossuth began to publish a journal which became the chief organ of the Magyar Liberals but alarmed the more moderate leaders of the party of reform by its inflammatory policy. Later he abandoned journalism and organized a society that encouraged the use of Hungarian products in preference to commodities of foreign origin. Under the influence of his burning oratory the wives and daughters of even the great nobles gave up, for a time, the choice fabrics of Parisian origin for the coarse cloth woven by the peasant looms of Hungary. The outbreak of the Revolution of 1848 thus found the Magyars greatly dissatisfied with Austrian rule and led by a man ready to resort to bold measures in order to realize the hopes of the Magyar nation.

The plans of the Magyars for the Kingdom of Hungary, however, did not enlist the coöperation of more than about half of the population. The Slovaks of northern Hungary dreamed of having a share in the glorious future prophesied for the Slav peoples by their Panslavist school-teachers and parish priests. The Rumanians of Transylvania and adjoining districts had already begun to think of political union with their kinsmen of Moldavia and Walachia. The Croats had commenced to plan for the severing of the bonds uniting the ancient Kingdom of Croatia to Hungary and for the union of Croats, Serbs, and Slovenes into a Southern Slav state.

The awakening of national consciousness among the Southern Slavs was the result of the organization of the Illyrian Provinces by Napoleon. The national movement found a leader in Ljudevit Gaj (1809–1872). In *The Illyrian National Journal* and its literary supplement he began in the thirties to advocate the use of the Serbian tongue as the literary language of all the "Illyrian" peoples, and on one occasion he published a map that made the Illyria of his visions include the present-day states of Bulgaria and Yugoslavia. Under his leadership the Croats founded a printing-press for the publication of books of interest to the Southern Slavs, established a literary club, and began to present Croatian plays. The Illyrian movement enlisted the support of the Croatian nobles, the Roman Catholic clergy, and the Austrian government and tended to spread to the neighboring provinces inhabited by Southern Slavs.

By 1842 the Illyrian party had attained sufficient strength to be victorious in the elections held for the purpose of choosing representatives of Croatia in the Hungarian parliament. In defiance of the Magyar majority of the Hungarian parliament, which was struggling to make Magyar the official language of the kingdom, the Croatian deputies insisted on addressing their colleagues in the parliament in the traditional Latin language, as a measure of defense against the threatened aggressions of Magyar nationalism. Their action precipitated a severe struggle. The Magyars howled down the Croatian deputies when they attempted to speak and made the use of Magyar as the official language the law of the land. The Croats retaliated by using their own tongue in their official reports and by resorting to mob violence against their political opponents. As a result of this struggle the Magyars found the Southern Slavs ranged against them in the political crisis of 1848.

By 1830 Bohemia was astir. The influence of Johann Gottfried von Herder, the French Revolution, the example of the people of Germany, and the attempt of Napoleon to arouse Czech national feeling, set the long-oppressed Czechs in motion. A group of literary men began to write of the past of the people, and to collect their songs and traditions. Their work aroused in the younger generation a pride in the history of the Czechs and hopes for a great future for the Czech nation. One scholar did much to awaken public interest in Slav antiquities. Another published a dictionary. In 1818 a Czech nobleman founded a museum for the preservation of Slavic books, documents, and manuscripts. In 1827 this institution started a learned journal, which became the chief organ of Czech erudition. Soon afterwards publications of a more popular character began to appear in Bohemia. In 1834 a small Czech theater was started at Prague. Finally the editor of the government journal published in the Czech language transformed the cultural movement into a political force. He hoodwinked the government censor by discussing events and conditions in Bohemia under the label of Irish affairs. This national movement among the Czechs enlisted the support of some of the nobles, a large portion of the middle class, and many of the peasants.

At first the Liberals among the strong German minority in Bohemia sympathized with the struggle of their Czech compatriots against Austrian absolutism. The Czech and German Liberals united in opposition to the censorship of the press, the secret police, and the centralizing policies of the Austrian government. Making embarrassing use of the material unearthed by František Palacký and other Czech historians, they protested against the appointment to official positions of persons from outside Bohemia and demanded larger powers for the diet, a broadening of the suffrage for the benefit of the middle class, and the establishment of schools in the Czech districts of the country.

This harmony of the Czechs and the Germans became disrupted over the question of the future of Bohemia. The Germans wished to maintain the ancient political bonds uniting them with their kinsmen in Germany. The Czechs, led by Jan Kollar and other prophets of Panslavism, dreamed of creating within the Austrian Empire a great Slav realm that would include the Poles, the Moravians, the Slovaks, the Illyrians, the Croats, and the Dalmatians. Under their leadership they foresaw a most brilliant future for the Western and Southern Slavs.

To the Austrian authorities in the first weeks of 1848 the situation in the Italian provinces seemed the point of greatest danger in the empire. The protests of the Congregations in Venetia and Lombardy and the collisions between the Austrian troops and the populace of Milan seemed to forebode a new revolutionary movement. In alarm the Austrian authorities arrested the Italian leaders, increased the watchfulness of the police, and sent military reënforcements into the two provinces. These measures left the Austrian government almost defenseless against the unexpected uprising that took place upon the arrival of the news of the Paris Revolution of 1848.

3

THE PROGRESS OF NATIONALISM IN THE BALKANS, 1829–1848

In the meantime the new spirit of nationalism was making rapid progress among the Serbian, Bulgarian, and Rumanian peoples of the Balkan peninsula. Stimulated by the success of the Greeks and the new influences coming in from western Europe, they began to study their national histories, languages, and literary remains, to found schools, newspapers, and periodicals, and to adopt the slogans and the programs of the Liberals of western Europe.

The Rumanians never suffered as severely from Turkish rule as did the other Christian peoples of the Balkan peninsula. The Rumanians of Transylvania only fell under the control of the Turks after the battle of Mohács in 1526 and before the lapse of two centuries they again came under the rule of the Austrian Empire. The Rumanians of Moldavia and Walachia always kept their local institutions and long retained a large measure of autonomy. Until 1711 the Sultan regularly chose the hospodars of the two provinces from the native nobility. From that date until the Greek revolt in 1821 he sold these offices to Phanariot Greeks, who exploited Moldavia and Walachia in order to recover the money they had paid in purchasing their positions. During this period the Rumanians of the two provinces sank into a state of mental and spiritual lethargy. In 1775 the Austrian authorities wheedled the harassed ministers of the Sultan into ceding to Austria the northwestern portion of Moldavia, thenceforth known as Bukovina, as a reward for their alleged diplomatic services. In 1812 Russia took Bessarabia from Moldavia as part of the booty of its war with the Ottoman Empire.

From this somnolent condition the Rumanians of the two provinces were awakened in 1821 by the invasion of Ypsilanti. Some of the boyars or nobles fled into Bukovina and Bessarabia in order not to compromise themselves in the rebellion. In exile they employed French tutors for their children and whiled away their idle hours in reading the revolutionary literature of western Europe. A few of the more adventurous traveled in western Europe, and sent their sons to school in France and Germany. These young men finally returned to their homes fired with the ambition to reorganize the life of Moldavia and

Walachia on Western models. The more courageous Rumanian nobles appealed to the Sultan for aid. They asked for the exclusion of the Greeks from the two provinces, the appointment of native hospodars again, and the promulgation of the laws in the Rumanian language. Upon receiving news of invasion of Ypsilanti the Turkish forces promptly occupied the provinces, suppressed the revolutionary movement, and replaced the discredited Greek hospodars with native nobles.

In 1829 the Treaty of Adrianople opened a new era in the history of the inhabitants of Moldavia and Walachia. This agreement provided that Russia should take the provinces under her protection, that the Black Sea should be open to the trading-vessels of all nations, that the two principalities should enjoy freedom of commerce, and that they should be assured against further Turkish misrule through the appointment of two hospodars for life, the restoration of autonomy, and the establishment of a fixed tribute.

Under the impact of these political and economic forces the two provinces began to lose their Oriental, patriarchal character. The Russian government immediately sent troops and administrators into the two principalities in order to reorganize them. Many of the Russian officers had been members of the allied army which had occupied France from 1815 to 1818. During their five years' residence in the two provinces they diffused among the Rumanians many of the new ideas with which they had come in contact in France and they formulated the organic statutes that regulated the political life of Moldavia and Walachia for the next three decades.

As a result of the stipulations of the Treaty of Adrianople concerning shipping in the Black Sea and freedom of commerce, trade and industry made rapid progress in Moldavia and Walachia after 1829. The improvement in economic conditions in turn made possible the founding of schools, the creation of a reading public, and the development of a native drama and literature. By 1861 the diplomats of Europe suddenly found themselves confronted by a matured nation determined to be independent.

The tiny Serbian state created by the Treaty of Adrianople, meanwhile, made slow progress at the work of transforming into a modern civilized nation a primitive population composed largely of pig-raising peasants. The lack of a seaport prevented rapid economic development. The descendants of the two heroes of the Serbian struggle for independence fought for possession of the throne and divided the country into two factions ready to gain their ends through assassination and the use of armed forces. The representatives of Austria, Russia, and Turkey intrigued with the rival factions in the hope of gaining some advantage for their respective states. In spite of these obstacles, the Serbs gradually learned the art of government, made some economic progress, and benefited culturally from contact with the more advanced Southern Slavs of the Austrian Empire. But in the middle of the nineteenth century no one dreamed that Serbia would ever become the nucleus of a great state that would include, eventually, the Southern Slavs of Serbia, Montenegro, Turkey in Europe, and the Austrian Empire.

During this period even the Bulgarians, who had suffered more from Turkish misrule than any of the other Christian peoples of the Balkan peninsula, felt the quickening influence of the forces awakening national consciousness among the peoples of Europe. Under Turkish rule the Bulgarian people had almost lost their identity. As a result of the Turkish conquest the Bulgarian provinces had been completely incorporated into the Ottoman Empire. With the decline of Turkish power they had suffered to the full the disadvantages of Turkish misrule. The soldiers and officials of the Ottoman Empire brutally mistreated them; the Greek clergy of the Eastern Orthodox Church shamefully exploited them in order to recoup themselves for the sums that they had advanced in purchasing their ecclesiastical offices, and strove to make the Bulgarians forget their language and their national history. As a result of these forces, Bulgarians often told inquiring travelers that they were Greeks.

Other forces, however, tended to counteract these proselyting tendencies. A feeble flame of Bulgarian nationalism flickered on in a few of the ancient monasteries. In the darkest period of Bulgarian history native merchants visited the trading-marts of Austria, where they came in touch with the ideas of western Europe. At the same time merchants from Ragusa, an independent Southern Slav republic on the Adriatic coast, traversed the Balkan peninsula distributing new ideas along with their wares of commerce. A few Bulgarian youths studied in the Austrian Empire and brought back to their countrymen the ideas current in the universities there. Expatriated Bulgarian merchants in Odessa and Bucharest gave material support to the reviving Bulgarian nation.

The pioneers of the national movement in Bulgaria were patriotic scholars. In 1762 a Bulgarian monk, roused by the jibes of his Greek companions in the monastery, embodied in a widely read volume his researches into the history of the Bulgarian people, in order to prove the injustice of the slurs heaped upon his nation. In 1806 a bishop published a collection of fables, stories, and proverbs still to be found in almost every Bulgarian household. In 1829 the first statistical and ethnographical account of the Bulgarian people appeared. In 1835 a group of merchants furnished the funds to found a Bulgarian school, and started a movement which resulted in the opening of thirteen other schools within the next six years. In the following decade the first periodical and the first newspaper made their appearance in Bulgaria.

The new Bulgarian nationalism soon expressed itself in a demand for the suppression of the abuses practised by the Greek clergy, and for the establishment of an independent Bulgarian Church. They asked for the appointment of Bulgarian bishops, the use of the Bulgarian language in the services of the Church, and the payment of definite stipends instead of fees to the clergy. In order to obtain their demands the Bulgarians resorted to rioting and violence. Their Greek clergy retaliated by refusing the malcontents the sacraments of the Church. In 1846 the Sultan finally ordered the Greek Patriarch at Constantinople to recall the Greek clergy and make the reforms necessary to quiet his Bulgarian subjects.

4

RUSSIA, 1812–1854

Russia emerged from the Napoleonic period with greatly enhanced prestige but confronted with vast problems of reform and reconstruction. The invasion of Russia in 1812 by the immense army of Napoleon created terrible conditions over a wide area between Moscow and the western border of Russia. Smolensk, Moscow, and a number of other cities had been burned. A large number of provinces had been devastated. Deadly epidemics followed in the wake of the military operations. The whole country suffered from the drain of the wars with France, Sweden, Austria, Turkey, and Persia, which disorganized the finances, increased the burden of taxation, and inflated prices through frequent issues of paper money. The Napoleonic wars alone are estimated to have cost the lives of a million and a half Russians and retarded the growth of population. The adherence of Russia to the Continental system of Napoleon had thrown the industry and commerce of the country into confusion.

The Napoleonic wars also added to the complexity and deferred the solution of many problems. Since the days of Peter the Great an educated class had slowly developed in Russia whose members knew something of conditions in other countries of western Europe, through reading or travel, and entertained hopes for the reform of conditions in their own state. At the time of the accession of Alexander I they had expected that he would give the Russian people a constitution which would substitute law for the will of the sovereign and institute the social and economic reforms needed to put Russia on a level with western Europe. Though the few reforms hesitantly made in the intervals of peace fell far short of their expectations, the news of his liberal views in regard to France and Poland revived their hopes that the Tsar would finally do something to reform conditions in his own country.

The problem of the peasants particularly demanded attention. Although they constituted almost 95 per cent of the population of Russia, they had no legal rights. Their lords sold them at will, interfered in their family life, subjected them to brutal corporal punishment, exiled them to Siberia for "insolent" behavior, and often cruelly maltreated them in other ways. This organization of society not only shocked the humanitarian sentiment of the time but also failed to meet the new demands made upon it. The devastation wrought by the campaign of 1812 caused many landowners to fall into debt. The rise in standards of living and the influx of new luxuries tempted others to mortgage their estates. The financial condition of the landlords increased their demands upon their serfs. At the same time the natural growth of the population increased the demands made on Russian agriculture, created a surplus of laborers in some regions, and intensified the burden of caring for the aged and the infirm. The economic organization, moreover, prevented any appreciable intensification of production. Both the peasants and the landowners had come to feel that the situation was intolerable.

In the years following the restoration of peace the breach between Alexander I and his subjects grew wider. He devoted most of his attention to the European congresses and the problems engaging their attention. His experiences with his Polish subjects, the revolt of one of his regiments against a brutal officer, and the coöperation of the Liberals in the revolutionary movements in southern Europe finally convinced the Tsar of the inherent connection between Liberalism and revolution. Thenceforth he abandoned his plans for a peaceful development of Liberal institutions and constitutional principles in Russia and docilely followed at home and abroad the policies advocated by Metternich.

This abandonment of Liberal principles by Alexander I caused the intellectual leaders of Russia to resort to secret organizations as a means of achieving their plans for the reform of the Russian state. Reënforced by officers familiar with conditions in western Europe through service abroad in the Napoleonic campaigns and in the army occupying the northern departments of France from 1815 to 1818, they organized a number of societies to work for social and political reform in Russia. Some of them sought the reorganization of the Russian state through peaceful development. Others took as a model the Italian Carbonari and other revolutionary societies of southern Europe.

In 1825 the sudden death of Alexander I presented the revolutionary societies with an unexpected opportunity to incite a revolt. Nicholas, the younger brother of the deceased Tsar, promptly ordered the garrison at St. Petersburg to take an oath of allegiance to his older brother, Constantine, commander of the military forces of Poland. Constantine, however, had no inclination to assume the burden of ruling over the huge Russian Empire, and three years before the death of his brother he had secretly renounced the throne. Now he insisted on the accession of his brother, Nicholas, to the vacant throne. The attitude adopted by the two brothers and the inadequate means of communication between St. Petersburg and Poland caused considerable delay and confusion.

The leaders of the revolutionary societies decided to make use of the unique situation to raise a revolt and demand a constitution. They told the ignorant soldiers that Constantine had been thrown into prison and persuaded half of one of the regiments to mutiny. Some soldiers and officers from other regiments joined the mutineers. For a time the situation placed Nicholas in some danger. In the end, however, loyal troops suppressed both the revolt at St. Petersburg and a weak rising in southern Russia. The revolutionary movement never had a real chance to succeed. A handful of conspirators could not set in motion the inert, ignorant masses of Russia. This experience made Nicholas I a steadfast opponent of Liberalism throughout his whole reign.

The new Tsar devoted the first months of his reign to tracking down and punishing those responsible for the revolt. His imagination exaggerated the conspiracy into a vast movement that imperiled the very existence of the Russian state. A special committee, directed by the Tsar, conducted the inquiry. After an investigation that made no provision for a legal trial, the committee sentenced five of the conspirators to be quartered and thirty-one to be shot. Before the condemned were actually executed, however, the Tsar reduced these severe sentences, the first to hanging and the second to imprisonment.

The inquiry into the causes of the conspiracy revealed to the Tsar an appalling need for administrative reforms. During the next few years he made a serious effort to remedy the faults and abuses that he found rampant in the administration. He devoted himself with the greatest diligence to the service of the state, attempted to fill the administrative posts with moderate Conservatives, and appointed a special committee to work out a general plan for the intended reforms. Before much had been achieved, however, the revolutionary movement of 1830 caused Nicholas I to abandon all his plans for modifying the institutions of the Russian Empire.

After the Polish Revolution of 1831 Nicholas I resolutely took up the task of defending orthodoxy, autocracy, and nationality in Russia from the influences of western Europe. From that time on the Russian government persecuted Jews and Uniates, the members of the Bible societies that had enjoyed the favor of Alexander I, the Lutherans of the Baltic provinces, and the Roman Catholics of Poland. It sought to capture the minds of its subjects by depriving the universities of self-government, limiting the number of students, regulating the studies offered in their curricula, supervising the reading and lecturing of their professors, and controlling the activities of the students. For the same reason it forbade travel abroad and the employment of foreign tutors.

It provided only the elementary and secondary educational facilities needed to supply the technical needs of the state.

The government did not dare to abandon its efforts to find a solution of the peasant problem. From the time of his accession peasant risings called the attention of Nicholas I sharply to the problem of ameliorating the condition of the serfs. During his reign they rose in revolt against their hard lot in five hundred and fifty-six villages or larger districts. In nearly half of these uprisings the situation demanded the intervention of military forces. A number of crop failures added to the misery of the peasants. At the same time the position of the land-owners grew steadily worse. In the more populous provinces the rapid increase of the population created a mounting surplus of laborers who must be fed and the continued rise in the standard of living forced into debt half of the owners of estates. Throughout the reign of Nicholas I a succession of committees and administrators made unsuccessful efforts to solve the problem of serfdom.

In spite of the repressive measures of the government, the educated class in Russia increased in numbers and in intellectual activity. In the fourth and fifth decades of the nineteenth century the Russian intellectual class split into two groups. One school of thinkers drew their inspiration from the French writers of the eighteenth century and centered its attention on social and political problems. The other group became followers of the leading German philosophers. The two groups met for the discussion of current problems in the homes of their leaders and published journals that reached a wider audience. As a result of this literary activity the possession of forbidden books from western Europe became the chief mark of good taste.

At the same time the closely supervised educational institutions grew in number and in quality. A brilliant group of university professors passed on to the younger generation the ideas they had garnered while in attendance at foreign universities. The number of secondary schools rose during the reign of Nicholas I from forty-eight to seventy-four. In spite of the repressive policy of the government the Russian universities and secondary schools managed to implant in the minds of their students many new ideas which ultimately undermined the traditions and institutions of Russia.

A survey of the history of Europe between the revolutions of 1830 and 1848 reveals the growing strength of the forces undermining the conservative organization of society. In France, Republicanism and Bonapartism revived and Socialism appeared for the first time as a force to be reckoned with. In Italy Mazzini and the neo-Guelphs brought the problems of Liberal reform and national unification out of the realm of conspiracy into the sphere of practical politics. In England the capitalist class created by the Industrial Revolution embodied its political and social philosophy in a series of important laws dealing with slavery, poor-relief, municipal reform, and free trade, while the laboring classes sought a panacea for the ills from which they suffered in trade-unions, the socialist ideas of Robert Owen, and Chartism. In Germany the Liberals found unexpected help in the new economic forces. In Austria the peoples of the empire steadily grew in national consciousness and increasingly threatened the unity of the monarchy. In Russia autocracy found itself fighting a losing battle against Western ideas and the peasant problem. In the Balkan peninsula the awakening nationalism of the Christian subjects of the Sultan foreshadowed the dismemberment of the Ottoman Empire in Europe and the creation of a group of new national states capable of checking further advances by Russia and Austria in southeastern Europe.

CHAPTER VIII

THE REVOLUTIONS OF 1848

The resistance of the Conservatives in control of Europe to the growing forces of Liberalism and nationalism made a resort to the arbitrament of arms almost inevitable. In 1848 a revolutionary movement broke out in France that rapidly spread to the countries lying to the north and the east.

I

THE REVOLUTION OF 1848 IN FRANCE

The revolutionary movement of 1848 in France grew out of the campaign of political banquets instituted by the party demanding parliamentary reform. A committee of the twelfth arrondissement of Paris announced a banquet for the twenty-second of February, 1848. To lend dignity to the gathering the committee obtained a promise from eighty-seven deputies of parliament to attend the banquet and invited the National Guard to appear in uniform without arms in order to receive the deputies as they marched into the banquet-room. The night before the proposed political demonstration the government forbade the committee to go on with its plans. The deputies obeyed the order but, as a result of the summons of two of the Republican journals, an aimless, leaderless mob, composed of students, workers, and shopkeepers, assembled at the appointed meeting-place on the night set for the banquet. As time went on the idle crowd became disorderly, lit a bonfire, started to raise barricades, and pillaged the shop of an armorer. From the neighborhood of the banquet-hall the disorder finally spread to the Republican quarters of Paris.

At this point Louis Philippe made a serious blunder. Although he reluctantly allowed Guizot to resign from the office which he had held since 1840, the King attempted to force an unpopular general on Thiers and the other leaders of the reform party, refused to dissolve the parliament or to surrender his pliant majority, and hesitated to promise measures of reform. While Louis Philippe temporized and the leaders of the reform movement negotiated, a collision took place in the vicinity of the residence of Guizot between the royal troops that were guarding the ex-minister and the Parisian mob. The incident caused the death of more than a score of persons and created great excitement throughout the whole city. The hesitating Republicans assumed leadership of the popular movement and the people of Paris threw up barricades in the narrow, crooked streets of the capital, seized arms where they could find them, and made a general attack on the royal forces. The army and the National Guard sympathized with the uprising and quickly showed that they could not be depended upon to quell the revolt. By sunrise on February 24 the armed mob had gained control of all the central part of Paris.

In order to avoid the establishment of a republic, the parliamentary leaders finally brought pressure to bear upon the King to abdicate his throne in favor of his grandson. The compliance of Louis Philippe with this demand left political power in France divided between the legally elected Chamber of Deputies and a self-constituted body of Republican leaders. Unable longer to look for guidance to the King or his ministers and divided by conflicting opinions, the deputies vacillated until the pressure of the mob compelled them to pass over the claims of the grandson of Louis Philippe and establish a provisional government composed of Republican leaders selected earlier in the day by a conference held in the office of one of the Parisian journals. In order to win the support of the Socialists, the new provisional government immediately proclaimed a republic and admitted Louis Blanc, the author of *The Organization of Labor,* and two other Socialists to offices in the government. This compromise joined together two inharmonious political elements—the Republicans, who regarded the establishment of a republic as an end in itself, and the Socialists, who considered the setting up of a republican form of government as merely a means toward the achievement of such a social reorganization as Louis Blanc had proposed.

The Republicans found themselves in a position that necessitated a conciliatory policy toward the Socialists. Intimidated by the invasion of its place of meeting by a mob of Socialist sympathizers, the provisional government agreed to adopt in principle the scheme of Louis Blanc, declared the Tuileries, the former royal palace, a home for incapacitated working-men, and set aside the income hitherto paid Louis Philippe as a fund to be used in redeeming goods pawned by destitute persons. On February 26 the provisional government decreed the immediate establishment of the national workshops advocated by Louis Blanc and his followers. Two days later it created a commission to inquire into the situation of the workers. Upon the recommendation of this body the government decreed the reduction of the working-day from eleven to ten hours at Paris and from twelve to eleven hours in the provinces.

These concessions never really affected the conditions of the French workers. The provisional authorities ignored the reasonable recommendations of the commission of inquiry and never made an honest trial of the scheme of Louis Blanc. They intrusted the management of the so-called national workshops to an avowed opponent of the proposal, who set the unemployed, without regard to their previous training, to work at making excavations. As the numbers of the unemployed mounted and useful tasks grew scarcer the director of the national workshops reduced the days of work per week and the scale of wages paid the workers. This policy created at Paris a large mass of idle men ready for desperate measures to relieve their situation.

Upon the election of a Constitutional Assembly by universal manhood suffrage in the latter part of April, the situation of the Socialists and their followers grew worse. The Socialists represented only a small minority in the nation. They owed their power entirely to the support of the armed working-men in certain quarters of Paris. The aristocrats, the bourgeoisie, and the peasants of France felt no sympathy for the ideas of the Socialists and elected a Constitutional Assembly that favored the establishment of a republic but opposed further Socialist experiments. This body replaced the provisional government with an executive committee of five members in which the Socialists had no representation. Discontented with the results of the election, the workers of Paris invaded the meeting place of the Constitutional Assembly, declared that body dissolved, and proclaimed a new provisional government composed of tried Socialist and revolutionary leaders. As soon as the irritated members of the Constitutional Assembly, with the aid of the National Guard, got the better of this mob, they decreed the arrest or exile of the leaders of the Parisian workers and the suppression of the national workshops. This action aroused the working class of Paris to a last desperate struggle that continued from the twenty-third to the twenty-sixth of June. The exacerbated combatants accused each other of massacring the wounded and the prisoners. The victorious Constitutional Assembly ordered the transportation of eleven thousand prisoners to penal colonies and the suppression of thirty-two journals. These measures temporarily destroyed the power of the Socialists and permanently embittered the relations between the bourgeoisie and the working class in France.

After it had broken the power of the Socialists for the time being, the Constitutional Assembly set to work at the task of drawing up a constitution for the Second French Republic. Upon its completion this document restored to the French people the right to form associations, to assemble peacefully, to petition the government, to express themselves freely orally and by the printed page, and freed them from arbitrary arrest, domiciliary visits, and extraordinary tribunals. It delegated executive power to a President elected by universal manhood suffrage, and the power to make laws to a legislative assembly of seven hundred and fifty members elected in the same manner as the chief executive. After adopting a constitution the Constitutional Assembly made the necessary preparations for the election of a President. In the electoral campaign three parties, the Socialists, the Republicans, and a Party of Order—composed of supporters of the Bourbons, the Orleanists, and the Catholic Church—put forward candidates for the Presidency. At first the Party of Order negotiated with the Republican candidate. After failing to reach a satisfactory agreement with him it decided to nominate Louis Napoleon, the heir of the Napoleonic tradition, who had returned to France after the outbreak of the revolution and had shown unexpected political strength in the supplementary elections to the Constitutional Assembly. Although his name had appeared frequently in popular demonstrations and several journals had rallied to his support, the leaders of the Party of Order do not seem to have realized either his ability or his ambition.

In the election Louis Napoleon won a great triumph. He received the support of the mass of the peasants and the workers, the royalists of every shade of opinion, and the Roman Catholics, and polled five and a half million votes. His Republican opponent obtained less than a million votes and the Socialist candidate only three hundred and seventy thousand ballots. As a result of this victory the Republicans lost control of executive power in the republic.

In May, 1849, the Constitutional Assembly made way for the legislative assembly provided for by the new constitution. This body differed greatly from the one which had preceded it. The Constitutional Assembly had contained an overwhelming Republican majority. The new legislative body was composed of about two hundred and fifty Republicans and five hundred Monarchists. This success of the Monarchists in gaining control of the Presidency and the legislative branch of the government foreshadowed a speedy overthrow of the Second French Republic.

2

THE SPREAD OF THE REVOLUTION OF 1848 TO SOUTHERN AND WESTERN GERMANY

The news of the events in France quickly started a revolutionary movement in southern and western Germany. On February 27 information concerning the rising at Paris reached Baden. Within a month the revolutionary movement had reached Hesse-Darmstadt, Bavaria, Hesse-Cassel, Nassau, Württemberg, Hanover, Saxony, Thuringia, Lippe-Detmold, Waldeck, Hohenzollern-Hechingen, Mecklenburg-Schwerin, Oldenburg, Bremen, and Hamburg. In most of these states mass-meetings forwarded petitions to the sovereign asking for such reforms as freedom of the press, the right to assemble freely, trial by jury, the right to present petitions, a national parliament, the right to arm, the grant of a constitution to states without constitutional rights, an oath of fidelity to the constitution by civil and military officials, and, occasionally, equality for all religious confessions, particularly for the Jews. Often threatening, tumultuous throngs accompanied the bearers of the petitions.

In almost every case the governments changed their political leadership, made profuse promises of reform, and pledged themselves to endeavor to effect fundamental changes in the organization of the German Confederation. In Hesse-Darmstadt, for example, a popular meeting took place at Mainz and drew up plans for a descent on the capital. To forestall the Liberals, the Grand Duke made his son coregent and summoned to office Heinrich von Gagern, long the recognized leader of the Liberals of Germany. In Hesse-Cassel the Elector, under pressure of deputations from Hanau and other places, appointed some Liberal ministers and promised to convoke the diet. Three days later a popular meeting presented an ultimatum that caused the Elector to establish a constitutional régime. These two examples well illustrate the course of events in the constitutional and the absolute states.

As soon as they had gained control of the individual states of southern and western Germany, the Liberals began to lay plans for the realization of their dreams of a national, centralized, constitutional, German state. On March 5, 1848, fifty-three Liberals from the states of southern and western Germany took counsel together at Heidelberg. This conference intrusted a commission of seven members with the task of convoking a preliminary parliament that finally assembled on the last day of March. The Liberal leaders realized from the first, however, that the success of their plans depended on the attitude of Austria and Prussia.

3

THE SPREAD OF THE REVOLUTION OF 1848 TO THE AUSTRIAN EMPIRE

The news of the uprising at Paris also incited to action the Liberals and the national groups within the Austrian Empire. In Austria proper members of the royal family, the intellectual leaders of Vienna, and the students of the university petitioned the government to abandon the political system of Metternich and adopt a policy of reform. The petitioners asked for the publication of the budget, periodical summoning of the provincial diets, removal of censorship of the press, concession of local government to cities, freedom of speech, and removal of restrictions on teaching and learning. The stubborn adherence of the government to its old repressive policy created great popular excitement. When the diet of Lower Austria met on March 13, 1848, a great crowd surrounded and invaded its place of meeting and demanded the removal of Metternich from office. The attempt of the military to restore order caused a collision between the troops and the crowd which resulted in the wounding of six persons. This incident aroused great popular indignation. In alarm Metternich resigned from office and fled from Austria, and the government promptly promised a constitution, abolition of censorship of the press, and the establishment of a National Guard. After the fall of the famous Chancellor a committee of twenty-four citizens took control of Vienna and a Liberal ministry assumed the herculean task of governing the Austrian Empire.

In Bohemia a self-constituted committee, representing both the German and the Czech elements in the population, took charge of political affairs and convoked a popular assembly that forwarded a petition to the Austrian authorities demanding freedom of assembly, a National Guard, the abolition of seigniorial dues, and, in rather vague terms, a closer union of Bohemia, Moravia, and Austrian Silesia, all three of these provinces being parts of the former Kingdom of Bohemia. By the time a deputation from Bohemia reached Vienna the Liberal ministry in power did not feel strong enough to refuse the Bohemian demands.

Upon returning to Prague, however, the bearers of the Bohemian petition found that the situation had changed. During their absence at Vienna the revolutionary movement had taken on a more national character. As a result of this development the Czechs gave the returning deputation a rather cool reception and forwarded to Vienna a new set of demands. They asked for a responsible Bohemian diet, a large degree of legislative autonomy, the right to examine the proposed Austrian constitution, and complete equality of the Czech and German languages. They found the Liberal ministry at Vienna still too weak to resist their demands.

The Magyars of Hungary demanded even greater concessions than the Czechs. A delegation from the Hungarian parliament persuaded the almost helpless Austrian government to permit the severing of most of the ties binding Hungary to the Austrian Empire. Its demands left only two bonds untouched, a Hungarian contribution toward the expenses of the Austrian court and the diplomatic service, and the right of the Emperor to exercise command of the Hungarian troops in time of war.

The Magyar Liberals, however, led by Louis Kossuth, demanded political reforms as well as national independence. During the absence of the Magyar delegation at Vienna, accordingly, they pressed through the lower house of the Hungarian parliament their social and political program. Practically ignoring the Conservative upper house, they voted for an independent ministry responsible to the Hungarian parliament, the incorporation of Transylvania into Hungary, annual sessions of the parliament, an extension of the suffrage, freedom of the press, trial by jury, the recognition of Magyar as the official language of the state, the abolition of tithes, the suppression of seigniorial dues with indemnification for the owners of estates, the abolition of the legal jurisdiction of the landlords, and equality in taxation. At the close of the session the Emperor came in person to give his sanction to these organic measures.

In planning for the future of Hungary, however, the Magyars disregarded the wishes and the interests of the Slovaks of northern Hungary, the Saxons and the Rumanians of Transylvania, and the Croats and the Serbs of southern Hungary. In Croatia the Illyrian party immediately formulated demands that threatened the unity of the Magyar state. In a national assembly held at Agram the Croats asked for the incorporation of Dalmatia and the military frontiers into the Croatian kingdom, a separate ministry, and the use of their own tongue in the army, the schools, and the administration. They elected as Ban of the kingdom Count Jellachich, a Croatian soldier and nobleman. The new leader immediately initiated a national struggle in Croatia against the Hungarian Government and its sympathizers by filling the administrative offices with Croatian patriots and forbidding all communication with the government of Hungary. In the meantime their Serbian kinsmen had met at Carlowitz and decided to demand the concession of their old privileges and to send a group of deputies to the Croatian diet.

Soon after it assembled in June, 1848, this body sent to the Austrian court a deputation headed by Jellachich and composed of representatives of both the Serbs and the Croats. The conflicting demands of the Magyars and these Southern Slavs put the harassed Austrian authorities in an embarrassing position. For a time they felt compelled to reaffirm the unity of the Kingdom of Hungary and to condemn the Southern Slav movement. The Southern Slavs, however, disregarded this rebuff and severed their relations with Hungary.

At Milan the leaders of the Italian national movement planned a formal demonstration in favor of a Civic Guard. A shot fired at the crowd by the military transformed this peaceful demonstration into an insurrection. Using the name of the new and liberal Pope as their battle-cry, the people of Milan invaded the royal palace and made the representative of the Austrian government a prisoner, erected numerous barricades, and raised the Italian tricolor. A battle ensued between the Austrian garrison of the city and the unarmed populace, lasting from the eighteenth to the twenty-second of March. After five days of fighting the Austrian commander withdrew his troops to the famous lines of the Quadrilateral because of a shortage of food and his fear of being cut off from his sources of supply by risings in the surrounding province. After the retreat of the Austrian forces from the city the Italian leaders established a provisional government in Lombardy. Simultaneously the people of Venetia declared their independence. In order to quiet the agitation at Venice the Austrian authorities freed the chief agitators and permitted the establishment of a small Civic Guard. On the same day that Count Radetzky withdrew the Austrian forces from Milan the new Civic Guard and the Venetian populace, led by Daniele Manin, captured the arsenal. After this incident Manin succeeded in persuading the Austrian military forces to evacuate Venice and the surrounding forts. After their withdrawal the revolutionists proclaimed the reëstablishment of the Venetian Republic and organized a provisional government headed by Manin.

The reports of the events at Milan and Venice stirred the whole Italian people to action against the domination of Austria in the peninsula. Impelled by patriotism, ambition, and the pressure of his Liberal subjects, and fearful lest the followers of Mazzini should take independent action, Charles Albert, King of Sardinia, assumed leadership of the national movement and prepared to attack the Quadrilateral. Under the pressure of the Liberals of the peninsula the other sovereigns of Italy made a pretense at least of rallying to the national cause. The Grand Duke of Tuscany immediately announced the forwarding of his regular troops to the front and the organization of a force of volunteers. At Rome the papal government reluctantly coöperated in the war against Austria, volunteers flocked to the colors, and princes and cardinals of the Church contributed to the national cause in defiance of the peaceful sentiments of the Pope. At Naples the reactionary King permitted bands of volunteers, the royal navy, and finally a small army to take part in the war for Italian independence. The Italian people seemed to be on the verge of achieving their aspirations for Liberal reforms and national independence.

4

THE SPREAD OF THE REVOLUTION OF 1848 TO PRUSSIA

On the fall of Metternich the reactionary government in Prussia lost control of the situation. After the arrival of this surprising news the popular agitation in East Prussia, Breslau, Berlin, and the Rhenish provinces began to assume a dangerous mien. From Breslau, Cologne, and Königsberg came deputations bearing to the King of Prussia petitions, couched in language of unwonted boldness, asking for Liberal reforms. At Berlin popular meetings demanded freedom of speech and the press, the summoning of the united provincial diets, the convening of a German parliament, improvement of the condition of the working classes, and the organization of a Civic Guard. The popular movement took a more and more threatening form as foreign agitators flocked to Berlin; the workers joined forces with the middle-class Liberals; and blood began to flow.

In order to conciliate his turbulent subjects Frederick William IV announced that it was his intention to summon the United Diets for the purpose of drawing up a constitution for Prussia, to give Germany a federal organization that would provide for the creation of a national army and navy and a federal judiciary and abolish internal customs lines and censorship of the press, and to do away with censorship of the press immediately in his own state. After reading this royal proclamation the populace began to press around the palace to express their gratitude for these concessions. As the day progressed, however, the peaceful demonstration transformed itself into an insurrection. The crowd began to doubt the loyalty of the government to its promises. Popular leaders commenced to harangue the assembled throng and the troops attempted to clear the palace. Two muskets went off and workers, citizens, and others seized arms and barricaded the streets. The wild ringing of bells, the thunder of cannon, and the rattle of musketry signaled to prince and people alike the outbreak of a revolution in Prussia. Courtiers, generals, officials, and deputations rushed to the royal palace to press upon the harassed sovereign their respective points of view. Amid the excitement the nerves of the unstable King gave way. To the indignation of his military advisers, he ordered the withdrawal of the royal troops from the city.

This decision left Frederick William IV for the time being at the mercy of the revolution and forced him to make concession after concession. On March 21 he had to stand bareheaded on a balcony of the palace and in a grim ceremony salute the dead bodies of one hundred and eighty-three persons killed in the street fighting. On March 29 he replaced his old advisers with a more liberal ministry. On April 6 it announced the principles of the proposed Prussian constitution. A few days later the Prussian people chose their representatives to the national parliament summoned to meet at Frankfort. This assumption of the leadership of the national movement by Prussia alarmed Austria, but she could make no effective protest until she had conquered the revolutionary movement in her own empire.

5
THE SPREAD OF THE REVOLUTION OF 1848 TO OTHER EUROPEAN STATES

Few of the states of Europe entirely escaped the revolutionary movement of 1848. In remote Moldavia the young Rumanian nobles, fresh from the schools of western Europe, felt chagrined at the medieval conditions still prevailing in their own province and on March 27 petitioned the reigning prince for freedom of the press, a Civic Guard, and a sincere observance of the organic statute. The presentation of this petition merely resulted in the exile or the imprisonment of the leaders of the movement. In Walachia the revolutionary leaders issued a proclamation directed against the influence of Russia in the province, marched at the head of a thousand men on Bucharest, and forced the reigning prince to sign a new constitution and to appoint a reform ministry. Russia replied to this challenge by inviting the Turkish Sultan to intervene. From that date until the Crimean War the two Rumanian provinces remained under the joint supervision of Russian and Turkish commissioners.

In Switzerland the twelve cantons dominated by the Unitary party took advantage of the preoccupation of the great powers with the revolution to transform the loose confederation established by the Federal Pact of 1815 into a more unified state. The new constitution of September 12, 1848, replaced the old directory with a federal executive of seven members elected by the two houses of the legislative body sitting jointly, substituted for the former diet a parliament of two houses modeled after the Congress of the United States, gave the central government control over external affairs, the army, weights and measures, coinage, the postal service, and customs, and guaranteed the Swiss people republican institutions, equality before the law, liberty of residence, religious freedom, and liberty of the press. The adoption of the new constitution paved the way for the abolition of cantonal customs lines, the establishment of a federal postal service, the adoption of a federal coinage system modeled after that of France, the introduction of uniform weights and measures, the creation of a unified electric-telegraph system, the initiation of great undertakings for the improvement of roads and rivers, and the opening of the Federal Polytechnic School at Zurich.

In the Kingdom of the Netherlands the combination of the blunders of William I in handling the Belgian provinces, the autocratic character of the government, and the potato disease had caused great discontent. The news of the revolutionary movements in other countries brought this dissatisfaction to a head. Alarmed for the safety of his throne, the King named a commission to draw up plans for reform. The new constitution drawn up by this body made the royal ministers responsible for all executive acts of the government, provided for freedom of worship, annual budgets, and reform of local and provincial government, and established a legislative body of two chambers, one elected by the provincial estates from the most highly taxed subjects of the state and the other chosen by the direct vote of all adult males paying a certain amount of taxes. The new constitution brought the Liberals into power and enabled them to democratize the suffrage, substitute direct for indirect taxes, reform the navigation laws, and abolish the excise on pork and mutton.

The revolutionary movement of the mid-century also affected the lands ruled by the King of Denmark—Denmark, Schleswig, and Holstein. The consultative assemblies established in 1831 had failed to satisfy the Liberals. The growth of national consciousness in Germany had given rise to a demand for free constitutions for Schleswig and Holstein and their complete separation from Denmark. The German national movement had evoked a counter Danish national movement that advocated the incorporation of Schleswig in Denmark and the abandonment of the Danish claims to Holstein. To propitiate Danish nationalism Frederick VII of Denmark had promulgated in January, 1848, a constitution that proclaimed the permanent union of the two duchies with Denmark and the creation of a common diet for his three territories.

Both the Danish and the German nationalists protested against the new constitution. In the two duchies the diets demanded the incorporation of Schleswig and Holstein into the proposed German Confederation as a single constitutional state. When the Danish sovereign ignored their demands, the German inhabitants of the two provinces rose in insurrection and established a provisional government and the Duke of Augustenburg, who hoped to rule the duchies after the death of the childless King of Denmark, hurried to Berlin to enlist the support of the Prussian government. The political leaders of Prussia seized the opportunity to restore its sadly dimmed prestige by intervening in a popular cause and marched troops into Holstein. A little later the German diet authorized them to occupy Schleswig also.

The intervention of Prussia in the two duchies threatened for a time to start a European war. Swedish troops came to the assistance of the Danes, the British government took steps toward sending its fleet, Russia made preparations to intervene, and Austria refused to support the German contentions regarding the two provinces. The attitude of Russia, in particular, caused the Prussian government to sign an armistice and commence diplomatic negotiations. After long efforts to reach a compromise—efforts that were interrupted by a temporary renewal of the war—the two contending parties came to an agreement that provided for the union of the two duchies with Denmark, the concession of increased parliamentary powers to the diets of Schleswig and Holstein, the settlement of the claims of the Duke of Augustenburg, and the recognition of the rights of the German Confederation in Holstein.

In the meantime, in response to the pressure of the Danish Liberals the King of Denmark had replaced the offending constitution of January, 1848, with a new constitutional document that limited his power in his Danish kingdom by a legislative body composed of a nominated upper house and an elected lower house and gave the Danish peasants a voice in their own government. They used their power during the next few years to put through the Danish parliament a series of measures that made Denmark a state of farm-owning peasants.

The Revolution of 1848 slightly affected a number of other countries. In Belgium the Liberal government felt compelled to reduce the property qualification for the suffrage. In Ireland some members of the Young Ireland party made an unsuccessful attempt to enlist the aid of France in a revolt against the British government. In Great Britain the Chartists circulated a monster petition and planned to march on Parliament, but the vigorous measures of the government caused them to abandon their plans.

6

THE BEGINNINGS OF SCIENTIFIC SOCIALISM

The general intellectual currents that produced the revolutionary movement of 1848 caused the development of a group of able writers, thoroughly committed to the idea of the need for a complete reorganization of society, who began to subject the Utopian schemes of men like Saint-Simon, Fourier, and Robert Owen to a merciless criticism. This group included two young Germans of Jewish origin, Karl Marx, a brilliant young doctor of philosophy from the University of Jena, and Friedrich Engels, a young business man residing in England. Together they founded the school of thought known as Scientific Socialism.

Karl Marx sprang from the Jewish community of Trier. When he was six years of age his father, as a result of official pressure, nominally adopted Christianity. After making a brilliant record at school and in the university the son turned to free-lance journalism, since he found an academic career closed to him on account of his radical economic and political views. In 1842 his trenchant writing brought him an invitation to become editor of the liberal *Rheinische Zeitung*. His acceptance of this position forced him to make a serious study of the economic problems and the Socialist literature of the time. His studies brought him to the conclusion that a revolutionary change in the organization of society must come about through the efforts of the class of industrial workers created by the Industrial Revolution. Finding that he could not continue his critical attitude toward the government longer in Prussia he went to Paris, where he edited a year-book in which he set forth most of the ideas that appear in his later works. In 1845 the Prussian government drove him from Paris to Brussels.

While he was in Paris Karl Marx came into contact with Friedrich Engels, the son of a partner in a textile firm with factories in both Germany and England. Engels early took a dislike to the religious and business environment in which he had grown up. Upon leaving home he fell under the same intellectual influences as his friend Marx and soon began to acquire a conspicuous place among the radicals of the period by his anonymous contributions to the social and economic controversies of the time.

Shortly after the beginning of their remarkable friendship, Marx and Engels became avowed Communists, as the Socialists were then called, and sought to organize the scattered Communists of Europe. Upon the initiative of the group in Brussels to which Marx belonged, a congress of Communists convened at London in 1847 which decided to work out a Communist statement of faith. A second congress commissioned Marx to draw up the proposed statement of Communist principles.

With the aid of Engels Marx thereupon wrote *The Communist Manifesto,* the first clear presentation of the ideas of Scientific Socialism. In the first of the four parts of this pamphlet the two friends discussed the rise and development of the capitalist class produced by the Industrial Revolution. They found that the discovery of America, the opening of Asia, and the consequent growth of world markets had revolutionized industry and had produced a class which had destroyed the old feudal relationships and made wages the only social tie. The very nature of this capitalist class caused an extension of the capitalist system all over the globe, a centralization of the means of production, an agglomeration of population, the concentration of property in a few hands, the periodic economic crises, and a proletariat steadily growing in numbers through the forcing down of the lower strata of the middle class. As a result of its increasing misery the proletariat was destined to become a revolutionary class that would ultimately destroy the capitalist system. The next part of the work defined the relations of the Communist party to the working class, defended it from the charges of preventing the individual from appropriating the products of society and communizing women, and demanded the immediate abolition of property in land, the application of land rents to public purposes, a graduated income-tax, the doing away with all rights of inheritance, the centralization of credit, production, and transportation in the hands of the state, the forbidding of child labor, and the compelling of all adults to work. The third part of the manifesto criticized the various forms of Utopian Socialism. The final section of the pamphlet asserted that Communists had no interest in the Liberal movement and urged the working-men of all countries to unite.

In 1848 the Communists did not have sufficient strength to influence the course of events. After the collapse of the revolutionary movement of 1848, Marx and Engels took refuge for a time in England. In order to enable his friend to continue his social and economic investigations Engels shortly resolved to resume his old "dog's trade," as he called business. Thenceforth Marx lived with his family in the most modest fashion on the income derived from an occasional article, the allowance sent him regularly by Engels, and, in his later years, from a small legacy left him by a Communist friend, and devoted himself to the preparation of his monumental work on capital and to the task of organizing the Socialist movement.

The revolutionary movement of 1848 temporarily destroyed the domination of the Conservatives in Europe. In France it replaced the bourgeois monarchy with the Second French Republic. In Germany it put the Liberals in power in southern and western Germany, started a movement that promised to realize the ambition of the German people for national unity, and finally caused the Prussian monarchy to concede Liberal reforms to its own subjects and to promise to place itself at the head of the German national movement. In central Europe it overthrew the political system of Metternich and gave promise of satisfying the aspiration of the peasants, the new industrial proletariat, the German Liberals, the Czechs, the Magyars, the Southern Slavs, and the Italians. In Walachia and Moldavia, the Swiss cantons, the Kingdom of the Netherlands, Belgium, the territories of the King of Denmark, and the United Kingdom of Great Britain and Ireland the revolutionary movement of 1848 caused popular disturbances and constitutional changes of greater or less significance. The permanent success of the movement depended on the ability of the revolutionists to carry on the work of reform after the subsidence of the first enthusiasm and to defend themselves against the counter-attacks of the still powerful Conservative forces in Europe.

CHAPTER IX

In spite of their success in the early stages of the revolutionary movement of 1848, the revolting nationalities and groups of Liberals soon commenced to reveal certain weaknesses. By taking advantage of these the politically far more experienced Conservatives of Europe regained much of the ground that they had lost.

I

THE DEFEAT OF THE REVOLUTION OF 1848 BY THE HAPSBURG MONARCHY

In the Austrian Empire particularly the failure of the various nationalities to present a united front to the Conservative forces of the monarchy finally proved their undoing. In the province of Bohemia the divergent interests of the Czechs and the Germans created a rivalry that finally prevented the two peoples from coöperating in the task of obtaining the hoped-for autonomy and Liberal institutions. Since medieval times the Kingdom of Bohemia had formed a part first of the Holy Roman Empire and later of the German Confederation which took its place. In 1848, consequently, the leaders of the movement for the unification of Germany invited the inhabitants of Bohemia to elect representatives to the proposed German national assembly to be held at Frankfort. The German element in the province desired to maintain the political ties uniting them to their kinsmen in Germany. The Czechs took an opposite position toward the invitation. Proudly flaunting his national origin, František Palacký, the historian of Bohemia, voiced the ambitions of the Czech nation. He asserted the necessity of maintaining the Austrian Empire and opposed the participation of the Czechs in the proposed German national assembly, on the ground that the maintenance of the political bond with Germany could only weaken the Hapsburg state. As a result of the refusal of the Czechs to coöperate in the German national movement, Bohemia sent to the National Assembly at Frankfort only thirteen of the sixty-eight deputies to which she was entitled.

Instead of taking part in the German movement, the Czechs convened in May, 1848, a great Slav Congress at Prague. Its membership included two hundred and thirty-seven Czechs and Slovaks, sixty-one Poles and Ruthenes, forty-two Southern Slavs, and one or two representatives from Russia and Serbia. The conflicting political principles entertained by its varied membership prevented the congress from translating its debates into effective action. In a petition to the Emperor of Austria, however, it demanded the subordination of the province of Moravia to Bohemia, the establishment of a Slovak national congress, the creation of a kingdom for the Slovenes, and the granting of the demands of the Croats and Serbs. The action of Czech leaders in summoning the Slav Congress aroused the fears of the German element in Bohemia. Fearing that they might find themselves overwhelmed by a Czech majority, the German minority in the province ceased to support the movement for Liberal reforms for Bohemia.

While the Slav Congress was still in session the Czechs suffered an unexpected defeat. Encouraged by the defection of the Germans, Prince Windischgrätz, the commander of the Austrian garrison at Prague, refused the demands of the Czech students for arms and cannon to protect their threatened constitutional freedom. As a result of this rebuff the populace of Prague crowded around the palace, mortally wounded by a chance shot the commander's wife as she stood looking out of a window, and erected barricades. Their action gave the Austrian commander the opportunity for which he had long been looking. Withdrawing his troops from the city, he bombarded Prague and quickly gained control of the situation. His cannon restored the Conservatives to power in Bohemia and encouraged the Hapsburgs and their advisers to attempt to master by military force the revolutionary movements in other parts of the empire.

In the meantime the successive Liberal ministries at Vienna, in an effort to regain control of Lombardy and Venetia, had been sending to the beleagured Austrian forces in the Quadrilateral all the military supplies and reënforcements at their disposal. The situation in the Italian peninsula made the task easier for the Austrians. Charles Albert, King of Sardinia, displayed no military capacity; the attitude of the Pope toward the national movement discouraged the contingent from the Papal States in the Italian army; and the disorder at Naples gave the hostile Neapolitan government an excuse for recalling its troops. The advocates of the union of Italy under the leadership of the Kingdom of Sardinia and the Republican followers of Mazzini mistrusted each other. Weakened by these conditions, the Italian forces began to lose ground. By the end of June, 1848, the Austrians had recaptured all of Venetia except the city of Venice. By August 9 they had driven the Italian forces back to the frontier of the Kingdom of Sardinia and compelled Charles Albert, its sovereign, to sign an armistice.

The Austrian victory created a confused situation in the Italian peninsula. The troops of Austria were in control of all Venetia except Venice, the province of Lombardy, the duchies of Parma and Modena, and the northern part of the Papal States. Behind his own frontier Charles Albert quietly watched the course of events in the peninsula. The people of Venice annulled the recently proclaimed union of Venetia and the Kingdom of Sardinia and reëstablished the Venetian Republic, with Manin as dictator. A democratic triumvirate came into power in Tuscany as a result of a revolt at Leghorn. The inhabitants of the Papal States drove the Pope into exile and established a republic. The reactionary King of Naples dismissed his parliament, returned to a régime of personal rule, and sent an expedition to reëstablish the royal authority in Sicily.

While these events were taking place in Bohemia and Italy the Liberal ministry at Vienna had been struggling with the problem of formulating a constitution satisfactory to the various social classes and national groups in the empire. In the latter part of April, 1848, the Emperor conceded to his subjects a constitution which left the privileged classes in control of the upper house of the proposed parliament and excluded artisans and servants from the suffrage. It satisfied only the upper-middle-class Liberals. The heroes of the March revolution, the students and the National Guard, protested, and demanded in an armed demonstration the summoning of a unicameral Constitutent Assembly elected by universal suffrage. After it convened this body encountered well-nigh insuperable obstacles. Less than 4 per cent of the eligible electors took the trouble to take part in choosing its members. Its session immediately disclosed a chaos of tongues and an irreconcilable clash of aims. As soon as their demands for freedom from seigniorial burdens had been met the peasant members withdrew. The victories of Windischgrätz at Prague and of Radetzky in Italy boded ill for the efforts of the Constituent Assembly to transform the Austrian monarchy into a constitutional state.

By October, 1848, the Conservative elements in the empire felt strong enough to risk an open break with the revolutionary leaders at Vienna. As the revolutionary movement became more radical the upper middle class began to be alarmed and lost its enthusiasm for reform. It began to regard its absent ruler as a mild benefactor and to sigh for the security it had known before the outbreak of the revolution. The military leaders of the empire demanded an opportunity to crush the existing disorder. In October, 1848, accordingly, the Conservative advisers of the Emperor used a new revolutionary rising as a pretext for commissioning Windischgrätz and Jellachich to move on Vienna with the military forces at their disposal. The mass of the Austrian people showed themselves openly hostile or wholly indifferent to the democratic elements that held control of the Austrian capital. A relieving force sent by the Magyars failed to raise the siege of the city. By November 1, 1848, consequently, the military forces of the monarchy had gained control of Vienna. With this victory, the hopes of the Liberals for constitutional freedom and of the workers for social reform vanished.

The Austrian Conservatives then proceeded to exploit their victory. They immediately transferred the Constituent Assembly to the little Moravian village of Kremsier, where the Liberals could be closely watched by the advisers of the Emperor. They put in control of the government a Conservative ministry headed by Prince Felix Schwarzenberg, a brother-in-law of Windischgrätz and a man of aristocratic, military, and diplomatic antecedents, who regarded the Constituent Assembly as a miserable group of bad and dangerous subjects. On December 2, 1848, they persuaded the feeble Ferdinand to abdicate in favor of his eighteen-year-old nephew, Francis Joseph I, who had made no promises to the revolutionary leaders. In March, 1849, just as the deputies had about completed the draft of a constitution, the Conservative ministry dissolved the Constituent Assembly and published a constitution of their own that never actually came into force.

The victories of the monarchy over the revolutionary movements in Bohemia and Italy enabled the advisers of the Emperor to abandon their ambiguous attitude toward the civil war going on in Hungary between the Magyars and the Southern Slavs. In order to conciliate the powerful Magyars the imperial government had at first formally deprived Jellachich, the Ban of Croatia, of all his honors and offices. After the victories of the Austrian military forces in Bohemia and Italy the advisers of the Emperor restored to Jellachich his honors and offices and pushed preparations for a campaign against the Magyars. In September, 1848, Jellachich crossed the Drave River with the military forces under his command and began a campaign against the Magyar national armies. In the following January Windischgrätz led a second Austrian force into Hungary. In the crisis the Magyar Liberals resorted to desperate measures. They declared Hungary a republic, appointed Kossuth a dictator, and prepared to resist to the last. Unable to crush the Magyars with their own forces, the Austrian authorities accepted the aid of Nicholas I, who considered himself the paladin of the absolutist principle. Weakened by the attitude of the more conservative Magyars and the hostility of the Slovaks and Rumanians, the Magyar forces finally surrendered unconditionally to the commander of the Russian troops in August, 1849.

Simultaneously Austrian and French troops were crushing the revolutionary movement in Italy. The establishment of the Republicans in power at Rome and at Florence exerted a great influence over the radical party in the Kingdom of Sardinia and threatened to destroy the popularity of Charles Albert both with his own subjects and with the refugees from Lombardy. To avert this danger he denounced the armistice that he had concluded with the Austrians and renewed the struggle for the independence of Italy. His second campaign for Italian freedom lasted only five days and ended in the crushing defeat of his troops in the battle of Novara (March 23, 1849) and his own abdication in favor of his son, Victor Emmanuel II. This victory opened the way for the overthrow of the Venetian Republic and the occupation of Tuscany. In order to prevent the whole peninsula from falling under Austrian control, Louis Napoleon, President of the Second French Republic, despatched an expeditionary force to overthrow the Roman Republic and restore to the Pope his temporal power. The victories of the Austrian troops over the revolutionary movement in Bohemia, in Italy, at Vienna, and in Hungary enabled the Austrian government to turn its attention to Germany.

2

THE FAILURE OF THE MOVEMENT FOR THE UNIFICATION OF GERMANY

On the last day of March, 1848, the preliminary parliament summoned by the Liberals of southern and western Germany met to draw up plans for the proposed German National Assembly. Composed of members and former members of the parliaments of the various German states, representatives sent by the German cities, and other distinguished Liberals chosen by the committee of seven, this assembly found itself confronted by problems of the greatest complexity. It had to determine the form and powers of the new central government and the boundaries of the new Germany and to make arrangements for the convening of the proposed National Assembly. The admittance of representatives from Schleswig might involve Germany in an international war. The inclusion of deputies from the eastern provinces of Prussia threatened to precipitate a war with Russia over the thorny Polish question. Austria with its Slavic, Magyar, and Italian provinces presented a serious problem. A decision of the question of the form of government would alienate either the princes of Germany or the German Republicans.

The sessions of the preliminary congress lasted four days. In the main it adopted the program recommended by the preparatory committee of seven, which provided for a federal executive with a responsible ministry, a Senate representing the states, a lower house representing the people of Germany, the surrender to the central government by the individual states of jurisdiction over the army, diplomatic affairs, commerce, navigation, customs, coinage, weights and measures, the postal system, and railroads, the establishment of a federal court and a civil and criminal code for all Germany, and the guaranteeing of the personal liberty of the German people. It postponed a decision concerning the boundaries of the new state, but declared in favor of the establishment of a constitutional monarchy. This decision caused the withdrawal of seventy-nine Republicans and led some of the Republican extremists to attempt to establish a republic in Germany by armed force. The preliminary parliament also decided that the members of the proposed German National Assembly should be elected by universal suffrage. It left the execution of its decisions in the hands of a committee of fifty persons.

After it assembled in the middle of May, 1848, the National Assembly took up the problem of creating a provisional government for Germany. In solving this question the inexperienced body made a serious mistake. In spite of the fact that the Liberals had come into power in Austria, the Austrian government had shown from the first an unfriendly attitude toward the proposal to reorganize Germany. The populous Austrian Empire had sent only two representatives to the preliminary parliament and had taken careful precautions to insure the election of deputies to the National Assembly who could be depended upon to oppose the plans for creating a strong centralized government in Germany under the leadership of Prussia. In face of these ominous signs of hostility, however, the National Assembly elected Archduke John, a member of the reigning house in Austria, Imperial Vicar, an office that might exert a decisive influence on the composition of the ministry and the execution of the laws. The readiness with which the diet of the old German Confederation surrendered authority to the new Imperial Vicar, however, began to open the eyes of the National Assembly to the significance of its action.

After creating the provisional government the National Assembly turned its attention to the task of drawing up a constitution. In achieving this work it displayed in an exaggerated form the faults common to all deliberative bodies. Although it was entirely dependent for authority and protection on a public opinion likely to be alienated at any time, the inexperienced deputies, tasting for the first time the sweetness of political and personal freedom, spent three precious months in protracted debates over the phrasing to be used in defining the fundamental rights of the German people. Five months after they had come together they attacked the problem of determining the form of government for the new Germany. They did not complete this part of their work until they had been in session almost a year.

Their deliberations finally resulted in the drawing up of a lengthy constitution of one hundred and ninety-seven articles. This document provided for the organization of the former states of the German Confederation into a highly centralized federal union with a government of broad powers. It intrusted the executive authority in the new state to an unnamed hereditary ruling house of Germany, which was to exercise it through a responsible ministry. It created a central parliament of two houses, an upper chamber composed of representatives chosen partly by the state governments and partly by the inhabitants of the states and a lower house made up of representatives of the people of the empire. It also provided for the establishment of a federal court.

The new constitution embodied the ideas of those deputies who felt that the new Germany must be organized under the leadership of Prussia. In the debates they found themselves opposed at every step by a party that opposed the elevation of Prussia over the other states of Germany. This group included the Austrian deputies, Roman Catholic members of the National Assembly, who had no desire to see a Protestant power supplant Roman Catholic Austria as the leading state of Germany, and representatives of the smaller German states, who feared that a political reorganization of Germany would deprive the smaller states of their cherished independence. The Prussian party refused to include in the new state the whole Austrian Empire with its great non-German population. Austria refused to surrender control of its German provinces to a government that it could not dominate. In consequence, the adoption of the new constitution really excluded Austria from the proposed German state and committed the National Assembly to offering the crown of Germany to the King of Prussia.

The adoption of the constitution, therefore, placed the fate of the proposed reorganization of Germany in the uncertain hands of the unstable, temperamental Frederick William IV of Prussia. As time passed, however, the Prussian sovereign felt more and more hesitation about accepting a crown from the people as Louis Philippe had done. The deputation that finally came from the National Assembly with the offer of the imperial crown received a discouraging answer. The King informed its members that he must obtain the crown from the aristocratic hands of his fellow-princes instead of from the plebeian hands of the people of Germany. In the formulation of this reply he had been guided in part by his own monarchical prejudices against revolution and in part by the attitude of Russia. His answer postponed for twenty-three years the attainment of the imperial crown of Germany for the Hohenzollerns. For while twenty-eight of the princes of the smaller states consented to his acceptance of the proffered office, the rulers of the larger German states refused to enter a political union that entailed the sacrifice of important powers and privileges. This outcome of their long labor discouraged the members of the National Assembly and caused a majority of the deputies to return to their homes.

While the King of Prussia was attempting the hopeless task of persuading his fellow-princes to surrender their highly valued independence, the Austrian government was conquering its rebellious nationalities and getting into a position to take vigorous action in Germany. As soon as it had restored order at home it invited the German powers to reëstablish the old German Confederation. At first only six German states sent representatives to the revived diet, but as time passed all the other states deserted Prussia and took their old places in the German Confederation. Prussia neither resumed her place in the old diet nor prepared to push through by military force her own plans for the reorganization of Germany. As the position of Austria improved, therefore, the relations of the two great powers of Germany grew steadily worse. In 1850 they finally reached a crisis over Hesse-Cassel, where the Elector had become involved in a struggle with his subjects as a result of his disregard of the constitution of the state. In response to an appeal of the Elector Austrian and Bavarian troops prepared to invade Hesse-Cassel in the name of the diet of the German Confederation. When Prussia protested against the proposed intervention and questioned the authority of the old diet, Austria demanded that Prussia should cease to oppose the federal execution in Hesse-Cassel, should abandon the position she had taken in the affairs of Holstein, and should restore the Prussian army to a peace footing. Fearing to venture a military struggle with Austria, the Prussian government accepted the humiliating Austrian terms and brought to a disheartening end the efforts of the German Liberals to reorganize Germany.

3

THE PERMANENT RESULTS OF THE REVOLUTION OF 1848

Notwithstanding the final success of the Conservative forces of Europe over the revolutions of 1848, the revolutionary movement effected some political and social changes. In the Austrian Empire the Conservatives restored the Ancien Régime as far as they could. In Austria they first disbanded the Civic Guard, then relieved civil servants of the crown from the obligation of swearing fidelity to the constitution, and finally in 1851 quietly suppressed the constitution that had been conceded by the Emperor. In Hungary they took a drastic revenge on the defeated Magyars. They sent as commander of the Austrian military forces in Hungary General Haynau, who, by his cruelty toward the defeated revolutionists, had just earned for himself in Italy the nickname of the Hyena of Brescia. With the approval of the Austrian government he caused the execution and imprisonment of the military and civil leaders of the Magyars, even incarcerating several bishops of the Church for long periods of time. The Austrian government also deprived Hungary of some of its border districts, reduced the rest of the kingdom to the status of a simple province of the empire, and let loose upon it swarms of foreign officials. The Southern Slavs received no reward for their indispensable aid in quelling the revolution. The Austrian government deprived Croatia of its diet for ten years. It did nothing to satisfy the demands of the Slovaks of northern Hungary or the Rumanians of Transylvania. It did not dare, however, to annul the legislation in behalf of the peasants. In both Austria and Hungary it suppressed serfdom without indemnifying the landlords but compensated them for all losses arising from the transformation of servile holdings into freeholds.

In Prussia the Revolution of 1848 finally resulted in the grant of a constitution which was far from fulfilling the hopes of the Liberals. Finding himself out of harmony with two constituent assemblies elected under the influence of the revolutionary excitement, Frederick William IV promulgated on his own authority a constitutional amendment that inaugurated in Prussia its famous three-class system of voting. The new suffrage arrangements classified the voters by the amount of taxes that they paid and permitted a comparatively small group of large taxpayers to choose as many of the electors—who actually selected the members of the lower house of the Prussian parliament—as the great mass of the small taxpayers. With the aid of the new electoral system the King obtained a constitution in harmony with his own conservative political views. The new constitutional document carefully guarded the supremacy of the crown, made the ministers responsible to the King instead of to the parliament, and intrusted legislative power to an upper house composed of hereditary and nominated members and a lower house that represented only the wealthy and the prosperous classes. Until after the Revolution of 1918 the Prussian parliament lacked some of the essential powers of a parliamentary body.

The revolutionary movement of the mid-century also completed the work of reform begun during the Napoleonic period by Stein and Hardenberg. The decrees issued by these two Prussian ministers freed the peasants on the royal domains but hardly affected the status of the peasants on the private estates. The War of Liberation of 1813 and the period of Conservative reaction that followed prevented the decree promulgated by Hardenberg in 1811 from being carried out on a large scale. By the middle of the century, however, improvement of the position of the peasants could no longer be postponed. In 1850, therefore, the Prussian government enacted legislation that abolished twenty-four different kinds of seigniorial dues, suppressed the hunting rights of the nobles, and made the peasants full proprietors of their lands. The work of indemnifying the landlords, however, dragged on for a number of decades.

In western and southern Germany the position of the peasants had been gradually improving since the latter part of the eighteenth century. Even prior to the French Revolution Baden had abolished serfdom on some of the royal domains and both Baden and Bavaria had made some efforts to improve the tenure of the peasants. The extension of French influence during the Napoleonic period resulted in the freeing of both the property and the persons of the peasants in these German lands on the left bank of the Rhine and along the North Sea which were annexed to France, and in the abolition of serfdom in Bavaria, the Grand Duchy of Berg, and the Kingdom of Westphalia. In 1817 Württemberg and three years later Baden completed the abolition of serfdom. The following decade saw the lot of the peasants further ameliorated in Baden, Hesse, Hanover, and Württemberg. The revolutionary movement of the mid-century completed the work of freeing the peasants in Baden, Hesse, Bavaria, and Württemberg. The legislation of this period in these states did away with the remaining relics of serfdom, transformed the peasant tenures into freeholds, indemnified the landlords for their losses, and abolished the hunting and fishing privileges of the nobility.

In Italy the Revolution of 1848 made the ruling house of the Kingdom of Sardinia the center of the hopes of most of the Italian patriots. They remembered that Charles Albert had twice sacrificed his resources and risked his throne in the cause of Italian independence. After his abdication his son had kept faith with his subjects and refused to annul the constitution granted by Charles Albert during the earlier days of the revolutionary movement. This policy tended to rally the majority of patriotic Italians around the royal house of the Kingdom of Sardinia.

In spite of their apparent failure, therefore, the revolutions of 1848 constitute one of the most significant movements in the history of the nineteenth century. That in France overthrew the régime of Louis Philippe and brought to the fore the Republicans, the Socialists, and Louis Napoleon. That in Italy caused the majority of the Italian patriots to cease to look to the Pope and to Mazzini for leadership and rallied them around the ruling house of the Kingdom of Sardinia. That in the Austrian Empire embittered and strengthened the subject nationalities and increased the difficulty of holding that polyglot, ramshackle monarchy together. That in Germany gave Prussia a Conservative constitution and discredited the Liberals. Throughout central Europe the revolutions of 1848 completed the work of freeing the peasants from the restrictions of the seigniorial system.

PART II

THE TRIUMPH OF LIBERALISM AND
NATIONALISM, 1848–1871

CHAPTER X

The Treaty of Adrianople, signed in 1829, did not solve the problem of the future of the Turkish Empire. On the contrary, the success of the Greeks in gaining their independence and of some of the Serbs and the Rumanians in gaining a large measure of autonomy disclosed the weakness of the Ottoman state. Thenceforth the history of the Near East becomes the story of the efforts of the Turks and of some of the European powers to bolster up the decaying empire and thwart the attempts of ambitious vassals, awakening nationalities, and avaricious neighboring states to break it up.

I

MEHEMET ALI AND SYRIA

The first threat to the integrity of the Turkish Empire after 1829 came from a remarkable adventurer named Mehemet Ali. Little is known about his early life. He seems to have been born in 1769 at Kavala, to have been the son of an Albanian peasant, and to have become an orphan while still quite young. Until he reached the age of twenty-nine he appears to have been half merchant and half irregular soldier, carrying on a tobacco business and commanding the body-guard of the Turkish governor of the region. In 1798 he went to Egypt with a contingent of Turkish troops to fight the expeditionary force led by Napoleon.

Not much is known about his rise to power in Egypt. He stayed in the country after the withdrawal of both the French and the British troops and participated in the confused struggle that took place between the representative of the Turkish Sultan, the nominal ruler of Egypt, and the Mamelukes, who had formerly been the real masters of the country. He won the loyalty of the Albanian troops under his command by his solicitude for their welfare and that of the inhabitants of Egypt by restraining his soldiers from plundering. By a skilful mixture of force and intrigue he then succeeded in expelling the representatives of the Sultan from Egypt and in defeating his rivals within the country. The long-enslaved natives offered no resistance to his plans. In 1807 he defeated a serious British attempt to gain control of the province.

In 1811 he trapped the Mamelukes with Oriental cunning and slaughtered them with great cruelty.

Upon obtaining control of Egypt Mehemet Ali proceeded to transform it into an efficient, lucrative despotism. He introduced an administrative system patterned closely after that of France and confiscated the estates of the Mamelukes, of the pious foundations, and of other great proprietors. On the lands acquired in this manner he dictated what crops should be raised and introduced the extensive cultivation of cotton, indigo, opium, and the mulberry. At harvest-time he took a portion of the crop in taxes, purchased most of the rest at a price set by himself, and left the cultivators of the soil only about one sixth of the yield of their fields. His efforts to establish factories for the manufacture of oil, silk, cloth, sugar, and indigo met with less success. He improved the irrigation system, made Alexandria a first-class port, and connected Cairo and Alexandria by a canal. Realizing the need of experts, he enlisted the services of French doctors and engineers, paid the expenses of Egyptian students at Paris, and established schools in Egypt. Having learned the value of Western military methods during the fighting between the Turkish troops and the expeditionary force of Napoleon, Mehemet Ali built up an army of ninety thousand men trained in European methods of fighting, established foundries, powder-mills, and factories for the manufacture of arms, cannon, and ammunition, and constructed a fleet that gave him command of the Red Sea and the eastern Mediterranean.

Master of Egypt and with a powerful army and navy at his disposal, Mehemet Ali soon attempted to widen the boundaries of his power. Between 1811 and 1818 he drove the schismatic Wahabis of Arabia into the desert and acquired control of the holy cities of Mecca and Medina. Next he attacked the Sudan, with the object of gaining gold and slaves and of putting a stop to the frequent forays of robber bands. From 1824 to 1829, spurred on by the promise of rule over the Morea for his adopted son, he aided the Sultan against the revolting Greeks, his expectations being thwarted only by the intervention of France, Russia, and Great Britain. From Greece Mehemet Ali turned his attention to Syria, a region always coveted by the rulers of Egypt, where the dissensions of the Turkish pashas invited his intervention. In 1831 his capable adopted son Ibrahim attacked the principal fortresses of Palestine and Syria with an army of eleven thousand men. By the middle of the following year he had captured Acre, Jerusalem, and Damascus and defeated a Turkish army in northern Syria. These victories opened the way for the advance of his army into the heart of Anatolia.

The prospect of an advance of the Egyptian army toward Constantinople caused the Sultan to ask the European powers for assistance. His appeal met with little response. At that time Great Britain was more interested in the Belgian question than in the Near East. France regarded Mehemet Ali as a protégé. Prussia and Austria made no move. Russia, however, sent a squadron to the Bosporus and disembarked troops on both sides of the Straits. This action alarmed the other European powers and caused the representatives of Austria and Great Britain at Constantinople to persuade the Sultan to offer Syria and Adana to his Egyptian vassal. This offer reëstablished peace in the Near East for the time being. Mehemet Ali accepted the terms of the Sultan in the Convention of Kutaya, and Russia withdrew its forces from the Straits.

After the departure of the Russian forces from the vicinity of the Turkish capital the news leaked out that Count Alexis Orlov, a member of the inner ring around the Tsar, had taken advantage of the situation created by the presence of Russian military and naval forces in the neighborhood of Constantinople to intimidate the Sultan into signing the Treaty of Unkiar-Skelessi (1833). This agreement ostensibly bound the Russian and Ottoman empires together for a period of eight years in a defensive and offensive alliance. In reality a secret and separate article relieved the Sultan from the obligations imposed by the published treaty, in return for his promise to close the Dardanelles to the warships of states at war with Russia. The fulfilment of this pledge would make Russia impregnable on the side of the Black Sea, convert the Ottoman Empire into a sort of Russian protectorate, give Russia control of some of the most important trade-routes in the world, and enable the Russian navy in time of war to issue from and retreat to the protection of the Turkish forts guarding the Dardanelles and the Bosporus.

2

THE CRISIS IN THE NEAR EAST, 1839–1841

At a meeting of representatives of the three Conservative powers which took place in Bohemia in 1833, Austria and Prussia gave their assent to the Treaty of Unkiar-Skelessi, but the British government had no intention of permitting Russia to obtain a preponderant position in the Near East without a protest. Because of the necessity of protecting British trade in the Levant and the British route to India Great Britain stood for the maintenance of the integrity of the Ottoman Empire and the preservation of the existing balance of power in Europe. As a result of this point of view the British government immediately made a formal protest against the Treaty of Unkiar-Skelessi, despatched a strong squadron to the Near East, and watched for an opportunity to break the hold on the government of the Sultan acquired by Russia.

In 1839 the British government saw an opportunity to destroy the hegemony of Russia over the Ottoman Empire. The agreement of 1833 between the Sultan and his Egyptian vassal had really settled nothing definitively. By 1839 the Sultan felt that his new army, trained under the eye of Count Helmuth von Moltke, was ready for battle, and renewed hostilities with Mehemet Ali. Again the campaign against the forces of his Egyptian vassal turned out badly. Within a month the new army of the Sultan had been defeated and his fleet had deserted him. These disasters left the fate of the Turkish Empire in the hands of Mehemet Ali and the European powers.

The ambassadors of the five great European powers advised the Sultan to conclude no peace without seeking their approval, but their home governments found themselves unable to agree on a policy. The British government had no desire to see Mehemet Ali gain a commanding position astride the shortest route to India and urged a blockade of the Syrian coast. The French government, on the contrary, felt a pride in the achievements of its Egyptian protégé and refused to coöperate in the suggested blockade. In July, 1839, nevertheless, the British, Austrian, Prussian, and Russian governments decided to act and offered Mehemet Ali the fortress of Acre and southern Syria for life and Egypt as an hereditary pashalik. For months war between France and the other four great powers of Europe seemed almost inevitable. Mehemet Ali refused the proposed terms, the French government took offense at not being formally invited to sign the agreement drawn up by the four powers, and the other four great powers maintained a blockade of the Syrian coast, gradually captured the strongholds of Syria, and finally invested Alexandria. In the end cooler counsels prevailed. Louis Philippe refused to risk his throne for Syria and, on account of their business interests, the French middle classes decided in favor of peace.

The five powers embodied the new settlement for the Near East in two treaties. One reëstablished peace between the Sultan and his Egyptian vassal and invested Mehemet Ali with hereditary rule over Egypt. The Convention of the Straits restored the ancient rule of the Ottoman Empire concerning the closing of the Bosporus and the Dardanelles to the war-ships of other powers. The two treaties really placed the Ottoman Empire under the tutelage of the five powers instead of under that of Russia alone and gave the government of the Sultan another opportunity to rehabilitate itself.

THE OTTOMAN EMPIRE
AND ITS SUBJECT PEOPLES
IN 1870

0   50   100   150   200   250
Scale of Miles

Turks
Rumanians
Bulgarians
Croats and Serbs
Greeks
Albanians
Boundary line of Ottoman Empire

MAX MAYER, THORNWOOD, N.Y.   20° Longitude   East   from   Greenwich   25°

© The Century Co., 1932

3

THE BEGINNING OF THE REFORM MOVEMENT IN THE
OTTOMAN EMPIRE

The successive defeats suffered by the military forces of the Turkish Empire finally set in motion a reform movement. The success of the various Christian peoples of the Balkan peninsula in gaining independence or autonomy and of Mehemet Ali in gaining control of Egypt seemed to foreshadow the ultimate dissolution of the Ottoman state. During these years, however, the number of Turkish students educated in western Europe increased rapidly, and upon their return to Turkey many of them took administrative posts. These Westernized advisers of the Sultan became convinced that the salvation of the Turkish Empire lay in the adoption of European institutions.

As a result of their influence the Turkish government announced in November, 1839, in a dramatic ceremony, the adoption of a new policy. Before an imposing assembly, composed of great officers and ministers of state, representatives of the different religious faiths of the empire, members of the diplomatic corps, and troops of the Royal Guard, the Sultan read a revolutionary state paper, known as the Tanzimāt of Gülhané, which ran counter to the rules of the Koran and to centuries of Turkish practice. This document promised all subjects of the Ottoman Empire, regardless of their religious affiliations, security of life, honor, and fortune, a regular assessment and collection of taxes, a just system of recruiting the army, and a definite term of military service.

During the next decade the reformers among the advisers of the Sultan made serious efforts to apply the new principles. They reorganized the Council of State, attempted to abolish the farming of taxes, promulgated a somewhat incomplete and incoherent penal code designed to repress corruption, exactions, and confiscations, intrusted to a French man of letters the task of compiling a civil code, established a national bank, prosecuted some abuses, and substituted for the old military system, with its unequal, irregular, and indefinite service, a new system modeled after those in use in western Europe. They also tried to improve the coinage and paper money, consulted with representatives of the different religious communities concerning the state of the empire, drew up an elaborate scheme for a free, secular, and obligatory system of public education, abolished feudal fiefs in Bosnia and Herzegovina, and established mixed tribunals for cases involving foreigners which accepted the testimony of Christians against Moslems. The old, semi-independent governors, who exercised the power of life and death over their subjects, disposed of the armed forces, and decreed taxes, they also replaced with officials carefully subordinated to the central government. The plans of the Turkish reformers encountered stubborn opposition from many elements in the population of the Turkish Empire and much interference from foreign powers.

4

THE CRIMEAN WAR

The great powers of Europe watched these developments in the Turkish Empire with the keenest interest. For three centuries France had maintained close political, commercial, and cultural relations with the countries of the Levant. Russia desired an outlet to the Mediterranean Sea and in her policy toward the Ottoman state vacillated between protection and partition. The British government felt that the preservation of the Turkish Empire was essential to protect its vital interests. Each of the great European powers, consequently, jealously scrutinized the moves made by its rivals in the Near East.

The interest of France in the Levant went back to the days of the Crusades. Thenceforward the Latin monks possessed certain privileges in regard to the Christian churches and shrines of Palestine. In 1535 and again in 1740 the Ottoman government had formally recognized these prescriptive rights. Later in the eighteenth century, however, the contemporaries and disciples of Voltaire and Diderot in control of the French government had been engaged in a great civil war and in a long struggle with foreign powers and had neglected to maintain the rights of France as protector of the Latin monks in the Near East and had allowed the Greek monks of the Eastern Orthodox Church to acquire control of the sacred places in Palestine. The Greek monks remained in unchallenged possession of these churches and shrines until the revival of Roman Catholic zeal in France resulted in 1822 in the establishment of a society for the propagation of the faith. From that time onward missionaries of the Roman Catholic Church, protected in many cases by French diplomats and marines, penetrated into Africa, Asia, and the islands of the Pacific. In Palestine they began a struggle to regain the favored position once held by the Latin monks.

In 1850 Louis Napoleon, as President of the Second French Republic, intervened in this squabble between the Greek and the Latin monks in the hope of retaining the support of the powerful Roman Catholic party in France and of winning prestige for his government by the adoption of an energetic foreign policy. He instructed the French ambassador at Constantinople to demand the exclusion of the intruding Greek monks, the reinstatement of the Latin monks as guardians of the keys of the chief door of the church at Bethlehem and of each of the two doors of the sacred manger and other sacred places, and the recognition of their right to place in the Sanctuary of the Nativity a silver star decorated with the arms of France. After a struggle lasting two and a half years the Sultan yielded to most of the French demands.

These concessions to France, however, aroused the wrath of the Tsar of Russia, the protector of the Greek monks. Feeling himself to be master of eastern Europe as a result of the part he had taken in the Revolution of 1848 and pushed on to a vigorous foreign policy by the rising tide of Panslavism, he refused to recognize the new imperial title of Louis Napoleon and resolved to reëstablish the Greek monks in their old position and to punish the Sultan for his concessions to the French. Early in January, 1853, therefore, he issued orders to concentrate Russian troops on the northern frontier of Moldavia. In the following month he sent a special envoy to Constantinople, who refused to have anything to do with the Turkish Foreign Minister responsible for the concessions to France, used insolent language to the Sultan, and demanded the restoration of the Greek monks as guardians of the holy places in Palestine, the negotiation of a secret alliance between Russia and the Ottoman Empire, and the recognition of a Russian protectorate over the twelve million or more adherents of the Eastern Orthodox Church among the subjects of the Sultan. The Tsar threatened to occupy the Turkish provinces of Moldavia and Walachia with Russian troops in case the Turkish government refused his demands.

Alarmed at the demands of the Russian government, the advisers of the Sultan sought the advice of the British chargé d'affaires at Constantinople. This official thereupon hastily summoned the British fleet from Malta to back up his recommendations. Upon learning of this movement of the British naval forces, the French government also despatched a fleet to the Near East. The arrival of the war-ships of Great Britain and France stiffened the resistance of the Turkish government. Upon the advice of the British and French governments the Sultan offered to compromise the quarrel between the Greek and the Latin monks but refused to concede to Russia a protectorate over her Christian subjects. Furious at this rebuff, the Tsar withdrew his special representative from Constantinople and demanded the acceptance of his ultimatum within eight days under penalty of a Russian occupation of Moldavia and Walachia. In June, 1853, his troops crossed the frontier of Russia and occupied the two principalities. Encouraged by the support of the British and French governments, the Sultan and his advisers demanded the evacuation of the two provinces.

The refusal of the Russian government to heed this demand precipitated the Crimean War. Turkish troops began to attack the Russian military forces occupying Walachia. The Russian government retaliated by destroying a Turkish fleet carrying supplies to the Turkish troops stationed on the Caucasus front. This so-called massacre of Sinope did much to raise the war spirit in France and Great Britain. In retaliation the French and British naval forces entered the Black Sea with orders to compel the withdrawal of the Russian ships of war to their base at Sebastopol in the Crimea. These orders and an unfortunately worded letter of Napoleon III touched the pride of the Tsar and caused him to withdraw his ambassadors from Paris and London. The British and French governments thereupon declared war on Russia. Their action met with the heartiest approval, particularly from the British people, who felt themselves to be champions of British commercial interests and defenders of popular liberty against the menace of political reaction.

The three allies—France, Great Britain, and the Ottoman Empire—first set themselves the task of expelling the Russian forces from the Turkish Empire. Their troops, therefore, attacked the Russian forces besieging the fortress of Silistria in the Dobruja and quickly compelled them to retire to the north bank of the Danube River. Their expulsion from the provinces of Moldavia and Walachia, however, was the work of Austrian diplomacy. Feeling its interests seriously threatened by the Russian occupation of these two principalities commanding the Danube, Austria forgot her indebtedness to Russia in 1849 and demanded the evacuation of Moldavia and Walachia. Not daring to add Austria to its enemies, the Russian government withdrew its troops from the principalities.

By this time, however, the British and French governments had increased their demands. In coöperation with Austria and Prussia they had proposed to the Russian government as a basis for the reëstablishment of peace the substitution of a European for a Russian protectorate over Serbia, Moldavia, and Walachia, freedom of navigation at the mouths of the Danube River, revision of the Convention of the Straits of 1841 concerning access to the Black Sea, and the conclusion of a European understanding for the safeguarding of the Christian subjects of the Sultan. Upon the refusal of Russia to accede to these four demands the French, British, and Turkish governments determined to attack the Russian military and naval base in the Crimea.

In September, 1854, the troops of the three allies disembarked a short distance north of Sebastopol. They faced the problem of holding a mobile Russian army in check while they besieged the great fortress. At the beginning no one seemed to realize the magnitude of the task. Russia had to scatter its forces on many fronts and to forward supplies and reënforcements to the Crimean peninsula by ox-teams traveling over almost impassable roads, but the forces of Great Britain, France, and Turkey had to contend with the Russian winter, the loss of forage, clothing, and medical supplies caused by a great storm that sank thirty allied vessels and with the resulting suffering and sickness, and to fight a series of bloody battles with the Russian field-army and carry on siege operations against Sebastopol for nearly a year. In October, 1855, the three allies, aided by a small contingent of Sardinian troops, finally captured the fortress.

Diplomatic and political developments, however, rather than military defeat, finally brought about the restoration of peace. During the siege of Sebastopol the stern and aging Nicholas I died and left the less resentful and more youthful Alexander II as master of Russia. Shortly afterward Sweden signed a treaty with the French and the British governments which menaced St. Petersburg with an attack in the campaign of 1856, and in addition to the four points, urged earlier as a basis of peace, Austria demanded the neutralization of the Black Sea. In January, 1856, the new Tsar yielded to the pleadings of the King of Prussia and accepted the five Austrian demands. His action opened the way for the negotiation of a treaty of peace.

In the following February representatives of Austria and the five belligerent powers met at Paris. Their negotiations resulted in the conclusion of treaties and conventions that provided for the restoration of all occupied territory, the admission of the Turkish state to the concert of Europe, the guarantee of its independence and territory by the European powers, the closure of the Dardanelles and the Bosporus to foreign war-ships, the cession of a portion of Bessarabia to Moldavia, the navigation and control of the Danube River, and certain important modifications of maritime law. The European powers also appreciatively recognized the promises of domestic reform promulgated by the Sultan just before the opening of the peace conference at Paris, but they did not put the Christian subjects of the Ottoman Empire under their protection.

For a time the seemingly needless struggle of the Crimean War changed the balance of power in Europe. In the Near East it halted for twenty years the advance of Russia toward Constantinople, gave the Ottoman Empire another opportunity to redress the grievances of its Moslem and Christian subjects, and made possible the development of autonomous and independent Christian states. In western Europe it relieved the anxiety of the British government over the route to India and strengthened the personal position of Napoleon III, who played a part in the affairs of Europe such as no French sovereign had taken since 1815. Within twenty-five years, however, most of the specific provisions of the Treaty of Paris had been abrogated.

The Crimean War marked the entrance of a number of new factors into European warfare. For the first time ironclads, the newspaper correspondent, the telegraph, and women nurses played a part in an armed conflict. Through the vivid despatches telegraphed to the London *Times* by William Howard Russell and other newspaper correspondents the

British public for the first time in history followed closely the progress of a military struggle. The accurate, colorful accounts of the aimless sacrifice of British lives in such heroic episodes as the charge of the Light Brigade and the needless suffering caused by the bungling and mismanagement of the British War Office led to the fall and rise of ministers and caused the sending of Florence Nightingale at the head of a band of women nurses to assume charge of the military hospitals. Also, through the new telegraph the home governments were able to subject the commanders in the field to closer supervision.

5

THE MAKING OF RUMANIA

The first Christian subjects of the Sultan to take advantage of the opportunity for national development created by the check of Russia were the Rumanians of Moldavia and Walachia. For some years the idea of uniting not only these two principalities but also the provinces of Bukovina, Bessarabia, and Transylvania into a single, independent state had been maturing in their minds. Some years after the conclusion of the Treaty of Adrianople they had succeeded in suppressing the tariff barriers between Moldavia and Walachia. After the Revolution of 1848 some of the Rumanian refugees living in Paris had succeeded in gaining the ear of Napoleon III and in persuading him that the union of the two provinces would be the best means of satisfying the Rumanians and checking Russian expansion in the Balkan peninsula.

As a result of this growth of Rumanian nationalism the Congress of Paris devoted considerable attention to the two principalities. The Treaty of Paris provided for a continuation of the suzerainty of the Sultan over Moldavia and Walachia under a guarantee of the contracting powers, for the maintenance of independent, national administrations and full liberty of worship, legislation, commerce, and navigation, for a revision of the laws and statutes, for the proposal of bases for their future organization by a special commission, composed of representatives of the signatory powers, and for the election of two Divans by the inhabitants of the two provinces. The conference failed to settle the question of the future organization of Moldavia and Walachia. The Turkish government opposed every proposal threatening the integrity of its empire and the Austrian government threw its influence against the proposed union of the two provinces because it would strengthen the nationalist agitation among its Rumanian subjects.

The failure of the conference at Paris to settle the problem of the future organization of Moldavia and Walachia inaugurated a struggle in the two principalities between the partizans of union and those of separation in which the powers of Europe repeatedly interfered. With the approval of Austria the Turkish government decided to intimidate the Unionists and named as rulers of the two territories persons interested in preventing their union. The new ruler of Moldavia, in particular, reëstablished censorship of the press, evicted the Unionists from the administration, and tampered with the election to the Divan. The ambassadors of France, Russia, Prussia, and Sardinia thereupon demanded new elections, which resulted in the selection in both Moldavia and Walachia of Divans favorable to their union.

The Unionists had yet to overcome the opposition of the European powers. The two Divans proposed to the commission of the powers the autonomy and neutrality of the two principalities and their uniting into a single state. Out of deference to the wishes of the Turkish and Austrian governments, however, the European powers decided that each province should have its own flag, ruling prince, legislative assembly, and tribute to the Sultan, but conceded to them a common court of appeals, a joint military organization, and a central commission for the preparation of measures of interest to both principalities. But in the elections held in 1859 the politicians of Jassy and Bucharest outwitted the European powers and elected Colonel Cuza, a soldier of noble birth with experience and considerable education, as ruler of both provinces. The breaking out of the war with France and Sardinia prevented the Austrian government from making an effective protest. In 1861, consequently, the union of Moldavia and Walachia as the Kingdom of Rumania was proclaimed with the consent of the Ottoman government and the European powers, with Cuza king as Alexander John I.

The new prince endeavored to improve the social and economic conditions of his state. He founded universities at the two provincial capitals, established a number of secondary and technical schools, and made elementary education gratuitous and nominally compulsory. He also attacked the problem of the monastic property, which had long troubled the two principalities. In earlier times the monasteries dotting the country had "dedicated" their foundations to the holy places of Jerusalem and other ecclesiastical corporations. This put extensive revenues and something like a fifth of the soil of Rumania under the control of foreign ecclesiastics. This situation aroused serious opposition among the Rumanian nationalists. Alexander solved the problem by secularizing the monastic property and transforming many of the monasteries into prisons and hospitals. The new prince likewise attempted to solve the agrarian problem by abolishing tithes and forced labor and making the peasants proprietors of their lands on payment of an annual sum to the state during a maximum of fifteen years. He failed to provide, however, for the growth of peasant families or for their protection against the rapacity of Jewish money-lenders.

This attack of the prince on the long-established seigniorial system stirred the opposition of the privileged classes. His opponents attempted to block the passage of the reform measures in the Rumanian assembly. Alexander replied by dissolving the parliament with the aid of a battalion of infantry, issuing a proclamation justifying his action, and promulgating a new constitution that placed most of the power in his own hands. In 1865, however, his aristocratic opponents achieved his overthrow. After carefully preparing Europe for the stroke by a campaign of propaganda, a group of officers broke into the bed chamber of the prince, compelled him to abdicate, and secretly hustled him out of the country. His Rumanian contemporaries quietly accepted his overthrow, but their descendants now recognize him as the founder of Rumania.

6

THE PROGRESS OF NATIONALISM AMONG THE SERBS AND BULGARIANS

During this period the Serbs and the Bulgarians continued their national development. After the conclusion of the Treaty of Adrianople the Serbs found the remaining signs of their former subjection to the Turkish Empire exceedingly irritating. In 1862 the people of Belgrade engaged in a riot that caused the withdrawal of the Moslem civilians still resident in the city. Five years later the ruler of Serbia persuaded the Sultan that a grateful nation would be a better protection for the Ottoman Empire against an Austrian attack than a few scattered Turkish garrisons surrounded by a hostile civil population, and gained the withdrawal of the last Turkish troops from Serbian soil. Their recall practically but not nominally completed the freeing of Serbia from Turkish rule.

In the Bulgarian regions of the Ottoman Empire nationalism expressed itself in an agitation for the removal of the Bulgarian Church from the jurisdiction of the Greek Patriarch at Constantinople. The Bulgarian priests began to omit the name of the titular head of their Church from their prayers and to agitate for the appointment of Bulgarian bishops and for ecclesiastical independence. Recognizing the advantage of weakening the influence of the Greeks and of setting the Greeks and the Bulgarians at enmity, the Sultan finally issued in 1870 a decree authorizing the establishment of an independent Bulgarian Church. Thereupon the Greek Patriarch and the new Bulgarian Exarch excommunicated each other and rival Greek and Bulgarian bands began to sack and murder in Macedonia in the name of religion and nationality.

From 1829 to 1870 the weakness of the Turkish Empire continued to menace the peace of Europe. From 1829 until 1841 Mehemet Ali of Egypt threatened to disrupt the Ottoman state. After 1850 the French and Russian governments took advantage of the feebleness of the empire to intervene in its domestic affairs and brought on the Crimean War. The defeat of Russia in this struggle by France, Turkey, and Great Britain gave the Ottoman Empire another opportunity to reform, halted the advance of Russia for a time, and permitted the Christian nationalities of the Balkan peninsula to continue their development.

CHAPTER XI

The defeat of the Italian revolutionary movement of 1848 by Austria and France did not kill the National movement in Italy. Guided by new leaders and employing new methods, the Italian patriots continued to hope and work for the union of Italy. Within twelve years after the defeat of the Roman Republic they succeeded in creating the Kingdom of Italy.

I

SARDINIA ASSUMES LEADERSHIP OF THE NATIONAL MOVEMENT

As has already been noted, after his disastrous defeat at Novara the enigmatic Charles Albert abdicated and this action made his son, Victor Emmanuel II, ruler of the little Kingdom of Sardinia. In many ways the new sovereign was not an attractive figure. He was indifferent to art and literature, quite superstitious, fond of plebeian dishes and not overnice in his relations with women. In spite of these traits, however, he showed himself to be of royal stature. He was a brave soldier, displayed sound common sense on more than one occasion, and had no fear of able advisers. These characteristics enabled him to play an important part in the work of unifying Italy.

Upon taking office the new sovereign found himself confronted by a difficult situation. His state had just been defeated by the military forces of Austria. The victorious Austrians, his own subjects, and the Italian Republicans regarded him with suspicion. The Austrian government demanded the retreat of his military forces, the disbandment of the Lombard volunteers in the Sardinian army, and the handing over of the fortress of Alessandria and the territory between the Sesia and the Ticino for temporary occupation. His politically inexperienced subjects refused to accept the inevitable and clamored through the voices of their loquacious representatives in the new Sardinian parliament for a continuation of the war. Mazzini even incited the inhabitants of Genoa to open revolt. The divided patriots in the other states of the peninsula waited to see what the new sovereign would do.

Victor Emmanuel II met the situation with his usual good sense. He accepted the hard terms of Austria and twice dissolved the noisy and irresponsible parliament which was trying to prevent the ratification of the treaty of peace. He took vigorous measures to suppress the revolt which had broken out in Genoa. In his policy toward the constitution conceded by his father, however, he showed himself to be a man of far different stamp from the other forsworn princes of Italy. In spite of the blandishments of the Austrian government, he maintained the Sardinian constitution in force and refused to allow his small state to become a political satellite of Austria. This loyalty to his pledged word won him the title of the Honest King.

After settling these pressing problems the Sardinian government took up the question of the relations of Church and State. In the Kingdom of Sardinia the Church still enjoyed privileges no longer conceded to it in most countries of western Europe. It still continued to protect criminals who sought safety in church edifices, to acquire property by deed and legacy, and to control marriage. The Sardinian government first tried to bring about the abolition of these privileges by negotiation with the papacy. After this method of attacking the problem failed, the advisers of Victor Emmanuel II pushed through the parliament legislation designed to do away with the right of asylum, to prevent the acquisition of property by the Church, and to make marriage a civil contract. In response to this challenge the Pope recalled his representative from Turin and the Sardinian bishops openly rebelled against the new policy of the state. The government replied by banishing one insubordinate bishop and fining and imprisoning another. In retaliation the Church refused the last consolations of religion to the dying Minister of Agriculture and Commerce because of the part he had played in putting the obnoxious laws through the Sardinian parliament. This punishment of a man at the point of death aroused public opinion to a high pitch.

The death of the Minister of Agriculture created a vacancy in the new cabinet. Although the court, the Conservatives, and the radicals all disliked Count Cavour, his training and proved gifts unmistakably pointed him out as the most suitable man for the post. He was born in 1810, the second son of a prominent noble family in the province of Piedmont. His parents had sent him at an early age to the Royal Military Academy. After his graduation from this institution at the age of sixteen he spent five years in the army. His Liberal views, however, soon brought him into disrepute with both his own family and his Conservative superiors and finally caused his resignation from military service. For the greater part of the next two decades he suffered from the lack of a definite purpose in life. His father put him in charge first of one and later of all the family estates, but he found time in the winter months to travel in Switzerland, France, and England, to lose considerable sums at cards and on the stock-exchange, and to philander with more than one French and Italian lady. As a result of his extensive reading, his observations abroad,

and his contact with men of all classes in France and England, Cavour
became the best-informed man in Italy on agriculture, railroads, banking,
the methods of manufacture, foreign affairs, and the working of parliamentary government. He took a prominent part in the agitation for
the introduction of the new economic methods in Italy and gradually
became one of the leading business men of the Kingdom of Sardinia. He
advocated the construction of railroads, built a large rice-mill on his
family estates, started a large chemical factory, and helped to establish a
bank at Turin. When his sovereign suddenly granted his subjects freedom of the press in 1847, Cavour took the initiative in founding the
famous journal *Il Risorgimento,* which exercised a powerful influence on
public opinion. His moderate views, however, made him unpopular during
the Revolution of 1848 with both the Conservatives and the followers of
Mazzini.

As soon as he took office as Minister of Agriculture in October, 1850,
Cavour began to display an energy that his chief in the cabinet once
described as diabolic. He frequently assumed functions that really belonged to his colleagues and made himself the principal defender of the
policy of the ministry. In 1851 he added the work of the Minister of
Finance to his duties. From this date until he became Prime Minister in
the following year Cavour followed a tortuous policy that confused
many of his contemporaries. In order to win the good-will of Louis
Napoleon, who by a successful coup d'état had just made himself master
of France, Cavour introduced in the Sardinian parliament a measure
that expelled some French refugees from the country and restricted the
freedom of the press to discuss policies of foreign states. The bill alarmed
Italian Liberals and incited the Conservatives to demand more repressive
measures. Next, without consulting his colleagues in the cabinet, Cavour
formed a new party composed of his personal followers among the Conservatives and the so-called Left Center, an action which broke up the
ministry.

The King quickly found himself forced by the political situation to
summon the dexterous Cavour to become head of the cabinet. Under
his leadership the Sardinian government initiated a program of reorganization. It negotiated with the other countries of Europe commercial treaties which tended to cheapen the necessaries of life and the
raw materials for industry, legislated concerning stock companies, co-
operative societies, agrarian credit, and banks of deposit and discount,
built eight hundred and fifty kilometers of railroad, established permanent
lines of Atlantic mail-steamers, projected the Mont Cenis tunnel, reorganized the army, and fortified the frontiers of the kingdom. These
measures quickened the whole life of the state but necessitated a policy
of heavy taxation that made Cavour one of the most unpopular men in
it. The more conservative nobles, most of the priests, and the uneducated

masses opposed his program. In 1853 the ignorant mob of Turin, holding him responsible for the bad harvests and a serious disease of the grape-vines, made an attack on his palace which endangered his life. A measure abolishing various ecclesiastical corporations and confiscating their property for the benefit of the treasury and the parishes aggravated the quarrel between State and Church and increased the natural opposition of the clergy.

Amid the press of domestic problems, however, Cavour did not forget the Italian question. By its harsh policy in the provinces of Lombardy and Venetia the Austrian government was arousing the hostility of Italian patriots everywhere in the peninsula. It ferreted out the participants in the Revolution of 1848, subjected them to a series of notorious political trials, harassed the whole population by espionage, fines, arbitrary imprisonment, and military executions, and finally in 1853 confiscated the property of former inhabitants of Lombardy and Venetia who had taken refuge in the Kingdom of Sardinia. Cavour made his government the champion of these refugees by making a strictly legal protest against the confiscation of the property of naturalized subjects of the Sardinian state. When the Austrian government made an ill-tempered reply to his protest he recalled the ambassador of Sardinia from Vienna. His policy tended to rally the partizans of Italian unity around the leadership of his sovereign.

2

CAVOUR ENLISTS THE AID OF NAPOLEON III

Unlike many of his enthusiastic compatriots, Cavour never believed that the Italian people could expel Austria from the Italian peninsula by their own efforts. From the time he assumed office he had endeavored to win the good-will of the French government for the cause of Italy. At one time he had advocated commercial concessions to France. A little later he had expelled French political refugees and muzzled the Sardinian press in order to please Louis Napoleon. After the outbreak of the Crimean War Cavour conceived the daring plan of gaining the sympathy of France and Great Britain for Italy by the intervention of the Kingdom of Sardinia in the conflict. His proposal struck the majority of his countrymen as absurd and dangerous but he finally convinced his sovereign of the feasibility of his plan and overcame the opposition of his reluctant fellow-ministers and the frightened Sardinian parliament. After long negotiations, consequently, the Kingdom of Sardinia became an ally of France and Great Britain and despatched to the Crimea at its own expense an expeditionary force of eighteen thousand men, which acquitted itself well and removed the stain on the honor of the army left by the inglorious defeat at Novara.

At the close of the Crimean War the Sardinian government began to reap the reward for its intervention in the struggle against Russia. During their visits to France and England Victor Emmanuel II and his Prime Minister received flattering receptions. At the congress held at Paris to conclude peace Cavour won a remarkable recognition for his small state. He obtained from the reluctant powers the right to sit at the council-table. In the deliberations of the representatives he attracted much attention by his fluency, the justice of his remarks, and the breadth and variety of his ideas. Between sessions he found many opportunities to ingratiate himself with persons of influence and to expose the wrongs of Italy and the oppression of Austria. In particular he caught the ear of Napoleon III and persuaded him by means of a memorandum and a personal interview to present the problem of Italy to the conference. The French Minister of Foreign Affairs, accordingly, brought the situation in the Italian peninsula to the attention of the conference and gave Cavour an opportunity to call the attention of Europe in a dignified way to the effete and corrupt rule of the Italian princes, the anomalous position of the Papal States, and the evils of Austrian rule. By his bold intervention in the Crimean War and his brilliant rôle at Paris he made himself a European figure and made the situation in Italy the most pressing international problem.

After being pilloried in this fashion before the eyes of Europe, the Austrian government attempted to conciliate public opinion in Lombardy and Venetia. At the end of the year 1856 it returned the property it had confiscated from the refugees in the Kingdom of Sardinia. In the following January Emperor Francis Joseph of Austria visited the two provinces and appointed the most amiable of his brothers, the ambitious but ill-fated Maximilian, as governor. The new Austrian policy, however, met with but little success. The illustrious Venetian exile, Daniele Manin, declared, "We do not want Austria to mend her ways in Italy, we want her to go." The city of Milan even erected in Turin at its own expense a monument to the Sardinian army.

At the same time Cavour had been rallying most of the forces opposed to Austrian rule under the leadership of the Kingdom of Sardinia. He urged his friends in Lombardy and Venetia to bring about a restoration of the state of siege in Milan. Gradually he enlisted the support of trusted followers of Mazzini, like Manin, the hero of the Venetian Republic of 1848, and Garibaldi, the defender of the Roman Republic of 1849, and a majority of the democratic party in Italy. Finally, with the connivance of Cavour the leaders of the revolutionary movement organized an Italian National Society that enrolled members and carried on an agitation in all parts of the peninsula.

Having gained the coöperation of many leaders of the democratic party, Cavour next attempted the difficult task of obtaining the assistance of their arch-enemy, Napoleon III. At the peace conference at Paris he had discovered the profound interest of the French Emperor in Italy. In the revolutionary uprising of 1831 he had fought for the freedom of the Italian peninsula. Throughout his life he had believed in the right of nationalities to independence. The attempt made in January, 1858, by the Italian conspirator Orsini to assassinate Napoleon III had the unexpected result of strengthening the French ruler's conviction that he must do something for the Italian cause. Cavour thus found the way prepared for him by the character and personal history of the French Emperor.

In June, 1858, Napoleon III invited Cavour to a secret conference at Plombières, a quiet resort in northeastern France. No one knows exactly what took place at the interview. But the French Emperor certainly promised to come to the assistance of Sardinia with the armies and resources of France provided Cavour succeeded in provoking Austria to declare war without making his little state appear to Europe to be the aggressor. The two conspirators apparently agreed that the objectives of the proposed war with Austria should be the expulsion of the latter power from Lombardy and Venetia, the addition of the two provinces and a small part of the Papal States to the dominions of Victor Emmanuel II, the formation of Tuscany and the duchies of central Italy into a kingdom, and the organization of the states of the peninsula into a confederation under the nominal presidency of the Pope. In return for the promised accession of territory Cavour undoubtedly agreed to the cession of Savoy and possibly Nice to France and to the marriage of the eldest daughter of Victor Emmanuel II to Prince Napoleon, the cousin of the French Emperor.

3

THE LIBERATION OF NORTHERN ITALY

Upon his return home Cavour immediately set to work at the double task of holding Napoleon III to his agreement and inciting Austria to adopt a bellicose policy. His efforts met with great success. At a reception to the diplomatic corps held on January 1, 1859, the French Emperor alarmed Austria and amazed Europe by publicly deploring to the Austrian ambassador that the relations between France and Austria had grown worse. In the following month the French and Sardinian governments concluded a formal treaty of alliance and Prince Napoleon married the daughter of Victor Emmanuel II. In the meantime Cavour had been following an extremely provocative policy toward Austria. In the speech from the throne at the opening of the Sardinian parliament he made the King dwell on the disturbed political conditions in Europe and assert that the Kingdom of Sardinia could not remain indifferent to the cry of pain arising from all over Italy. In addition he asked the parliament to authorize a war loan and commissioned Garibaldi to recruit a force of volunteers from the whole peninsula. As a reply to these provocative measures Austria sent reënforcements to Italy and massed her military forces on the Sardinian frontier.

In alarm at the prospect of war in Italy, the European powers intervened. Though the British public generally sympathized with the idea of liberal reforms in the Italian peninsula, the British government had no wish to further the ambitions either of France or of the Kingdom of Sardinia and consequently exerted all its influence on the side of peace. Russia unexpectedly proposed a congress of the five great powers of Europe. In reply to this proposal Austria stipulated that all the Italian states should be admitted to the suggested congress, that there should be no territorial changes in the Italian peninsula, and that the Kingdom of Sardinia should disarm. The Sardinian government, however, refused to consent to leave itself at the mercy of the Austrian military forces massed on the frontier. The British government, recognizing the justice of the position taken by Cavour, then insisted that the government of the Kingdom of Sardinia should be given a guarantee against attack. The refusal of the Austrian government to insure the Sardinian government against attack brought the negotiations to a standstill and the danger of war steadily increased.

When he was finally certain that he had aroused the Austrian government to a state of unreasoning fury, Cavour offered by telegraph to disarm his state. His despatch came too late to avert war. The war party had gained the upper hand at Vienna and the Austrian government peremptorily demanded the disarmament of the Kingdom of Sardinia within three days. When Cavour disregarded this ultimatum the Austrian government declared war (April 27, 1859).

On the same day that war was declared the Austrian troops began to cross the boundary between Lombardy and the Kingdom of Sardinia. They moved with such incredible slowness, however, that they gave the French troops time to pour into Italy and save the little Sardinian state from being overrun. Upon the arrival of the French forces the Austrian troops began to retreat. At Magenta, just across the western frontier of Lombardy, the advancing French and Sardinian troops overtook and defeated the retreating Austrian army in a great battle (June 4, 1859) in which neither side displayed much generalship but the French and their Italian allies outfought the Austrians. This victory caused the Austrian army to evacuate the whole province of Lombardy and to retire behind the lines of the famous Quadrilateral. In the meantime Garibaldi had led his small force of volunteers on a dangerous and spectacular raid into northern Lombardy which diverted the attention of much-needed Austrian troops and caused a rising of the civilian population against

THE UNIFICATION OF
ITALY
1859-1866

NOTE: *The dates* **(1860)** *indicate the accession to the Kingdom of Sardinia and after 1861 to the Kingdom of Italy*

0 25 50   100   150   200

Scale of Miles

MAX MAYER, THORNWOOD, N.Y.

10°   12° *Longitude East* 14° *from Greenwich* 16°

© The Century Co., 1932

Germany · Munich · Danube R. · Vienna · France · Austria · Salzburg · Zürich · Switzerland · Bern · Innsbruck · Graz · Hungary · Rhône R. · Tyrol · Bozen · Geneva · Savoy (To France 1860) · Trent · Udine · Gorizia · Trieste · Istria · Fiume · Croatia · Bosnia · Magenta 1859 · Lombardy · Brescia · Vicenza · Treviso · Verona · Villafranca 1866 · Venice · Novara · Peschiera · Solferino · Custozza · Mantua · Po R. · Pola · Milan · Casale · Montebello · Alessandria · Parma · Guastalla · Ferrara · Sardinia · D. OF PARMA 1860 · Modena · Bologna · Adriatic Sea · Genoa · D. OF MODENA 1860 · Romagna 1860 · Rimini · Rep. of San Marino · Dalmatia · Pontremoli · Spezia · D. OF LUCCA (To Tuscany 1847) · Lucca · Pisa · Florence · Pesaro · Nice (To France 1860) · Monaco · Nice · Leghorn · Arno R. · Marches · Ancona · Castelfidardo · Urbino 1860 · Macerata · Bastia · I. of Elba · GR. D. OF TUSCANY 1860 · Umbria · Spoleto · PAPAL · Corsica (To France) · STATES 1870 · Rieti · Tiber R. · Ajaccio · Civitavecchia · Mentana · Rome · Caprera · Pontecorvo · Capua · Gaeta · Benevento · Bari · Volturno R. · Naples · Salerno · Brindisi · Sassari · Castellamare · 1860 · Taranto · Sardinia · Tyrrhenian Sea · Cagliari · Lipari or Aeolian Is. · Pizzo · Monteleone · Kingdom of the Two Sicilies · Messina · Aspromonte · Reggio · Palermo · Marsala · Sicily 1860 · Catania · Girgenti · Syracuse · Pantellaria I. · Mediterranean Sea · Malta (Br.)

Austria. Undiscouraged by these defeats, the Austrian military leaders formulated a plan to use their entire military strength in a surprise attack against the slowly advancing French and Italians. This decision led to the battle of Solferino, in which the superior valor and discipline of the French common soldier again won the struggle. This victory assured the French and Sardinian troops control of the province of Lombardy.

Napoleon III, however, made an unexpected use of his success. To the surprise of friend and foe he opened negotiations for peace. A number of considerations moved him to adopt such a policy. The sight of the wounded on the battle-fields of Magenta and Solferino had horrified him. He had gained the province of Lombardy more through good fortune than skilful generalship and the well-nigh impregnable Quadrilateral yet stood between him and the province of Venetia. The patriots of Parma, Modena, Tuscany, and the Romagna had driven out their rulers and promised to become unmanageable. The Catholic supporters of Napoleon III in France, who had made possible his rise to power, opposed his policy in Italy because they feared lest it should injure the interests of the Pope. Prussia had mobilized her military forces on the French frontier. The French Emperor, accordingly, sent a subordinate on a secret mission to the Emperor of Austria with a request for a personal interview and for the conclusion of an armistice. The requested interview opened the way for the negotiation of the Armistice of Villafranca. In this treaty the French and Austrian governments agreed to the cession of the province of Lombardy (with the exception of Peschiera and Mantua, two of the four cities in the Quadrilateral) to Napoleon III, who was expected to hand the ceded territory over to his Sardinian ally; to the restoration of the former rulers of Modena and Tuscany; to the formation of an Italian Confederation under the presidency of the Pope; and to the making of a joint demand on the Pope for the introduction of reforms.

The agreement came far from fulfilling the promises made to Cavour at Plombières and placed the Sardinian government in a difficult and exasperating position. Cavour for a moment lost his usual poise and sense of realities and hastened to the King to demand a continuance of the war without French assistance. When the cooler-headed King told him that this was impossible the Prime Minister forgot the respect owed by a minister to his sovereign, roundly upbraided Victor Emmanuel II, and resigned from office. The King, on the contrary, displayed extraordinary dignity and self-control. He accepted the resignation of Cavour, signed the disappointing armistice so discourteously negotiated behind his back, and thanked Napoleon III for the sacrifices that he had made in the cause of Italian independence.

The conclusion of the hasty Armistice of Villafranca, however, did not extricate Napoleon III from his difficult situation. In Tuscany the provisional government, set up by the revolutionary leaders after the expulsion of the Grand Duke, fell under the control of Baron Ricasoli, the last scion of a famous family. His noble origin and his landed estates gave him the prestige necessary to force his policy on the discordant factions of Liberals in the Tuscan cities, on the hostile clergy, and on the ignorant, conservative peasantry. Convinced of the necessity of fusing Tuscany and the Kingdom of Sardinia into a new state, he disregarded the timid counsels of the successors of Cavour and defied the threats of Napoleon III. During the critical months following the signing of the preliminary arrangement of Villafranca he resisted with the zeal and inflexibility of a fanatic all efforts to restore the former ruler of Tuscany or to merge his state into a new Central Italian Kingdom that would ultimately be an obstacle to the unification of the peninsula. In carrying out his policy he employed methods that were far from democratic. He kept order with an iron hand, prevented his opponents from presenting their case in journals and pamphlets, and finally instructed the landlords to march their peasants to the polls to vote for the union of Tuscany with the Kingdom of Sardinia. In all probability he hardly understood the point of view of his opponents or the intricacies of the diplomatic situation, but a Cromwellian assurance of the rightness of his cause and a certainty of ultimate success upheld him in his struggle.

In Parma, Modena, and the Romagna Luigi Farini carried out the same policy. Though he had been educated as a physician and had attained considerable success in his profession, he had devoted the greater part of his life to the cause of Italian unity. He had taken part in the revolutionary movement of 1831, had suffered expulsion from the Papal States in 1843 because of his Liberal views, and had served as minister of the Roman state during the Revolution of 1848. After the defeat of this movement he had established himself in the Kingdom of Sardinia and had become one of the trusted friends of Cavour. So when the patriots of central Italy drove away their rulers Cavour selected Farini for the difficult post of commissioner of the Sardinian government. After the conclusion of the Armistice of Villafranca he disregarded the orders for his withdrawal and stayed on in the Duchy of Modena as leader and dictator of the revolutionary movement. Later he assumed the same position in Parma and the Romagna. He organized the three territories under his control into the temporary state of Emilia and held them for Victor Emmanuel II.

The situation in central Italy put Napoleon III in a delicate position. With his own power in France founded upon plebiscites, he could not entirely ignore the expressed will of central Italy for union with the Kingdom of Sardinia. He had no desire to see the British government under the leadership of Palmerston capture the place in the hearts of the Italian people that he had just voluntarily vacated. Neither could he simply stand aside and let Austria regain control of Italy. On the other hand the French Catholics resented the threatened spoliation of the temporal possessions of the Pope and the French nationalists opposed the creation of a new European power. Napoleon III, consequently, could do nothing but stand aside and watch Italy flout his wishes.

Finding himself unable to coerce the two dictators of central Italy, the French Emperor decided to salvage what he could from the wreck of his plans. As soon as Cavour returned to office in January, 1860, Napoleon III concluded a treaty that provided for the union of central and northern Italy into a single kingdom under the rule of Victor Emmanuel II at the price of the cession of the Sardinian territories of Nice and Savoy to France. This agreement by no means ended the difficulties of Napoleon III. His action in signing the treaty roused the anger of the Pope and the British government, did nothing to placate public opinion in France, which long regarded the new acquisitions as a few bare rocks and a miserable strip of shore, and failed to prevent the spread of the revolutionary movement to southern Italy.

4

THE MAKING OF MODERN ITALY

For months ardent Sicilian patriots had been urging the leaders of northern Italy to undertake an expedition for the liberation of Sicily from the rule of the Bourbons. All the Italian factions, consequently, commenced to consider the problem. The Italian National Society began to plan an expedition of volunteers to the island. Those still loyal to Mazzini hoped to offset the victories of the Monarchists in northern and central Italy by a Republican success in the Papal States or in southern Italy.

All the Italian factions looked upon Garibaldi as the inevitable leader of the proposed expedition to Sicily. This picturesque individual had been born at Nice in 1807. After he had fallen under the influence of Mazzini in 1833 he had thrown all his energies into the cause of Italian independence. His participation in a revolutionary rising at Genoa forced him to leave his native country for a time and to sail for South America, where he had a romantic career as a revolutionist. During the Revolution of 1848 he had fought in the Sardinian army and unsuccessfully attempted to defend the short-lived Roman Republic. After the defeat of the Republican forces at the hands of the troops of the Second French Republic he had eluded his pursuers in a most dramatic manner. After a decade of inaction he had organized a band of volunteers and led them in a brilliant raid into northern Lombardy. Throughout his career he had shown great gifts as a leader of volunteer troops.

Early in 1860 Garibaldi began to consider seriously the idea of leading an expedition to Sicily. At first he doubted the advisability of taking a band of volunteers to the island and asked for proof of the readiness of the Sicilians to do something to win their freedom. Upon the arrival of a report that they had actually risen in revolt he determined to go to their assistance and began to collect money and recruits for the proposed expedition. His preparations and resources seemed entirely inadequate for the formidable task of overthrowing the Neapolitan government. He obtained from the Italian National Society some antiquated muskets. Through the connivance of the official of an Italian steamship company he seized two ships in the harbor of Genoa for the transportation of his eleven hundred and fifty followers, later popularly known as The Thousand. On his way down the Italian coast he obtained from a patriotic officer of the regular army a scanty supply of powder. Cavour permitted the expedition to depart but stood ready to repudiate the madcap adventure if it failed.

Within a few weeks Garibaldi and his volunteers had accomplished the seemingly impossible task of gaining possession of all Sicily. Eluding the watchful Neapolitan cruisers patrolling the coast, he effected a landing in the western part of the island. Once safely ashore he defeated a considerable Neapolitan force at Calatafimi and seized the city of Palermo before the eyes of twenty thousand regular troops. After this astonishing success recruits and supplies began to arrive from northern Italy. With their assistance Garibaldi soon gained control of the whole island. He owed his success to his own gifts as a leader of volunteers, the bravery of his men, and the hesitancy and stupidity of his opponents.

In August, 1860, Garibaldi and his volunteers succeeded in crossing over to the mainland and started a march up the coast toward the city of Naples. As they advanced Liberal nobles and hardy mountaineers joined their ranks in considerable numbers, and some sharp but ineffective fighting caused the King and his loyal troops to withdraw from the Neapolitan capital toward the northwestern part of the kingdom. Upon hearing of this movement of the royal troops Garibaldi pushed ahead of his volunteers and entered Naples, where the volatile population gave him a tumultuous welcome. Setting up a provisional government in the capital, he next led his troops in pursuit of the retreating royal army. His volunteers, however, found themselves unequal to the task of destroying the royal forces and even checked their advance toward Naples only after desperate fighting.

Cavour watched the progress of events in central and southern Italy with the greatest apprehension. In spite of the repeated assurances given by Garibaldi of his loyalty to Victor Emmanuel II, Cavour did not feel sure of him. He had seen the unwillingness of Garibaldi to surrender his dictatorship in Sicily and his tendency to heed the suggestions of the fol-

lowers of Mazzini who flocked round him. He threatened to delay the
union of southern and northern Italy indefinitely and to cause the intervention of Napoleon III by an invasion of the Papal States. In the Papal
States the Pope and his ardent supporters resented the loss of the Romagna. The Pope appointed an enemy of Napoleon III as commander of
his troops; a clerical visionary proposed a crusade against the French
Emperor; and volunteers flocked to Rome to defend the Roman Catholic
religion and to restore the rule of the Bourbons in France.

These developments finally caused Napoleon III to give his consent to
the intervention of Sardinia in the Papal States and in southern Italy.
In September, 1860, accordingly, the troops of Victor Emmanuel II entered the territory of the Pope. One column overran Umbria; the other
defeated the main papal army at Castelfidardo and captured Ancona.
These victories left the Pope only the little Patrimony of St. Peter. From
the Papal States the victorious forces of Victor Emmanuel II marched
into the Kingdom of the Two Sicilies and completed the task of defeating
the Loyal Neapolitan troops. These victories settled the Italian question.
In October and November, 1860, the inhabitants of Sicily, Naples, the
Marches, and Umbria voted overwhelmingly for union with the other
provinces of Italy and in March, 1861, a parliament composed of representatives of all the provinces of the peninsula except Rome and Venetia
proclaimed Victor Emmanuel II of Sardinia King of the new Kingdom of
Italy.

In 1861 the Italian nationalism awakened by Napoleon Bonaparte
finally created the Kingdom of Italy. The adroit policy of Cavour first
rallied the contending patriotic factions to the leadership of Victor Emmanuel II and enlisted the powerful assistance of Napoleon III. Then the
intervention of France, the diplomatic situation, the stubborn insistence
of central Italy on union with the Kingdom of Sardinia, and the romantic
exploits of Garibaldi and his adventurous band of volunteers coöperated
in achieving the tremendous task of breaking the grip of Austria on the
peninsula, overthrowing the Italian rulers, and unifying all the provinces
of Italy except Rome and Venetia into a national kingdom.

CHAPTER XII

The French people had used the power given to them by the Revolution of 1848 to put Louis Napoleon, the heir to the imperial tradition, in control of the executive machinery of the Second French Republic. From the time of his election in 1849 until his defeat and overthrow in 1870 his character and ambitions colored the whole history of France. Until 1859 he seemed to be a child of fortune and a benefactor of France.

I

THE FIRST MEASURES OF THE NEW PRESIDENT

Louis Napoleon owed his elevation to the Presidency of the Second French Republic to a political combination composed of supporters of both the Bourbon and the Orleanist claimants to the throne of France. This Party of Order laid great stress on the protection of the interests of the Roman Catholic Church and of the French upper classes. They selected Louis Napoleon as their candidate for the Presidency solely because of the prestige attached to his name. They had no just realization of his ability or his ambitions.

The interests of his supporters determined the early policies of the new President. He sent a French military expedition to Italy with the object of restoring to the Pope his temporal possessions and of forestalling the action of Austria, the Neapolitan Bourbons, and Spain. Not daring to avow openly to the French Republicans the object of the expedition, he merely asked for authority to despatch a military force to the Mediterranean. Secretly, however, he gave its commander a commission to overthrow the Roman Republic, restore the Pope, and compel him to reform the administration of his state. With the aid of reënforcements, the French expeditionary force fought its way into Rome in spite of the heroism of its Republican defenders, but relying on the support of Austria, Spain, and the Kingdom of the Two Sicilies, the Pope refused to concede to his subjects any administrative reforms. His policy of intervention in the Papal States won for Louis Napoleon the implacable hostility of both French and Italian Republicans, but strengthened his influence over the French army.

At home the new President of France made important concessions to the Party of Order in regard to education. The Republican party had intended to make primary education free, obligatory, and under the control of lay teachers appointed by the state. The Party of Order wished to put an end to the propaganda of the Republicans and the Socialists and prepared a measure designed to place the primary teachers under the supervision of the ecclesiastical authorities who favored the existing social order. The proposed law provided for the abolition of the monopoly of the state over education by authorizing the establishment of schools by private persons and religious associations, the limitation of the rôle of the school-inspectors appointed by the state, and the placing of primary teachers under the supervision of the mayor and the parish priest of the commune. In 1850 the French parliament finally passed the proposed law by a large majority. The passage of this measure resulted in the setting up of rival institutions to compete with the universities, the establishment of many secondary schools for the education of the sons of the aristocracy and the bourgeoisie under the supervision of the Jesuits and other ecclesiastical orders, the gaining of control of a large number of primary schools for boys and all the primary schools for girls by the teaching orders, and the separation of French Catholics and French Protestants from infancy.

The first measures of the régime aroused the bitter enmity of the French Republicans. The conservative President and the Party of Order, consequently, worked hand in hand to protect themselves from their Republican enemies. After the Republican demonstrations against French intervention in the Papal States the French government dissolved units of the National Guard, suspended the publication of several newspapers, brought to trial or drove into exile Republican leaders, sent soldiers with Republican sympathies to service in Algeria, broke up public meetings, disbanded political associations, adopted severe measures in districts placed under military law, and subjected the whole press to a severe censorship. The success of the Republicans in electing candidates particularly odious to the Party of Order to vacant seats in the French parliament stirred the government to further measures of repression. It destroyed the Republican newspapers with fines and lawsuits, forbade the distribution in rural districts of pamphlets and almanacs containing Republican propaganda, disciplined subordinate officials, postmen, school-teachers, and railway employees by fines and dismissal, and prosecuted private individuals for shouting Republican slogans or wearing Republican emblems. In 1850 the President, with some reluctance, and the Party of Order, with greater eagerness, crowned their campaign against the Republicans by the passage of a law that practically excluded a third of the voters of France from elections by requiring them to be domiciled for three years in a canton before voting. This legislation particularly affected the artisans, who constituted the rank and file of the Republican party.

2

THE SEIZURE OF POWER BY LOUIS NAPOLEON

The position of Louis Napoleon, however, was far from satisfactory. The Party of Order regarded him as an incapable adventurer, forced ministers upon him whom he disliked, excluded him from their political conferences, and regarded with satisfaction the approach of the end of his four-year term of office. To meet this situation Louis Napoleon set to work to build up a personal following. At first he had only a handful of loyal adherents, but he seized every opportunity to increase their numbers. With this end in view he conversed democratically with artisans as he walked the streets of Paris, and frequently reviewed the troops.

After the Republicans had been crushed the President felt strong enough to break with the Party of Order. Finding himself at odds with its leaders over the reactionary policy of the Pope toward his subjects in the Papal States, Louis Napoleon dismissed his old ministers, announced his intention of choosing advisers responsible to himself rather than to the parliament, and selected a new ministry from his personal followers. The adoption of the new policy precipitated a struggle between the President and his former supporters. Though he was badly in debt, his opponents in the parliament increased his income with the greatest reluctance. They refused absolutely to give him authority to nominate the mayors of French communes. His former Bourbon and Orleanist supporters made an unsuccessful attempt to compromise their differences and unite on a common candidate for the throne of France, and voted down a proposed revision of the constitution that would have extended his term of office. On his part the President toured the provinces, held reviews, wrote letters to the generals, and gave banquets to the officers of the army in an effort to increase his popularity, and thwarted the attempt of the parliament to gain control of the garrison at Paris. To both sides it began to seem that a coup d'état would be the only solution of the conflict.

The President and a small group of his advisers, therefore, finally decided to seize control of the state by the use of force. He attached some of the officers of the army to his personal fortunes by promises and promotions and placed them in command of the troops stationed at Paris, took pains to have impressed on the garrison of the capital the duty of a soldier to obey without hesitation the commands of his officers, and appointed a cabinet of practically unknown men selected from his personal followers. These measures gave him control of both the army and the police. In the hope of placating the Republicans and dividing his opponents in the parliament, he proposed the abrogation of the recent law disfranchising a third of the voters of France.

After postponing the proposed coup d'état a number of times, Louis Napoleon and his fellow-conspirators finally decided to seize control of the machinery of government on the night of December 2, 1851, the anniversary of the famous Napoleonic victory at Austerlitz. Late that evening he disclosed his plans to the small group of men whom he had chosen to execute the plot. During the night the national printing-office set up a proclamation to the French people, the police seized the leaders of the Monarchists and the Republicans, troops upon whom the President felt that he could rely occupied strategic points in the city of Paris, the military authorities closed the meeting-place of the legislative assembly, and subordinate agents of the President posted the proclamation justifying the seizure of power.

The proclamation that met the astonished gaze of the Parisians on the following morning accused the opponents of the President of trespassing on the sphere of the chief executive and asked the French people to judge between Louis Napoleon and the parliament. It charged them with plotting the overthrow of the Republic and urged the French people to give their President the means to carry out the mission intrusted to him by the nation at the time of his election to the Presidency. As specific means for the carrying out of the task intrusted to him, the proclamation proposed as bases of a new constitution an executive elected for a term of ten years, a ministry responsible to the President, a Council of State composed of distinguished citizens and authorized to discuss and prepare the laws, a Senate, and an Assembly elected by universal suffrage. In closing, the proclamation recalled the glories of the régime of Napoleon I and asked the French people to ratify the coup d'état.

The country accepted the seizure of power by the President with comparatively little open opposition. Neither the two Monarchist factions nor the weakened Republicans could offer an effective resistance. The troops broke up the attempt of the high court and the parliament to make a legal protest, overpowered the Republican opposition in the working-class quarters of Paris, and put down the scattered local movements of protest in the provinces. In the plebiscite held on December 21, 1851, the French people formally ratified the seizure of power by a vote officially announced as seven million four hundred and thirty-nine thousand two hundred and sixteen. Less than a half-million persons ventured to vote against the coup d'état. The supporters of the Bourbons abstained entirely from voting. The Orleanists and the Catholics, frightened by the armed risings in different parts of France, quite generally supported the President. The peasants voted for him because of the part Napoleon I had played in freeing them from the burdens of the seigniorial system. The government, on the other hand, gave the opponents of the President no opportunity to agitate against the proposed changes in the constitution. According to the statement of Louis Napoleon himself the government made "resolute and consistent use of every allowable means of influence and persuasion."

Even after the plebiscite the government took every precaution against a revolt. The authorities sought out and arrested suspected persons in all parts of France, deported five members of the parliament, expelled sixty-five Republican leaders from the country, arrested and tried over twenty-eight thousand individuals and imprisoned, transported, exiled, or put under surveillance the greater part of the accused, required publishers to obtain approval not only of the whole journal but also of each separate article, disbanded the National Guard, and carefully regulated the cafés and wine-shops to prevent their becoming centers of disaffection. By these measures the government removed and disarmed its opponents.

Meanwhile a commission had been engaged in the task of drawing up a constitution. By the middle of January, 1852, it had finished its work. The new fundamental law of France followed closely the constitution drawn up at the dictation of Napoleon I after his seizure of power in 1799. It gave the President control of the French state for a term of ten years and granted him the right to command the army, to declare war, to make treaties, to appoint the functionaries of the government, to initiate, sanction, and promulgate the laws, to select ministers and remove them from office, and to choose the members of the Senate and the Council of State and to fix their salaries. It entrusted to the Council of State, a body composed of state functionaries appointed by the President, the duty of preparing legislation and the power of granting and withholding its assent to amendments. The granting of these wide powers to the chief executive and the Council of State reduced the legislative body to the rôle of merely accepting or rejecting the measures proposed by the ministers. The Senate, composed of such ex-officio members as cardinals, marshals, and admirals and of persons appointed by the President, examined measures passed by the Assembly and annulled those it found to be unconstitutional. In theory the new constitution made the President responsible to the French people; in reality it gave them no control over the all-powerful head of the state.

The new régime entirely destroyed political life in France. The new constitution admitted the public to the sessions of the Assembly but prohibited the publication of parliamentary debates. The government gerrymandered election districts, threw the influence at its command in favor of official candidates, and displayed a preference for men of only local reputation desirous of recognition and advancement. It likewise throttled the press by requiring governmental approval for the establishment of a new journal and for every change in its ownership, management, and editing, by increasing the amount of the preliminary deposit demanded of all newspapers, and by suspending or suppressing those which opposed the government and its policies. It subjected university professors to the closest surveillance. The government left no legal means of opposing it. No one dared to print or distribute the placards and handbills of opposition candidates. Government officials refused the opposition permission to hold political meetings on the ground that they interfered with the liberty of citizens. Voters who were opposed to official candidates had to purchase their ballots. The government appointed mayors of communes, took charge of elections, and at times manufactured the returns. For the greater part of a decade the policy of the government produced a condition of almost complete political torpor.

But Louis Napoleon yearned for the trappings as well as the substance of power. In the fall of 1851 the Prince-President, as he was called after the coup d'état, made an extended tour of central and southern France for the purpose of testing public opinion on the question of the restoration of the empire. The obsequious prefects, accordingly, took great care to have him received everywhere with cries of *"Vive l'empereur!"* and *"Vive Napoléon III!"* Although the tour, because of this fact, left the real sentiments of the French people a matter of the greatest doubt, those close to Louis Napoleon asserted at the close of the presidential journey that the popular demonstrations for a restoration of the empire imposed on the Prince-President the duty of consulting the Senate. The consultation resulted in the docile senators' proposing the submission to a popular vote of the question of making Louis Napoleon Emperor of the French. In the plebiscite held in November, 1852, the French people ratified the proposed reëstablishment of the empire by an enormous majority. On December 1, 1852, the spokesman of the Council of State, the Senate, and the Assembly addressed the President for the first time as "Sire" and officially informed him of the results of the plebiscite. The Prince-President thereupon assumed the title of Napoleon III, with the formal approval of the Council of State, the Senate, and the Assembly, and the Second Empire replaced the Second French Republic.

3

THE DOMESTIC POLICIES OF NAPOLEON III

Even before he gained the imperial title Napoleon III had begun to create a court. He installed himself in the old royal palace of the Tuileries and revived the forms and ceremonies in use during the days of the monarchy. When the long-established royal families of Europe showed no inclination to provide him with an empress the new Emperor surprised his subjects by marrying Eugénie de Montijo, the daughter of a Spanish grandee, a lady whose beauty and dignity added much to the splendor of the new court.

Napoleon III made great efforts to gain the support of the army. Hitherto the government had permitted the sons of the upper and middle classes to escape military service by hiring substitutes. The Emperor put an end to this practice. He ordered that henceforth conscripts should obtain exemption from the army only by paying the government a stipulated sum. With the money thus obtained Napoleon III recruited from old soldiers willing to reënlist a professional army devoted to his personal fortunes.

The Emperor likewise assiduously courted the good-will of the Church. At his instigation the government replaced crosses that had been destroyed, simplified the laws regulating the recognition of monastic institutions, sent official representatives to the festivals of the Church, and permitted the clergy to increase their hold on the universities and the secondary and primary schools.

With the aim of stirring French pride, giving work to the dangerous working classes, and making impossible a repetition of the barricades and the street fighting that had caused the overthrow of Charles X in 1830 and of Louis Philippe in 1848, the Emperor sponsored an extensive program of public works. At Paris Baron Haussmann ruthlessly carried to completion the imperial schemes for the embellishment of the city. He improved the Louvre and the great central market, bettered facilities for traffic, made the present magnificent approaches to many of the public buildings of the capital, and pierced and encircled old Paris with wide boulevards. The imperial policy transformed Paris and the principal provincial towns into modern cities.

Under the empire the French government did a great deal to develop credit institutions. In 1852 it authorized the establishment of a land bank for making long loans to proprietors on first mortgages at a low rate of interest and two years later it transformed this enterprise into a state institution. With the purpose of fostering the extension of credit to industry, the government authorized an extension of the activities of the Bank of France and approved of the establishment of the Crédit Mobilier. It finally ordered the Bank of France to establish at least one branch in every French department.

As a result of the growth of credit and the encouragement of industry the economic life of France developed marvelously during the Second Empire. The Bank of France and the Crédit Mobilier financed new railways, a transatlantic steamship company, and an amalgamation of the various gas-works of Paris. By 1855 the electric telegraph reached every prefecture. Between 1851 and 1858 the mileage of French railways increased from three thousand six hundred and twenty-seven to sixteen thousand two hundred and seven kilometers. In the twenty years from

1847 to 1867 the horse-power of the steam-engines in France grew five-fold and the number of patents issued annually by the government doubled in number. The iron and steel industry developed sufficiently to meet all the demands made upon it by the construction of the new railways and the cotton industry doubled its consumption of raw material. The exhibition held at Paris in 1855 first called the attention of the general public to this great economic development. For a time their prosperity caused the French middle classes to forget the loss of their political liberty.

A number of features in the general situation of France, however, created discontent with the imperial régime even during its apparent prosperity. In 1853 bad harvests plagued the state. In the following year cholera ravaged both Paris and the provinces. During the next two years terrible floods inundated large areas and seriously interfered with the economic life of France. Further, the great economic development witnessed by the country increased the cost of living 50 per cent and gave rise to a wave of speculation that alarmed the Emperor.

These unfavorable conditions caused the government great uneasiness. In an effort to check the threatened spread of Republican propaganda among the discontented working classes concentrated in the industrial centers, the government reformed the pawnshops patronized by the poor, applied the funds that it had acquired through the confiscation of the property of the Orleanist family to the improvement of the dwellings of the working classes, contributed money generously in times of scarcity and disaster, and encouraged the organization of insurance societies. In spite of the efforts of the government, however, the working-class quarters became the recruiting-ground for the Republicans, the Socialists, and the Revolutionists.

4

EARLY DIPLOMATIC AND MILITARY SUCCESSES

Warned by the ennui felt by the French people because of the cautious diplomacy of Louis XVIII, Charles X, and Louis Philippe, Napoleon III strove to strengthen his position in France by the adoption of a vigorous foreign policy. In 1850 he intervened in the quarrel of the Latin and the Greek monks over the guardianship of the holy places of Palestine, a policy which appealed to the Roman Catholics, the nationalists, and the army. In all probability he would have been satisfied to have gained merely a striking diplomatic success, but after he noted the reawakening of French patriotism that resulted from his policy of intervention in the Near East he did not hesitate to let the diplomatic struggle develop into the Crimean War. The success achieved by France as a result of the policy of the Emperor gave general satisfaction. The French army acquitted itself well in the conflict around Sebastopol and representatives of

France played a striking part in the subsequent negotiations at Paris. The French people felt that they had again taken their rightful place as the first power in Europe.

His perennial interest in nationalities caused the Emperor to take up next the Rumanian quesion. He energetically supported the Unionists in Moldavia and Walachia. He caused the first elections held in the two provinces to be annulled on the ground of Turkish intimidation and gave the inhabitants of the two principalities an opportunity to elect constituent assemblies free from both Austrian and Turkish interference. At the conference of the European powers held at Paris in 1858 for the discussion of the Rumanian question the French government pursued a policy that favored the formation of Moldavia and Walachia into the Kingdom of Rumania. By this action the French government strengthened the ties already linking the French and Rumanian peoples.

Next the Emperor turned to Italy. In the Italian peninsula, however, his good fortune came to an end. Notwithstanding military successes obtained by the French armies, the intervention in northern Italy had disastrous results for the prestige of Napoleon III. In Italy he started a movement that he could not control. Instead of merely driving out Austria and strengthening the Kingdom of Sardinia he unloosed forces that created the Kingdom of Italy. His desertion of Cavour when the task was but half completed killed the gratitude kindling in the hearts of Italian Liberals. His annexation of Nice and Savoy aroused suspicion in the foreign offices of Europe. The territorial spoliation of the Pope resulting from his Italian policy stirred the resentment of his Roman Catholic subjects. The Pope issued an encyclical against the French imperial policy in Italy. Spurred on by their bishops, French Catholics penned a succession of hostile pamphlets and articles. The usually docile members of the Senate voiced their displeasure with the foreign policy of the government. The creation of a new power of the first rank on the frontier of France alarmed French nationalists.

In an effort to allay the irritation of the British government caused by his Italian policy, Napoleon III stirred up opposition in a new quarter. The experience of Great Britain with free trade had convinced the Emperor that the adoption of a similar policy would promote the best interests of France. He thought that adoption of free trade would encourage each state to develop its own resources in a rational way, draw the peoples of Europe together through commercial intercourse, and win for himself the gratitude of the French working classes by assuring them cheap food. Knowing that his ideas ran counter to the protectionist traditions of French industry, he began to advocate a policy of free trade with great caution. In 1859 he decided to rally the free-traders of Great Britain to the support of Palmerston, who favored the conclusion of an alliance with France, by offering the British government commercial concessions.

At the close of the year he authorized a confidant to negotiate secretly a treaty that suppressed all prohibitions on British goods, limited Franch duties on British imports to 25 per cent of their value, and admitted French products into Great Britain free of duty unless similar articles of British manufacture were subject to taxation by the British government. Early in the following year the French government announced the new tariff policy and the obedient French parliament passed the legislation necessary to put the treaty with Great Britain into effect. French manufacturers, however, denounced the agreement as a national disaster.

For ten years fortune seemed to smile on Louis Napoleon. The French people elevated him to the Presidency of the Second French Republic, approved of his seizure of the state in 1851, and in the following year gave him the imperial dignity. After his installation as Emperor success continued to attend his policies for a number of years. Abroad he obtained military glory for France in the Crimean War and diplomatic successes at the subsequent peace conference and in the Rumanian question. At home a period of striking economic development overshadowed the effects of bad harvests, disastrous floods, and rising prices. Crowds of foreign visitors acclaimed the exhibits of French culture and prosperity at the exhibition held at Paris in 1856. The birth of an heir seemed to insure a continuation of his dynasty. In 1859, however, he initiated a policy in Italy and negotiated a commercial treaty with Great Britain that aroused ominous opposition both at home and abroad.

CHAPTER XIII

THE DECLINE OF FRENCH PRESTIGE AND THE LIBERALIZATION OF THE SECOND EMPIRE

The intervention in Italy and the negotiation of the commercial treaty with Great Britain proved a turning-point in the career of Napoleon III and in the history of France. After 1859 he seemed to lose the magic touch that had appeared to bring success and prestige to his country. To allay popular discontent and regain his former position of power he alternately made concessions at home and attempted unsuccessfully to repeat his early diplomatic and military triumphs abroad.

I

THE CONCESSIONS OF NAPOLEON III TO HIS POLITICAL OPPONENTS

The strength shown by the opponents of his Italian and his free-trade policies caused the Emporor to make political concessions to the Republican and Liberal elements in France, which had hitherto opposed him. In April, 1860, on the eve of the break with his former Roman Catholic supporters Napoleon III granted a complete amnesty to all persons who had been sentenced for political crimes. This action permitted the most uncompromising enemies of the imperial régime among the proscribed Republicans to return to France. In November of the same year the Emperor conceded more freedom to the orators of the French parliament. He granted the Senate and the Assembly the right to discuss and vote each year a response to the speech from the throne in the presence of representatives of the ministry authorized to explain the policies of the government. He created several ministers without portfolio to defend government measures before the Assembly, and permitted full stenographic reports of parliamentary discussions to be published in the official journal. The government also remitted some of the fines that had been levied on the press and permitted the establishment of an opposition newspaper, the French journal *Le Temps*. In 1861 the Emperor pretended to give up the practice of borrowing money and shifting funds from one section of the budget to the other without the consent of the Assembly. In reality he continued to borrow and met the resulting deficits by succeeding budgets.

The concession of freedom of speech and publicity of debates to the parliamentary opposition reanimated political life in France. The removal of restrictions gave an opportunity for the expression of the growing popular discontent and fostered the development of opposition parties. Even official candidates ventured to criticize the Italian and commercial policies of the Emperor, sixty-one members of the Senate and ninety-one deputies of the Assembly having demanded, for instance, the maintenance of the temporal power of the Pope. The Roman Catholics vigorously insisted on freedom of the press and the right of association and protested against the surveillance exercised by the government over the religious orders. The five Republican members of the Assembly commenced to play the part of a parliamentary opposition. At every opportunity they asked for a genuine and independent universal suffrage, freedom to hold public meetings, liberty of the press, ministerial responsibility to the parliament, and parliamentary control of finances. Old politicians like Thiers began to take part in politics again. At the instigation of Prince Napoleon, the nephew of the Emperor, the working-men of France commenced an agitation for an improvement of their condition. In 1862 a delegation of French workers visited England and found the British laboring classes enjoying higher wages, shorter hours, and greater protection against injuries and disease than they themselves enjoyed, and having the legal right to organize for the purpose of improving their situation. The visit stimulated the more active French working-men to resume political activity and to demand the right to organize. The new generation of students professed a hatred of the religious and intellectual tyranny of the government and the more radical members of the student body joined with some of the workers of Paris in organizing a Revolutionary party. After 1863 a new opposition, known as the Third party, composed of discontented official deputies, Roman Catholics irritated at the treatment accorded the Pope by the Emperor, and protectionists alarmed at his free-trade policy, began to demand additional political concessions.

The new spirit of opposition made itself felt in many ways. In 1861 the debates on the response of the Assembly to the speech from the throne drew large crowds. At a general assembly of the Society of St. Vincent de Paul a French bishop openly referred to the Emperor as Judas. The students frequently demonstrated against conservative professors and the government and founded literary reviews that attacked morality, religion, and the existing order of society. In the electoral campaign of 1863 the Legitimist supporters of the Bourbons, the Orleanists, the Roman Catholics, and in some cases even the Republicans forgot their differences and joined in opposing the official candidates. At Paris the opposition succeeded in electing the old Orleanist Thiers and eight Republicans as members of the Assembly. In most of the French provincial cities the opposition obtained majorities and in the whole country its candidates received about two sevenths of the total vote.

2

THE LATER FOREIGN POLICY OF NAPOLEON III

In the hope of allaying popular dissatisfaction and recapturing the imagination of the French people, after 1860 the Emperor intervened, or at least interfered, in Poland, Schleswig-Holstein, Mexico, Italy, and Germany. In each case he failed to maintain a consistent policy and repeatedly he displayed an inability to see all the consequences of his policies. As a result he irritated every important political element in France, alienated the good-will of the principal European powers, and gained nothing but humiliation and loss of prestige for himself and his empire.

In Poland the reforms inaugurated by Tsar Alexander II of Russia after the close of the Crimean War had aroused the hopes of the Poles. Their peaceful agitation for a relaxation of the oppressive régime imposed on them after their unsuccessful revolution of 1831 awakened the sympathy of all French parties. French Catholics sympathized with their Polish fellow-religionists. French Republicans regarded them as an oppressed people. French nationalists remembered the historic alliance between France and Poland in the days of the Ancien Régime. In 1863 the peaceful agitation of the Poles became transformed into a revolutionary movement. Out of deference to French public opinion the Emperor intervened diplomatically in behalf of the Poles, but he felt unprepared to resort to arms in the cause of Polish independence. This futile intervention in a question that he considered a purely domestic matter angered the Tsar without bettering in any way the condition of the Poles.

In the same year the Danish government, relying on the support of France, Great Britain, and Sweden, ventured to revive the question of the future of the two provinces of Schleswig and Holstein and finally defied both Prussia and Austria. In the crisis Napoleon III toyed for a time with his favorite remedy for the ills of Europe, a congress of the powers, but finally, fearing to involve France in an armed struggle, he refused even to allow the French fleet to accompany a British fleet into Danish waters. His weak, hesitant policy allowed Prussia and Austria to gain complete control of Schleswig-Holstein.

The Emperor next turned his attention to Italy, where the maintenance of a French garrison at Rome embittered the relations of France and the new Kingdom of Italy without improving the position of Napoleon III with either the Pope or the French Catholics. Upon learning of the intention of the Italian government to remove the capital of Italy from Turin, the Emperor attempted to tie together the question of the with-

drawal of the French garrison from Rome and the problem of the removal of the seat of the Italian government. In a convention concluded
in September, 1864, he promised to complete the evacuation of Rome by
the French troops within two years provided that the Italian government
would move its capital to Florence, renounce its hopes of making Rome
the political center of Italy, and promise to protect the Pope from attack.
The treaty angered Italian patriots and inspired no confidence in Napoleon on the part of either the Pope or the Roman Catholics in France.

Napoleon III mismanaged his foreign policy as badly in America as
in Europe. When the Civil War broke out in the United States in 1861,
the majority of the French people sympathized with the North; Napoleon III and his court felt more sympathy with the more aristocratic
South and hoped to obtain for French industry the raw cotton kept in
the Southern ports by the blockade maintained by the North. As a result
the Emperor received three different times the diplomatic representative
sent to France by the government of the Confederacy, proposed to the European powers joint intervention in America, and permitted the Southern
States to build commerce-destroyers, only one of which actually ever
sailed from France. In the end he found that he had supported the losing
side in the conflict.

His mismanagement of the problem of the Civil War in the United
States had an unfortunate influence on his Mexican venture. Since 1858
the Conservatives and the Liberals of Mexico had been carrying on a
struggle for the control of the state. Upon gaining the Presidency, the
Liberals had secularized the property of the Church and abolished the
clerical courts. The Conservatives, headed by the clergy and the great
landed proprietors, had thereupon taken up arms in behalf of the Church
and of a more centralized form of government. In the ensuing civil war
the Liberals had defeated the Conservatives, but they had found it impossible to meet the interest payments on the foreign debt of Mexico. The
European investors in the Mexican bonds had therefore appealed to their
respective governments to use military pressure to force the government
of Mexico to meet its financial obligations.

The diplomatic representative of France in Mexico and his Conservative Mexican friends formulated a plan for using the proposed British,
French, and Spanish expeditions to overthrow the Liberal government
of Mexico. With this end in view the Mexican Conservatives sent an
envoy to Paris who represented to Napoleon III that the Liberal régime
had been imposed on Mexico by the government of the United States
and that the Mexican people would welcome the establishment of a
monarchy. The idea appealed to the imagination of the Emperor. He vi-
sioned an empire Latin, Catholic, and centralized, confronting the hostile
Anglo-Saxon and Protestant republic of the United States. With this
end in view he offered the throne of the proposed empire to Maximilian,

brother of Francis Joseph of Austria, in the hope of conciliating Austria and facilitating the cession of the Austrian province of Venetia to the new Kingdom of Italy, and negotiated a convention with Spain and Great Britain that provided for a military demonstration by the three powers to compel the Mexican government to meet its financial obligations.

Upon the arrival of the three expeditions at Vera Cruz, however, the French began to disclose their real purpose in urging the use of military force against Mexico. They made such exorbitant demands on the Mexican government and showed such marked sympathy for the Mexican Conservatives that the British and Spanish expeditionary forces soon withdrew from the country. The French troops pushed on into the interior of Mexico, defeated, with the aid of reënforcements sent from France, the poorly armed and badly trained troops of the Mexican Liberals, gained control of the greater part of the territory of Mexico, and set up the proposed empire. Only in the extreme north and in the southern part of Mexico did the Liberals still maintain an armed resistance.

Put in power by the military forces of France, Emperor Maximilian immediately began to discover the difficulties inherent in his new position. The Roman Catholic clergy demanded as the price of their support the repeal of the laws enacted by the Liberals abolishing the clerical courts and secularizing the property of the Church, supervision of the schools by the clergy, and recognition of Roman Catholicism as the sole religion of the state. The refusal of the Emperor to concede these demands embroiled the new empire in a quarrel with the Roman Catholic clergy. The Mexican officials and the officers of the French expeditionary force quarreled. Maximilian disagreed with his patron, Napoleon III, over finances. Finally, at the close of the American Civil War the government of the United States protested vigorously against the presence of French troops in Mexico and seemed ready to mobilize its veteran soldiers on the Mexican border. Developments in Schleswig-Holstein impressed on Napoleon III the need of having all his resources at his disposal. The situation left the ambitious French Emperor no recourse but to withdraw his troops from Mexico under the pretext that the government of Maximilian had failed to pay their expenses.

The withdrawal of the French forces in 1867 sealed the fate of the unstable Mexican Empire of Napoleon III. No substantial portion of the Mexican people had ever favored the plans of the French Emperor. The defense of his empire in Mexico fell to the lot of a few thousand Austrian, Belgian, and Indian troops entirely unequal to the task. As a result the Mexican Liberals had little difficulty in defeating the troops of Maximilian, capturing, trying, and executing the unfortunate young Emperor, and regaining control of the whole country.

The Mexican venture had many injurious effects on the political position of Napoleon III. Many Frenchmen lost their Mexican investments. France wasted on the expedition men, money, and other resources that she could ill spare. The expedition to Mexico aroused the hostility of the United States and diverted troops needed to give weight to French diplomacy in Italy and Germany.

In both these countries the French Emperor misjudged the situation badly. With the idea of conciliating Italian public opinion by bringing about the annexation of Venetia and of insuring France the dictatorship of Europe by a long and exhausting war between Prussia and Austria, he watched with benevolent neutrality the preparation of the two countries for a struggle for the supremacy of Germany, and facilitated the conclusion of a military alliance between Prussia and Italy with the idea of equalizing the contending forces. But when the War of 1866 actually broke out Prussia surprised the Emperor by promptly defeating Austria at Königgrätz. His failure to estimate correctly the relative strength of the two states contending for the hegemony of Germany had serious results for both France and Napoleon III. As a result of her victory Prussia annexed a large amount of territory and organized the states north of the Main River into the North German Confederation. The French people, in consequence, considered the battle of Königgrätz as much a defeat of France as of Austria. Thiers declared it the greatest disaster experienced by the French nation in four hundred years. Compelled to take Venetia as a gift instead of by arms, the Italian people felt no gratitude toward Napoleon III for his aid in bringing about its annexation to the Kingdom of Italy. The Emperor uselessly irritated Prussia by preventing the inclusion in the new confederation of the states south of the Main River. By his futile demands for the frontier of 1814 or the principality of Luxemburg as compensation for his neutrality in the war he discredited himself with the Russian, Belgian, and British governments and drove the South German states into an offensive and defensive alliance with Prussia.

In this same year of the war between Prussia and Austria Napoleon III suffered a number of other humiliations. Out of deference to public opinion in Germany Bismarck vetoed a plan for permitting the King of the Netherlands to cede the Grand Duchy of Luxemburg to France. When Napoleon III pressed Prussia to execute the promise to submit to a plebiscite the question of the annexation of the Danish districts of Schleswig, Bismarck reminded him that the promise had been made to Austria and not to France and refused to put the question of annexation to a vote. To prevent the seizure of Rome by Garibaldi Napoleon III reoccupied the city and added to the ill-will already felt toward him by the Italian people. This succession of defeats and failures in his foreign policy inevitably reacted unfavorably on his position in France.

3

FURTHER CONCESSIONS TO DOMESTIC DISCONTENT

The diplomatic reverses suffered by France after 1859 convinced nearly every one that the absolutist régime established by the coup d'état of 1851 could no longer be maintained. Napoleon III, by this time a sick man, lost confidence in himself, and his old associates advised him to make some further concessions to the insistent demands of the opposition. Early in 1867, consequently, the Emperor demanded the resignation of his old ministers and announced a change of policy. He substituted for the time-consuming debates over the response to the speech from the throne the right of the parliament to interpellate his ministers, liberalized the policy of his government toward the press, and removed many of the restrictions on public meetings. But he largely neutralized these concessions by retaining many of his conservative advisers, placing cumbersome restrictions on the new right of interpellation, and enlarging the powers of the appointed Senate. In consequence his concessions merely disquieted his supporters without satisfying his opponents.

The opposition took advantage of the relaxation of the restrictions on the press and public meetings, moreover, to intensify its agitation. In Paris the workers held public meetings for the discussion of politics under the guise of social and economic questions. Journals sprang up that criticized and ridiculed the imperial régime. The opponents of the Emperor attacked him at his weakest point, the origin of his empire in the coup d'état of 1851. They made a martyr to the cause of liberty of Jean-Baptiste Baudin, a Socialist deputy who died on the barricades during the armed protest of the working-class quarters of Paris against the seizure of power by Louis Napoleon. When one of the opposition journals brought upon itself prosecution by the government for starting a subscription to be used for the purchase of a monument to mark the tomb of Baudin, Léon Gambetta, a fiery young Republican lawyer, made himself a public figure in France and aroused great popular indignation against the imperial régime by his defense of the offending newspaper and his scathing indictment of the Second Empire.

In 1869 the elections for the renewal of the Assembly unmistakably showed the effect of this agitation against the Emperor. In spite of the pressure exerted by the government in behalf of official candidates and its manipulation of the electoral machinery, the opposition won by an enormous majority in Paris, carried most of the other large cities of France, and obtained three eighths of the popular vote in the whole country. The new deputies included the fiery Gambetta. In three years the opposition had cut down the majority of the government from three million to one million votes.

The success of the opposition in the elections thrust sharply on the attention of the hesitant Emperor the question of further political concessions. The leaders of the Third party circulated a petition for the establishment of a ministry responsible to the parliament and for a greater participation of the French people in the work of government, and it obtained the signatures of one hundred and sixteen deputies. The signers of the petition and the Republicans constituted a majority in the Assembly. The Emperor, accordingly, dismissed Eugène Rouher, an unpopular minister who had become a symbol of absolutism, conceded to the Assembly the right to elect its own officers, initiate legislation, interpellate the government, and vote the yearly budget by chapters, and made the Senate again a legislative body with its sessions open to the public.

The new concessions only increased the popular agitation. The working classes engaged in a number of serious strikes; the Socialists and the revolutionary Republicans demanded more vigorous measures; the moderate Republicans insisted on the grant of full parliamentary government; and the Third party finally obtained one hundred and sixty-three signatures to its petition. In response to this agitation the Emperor summoned Olivier Ollivier, one of the five members of the original opposition in the Assembly, to organize a new ministry and reëstablish parliamentary government in France.

The new ministry compelled the Emperor to revise the constitution. A decree of April 20, 1870, took from the Senate its power over the constitution and reduced it to the rôle of an upper house of the parliament, and gave both the Senate and the Assembly the right of interpellating ministers and amending the laws, but retained the plebiscite and left the ministers still dependent on the Emperor. For a moment Napoleon III seemed to have reëstablished his power on a firm foundation. Paris and the larger provincial cities voted against the new constitution, but the country as a whole ratified the constitutional changes by seven million three hundred and fifty-eight thousand to one million five hundred and seventy-two thousand votes. However, the new ministry immediately embarked on a foreign policy that ended in the defeat of France in the Franco-Prussian War and the overthrow of the imperial régime.

4

THE FALL OF THE SECOND EMPIRE

The policy adopted by the new ministry toward the question of the candidacy of Leopold of Hohenzollern-Sigmaringen for the Spanish throne finally involved France in a disastrous war with Prussia and the other German states. The Spanish Revolution of 1868 created a vacancy on the throne of Spain. At the instigation of Bismarck, the Prussian Foreign Minister and Chancellor of the North German Confederation, the army officers in control of Spain offered the position of king to Leopold, a distant relative of the reigning house of Prussia. The offer greatly alarmed Napoleon III and his advisers. They assumed that the Hohenzollern candidate would be little more than an agent of Prussia. French newspapers, consequently, began to refer to him as the Prussian proconsul and to talk of the revival of the empire of Charles V. Though the proposed candidate twice refused the offered throne, the French ministry became greatly disturbed at the news of a third proffer of the vacant office. It instructed Count Vincent Benedetti, the French ambassador to Prussia, to proceed to Ems, where William I, King of Prussia, was spending some time, and induce him to persuade his relative to refuse the Spanish kingship a third time. At first the Prussian sovereign took the position that his government had no direct interest in the question, but when the French government, desirous of obtaining a striking diplomatic success, instructed its ambassador to ask William I to forbid the acceptance of the Spanish throne by his relative, he finally authorized the French ambassador to telegraph his government that the King of Prussia expected to receive a message from his relative on the following day, and invited Benedetti to dine with him. On that very day the father of Leopold, exercising his rights as head of the family, declined the new Spanish offer in the name of his son. His refusal of the throne thwarted for the moment Bismarck's plans for a war between Prussia and France.

This striking success, however, did not satisfy certain elements in French political life. The Conservatives at court and in the parliament urged the French Foreign Minister to attempt to obtain from the Prussian sovereign a promise that his relative would refuse to accept any future offer. On July 13, 1870, accordingly, the French ambassador to Prussia presented this demand of his government to William I at a chance meeting in the public park of Ems. Acting upon the advice of Bismarck, the Prussian sovereign broke off the interview with considerable irritation, refused to grant the French ambassador another audience or to give him the desired assurances for the future, telegraphed his Chancellor an account of the final interview, and authorized him to publish it.

Bismarck made skilful use of the telegram of his sovereign. Revising it in a way calculated to inflame public opinion in both France and Germany, the Chancellor published the despatch in an official newspaper and sent an account of the interview at Ems to the Prussian representatives at the various courts of Europe. Upon the arrival of news of the Ems episode, the publication of the telegram of the Prussian King, and the sending of the circular note, the French ministers lost their heads and

decided on war with Prussia (July 15, 1870). Ignoring the advice of
Thiers and the opposition of many of the Republicans, the French parliament immediately voted a war credit. In form the French ministry went
to war over the question of the candidacy of Leopold of Hohenzollern-
Sigmaringen for the Spanish throne; in reality it precipitated the Franco-
Prussian conflict in an attempt to recapture the position of dominance
that it had lost through the long succession of blunders in foreign policy
made by Napoleon III.

From the moment of the declaration of hostilities the war went badly
for France. Disregarding some vague promises made in the previous
year, the Austrian government deferred to public opinion among its
German and Magyar subjects and refused to send an army into Bohemia
to immobilize a substantial portion of the Prussian army. The Italian
government made the evacuation of Rome by French troops a condition
of its coöperation with Austria and France against Prussia. The South
German states, on the contrary, fulfilled their treaty obligations and co-
operated in the campaign with the North German Confederation.

The mobilization of the military forces quickly revealed that Prussia
was better prepared for war than was France. Prussia put into the field
with greater rapidity a larger number of trained troops, displayed greater
skill in handling large masses of men, proved superior in artillery, used a
superior system for feeding and sheltering her troops, and showed more
knowledge of the theory of war. In France, on the other hand, the order
for mobilization threw everything into confusion. Reservists had to await
the arrival of arms and equipment. Regiments arrived at the front without their full complements of men. Commanders lost track of their troops,
and military units made useless journeys to different parts of France.

The unpreparedness of France gave the German forces the initiative
in the campaign. Two German armies moved toward Lorraine and a
third army, composed largely of troops of the South German states,
marched into Alsace. At the beginning of August the latter army surprised a French force at Weissenburg. Two days later it defeated the
main French army at Wörth and drove it in confusion across the Vosges
Mountains. The fortress of Strasbourg, however, held out until the end
of September. In the meantime the campaign in Lorraine had been going
badly for the French. After one or two indecisive encounters the French
commander learned of the French defeat in Alsace and began to retreat.
After one or two battles he fell back to the protection of the guns of
Metz. Thereupon the German troops not needed for the investment of
Metz pushed on toward Châlons, where a new army, composed of old
soldiers, inexperienced recruits, and troops defeated in Alsace, had been
organized. On September 2, 1870, the German forces compelled the
Emperor and the new French army to surrender at Sedan.

The capture of Napoleon III and the defeat of his armies caused the overthrow of his empire. Even the close advisers of the Emperor realized that he could not continue to govern France. But while the hesitant leaders of the parliament deliberated on the best method of terminating the imperial régime, the Parisian mob took control of the situation. Two days after the surrender of Napoleon III and his army at Sedan a crowd broke into the hall occupied by the Assembly and demanded the proclamation of the fall of the Second Empire and the establishment of a republic. They had no difficulty in intimidating the deputies into proclaiming the Third French Republic; the Empress fled to England; and a self-constituted provisional government, known as the Government of the National Defense, composed mainly of Republican deputies from Paris, took charge of the conduct of the war. In view of the grave situation the French people accepted the new government with comparatively little protest.

Between 1859 and 1870 Napoleon III suffered a succession of reverses both at home and abroad. In an effort to recapture the imagination of his subjects by a brilliant stroke of foreign policy he intervened or interfered unsuccessfully in Poland, Schleswig-Holstein, Mexico, Italy, and Germany. His reverses in foreign policy weakened his position at home. In the hope of allaying domestic discontent he gradually reëstablished a parliamentary régime. No sooner had parliamentary government been set up, however, than the French cabinet embarked on a foreign policy that ended in the defeat of France and the overthrow of Napoleon III.

CHAPTER XIV

The conquest of the Revolution of 1848 by Austria settled definitely none of the problems of central Europe. The victorious Austrian government still found itself confronted by four potential enemies—the nationalities of the Austrian Empire, the Italian people, Prussia, and the new economic forces of Germany.

I

THE NEW PERIOD OF REACTION

After the defeat of the revolutionary movement of 1848 reaction became again the watchword for the masters of central Europe. In Austria the advisers of the young Emperor Francis Joseph inaugurated a new form of absolutism. The Emperor lacked imagination and firmly believed that the simple principles of discipline effective in the army would solve the more complex problems of the Austrian Empire. He gathered around him a group of advisers who aimed at the centralization and the modernization of the state. They felt no sympathy for the historic rights of the nobles, the autonomy of the provinces, or the ambitions of subject nationalities. They strove for the complete centralization of political authority in the hands of the Emperor. With this end in view they refused to restore to the great landlords their patrimonial courts and police powers, and replaced the nobles with a docile middle-class bureaucracy. Asserting that a constitution was incompatible with the monarchical principle, they revoked in 1851 the constitution granted two years earlier and thenceforth denied Austrian subjects the right of assembly, trial by jury, and freedom of the press. Thereafter they relied on the loyalty and watchfulness of the police, the army, the Church, and the bureaucracy to hold the discordant nationalities together.

As a result of the influence of his mother and his belief that the Church was an effective check on Liberalism and nationalism the Emperor made important concessions to the Church. Since the days of Joseph II the state had carefully regulated the relations of the Austrian bishops and the monastic institutions with the Pope and with other foreign ecclesiastical superiors, the publication of papal and episcopal pronouncements, and the administration of Church property. By the Concordat concluded with the Church in 1855, however, the Austrian government freed the Church almost entirely from the supervision of the state, gave the canon law a decisive voice in governing the relations of Church and State, handed over to the clergy the supervision of education, reëstablished censorship of books, placed in the hands of the Church control of marriage, and removed restrictions on the acquirement of property by the Church. In concluding this agreement the Austrian government followed a policy that ran counter to the trend in other countries.

Notwithstanding its reactionary tendencies, the new régime benefited the inhabitants of the Austrian Empire in many ways. The new advisers of the Emperor executed the revolutionary decrees freeing the peasants from their seigniorial dues, stimulated commerce by removing provincial customs lines and lowering the tariffs on imports, established chambers of commerce, fostered the building of highways and railroads, and put the universities and secondary schools of Austria on a par with those of Germany.

In Prussia the government did not restore absolutism as completely as it was restored in Austria. After the subsidence of the revolutionary movement of 1848 it revised the new constitution in a Conservative direction and excluded the Prussian people as far as possible from political life. It restored to the great landholders their police powers and the right of entailing their estates, deprived local administrative districts of many rights of self-government, and made the upper house of the Prussian parliament a docile political instrument. It removed judges from office for showing independence in their political decisions, refused promotion to royal employees with Liberal opinions or dismissed them entirely from the service of the state, restricted freedom of the press, encouraged the secret police to tamper with private correspondence and to spy on the daily lives of Prussian subjects, and persecuted prominent Liberals. By the educational regulations of 1854 it subordinated all other branches of the curriculum to religious instruction, placed the popular schools under clerical supervision, and forbade the reading of many German classics. It made a display of religious orthodoxy the test of advancement for state employees. Until the establishment of the Regency in 1858 an irresponsible camarilla, recruited from the clergy and the most reactionary elements in the state, struggled with the bureaucracy for control of the royal policy.

Most of the other German states voluntarily followed the leadership of Austria and Prussia. Saxony, Württemberg, and some of the other smaller states annulled the constitutions that they had adopted under the pressure of the revolutionary movement of 1848. If they showed a tendency toward a Liberal policy, the largest states of the German Confederation compelled them to adopt a Conservative policy. Upon the initiative of Austria and Prussia the diet of the Confederation established a committee in 1851, popularly known as the Reactionary Committee, for the purpose of preventing the individual states from maintaining institutions incompatible with peace and order as defined by the Conservatives. This body proceeded first against the smaller states and then took in hand those of larger size. It forced Hesse-Darmstadt, for example, to reestablish the upper chamber abolished by the Revolution of 1848 and to annul its liberal legislation concerning local government; practically restored absolutism in Hanover; and compelled Hesse-Cassel to annul the constitution granted by its Elector after the Revolution of 1830. In all the German states the committee took action against political societies, forced printers to obtain a special concession, compelled publishers to make a precautionary deposit, and abolished trial by jury for cases involving censorship of the press.

The policy of Austria and Prussia produced a condition of almost complete political stagnation. The leaders of the Liberals suffered from persecution and tens of thousands of Germans emigrated like Carl Schurz to the freer air of the United States. The rigid censorship prevented all political agitation. The parliaments of the smaller states concerned themselves exclusively with local questions. The Conservatives obtained their objectives by resort to intrigue rather than by political action. During this period the Roman Catholic deputies in the state parliaments did form the habit of discussing together the interests of their church and laid the foundation of the later Center party of the German Empire.

The political reaction, however, could not stay the economic transformation of Germany. In the decade following the Revolution of 1848 Germany rapidly changed from an agricultural to an industrial state. The mileage of her railroads doubled; the electric telegraph came into general use; and German capitalists established many banks and stock companies. Cotton manufactures developed in southern Germany, textile and metallurgical industries in Saxony, and mining and iron and steel manufacturing in the Rhineland, Westphalia, and Upper Silesia. Industrial plants greatly increased in size and doubled and trebled their output.

The growth of German industry and commerce called the attention of the German people sharply to the obsolete political machinery of the German Confederation. The air became filled with proposals for its reform. Austria proposed the admission of all its provinces to the Prussian tariff union. The South German states advocated an extension of the powers of the German Confederation to include coinage, weights, and measures. These proposals quickly disclosed the conflicting points of view of the different states. Prussia had no intention of expanding her tariff union so far that Austria and the smaller German states would acquire control of its policies. Neither Prussia nor Austria had any thought of surrendering essential political powers to the German Confederation. Hanover, Oldenburg, Bremen, Hamburg, and Lübeck, however, did decide that their interests dictated their joining the Prussian Zollverein.

2

PRUSSIA ASSUMES THE LEADERSHIP OF GERMANY

In 1858 an event of great significance for the future of Germany occurred. The mentally sick Frederick William IV of Prussia resigned his power into the hands of his brother, Prince William, who governed Prussia for three years as Regent and then became sovereign in his own right under the title of William I. The new Prussian ruler took office in his sixty-first year. As a child he had seen the breakdown of Prussia after the battle of Jena, had then taken part in the flight of the royal family to East Prussia, and had later witnessed the humiliation of his state at Tilsit. These experiences bred in him a feeling of hostility to France and Napoleon. His birth and training made him a monarchist and a Conservative. He had spent the greater part of his life in the army and believed that the power of Prussia rested on command of the army and control of the political policy of the state by its sovereign. He openly disapproved of the camarilla that surrounded his brother. Upon assuming control of the government, consequently, he dismissed the advisers of his predecessor, announced his adherence to sound, conservative principles of government, condemned the practice of using religion as a cloak for politics, and asserted the readiness of Prussia to defend its rights.

As a result of his training he naturally turned his attention first to the Prussian army. He considered the military forces of Prussia too small for the size of its population. While the number of his subjects had mounted since 1820 from eleven to eighteen millions, there had been no corresponding increase in the number of recruits. By 1858 a third of the youth of Prussia entirely escaped military service. This situation did an injustice to the conscripted young men, violated the principles of the Prussian military system, and compelled the government in times of danger to mobilize men with families who were deeply enmeshed in the economic life of the country. Both the officers and the men of the reserve forces lacked the necessary professional training. As a remedy for this situation Prince William proposed the conscription each year of twenty-five thousand additional recruits, the formation of forty-nine new regiments in the standing army, and the creation of a reserve that should train with the standing army for a few weeks each year. At the end of 1859 he entrusted General von Roon with the task of carrying out the proposed army reforms.

The chief obstacle to the adoption of the proposals of Prince William proved to be the Liberals. They looked upon the appointment of Von Roon as an indication of a swing toward Conservatism, regarded the standing army as a relic of absolutism, desired to reduce the period of military service in the army from three to two years, and looked upon the proposed reforms of the Regent as an attack on the militia, an institution that gave the young men of the middle class a position in society which they valued greatly. Left free after the accession of Prince William to carry on a political agitation, and encouraged by the success of the Italians against Austria, they had gained many seats in the Prussian parliament. In the session of 1860, consequently, probably with the hope of gaining a decisive voice in military matters and of preventing the Regent from throwing himself completely into the arms of the Conservatives, the Liberals took the serious step of voting the funds necessary to carry out the proposed reorganization of the army for a period of fourteen months. As a result of this vote the Regent and his Minister of War put into force the new military reforms.

At the end of two years, however, the Prussian parliament refused to continue its support of the new regiments. In the session of 1861 nineteen Liberals had separated from their party and voted against the proposed army reforms. They finally constituted themselves a separate party known as the Progressives and drew up a political program that demanded the establishment of a constitutional régime, the reform of the upper house of the Prussian parliament, a responsible ministry, and a discontinuance of the new units of the army unless the government retained the institution of the militia and reduced the period of military service to two years. In the election of 1861 the new party won a great success. Upon the refusal of Von Roon to reduce the term of service in the army to two years, the new party, with the aid of the Liberals, refused to grant the funds needed to continue the new regiments.

This action of the Liberals and the Progressives produced a constitutional crisis. Relying on English precedents, the lower house of the Prussian parliament contended that it had the power of the purse. King William took the position that in case of disagreement between the two houses of the parliament the government had the legal right to collect through taxation a sum equal to the amount voted at the previous session. Opposed by the Queen, the heir to the throne, most of the royal ministers, and a majority of his subjects, the King for a time thought seriously of abdicating. At the urgent solicitation of Von Roon, however, he finally decided to stick to his own interpretation of the constitution and invited Prince Bismarck, the Prussian minister at Paris, to become head of the Prussian government and defend the royal point of view concerning the army.

The new minister had sprung from the Junker class, the governing caste of Prussia. He had been educated at schools in Berlin and at the

University of Göttingen but none of his teachers and professors seems to have made any impression upon him. After leaving the university he had spent several years in the Prussian bureaucracy. Disliking the life of an administrative official, he had resigned from the service of the government and had taken over the management of one of the family estates. During the next few years he had found time to read widely in the fields of history, philosophy, and literature and to travel in France and England. In 1847 his neighboring landlords had sent him as their representative to the United Provincial Diets at Berlin. Two years later they had elected him a member of the Prussian parliament.

In these bodies he attracted much attention by his bold defense of the conservative point of view. At a time when Liberalism was in the saddle he defended the Christian state, the gild system, and the Junker class, opposed the plans of the Liberals for Prussia and Germany, and approved the action of Prussia at Olmütz. As a result of his speeches Frederick William IV appointed him in 1851 as the representative of Prussia to the diet of the German Confederation. During the eight years in which he occupied this post he served his diplomatic apprenticeship and gradually formulated his ideas. He went to Frankfort a partisan of the traditional Prussian policy of coöperation with Austria. His experiences there taught him the selfishness of Austria and convinced him that Prussia must adopt an independent policy, oppose all plans for strengthening the German Confederation, and eventually fight Austria in order to gain a free hand in the reorganization of Germany. After he left Frankfort his government sent him as its diplomatic representative first to St. Petersburg and then to Paris. In both posts he gained a knowledge of men and conditions which later proved valuable. The King thus summoned to the leadership of Prussia in the midst of the constitutional crisis an experienced diplomat forty-seven years of age, at the height of his physical and mental powers, and with clear-cut ideas about the Prussian constitution, the reorganization of Germany, and the foreign policy of Prussia.

3

THE FIRST MEASURES OF BISMARCK

Upon taking office Bismarck quickly made himself most unpopular. In Germany he soon gave the parliamentary opposition to understand that he would make no fundamental concessions in regard to the reorganization of the army and bluntly told his opponents that Germany gave heed to Prussia not because of her Liberalism but on account of her power, and that the great questions of the time would be decided not by speeches, which was the mistake of 1848, but by blood and iron. In an effort to intimidate the opposition he resorted to many unconstitutional measures. He prorogued the parliament, destroyed freedom of the press, forbade municipal governments to discuss political questions, and punished Liberal judges and administrative officials for political agitation. In the election held in October, 1863, he vainly attempted to defeat the opposition candidates.

In the same year he gave Austria warning that a new pilot was at the helm in Prussia. In December, 1863, he informed the Austrian ambassador at Berlin that henceforth Austria must recognize Prussia as an equal. As a sign of her new position he demanded command of the military forces of northern Germany for Prussia and permission, in case of war, for a Prussian occupation of Hanover and Hesse-Cassel. He also told the Austrian ambassador that he considered a war between Prussia and Austria for the leadership of Germany inevitable and advised Austria to turn her attention from Germany to the Balkan peninsula.

At the same time he adopted a policy toward the revolt of the Poles that confirmed the worst suspicions of the opposition. In defiance of the sympathy felt for the Polish revolutionists by the Liberals and the Roman Catholics of Germany, he closed the Prussian frontier to Polish refugees, and offered the Tsar the aid of the military forces of Prussia. As yet, however, no one saw the real significance of his domestic and foreign policies.

4

THE SETTLEMENT OF PRUSSIA WITH AUSTRIA

The reopening of the Schleswig-Holstein question almost immediately gave Bismarck an opportunity to begin the reorganization of Germany. The conference held at London in 1852 by the European powers had by no means settled the problem of the future of the two duchies. Their representatives had hardly separated before the King of Denmark began to show signs that he had no intention of respecting the independence of the two provinces. Pushed on by the Danish nationalists and the vaguer Scandinavian movement, he punished the inhabitants of Schleswig and Holstein involved in the Revolution of 1848, persecuted the Germans living in the two duchies, withdrew control of the domain lands from the provincial diets, subjected some branches of the administration to the ministry in Denmark, and filled the two provinces with Danish officials, pastors, and school-teachers. In 1863 his successor issued a constitution that completely incorporated Schleswig into Denmark.

The policy pursued by the Danish goverment in Schleswig and Holstein aroused intense excitement in Germany. The diet of the German Confederation ordered Saxony and Hanover to intervene in Holstein and to compel the Danish sovereign by the use of force to grant the two duchies a new constitution; and the heir of the Duke of Augustenburg revived the claims of his family to the two provinces. In December, 1863, an assembly of nearly five hundred deputies from the different German parliaments met in Frankfort and organized a commission to work in behalf of the Augustenburg claims. The sovereigns of the smaller German states welcomed the prospect of an increase in their numbers and joined in the popular agitation. In the following January the Saxon and Hanoverian troops took possession of Holstein. Under their protection the Augustenburg claimant entered the duchy, set up a government, and declared the Liberal constitution of 1848 in force in the duchy.

Austria and Prussia, however, adopted a different policy. After long negotiations, in January, 1864, the governments of the two states presented Denmark with an ultimatum that demanded the withdrawal within forty-eight hours of the constitution incorporating Schleswig into the Kingdom of Denmark and permission for the two powers to occupy Schleswig and Holstein with their troops. Upon the refusal of the Danish government to comply with these demands the military forces of Prussia and Austria defeated the Danish troops in Schleswig, seized three key fortresses in Holstein in spite of the protests of the commander of the Saxon and Hanoverian troops, and finally occupied most of Jutland.

These successes reopened the question of the future of Schleswig and Holstein. Bismarck regarded the agreement reached by the European powers at the conference held at London in 1852 as nullified by Denmark and sought to annex the two duchies to Prussia or at least to bring them under Prussian control. Austria would consent to this solution of the problem only on condition that she should receive a portion of the Prussian province of Silesia in compensation. Popular opinion in Germany advocated the separation of the two duchies from Denmark and their formation into an independent German state ruled by the Augustenburg family. The European powers proposed the union of the Danish districts of Schleswig to Denmark and the formation of the rest of the territory of the two provinces into an independent German state.

The Austrian and Prussian governments reached even a temporary settlement of the question only with the greatest difficulty. The Danes blindly insisted on the fulfilment of their extreme demands. The heir of the Duke of Augustenburg failed to come to terms with Bismarck. Austria refused to permit Prussia to annex the two duchies. In 1865, however, the two powers finally reached an agreement known as the Treaty of Gastein, which recognized the joint sovereignty of the two powers over both provinces, gave Austria provisional administration of Holstein, conceded to Prussia control of Schleswig and the right to maintain a military road and a telegraph-line across Holstein, to build a canal from the North Sea to the Baltic Sea, and to purchase the little Duchy of Lauenburg, and included both Schleswig and Holstein in the Prussian Zollverein.

The agreement concluded at Gastein neither gave a satisfactory solution to the problem of the permanent future of Schleswig and Holstein nor decided the burning question of the political leadership of Germany. Bismarck, consequently, commenced at once to make diplomatic preparations for the war with Austria that he considered inevitable. He attempted to win the support of Bavaria, visited France to assure himself of the attitude of Napoleon III, and, with the assistance of the French Emperor, negotiated an agreement that obligated Italy to take part in the anticipated war with Austria provided hostilities should commence within three months, in the hope of receiving the province of Venetia for her sacrifices.

Bismarck was too clever a minister, however, to allow himself to appear to be precipitating a war with Austria over such a minor question as the future of Schleswig and Holstein. In order to enlist public opinion in Germany on the side of Prussia he pushed the problem of the future of the two duchies into the background and brought forward again the question of the reorganization of Germany. He therefore instructed the Prussian representative at Frankfort to propose to the diet of the German Confederation the summoning of a German parliament elected by equal, secret, and universal suffrage, and the conferring on Prussia and Bavaria of command of the military forces of the Confederation in northern and southern Germany. Upon being pressed for details, the Prussian representative sketched a plan of reorganization which gave the new German parliament an equal voice with the old German diet, abolished the rule requiring the unanimous consent of the German states as a prerequisite for common action, and extended the competence of the German Confederation to include economic questions, diplomatic representation abroad, and military and naval affairs. He left it to be inferred that Austria would have no place in the new Germany.

The policy of Bismarck frightened Austria into adopting measures that made war inevitable. In March, 1866, the Austrian government strengthened its military forces on the northern frontier of Bohemia. Its action gave Bismarck a plausible excuse for mobilizing the Prussian army. At this point the Tsar, Queen Victoria, and the Bavarian government intervened. At first Austria agreed to reduce her military forces to a peace footing, but she finally refused to demobilize because of the threatening situation in Italy. After the breakdown of these negotiations both Austria and Prussia called to the colors all their military reserves.

Mobilization created a situation that finally produced war. Faced by the prospect of war with Austria, Bismarck negotiated with the opposition parties in the smaller German states and with the disaffected Magyars in Hungary. Austria made a bid for the support of the lesser German states by announcing her willingness to summon the diet in Holstein and to leave the question of the future of Schleswig and Holstein to the decision of the North German Confederation. Not being willing to leave the question of the future of the two duchies to a body in which she would be outvoted, Prussia refused to accept this solution of the problem, declared the Treaty of Gastein annulled by the action of Austria, and instructed the Prussian commander in Schleswig to occupy Holstein. Austria thereupon evacuated Holstein and appealed to the German Confederation; Prussia declared the German Confederation dissolved and invited the smaller German states to adhere to the Prussian plan for the reorganization of Germany.

The resulting war was fought in three areas. Upon the refusal of the governments of the smaller German states to heed an ultimatum demanding the demobilization of their military forces and their adherence to the Prussian plan for the reorganization of Germany, a Prussian army promptly occupied Saxony, Hanover, and Hesse-Cassel, drove the Saxon army into Bohemia, captured the Elector of Hesse-Cassel, and forced the royal family in Hanover to take flight and the Hanoverian troops to capitulate. From central Germany the Prussian troops advanced into the South German states and defeated the military forces of Bavaria. The particularism of the smaller German states made their defeat by Prussia inevitable.

The ally of Prussia did not meet with similar success in Venetia. As a result of a division of opinion among the Italian generals the Italian military authorities divided their forces and marched into the province both from the west and from the south. The Austrian commander in Venetia quickly seized the opportunity presented to him by the blunder of his opponents, struck the advancing Italian armies before they could unite, and won a brilliant victory that compelled the armies of Italy to evacuate Venetia.

The decisive operations of the war, however, took place in Bohemia. From the beginning the Austrians seem to have been fearful of defeat. At first they decided to defend the road to Vienna at a strong position near Olmütz in Moravia. On the other hand Von Moltke, the chief of the Prussian general staff, planned a bold offensive campaign and sent armies across the Bohemian frontier at three different points. Finding that they had misjudged the intentions of the Prussians, the Austrians abandoned their defensive campaign, advanced into Bohemia, and came into touch with the oncoming Prussians at Königgrätz. In the battle that followed the Prussians almost destroyed their Austrian opponents. The Prussian military authorities owed their victory to their superior generalship and to the new needle-gun with which they had equipped the infantry.

The defeat of its military forces at Königgrätz caused the Austrian government to sue for peace. In drawing up his demands on Austria Bismarck had to take into consideration the influential group in France that opposed the aggrandizement of Prussia and advocated the intervention of France in the war. He asked Austria to cede Venetia and pay a moderate indemnity and to permit the annexation by Prussia of Nassau, Hanover, Hesse-Cassel, the city of Frankfort, and Schleswig and Holstein. To save the pride of Austria he permitted the Austrian government to hand Venetia over to France for cession to Italy ; and out of deference to French public opinion he left the states south of the Main River out of the proposed North German Confederation.

5

THE SETTLEMENT OF PRUSSIA WITH GERMANY

The victory of Prussia suddenly made Bismarck a popular man and solved the question of the leadership of Germany. The military success of Prussia thrust the constitutional problem into the background for many Germans. Even the Liberals saw that the policies of the Prussian Chancellor were bringing about the unification of Germany so much desired by them and began to feel that they should compromise with the government. This change in public opinion first revealed itself in the election for the choice of members of the lower house of the Prussian parliament, held on the day of the battle of Königgrätz. The Conservatives increased their representation from thirty-eight to one hundred and forty-two members and the Liberals and Progressives ceased to have a majority. Their defeat increased their readiness to effect a compromise with Bismarck. Bismarck, on his part, had no desire to continue in the proposed North German Confederation the antagonisms of the Prussian parliament or to drive into the opposition the Liberal parties in the states which he planned to annex to Prussia or to include in the new North German Confederation. Accordingly he asked the Prussian parliament to approve the policy that he had followed in the constitutional crisis. His request for a law of indemnity met with general approval and the Prussian parliament passed by a large vote the legislation asked for.

The conciliatory policy of Bismarck caused a general political realinement in Germany. A minority of the Prussian Conservatives, composed of great nobles and higher administrative officials, continued to support the government under the name of Free Conservatives. A majority of the party disapproved of the request of Bismarck for political indemnity, the failure of the government to crush the Liberal opposition, and the deposition of three legitimate dynasties in Germany and the annexation of their states to Prussia. In the states annexed to Prussia the Conservatives for the most part remained loyal to their dethroned rulers and opposed the Prussian government. The Liberal and Progressive parties, likewise, broke up. The doctrinaires in the two groups continued to oppose Bismarck. The opportunists united with like-minded elements in the recently annexed provinces and in the other German states to form the National Liberal party. This group abandoned the constitutional struggle and turned its attention to the practical problems confronting Germany.

The first question facing them was the organization of the proposed North German Confederation. Immediately after he had concluded peace with Austria Bismarck negotiated a treaty with the allies of Prussia in northern Germany that guaranteed their territorial possessions and pledged them to coöperate in the formation of the proposed confederation. He then made adherence to this alliance one of the conditions of peace for the North German states that had opposed Prussia in the war. In December, 1866, he submitted to representatives of the states belonging to this alliance a constitution drawn up by himself and his technical advisers. In the following March he submitted the proposed constitution and suggested amendments to a parliament representing all the states of the new alliance. After compelling the Prussian government to make some further amendments the several states and the Bundesrat and the parliament of the new German confederation finally ratified the new constitution.

This constitutional document organized the states of northern Germany into a federal union, known as the North German Confederation, under the hegemony of Prussia. It gave the new federal union, in contrast to the old German Confederation, control of taxation, customs duties, the army, the navy, the consular service, foreign commerce, the post-office, telegraphs, roads, canals, transportation on interstate rivers, change of residence, the licensing of trades, weights and measures, coinage, paper money, banking, patents, copyrights, medical and veterinary police, the press, and civil and criminal law. It vested legislative power in a Bundesrat, which represented the states of the Confederation, and a Reichstag, composed of members elected by universal suffrage for a term of five years. The constitution empowered the Bundesrat to give or withhold assent to legislation, to make administrative regulations, to issue ordinances for the completion of laws, to act as a chamber of accounts, to make many appointments, to act as a court of appeal, and to decide disputes between the states and the Confederation. It held its sessions behind closed doors and initiated all important legislation. The Reichstag lacked the power of the purse and in consequence played a far less important rôle. It gave expression, however, often in a rather futile way, to the prevailing public opinion. The new constitution made the King of Prussia, under the title of President, the chief executive of the new Confederation. It gave him command of the army and control of foreign relations but left the execution of the laws to the governments of the separate states. As King of Prussia, however, the President of the Confederation really executed the laws in the greater part of the new federal state. The titular head of the North German Confederation acted through a unique official, known as the Chancellor, who presided over the Bundesrat, defended the policies of the government in the Reichstag, controlled the administrative machinery of the Confederation, and usually headed the Prussian ministry. The new constitution attempted to effect a compromise between the conflicting political forces of Germany by making concessions to the dominant position of Prussia, the particularism of the smaller states, and the new currents of political thought.

Although for the time being he could not include Baden, Bavaria, Württemberg and the southern portion of Hesse-Darmstadt in the Confederation because of the particularist spirit in these states and the opposition of Napoleon III, Bismarck soon succeeded in establishing military and economic bonds between the new federal union and the states of southern Germany. The demands made by France for territorial compensation at the close of the War of 1866 frightened the South German states into concluding secret military alliances with Prussia. In the following year Bismarck proposed the reëstablishment of the Prussian Zollverein, which had been destroyed by the war, the creation of a parliament for the discussion of tariff questions—composed in practice of the Bundesrat and the Reichstag of the North German Confederation enlarged by the addition of representatives of the South German states—and the decision of economic questions by a majority vote instead of by the unanimous consent of all the states in the tariff union. By threatening them with the loss of the military protection of Prussia and exclusion from the Zollverein, Bismarck forced the states of southern Germany to adopt his proposals. He foresaw that coöperation in military and economic affairs would eventualy break down the political barriers between northern and southern Germany.

6

THE COMPLETION OF GERMAN UNIFICATION

Bismarck did not have to wait long to see the anticipated political union of Germany completed. In contrast to that regarding the conflict of 1866 with Austria, German public opinion generally approved of the War of 1870 with France. On the railroad journey from Ems to Berlin, after his interview with French ambassador, the Prussian people staged at every station great demonstrations for their sovereign. The governments of Baden, Württemberg, and Hesse-Darmstadt immediately recognized their obligation to come to the military assistance of Prussia. After a moment of hesitation the Bavarian government followed their example. In the war the South German troops played an important part in the campaign in Alsace, crossed the Vosges Mountains, and fought around Sedan. The whole German people felt that the day of reckoning had come for the power that had dominated and humiliated them for three centuries.

This enthusiasm engendered a conviction that military coöperation must lead to a common political organization. The Grand Duke of Baden and his people had long desired to join the North German Confederation. After the great victory at Sedan the subjects of the King of Württemberg gave him to understand that he must take steps to merge his state with the rest of Germany, and even many Bavarians in the cities and in the Protestant districts decorated their houses with the flags of the Confederation. In Bavaria, however, the spirit of particularism still showed its strength. Before intrusting his troops to the command of the King of Prussia the King of Bavaria stipulated that no attempt should be made to compel him to unite his state in a political union with the other states of Germany. The Roman Catholics of Bavaria, too, hesitated to place their state under the leadership of the Protestant King of Prussia, and the Bavarian peasants cared little about the whole question of the political unification of Germany.

Bismarck promptly took steps to utilize the popular enthusiasm to overcome the particularism of Bavaria and Württemberg. First, by a skilful mixture of persuasion and intimidation he maneuvered the two governments into opening preliminary negotiations through various agents. Then at his invitation they sent diplomatic representatives to Versailles to open direct negotiations with the North German Confederation. They feared that a refusal to negotiate would be punished by exclusion from the Zollverein. In November, 1870, Bismarck finally obtained the signatures of each of the South German states to the treaties uniting them with the North German Confederation. Baden and Hesse-Darmstadt put few obstacles in the way of the negotiations, but Bavaria and Württemberg extorted important concessions from Bismarck as the price of their adherence to the new German Empire. In the following month the King of Bavaria gave his consent to the adoption of the imperial title by the King of Prussia.

Before they could become effective the treaties had to be ratified. Both in northern and in southern Germany they encountered considerable opposition. Many German Conservatives advocated the creation of an aristocratic House of Peers as a check on the popularly elected Reichstag. The Liberals of Germany thought the time ripe for the establishment of a ministry responsible to the elected representatives of the German people, to take the place of the all-powerful Chancellor. Many Bavarian Catholics opposed the merging of their state in a union dominated by Protestants. During December, 1870, however, the Bundesrat and the Reichstag of the North German Confederation and the parliaments of Baden, Württemberg, and Hesse-Darmstadt ratified the treaties. The upper house of the Bavarian parliament withheld its approval until the following February.

The conservative William I, however, wished to have his new imperial title proclaimed by his fellow-princes rather than by the elected representatives of the people. For this purpose Bismarck staged an imposing piece of pageantry in the heart of defeated France. On January 18, 1871, in the Hall of Mirrors of the Château of Versailles, the palace of Louis XIV and a symbol of French aggression against Germany, amid the flags and standards of the victorious German armies and surrounded by the princes, military leaders, and other representatives of Germany, Bismarck read a proclamation announcing the establishment of the German Empire, and the elderly King of Prussia heard himself proclaimed German Emperor by his peers.

The expansion of the North German Confederation into the German Empire necessitated few constitutional changes. The President of the confederation became German Emperor but exercised the same powers and privileges. The Bundesrat and the Reichstag enlarged their membership by the inclusion of representatives of the governments and peoples of southern Germany. The revised constitution recognized the concessions made to the South German states. Bavaria retained control of her troops in times of peace and Württemberg exercised more than the usual power over her military forces. Both states maintained their own postal and telegraph systems. Baden, Bavaria, and Württemberg reserved the right to tax beer and brandy. In the main, however, the formation of the German Empire left the essential features of the constitution of the North German Confederation untouched.

For a time after the revolutions of 1848 Germany seemed to be satisfied to allow Austria to reëstablish the former political régime. The Austrian political system, however, ran counter to the new economic forces of the time and to the interests of Prussia. After 1858 the rulers of Prussia abandoned the old policy of coöperation with Austria and assumed leadership of the movement for the political reorganization of Germany. Guided by Bismarck, they fought three wars for the purpose of furthering the interests of Prussia. By the war with Denmark Prussia obtained control of Schleswig and Holstein for herself and Austria. By a war with Austria she settled the Schleswig-Holstein question in her favor, excluded Austria from German affairs, and opened the way for the annexation of Nassau, Hanover, Hesse-Cassel, Frankfort, and Schleswig-Holstein to Prussia, and the reorganization of the states north of the Main River into the North German Confederation, a union dominated by Prussia. By the War of 1870 with France she completed the unification of Germany into the German Empire through the annexation of the states of southern Germany.

PART III

THE DOMESTIC DEVELOPMENT OF THE
EUROPEAN STATES, 1870–1914

CHAPTER XV

THE THIRD FRENCH REPUBLIC, 1870–1914

The self-constituted provisional French government, set up in Paris after the capture of Napoleon III and his army at Sedan, assumed a task of the greatest difficulty. The victorious Germans had occupied all northern France and had closely invested the last of the imperial armies in Metz, and they were preparing to march on Paris and besiege the city. The new French government, on the other hand, had no organized military forces at its disposal and had no assurance that it really represented the political sentiments of the majority of the French people.

I

THE WORK OF THE PROVISIONAL GOVERNMENT

The most pressing problem confronting the provisional government was the defense of Paris. Within the city it succeeded in assembling a motley but numerous force of defenders, composed of marines, regular troops, reserves, and National Guards, but one sadly in need of experienced officers and military training. In the provinces the French people, led by Gambetta (who escaped from Paris by balloon after the investment of the city by the Germans), recruited, armed, and equipped six hundred thousand men and made a heroic but unsuccessful effort to relieve the capital. These improvised forces proved to be no match for the trained armies of Germany. At the end of January, 1871, after a siege of five months, the provisional government, threatened by famine and revolution, surrendered the beleaguered city and signed an armistice.

In order to have a representative body with which to conclude a permanent peace, Bismarck stipulated that the French people should elect a National Assembly by universal suffrage. The elections held in compliance with this stipulation turned on the issue of peace or war. Gambetta and his followers repudiated the action of the provisional government in concluding the armistice and advocated a continuance of the war. The majority of the French people desired peace. The voting, consequently, resulted in the defeat of the Republican adherents of Gambetta and the election of a National Assembly—composed of some four hundred Monarchists, thirty Imperialists, and only about two hundred Republicans—favoring the conclusion of a permanent peace.

2

THE FIRST MEASURES OF THE NATIONAL ASSEMBLY

When the newly elected National Assembly met in February, 1871, it took up the difficult problems left unsolved by the self-constituted provisional government. It found the country disorganized by the war. The conflict with Germany had killed one hundred and forty thousand Frenchmen, disabled, temporarily or permanently, many more, and brought industry and commerce to a standstill. The business situation threatened the working classes with unemployment and the well-to-do with bankruptcy. The Republican minority in the National Assembly hated and suspected the Monarchist majority. The majority, divided by dynastic loyalties, found themselves unable to unite on a common program. The victorious Germans were occupying a large part of the country.

The situation called for a strong executive, capable of inspiring general confidence. In the crisis the National Assembly turned instinctively to Thiers. Under the Bourbons he had attracted attention to himself by his work as a journalist and as a historian of the French Revolution. During the reign of Louis Philippe he had held a succession of political offices and had finally risen to the position of first minister. After his retirement from the premiership in 1840 he had added to his literary fame by writing his history of the Consulate and the Empire. During the rule of Napoleon III he had been an opponent of the Empire and had been banished from France for a time. In 1870 he had made an unsuccessful attempt to prevent a declaration of war against Germany and had then patriotically undertaken a fruitless diplomatic mission in search of aid for his country. In the elections for the National Assembly twenty-six districts had chosen him as a deputy. His political experience, fervent patriotism, and great prestige caused his fellow-deputies to intrust to him, under the title of Chief of the Executive Power, a large share of the authority just surrendered by the provisional government, and authorized him to exercise it under the supervision of the National Assembly and in coöperation with ministers chosen by himself.

Upon assuming office Thiers immediately took up the problem of concluding a permanent peace. He conducted the negotiations with great skill. Because of the pressure of the military party in Germany Bismarck demanded the cession of a third of Lorraine and all of Alsace and an indemnity of six thousand million francs. Thiers declared the German demands impossible and threatened to conclude no treaty of peace. In a personal interview he attempted in vain to convince the German Emperor of the danger of incorporating in his empire an unwilling population and of making a reconciliation between France and Germany impossible. He succeeded in reducing the sum demanded from France to five thousand million francs and saved for his country the fortress of Belfort in the gap between the Vosges and the Jura mountains. The German government also agreed to withdraw its troops from France as fast as the French government paid off the imposed indemnity. These terms of peace were embodied in two diplomatic agreements, the preliminary Treaty of Versailles (February 26, 1871) and the Treaty of Frankfort (May 10, 1871).

3

THE COMMUNE

Thiers and his associates displayed far less dexterity in handling domestic problems. They caused the people of Paris to suspect the existence of a plot to restore one of the former dynasties to power, rewarded them ill for their sacrifices and sufferings during the siege, and injured their material interests by making Versailles, with its Monarchist traditions, instead of Republican Paris, the permanent seat of the government. Later, deaf to their pleas for a continuance of the moratorium declared during the siege, the government exposed thousands of Parisians to prosecution for debt by ordering them to pay their rents, debts, and notes within forty-eight hours. It also humiliated them by permitting the victorious Germans to enter Paris and deprived many of them of their principal means of support by suppressing the National Guard. These policies set in motion all the radical elements in the city, the anarchists, International Socialists, and embittered Republicans, and the disbanded National Guard organized a central committee to watch over the republic, which body gradually usurped the powers of the municipal government.

The conservative leaders of French political life urged Thiers to take action against those arrogating to themselves the control of Paris and hindering by their policies a resumption of normal conditions. The self-constituted leaders of the city suspected every move of their opponents. When the government at Versailles attempted to gain control of some cannon at Paris the former National Guard and all the radical elements of the city resisted. They organized a provisional government and an army, adopted the red flag of the Socialists and the revolutionary calendar of the first French Republic, announced the abolition of the militarism, officialdom, exploitation, stock-jobbing, monopolies, and privileges responsible for the servitude of the French proletariat and the misfortunes of France, and declared for a decentralized France, composed of federated communes. They seem to have hoped that the movement would give the Republicans of the larger cities more independence and the Socialists of France an opportunity to introduce in some places the social and economic revolution at which they aimed.

After making some unsuccessful attempts to negotiate with leaders at Paris, Thiers and his associates prepared to crush an insurrection that seemed to them to be a threat against the existing social order and a betrayal of France in the presence of the invading Germans. In imitation of the tactics used by Windischgrätz at Prague in 1848, they temporarily withdrew the regular troops from Paris to isolate them from revolutionary influences and collected an army of one hundred and forty thousand men, recruited from troops in the departments, volunteers, and repatriated prisoners. With these forces the government at Versailles defeated an attempt of the leaders of the Parisian Commune to disperse the National Assembly, fought its way step by step into Paris, and finally overcame the Commune. The siege of the city lasted through the greater part of April and May, 1871. The attacking troops bombarded the city and gave their opponents no quarter. The infuriated insurgents, in revenge, executed a number of prominent persons held as hostages and set on fire many public buildings and historic monuments.

The capture of the city did not put an end to the slaughter. The victorious troops mercilessly shot down armed communists at sight and the courts hastily set up convicted and sent to execution without much discrimination both insurgents and those innocent of opposing the government at Versailles. Contemporaries estimated that after the close of the massacre seventeen thousand or more nameless corpses found burial in trenches hastily dug in cemeteries, public squares, and public and private gardens. The prosecution of communists continued for years. By 1875 the government had condemned over thirteen thousand to deportation and imprisonment and had arrested in all thirty-eight thousand persons.

4

THE REORGANIZATION OF FRANCE

After this national disaster the French government took up the problem of freeing France from German troops. Their presence on French soil wounded the national pride, imposed a heavy financial burden, and threatened the peace of the country. To meet the indemnity payments stipulated by the treaty of peace the French government resorted to popular loans. The response of the French people to its appeals amazed Europe. They oversubscribed the first loan twice, and the second fourteen times. Their response enabled the government to free France of German troops six months before the end of the three-year period stipulated in the peace treaty.

In the meantime the plans of the Monarchists had gone awry. They had expected to let the Republicans assume the odious task of concluding a peace treaty dismembering France and then to effect a compromise that would unite the Orleanists and the Bourbon Legitimists behind a single candidate for the French throne. For a few weeks in the summer of 1871 they seemed to be on the verge of success. The most respected of the Orleanist princes agreed to recognize the Count of Chambord, the Bourbon claimant to the throne, as head of the royal family. The compromise candidate, however, ruined the plans of his supporters for a restoration of the monarchy by issuing a proclamation that asserted in a dramatic manner that Henry V could not give up the white flag of Henry IV. The Orleanists knew that the French people, the heirs of the French Revolution, would never support a candidate for the throne who refused to accept the tricolor flag, the symbol of French liberty and the standard under which the armies of France had won their most remarkable victories. They consequently withdrew their support from the Count of Chambord. In August, 1871 the baffled Monarchists conferred on Thiers, by the Rivet Law, the title of President. The latter remarked that the Legitimist candidate deserved to be called the George Washington of the Third French Republic.

Even before the German troops had gone from France, the National Assembly took up the problem of national defense. The French people felt that they must create a new army to take the place of the discredited imperial military system. The law finally enacted in 1872 represented a compromise between the German system and the convictions of Thiers concerning the superiority of a professional army. In principle it made every able-bodied Frenchman subject to military service for twenty years, in the active army and the reserve. In practice only a part chosen by lot from those subject to military service spent the stipulated five years in the active army. The rest served only six months in the active army, in order to lighten the burden of the French treasury. By volunteering ahead of time at their own expense and paying a sum of fifteen hundred francs to the government, young men of the upper classes could reduce their term in the active army to one year. This reorganization of the army made the French people feel that they had taken an important step toward the restoration of France as a great power.

In the meantime the Monarchists had felt increasingly disquieted. The recurring elections for the filling of vacant seats in the National Assembly plainly indicated a swing of public opinion in France toward the republic. Gambetta had alarmed them by carrying on a great political agitation in all sections of France in which he defended the Republican régime, demanded the dissolution of the National Assembly, advocated the education of the masses and the separation of Church and State, and appealed for support to the workers of the cities and rural France, who had just been enfranchised by the Third French Republic. Though originally an Orleanist, Thiers had expressed with growing boldness his belief in the necessity of maintaining the republic and had finally declared a reëstablishment of the monarchy impossible, since three candidates desired the same throne. As long as the Germans continued to occupy northern France the Monarchists tolerated Thiers in office. As soon as the Germans withdrew from French soil the Monarchists passed a vote of censure on his general policy and in conformity with the principles of parliamentary government Thiers resigned the Presidency. As the ideas of the Count of Chambord continued to prevent a reëstablishment of the monarchy, the Monarchists elected Marshal MacMahon President.

The election of MacMahon gave the signal for a renewal of Monarchist activity. The marshal chose a Conservative ministry, which removed Republican emblems from many public buildings, omitted mention of the republic in official documents, maintained martial law in Republican centers, and prosecuted and harassed Republican journals. The clergy intervened actively in politics. The Count of Paris, the Orleanist claimant for the throne, recognized the Count of Chambord as head of the royal family and the Monarchist deputies pushed forward their plans for a restoration of the monarchy. The overthrow of the republic seemed imminent.

The plans of the Monarchists, however, encountered unexpected difficulties. MacMahon suddenly revealed that he considered himself committed to the maintenance of a conservative republic by his election as President and he asserted that he could not answer for the preservation of order if the white flag of the Bourbons should be adopted, instead of the republican tricolor, out of deference to the principles of the Count of Chambord. The National Assembly, consequently, resigned itself to a continuance of the republic and made the term of office for the President seven years.

As a result of this turn of affairs and of the renewal of political activity by the Imperialists, even the Monarchists began to feel the need of terminating the provisional political régime and giving France a permanent form of government. Preferring a conservative republic to a reëstablishment of the Napoleonic régime, a group of Orleanists united with the moderate Republicans in giving the Third French Republic a definite constitution. The three constitutional laws enacted in 1875 made no attempt to describe completely the organization of the republic and the functions of its political machinery. They created a bicameral legislative body consisting of a Senate, composed of seventy-five senators elected for life and two hundred and twenty-five members chosen for a term of nine years, and a Chamber of Deputies selected by universal suffrage. By these provisions the Monarchists hoped to be able to retain control of at least the Senate, through the influence of the large landed proprietors over the rural communes. The new constitution intrusted the executive power, nominally, to a President elected for a term of seven years by the Senate and the Chamber of Deputies sitting together as a National Assembly. In practice his executive acts required the signature of a minister responsible to the Chamber of Deputies. The constitution also conceded to the National Assembly the right to revise the constitutional laws. As in England, unwritten customs and precedents determined many things.

5

THE REPUBLICANS GAIN CONTROL OF THE REPUBLIC

In the ensuing elections the Monarchists captured a majority of the seats in the new Senate but the Republicans gained control of the new Chamber of Deputies. The President and the Republicans, consequently, quickly clashed over the question of the responsibility of the ministry. The Republican majority in the Chamber of Deputies adopted a vote of censure of the Monarchist ministry selected by MacMahon. With the aid of the Senate, the President thereupon dissolved the lower house of the parliament. In the subsequent electoral campaign the Monarchists used every means at their disposal to influence the results of the election. In spite of their revival of official candidatures, the pressure of administrative officials upon the voters, the interference with the distribution of Republican journals, the closing of places of business that served as centers of Republican agitation, and the condemnation of Gambetta to fine and imprisonment, the Republicans won a majority of seats in the new Chamber of Deputies. Their victory compelled the President to choose his ministers henceforth from the dominant party in the lower house of the parliament.

In the elections of 1879 the Republicans finally gained control of the Senate. They immediately demanded that thereafter the civil and administrative posts should be filled by persons loyal to the republic. President MacMahon, however, refused to displace his old comrades in the army and resigned his office. The National Assembly thereupon elected Jules Grévy, a man devoted to the republic for more than thirty years, to fill the vacant post. With his election the Republicans gained control of all the machinery of the government.

6

THE EMBODIMENT OF THE REPUBLICAN PROGRAM IN LEGISLATION

The new President carefully established the precedents that have since governed his successors in the office. In order to make it impossible for a head of the republic to transform the Presidency into a dictatorship, Grévy attempted no personal policy and left the initiation of administrative measures to his ministers. His manner of conducting his office made the French President the ceremonial head of the state and deprived him of independent authority. The associates of Grévy, meanwhile, set to work at the task of reviving the republican symbols. They transferred the seat of government from Versailles to Paris, revived the celebration of the anniversary of the storming of the Bastille, July 14, as the national holiday, and made the "Marseillaise" once more the national anthem.

The Republicans also attempted to embody their political program in legislation. One measure abrogated a law of 1814 forbidding work on Sundays and Catholic holidays. Another put an end to the discretionary power exercised by the government over places dispensing alcoholic liquors. A law of 1880 granted all French citizens the right to sell books, pamphlets, and journals. Two measures passed in the following year established freedom of the press and permitted the holding of public meetings without preliminary authorization of the government. A law of 1884 enabled French workers to organize trade-unions.

Other legislation struck at the control of the Church over the schools. A law of 1880 excluded bishops of the Church and other non-professional members from the Superior Council of Instruction. Another measure of the same year pretended to establish freedom of teaching for all Frenchmen but deprived the higher institutions of learning under the control of the Church of the right to grant degrees or to call themselves universities. By administrative decrees the Republicans dissolved the Jesuit order and required other non-authorized teaching orders to apply within three months for authorization from the state. These measures finally resulted in the closing of all the schools conducted by the Jesuits and most of those operated by the non-authorized teaching orders. Another law of 1880 created a system of secondary schools for girls. A series of measures made elementary education gratuitous for all and obligatory for children between the ages of six and thirteen and allowed laymen to teach in the elementary schools.

In 1884 the Republicans slightly revised the constitution adopted in 1875. They made illegal any proposal to change the republican form of government in France, declared members of former ruling familes ineligible for the Presidency, and provided for the gradual transformation of the seventy-five life senatorships into ordinary senatorships.

7

THE REVISIONIST MOVEMENT

After the embodiment of the Republican program in legislation, French political life became increasingly unsatisfactory. The old Republican leaders died or became discredited. The split of the Republicans into four jealous, hostile groups turned French politics into a meaningless succession of ministries too short-lived to carry through any political policy. Many felt that the conservative constitution adopted during the dominance of the Monarchists should be thoroughly revised. To many persons the French government seemed to be devoting the strength of France to colonial ventures instead of taking a firm tone with Germany. This situation gave rise to the Revisionist movement.

This movement is inextricably intertwined with the career of the dashing General Boulanger. A contemporary described this army officer as a man incapable of doing the most ordinary act in any but a striking way. After spectacular service in the army he was appointed Minister of War at the suggestion of Clemenceau, the leader of the Republican group known as the Radicals. In this position he quickly began to attract the attention of the general public. He removed from the vicinity of Paris some regiments whose officers displayed royalist opinions, demanded supplementary credits for war material, built barracks near the German frontier, and showed sympathy with the idea of a rapprochement with Russia. His policy divided the French people. His partizans began to call him the general of the "revenge" against Germany and the indispensable officer, acclaimed him with wild enthusiasm on public occasions, and finally organized a political party. The Parisians sang popular songs about him and bought his portrait and his biography from the street venders. His opponents denounced him as an ambitious individual who aspired to a dictatorship and caused the government first to order him to a post away from Paris and finally to dismiss him from the army, as a punishment for his political activity.

His dismissal left Boulanger free to carry on a spectacular political campaign designed to prove his popularity in France. In 1888 he stood as a candidate for the parliament in a number of French departments and obtained a great personal triumph in a succession of by-elections. In his campaign and his parliamentary speeches he summarized his political ideas in the vague phrase "Dissolution, Constitutional Assembly, and Revision." He seems to have planned for a responsible President of the republic, governing directly, for a Chamber of Deputies to vote without discussion, and perhaps for some generals to take the place of the prefects. As he hoped to obtain office finally by legal means, he put aside the suggestions of his partizans for a coup d'état and never attempted to seize political power by force.

Faced by this grave danger, a majority of the Republicans rallied to the defense of the existing Republican régime. They passed a law requiring candidates to run for office in a single parliamentary district. The government then made Boulanger believe that he was about to be arrested and caused him to fly to Belgium for safety. Later the Senate, sitting as a high court, found Boulanger, his principal political agent, and one of his principal supporters among the French journalists guilty of a plot to change the form of government in France and condemned them to imprisonment. After this vigorous action the position of the government improved rapidly. In the elections of 1889 the Republicans defeated the Monarchists and the Revisionists. Then the success of the Paris Exposition celebrating the hundredth anniversary of the French Revolution tended to make the public forget General Boulanger, and later revelations concerning his negotiations with the Imperialists and the Monarchists completed his political ruin. In 1891 the discouraged and discredited man finally committed suicide.

8

THE CHURCH RALLIES TO THE REPUBLIC

The victory of the republic over the Revisionists gave an impetus to an important movement in the Roman Catholic Church. For a long time some devout Catholics had felt that the communicants of their Church should abandon their traditional alliance with the Monarchists and organize themselves into a constitutional party loyal to the republic. By 1890 Pope Leo XIII judged the time ripe for action and bade the respected head of the Church in Tunis to assume leadership of the movement for the reconciliation of Church and State in France. The new policy divided both the Monarchists and the Republicans. Many devout Catholics refused to abandon the Monarchist cause and the Republican extremists harbored a deep suspicion of the sudden conversion of the Roman Catholic Church to Republicanism. In spite of these divisions, however, the new movement made steady progress. In 1892 seventy-five French bishops signed and published a declaration of their adherence to the republic. Shortly afterwards the Pope openly declared the French Republic a legitimate form of government. Thenceforth the Church opposed only the secularizing tendencies of the French government.

9

THE DREYFUS AFFAIR

In September, 1894, an incident occurred that in the end stirred the French nation to its depths. The War Department obtained possession of an unsigned document which indicated that some artillery officer connected with the general staff had transmitted French military secrets to an attaché of the German embassy. Because of the bitter campaign being waged at the time against Jews, suspicion pointed to Captain Alfred Dreyfus, a Jewish officer of Alsatian origin, as the one guilty of betraying French military secrets. After some hesitation the Minister of War caused his arrest and his trial by a military court. On the evidence of a majority of the five handwriting experts consulted, and of material never submitted to the accused, the court condemned Dreyfus to expulsion from the army and imprisonment for life. The military authorities thereupon publicly humiliated him in the courtyard of the military school that he had attended, by breaking his sword and tearing the insignia of his military rank from his uniform, and then transported him to Devil's Island off the coast of Guiana, to be kept in solitary confinement for the rest of his life.

At first only the immediate family and close friends of Dreyfus believed his steadfast protestations of innocence. In 1896, however, a French journal directed the attention of the general public again to his case by revealing that he had been condemned on the basis of evidence never communicated to the accused man or his counsel at the trial. As a result of this revelation the wife of the unfortunate officer made an unsuccessful appeal for a retrial of his case. In the following year the vice-president of the Senate brought the case to the attention of the parliament on the basis of evidence discovered by a conscientious officer attached to the general staff, Lieutenant-Colonel Picquart, and on the advice of this distinguished senator the brother of Dreyfus accused Count Walzin Esterhazy, an officer of Hungarian origin, of being the real author of the unsigned document. The subsequent acquittal of Esterhazy on the charge by a military tribunal and the imprisonment of Picquart by no means silenced the agitation. Two days later the eminent novelist Émile Zola published in the French press a sensational letter to the President of the Republic entitled *I Accuse,* in which he charged the military authorities with having suppressed evidence of the innocence of Dreyfus, the first military court of having condemned him on the basis of evidence never presented to him, and another court of having knowingly aquitted the man really guilty of the treason.

The daring accusations of Zola made the Dreyfus case the most pressing question before the French public. The Protestants, the Freemasons, the Jews, and many writers, professors, Radicals, and Socialists sought to have the case revised. The clergy, the Conservatives, and most of the army officers opposed a reconsideration of the matter. The military authorities regarded the steadily growing agitation as an attack on the honor of the army. They caused Zola to be tried and condemned for his attack, and finally drove him to England in exile. The Minister of War even brought forth three new documents alleged to prove the guilt of Dreyfus and prosecuted Picquart for communicating the contents of a secret document.

The effort to repress the agitation did not succeed, however. Lieutenant-Colonel Picquart asserted that he could prove that two of the alleged new proofs did not apply to Dreyfus, and that the third appeared to be a forgery. Shortly afterwards an officer of the general staff avowed his authorship of the forgery and committed suicide, and Esterhazy retired to London. This new evidence made a retrial of Dreyfus imperative. The partizans of the condemned officer, who now included most of the Republicans, forced the military authorities to give him a new trial. The retrial of the case only resulted in a reduction of the original sentence to ten years' imprisonment, but the government, in an effort to put an end to a discussion that was splitting the French nation asunder, released Picquart, permitted the return of Zola to France, pardoned Dreyfus, and issued a general amnesty.

The action of the government did not satisfy the partizans of Dreyfus. They demanded not amnesty but vindication. In 1906 their efforts finally resulted in the complete clearing of the name of Dreyfus by the highest court in France. The French government thereupon did its utmost to compensate the principal victims of the affair. It restored Dreyfus to his rank in the army and conferred upon him the ribbon of the Legion of Honor, gave back to Picquart his rightful military rank and soon made him Minister of War, and removed the body of Zola, who had died in the meantime, to the Panthéon, the national shrine of Republican France. The bitterness engendered by the prolonged struggle, however, long lingered in the hearts of the French people.

10

THE SEPARATION OF CHURCH AND STATE

The Dreyfus Affair united the Republican factions in defense of the republic. In 1899 a ministry came into power that contained representatives from each of the Republican groups and even included Alexandre Millerand, the first Socialist to take a ministerial post in France. The new cabinet set to work at the task of punishing those responsible for the recent agitation of the country. It made important changes in the personnel of the army and the judiciary, dissolved three societies particularly responsible for the violent agitation against the Jews and the treasonable demonstrations against the republic and its elected officials, and prosecuted and convicted a number of the leaders of those opposed to a revision of the Dreyfus case.

The government also initiated an attack on the religious orders for their hostility to the republic. It first attacked the Assumptionist Fathers. Founded in 1850, this order had been expelled from France thirty years later by an administrative decree on the ground that it had never been authorized by the government. Within a few years, however, its members reëstablished themselves in France and founded a number of journals that attacked Jews, Freemasons, and the republic, and aided in the election of deputies hostile to the government. After 1894 they had made themselves conspicuous by a campaign against the proposed revision of the Dreyfus case.

The sympathy publicly manifested by the Catholics of France for the Assumptionist Fathers coöperated with a number of other causes to stir the government to action against all the unauthorized orders. The anticlerical Republicans looked with disfavor upon the monastic orders because of the increase of their property holdings, the growth of their business enterprises, and their control of secondary education. The orders carried on a flourishing trade in liqueurs, chocolate, sweetmeats, and perfumes, and educated the children of almost all the nobility, the richer members of the middle class, and the officers in the army. In July, 1901, the French Republicans, consequently, struck at them in the Law of Associations passed by the French parliament. This piece of legislation provided that no religious order could be established without the authorization of a special law, that no house of an order could be opened without a decree of the government, and that the existing unauthorized orders must apply to the state for authorization within a period of three months. The law affected seven hundred and fifty-three houses or congregations, one hundred and forty-seven of men and six hundred and six of women. Less than half of the congregations of men and only a third of those of women made the required demand for authorization. Most of the remaining houses made a pretense of dissolving. After the elections of the following year had demonstrated that the electorate approved its policy, the government began to enforce the law. It dissolved all the unauthorized orders, finally closed all their schools except those in localities not supplied with other schools, and forbade the members of the orders to preach or to teach. In carrying out the law the agents of the government encountered some resistance. Ardent Catholics barricaded themselves in some of the houses of the unauthorized orders and a group of Catholic women attempted to carry a petition to the wife of the President of the republic.

In 1904 the determination of the Republicans to take the schools out of the hands of the clergy led to the enactment of a law directed against the authorized teaching orders. This piece of legislation forbade the authorized orders to recruit their membership, provided for the closing within a period of ten years of all schools taught by the clergy, and applied the property of the orders to other public purposes. The law permitted the orders to continue their activities in the French colonies and protectorates.

The Republican campaign against the Catholic orders naturally accentuated the existing friction between the French government and the papacy. The Concordat of 1800 had stipulated that the Pope should confer French bishoprics upon persons nominated by the government, but after the establishment of the republic the Pope had accepted the nomination of the state only after there had been a preliminary discussion. The Republicans felt that the Pope made a practice of refusing to accept as nominees of the government those suspected of favoring Gallican or Republican doctrines. In 1902, accordingly, the Republican leaders decided to insist on the rights of the government and presented the names of three men to vacant French bishoprics without coming to a preliminary agreement with the Pope. When Leo XIII refused to institute them in office, the Prime Minister accused him of rejecting the nominees of the government because they were Republicans. In 1904 the intervention of the Pope in favor of the teaching orders and his protest to the Catholic powers of Europe against the visit of the President of France to the King of Italy increased the irritation of French Republicans with the papacy. The French government answered the action of the Pope by withdrawing its ambassador from the papal court and leaving the conduct of its diplomatic business to a chargé d'affaires. When the Pope attempted to remove two French bishops from office, the French government took the ground that the papacy had nullified the Concordat and broke off diplomatic relations completely.

The break of the French government with the Pope opened the way for the separation of Church and State in France, the logical culmination of the secularizing legislation sponsored by the Republicans in previous decades. In 1905 the government pushed through the parliament a law that provided that the state should no longer pay the salaries of the French clergy or nominate them to office, that the property used by the various religious denominations should return to the control of the state, that the control of buildings actually used for religious services should be transferred to associations of laymen formed to provide for the cost, maintenance, and public exercise of religion, and that the clergy who had been in service for a long period should be pensioned. The law aimed to establish in France the American system of relations between Church and State.

In their attempts to execute the law the Republicans met with considerable opposition. The Pope condemned it as an attack on the order established in the world by God and criticized the transfer of the property of the Church to the control of associations of laymen. To put into effect this statement of principles, the Pope promptly prohibited French Catholics from forming the required religious associations, and at various points in France crowds of hostile Catholics prevented the agents of the government from making the prescribed inventories of Church property. In order to avert a complete cessation of Catholic worship in France, the government passed a law in 1907 that permitted the Catholic clergy to hold public worship in their former churches without organizing lay associations.

II

THE GROWTH OF RADICAL PARTIES

After the establishment of the Third French Republic, public opinion in France steadily drifted away from the point of view of the Monarchists. In 1879 the death of the Prince Imperial, the heir of Napoleon III, in the Zulu War caused the Imperialists to divide and disintegrate. The rallying of the Roman Catholic Church to the republic had caused many of the Monarchists to aline themselves with the conservative Republicans and had greatly weakened the monarchical parties. By 1914, consequently, the avowed Monarchists in the Chamber of Deputies numbered only twenty-eight.

The old Republican political program, however, did not long satisfy the more radical members of the Republican party. In 1881 a Radical group of deputies organized itself in the parliament under the leadership of Clemenceau. It stood for the suppression of the Senate and the Presidency, the submission of the constitution to the people; liberty of assembly, association, the press, and the individual; separation of Church and State; free, lay, and obligatory education; nationalization of mines, canals, and railroads; progressive taxation of property and incomes; reduction of the length of the legal working day, prevention of child labor; and old age, invalidity, and accident insurance. Between 1881 and 1910 its representation in the lower house of the French parliament rose from forty-six to two hundred and fifty-two seats. After 1899 it became the principal political group in the Chamber of Deputies.

The defeat of the Commune had destroyed for a time the Socialist agitation in France. But in 1876 the working-men of France succeeded in organizing a national association committed to the formation of co-operative societies and trade-unions as the best means of ameliorating their condition. When the government permitted their leaders to return to France in 1879, the Socialists captured the new party and persuaded it to adopt a program drawn up with the coöperation of Karl Marx. Many French Socialists, however, felt that the Marxian ideas were alien to France and advocated a policy of accepting such social changes as proved immediately possible. As a result of their opposition to the newly adopted program the Socialists split first into a Marxian and a Possibilist faction, and later into five factions. In spite of their divisions, however, the Socialists became an important political force in France. In 1893 they elected forty-nine deputies. Under the leadership of Jean Juarès they played a significant rôle in the struggle for the revision of the Dreyfus case and in the campaign for the separation of Church and State. After 1900 Socialists began to accept posts in the cabinet. In the elections of 1910 they obtained one hundred and four seats.

The Socialists did not succeed in maintaining control of the whole labor movement. Many French workers harbored a deep distrust of political methods. This element in the trade-unions organized the General Confederation of Labor. This organization advocated the use of the general strike, the boycott, and sabotage, and opposed all efforts to better the lot of the working classes by legislation. During the first decade of the twentieth century it kept the country in turmoil through widespread strikes.

12

THE ECONOMIC DEVELOPMENT OF THE THIRD REPUBLIC

Even down to the days of the World War France remained an agricultural state to a far greater extent than did England or Germany. Although the rural population declined somewhat in numbers after 1871, a half-century later nearly 56 per cent of the population of France still lived in communes classed as rural. Under the Third French Republic the framework of rural life continued unchanged. The average farm remained small in area and consisted of scattered plots of ground lying in uninclosed fields. On account of the small size and the dispersion of the holdings and the cheapness of labor agricultural machinery came into use very slowly. As late as 1892 many small holders owned no plows, not even the primitive bough of a tree shod with iron, and sowing and haymaking by hand predominated even on the larger estates. Poorly paid temporary immigrants from Belgium, Spain, Italy, Germany, and even Poland furnished much of the required manual labor. As time passed, however, French farmers left less and less land lying fallow, the production of wheat, the master cereal crop of France, steadily increased, and the potato came into general use. As a result of the building of railroads market-gardening and dairying became more and more important industries. In the seventies, however, the phylloxera, a plant-louse, attacked and nearly destroyed the vineyards of France. In the next decade French agriculture began to feel keenly the competition of the agricultural products imported by the new railway and steamship lines. As remedies for this situation French agriculturists turned to a protective tariff, coöperative enterpises, and agricultural education.

The treaty of peace with Germany dealt French industry a serious blow. By the cession of Alsace and Lorraine France lost the iron and steel plants of two of her most important firms, nearly half of her cotton-looms, and important iron deposits. For the next two decades French industry stagnated. French manufacturers felt uncertain about the future, French coal was poor in quality and expensive in price, and for economic reasons manufacturers exported much French iron ore to smelting establishments in the vicinity of the German coal deposits. After 1890, however, France adopted a high-tariff policy that gave French manufacturers a monopoly of the domestic and colonial markets. Under the stimulus of the new economic policy certain French industries expanded rapidly. Between 1869 and 1913 the output of French coal-mines mounted from thirteen million to forty-one million tons, the production of cast-iron quintupled, and France took rank as the third most important state in Europe in the manufacture of iron and steel. In the cotton industry the number of power-looms more than doubled and most of the hand-looms disappeared. France failed to develop shipbuilding and the chemical and electrical industries. Her characteristic manufactures continued to be articles of luxury that required a high degree of training and skill for their production.

The domestic history of France from 1870 to 1914 is a story of recovery from defeat and civil war, of a swing from Conservatism toward the Left, and of growing strength. Born amid the disasters of the war with Germany, the Third French Republic brought the foreign war to an honorable conclusion, survived a fratricidal civil war, freed the soil of northern France of German troops, created a national defense, drew up a new constitution, and stood such severe tests as the Revisionist movement and the Dreyfus case. During these years France became more radical and more secular. The Republicans wrested from the grasp of the Monarchists in turn the Chamber of Deputies, the Senate, and the Presidency, and then began to embody their political program in legislation. They made France democratic and secular. In the meantime the Monarchists and the Imperialists steadily lost ground, the Church rallied to the republic, the Republicans split into factions, new radical parties and groups made their appearance, and the country slowly grew in economic strength.

CHAPTER XVI

In 1871 the new German Empire found itself confronted by a variety of complicated problems. The new political machinery had to be set in motion; the formation of the empire had left many old problems unsolved and created many new ones; and the interesting experiment of attempting to adjust a conservative social structure to the new economic forces had to be carried to completion.

I

THE EFFORTS TO COMPLETE THE UNIFICATION OF GERMANY

After the reëstablishment of peace with France in 1871, Bismarck, as Chancellor, immediately directed his attention to the task of completing the unification of the recently formed empire. Under his leadership the new imperial legislative bodies, the Bundesrat and the Reichstag, passed a mass of legislation designed to merge the South German states in the empire and to centralize authority in the hands of the imperial government. They established the present German postal system, created an imperial consular service, adopted a uniform system of weights and measures, adapted the criminal code of the North German Confederation to the needs of the empire, organized a central bureau of accounts and an imperial railway bureau, and adopted a uniform coinage system for the empire. They also gave the central government control of navigation on interstate rivers, extended the Prussian military system to the South German states, enacted a press law for the empire that tended to liberate the newspapers of Germany, organized an imperial bank to end the bank-note anarchy, adopted a uniform judicial organization and civil and criminal procedure, and created a commission for the compilation of a civil code, which did not complete its work for a quarter of a century. The adoption of these prosaic institutions affected the daily life of the German people in innumerable ways and did more to modernize German life than the more dramatic episodes of recent German history.

In 1872 the Prussian government took up the problem of modernizing the local government in the five conservative agricultural provinces east of the Elbe River. In this region the landholding Junkers still exercised a patriarchal authority. They retained police and administrative powers over their own estates, the neighboring villages, and the larger administrative areas known as circles and provinces. However, the reform of city government by Stein, the extension of French institutions to Rhenish Prussia and Westphalia, and the growth of industrial and commercial cities in East Prussia finally forced the Prussian government to reform the machinery of local government in its five eastern provinces. The legislation enacted for this purpose in 1872 deprived the Junkers of their police and administrative powers, gave the parishes the right to elect their own officials, grouped parishes and private estates into districts administered by appointees of the central government, created assemblies for the circles in which the Junkers found themselves outnumbered by the representatives of the cities and the small property-owners, and placed the higher administrative posts of the circles under the control of the Prussian bureaucracy.

2

THE KULTURKAMPF

In the same year in which he reformed local government in East Prussia Bismarck inaugurated a campaign against the Roman Catholic Church in Germany. Since the outbreak of the French Revolution the Church had been an object of attack. In France the revolutionary movement had deprived it of its property and its privileges and dissolved its monastic institutions. The Napoleonic period had extended these policies to Italy, Spain, Germany, and the Netherlands. As the nineteenth century had progressed, the Liberals of Europe, the spiritual heirs of the French Revolution, had threatened the control of the Church over marriage, divorce, and the schools. At the same time they had held up for execration the administration of the Pope in the Papal States and that of Austria, the chief Roman Catholic power in Europe. These attacks had culminated in the spoliation of the Pope of his temporal possessions, the defeat of Austria at Königgrätz, and the discrediting of the Roman Catholic party in Germany.

The Church reacted vigorously to the menace of Liberalism. Under the leadership of men who had risen from the people—one of the results of the secularization of ecclesiastical property—the Church took the offensive against its enemies. In 1864 the Pope, as official spokesman of the Church, strongly condemned the whole Liberal movement and its achievements in the *Syllabus of Errors*. In 1870 the Vatican Council threw down the gantlet to the Liberals by solemnly asserting the doctrine of papal infallibility. In all Catholic countries the clergy and laity eagerly seized the weapons unwittingly furnished them by their opponents—the ballot, liberty of the press, and freedom of assembly and association. In Germany they formed the Center party to defend the interests of the Church. Its program called for a restoration of the former Papal States to the Pope, the maintenance of the independence of the Church in Germany, and the preservation of its control over primary education. The new party immediately gained over one eighth of the seats in the Prussian lower house and nearly a fifth of the membership of the new imperial Reichstag.

Bismarck watched the development of the new party with growing suspicion. He disliked its leadership, the evidences of its strength and discipline, and its alliance with the unassimilated Poles of East Prussia and the hostile adherents of the disinherited House of Hanover. He feared that it might embroil Germany with the new Kingdom of Italy over the question of the restoration of the temporal power of the Pope and with Russia by its demands for autonomy for the Prussian Poles. He considered it to be mobilizing against the empire that he had just organized, and decided to combat it.

The Chancellor began his attack on the Church by the publication of an article in a semi-official newspaper accusing the Center party of being led by the Jesuits at Rome. As the conflict developed he placed the control of ecclesiastical affairs in the hands of a bureau manned principally by Protestants, favored the Old Catholics, who refused to accept the doctrine of papal infallibility, and finally, in imitation of the Kingdom of Italy, persuaded the Bundesrat and the Reichstag to enact a law that forbade the clergy to use their position to attack the agents and policies of the government.

The new policy divided the German people. The old opponents of Bismarck, the National Liberals and the Progressives, considered the conflict a battle of science, Liberalism, and Protestantism against particularism, Roman Catholicism, and medieval obscurantism, and gave the Chancellor their enthusiastic support. The Conservatives, on the contrary, considered the attack on the Church a blow at the old alliance between the altar and the throne and almost as much of a menace to the Lutheran as to the Roman Catholic Church. Each side rallied to the defense of its point of view with resolutions, petitions, pamphlets, books, and newspaper articles.

In 1872 Bismarck attacked the Jesuits and the control of the Church over the lower schools. The Prussian government passed legislation taking the inspection of the primary schools out of the hands of the clergy, making school-inspectors agents of the state, and excluding Catholic orders from teaching. The laws against clerical control of the schools injured the Lutheran clergy as much as the Roman Catholic and

224 DOMESTIC DEVELOPMENT OF EUROPEAN STATES

completed the break between the Chancellor and the Conservatives. In response to the widespread popular antipathy toward the order the Prussian and imperial governments adopted a policy that destroyed the Jesuits as an organization in Germany and drove their members of foreign origin out of the country.

In the May Laws passed by the Prussian parliament in 1873 Bismarck attempted to subject the Church to the state. One of these famous laws provided that henceforth there should be installed in Prussian parishes only Germans who had attended a state gymnasium and a three-year theological course at a secular university, had passed an examination in history, philosophy, and German literature set by the government, and had received the approval of the secular authorities. Two other measures attempted to limit the jurisdiction of the Pope over the Church in Prussia. A fourth law expedited the withdrawal of the laity from the Church and freed them from further obligation toward the parishes.

The Roman Catholics of Germany replied to these attacks on the Church by adopting a policy of passive resistance. The Prussian bishops refused to obtain the recognition of the state for their seminaries for the training of young priests and installed parish priests without previously notifying the secular authorities. The candidates for the priesthood failed to present themselves for the required examination. The government retaliated by withholding its contributions to the clergy and the seminaries, punishing the bishops and priests by fines, imprisonment, the confiscation of their property, and banishment from the country, and enacting legislation introducing civil marriage and civil registration of births, deaths, and marriages. The policy of the government deprived over a thousand parishes of the comfort of the sacraments. But repression only increased the determination of the Roman Catholics. In the elections of 1873 the Center party increased its representation in the Reichstag from fifty-two to eighty-nine seats.

The struggle known as the *Kulturkampf* did not rage with equal fury in all the states of the empire. In Bavaria the government recognized the futility of imitating the Prussian legislation against the Church and confined itself to refusing to allow the publication of the doctrine of papal infallibility and to protecting the Old Catholics from attacks. In Württemberg the National Liberal party constituted a minority and the secular and ecclesiastical authorities lived in peace. In Baden the government had initiated a struggle with the Church four years before Bismarck began the *Kulturkampf*. In Hesse-Darmstadt the political leaders passed legislation against the Church that closely imitated the Prussian May Laws.

By 1878 the efforts of Bismarck and the National Liberals to exalt the state at the expense of the Roman Catholic Church had wrought great havoc among the German people without breaking the power of either the Church or the Center party. At the same time the victory of the anticlerical Republicans in France and the improvement of relations between Austria and Germany, which foreshadowed the conclusion of the Dual Alliance of 1879, relieved Bismarck to a large extent of his fear of a coalition of the Catholic powers of Europe against Germany. As a result of these changes in the political situation, Bismarck modified his policy toward the Church and attempted to separate the Catholic masses from their leaders by conciliatory measures. In 1880 the Prussian government pushed through the parliament legislation empowering it to disregard the injunctions of earlier laws concerning the education of the clergy, the oath of loyalty required of the bishops, and the withholding of contributions to the Church. These measures restored in most of the vacant parishes the ordinary religious services. Two years later the Prussian government reëstablished diplomatic relations with the papacy. During the next few years the government of Prussia passed laws restoring the bishops to their sees, abolishing the state examination in history, philosophy, and literature, permitting the education of candidates for the priesthood in episcopal seminaries, and allowing the religious orders (with the exception of the Jesuits) to return to Prussia. The Prussian government still maintained in force the legislation prohibiting the use of the pulpit for religious agitation, requiring that the state should be informed about clerical appointments, giving the state supervision of the schools, and establishing civil marriage and civil registration of births, deaths, and marriages. The furious struggle thus really ended in a compromise.

3

THE PROBLEM OF NATIONAL MINORITIES

From the first the Danes of Schleswig, the former subjects of France in Alsace and Lorraine, and the Poles of East Prussia constituted a serious obstacle to the spiritual unification of the new empire. The Poles formed a substantial proportion of the population in the provinces of Posen, Silesia, and East and West Prussia, and had been incorporated into the Prussian state in the eighteenth century as a result of the conquest of Silesia from Austria and the three partitions of Poland. At first the Polish national movement affected only the clergy and the nobility. Jews and Germans performed the functions of a middle class and the peasants remained untouched by national sentiment. As the nineteenth century progressed, however, the Prussian schools began to reduce the illiteracy of the Poles, the social legislation of Prussia released the Polish peasant from the restrictions of the old seigniorial system, and the economic revolution opened opportunities for engaging in new crafts and trades. The sons of the Polish peasants took administrative positions in the new postal and telegraph systems and began to enter business and to prepare for the professions of law, medicine, and teaching. With the growth of a middle class the Polish national movement became democratized and stronger. In 1864 the Poles succeeded in electing twenty-six deputies to the Prussian diet. After the formation of the empire they regularly sent fourteen members to the imperial Reichstag.

Confronted by the menace of this growing Polish nationalism, the Prussian government adopted a series of measures designed to avert the danger. In undertaking the struggle with the Church Bismarck undoubtedly had in mind the Polish provinces of Prussia. The regulations concerning the use of the Polish language struck directly at the Polish national movement. By the legislation concerning their Church and their language Bismarck hoped to open the minds of the Polish masses to German influences. In 1886 the Prussian government created a settlement commission for the purpose of Germanizing the Polish districts of Prussia by establishing German colonies in their midst through the inducement of land improvements and building loans. The Prussian authorities planned to acquire the land for these colonies by buying up the estates of the impecunious Polish nobles, thus depriving the Poles at the same time of their land and of their natural leaders. The plan, however, had the unexpected result of stimulating the Polish national movement. The Poles founded banks and coöperative societies, which taught the people thrift and rescued them from usurers, and bought more land for settlement than the government-aided Germans.

The imperial government realized at once that it could not put the provinces of Alsace and Lorraine on an equal footing with the other German states. It attempted to meet the situation by putting the two conquered provinces under an arbitrary government authorized to declare martial law on the slightest provocation. The policy of the new German authorities caused the greatest dissatisfaction. They enforced conscription in the two provinces after 1872, expelled from Alsace all inhabitants who decided to remain French citizens, made German the language of the elementary schools, applied the *Kulturkampf* legislation in the two provinces, forced the social organization in Alsace and Lorraine to admit German immigrants, forbade the use of French words and signs, tampered with the mails, instituted a passport system that isolated the provinces from France, and persecuted all who displayed French sympathies. Consequently, when they were given an opportunity in 1874 to send fifteen deputies to the imperial Reichstag the inhabitants of Alsace and Lorraine sent a delegation hostile to the German government, which demanded as its first official act the submission of the question of annexation to a referendum. Because of the attitude displayed by a majority of the population, the German authorities never dared to grant the two provinces complete self-government. The civil government finally established by them in Alsace and Lorraine consisted of a governor appointed by the Emperor, a ministry responsible to the governor, and a consultative body that lacked the essential powers of a legislative body.

The Danish problem grew out of the annexation of Schleswig by Prussia in 1866 and the subsequent failure of the Prussian government to keep the promise made to Austria in the treaty of peace to hold a plebiscite in the province on the question of annexation. The Danes of both Denmark and northern Schleswig felt aggrieved because of the failure of the Prussian government to keep its word. In Denmark the Danes organized South Jute associations to keep alive the flame of Danish nationalism in northern Schleswig. In Schleswig they established loan associations and social, gymnastic, and language clubs to combat Germanizing influences. The question of the status of the Schleswig Danes who opted to remain Danish citizens continued to plague the Prussian government until the settlement of the problem at the close of the World War.

4

THE ECONOMIC DEVELOPMENT OF THE NEW EMPIRE

The failure of Bismarck to conquer the Church and the national minorities did not prevent a rapid economic development of the new empire that transformed it into an industrial state and greatly influenced its later history. During the first three years of the new imperial régime more establishments for iron smelting and working started up in Germany than had come into existence in all the previous years of the century. In the eighties, while the iron and steel industry practically stood still in France, Belgium, and Great Britain, the iron and steel furnaces and mills of Germany nearly doubled their output. In 1910 the German iron and steel industry produced twenty-eight times as much as in 1860 and held first place in Europe.

After 1871 Germany also won an important place in textile manufacturing. Though the linen industry declined as a result of the competition of Ulster, cotton and woolen manufacturing made great progress. About 1850 Germans began to wear cotton instead of woolen clothing and the change stimulated the cotton industry. Centers for the manufacture of cotton developed in Silesia, Bavaria, and Württemberg. In 1871 Germany annexed the highly developed textile plants of Alsace. As a result of these developments the consumption of cotton doubled in Germany between 1866 and 1875.

After the establishment of the empire Germany likewise became a great chemical and a great electrical center. In the early decades of the nineteenth century German investigators had laid a broad foundation of scientific knowledge for the development of these industries. In Saxony, Thuringia, and Hanover, Germany possessed unique deposits of potash salts. From her abundant beds of iron pyrites she began to extract sulphur, sodium chloride, and potassium salts. Her rich deposits of coal and coal-tar furnished the raw materials for a great dye industry. The development of the telegraph, the telephone, and the submarine cable, and the progress in the use of electricity for power, lighting, and transportation, gave rise to a great electrical industry. The census of 1882 ignored this branch of industry. A quarter of a century later electrical establishments gave employment to over a hundred thousand persons.

The industrialization of Germany stimulated the mining of coal. While the production of coal merely doubled in Belgium and trebled in France and Great Britain, the output of the coal-mines of Germany increased nearly 800 per cent between 1871 and 1914. By the end of the nineteenth century Germany had become a regular exporter of coal to surrounding countries.

The growth of German industry finally gave rise to a large expansion of German commerce and a great development of shipping. Every coast and river port improved its facilities for trade. The two great shipping-lines, the Hamburg American and the North German Lloyd, substituted frequent and regular sailings for the tramp style of steamer and built larger and larger ships, which provided all the luxuries and comforts of modern life. Between 1871 and 1905 the number of German steamships rose from one hundred and forty-seven to one thousand seven hundred and sixty-two, their net tonnage from eighty-two thousand to almost two million tons, and their crews from less than five hundred to over fifty thousand men.

The German Empire owed its remarkable industrial and commercial development to its persistent application of intelligence to the problems of manufacture and trade. The industrialists of Germany developed relatively large manufacturing units, adopted mass-production, standardized their commodities, maintained staffs of scientific investigators and large laboratories, and applied the results of scientific discoveries much earlier and more systematically than did their competitors. They organized cartels that divided the market between the competing German firms and assured each a profitable return on its investment. German exporters made a thorough study of foreign markets, sent trained representatives abroad, adapted their commodities to the demands of their customers, and adopted terms of payment in harmony with the financial customs of the latter. The banks of Germany lent money to German business men because of their character and prospects of success as well as on account of the security offered, and established branches all over the world. The state maintained schools that prepared their students well for trade and industry, promoted the building of a network of canals and railroads in Germany, and granted exporters very low freight-rates on commodities shipped abroad.

The industrial and commercial growth of the empire also caused a development of German banking. Prior to 1848 there had been in the German states only family and private banks like that of the Rothschilds at Frankfort. After that date banks owned by groups of stockholders began to make their appearance and to finance the construction of railways in Germany, Austria, and Russia. After the formation of the North German Confederation these early banking institutions began to increase their capital and to establish branches in other countries. For example, the Deutsche Bank, founded in 1869, started branches at Bremen and Hamburg in 1871, opened an agency in London two years later for the benefit of German exporters and importers, and finally established subsidiary banking institutions in South America, absorbed a bank in Brussels, and started a branch in Madrid.

This rapid economic expansion of Germany affected her social and political development in many ways. It gave rise to a change in German tariff policy, created a large city proletariat which sought in Socialism a remedy for its unfavorable economic situation, brought to the fore such social problems as unemployment, protection of industrial workers, and provision for old age, sickness, and disability, and caused a demand for the acquisition of colonies as markets for the expanding German industry.

5

THE CHANGE IN THE FINANCIAL POLICY OF THE EMPIRE

Toward the end of the seventh decade of the nineteenth century the free-trade movement initiated in England began to lose its appeal in Germany. A period of unsound speculation, aggravated by the indemnity paid to Germany by France, followed the Franco-Prussian War. Badly built railroads and unsound industrial concerns multiplied. Then in 1873 the world-wide financial panic destroyed public confidence in the continuance of German prosperity. Railroad, industrial, and commercial shares suddenly slumped or became entirely worthless on the market, and business failures, limitation of purchases and production, and unemployment followed hard on the heels of the decline in the value of stocks. At the same time the Junkers of eastern Germany began to suffer from the competition of Russian meat and of wheat from the Balkans, Austria-Hungary, Argentina, and the United States, as a result of railway construction and the development of ocean steamship-lines. The economic depresssion and competition converted the harassed industrialists and landholders to the principle of protection and finally created in the Reichstag a majority—composed of Roman Catholics, Conservatives, and a part of the National Liberals—that began to demand a high tariff.

The advocates of a high-tariff policy found Bismarck ready to cooperate with them. He appreciated the votes of his political allies, the National Liberals, but he disliked their ideas about a responsible ministry and desired to free the imperial government from its dependence on the grudgingly given contributions of the separate states. At first he had hoped to find a solution for the latter problem in the purchase by the empire of the private and state-owned railroads, the creation of an imperial monopoly on tobacco, and the taxation of brandy, but the opposition of the Reichstag and the states prevented him from carrying out his plans. The proposed high tariff offered him an opportunity to obtain through one measure protection for German products and a larger revenue for the empire. In 1879, accordingly, Bismarck pushed through the Bundesrat and the Reichstag a tariff bill which taxed practically all imports except commodities not produced in Germany. The new economic policy tended to free the imperial government from the control of the states, to tie the manufacturers and landholders to the new imperial régime, to make food and clothing dearer for the working classes, and to stimulate economic rivalries and national feeling.

6

THE WAR ON SOCIALISM

Before he had brought his struggle with the Church to a conclusion Bismarck involved the imperial government in a new conflict. For some years he had watched the growing strength of the Socialists. In the sixties the working classes of Germany began to recover from their defeat in 1848 and commenced to organize labor-associations throughout Germany. In 1863 a group of these associations found a brilliant leader in Ferdinand Lassalle, the son of a wealthy wholesale merchant of Jewish birth at Leipzig, who maintained that credit unions and cooperative societies were mere palliatives and advocated the organization of productive associations and the formation of an independent political party composed of the workers of Germany. At the invitation of a congress of working-men held at Frankfort-on-the-Main, he organized the Universal German Working-men's Association and started a remarkable campaign of agitation, marked by great meetings and tremendous ovations; but this was cut short by his death in a duel fought with a rival for the affections of the beautiful but fickle daughter of a Bavarian diplomat. Before his death, however, another group of workers' associations had been formed in Saxony and southern Germany under the leadership of Wilhelm Liebknecht—a friend and disciple of Marx and Engels—and August Bebel, a turner who knew the misery of abject poverty by experience and incarnated the spirit of working-class revolt. In 1868 this group accepted the main tenets of Karl Marx. In 1875 the two groups of Socialists finally united to form the Social Democratic party of Germany.

After the formation of the empire the Socialists had shown greater strength in each succeeding election. In 1871 they cast only one hundred and two thousand votes and obtained only two seats in the imperial Reichstag. But the increasing industrialization of Germany and the economic depression which followed the crisis of 1873 drove thousands of persons in the Protestant districts of Germany into the ranks of the Socialists. In 1877, in consequence, their popular vote rose to four hundred and ninety-three thousand and the number of their representatives in the lower house of the imperial parliament to twelve. As a result of this growth of strength they became the third strongest party in the empire.

As early as 1874 Bismarck sought from the Reichstag the grant of wide and indefinite powers for combating the Socialists, but without success. In 1878, however, the situation changed. Two attempts on the life of the aged and respected Emperor William I by alleged Socialists frightened the German public with the specter of revolution and the Chancellor seized the opportunity to dissolve the Reichstag. The subsequent elections, held amidst great popular excitement, resulted in the loss of twenty-nine seats by the National Liberals and of three by the Socialists and an increase in the number of deputies returned by the Center and Conservative parties. The new Reichstag readily enacted legislation that authorized the imperial government to prevent the meetings, dissolve the organizations, and suppress the publications of the Socialists. Armed with these powers, the government initiated a protracted campaign that drove the leaders of the Socialists into exile and forced their party to resort to secret methods of propaganda. During the twelve years that the struggle against the Socialists continued the government is estimated to have suppressed some thirteen hundred publications, broken up three hundred and thirty-two organizations, and expelled nine hundred persons from the country.

Even the conservative Chancellor recognized, however, that the appeal of Socialism to the working classes of Germany was due to certain defects in the social organization of the empire. In 1881, therefore, the speech from the throne announced a program of social insurance designed to remedy the worst evils in the lot of the proletariat. The next year

Bismarck pushed through the Reichstag and the Bundesrat a Health Insurance Act that provided the sick worker who had an income of less than two thousand marks with free medical care and half-pay for a period of thirteen weeks. In the following year Bismarck persuaded the imperial parliament to establish accident insurance for industrial workers. Finally, in 1889 he pressed through the two imperial legislative bodies a measure providing for the workers of Germany insurance for old age and invalidism. Amended from time to time until they affected all classes receiving less than two thousand marks a year in wages, the three laws finally assured the German worker free medical care and half-pay for twenty-six weeks when he became sick, a yearly income ranging from one hundred and fourteen to four hundred and fifteen marks if he became an invalid, and a small income after he reached the age of seventy, and provided somewhat for his wife and children after his death. The cost of the new system of social insurance was met almost wholly by the contributions made by the worker and his employer. But neither the repressive measures nor the social-insurance program of the government stayed the growth of the Social Democratic party.

7

THE DISMISSAL OF BISMARCK

In March, 1888, death brought to an end the reign of William I, the titular founder of the new German Empire. Under normal conditions his son Frederick III would have served as head of the state until some time in the twentieth century. He came to office, however, mortally ill and survived his father only ninety-nine days. His death made the youthful William II King of Prussia and German Emperor.

In a state as undemocratic as Germany the character and training of the new sovereign meant much for the weal or woe of his subjects. In his earlier years his mother had surrounded him with English influences. He learned to speak the English tongue, adopted the customs of the English people, and often visited his grandmother, Queen Victoria. As he grew older he came under the supervision of a tutor who disregarded art and music and emphasized piety and discipline. Later he attended a gymnasium at Cassel and the university at Bonn. After completing his formal education he entered the Potsdam Guards. Among their officers he learned the military traditions of Prussia and absorbed the conservative point of view. As a result of his natural endowment and his training he came to power rash, immature, with an interest in many things, given to sudden changes of policy, fond of military display, and imbued with the conservative traditions of his family and his state.

The young Emperor and his aging Chancellor soon found themselves in disagreement over a number of matters. William II felt that he had been poorly served by Bismarck at the time of the publication of selections from the diary of Frederick III. The two men differed in regard to the policy to be followed in respect to the series of strikes that broke out in various mining regions in Germany after 1889 and as to the renewal of the repressive legislation against the Socialists. The Chancellor desired to crush the strikes and to destroy the Socialists by military force. The Emperor wished to settle the social problem through the summoning of an international conference and the adoption of measures forbidding Sunday work, the labor of women at night, and child labor. They disagreed also over the question of increasing the size of the standing army and differed over the question of a parliamentary majority. Furthermore, a crowd of flatterers surrounded the Emperor and urged him to oppose the policies of Bismarck.

Back of these specific differences lay the fundamental question of power. Bismarck desired to retain his old dominant position in the state. The Emperor chafed at the opposition of the Chancellor. When the subordinates of Bismarck, scenting the fall of their chief, began to discuss questions of policy directly with William II, the Chancellor produced a royal order of 1852 and demanded that he should henceforth be the sole channel of communication with the Emperor. William II, however, refused to be excluded from the control of affairs and insisted that he be kept informed of the actions and plans of his chief minister. After an open quarrel in the residence of Bismarck, the Emperor, egged on by his confidants at court, demanded the surrender of the cabinet order of 1852 or the resignation of the Chancellor. After an unsuccessful effort to delay his resignation, Bismarck yielded to the repeated demands of his youthful master and resigned his offices and his power. This brusk dismissal of the founder of the German Empire astonished the people of Germany and of Europe.

8

THE NEW COURSE

Immediately after his dismissal of Bismarck the Emperor dramatically telegraphed to the Grand Duke of Weimar: "The post of pilot on the ship of state has fallen to me. The course remains the same. Full steam ahead." In spite of this bombastic message, however, the resignation of the old Chancellor inaugurated a new era in German history marked by the subordination of the imperial chancellors to the will of the Emperor, sudden changes of policy and advisers, a great material development of the empire, and a determination to have Germany take a conspicuous place in the world. The Emperor attempted to charm all by his pleasing address, his quick powers of perception, and the variety of his interests. He took a naïve pleasure in posing as a military chieftain but alienated many army officers by meddling in technical matters which he hardly understood, showing a lack of deference to experienced officers, favoring certain units of the army, and playing a spectacular rôle at army maneuvers. He intervened dramatically in social and political movements, traveled extensively, made provocative speeches, and treated his chancellors like subalterns. He allowed a Count Botho Eulenburg to decide the fate of policies and of persons by the arts of the courtier and for nearly twenty years permitted the foreign policies of the empire to be shaped by the suspicious and mistrustful Baron Holstein.

After his fall Bismarck adopted the part of a bitter critic of the policies of his successors. He expressed himself freely in the press and in conversation. In retaliation the Emperor resorted to means that shocked the German nation. In 1892 the quarrel reached its climax when William II used his influence to prevent the Emperor of Austria from granting Bismarck an interview at the time of the marriage of his son to an Austrian subject. Later an interchange of courtesies relieved the strain somewhat but did little to heal the deep wounds left by the conflict.

9

THE EMPEROR AND THE SOCIALISTS

The young Emperor first directed his attention to the social problems of the working classes that had been created by the industrialization of Germany. In the hope of undermining their position, he relaxed the harsh laws against the Socialists and sponsored the meeting of an international conference for the protection of labor. But his social policy brought him nothing but disappointment. The conference resulted in the adoption by Germany of legislation concerning work on Sunday, the employment of children of school age in factories, and the protection of women workers, but did nothing to stop the growth of the Social Democratic party. In the elections of 1890 the Socialists gained thirty-five seats in the Reichstag. From that date onward their representation in the German parliament steadily increased until in the elections of 1912 they won one hundred and eleven seats and became the strongest party in the empire.

Their failure to yield to his blandishments made the Emperor regard the Socialists as enemies. Thenceforth he summoned the conservative elements of German society to do battle against the party of revolution in behalf of morality, religion, and the social order. In 1894 and again in 1897 he made unsuccessful attempts to have the Reichstag adopt new repressive legislation against the Socialists. He personally intervened against them in electoral contests and refused to modify the Prussian three-class system or to readjust the electoral districts, for fear of increasing their political strength in the Prussian and imperial parliaments. In all struggles between capital and labor the government saw harbingers of the revolution foretold by the Socialists and energetically supported the employing classes.

Meanwhile, however, the Socialists were ceasing to believe in the inevitability of the social revolution foreseen by Karl Marx. In 1890 Eduard Bernstein published the results of a long study of the principles of the founder of Scientific Socialism. He came to the conclusion that improvement of social conditions must come through a peaceful social evolution and that the Social Democratic party must consciously work for the realization of its objectives. Those who accepted this point of view became known as Revisionists and gradually transformed the Socialists into a reform party.

10

THE STRENGTHENING OF THE ARMY AND THE NAVY

The new course adopted by Germany necessitated a greater emphasis on the army. Bismarck had depended for security primarily on a complicated system of alliances and only secondarily on the army. The abandonment of the Reinsurance Treaty with Russia weakened the diplomatic defenses of the empire and made necessary a greater reliance on armaments. The new situation was revealed by the speeches of the Emperor, a somewhat more threatening and aggressive attitude in diplomatic relations, and an increase in the size of the standing army.

The new course affected the navy as well as the army. Bismarck had always carefully avoided any appearance of challenging British sea-power. William II, on the contrary, showed from the time of his accession an interest in the development of the German navy. At first the German naval authorities seemed to regard the navy as merely an additional weapon against France. As time passed, however, they began to take into consideration the possibility of a conflict with Great Britain and to work for a great expansion of the German naval forces. In inflammatory speeches the Emperor asserted that bitter need forced an increase of naval strength and that the trident belonged in the fist of Germany. The campaign in behalf of a larger navy gradually broke down the opposition of the Reichstag and caused the empire to adopt the policy that led in the early years of the twentieth century to the naval rivalry with Great Britain.

The Emperor also became spokesman of the widely felt conviction that henceforth Germany must take an important part in the affairs of the world. The movement found recruits and leadership among professors, officials, army and navy officers, and the industrial and commercial leaders of the empire. It found expression in the Alliance of All the Germans established in 1891 as a result of the dissatisfaction felt over the treaty ceding Helgoland to Germany, in the German Society for North Schleswig, organized in 1890 to combat Danish nationalism, in the East Mark Society, formed in 1894 to fight Polish nationalism, in the Anti-Semitic Society, founded in the same year to check the Jews, in the German Navy League, started in 1898, in the German School Society, established to give support to German culture in neighboring countries, and in German foreign policy. This feeling that Germany must play a part in the world increased the tension between the European powers and contributed toward the creation of the state of mind that brought on the World War.

II

THE EMPEROR AND THE NATIONAL MINORITIES

The new pilot had no more success in solving the problem of Polish nationalism than the old Chancellor had had. Bismarck had considered the possession of the Polish provinces necessary for the defense of the empire and the friendship of Russia more important than the contentment of the Polish subjects of Prussia. After William II assumed control of the government he attempted a policy of conciliation in the hope of gaining the support of the sixteen Polish deputies in the Reichstag. He permitted a Pole to be selected for the vacant archbishopric of Posen-Gnesen and allowed the Polish language to be used again in the popular schools. But neither the conciliatory policy of the Emperor nor the colonization policy of the East Mark Society could halt the march of the Polish national movement. The new middle class joined forces with the nobility and carried the Polish agitation into Upper Silesia and the majority of German emigrants preferred to go overseas rather than to the German colonies in the Polish provinces of Prussia.

In Alsace-Lorraine German pressure ultimately began to have an effect on the former subjects of France. Long years of fruitless protest convinced the older inhabitants of the two provinces of the hopelessness of the policy of active resistance; a new generation, trained in German schools and disciplined by the German army, grew up; and the Socialist and Center parties of Germany gradually won a considerable following in both Alsace and Lorraine. The political leaders of the two provinces, in consequence, began to substitute for the old program of reunion with France the idea of autonomy within the German Empire.

The imperial government, however, never felt that it could put Alsace and Lorraine on the same basis as the states of the empire. The new constitution of 1910, therefore, attempted only to effect a compromise between statehood and subordination to the imperial government, by providing for an appointed governor and the representation of the provinces in the Bundesrat by three members, by giving the Emperor a veto over the legislation of the provincial diet, and by making half the members of the upper house of the provincial legislative body imperial appointees. The granting of this constitution, consequently, did little to strengthen the loyalty of the inhabitants of Alsace-Lorraine to the empire.

The ink had hardly dried on the proffered constitution when a clash at Zabern between the German military authorities and the civilian population reawakened the slumbering hostility of the two provinces toward German rule and stirred the democratic elements of the whole empire against the autocratic government. In the town of Zabern a young lieutenant, sprung from the Junker class, made himself so obnoxious to the Alsatian recruits that he became an object of public scorn and derision. The taunts of street gamins and rowdies resulted in a series of clashes between the military forces and the civilian population. In one of these the arrogant young lieutenant slashed with his sword a crippled, unarmed shoemaker as the latter was being held by two soldiers. The protection extended to the aggressor by the military authorities aroused public opinion in the two provinces to the highest pitch and gave rise to vigorous protests from German Liberals who realized the harm being wrought by the military authorities.

12

THE PROGRESS OF THE DEMOCRATIC PRINCIPLE

During these years the democratic principle made considerable progress in Germany. As a result of a law of 1906 the members of the imperial Reichstag received thenceforth a yearly stipend of three thousand marks. This innovation made it somewhat easier for the popular parties to find representatives. Contemporaneously a number of the German states liberalized their political machinery. In Bavaria the Center and Social Democratic parties forced the adoption of a law providing for direct election of members of the lower house of the Bavarian parliament and a rearrangement of electoral districts. In 1909 Saxony abandoned its three-class franchise, adopted in 1896, for one that permitted certain classes a plural vote on account of such qualifications as education, income, and age. In 1911 Hesse adopted direct election and a suffrage which gave an extra vote to voters over fifty years of age. The

Socialist demonstrations grew more and more impressive each year and the democratic element in the Center party steadily gained ground. Under the leadership of Matthias Erzberger the Catholics of Germany did not hesitate to coöperate with the Socialists for the attainment of a particular objective. The democratic principle, however, made no headway against the Prussian three-class system or toward a readjustment of the electoral districts of the empire.

With the development of the democratic elements of the empire the dissatisfaction with the Emperor and his bombastic manner of intervening in foreign and domestic affairs grew stronger. This feeling came to a head at the time of the publication of the interview with the Emperor in which he boasted of his personal services to England on various occasions and particularly at the time of the Boer War. Its appearance threw Germany into an uproar. In newspaper articles and parliamentary speeches the German people expressed their disapproval of the personal policy of the Emperor. The Chancellor Prince von Bülow, seized the opportunity to put an end to the irresponsible intervention of William II in governmental affairs and assured the Reichstag that henceforth the Emperor would observe in public and private intercourse the reserve indispensable to a continuity of political policy and the dignity of the crown. After an audience with the Chancellor the Emperor confirmed these declarations and assured him of his continued support. The incident made the question of the abdication of William II a matter of general discussion and cast a shadow on the monarchy from which it never entirely escaped.

During the half-century between the formation of the German Empire and the opening of the World War the imperial government made the experiment of attempting to preserve the political organization and social structure of the Ancien Régime by adapting them to the new forces astir in the world. Animated by this ideal, it carried on vainly great struggles with the Church and the Socialists, waged futile conflicts with French, Danish, and Polish nationalism in the border provinces of the empire, transformed Germany from an agricultural state to the greatest industrial and commercial state of the Continent, built up a powerful army and navy, and attempted to play a great rôle in the world. In this development Germany found leadership first in the accomplished conservative diplomat, Bismarck, and then in the vain, impulsive William II. In spite of their efforts to maintain existing political and social institutions, however, the Church, the national minorities, and the democratic forces of the empire strengthened their positions.

CHAPTER XVII

THE AUSTRIAN PROBLEM, 1860–1914

For a decade after the Revolution of 1848 had revealed to the rest of Europe the difficulty of maintaining the ancient authority of the Hapsburg monarchy and its agents over the numerous peoples of Austria, the Austrian government attempted to solve the problem by a resolute continuance of absolutism. But the defeat of its military forces in 1859 by the armies of France and Sardinia compelled the Austrian government to seek a new solution of the question. After the battles at Magenta and Solferino even Emperor Francis Joseph and his conservative advisers realized that absolute government could no longer be maintained. The regiments recruited in the Magyar and Italian provinces of the empire had proved to be unreliable. Public opinion at Vienna singled out the Emperor, the court, the Concordat, and the military system for the severest criticism, and at times seemed to threaten the security of the whole autocratic system. The growing middle class demanded concessions to the Liberal spirit of the century. The ten pent-up nationalities clamored for a reorganization of the empire that would recognize their national claims. The Magyars were making preparations for resistance that threatened to get beyond the control of the imperial authorities. The condition of the Austrian finances made the raising of further loans impossible. The whole situation called for immediate action.

I

THE OCTOBER DIPLOMA

In this crisis the Emperor turned for assistance first to an assembly of the notables of the empire, the representatives of the great noble families of Hungary, Bohemia, and the other hereditary provinces. Upon their advice Francis Joseph issued the October Diploma. This document aimed to maintain the unitary realm created by Schwarzenberg by giving it a federal form which recognized the individuality of the historic provinces of the empire. In the old Kingdom of Hungary it suspended the régime of absolutism set up in 1850, reëstablished the parliament, and restored self-government in the counties and municipalities. These concessions gave back to the Magyar aristocracy much of its former political authority. In the rest of the empire the new constitution set up seventeen provincial diets largely under the control of the German aristocracy. Those responsible for the new organization of the state planned to bind the kingdoms and provinces of the empire together by creating a central parliament of one hundred members, composed of delegates from the various provincial diets and endowed with authority to vote supplies and to exercise a deliberative voice in legislation. They entirely disregarded the Liberal and national forces at work in the empire.

The promulgation of the October Diploma started an agitation which astounded every one. The new constitution pleased only the Czechs and the Poles. The majority of the Magyars refused to permit the establishment of a régime that subordinated the Kingdom of Hungary to an imperial parliament. As a result of their opposition great demonstrations took place in Budapest and other Hungarian cities, riotous proceedings marked the meetings of the reëstablished county and municipal councils, and rural and urban inhabitants refused to pay their taxes. Only the presence of strong military forces prevented the outbreak of a revolution among the Magyars. In Vienna and the German cities of western Austria, the middle classes, encouraged by the higher bureaucracy, turned against the policy of the nobles. The agitation carried on by the Magyars and the German middle classes finally convinced the Emperor and his advisers that the October Diploma was unworkable.

2

THE CONSTITUTION OF 1861

In February, 1861, under the pretext of supplementing the October Diploma, Francis Joseph promulgated a new constitution. This document provided for a parliament of two houses, an aristocratic chamber consisting of the members of the royal family, dignitaries of the state and the Church, and representatives of the great noble families, and a lower house composed of deputies elected by the provincial diets. When it included the one hundred and twenty deputies of Hungary and the dependent kingdoms of Croatia and Transylvania the proposed parliament was to legislate for the whole empire. When they were excluded it constituted a central legislative body for the non-Hungarian provinces of the monarchy. The new constitution therefore placed authority in the hands of the Austrian Germans and ignored the demands of the Magyars, the Slavs, and the other minor national groups of the empire.

Under the leadership of Francis Deák the Magyars refused to send representatives to the new imperial parliament and the Hungarian diet declared its decrees of no force within the limits of the Kingdom of

Hungary and demanded a restoration of the Hungarian constitution of 1848 and a restitution of Croatia, the port of Fiume, the Serbian Military Frontiers, and Transylvania to the Magyar state. The imperial authorities responded to their demands by dissolving the Hungarian diet and reëstablishing a régime of absolutism. However, the stubborn resistance offered by the Magyars to Austrian rule finally induced the Emperor to begin negotiations with their leaders. In the course of the ensuing discussions Deák proposed a solution of the Austrian problem that foreshadowed the creation of a dual monarchy in which the Magyars and the Germans should divide the rule of the empire between themselves. But the imperial authorities and the recalcitrant Magyars did not reach a compromise until after the defeat of the monarchy in the War of 1866 with Prussia.

The relaxation of the régime of absolutism stirred other peoples of the empire into political activity. The Croats of Croatia refused to send representatives to the imperial parliament, demanded the union with Croatia of Slavonia, Dalmatia, and the districts occupied by the Slovenes, and asked for an independent administration and complete freedom from the control of both the Hungarian and the Austrian governments. They found an able champion in Bishop Joseph Strossmayer, the chief ecclesiastical dignitary of Croatia, who could speak for the Croats at both Rome and Vienna. Though a firm believer in the necessity of maintaining the Hapsburg monarchy, he stood resolutely for the historic rights of the Kingdom of Croatia and dreamed of the expulsion of the Turks from Europe and the union of the Croats, Serbs, Slovenes, and Bulgars into a single Southern Slav state. He gave his people the noble slogan, "Through education to freedom," founded an academy at Agram in 1862, began the agitation which finally resulted in 1874 in the organization of a university in the same city, fostered the establishment of schools, extended his patronage to struggling scholars and writers, and started a society for the diffusion of good reading. The national academy furthered the Southern Slav movement by the publication of a yearbook, a dictionary, and historical documents.

Even the backward two million Slovaks of northern Hungary began to show signs of national consciousness. In 1861 their leaders presented a memorandum to the Hungarian parliament which appealed for harmony and understanding between the Slovaks and the Magyars, asserted the individuality of the Slovak people, and demanded supremacy for them in northern Hungary. Though their demands received scant consideration from either the Magyars or the Emperor, many signs indicated their growing national consciousness. In 1862 the Slovaks opened their first schools and organized a society and raised funds to promote the publication and circulation of Slovak books and to encourage Slovak authors and artists. The society published a chronicle of national events, stories and proverbs, important documents, popular songs, scholarly works, and manuals of agriculture, and started one hundred and fifty reading clubs and circulating libraries. Under this stimulus Slovak reviews and journals rapidly increased in number.

In the province of Transylvania the Saxons and the Rumanians seized the opportunity to get an advantage over the dominant Magyars. The former favored the constitution of 1861 because it favored the Germans. The latter regarded the revival of Transylvanian autonomy as a step toward their union with the rest of their nation on the eastern slopes of the Carpathian Mountains. As a result of the manipulations of the Austrian government the two peoples obtained a majority in the diet of Transylvania and sent representatives to the central parliament.

The Czechs of Bohemia and Moravia consciously imitated the policy of the Magyars of Hungary. They desired a considerable degree of political autonomy, administration of the laws by officials using the Czech language, a fair proportion of the administrative and military offices, and educational institutions equal in number and equipment to those provided for the German minority in Bohemia in which instruction should be given in the Czech language. In 1863, consequently, the Czech deputies ceased to attend the imperial parliament. In the same year in which the plan of Francis Deák for a dual monarchy appeared, Palacký, the famous Czech leader, published *The Idea of the Austrian State,* which advocated for Austria a federal organization with a central government of restricted authority and state governments with wide powers. His conservative leadership, however, did not satisfy the more radical of the Czechs and the Czech national party began to separate during this period into the groups later known as the Old Czechs and the Young Czechs.

The issuing of the constitutions of 1860 and 1861 aroused other class and national conflicts. In Galicia the Polish nobles in control of the provincial diet abstained from electing deputies to the parliament at Vienna in order to maintain the autonomy of the province and to retain their position of dominance over the Polish and Ruthenian peasants. In Venetia the Italians refused to send deputies to an Austrian parliament. Even the German Liberals began to see that they had sold the opportunity for constitutional liberty for an illusory domination over the remaining peoples of the empire.

The policy of abstention from participation in the central parliament employed by the Croats, the Czechs, the Italians, and the Magyars destroyed the moral authority of the constitution of 1861 and convinced the Austrian government of the necessity for attempting another solution of the Austrian problem. Since the Magyars were the strongest and the most resolute of the refactory nationalites, the imperial authorities entered into negotiations with them. The defeat of Austria by Prussia in the War of 1866, before the completion of these negotiations, compelled the Austrian authorities to accept the terms of the Magyars and agree to the Compromise of 1867.

3

THE COMPROMISE OF 1867

The agreement with the Magyars organized the heterogeneous provinces and the polyglot peoples of the empire into two states, the ancient Kingdom of Hungary with its dependencies of Croatia and Transylvania and the lands and provinces subsequently designated for the sake of convenience as Austria. This arrangement placed the Croats and Serbs of Croatia, Slavonia, and southern Hungary, the Saxons and Rumanians of Transylvania, and the Slovaks of northern Hungary under the control of the Magyars, and the Croats and Serbs of Dalmatia and the Serbian Military Frontier, the Slovenes around the head of the Adriatic Sea, the Italians of Southern Tyrol, Trieste, and Dalmatia, the Czechs of Bohemia and Moravia, the Poles and Ruthenians of Galicia, and the Rumanians of Bukovina under the control of the Germans. Henceforth the maintenance of their political supremacy became the chief aim of the dominant Magyars and Austrian Germans. The reorganized state took the name of Austria-Hungary.

The Compromise of 1867 created unique political machinery for the conduct of the common affairs of the two states of the new Dual Monarchy. It provided that the joint sovereign of the two states should indicate their equality by styling himself Emperor of Austria and King of Hungary. It established common ministries for foreign affairs, war, and finance and invented an extraordinary deliberative body consisting of two delegations—one from Austria and one from Hungary—each composed of twenty members of the upper house and forty members of the lower house of the parliament. The two delegations were to meet alternately at the two capitals but they were to debate and to vote separately. In case of disagreement, however, the two delegations were to hold joint sessions and vote on disputed questions without debate. The compromise restricted the jurisdiction of the delegations, for the most part, to the voting of supplies and the control of administration and left the work of legislation mainly to the Austrian and Hungarian parliaments.

The compromise also stipulated that certain questions should be settled by special agreements between the Austrian and the Hungarian parliament. At intervals, consequently, representatives of the two states negotiated concerning such common affairs as defense, tariff, railroads, money and coinage, and indirect taxes affecting industry. In these negotiations the Magyars enjoyed a great advantage. With its compact territories the Kingdom of Hungary could maintain an independent political existence. The Germans, on the other hand, with such sprawling, indefensible provinces as Galicia, Bukovina, the Tyrol, and Dalmatia, and with their control of the empire constantly threatened by their dissatisfied subjects, could not maintain their position without the Hungarian alliance.

4

AUSTRIA AFTER 1867

After making these concessions to the Magyars the Emperor recognized the impossibility of maintaining any longer the Austrian régime of absolutism. In December, 1867, therefore, he granted his Austrian subjects a constitution which was largely an adaptation of the constitutional document of 1861 to the needs of the Austrian part of the Dual Monarchy. It gave the Emperor control of the ministers and power to proclaim a state of siege, to suspend the constitutional rights of citizens, and, in times when the parliament was not in session, to issue ordinances with the force of law. It placed the administration of the Austrian provinces in the hands of an irresponsible bureaucracy. It created a legislative body, known as the Reichsrat, composed of two houses, an upper house made up of princes of the royal family, prelates, and hereditary and life members, and a lower house consisting of members elected by the provincial diets. The new constitution gave Austria an arbitrary, undemocratic government under the control of the German Liberals, a party recruited in the main from the upper middle class of the cities of Bohemia, Moravia, and Upper and Lower Austria.

The political situation created in Austria by the Compromise of 1867 and by the new Austrian constitution aroused great opposition among the subject races. In the hope of emulating the success of the Magyars, the leaders of the Czechs refused to attend the sessions of the Bohemian diet, asserted that the Kingdom of Bohemia had only the dynasty in common with the other provinces of the monarchy, declared that the new Austrian parliament had no authority to legislate for Bohemia, Moravia, and Austrian Silesia, and demanded the establishment of a responsible central government at Prague. A group of Czech leaders made an ostentatious pilgrimage to Moscow and began to revive the idea of Panslavism. When the Emperor visited Prague in 1868 crowds of people left the city, and in other parts of Bohemia the Czechs staged popular demonstrations to indicate their disapproval of the existing political situation. The Czechs of Moravia made a somewhat similar protest.

The other non-German nationalities of Austria also protested against the establishment of the Dual Monarchy. The Poles refused to attend the Austrian parliament but proved more fortunate than the Czechs in obtaining concessions from the central government. In return for their abandonment of their demands for a federal organization of Austria they obtained an official status for their language in Galicia and autonomy for their school system. These concessions tended to put the Ruthenians of eastern Galicia at the mercy of the Poles. The majority of the Southern Slavs of Dalmatia demanded union with Croatia and some inhabitants of the province offered serious opposition to the conscription of their sons for the Austrian army. In the city of Trieste the Italians and the Slovenes engaged in bloody disputes, and in Laibach the Slovenes and the Germans did the same. In western Tyrol the diet demanded full autonomy. These disturbances endangered the success of the Dual Monarchy.

The victory of Prussia, the rival of Austria, in the Franco-Prussian War, impressed on the political leaders of Austria the necessity for finding a solution for the internal situation of the monarchy. In September, 1871, therefore, they made overtures to the Czechs, the strongest of the nationalities opposing the dominance of the Austrian Germans. The Emperor solemnly promised to recognize the rights of the Kingdom of Bohemia by coming to Prague to be crowned and to grant to the Bohemian kingdom legislative control over all questions not common to all the Austrian provinces. In order to placate the German minority in Bohemia the Austrian authorities proposed to put the Czech and German languages on an equality and to create administrative districts that would segregate the Czechs and the Germans.

The concessions promised to the Czechs stirred violent protests. The German minority in Bohemia protested against being subjected to the political control of the Czechs and absented themselves from the Bohemian diet. From sympathy with the German minority in Bohemia the Germans in the other Austrian provinces held great political demonstrations. The Magyars of Hungary also regarded the maintenance of German supremacy in Austria as indispensable for the preservation of the Dual Monarchy and consequently opposed the concessions. In deference to these varied protests the Emperor broke his word to the Czech leaders and failed to reëstablish the autonomy of the Kingdom of Bohemia. The episode, of course, only increased the mutual ill-will of the Czechs and the Germans.

In 1873, the boycotting of the Austrian parliament by the minor nationalities led to an important change in the method of electing deputies to the lower house. Prior to that date the provincial diets selected them. This arrangement left the dominant nationality of the province in complete control of the provincial delegation to the Austrian parliament and permitted it to embarrass the central government by a policy of passive resistance. In order to break up the practice, the Austrian government introduced direct elections to the central parliament. The new electoral system broke up the national blocks in the provinces and ultimately favored the minor nationalities.

In 1879, the strength shown by the minor nationalities of Austria and the break-up of the dominant Germans into discordant parties led to the rise to power of Count Taaffe, a boyhood friend of the Emperor. He tried to compromise the conflicting national interests and to govern through the support of a coalition composed of Czechs, Poles, Slovenes, and German Clericals. His fourteen years of rule postponed a crisis but did not settle the Austrian problem. He won the coöperation of the Czechs by conceding to them a Czech university at Prague and for their language a position of equality with German in the administrative system of Bohemia. In Galicia he gave the Poles complete control over the Ruthenians. However, his policy of playing one nationality off against another failed to satisfy any of his supporters completely. In 1890 the victory of the Young Czechs, the more democratic wing of the Czech national party, greatly weakened his position. In 1893 his proposal to introduce into the suffrage system a fifth electoral class, composed of all adult males in Austria, aroused such great opposition among his supporters as to cause his resignation from office. He left the Emperor in a much stronger personal position than he had found him, but his period of rule contributed nothing toward a solution of the Austrian problem.

In the sixties Austria began to be really affected by the Industrial Revolution. Old industries increased their output, new manufacturing establishments developed, large-scale factories made their appearance, many stock companies and banks came into existence. The Austrian provinces, particularly Bohemia, became a center for the manufacture of textiles, glassware, porcelain, chemicals, and paper. Large breweries, operated by steam-power, drove out the former small establishments. About 1860 Austria began to produce refined mineral oil and paraffin. As in other countries, the development of manufacturing stimulated the mining of coal and iron ore, the building of machinery, and the spread of the new means of transportation and communication. After 1852 shipping, aided by government subsidies, rapidly increased on the Danube and its tributaries. Three years later the government began to subsidize the Lloyd Line of steamships. After 1870 this steamship company began to send vessels to the Far East and to America.

The economic transformation of Austria greatly modified the political situation. The government found itself unable to refuse the demand for a democratization of the suffrage. In 1896 it added a fifth class of voters to the suffrage by giving the vote to all male subjects of the Emperor who were twenty-four years of age. Ten years later it abandoned the complicated system of five electoral classes and established universal manhood suffrage. New parties, Agrarian, Socialist, and Christian Socialist, for the achievement of definite economic programs, also made their appearance. After 1906, however, national feeling made it impossible for the Socialists of the different nationalities to meet together in harmony.

5

HUNGARY AFTER 1867

In Hungary the Compromise of 1867 put in force again the constitution formulated in 1848. In his Hungarian Kingdom, consequently, Francis Joseph enjoyed only the powers of a carefully restricted constitutional monarch. Ministers responsible to the Hungarian parliament controlled the administration of the country and a parliament of two houses, known as the Table of Magnates and the Table of Deputies, exercised legislative power. The regulations concerning the suffrage made the Magyars dominant over the Slovaks of northern Hungary, the Rumanians of Transylvania, and the Croats and Serbs of southern Hungary.

Immediately after the adoption of the Compromise of 1867 the non-Magyar peoples of Hungary began to protest against their domination by the Magyars. The Croats demanded the historic rights of Croatia. The Rumanians protested against the destruction of the separate institutions of Transylvania and refused to take part in the Hungarian political life. In 1869 representatives of the Slovaks, the Ruthenians, and the Rumanians met and proclaimed the federation of the non-Magyar nationalities. The strength of this movement of protest forced the Magyars to compromise with the Croats, the strongest of the protesting nationalities.

The compromise concluded in 1868 between the political leaders of the Croats and the Magyars purported to safeguard the interests of the Southern Slavs of Croatia and Slavonia. It provided that the Kingdom of Croatia should have five representatives in the Hungarian contingent to the Austro-Hungarian Delegations, three members in the Hungarian Table of Magnates, and forty in the Table of Deputies. It limited the authority of the Hungarian parliament over the Kingdom of Croatia to such matters as the army, trade, and finance, recognized the Croatian tongue as the official language of Croatia, and gave the subordinate state a large measure of autonomy.

The Compromise of 1868 by no means satisfied the political ambitions of the Croats. They desired to annex to their state the port of Fiume, the district known as the Serbian Military Frontier, and the Austrian province of Dalmatia, and to transform the Dual Monarchy into a triune state in which the Southern Slavs would hold a position of equality with the Magyars and the Germans. The lack of unity between the Croats and Serbs and the opposition of the Magyars and the Austrian Germans stood in the way of the dreams of the Croats until the break-up of the Dual Monarchy in 1918.

As long as Francis Deák lived the Magyar leaders made some show of treating the minor nationalities of Hungary with consideration. At his insistence, in 1868 the Hungarian parliament passed a law that conceded to the minor nationalities of the kingdom the right to use their own language, to found schools and societies, and to be judged and administered by officials able to converse in the tongue of the litigant and the taxpayer. After the death of Deák in 1875, the selection of Count Andrássy for the post of Chancellor of Austria-Hungary, and the rise of Count Tisza to political leadership in Hungary, the Hungarian government began a policy of Magyarization designed to exterminate the identity of the other nationalities of the state and to incorporate their members into the Magyar nation. It began to treat educated men who failed to use the Magyar tongue as traitors, to close the Slovak and Rumanian schools, to confiscate the funds devoted to the propagation of the language and literature of the minor nationalities, to gerrymander parliamentary districts and manipulate elections in favor of the Magyars. In order to force the subject nationalities to learn the official language of the state the government used only Magyar in the railroad, post-office, and telegraph services. The political leaders of the Magyars continued to follow this policy until the dismemberment of Hungary at the close of the World War.

The policy of Magyarization, however, failed to achieve its purpose. For a time after the formation of the Dual Monarchy political discrimination, heavy taxes, the competition of American agricultural and industrial products, the destructive effect of large-scale manufacturing on hand-industries, and the usury of Jewish money-lenders threatened to overwhelm the Slovaks. After 1874, however, the Slovaks began to emigrate to America and their situation in northern Hungary began to improve. The returned emigrants and the money sent back by those who stayed in America stimulated the resistance of the Slovaks. Newspapers multiplied in spite of press trials and heavy fines and court expenses, education increased, and the Slovaks began to prosper. By the end of the World War they were ready to take a place beside the kindred Czechs in the new state of Czechoslovakia.

In 1883 the Hungarian government suspended the Compromise of 1868, but the repressive régime introduced in the province failed to prevent the growth of the Southern Slav movement. In Transylvania the Rumanians also kept up the struggle against Magyarization. In 1881 an assembly of one hundred and fifty Rumanian delegates drew up a political program that called for a loyal fulfilment of existing laws, state aid to Rumanian schools, the appointment of Rumanians as officials, and the restoration of autonomy to Transylvania. Later the Rumanian leaders made an unsuccessful attempt to present their grievances directly to their sovereign; this brought down upon them a famous trial for the crime of "incitement against the Magyar nationality." About the same time they founded the League for the Cultural Unity of all Rumanians. Like the Slovaks, the Rumanians founded banks and coöperative societies to promote their economic advancement, and an intellectual class proud of its national origin began to develop. After 1906 the Rumanians ceased their policy of passive resistance and began to participate in Hungarian politics. The policy of Magyarization thus merely widened the breach between the dominant Magyars and the subject nationalities.

6

AUSTRIA-HUNGARY AFTER 1867

The two halves of the Dual Monarchy had a common history as well as separate histories. As soon as the political leaders of the monarchy had set in operation the new political machinery in Austria and Hungary they began to consider the question of expansion in the Balkan peninsula. The decisive victory of Prussia over France in 1870 seemed to put an end to Austria's hopes of regaining her former position in Italy and Germany. The opening of the Suez Canal, the weakness and disorders of the Turkish Empire, and the opportunities for economic expansion seemed to beckon Austria-Hungary eastward. From the outbreak of the revolt in Bosnia and Herzegovina in 1875 the political leaders of the Dual Monarchy scrutinized with the closest care every political and military move affecting the Balkan peninsula. They opposed the Treaty of San Stefano, dictated by Russia at the close of the war of 1876 to 1877 with Turkey, forced the Russian government to submit the Balkan problem to the Congress of Berlin in 1878, and finally persuaded the assembled powers to authorize the occupation of Bosnia and Herzegovina by Austria-Hungary.

The new foreign policy increased the difficulties of the political leaders of the Dual Monarchy. The army sent into the two provinces met with stubborn resistance from the Moslems and the Orthodox Serbs. Many of the Magyars and the Austrian Germans opposed the strengthening of the Slavic element in the monarchy. The Serbian government watched with the greatest indignation the seizure of lands that it had long looked upon as its rightful heritage.

From the time of their occupation in 1879 until their formal annexation in 1908 Bosnia and Herzegovina had a peculiar political status. They remained under the nominal suzerainty of the Ottoman Empire but under the actual control of Austria-Hungary. As neither half of the Dual Monarchy desired to increase the number of its Slavic deputies in the parliament, Austria and Hungary governed the two provinces jointly. The common Minister of Finance supervised their administration and the Austro-Hungarian delegations defrayed any administrative expenses not met by local taxation. In the thirty years of its rule Austria-Hungary transformed the wild provinces into a civilized state.

The occupation of the two provinces increased the danger from the Southern Slav movement. In books, pamphlets, and the press the Southern Slavs urged the necessity of revising the Compromise of 1867 and reorganizing the Dual Monarchy. British, French, German, and Austrian publicists brought the problem to the attention of the general public. All agreed on the impossibility of maintaining the Dual Monarchy, but they seriously disagreed as to the proper solution for the problem. A majority of the Southern Slavs within Austria-Hungary carried on an agitation for a union of the Southern Slav provinces into a third state of the monarchy. This proposal seems to have won the sympathy of the heir to the Austro-Hungarian throne but encountered the determined opposition of the Magyars. The latter regarded the proposal as a threat to the unity of the Magyar state and to the power of the Magyar nation in the Dual Monarchy.

After 1903 the various branches of the Southern Slavs showed signs of forgetting their differences and drawing together. The Croat and Slovene students of Professor Thomas Masaryk at the University of Prague gradually came to regard each other as brothers. In 1905 a conference of Croatian deputies from Croatia, Istria, and Dalmatia met at Fiume and adopted a resolution demanding national unity. A few days later a group of Serbian deputies from Dalmatia met at Zara and confirmed the Fiume resolution on the condition that the equality of the Serbs and the Croats should be recognized. A month later representatives of both groups met at Zara and declared that the Serbs and Croats formed one nation. They followed up this action by forming a political coalition which thereafter dominated the Croatian parliament. In 1912 the Southern Slav agitation began to affect the less demonstrative Slovenes. In that year an assembly met at Laibach and resolved to work for the union of the Slovene lands with the Kingdom of Croatia.

After 1903 the leaders of Austria-Hungary began to fear that the development of Serbia would attract their Southern Slav subjects and ultimately break up the monarchy. In that year a band of army officers broke into the palace and murdered the pro-Austrian King of Serbia and his unpopular wife and put in his place King Peter of the Karageorgevich family, who followed an independent political policy. Great numbers of Southern Slavs from Austria-Hungary flocked to the coronation of the new Serbian sovereign who had fought to free Herzegovina from Turkish oppression, and many Southern Slavs of the Dual Monarchy came to look upon a union of all the Southern Slavs under the leadership of Serbia as the best solution of their difficulties.

In alarm at this development, the leaders in Austria-Hungary decided to take vigorous action against the leaders of her Southern Slav subjects. In the latter part of 1908 they brought a charge of conspiracy against fifty-three members of the Croatian parliament and convicted thirty-one of them by the use of methods and evidence that created a scandal. In self-defense the government submitted the evidence to a patriotic historian, who became convinced of the disloyalty of the leaders of the Southern Slavs to the monarchy. The opponents of the Austro-Hungarian authorities, however, immediately proved by a libel suit the inaccuracy of the documents, forced the learned historian to make a public apology, and finally demonstrated that the documents were forgeries originating in the Austro-Hungarian legation at Belgrade. The exposure of the fraudulent methods employed by the government increased the unrest of all the Southern Slavs of the monarchy and led to the passage, in 1912, of a resolution in the Croatian parliament demanding the separation of Croatia from Hungary.

The Balkan Wars of 1912 and 1913 greatly increased the anxiety of the leaders of Austria-Hungary. Upon the outbreak of the wars Southern Slav volunteers in large numbers slipped over the Serbian border, and Croats, Serbs, and Slovenes collected funds and staged political demonstrations. The unexpected victories of Serbia against the Turks and the Bulgarians aroused their pride and caused many of them to turn their eyes toward the rising Serbian state for political salvation. By 1914 the political leaders of the Dual Monarchy found themselves confronted with the alternative of political dissolution or a revolutionary reorganization.

The domestic history of Austria-Hungary from 1860 to 1914 conclusively demonstrated the inability of the imperial authorities to solve the Austrian problem. They could find no form of government that satisfied the ten nationalities of the empire. The October Diploma pleased only the Czechs and the Poles. The constitution of 1861 satisfied only the Austrian Germans. The compromise of 1867 met the demands of only the Magyars and the Austrian Germans. All the subject peoples—the Czechs, the Slovaks, the Poles, the Italians, the Rumanians, and the Southern Slavs—created difficult problems for the two ruling nationalities to solve. After 1903 the Southern Slav problem threatened the Dual Monarchy with the alternative of reorganization or dismemberment.

CHAPTER XVIII

ITALY, 1861–1914

The stirring events of the years of political and territorial unification left the Italian people with many vital problems to be solved. They looked upon several of the adjoining provinces as parts of their rightful heritage. They still had to achieve spiritual unity and lacked many modern institutions. Their pride stimulated them to attempt to be a great power.

I

ITALY IN 1861

The series of dramatic events that occurred in the Italian peninsula between 1859 and 1861 placed under the rule of one government a people divided by geography, history, culture, and language. They had been separated politically for centuries. They spoke seventeen different dialects and frequently could scarcely understand each other. The population of northern and parts of central Italy had long enjoyed good government and a relatively high stage of culture. The inhabitants of southern Italy had suffered for hundreds of years from oppression, misgovernment, and exploitation. There had not been sufficient development of the press, literature, the railroad, the telegraph, and commerce to fuse the Italians into one people.

The new state inherited terrible social and economic conditions. In southern Italy brigandage flourished. Many districts suffered from malaria. The whole peninsula lacked hospitals, medical service, and schools; 68 per cent of the people over five years of age were unable to read or write. The mass of the people maintained a very low standard of living. The general ignorance of the people, the character of the soil, and the lack of resources all stood in the way of industrial and agricultural progress. One tenth of the soil was entirely sterile and three fifths of it produced very little. The country lacked cattle, agricultural machinery, iron, coal, and capital. The numerous tariff barriers had hindered the development of commerce. Only two thousand one hundred and eighty-nine kilometers of railway, nearly half of which were in the province of Piedmont, had been built.

The process of unifying Italy had created difficulties for the new state. Garibaldi, the popular hero, sulked on his little island estate because of the treatment accorded to himself and his volunteers by the regular Sardinian army. Loyal Roman Catholics held aloof from national politics because of the seizure of papal territory. The partizans of the former governments of the peninsula plotted against the new state and abetted the lawless brigands of southern Italy in their crimes. The Austrian government had not forgotten the dismemberment of its empire for the benefit of the new kingdom. The Pope and the Catholic political parties and states of Europe resented the seizure of the Papal States by Italy and held over the new kingdom the menace of foreign intervention. The majority of Frenchmen considered the creation of the new Italian Kingdom a blunder on the part of Napoleon III and regarded it with unconcealed hostility. The desire of the majority of the Italian people to complete the unification of Italy by the annexation of the city of Rome, a territory held for the Pope by a French garrison, and the Austrian provinces of Venetia, Trieste, and Southern Tyrol complicated a situation already highly delicate.

Before the Italian people had time to turn their attention to these difficult problems they lost their accomplished leader. On June 6, 1861, death struck down Cavour, the creator of Italian unity. A succession of men of lesser mold struggled with only moderate success with the problems which he left unsolved.

2

THE DOMESTIC POLICIES OF THE NEW GOVERNMENT

The new Italian state took over the laws and political system of the Kingdom of Sardinia. The constitution which Charles Albert had granted in 1848 to meet the demands of his agitated subjects was extended to the new kingdom. This gave the new Italian state a ministry responsible to a parliament composed of a Senate made up of ex-officio and appointed members and a Chamber of Deputies elected by a franchise that permitted only about 2.5 per cent of the population to vote. The Napoleonic traditions of the peninsula and the need of consolidating the new kingdom caused the new government to adopt the French administrative system with its hierarchy of administrative divisions and its centralization of authority in the hands of the Minister of the Interior. Because of the great power wielded by this official and the multiplicity of parties, the parliamentary system often failed in practice to work satisfactorily in Italy.

As soon as it had been set up the new government commenced an attack on the brigandage rampant in southern Italy. Economic poverty and chronic misgovernment had long made the bandit a common and popular figure in the former Kingdom of Naples. In spite of its ignominious record, the former government also left many partizans in southern Italy. Under the protection of the French garrison at Rome the Neapolitan Bourbons used these rebels and brigands to foment trouble for the new Italian government. Unable to strike directly at the root of the trouble and hampered by lack of money and by the attitude of the civilian population, the government found itself forced to carry on its war against brigandage for several years.

The balancing of the budget proved an even longer and more difficult task. The new Kingdom of Italy assumed the debts of the states and provinces that it incorporated and made heavy expenditures for the army and navy, public education, the construction of roads, railroads, and telegraph-lines, the War of 1866 against Austria, and the campaign of 1870 against Rome. Taxation did not meet these demands on the treasury and the government resorted to loans and to issues of paper money to balance the budget. It did not succeed in making the revenues equal the expenditures until 1875.

Another difficult problem for the government was the demand of a determined party of Italian patriots, headed by Garibaldi, for the immediate annexation of Rome and Venetia. Disregarding the certainty of provoking war with Austria and France, the leaders of this party formed a committee to collect funds and to enroll volunteers. In 1862 they organized a society for the emancipation of Italy and prepared for an attack on Rome and Venice. The government averted the danger only by despatching an armed force to stop the northward march of Garibaldi from Palermo. Two years later it negotiated an agreement with the government of France which provided that during the next two years the French garrison should gradually evacuate the city of Rome, on condition that Italy agreed to establish its capital permanently at Florence. This compromise settled nothing. The partizans of the Pope in France criticized the concessions made by Napoleon III to the Italian government. The Italian people resented the intervention of the French Emperor in an Italian domestic question and looked upon the removal of the capital to Florence as merely a step toward Rome. The inhabitants of Turin, the old capital of the Kingdom of Sardinia, broke out into disastrous riots over the blow to their dignity and prosperity. The Pope issued a sweeping condemnation of modern ideas and institutions known as the *Syllabus of Errors*.

3

THE ACQUISITION OF VENETIA AND ROME

Just at the moment when the prospects for acquiring the unredeemed provinces seemed darkest, however, Bismarck gave the Italian government an opportunity to annex Venetia. In 1866 he offered the province to Italy as a reward for her assistance in the war brewing between Austria and Prussia for the hegemony of Germany. Although the Italian military and naval operations against Austria ended disastrously, the spectacular Prussian victory at Königgrätz enabled Bismarck to force the Austrian government to agree to hand over the province of Venetia to Napoleon III for cession to the Kingdom of Italy.

The unexpected acquisition of Venetia intensified the agitation in Italy for a solution of the Roman question. In 1867 Garibaldi left his solitary home on the island of Caprera and led a band of volunteers against Rome. The expedition succeeded in defeating the papal troops but proved unequal to the task of warding off the attacks of the French troops that had occupied the city. To avoid foreign complications, the Italian government again intervened, disbanding the volunteer force gathered by Garibaldi and temporarily imprisoning its leader. In spite of this defeat, however, the Italian patriots had to wait only three years for the annexation of Rome. The defeat and capture of Napoleon III and his army at Sedan in 1870 forced the new provisional government of France to withdraw the French garrison at Rome. This enabled the Italian government to seize the city and transfer the capital of the state from Florence to Rome.

4

THE RESULTS OF THE SEIZURE OF ROME

The occupation of Rome by the military forces of Italy gave great satisfaction to a large section of the Italian people but embittered relations between the Church and the new Italian state. The Pope took the natural position that he had been illegally deprived of his temporal possessions. The Italian government attempted to placate the Pope by passing the Law of Papal Guarantees. This legislation recognized the papal claim to sovereign honors and prerogatives, declared the person of the Pope sacred and inviolable, conceded him a large annual revenue and the use of the Vatican and Lateran palaces and the villa Gandolfo, assured conclaves and ecumenical councils the fullest liberty, absolved Italian bishops from taking an oath of allegiance to the King of Italy, promised the Pope complete freedom in the exercise of his spiritual functions, gave foreign envoys accredited to the papal court the usual diplomatic privileges, and permitted the presence of postal and telegraphic services in the Vatican free of tax or expense. But the Pope refused to accept the compensation proffered by the Italian government and in a note issued two days after the publication of the law called on the European powers to restore his temporal power. Thenceforth he regarded himself as a prisoner in the Vatican and refused to accept the offered annual income.

The adoption of this policy by the Pope created difficulties for the Italian government. The papacy forbade Catholic rulers to return the official visits of the sovereign of Italy and made it hard for the Italian government to cultivate good relations with neighboring states. The papal appeal obtained a sympathetic hearing from the Catholic parties of Europe and caused the Italian government for years to fear foreign intervention in Italian affairs. The attitude of the Pope also made Italian Catholics hesitate to participate in the political life of the kingdom. In 1878 the papal authorities declared it inexpedient for Italian Catholics to take part in parliamentary elections. The failure of the Italian government to come to terms with the papacy isolated and hampered it at every turn and removed from Italian political life some of the best elements in the Italian nation.

The occupation of Rome also gave an impetus to the demands for the acquisition of other lands of Italian speech not yet incorporated in the Kingdom of Italy. The movement numbered among its adherents the leaders of all the parties not in power and its secret sympathizers included men of every rank, from the King to the humblest of his subjects. In the name of Italian unity the leaders of the agitation laid claim to Trieste, Southern Tyrol, and much of the eastern shore of the Adriatic Sea.

5

ITALIAN POLITICS AFTER 1861

Upon the death of Cavour his followers divided into parliamentary groups known as the Right and the Left. At first the Right controlled the government. Its members belonged to the aristocracy and came for the most part from northern Italy, a region that had long enjoyed good government and orderly society. During their tenure of office the leaders of the Right continued to some extent the political traditions of the Kingdom of Sardinia. However, after they had set in motion the new political machinery, suppressed brigandage, annexed Venetia and Rome, and balanced the budget, they seemed to regard their work as completed.

In 1876 they made way for the Left. The coming into office of this party inaugurated a new era in Italian politics. Originating in southern Italy and starting political life as followers of Mazzini, the members of the party inherited a different political tradition. While in opposition to the government they had declaimed much concerning the reduction of taxes and the enlargement of personal liberty. After assuming office they did little to fulfil their promises and much toward the introduction into Italian politics of the unhealthy political life of southern Italy. They used the governmental machinery to influence elections, bought constituencies with railways and public works, bribed members of the parliament, and intrigued with the different parliamentary groups. At times strikes, bank scandals, and the Socialist agitation seemed to threaten the foundation of the state and necessitated the proroguing of the parliament, the illegal collection of taxes, and the proclamation of martial law.

In spite of inadequate leadership, however, the Italian people made progress after 1861 toward the solution of the perplexing problems confronting them. The adoption of the principle of universal military service in 1875 threw the recruits from different regions together and acquainted them with their country by transferring them from garrison to garrison. The development of a railway system bound the various provinces together with bands of steel and promoted the movement of the population. The spread of education gave the Italian people a common literary language and a common intellectual heritage. Foreign wars and colonial ventures stimulated the growth of national pride. These forces gradually knit the Italian people together into a nation.

6

THE ECONOMIC DEVELOPMENT OF ITALY

The new Kingdom of Italy made slow progress in its struggle against the obstacles that hampered its economic development. Until 1873 the statistics of agriculture, manufactures, and commerce indicated a steady improvement of economic conditions. The world-wide financial crisis of that year, however, affected production and trade unfavorably for the next half-decade. Then from about 1878 until 1887 Italy resumed her economic development. In 1888 the progress made by the doctrine of protection and strained diplomatic relations led to the outbreak of a tariff war between France and Italy, which lasted twenty-two months and caused a marked economic depression for the next ten years. As a result of the loss of the French market both exports and imports declined and agriculture suffered severely. Protection, however, enabled certain industries to capture the home market. From about 1898 until the severe depression of 1907 Italy shared in the general improvement of world business conditions. Nevertheless a half-century of economic development left Italy still a poor country.

Throughout this period agriculture, the basic Italian industry, improved steadily. The central and local governments drained over a million and a half acres of swamp and marshland and made many malarial areas usable for agriculture. In northern Italy, particularly, the peasants improved their stock, adopted better implements, practised rotation of crops more extensively, and increased their use of fertilizers. In 1872 a village priest started a coöperative dairy and initiated a movement that gradually revolutionized the production of butter and cheese in the northern provinces of Italy. After 1883 village banks began to loan money to responsible peasants at low rates of interest. About the same time the peasants commenced to organize coöperative societies for the purchase of seeds, implements, and fertilizers at cost. As a result of these developments Italy produced 30 per cent more wheat in 1911 than in 1861, 50 per cent more wine, doubled the value of its agricultural products, and tripled the value of its cattle.

The Italian Industrial Revolution scarcely got under way until after the adoption of a protective-tariff policy. The manufacturers of silk gradually developed an industry that consumed most of the raw silk produced in Italy and considerable quantities of imported silk. In the thirty years preceding the World War the output of the cotton-mills of Italy increased fifteenfold. Her iron and steel establishments eventually supplied the domestic demand for railway equipment, armor, and artillery. In time the Italian electrical industry met the needs of the home market. Turin, Milan, and Genoa finally became centers for the manufacture of automobiles. Italy, however, never attained the industrial strength of France, Germany, or Great Britain.

Italy also made great strides in the development of means of transportation and communication. Between 1861 and 1911 the mileage of her roads tripled, the number of her steamers rose from fifty-seven to six hundred and fifty, the length of her telegraph-lines mounted from five thousand to thirty-five thousand miles, and the trackage of her railroads increased nearly tenfold. This improvement in transportation and communication opened the way for the development of a stronger national feeling, an improvement in economic conditions, the penetration of new ideas, and the emigration of the surplus population.

7

THE SOCIAL DEVELOPMENT OF ITALY

The poverty of the country, the slowness of its economic development, the diversion of available funds to the construction of public works, the increase in armaments, and the attempt to develop a colonial empire prevented a rapid conquest of Italian illiteracy. In 1861, 68 per cent of the population could not read or write, the government spent a wholly inadequate sum on elementary education, and among European countries only Portugal ranked higher than Italy in illiteracy. Education was only nominally compulsory for children between the ages of six and ten. As late as 1895 the elementary schools reached only 74 per cent of the children and whole districts lacked regular school buildings and adequate equipment. In 1901 statistics indicated that nearly half of the population was still unable to read and write. The illiteracy of the different regions, however, varied from 3 per cent in certain parts of northern Italy to 75 per cent in some provinces of southern Italy. In 1911 the Italian parliament lengthened the school year, transferred the control of elementary education from the hampering influence of the communes to the central government, and improved the situation of the teachers in the elementary schools. By that year the government was spending seven times as much for elementary education as it had fifty years earlier.

The Italian government also met with considerable success in its efforts to improve the health of its subjects. In fifty years it lowered the death-rate from thirty to twenty per thousand. It decreased the deaths from smallpox from five hundred and thirty-four to thirteen per million, those from scarlet fever from three hundred and thirty-seven to eighty-seven, those from diphtheria from eight hundred and twenty-five to one hundred and sixty-seven, those from typhoid fever from eight hundred and eighty-six to two hundred and twenty-five, and those from malaria from five hundred and ninety-five to one hundred and twenty-five. Italy owed these remarkable improvements in health to the draining of her swamps and marshes, the distribution of quinine in malarial regions, the substitution of trained scientists for politicians in the enforcement of health regulations, the building of three thousand aqueducts for the improvement of water-supplies, the inspection of food, housing, and cemeteries, and by requiring the residence of a doctor in every town.

8

THE GROWTH OF A SOCIALIST PARTY

The slow growth of manufacturing hindered the progress of Socialism in Italy. At first the party included quite diverse elements—anarchists, Socialists, and followers of Garibaldi—and numbered only about ten thousand persons. In 1872 it held its first national conference. After the extension of the suffrage in 1882 the Socialists succeeded in electing a number of deputies to the parliament. In 1891 they definitely separated themselves from the anarchists and organized a veritable political party and established a Socialist journal. Four years later the Socialist Congress voted in favor of political coöperation with Republicans and Radicals. In 1904 this question split the party asunder into a Reformist and a Revolutionary wing, but the believers in political evolution triumphed over the orthodox followers of Karl Marx. In 1911 a member of the Reformist wing of the Socialist party entered the ministry and two years later the King named three Socialists as senators. In the meantime the popular vote of the Socialists and their representation in the parliament grew steadily. By the time of the outbreak of the World War they could command forty-four seats in the Chamber of Deputies and a quarter of the popular vote.

This growth of Socialism caused the papacy to change its policy toward the participation of Roman Catholics in Italian politics. Many earnest Catholics had long resented the hostility of the Pope toward the new Kingdom of Italy and the passage of time had softened somewhat the irritation of the papacy over the seizure of the temporal possessions of the Pope and its unheard demands for compensation. With the growth of the Socialists in numbers both the Church and the propertied classes felt menaced. In the face of the supposed danger many Roman Catholics began to support government candidates against representatives of the radical parties. Finally in 1893 the Pope practically revoked his earlier prohibition against the participation of Roman Catholics in parliamentary elections and enjoined them to rally to the defense of the existing social order. As a result of this change of policy a Catholic party came into being, which in 1913 obtained thirty-five seats in the Chamber of Deputies. The new party opposed Socialism, divorce, and the secularization of the state. The entrance of both the Socialists and the Catholics into the political life of the state tended to purify and improve Italian politics.

The growth and coöperation of the Republican, Radical, and Socialist parties resulted in further extension of the suffrage. In 1912 a new electoral law practically established adult male suffrage. This legislation trebled the electorate but thrust the ballot on an illiterate population unprepared to vote intelligently.

9

ITALIAN EMIGRATION

The economic situation in Italy, the steady increase in Italian population, the development of better means of transportation, and the opening of opportunities for work and settlement led to a remarkable movement of emigration that resulted within half a century in the departure of sixteen to seventeen millions of Italians for the neighboring countries of Europe, northern Africa, and North and South America. Four million of this immense host remained permanently in the countries to which they emigrated. The remainder finally returned to Italy.

In Europe great numbers of Italians sought temporary employment in France, Germany, Switzerland, Austria-Hungary, and the Balkan states, after the opening of railway connections along the French and the Italian Rivieras and through the passes of the Alps. They established large colonies in France at Marseilles, at Paris, and in the mining districts of Lorraine, replaced the diminishing agricultural labor forces of France, and did much of the heavy toil in French industries and construction work. By 1911 nearly half a million Italians had found their way into the country. In Germany they migrated particularly into southern and western Germany, nearly two hundred thousand finding work in German mines and industries. An equal number penetrated into Switzerland to do much of the heavy labor on the new tunnels and railways and in the mines and factories. By 1914 nearly one hundred thousand Italians found permanent employment in Austrian territory, in spite of their traditional hostility for the Hapsburg state. In the Balkan peninsula Italians did much of the hard work of constructing railroads and public works. The great majority of these emigrants to neighboring European states were seasonal workers, seeking to buy a patch of ground or to improve their economic status in other ways, by finding temporary employment. Not more than a tenth of them found permanent homes abroad.

Northern Africa attracted great numbers of other Italian emigrants. In Egypt they helped to construct the Suez Canal and the great dams and bridges across the Nile and added an important contingent to the motley throng of clerks, retail dealers, and adventurers. In Tripoli few Italians found a foothold until after the conquest of the province by Italy in 1911. In Tunis they largely built the railroads and public works, fished the adjoining waters, and settled in the cities as professional men, merchants, and craftsmen. By 1914 the presence of possibly one hundred and thirty thousand Italians in the province gave rise to the saying that Tunis was an Italian colony guarded by French soldiers. In Algeria the Italians numbered more than forty-four thousand.

In South America the immigrants from Italy obtained a remarkable foothold in Argentina and Brazil. In the former state they and their children probably constitute a third of the whole population. Enticed by the circulars and agents of the Argentine government and fired by the prospect of better economic conditions, they largely made possible the economic renaissance of Argentina. They made their adopted country one of the great wheat-exporting countries of the world, controlled the shipping of the La Plata River and its branches, furnished most of the unskilled labor in the cities, and made important contributions to the crafts, trades, and professions. One member of the Italian race rose to the Presidency of Argentina. In Brazil the Italian immigrants met with less social and economic success. They suffered from the over-production and patriarchal organization of the coffee-plantations and often encountered insuperable obstacles in pioneer farming. In 1910 an authority estimated the total number of Italians in Brazil at a million and a half.

Italian emigrants came in immense numbers to the United States, but they arrived too late to modify its civilization seriously. In the first ten years after 1861 only a few over twelve thousand came to the United States. They came with the intention of becoming permanent residents. Later a large proportion of the Italian immigrants came with the purpose of accumulating a small fortune and returning home. In spite of a steady increase in Italian immigration after 1870, the census-enumerators of 1900 found less than half a million Italians in the United States. Although two million arrived during the next decade, ten years later the census-takers discovered only a little over one million three hundred thousand Italians still in the country. In the main they have done the heavy tasks and the unskilled work; they have suffered from oppression, exploitation, and their own lawlessness; and they have con-tributed to the congestion and insanitation of many American cities.

This great tide of emigrants profoundly affected the country from which they departed as well as the states to which they went. They either sent or brought back to Italy considerable amounts of capital. The returning emigrants came back to their homes with new ideas and new experiences. They no longer naïvely assumed that they be-longed to the first nation of the world, but in many cases recognized the superior conditions which they had found in other countries. The steady flow of emigrants abroad stimulated the development of a mer-chant marine, increased the importance of Italy as a world power, gave rise to diplomatic disputes with other states, furnished a powerful ar-gument for the acquisition of a colonial empire, reënforced the claims of Italy to the eastern coast of the Adriatic Sea, and supplied an ex-panding market for Italian commodities.

After 1861 the Italian people turned from the task of achieving the political unification of their state to the work of achieving spiritual unity and acquiring modern institutions. They found themselves handi-capped at first by disunion, political corruption, lack of resources, brigandage, ignorance, disease, and poverty. In the end they conquered banditry, diminished disease and ignorance, balanced the budget, im-proved agriculture, developed modern industries, acquired important parts of unredeemed Italy, welded themselves into a nation, and sent a vigorous stock to aid in the building of other states in Europe, Africa, and America. By depriving the Pope of his temporal possessions, however, the Italian government created a problem of the greatest difficulty.

CHAPTER XIX

RUSSIA, 1856–1914

Until the disasters of the Crimean War the power of Russia seemed indisputable both to the Russian ruling classes and to the other states of Europe. That conflict disclosed to all the defects of the political and social system maintained by Nicholas I. With a million soldiers and the resources of Russia at his disposal, he found himself unable to prevent the capture of the fortress of Sebastopol by an allied army of seventy thousand men. The ox-carts of Russia could not compete with the locomotives and steam-driven vessels of France and Great Britain in supplying the needs of the fighting front. The backward medical and sanitary services of the Russian Empire could not cope with the diseases let loose in the southern provinces by the war. The repressive political system deprived the army of the needed technical experts and of commanders of initiative, and fostered ignorance and corruption. The sudden revelation of these facts convinced even the ruling classes of Russia of the necessity of making concessions to the demands for reform.

I

A DECADE OF REFORM

The imperial government took up first the problem of the freeing of the serfs. It initiated the movement by requesting the nobles to present their ideas on the subject to a main committee. This action started a discussion that quickly disclosed the complexity of the problem. The landowners of the fertile, densely populated districts of central and southern Russia advocated the freeing of the peasants without compensation. This would relieve the owners of the large estates from the heavy burden of maintaining the peasants, permit them to retain their valuable lands, and insure them a plentiful supply of cheap labor. In the northern provinces of Russia, on the contrary, the landlords derived most of their income from the payments made by the peasants for permission to leave the estates and work in the towns and factories. The owners in this region, consequently, although they offered no objection to the assignment of a portion of their estates to their peasants, asked for a high compensation for the threatened loss of income. Many proprietors also still opposed the whole idea of freeing the serfs. These conflicting points of view made extremely difficult the work of the officials, committees, and commissions charged with drafting the legislation designed to free the serfs.

On February 19, 1861, in a long and complex decree containing hundreds of articles, the imperial government finally proclaimed the emancipation of the serfs. This piece of legislation abolished serfdom but did not give the Russian peasants the same civil rights as other classes of society. It freed, after two more years of service, the peasants personally attached to the nobles but transferred to the communes, working under the supervision of an agent of the central government, much of the authority hitherto exercised by the landlords over the peasants on private estates. These administrative units henceforth assessed the share of the peasant in the common burden of taxation and controlled the granting of the passport indispensable to the peasant wishing to seek work outside of his village. In cases where the land had been held in common the commune assigned to each peasant household a share in the communal lands to cultivate. The peasants in the newly colonized steppe region of southern Russia and in the industrial provinces of the north received more arable land than those living in the rich, densely populated black-soil area. In most cases the freed peasant obtained less land than he had cultivated as a serf and found himself compelled to supplement his income by working for his former master. On an average the nearly ten million serfs on the private estates each received about nine acres of arable land. The government compensated the landlords for their losses by advancing them a sum equal to the income for a period of sixteen and two-thirds years of the lands assigned to the peasants and recovered its outlay from small annual payments made by the peasants. The nearly one million serfs on the royal appanages and the nearly eleven million on the state domains, always more fortunate than their fellow-peasants on the private estates, obtained their freedom in 1863 and 1866 and received on an average twelve and seventeen acres of land respectively.

The imperial authorities foresaw that the emancipation of the serfs would necessitate changes in the system of local administration. To allow the proprietors to continue to maintain their monopoly of the police and the judicial posts in the local administration would jeopardize the new freedom of the peasants. The imperial government therefore replaced the patriarchal rule of the landlords with a system of district and provincial zemstvos. By a sort of three-class electoral system the landlords, the townsmen, and the peasants of a district chose delegates to a district council meeting once a year. This body elected an executive board for the district and the representatives of the districts to the provincial councils. These district and provincial zemstvos looked after the roads and the needs of agriculture, provided relief in famine years, and maintained elementary schools, hospitals, and charitable institutions. They enlisted the participation of the living forces in Russian society in the work of local government and gave the people of Russia some training in self-government.

In the same year in which it created the zemstvos the Russian government transformed the judicial system. The old courts differentiated between classes, subordinated the judiciary to the administration, permitted secret proceedings and archaic inquisitorial processes in criminal cases, reached a verdict without arguments from attorneys or parties to a suit, and reeked with bribery and abuses. The new legislation made trials public, provided for the formulation of accusations and the defense of the accused by an attorney, established trial by jury in most cases, and created the office of justice of the peace for the hearing of petty cases.

The decade following the Crimean War also witnessed some improvements in education. The government granted the universities a greater degree of autonomy and permitted students to have their meetings and organizations and to publish their own periodicals. In 1859 a few private secondary schools, supported by voluntary contributions, opened for women and a movement began among students, progressive army officers, and wealthy women for the opening of Sunday Schools for the secular and religious education of adults of the poorer classes. In 1862, however, the government suppressed these last schools because they were being employed for the spread of political propaganda. In the same year schools for women supported by contributions of the state began to be created. After 1864, also, the zemstvos began to do something for primary education, hitherto almost entirely neglected except by an occasional philanthropic proprietor. In 1870 a college for women was started at St. Petersburg and two years later one at Moscow.

In 1865 the government likewise slightly modified its rules and practice in regard to the censorship of books and periodicals. The new regulations freed books and the journals of St. Petersburg and Moscow from preliminary censorship. The shackled press welcomed even these slight concessions as a harbinger of better times.

The Crimean War disclosed the economic as well as the social and political defects of Russian society. In the three years immediately following that conflict, consequently, the government made a successful effort to improve transportation, credit facilities, and the economic organization of Russia. Although the construction of railways was begun in 1837, the line between Moscow and St. Petersburg was the only long railroad in operation in Russia at the time of the outbreak of the war in the Crimea. After the close of that struggle the government began to plan a network of railways for its European provinces. After 1866 Russian capitalists eagerly sought railway concessions. As a result of the efforts of the government and private individuals Russia possessed by 1875 a net of railways connecting the plains and coal-fields of Russia with the principal Russian cities and ports. In 1860, also, the government established the Imperial Bank and began to encourage Russian capitalists to establish private banks and societies of various sorts to extend credit. By introducing the principle of limited liability the government gave a great impetus to the formation of joint-stock companies. In the four years subsequent to 1859 the number of such companies quadrupled.

In the years following the Crimean War Russian industry did not keep pace with transportation and finance. The American Civil War and the abolition of serfdom both interfered with the progress of Russian manufactures. The struggle in America cut off the cotton-factories of Russia from their regular supplies of raw material and caused an actual decline in the number of such establishments. The freed serfs, employed in industry and mining, often proved to be lazy, drunken, and dishonest and showed a tendency to return to the land. These developments particularly hurt the mines and iron-works of the Ural region. After 1866, on the other hand, the Russian government gave a great impetus to manufacturing by requiring that the material and equipment needed for the new railways be purchased in Russia.

2

A NEW PERIOD OF REACTION

In 1866 an event occurred that put an end to the period of political and social reform. An unbalanced member of a society that advocated communistic ideas came to St. Petersburg from Moscow and fired a pistol at the Tsar. The attack convinced Alexander II, who at heart had always shared the views of his father, Nicholas I, of the danger of making concessions to the demands of the Russian reformers and initiated a period of reaction that lasted until the Revolution of 1905.

From 1866 onward, consequently, the imperial government attempted to hold the growing Liberal movement in check by control of the schools, the new zemstvos and law-courts, and the press. Its new program for secondary education banished science from the curriculum, reduced the time devoted to modern languages and literatures, history, and geography, and emphasized mathematics, Latin, Greek, and Church Slavonic. It completely deprived the teachers of their independence, encouraged students to spy on their instructors and fellow-students. It curtailed the activities and independence of the newly established zemstvos, and attempted to limit their discussions, to censor the accounts of their annual meetings, and to limit the attendance of the public at their sessions. It threatened the freedom of the newly created law-courts by supervision of appointments, restrictions on the freedom of lawyers, attacks on the jury system, and removal of political cases from the jurisdiction of the courts. It subjected the provincial press to a strict preliminary censorship and watched the journals of Moscow and St. Petersburg with the greatest vigilance. This reactionary policy of the government produced a crisis among the advocates of reform.

As a result of the spread of education and the increased contact of Russia with western Europe the Russian reformers had been steadily growing in numbers. Their protests against existing conditions took many forms. The more enlightened and more generous of the nobles hoped for the gradual adoption by Russia of the political and social institutions of France and Great Britain and welcomed the freeing of the serfs, the organization of the zemstvos, the reform of the judicial system, and the removal of some of the restrictions on the press and the universities. They deprecated the abandonment of the policy of reform, but found themselves deprived of legal means to carry on a conflict with autocracy. The more moderate elements among the educated class continued the struggle through petitions and the zemstvos. The more radical defied the government and resorted to illegal propaganda and violence.

About 1861 an intellectual movement that came to be known as Nihilism had made its appearance in Russia. Its adherents aimed at the freeing of the individual from the prejudices, superstitions, and conventions of Russian life. Under the influence of the current scientific ideas of the day the Nihilists attacked mercilessly the family, society, and religion. They found many followers among the educated classes. The government replied to their attacks by suppressing their publications, banishing them from the universities, exiling them to Siberia, or driving them from the country.

But a policy of simple protest against existing conditions and institutions could not long satisfy the generous spirit of Russian youth. The younger generation began to discuss the duties of the individual. A literary school arose, in consequence, which described in a brilliant fashion the difficult position of the peasants who had just emerged from serfdom and emphasized the responsibility of the educated class to the people. It made the "embodiment of truth and justice in social forms" the slogan of the youth of Russia. Starting from this general principle, many schools of thought arose. Mikhail Bakunin maintained that the individual could become free only by liberating himself from religious beliefs and that economic and social freedom could be achieved only by the annihilation of the state, the abolition of the institutions of hereditary property, marriage, and the family, the transfer of the land to agricultural communes and of factories, capital, and the means of production to labor associations, the granting of equal rights to women, and the handing over of the education of children to the state. Another Russian leader maintained that the revolutionist was justified in ignoring all moral principles, and he organized a secret society which threw much discredit on the whole radical movement.

Under the influence of these writers generous-spirited young men and women began to go "to the people." They went to the villages of Russia as physicians, school-teachers, clerks, day-laborers, and nurses, for the purpose of helping the peasants out of their misery and ignorance. Their efforts at peaceful propaganda met with little success. The peasants failed to respond to their appeals and in some cases betrayed them to the police. The agents of the government tracked them down and arrested them in large numbers. The failure of this peaceful agitation caused the Russian radicals to split into two distinct parties, the advocates of peaceful propaganda and the Terrorists.

After 1878 acts of terrorism became increasingly frequent in Russia. Murders of spies and policemen became common and there were even attempts on the life of the Tsar. In November, 1879, the Terrorists tried to blow up the train bearing the ruler of Russia from the Crimea to St. Petersburg. A few months later they almost succeeded in destroying the whole royal family as they entered the dining-room of the Winter Palace. The Tsar attempted to meet the crisis by giving dictatorial powers to a commission headed by Loris Melikov and charged with the task of rooting out the revolutionary movement. This body respected the rights of the people, abolished unnecessary restrictions, and drew up plans for the organization of commissions for the drafting of new legislation and the submission of their proposals to consultative bodies composed of representatives of the zemstvos and the towns and commissioned to defend their projects before the Imperial Council—reforms which would have gone far toward satisfying the demands of the moderate Russian reformers. Before the new plan was published, however, the Terrorists succeeded in mortally wounding the Tsar by the explosion of a bomb as he was driving home from a military review.

3

REACTION FORMULATED INTO A POLITICAL THEORY

The assassination of Alexander II turned public sympathy away from the revolutionists and threw the government under the control of an extremely reactionary group of political leaders. The chief adviser of the new Tsar, Alexander III (1881–1894), and of his son and successor, Nicholas I, was Pobyedonostsev. He formulated reaction into a political theory. He asserted political liberty to be a failure, freedom of thought a humbug, education a dangerous thing, parliaments and other organs of self-government places for talk and nests of sordid selfishness, the new law-courts fields for the practice of the arts of casuistry, and the press an instrument for the spread of falsehoods and the arousal of public passions. Another theorist of reaction found the root of all the troubles of Russian society in the breaking down of the barriers between social classes that followed the emancipation of the serfs, and the remedy for the existing situation in the restoration of class distinctions. Under the influence of these reactionaries the government returned to the watchwords of Nicholas I—autocracy, orthodoxy, and nationalism.

Almost immediately the schools of Russia felt the effect of the new policies of the government. A new statute deprived the universities of their last vestige of autonomy, forbade student organizations, and ruthlessly punished by dismissal, imprisonment, and exile student activity in behalf of reform or revolution. In the secondary schools the government attempted to discourage the attendance of the members of the lower classes. Only its lack of funds prevented it from taking the primary schools out of the hands of the zemstvos and placing them under the control of the Church.

The government also openly displayed its hostility to the institutions created during the period of reform that followed the Crimean War. It issued decrees that carefully subordinated the zemstvos to the central government and insured the nobles a preponderance over the peasants in the district and provincial assemblies. It modified the new judicial system by restricting the authority of juries and handing over the work of the justices of the peace to administrative officials belonging to the nobility. It placed restrictions on the press that destroyed all but the most docile organs of opinion. It subjected journals to a preliminary censorship, stopped publications on account of "pernicious tendencies," and inflicted heavy penalties on editors and owners of papers that ventured to criticize the government.

The reactionary authorities persecuted all elements of Russian society that failed to conform in all particulars to Russian standards in origin, language, and religion. It denied the dissenters of Russia the right to practise freely the forms of their religion. In the Ukraine it suppressed the geographical society and forbade the use of the Little Russian language in journals or on the stage. In the Baltic provinces the Lutherans and the Germans lost many of the privileges that they had previously enjoyed. Alarmed by the unification of Germany in 1870, the Russian government incited the Esths and the Letts, who constituted the mass of the population in this region, to push forward the claims of their own languages, made Russian instead of German the official speech, made the building of Lutheran churches dependent on the consent of the head of the Russian Eastern Orthodox Church, assumed control of the Lutheran schools, and transformed the University of Dorpat into a Russian institution. In western Russia it forcibly converted the Uniates to the state church. The government also imposed many new restrictions upon the Jews. It compelled them to live within the Pale of Settlement, expelled some seventeen thousand Jewish artisans from Moscow, forbade Jews to buy real estate in the villages anywhere, did little to protect them from pogroms started by the lower classes in the cities, limited the number of Jewish children that could enter the schools and thus closed many professions to members of the Jewish race, and took a disproportionate number of Jewish recruits for the army.

As a result of the revolt of the Poles in 1863 the Russian government made a special effort to crush their national spirit. It made Russian the official language, forbade the use of the Polish tongue, first in the secondary schools and later in the primary schools, and even declared illegal the giving of religious instruction in the Polish language. It compelled the Poles to use the Russian language on trade signs, deprived the Roman Catholic Church in Poland of its revenues, made the parish priests salaried state officials, and excluded the Poles from government posts in their own country.

However, the incorporation of Poland into the Russian Empire brought the Poles some advantages. Agrarian reforms created a small class of peasant farmers and promoted progress in agriculture. The removal of customs barriers opened up the vast markets of the Russian Empire to the Polish coal-mines and manufactures and the Russian tariff shielded Polish industry from the competition of western Europe. Warsaw quadrupled its population within forty years and other Polish cities grew even more rapidly. The development of trade and industry caused the growth of a middle class and an industrial proletariat with political aims quite different from those of the Polish aristocracy. The immediate goal of the new middle class became autonomy within the Russian Empire rather than independence.

The Russian government likewise strove to destroy the autonomy conceded to Finland by Alexander I at the time of her conquest by Russia. The policy of Russification began in this province in the early nineties. Russians began to take the places of the Finns in the higher administrative posts and a knowledge of the Russian language became a prerequisite for appointment to the lower posts in the administration. In 1899 the imperial government issued a manifesto that reduced the Finnish diet to a mere consultative body and a Russian took office as Secretary of State for Finland in complete disregard of the provisions of the Finnish constitution. In 1900 Russian became the official language of Finland. The next year a new military law abolished the hitherto independent Finnish army and established in the Finnish provinces the same conditions enforced in the rest of the empire. Although in practice the Russian government asked for only an insignificant number of recruits, its action added to the irritation of the Finns. In 1902 the Russian government threw open all Finnish administrative posts to Russians but the number actually appointed was small. In the following year the government introduced in Finland the policy of domiciliary searches and arbitrary arrests and imprisonments that had long been applied to the rest of Russia. These attempts to make the religious sects and national minorities conform to the Russian national standard aroused a mounting tide of resentment against the imperial régime.

4

THE INDUSTRIAL REVOLUTION IN RUSSIA

Though successful for a time in crushing the revolutionary movement, the Russian government could not prevent the transformation of old Russia by the Industrial Revolution. The Russian tariff on imports steadily mounted until by the last decade of the nineteenth century the empire found itself surrounded by a high wall of protection from foreign competition. The government encouraged foreign investments in Russia by stabilizing the currency and introducing the gold standard, and contracted large loans abroad for financing industrial undertakings. Under the influence of the high tariff, an improved currency, and foreign capital, Russian industry enjoyed large profits, foreign capital poured into the country, and mining, manufacturing, transportation facilities, and commerce developed with great rapidity. Between 1881 and 1894, the mileage of Russian railways increased 66.66 per cent, and in 1891 Russia began the construction of a railroad across Siberia. Between 1887 and 1897 the number of factories in Russia increased about 25 per cent, the total value of the goods produced in all branches of industry more than doubled, the output of the coal-mines of Russia increased fivefold, and the production of iron ore quadrupled. Much of this industrial development took place in southern Russia, where the output of the coal-mines finally became 70 per cent of the total production of Russia and the iron industry became far more important than the older iron establishments of the Ural Mountains. This industrial development, however, greatly increased the burdens of the peasants by forcing them to pay two and a half times as much for cotton and sugar as the German peasant, four and a half times as much for iron, and six times as much for coal.

5

THE REVOLUTION OF 1905

In 1904 the adventurous foreign policy in the Far East finally precipitated a disastrous war with Japan that fully disclosed the corruption and incompetence of the reactionary Russian government. The dishonest and incompetent officials of the bureaucracy proved unable to supply the army with the indispensable ammunition, equipment, and supplies. Incapable officers led the troops. The resulting series of military and naval defeats revealed the weakness of the government. By the end of the campaign of 1904 the government had hardly an avowed supporter left in the country.

By this time the opposition to autocracy was much stronger and better organized than it had been a generation earlier. From the beginning the moderate reformers active in the zemstvo councils had shown a tendency to coöperate for the attainment of local and national reforms. In spite of the hostility of the reactionary authorities, they continued to present to them respectful petitions, to carry on useful administrative functions, and to defend themselves from the attacks of the government. In face of the danger of dismissal from office, of arbitrary arrest, and of exile, councils and congresses of zemstvos discussed the problems of the peasants, the hindrances to the development of education, the restrictions on the zemstvos, the unfairness of the electoral system, the need of a free press, and the financial policy of the government. In June, 1903, secret conferences, held in Germany between the Liberals in the zemstvos and members of the professional classes resulted in the organization of a Union of Liberation, which declared for the political emancipation of Russia through the abolition of autocracy and the establishment of a democratic constitutional régime. The union organized branches in the provinces and soon became the rallying-point for the Liberal elements among the Russian people. At a congress held at St. Petersburg in November, 1904, the leaders of the reform party urged the need of protecting the inviolability of person and domicile in Russia, of making officials responsible to the ordinary law-courts, of establishing liberty of conscience and freedom of the press, meeting, and association, of reorganizing the zemstvos on a more democratic basis, and of creating a national assembly. The resolutions of the congress met with widespread approval and stimulated public demonstrations and discussions in favor of reform.

The development of an urban proletariat as a result of the growth of industry opened the way for the growth of Marxian Socialism in Russia. The Marxian Socialists helped the exploited workers of the cities to organize strikes in 1895 and 1896 and two years later they formally founded a Social Democratic party. Almost immediately a struggle began within the party between the advocates of the establishment of a political dictatorship, who were led by Nikolay Lenin, and a moderate group that believed in peaceful methods of agitation and even stood ready to make use of parliamentary institutions and to cooperate with other parties. At a congress convened in 1903 in Brussels and later shifted to London the conflict between the extremist followers of Lenin and the more moderate elements split the Russian Social Democratic party into a majority group, the Bolsheviki, and a minority group, the Mensheviki.

Another party purely Russian in origin, the Social Revolutionaries, attempted to win the support of the peasants and the professional classes as well as of the urban proletariat. They looked upon terrorism as a useful weapon for stimulating the masses to action. Their doctrines appealed particularly to the younger generation among the educated classes.

In the hope of diverting the attention of the workers from the political struggle, the government permitted the formation at St. Petersburg of a society of factory workers, headed by Father Gapon. In January, 1905, thirteen thousand metal-workers at the Putilov works struck for a shorter working day, increased wages, and better treatment. When their demands were rejected they decided to march under the leadership of Father Gapon, accompanied by their families, to present a petition to the Tsar that contained both economic and political demands. In handling the peaceful demonstration the authorities made a terrible blunder. The troops fired on the unarmed workers, killing and wounding several hundred persons. This so-called Bloody Sunday did much to alienate the Russian people from their rulers.

After this event the signs of discontent with the absolute government multiplied. Under the leadership of the Social Democrats political strikes stopped the larger factories and the principal railway-lines of the country, and street demonstrations took place in many cities. Assassinations of officials and policemen became frequent. The zemstvos and the town governments held meetings for the discussion of national problems and organized the professional classes, the skilled workmen, and even the government employees into unions. After every military defeat in the Far East the demands of the Russian public grew bolder. After the destruction of the Baltic fleet a congress of zemstvos sent a delegation to the Tsar that described the situation of the country in plain terms and asked for the summons of representatives of the people, equally elected by all classes, and for the abolition of the bureaucratic wall between monarch and people. Student strikes closed the doors of the universities. In October a general strike took place that suspended traffic on twenty-six thousand miles of railroad, stopped the street railways, the telegraph services, and the power and water plants of the cities, and closed offices, stores, and factories. Sailors and soldiers began to mutiny. Conflicts between the public and the troops became frequent. A council of workmen's delegates, composed of representatives of the St. Petersburg factories and largely dominated by the Social Democrats, finally assumed leadership of the spontaneous movement and began to organize the workmen for effective resistance and to formulate their political demands. At the same time the peasants, instigated by the Social Revolutionaries, rose in many provinces. Whole villages marched to the country houses of their landlords and cut down timber, wrecked the gardens, pillaged the houses and barns, and drove off the cattle. From the peasants in all sections came petitions to the central government asking for land, relief from taxation, remission of redemption dues, and freedom to leave their villages.

With the greater part of the troops thousands of miles distant in Manchuria, the general strike found the government unprepared and helpless and faced with bankruptcy and disintegration. The Tsar and his advisers, consequently, decided to make concessions to his determined people. In August they promised to establish a state Duma, with consultative powers, based on a very limited suffrage. The Tsar dismissed Pobyedonostsev and appointed in his place Count Sergius Witte, a man who believed in appeasing the moderate majority by the introduction of necessary reforms. On October 17 Nicholas II promised his subjects civil liberty, an extension of the suffrage, and a voice in the making of the laws. But massacres of Jews and members of the educated classes, instigated and directed by reactionary officials close to the Tsar, almost neutralized the effect of the imperial manifesto. A little later the Russian government restored to Finland its former liberties, granted political prisoners a partial amnesty, reduced the redemption dues of the peasants one half for the year 1906 and promised to abolish them entirely after January 1, 1907.

After gaining these successes the revolutionary movement began to lose its force and solidarity. The opponents of the revolution, led by officials, proprietors, a physician, two or three merchants, and members of the clergy, and supported by the lower strata of the urban proletariat, began to organize and to incite attacks on strikers, Jews, and students. Disturbed by the agrarian disorders and the revolutionary excesses, the more moderate elements among the reformers organized a separate party, which advocated support of the governmental program that had been announced in October. Even the Constitutional Democrats, the party that grew out of the zemstvo movement, became more moderate in their demands. The general strike called by the Council of Workers' Delegates in November proved a failure. Encouraged by these developments, the government began to arrest its chief opponents, repress strikes, prevent the holding of public meetings, declare martial law, and suspend journals. In December a third general strike proved a complete failure. The army, in the main, remained loyal to the government and crushed with unnecessary harshness, the revolutionists. Military detachments burned whole villages to the ground, beat the peasants cruelly, and executed great numbers of persons without trial.

6

A NEW PERIOD OF REACTION

The government utilized its victory to curtail the concessions that it had made to the Russian people at the height of the revolutionary movement. A decree published late in December, 1905, regulated the elections to the new Duma in such a way that they were neither equal nor direct. This piece of legislation divided the voters into groups isolating the peasants and the workers, and gave the nobles a disproportionate influence in the election of representatives to the Duma. A decree issued in February, 1906, reorganized the Council of State as an upper chamber with legislative rights equal to those of the promised Duma and with half of its members appointed by the Tsar and half elected from the universities, commercial committees, the zemstvos, the clergy, and the nobility. A decree promulgated three days before the opening of the legislative body forbade the Duma to discuss the fundamental laws and reserved for the Tsar his old authority in questions of peace and war, international relations, expenditures for the army and the navy, contracting loans (in certain cases), and summoning and proroguing the Duma. These decrees virtually deprived the Russian people of the parliamentary institutions that they had been promised, but left them a constitutional régime resembling those in Japan and Germany.

In spite of the manipulation of the franchise by the government the voters elected to the new Duma a majority strongly opposed to the reactionary policy of the Tsar and his advisers. It consisted of one hundred and seventy-nine Constitutional Democrats and about a hundred Labor members out of a total membership of five hundred and twenty-four. The Socialist parties boycotted the election. The supporters of the government included only a small number of Octobrists and moderates and a handful of reactionaries. Immediately after the opening of the Duma the opposition asked in a forceful petition for ministerial responsibility, abolition of the Council of State, enlargement of the powers of the Duma, full civil liberties for all peoples and classes, expropriation of state and private land for the benefit of the peasants, and amnesty for those imprisoned for political or religious convictions or for agrarian disturbances. The petition precipitated a struggle that lasted for the rest of the session. The Duma refused to pass the small amount of legislation asked for by the government. Its members used the right of interpellation to reveal day after day the abuses of the administration. The government opposed the project of the opposition for appropriating land for the peasants. When the opposition prepared to appeal to the Russian people against the government the imperial authorities dissolved the Duma. In reply, two hundred of the dismissed deputies assembled at Viborg in Finland and asked the Russian people to refuse to pay taxes or to answer the summons of the government to military service. The government punished the recalcitrant deputies by sentencing them to three months' imprisonment and depriving them of electoral rights.

The ministry felt under compulsion to conciliate European public opinion by appearing to maintain a parliamentary régime but made great efforts to insure a more pliable Duma. It disfranchised certain classes of the population, imprisoned or exiled undesirable candidates, and prevented the opposition parties from conducting a political campaign. In spite of all the efforts of the government to manipulate the elections, the opposition increased its strength in the new Duma, the Socialists having reversed their political tactics and elected eighty-three members. In the second Duma, which assembled in March, 1907, the Constitutional Democrats tried to avoid useless conflicts with the government and to accomplish as much practical work as possible. The government, however, demanded that the pacification of the country should precede the concession of reforms and insisted on the surrender by the Duma of fifty-five of its Social Democratic members, on the pretext that they had been organizing a military plot. The reference of the question to an investigating committee caused the government to dissolve the Duma and to change the electoral law in such a way as to reduce the representation of regions of the empire not inhabited by Russians and to give a preponderance to the large landowners.

The new electoral law insured the government a moderate majority in the Duma. Petr Stolypin, the head of the government, used his favorable position to pacify the empire. The government subjected non-Russians to more restrictions than ever before. Finland again lost her autonomy in all matters except local affairs. The tyranny and arbitrariness of governmental officials increased greatly. Between 1906 and 1913 three thousand two hundred and eighty-two persons were sentenced to be executed, and the government successfully prosecuted the journals of Russia for offenses against the press laws one thousand six hundred and thirty-four times. Opposition newspapers, however, were tolerated. The universities again lost their autonomy. Yet on the whole the new régime was an improvement over those which had preceded it.

For a time the Russian people, weary of disorder and lacking in political training, seemed to accept the repressive policy of the government. Finally, however, even the moderate Octobrists became an opposition party, and popular discontent began to manifest itself more openly. By the summer of 1914 many felt that a second revolution was inevitable.

Notwithstanding the policy followed by the government, the years subsequent to the Revolution of 1905 witnessed considerable social progress in Russia. In 1906 the cabinet, with the assent of the Duma, promulgated an agrarian law that permitted and encouraged the peasants to transform their communal holdings into private property. By this measure the government hoped to prevent Russian villages from rising in the future as a unit. The government placed state lands on sale, attempted to reduce the congestion in the more populous regions, and restored the jurisdiction of the justices of the peace over the peasants. The sums allotted to education mounted steadily and something like a hundred private institutions for higher education opened their doors. The Duma also adopted a plan for introducing universal education by 1922. Agriculture and industry made rapid progress. Coöperative societies for promoting mutual loans, for the acquisition of cattle and agricultural implements, for obtaining the necessaries of life at cost, and for the production of dairy products multiplied.

The impact of western Europe on the Russian Empire made itself increasingly felt from the time of the Crimean War onward. Discredited by its defeat in that struggle, the government for a decade made important concessions to the demands for reform. An attempt on the life of the Emperor in 1866, however, put an end to the period of reform and inaugurated a policy of reaction that was maintained in force until 1905 and was resumed in 1915. The abandonment of the policy of reform caused the extremists among the reformers to resort to acts of terrorism against the royal family and its political agents. After the assassination of Alexander II in 1881 the government broke up the organizations of the Terrorists, reduced the moderates to silence, and followed a policy that favored autocracy, orthodoxy, and nationalism. In 1905 the war with Japan revealed the corruption and inefficiency of the autocracy, brought the opposition to the point of revolution, and prevented the government for a time from resisting the demands of the Russian people. Lacking troops and confronted by the Russian nation, the government promised important political reforms. But the breaking up of the solidarity of the opposition and the termination of the war finally enabled it to resume its repressive policies and to reduce the new political institutions to becoming docile tools of the autocracy.

CHAPTER XX

THE BALKAN STATES, 1870–1909

The continued decline of the Ottoman Empire in the nineteenth century aroused both the cupidity of neighboring states and the hopes of the Christian peoples of the Balkan peninsula. For a time defeat in the Crimean War put a stop to the intervention of Russia in Balkan affairs and gave the Christian nationalities an opportunity to develop. By 1870, however, Russia was again ready for a forward policy.

I

RUSSIA RESUMES ACTIVITY IN THE BALKANS

The Franco-Prussian War offered the political leaders of Russia an opportunity to free themselves from the conditions imposed on the Russian government as a result of its defeat in the Crimean War. While France and Prussia were engaged in a military struggle the Russian Chancellor, in a circular note to the powers, announced that his government would no longer consider itself obligated to maintain the neutrality of the Black Sea. This declaration resulted in the negotiation of a convention in 1871, at London, which gave the force of international law to the declaration of Russia. Thereupon the Russian government reestablished Sebastopol as a naval base and created an armed fleet on the Black Sea.

2

THE CHRISTIAN PEOPLES OF THE BALKANS RISE AGAINST TURKISH MISRULE

For a few years after this action of the Russian government the attention of Europe was diverted from the Balkans. In 1875, however, the desperate peasants of the province of Herzegovina rose in revolt and again drew the eyes of the political leaders of the chief European states to the Balkan peninsula. Unable to meet the demands of the Turkish tax-gatherers, owing to the bad harvest of the preceding year, the peasants of one village offered armed resistance to their Moslem landlords and local authorities. The rising spread rapidly over Herzegovina and the neighboring province of Bosnia and developed into a revolt against Turkish misrule. The peasants demanded that a third of the land be given to them, and thwarted the efforts of the foreign consuls stationed in the two provinces to effect a conciliation with the Turkish government. Through sympathy for their fellow-Christians the Serbians of both Serbia and Montenegro, and many Bulgars, joined the revolt against Turkish rule.

The Turks aroused the horror of the civilized world by the manner in which they put down the rising among the Bulgars. A detachment of Turkish irregular troops, known as Bashi-bazouks, swooped down upon the Bulgarian village of Batak and in spite of a promise to spare their lives killed approximately five thousand of the seven thousand villagers, and put to death thousands of the Bulgarians living in the surrounding province. The Turkish soldiers killed some in cold blood and burned others to death after they had taken refuge in a school and a church. An alert English newspaper correspondent promptly informed his journal of the massacre. The news inflamed public opinion everywhere in western Europe, the popular indignation finding its fullest expression in the famous pamphlet of Gladstone on the Bulgarian atrocities.

In the meantime the Turkish military forces made steady progress in quelling the revolt in other provinces of the empire. Poorly led and without experience in warfare for two generations, the Serbians proved no match for the Turkish troops. To prevent Serbia from being completely overrun Russia intervened and forced the Turkish government to grant an armistice.

At this point the British government succeeded in persuading the great powers of Europe to hold a diplomatic conference at Constantinople to discuss the Turkish problem. On the day the diplomats were to assemble, however, the new Sultan of Turkey, Abdul Hamid II, who had just been put in office by a revolution at the Turkish capital, proclaimed a constitution that created a parliament of two chambers, declared all Turkish subjects equal before the law, and asserted the integrity of the Ottoman Empire. This skilful move kept the conference from achieving any tangible results. The new Sultan refused, on constitutional grounds, to make any cessions of territory, and he never executed the promised reforms.

3

THE INTERVENTION OF RUSSIA

The failure of the Turkish authorities to make any of the promised reforms gave Russia a pretext for intervention in behalf of its oppressed "Little Slav brothers." Late in April, 1877, Russian troops crossed the Turkish frontiers both in Europe and in Asia. In June they crossed the Danube River. During the year 1877 the Turkish troops succeeded in preventing further advances, but in the following year the Turkish defense crumpled under the attacks of the Russian, Rumanian, Serbian, and Montenegrin armies. The Russians entered Adrianople in European Turkey and captured important border cities in Asiatic Turkey; the Serbians took Nish; the Montenegrins captured the port of Antivari and an outlet to the Adriatic Sea; and the Greeks of Epirus, Crete, and Thessaly rose in revolt. At this point the attitude of the British government forced the conclusion of an armistice.

Victorious Russia imposed the Treaty of San Stefano on the defeated Turkish Empire. A large number of articles in this document attempted to regulate the future of the Bulgarian people. They provided for the establishment of a large, independent Bulgaria with boundaries extending to the Danube, the Black Sea, and the Ægean Sea, the election of a ruling prince by popular vote, and the organization of an administrative system by an assembly of notables under the supervision of a Russian commissioner. Other articles extended the boundaries of Serbia and Montenegro considerably. Rumania, on the contrary, received most ungenerous treatment at the hands of Russia. While she obtained her freedom from Turkish suzerainty, Russia compelled her to hand back the portion of Bessarabia she had acquired at the end of the Crimean War and take in exchange the Dobruja, a barren, infertile Turkish province lying just south of the Lower Danube. The treaty also provided for the autonomy of Bosnia and Herzegovina under the administration of a Christian governor-general and for some protection for the Christian inhabitants of Epirus, Thessaly, Crete, and the Armenian provinces.

4

THE CONGRESS OF BERLIN

The Treaty of San Stefano pleased only the Russians and the Bulgarians. The Turks protested against the dismemberment of their empire. The British and Austro-Hungarian governments feared that the proposed Bulgarian state would become to all practical purposes a province of Russia. Austria-Hungary in addition coveted the provinces of Bosnia and Herzegovina and desired to prevent the creation of a Bulgaria that would block the expansion of the Dual Monarchy toward Saloniki, and the establishment of a Montenegrin port on the Adriatic that might serve as a Russian naval base. The Albanians objected to the cession of districts in northern Albania to Montenegro. The Greeks felt that their legitimate demands had been neglected. The Rumanians felt aggrieved at the forced exchange of Bessarabia for the Dobruja.

THE PEOPLES OF
SOUTHEASTERN EUROPE
1878-1885

0   50   100   150   200   250
Scale of Miles

Turks

Rumanians

Bulgarians

Croats and
Serbs

Greeks

Albanians

RUSSIA

Dniester R.

Bug R.

Bessarabia

Bukovina

Pruth R.

Kishinev

Jassy

Moldavia

Akkerman

HUNGARY

Drave R.

Fünfkirchen

Danube R.

Save R.

Temesvár

Transylvania

Kronstadt

Galatz

BLACK SEA

BOSNIA
Administered by
Austria-Hungary
Sarajevo
since 1878
Herze-
govina

Belgrade

SERBIA

Morava R.

Morava R.

Nish

WALLACHIA

RUMANIA

Danube R.

Iron Gate

Bucharest

Dobruja

Constantsa

NOVI
BAZAR

MONTE
NEGRO

Cattaro

Vidin

Danube R.

Silistria
Rustchuk

BULGARIA

Shumla

Varna

Sofia

Eastern Rumelia

Philippopolis

Maritza R.

Burgas

ADRIATIC SEA

TURKEY

Uskub
(Skoplje)

EMPIRE

Adrianople

Constantinople

Bosporus

Shkatari

ITALY

Brindisi

Monastir
(Bitolia)

Salonika

Gallipoli

San Stefano

Marmara
Sea

Brusa

Strait of Otranto

Corfu

Ionian Islands

Larissa

Lemnos

Dardanelles

AEGEAN SEA

Mytilene

Asia Minor

Chios

Smyrna

Patras

Athens

Samos

Morea

GREECE

Cyclades

Rhodes

MEDITERRANEAN SEA

Crete

MAX MAYER, THORNWOOD, N.Y.

20°   Longitude   East   from   Greenwich   25°

© The Century Co., 1932

Under the pressure of these protests the Russian government finally agreed to submit the Balkan problem to a congress of the powers to be held at Berlin. Its sessions actually opened in the middle of June, 1878, and lasted for a month. The great powers sent to the congress their ablest diplomats and ministers. These finally embodied the results of their deliberations in the Treaty of Berlin. This agreement created a small, autonomous Bulgaria, bounded by the Black Sea, the Danube River, and the Balkan Mountains, and left her still under the suzerainty of the Turkish Empire. It organized the central part of the Great Bulgaria proposed by the Treaty of San Stefano as a small autonomous principality, known as Eastern Rumelia, under the rule of a Christian governor-general appointed by the Turkish Sultan for a term of five years. It left in the Ottoman Empire the rest of the territory occupied by Bulgarians. The Treaty of Berlin also gave Austria-Hungary the right to occupy and administer Bosnia and Herzegovina and to maintain military and commercial roads in the Sanjak of Novibazar, the Turkish province between Serbia and Montenegro pointing like an index-finger toward the valuable Ægean port of Saloniki. The treaty likewise granted complete independence to Serbia, Montenegro, and Rumania, ceded to Serbia the territory around Nish, gave Montenegro the use of the Adriatic port of Antivari for commercial purposes, forced Rumania to make the hated exchange of Bessarabia for the Dobruja, and promised Greece a rectification of her northern frontier. These important modifications of the Treaty of San Stefano were regarded by contemporary opinion as a great victory for British diplomacy.

5

THE DEVELOPMENT OF BULGARIA AFTER 1878

After the Congress of Berlin Bulgarian affairs continued to attract the attention of Europe. In 1879 a Constitutional Assembly drafted a constitution and selected a ruler for the new state. This new organic law provided for a unicameral National Assembly elected by the male citizens thirty years of age and able to write, but left a number of questions concerning the acquisition and cession of territory, vacancies on the throne, regencies, and the revision of the constitution to a special assembly twice as large as the National Assembly. The Constitutional Assembly chose as ruler of Bulgaria an attractive but inexperienced young man of twenty-two, Prince Alexander of Battenberg, a nephew by marriage of the Tsar.

From the first the inhabitants of Bulgaria and Eastern Rumelia considered the decisions of the Congress of Berlin in regard to Bulgarian affairs as only a temporary arrangement. Both their national and their economic interests demanded the fusion of the two states. For several years after the congress, consequently, the national leaders in Bulgaria and Eastern Rumelia carried on an agitation for a union of the two provinces. After having prepared the way in this fashion, a group of conspirators finally seized the governor-general of Eastern Rumelia in 1885, sent him back to Constantinople, and proclaimed the union of Bulgaria and Eastern Rumelia. At news of this bloodless revolution public opinion in Bulgaria approved the action of the conspirators. Stefan Stambulov, the president of the National Assembly, bluntly told his sovereign that two paths lay before him, "one to Philippopolis and as far beyond as God may lead, the other to Darmstadt." After this warning Prince Alexander proclaimed his acceptance of the throne of united Bulgaria and ordered the military occupation of Eastern Rumelia.

This aggrandizement of Bulgaria alarmed her Balkan rivals. Already at odds with her over tariff and boundary questions, Serbia seized upon the expansion of Bulgaria and the consequent upsetting of the balance of power as a pretext for armed intervention. The Serbian sovereign left his capital for the frontier amid the cheers of the populace for "the King of Serbia and Macedonia." But the ensuing military struggle lasted only fourteen days. The Bulgarians of Bulgaria, Eastern Rumelia, and Macedonia rallied to the national cause and the new Bulgarian army promptly invaded Serbia and decisively defeated the Serbian military forces. Only the intervention of an Austro-Hungarian army put an end to the advance of the Bulgarian troops and the dreams of the Bulgarian nationalists concerning the incorporation of Serbia into Bulgaria.

This demonstration of Bulgarian military strength terminated the diplomatic uncertainty created by the revolution in Eastern Rumelia. Under the pressure of Great Britain, which aimed at the strengthening of the Balkan states as a bulwark against Russian expansion, the Sultan of Turkey formally recognized the union of the two Bulgarian principalities and appointed Prince Alexander governor-general of Eastern Rumelia. The revolution in Eastern Rumelia, the victory over Serbia, and the diplomacy of Great Britain thus created the Bulgarian state that Europe knew from 1885 until the outbreak of the Balkan Wars in 1912.

After his accession to office Prince Alexander found himself exposed to the conflicting demands of the agents of the Russian government and the members of the inexperienced National Assembly. As the years passed he showed himself more and more inclined to follow an independent policy. In consequence, after the accession of Tsar Alexander III in 1881 the Russian government more and more openly avowed its hostility to the young Bulgarian prince and began to lay plans to recover the position it had lost in Bulgaria. The success of the Bulgarian nationalists in annexing Eastern Rumelia determined the Russian government to take decisive action against Prince Alexander. It easily found a group of discontented Bulgarian army officers ready to carry out its plans. In August, 1886, accordingly, these conspirators forced their way into the royal palace at Sofia, compelled Prince Alexander to abdicate, and then hustled him down the Danube and across the Russian border into Bessarabia.

Events quickly proved that Russia had not gaged correctly the strength of the Bulgarian national movement. The provisional government set up by the conspirators stayed in power only three days. Loyal regiments recaptured the capital and enabled Stambulov to gain control of the situation. At his solicitation Prince Alexander returned to his subjects but, prompted by a Russian agent, he weakly telegraphed the Tsar as he regained Bulgarian soil, "Russia gave me my crown and I am ready to return it into the hands of her sovereign." Seizing the opportunity offered to him, the Tsar replied "I cannot approve your return to your country." Upon receiving this message Prince Alexander resigned his throne.

His removal did not, however, restore the influence of Russia in Bulgaria. Stambulov refused to heed the orders of the Russian authorities and for the next few years he practically controlled Bulgaria. Intensely patriotic, ambitious, and determined, and possessed of a grim face that frightened his opponents, he took the measures necessary to insure his control of the government, imprisoning important opponents and stationing armed sentries at the ballot-boxes. Assured by these means of the support of the National Assembly, he began a search for a new sovereign and finally persuaded Ferdinand of Saxe-Coburg-Gotha to defy Russia and accept the throne.

Until 1894 this astute prince left the conduct of affairs in the hands of his all-powerful minister. The policies of Stambulov, however, aroused a growing antagonism, and in 1894 Ferdinand surprised his unpopular minister by accepting his proffered resignation. Thenceforth the Tsar of Bulgaria played an important part in shaping the policies of his state. His gifted mother contributed much to his success by her tact and philanthropy. His own diplomatic talents finally restored good relations with Russia and established cordial ties with Austria-Hungary. The growing material prosperity fostered by the orderly government initiated by Stambulov made for the contentment of the subjects of the prince.

6

THE DEVELOPMENT OF SERBIA AFTER 1878

In Serbia civil and dynastic dissensions prevented a corresponding development. Cut off from Saloniki by Turkey and from the Adriatic by the provinces of Bosnia, Herzegovina, and Dalmatia, Serbia depended for her prosperity largely on the good-will of Austria-Hungary. One party in Serbia favored Prince Nicholas of the ruling dynasty of Montenegro. Another growing faction supported the pretensions to the throne of Serbia of the descendants of Karageorge, one of the leaders in the Serbian struggle for liberty. A stronger ruler than Obrenovich IV, later Milan I (1868–1889), might have found a solution for these perplexing problems without endangering the dignity of himself or his state. But, fearful for his personal safety and far more interested in the pleasure to be derived from his official position than in his political duties, he signed a secret agreement with Austria-Hungary which bound him to tolerate no intrigues against the Dual Monarchy, to observe a friendly neutrality in case Austria-Hungary became involved in war, and to conclude no treaties with foreign powers without her approval. This agreement made Serbia a tributary state, in spite of the assumption of the royal title by its ruler in 1881. Notwithstanding the support extended to him by Austria-Hungary the new King soon damaged his position in Serbia irretrievably. His philandering involved him in quarrels with his pro-Russian Queen that created a public scandal; his orthodox subjects considered illegal the divorce that he finally obtained, and the unsuccessful war of 1885 with Bulgaria completed the ruin of his prestige. In 1889, consequently, he resigned his throne in favor of his son, Alexander. For years, however, he continued to hinder the moral and economic progress of the country by his unseemly quarrels with his divorced wife and by the resulting fruitless political strife.

His successor added to the disrepute of his house by an unfortunate marriage. While on a vacation at the French coast resort of Biarritz, King Alexander fell violently in love with the beautiful divorced wife of a Serbian officer. The whole Serbian nation opposed the proposed match because of the past of the lady, her known inability to have an heir, and the disparity in the ages of the two individuals. Coming as it did at the end of thirty years of quarrels in the royal family, political insecurity, disorganization in the finances, and subservience to Austria-Hungary, the rash marriage of the King completed the ruin of the prestige of the royal family and gave rise to a conspiracy against Alexander and his unpopular Queen. During the night of June 10, 1903, the conspirators, assured of the support of a group of politicians and a part of the army, broke into the palace and assassinated the royal couple with hideous brutality.

This terrible deed, nevertheless, proved a turning-point in the history of Serbia. The National Assembly elected to the vacant throne Prince Peter, the heir of the claims of the Karageorge family, a man fifty-nine years of age and endowed with fine personal qualities. Although the powers of Europe for years looked askance at the new sovereign of Serbia, he gradually led his state along the path of rehabilitation and made himself a center around which the hopes of the Southern Slavs began to turn. Within three years he succeeded in retiring from office all persons implicated in the assassination of his predecessor. He maintained constitutional government and gave men educated in the great universities of western Europe an opportunity to enter political life. His record of service in the Serbian revolt against Turkey in 1875 made him "our King" to many a Southern Slav beyond the Serbian border.

In foreign affairs he abandoned the policy of dependence on Austria-Hungary and turned to Russia for support, a state more remote and in consequence less likely to destroy Serbian independence. In 1906, during the negotiations for a renewal of the tariff treaty with Austria-Hungary the Serbian government gave the first striking indication of its new policy. The government of the Dual Monarchy demanded a monopoly of supplying Serbia with munitions. Compliance with this demand would have put Serbia at the mercy of her powerful neighbor. When the Serbian government refused to comply the government of Austria-Hungary placed a prohibitive duty on the importation of Serbian meat and live stock. This punitive measure unexpectedly contributed to the development of Serbian commerce and industry. Shut off from her former market by the action of Austria-Hungary, Serbia negotiated commercial treaties with a number of other European countries, commenced to develop industries for the conversion of raw materials into manufactured goods, and persuaded Turkey to free Serbian imports and exports from transit dues at the port of Saloniki.

Meanwhile the Serbian leaders had begun to dream of a Greater Serbia which would eventually include Serbia, part of Macedonia, Bosnia and Herzegovina, Dalmatia, and Montenegro, and possibly all the Southern Slavs of Austro-Hungary, and give Serbia a much-needed port on the Adriatic Sea. With this end in view they kept up an active agitation among the Southern Slavs of both Turkey and Austria-Hungary. The agitation aroused fears of dismemberment in Austria-Hungary and made the Serbian people sensitive to every political development affecting the status of the Southern Slavs.

7

GREECE AFTER 1878

For fifty years after Greece obtained her independence she stagnated and dreamed. As late as the time of the Congress of Berlin, Greece lacked railroads, roads, bridges, and port facilities. Brigandage still flourished. Foreign capitalists doubted the wisdom of investing in the country. The Greek treasury hovered on the verge of bankruptcy.

Dreams of future political greatness prevented the material development of the country.

The political thinking of the Greeks was dominated by the fact that the Greek state created in 1829 by the Treaty of Adrianople included only about one third of the Greek people. In the name of nationality the Greeks claimed the provinces of Thessaly and Epirus, the coast region of Turkey in Europe, the islands in the Ægean Sea, and the littoral of Asia Minor. They devoted the greater part of their energies to the achievement of this dream of a Greater Greece. In 1881 they obtained Thessaly and Epirus as a result of the promises made to them by the Congress of Berlin. In 1897 the question of Cretan independence precipitated a disastrous war between Greece and Turkey that destroyed the prestige of the Greek army, completed the bankruptcy of Greece, and caused the loss of strategic points on her northern frontier.

8

THE DEVELOPMENT OF RUMANIA AFTER 1866

After the forcible removal of Cuza (Alexander John I) from power, the political leaders of Rumania finally persuaded Prince Karl of Hohenzollern, a distant relative of the Prussian royal family and a descendant of both Murat and the Beauharnais, to defy the powers of Europe and accept the Rumanian throne. The new ruler, Charles I, often called Carol, was a soldier by training, a cautious man, and one endowed with great political sagacity. These qualities caused him to abandon for the time all dreams of territorial expansion in order to devote himself to the political and material development of the state.

Shortly after his accession, Rumania received a new constitution. This vested executive power in the sovereign acting through ministers responsible to the parliament. The legislative body, however, was far from democratic. The Senate was composed of members who had reached the age of forty and possessed a considerable annual income. The Assembly was elected by a system of three colleges that gave 86 per cent of the population only thirty-eight out of a total of one hundred deputies. The King had an absolute veto over legislation. The constitution also contained the usual guarantees of liberty and protection.

Public opinion made the Jewish problem acute in Rumania. The Jews had obtained a position of great economic power in the country. They had captured most of the trade of the state and had come to hold a position as middlemen between the peasants and the capitalists and large landowners. In response to popular feeling the government attempted to counteract the economic power acquired by the Jews by excluding them from political life.

As might have been expected of one of his training, the soldierly King gave much attention to the improvement of the army. He increased its numerical strength, imported German instructors, introduced higher standards of training, and bettered its equipment. The new army gave a good account of itself in the war that broke out between Russia and Turkey in 1876, and caused Rumania to be recognized as the strongest of the Balkan states.

9

THE DECLINE OF TURKEY

The realization of the hopes of Serbs, Greeks, and Bulgars depended largely on the fortunes of the Turkish Empire. For a long time the international situation favored its preservation and the postponement of the realization of the dreams of the Christian peoples of the Balkans concerning expansion. Most of the great powers opposed the aggrandizement of Russia, Austria-Hungary, or the Balkan states. This international rivalry left the Turkish government free to continue its misrule of its Christian and its Moslem subjects.

The Revolution of 1876 at Constantinople placed in power in the Ottoman Empire Abdul Hamid II. He was born in 1842. In his youth he showed few attractive qualities. He cared nothing for sport or for study. He grew up ill-informed, self-willed, mistrustful, avaricious, and extravagant. Upon reaching maturity he was given no opportunities to take part in public functions or to become acquainted with public men. He came into power ignorant of political history and foreign politics and with a strong dislike for both his Christian subjects and the idea of political reform. Once established as Sultan, Abdul Hamid took steps to get rid of the reformers who had placed him in power and to nullify the constitution that they had forced upon him. The reform party in Turkey had hoped to establish in the empire parliamentary government and equality between Christians and Moslems. As long as he needed the support of this party the new Sultan professed complete sympathy with its plans. As soon as he felt sure of his position, he got rid of the parliament proclaimed in 1876 to forestall the danger of foreign intervention in Turkey, forced Midhat Pasha, the leader of the reform party, from office, and finally caused him to be strangled.

After destroying the work of the reform party in Turkey, Abdul Hamid endeavored to evade the provisions of the Treaty of Berlin. Though he felt compelled to withdraw his troops from Bosnia and Herzegovina, his agents fomented an insurrection in the two provinces that required the efforts of one hundred and fifty thousand Austro-Hungarian troops to suppress. He secretly stirred up the Albanians to protest in the name of nationality against the cession of Albanian districts to Montenegro and to organize a league for the preservation of Albania against the designs of the Serbs, the Greeks, and the Montenegrins. He abandoned his opposition to the fulfilment of clauses of the Treaty of Berlin dealing with Montenegro only under the threat of a British occupation of Smyrna. He put off the promised rectification of the northern frontier of Greece until the great powers finally forced him to cede Thessaly and the southern part of the province of Epirus.

Throughout his reign Abdul Hamid misgoverned both his Moslem and his Christian subjects. He allowed the army to become demoralized and the navy to deteriorate. He failed in his attempt to establish a Turkish postal system. He subjected the native and the foreign press to a censorship that kept Turkish subjects in ignorance of many matters. He maintained a system of espionage that kept him fully informed of the acts and sayings of his subjects. He prevented the installation of both telephones and electricity at Constantinople. He did nothing to lessen the corruption and misrule of his officials. His misgovernment alienated both his Christian and his most enlightened Moslem subjects.

The dissatisfaction and sufferings of certain peoples and provinces of the empire kept the misrule of the Turkish government steadily before the eyes of Europe. As early as the Treaty of San Stefano the situation of the Armenians had begun to attract attention. They played an important part throughout the empire in occupations and professions calling for intelligence and industry, and they constituted nearly half of the population in six of the northeastern provinces of the empire. They suffered from the exactions of soldiers and tax-gatherers and the raids of Kurds and Circassians, and the government did nothing for the protection of their property, their honor, or their lives. In spite of promises of reforms their situation grew steadily worse after the Congress of Berlin. The half-savage Kurds from the hill districts plundered at will the unarmed Armenians of the plains, even the Turkish tax-gatherers recognizing the impossibility of collecting any revenue from the victims of these raids. The protests of the Armenians grew louder, and many of them fled to the adjoining provinces of Russia and to other countries, where they organized committees to work for the redress of their grievances; and representatives of the European powers made ineffectual protests against Turkish misgovernment.

Unable or unwilling to remedy conditions in Armenia, Abdul Hamid determined to solve the problem by exterminating the hated people. For a period of three years massacres of Armenians took place in the provinces and at Constantinople. The first of these massacres occurred in 1894 as a result of the refusal of the Armenian peasants to pay taxes. Having already paid exorbitant blackmail to the Kurds, they seem to have depended on the latter for protection. When the Armenians refused to pay their taxes, Turkish troops killed several thousand of them and burned twenty-five of their villages. In the following year agents of Abdul Hamid appeared in the Armenian provinces, collected the Moslems in the mosques, and invited them to seize the property of their Armenian neighbors and to cut down all who offered resistance. These appeals to cupidity in the name of religion precipitated a series of terrible massacres both in Turkish Armenia and at Constantinople. In the following year there were unspeakable outrages, which destroyed an immense amount of property, permanently injured the commerce and industry of the empire, and cost the lives of one hundred to three hundred thousand victims. Only his keen remembrance of the effect on European public opinion of the Bulgarian atrocities of 1876 prevented Abdul Hamid from completing the work of exterminating the Armenians.

In the province of Macedonia in European Turkey a far more complicated situation existed. Moslems, Jews, Albanians, Bulgars, Serbs, Greeks, Rumanians, and hundreds of persons unconscious of all national ties lived inextricably intermingled. From the time that the Turks had established themselves in Europe the inhabitants of the province had suffered from the same misrule as the other Turkish provinces. The loss of Serbia, Rumania, and Bulgaria as a result of misgovernment brought no amelioration in the situation of the Macedonians. They suffered from the exactions of the unpaid Turkish soldiers and from the incursions of Albanian brigands. After the Congress of Berlin they became the victims of the propaganda of the Serbs, the Bulgars, and the Greeks. The Greeks claimed the Ægean coast on historical, ecclesiastical, and national grounds. The Serbs wished to acquire as much of Macedonia as possible. The Bulgars claimed most of the province on the ground of nationality. Each Balkan people sympathized with its fellow-nationals in Macedonia, and sought to strengthen its position in the provinces through schools, the Church, and armed bands. The Turkish misgovernment and foreign intervention produced an indescribable anarchy, which drove large numbers of the inhabitants of the province into exile and compelled the great powers of Europe to devote some attention to the problem of Macedonia. The rivalry of the great powers, however, prevented them from effective intervention in the province.

10

THE TURKISH REVOLUTION

A few enlightened Turks had long realized that the misrule of Abdul Hamid would eventually destroy the Turkish Empire. As the misgovernment continued the numbers of the discontented Moslems grew rapidly. They found recruits in Macedonia and among the refugees abroad. In 1906 these malcontents established a central committee, which met at Saloniki. In the following year the refugees organized a committee at Paris also. The two committees took the name of the Committee of Union and Progress. From 1906 to 1908 this organization carried on revolutionary propaganda that met with great success.

The character and methods of the revolutionists is well illustrated by Niazi Bey. As a young army officer stationed at Constantinople he became disgusted with the jobbery, favoritism, and injustice that he found in the army and the civil service, the enrichment of the commissariat officers at the expense of the troops, and the oppression of peaceful peasants. His expressions of indignation came to the ears of the Sultan through spies, and he was forced to flee to Paris to escape arrest. Returning from there he began an active propaganda against the rule of Abdul Hamid. Disguised as a hawker or a begging dervish, he boldly approached the discontented officers and soldiers in many of the garrisons of Asia Minor and gained many recruits for the revolutionary movement. By such methods the Committee of Union and Progress gradually won over the leading employees of the Macedonian railways and telegraph-lines, a good many officers in the army, and many other persons, Christians as well as Moslems.

At first the Committee of Union and Progress planned to begin the revolution on September 1, 1908. In July, however, news of the approaching meeting between the King of England and the Tsar of Russia to discuss the Macedonian question and the fear of Austro-Hungarian intervention in Macedonia as a result of Albanian attacks on an Austrian consul forced the revolutionary leaders to take immediate action. They persuaded the Albanian chieftains, hitherto favored by the Sultan, to join the revolutionary movement and demand the revival of the constitution of 1876. At Resnja a major seized the military chest and arms and led a band of Young Turks, as the reform party was called, into the mountains. Assassinations of a number of reactionary army officers were reported. Enver Bey won over to the revolutionary cause a number of garrisons in Turkey in Europe. On July 23 the Committee of Union and Progress proclaimed the constitution of 1876. Threatened with a march of his rebellious troops on Constantinople, Abdul Hamid abandoned all idea of open opposition and announced the reëstablishment of constitutional government, the abolition of censorship of the press and the spy system, and the summoning of a parliament. For the time being all political power passed into the hands of the Committee of Union and Progress.

At first the European powers and most of the subjects of the Sultan received the news of the success of the revolution with enthusiasm.

Enver Bey declared that henceforth all the subjects of the Sultan—Bulgars, Greeks, Jews, Rumanians, and Moslems—were brothers and gloried in the name of Ottomans. The president of the Bulgarian committee embraced the Greek archbishop and the revolutionary leaders imprisoned a Turk for insulting a Christian. Turks and Armenians joined in prayers in an Armenian cemetery for the victims of the Armenian massacres. The powers hoped for a moment that the Macedonian question had been solved, and removed many of the signs of foreign control.

Bulgaria and Austria-Hungary, however, seized the opportunity offered by the revolution in Turkey to further their own interests. Alarmed at suggestions in the Turkish press concerning the extension of the revived constitution to such provinces of the Turkish Empire as Eastern Rumelia and Bosnia and Herzegovina, the two powers came to an understanding and promised each other support. On October 5, 1908, Prince Ferdinand proclaimed himself Tsar of the Bulgarians. Two days later Austria-Hungary formally annexed Bosnia and Herzegovina. Although the connection of these provinces with the Turkish Empire had been only nominal for thirty years, the severance of the last connecting tie tended to discredit and embarrass the Young Turk party.

In the end the Turkish government resigned itself to the loss of Bulgaria and Bosnia and Herzegovina. The Ottoman Empire was not in a position to resort to arms successfully. Russia, the power which had long posed as the friend of the Balkan Slavs, had not recovered sufficiently from the exhausting struggle with Japan to risk a conflict with Austria-Hungary and Germany over Bosnia and Herzegovina. Serbia and Montenegro could only watch in impotent rage the annexation of the two provinces by the Dual Monarchy. In face of this situation the Turkish government made the best terms possible with Austria-Hungary. By an agreement concluded with Turkey in February, 1909, the Dual Monarchy renounced its rights to Novibazar, permitted its Moslem subjects in Bosnia and Herzegovina to recognize the Turkish Sultan as their spiritual head, and promised to pay for the domain lands acquired as a result of the annexation of the two provinces. In April of the same year, Turkey and Bulgaria came to terms. In return for the payment of a large money compensation to Turkey, the Turkish government recognized the recently proclaimed independence of Bulgaria.

The Turkish Revolution of 1908, however, did not meet with the approval of all elements in the Ottoman Empire. Former government employees, dismissed spies of the old régime, and conservative Moslems finally formed a secret society to oppose the Committee of Union and Progress. As a result of its propaganda and its distribution of money, a revolt broke out on April 13, 1909, which eventually gave the mutinous troops control of Constantinople for a moment and put in power a cabinet opposed to the Young Turks. All the prominent members of the government and the Committee of Union and Progress sought refuge in foreign consulates or in friendly private houses. After the disorders quieted down they withdrew to the village of San Stefano and awaited developments. Fearful for his personal safety, Abdul Hamid made no move toward taking advantage of the counter-revolution. Outside of Constantinople the troops remained loyal to the revolution. After a delay of a few days, an army, composed mainly of Albanians and Christians, started from Saloniki for Constantinople and after overcoming some slight resistance occupied the Turkish capital. The Committee of Union and Progress used this victory to compel Abdul Hamid, whom they credited with originating the plans for the counter-revolution, to abdicate.

II

THE PROBLEMS OF THE YOUNG TURKS

The defeat of the counter-revolution by no means solved the vexing problems confronting the Committee of Union and Progress. Under Abdul Hamid there had been no uniformity in the status of the various subject peoples. Even the Christians enjoyed many special privileges as members of their several national churches. The Young Turks, on the contrary, adopted a policy of Turkification that threatened to reduce the peoples and provinces of the empire to a dead level of uniformity. The new policy aroused much protest. The Christians hesitated to give up their privileged position. The Bulgars of Macedonia protested against the immigration of Moslems from Bosnia and renewed their revolutionary organization. The Greek Patriarch declared his church to be in danger. The Cretan Christians kept up their efforts to bring about a union of their island with Greece. The Druses, the Arabs, and the Albanians revolted.

The insurrection in Albania reached serious proportions. The military uprisings continued from 1909 to 1911. The mountainous nature of Albania made the pacification of the country difficult and enabled the Albanian tribesmen to inflict severe losses on the Turkish military forces sent against them. For a time sympathy for their neighbors threatened to involve the Montenegrins in the conflict. Finding the Albanian refugees a heavy burden, King Nicholas finally compelled the Albanians to accept the Turkish terms. These included amnesty, the limitation of military service to Europe, freedom from taxes for two years, permission to bear arms outside the towns, roads, schools, and compensation in cash and in maize.

12

THE REVIVAL OF GREECE

The Christians of Crete attempted to take advantage of the disturbances in the Turkish Empire to bring about the long-desired union of the island with Greece. They appointed a provisional government, which included Eleutherios Venizelos, to carry on the administration in the name of the Kingdom of Greece, took an oath of allegiance to King George of Greece, and identified themselves as far as possible with the Greeks of the mainland. If the Greek government had acted promptly it might possibly have annexed the island without serious opposition. But after the suppression of the counter-revolution of 1909 at Constantinople the Young Turks took a stiffer tone and threatened Greece with war. As a result of this change in the situation the Greeks and the Cretans found themselves compelled to postpone the union of Greece and Crete and to continue the maintenance of the island as an autonomous political unit under Turkish suzerainty and the supervision of the powers.

The humiliation felt in Greece over the outcome of the Cretan revolt led a group of younger army officers to form a Military League. Protesting their loyalty to the crown, the members of the new organization demanded radical reforms, particularly in the army and the navy. Their program won widespread support and led throughout the country to popular demonstrations against the existing political corruption. Emboldened by this show of support, they forced compliance with their demands, gave orders to the Greek parliament, and finally induced the King to invite Venizelos, whose career in Crete had attracted widespread attention, to come to Athens as the principal minister of the kingdom.

After 1870 the Turkish Empire continued to decline. This situation produced a constant succession of episodes that kept the Balkan peninsula in turmoil. In 1875 a revolt broke out among the Christian inhabitants of Bosnia against Turkish misrule that finally enlisted the support of the Serbs of Serbia and Montenegro, many Bulgarians, and the Russian government. As a result of its victory in the war Russia imposed the Treaty of San Stefano on the defeated Turkish Empire, but the powers forced the submission of the Balkan problem to a congress held at Berlin in 1878. Its decisions freed Serbia, Montenegro, and Rumania from Turkish rule and created an autonomous Bulgaria. After 1878 Bulgaria acquired Eastern Rumelia and steadily grew in strength; Serbia found herself long hampered by civil and dynastic strife; Greece dreamed of future greatness but long remained a backward state; Rumania followed a cautious policy that made her the strongest of the Balkan states; and Turkish misrule continued to scandalize public opinion in western Europe. After the turn of the century a new dynasty led Serbia to improve conditions and made her a rallying-point for the Southern Slavs; the reform party in the Turkish Empire plotted and successfully carried out a revolution; and the Greek people suddenly began to take steps to make their dreams of future greatness come true.

CHAPTER XXI

From 1815 to 1850 there was at least a superficial similarity between the course of events in Great Britain and that on the European continent. After the middle of the century this parallelism ceases. The insular position and the imperial interests of their country hold the British people somewhat apart from Continental movements.

I

A PERIOD OF PROSPERITY AND COMPLACENCY

The years from 1846 to 1867 were a period of prosperity and complacency for the British people. The reforms of the previous period had brought real progress and to a large degree had restored contentment. The economic supremacy of Great Britain seemed impregnable. The towns were getting rid of many of the evils that had attended their earlier growth and were introducing sound methods of sanitation and equipping themselves with parks, new water-systems, public halls, libraries, and art galleries, largely by the labor of public-spirited citizens. The parliamentary system seemed to be working smoothly and inspired John Stuart Mill to write his *Representative Government* and Walter Bagehot his *English Constitution*.

British political life was stirred by no great issues. The Conservative party had been shattered by the struggle over the repeal of the Corn Laws and a group of free-trade Conservatives attempted to maintain a separate existence but found themselves forced to form a coalition with the Liberal party. With the exception of three short intervals the Liberals held office during the whole period. The dominating political figure was Lord Palmerston, who held the office of Foreign or Prime Minister for his party whenever it was in power between 1830 and 1865. He established the tradition of hostility to Russia and patronage of Turkey and through his incessant and meddlesome activity maintained the right of Great Britain to uphold free government and protect its citizens everywhere. In the Liberal party William Ewart Gladstone was laying the foundation for his later career, by his able conduct of the office of Chancellor of the Exchequer. In the opposition Benjamin Disraeli was calling attention to himself and educating his party to a new conception of Toryism, by his gift of irony, his mastery of the arts of politics, and his humorous appearance of detachment from affairs.

These years witnessed the realization of two minor political reforms. In 1853 Gladstone secured the appointment of a Civil Service Commission which recommended that all civil-service posts should be filled by competitive examination. Its recommendations were first applied to the civil service in India. After 1868 Gladstone put them into full effect in nearly all the departments of the British government. In 1858 Parliament opened the opportunity of a political career to Jews by permitting the House of Commons to frame an oath for admission that did no injury to the religious convictions of persons belonging to the Jewish faith.

During these years British industry was at the zenith of its industrial and commercial supremacy. It enjoyed the advantage of a generation's start over its rivals. In consequence the newer industrial establishments of the Continent bought their machinery and borrowed experts and skilled workmen from Great Britain. In addition, new inventions, such as the Bessemer process of making steel from non-phosphoric iron, continued to come mainly from Great Britain. The British state enjoyed a like advantage in regard to railways. Its longer experience in the management and construction of railroads caused the more backward countries to turn to Great Britain for rails, locomotives, and rolling-stock, for contractors to supervise the work of construction, and for capital to finance the lines of railroads. No other country had begun to rival Great Britain in the production of coal, and consequently her factories and her steamships enjoyed the great advantage of cheap and abundant motive power. British shipping continued to outstrip all its rivals. The opportunities for safe and profitable investment had stimulated the accumulation of new capital.

After the failure of the Chartist movement the workers of Great Britain turned for help to the coöperative movement and trade-unionism. In 1844 twenty-eight working-men opened a modest shop at Rochdale with the idea of supplying their own needs and intercepting the profit of the middleman. Their success caused coöperative stores to spring up rapidly in all parts of England, especially in the north. But the new start made by trade-unionism was of far greater significance. In place of little local clubs, managed in spare moments by men actually at work, the workers began to organize powerful national unions, served by officials who gave their whole time to the task. These leaders considered the policy of constant strikes wasteful and harmful, and looked forward to the establishment of conciliation boards that would enable them to deal on equal terms with employers and to coöperate in the control of industry. As in the earlier period, however, the trade-unions suffered from the opposition of the employers and the excesses of workmen made desperate by such periods of depression as the panic of 1857.

2

THE EMPIRE, 1852–1880

Until comparatively late in the nineteenth century, most British political leaders continued to believe that the ultimate goal of the British colonies was independence. As a result of this view the colonies were left to govern their own affairs. They were allowed to establish fiscal independence and even to raise tariff barriers against British goods, as Canada and some of the Australian colonies did. In 1862 Parliament ordered the withdrawal of regular troops from the self-governing colonies and urged them to organize their own military and naval forces for home defense. Not until the seventies did the interest of the general public in the empire revive.

Under the magic touch of self-government stagnant and unprogressive British North America suddenly awoke and began to make rapid advances. The population of Canada grew between 1840 and 1871 from a million and a half to three million and a half. The building of roads, canals, and railways went forward feverishly. The discovery of gold on the Fraser River in 1857 led to the organization in the following year of the colony of British Columbia. Though nine out of ten Canadians disliked the idea of annexation, their leaders began to realize that something must be done to counteract the growing economic dependence of the Canadian colonies upon the United States. Immigration also threatened the equipoise established between the British and French stocks in Canada by the Union Act of 1840, which embodied some of the recommendations of the report of Lord Durham. The Canadian leaders found a solution for these two problems in federation. In 1864 representatives of Upper and Lower Canada and the maritime provinces met to discuss the question and drew up a complex agreement. After the provincial legislatures had taken favorable action on the proposed union the British Parliament enacted the agreement into law in 1867, under the name of the British North America Act. The scheme of federation adopted by the Canadian provinces reserved to the central government all powers not specifically allotted to the provinces and made the executive branch of the government dependent on Parliament. In 1869 the Hudson's Bay Company ceded to the new dominion the vast area which it had previously controlled. In 1871 British Columbia joined the Canadian federation. In 1876 a railway-line finally united the maritime provinces with Quebec and Ontario.

The slowing up of immigration in the forties checked for a time the growth of the Australian colonies. In 1851, however, gold was discovered in New South Wales and shortly afterwards still richer deposits were found in Victoria. The discovery of gold caused an extraordinary inrush of adventurers and the population grew by leaps and bounds, the number of inhabitants in New South Wales rising in the twenty years after the discovery of gold from seventy-seven thousand to seven hundred and twenty thousand. Although many of the new-comers were turbulent and made the colonial authorities much trouble, their coming stimulated agriculture and manufactures.

During these years the New Zealand settlements also steadily developed. Between 1856 and 1878 the population grew from less than sixty thousand to about three hundred and fifty thousand. In 1876 New Zealand abolished the six provincial legislatures established in 1856 and became a unitary state. Between 1861 and 1870 wars with the Maoris, caused in the main by disputes about land sales, interfered with the growth of settlements in North Island. After 1856 gold was discovered in a number of regions, with the same results as in Australia. After the end of the Maori wars New Zealand developed rapidly.

In South Africa the policy of letting the Boers go their own way seemed for a time to work well. Cape Colony, Natal, the Orange Free State, and the Transvaal appeared to have each a separate development. In Cape Colony the period witnessed a real advance. Between 1849 and 1875 the white population grew from seventy-six thousand to two hundred and thirty-seven thousand. Amicable relations existed between the Dutch and the British inhabitants of the province, and the natives, in the main, remained at peace. In 1854 the British government conceded the colony an elective legislature and in 1872 full responsible government. Natal, on the other hand, remained a crown colony because of the slow growth of the white population and the great numbers of natives resident in the province. Events occurred, however, which showed that it was impossible for the two predominantly British colonies and the two Boer colonies to live apart. The native problem led to constant friction. In 1877 the British Colonial Secretary, Lord Carnarvon, attempted to hasten the union of South Africa by annexing the Boers of the Transvaal.

In India the impact of European culture finally led in 1857 to the Indian Mutiny. In spite of the opposition of the British government, the ambitious governors whom it sent to India felt compelled to intervene in native affairs for the maintenance of order and the preservation of British prestige. Lord Dalhousie, who ruled India from 1848 to 1856, labored with fierce zeal to accelerate the introduction of Western civilization and to annex dependent and misgoverned states. During his administration he brought no less than seven states, with a total area of one hundred and fifty thousand square miles, under the direct rule of the British government. He equipped India with roads, steamboats, new harbors, telegraphs, and a postal system, drew up a well-planned scheme for a railway system, explored the coal and iron resources of the country, and attempted to improve its agricultural methods. With the country humming with unrest as a result of these policies, the British authorities unwittingly created unrest in the army, the very foundation of its power in India. As a result of its experiences in the Second Burmese War the British government refused to enlist in the army native soldiers, who were unwilling to cross the sea from fear of losing caste, and thus excluded many Hindus from the only trade they could lawfully follow. It then brought the unrest in the army to a climax by introducing a new cartridge alleged to be incased in paper smeared with the grease of pigs and cows, which the Hindu and Moslem troops could not use without violating their traditions and their religious beliefs.

In May, 1857, the Sepoys in the neighborhood of Delhi suddenly mutinied, murdered their British officers and many British civilians, and proclaimed the old Mogul as Emperor of India. In June the military mutiny spread through the Upper Ganges Valley and into central India. The mutinous troops struck at a time when India had been denuded of large contingents of British troops but, aided by loyal Sepoys and reënforcements, the British forces recaptured one by one the places won by the mutineers. The last of the mutinous troops were not defeated until after the lapse of a year that was marked by the terrible excesses of the Hindu soldiers and barbarous retaliation by the infuriated British forces.

The fearful sacrifices caused by the rising were not made entirely in vain. The revolt called the attention of the British public to the anomaly of intrusting the rule of vast numbers of subject peoples to a trading company and resulted in the transfer of the remaining political powers of the East India Company to the British crown. Indian affairs thenceforth came under the direct control of a member of the British cabinet responsible to Parliament—not as beneficial a change for India as it might seem. The rising also put a stop to British annexations in India and made the British authorities far more cautious in making innovations.

The mutiny, however, did not put an end to the introduction of western civilization. The problem of the recurring famines began to be seriously studied. The great trunk railway-lines were constructed. Secondary schools and universities developed rapidly and began to educate a generation which felt competent to take a greater part in the management of its own affairs. To cap all this, Disraeli conceived the dramatic plan of having his Queen crowned Empress of India. In 1877, accordingly, the British Viceroy announced the new title in a stately and ceremonious durbar held at Delhi, the old capital of India.

3

BRITISH POLITICS AFTER 1865

In the three years after 1865 death and retirement suddenly took from the stage of British politics the jaunty Palmerston, Lord Derby, and Lord Russell. Their passing opened the way to political leadership to Gladstone and Disraeli, the two dominant figures in British politics during the next twenty years. Starting his political career in 1833 as a Conservative, Gladstone had first become a follower of Sir Robert Peel and finally an advanced Liberal. During his parliamentary life he displayed a powerful mind, great talent as an orator, and an extraordinary capacity for hard work. His high moral tone appealed strongly to the British respectable classes but often caused him to assume the attitude of a good man struggling against wicked adversaries. His great opponent, Disraeli, possessed qualities strikingly different. At first the members of his party had considered him an erratic and impudent Jew. In time, however, his ability and brilliance overcame their suspicion and made him the leader of his party. As head of the Conservatives in the House of Commons he assumed a pose of practicality, relied on wit and brilliant epigrams, and showed little regard for political consistency. In contrast with Gladstone he appealed to the sense of romance latent in the British people.

The first achievement of the two new leaders of British politics was a further extension of the suffrage. The question had been before Parliament since 1851 but the conservatism of the British political leaders and their engrossment with foreign and imperial problems had prevented the actual passage of a bill extending the right to vote to new classes. In 1866 Gladstone introduced a measure providing for a moderate extension of the suffrage to town artisans, which encountered defeat at the hands of a coalition of Conservatives and discontented Liberals. But the widespread popular resentment over some of the phrases used in the parliamentary debates and the huge demonstrations held in London and other towns convinced Disraeli that he had an opportunity to benefit his party by meeting the popular demand. With the aid of the followers of Gladstone, therefore, he pushed through Parliament a suffrage measure that transferred a few seats from small boroughs to larger towns and counties and extended the privilege of voting to nearly all adult householders in the towns. This legislation of 1867 nearly doubled the electorate.

In 1868 the Liberals, headed by Gladstone, returned to power and presented to Parliament a series of reform measures of the greatest importance. They began by introducing two bills designed to redress the wrongs of Ireland, which the Fenian movement had just forced upon the attention of the British political leaders. The first disestablished the Church of England in Ireland, deprived it of many of its great endowments, put it on a voluntary basis, and relieved the Irish people of the burden of supporting a church which possessed the allegiance of not more than 8 to 12 per cent of their number. The second attempted—unsuccessfully—to protect the tenants of Ireland against unjust evictions from their little holdings and to insure them compensation for improvements which they had made.

Another great act revolutionized the British system of elementary education. Until 1833 the government had done nothing to promote elementary education. Private persons managed the lower schools and financed them by the income from fees, gifts, and endowments. After 1833 the government began to contribute toward their support, but these voluntary schools did not provide educational facilities for more than half of the children of Great Britain. The legislation of 1870 authorized the local authorities to establish and maintain public schools where these private, voluntary schools did not provide adequately for the education of the children of a locality, divided the expense of the new schools between the national government, the local government, and the patrons, and enabled local authorities to make attendance at school compulsory. The act also increased the aid given by the central government to the voluntary schools.

In 1872 Parliament provided against the intimidation of the new mass of voters by adopting the Australian ballot. Prior to this time the voter had to express his preferences between candidates publicly. The adoption of the secret ballot protected employees from pressure by their employers.

In 1873 the government initiated legislation designed to effect sweeping reforms in the judiciary. The court system of Great Britain made justice costly and vexatious. The Judicature Act reorganized the central courts, reformed their procedure, did away with much confusion, and made justice easier, more certain, and less expensive.

The Liberals made a number of other reforms. They aroused a storm of protest in aristocratic circles by abolishing the purchase of commissions in the army, a practice which had limited the attainment of these to the wealthy classes. They did away with religious tests at the universities, except for theological chairs, and introduced a licensing bill that aroused the opposition of both the temperance advocates and the brewers and publicans. By 1874 they had alienated a sufficient number of groups by their reform policies to drive the cabinet of Gladstone from office.

From 1874 to 1880 Disraeli was at the head of the British government. In the main he subordinated domestic questions to foreign and imperial problems. His first brilliant stroke was the purchase of nine twentieths of the shares of the Suez Canal, an action which gave Great Britain in reality a controlling interest. Opened in 1869, this waterway was of vital interest to the British government, since it constituted the shortest route to India. In order to prevent the purchase by France of the shares owned by the bankrupt Khedive of Egypt, Disraeli negotiated the purchase of the shares with the aid of London bankers and then subsequently obtained the approval of Parliament for his action. This bold transaction appealed to the popular imagination as a masterly stroke in behalf of the empire. In 1876 Disraeli attempted to stir the emotions of the British people and to enhance British prestige in Asia by inducing Parliament to confer upon Queen Victoria the title of Empress of India. Two years later he managed British interests at the Congress of Berlin so skilfully that he could assure the British people that he had returned bringing peace with honor. His imperial policy, however, involved the empire in costly wars with Afghanistan and with the Zulus of South Africa which finally caused a popular reaction and brought the Liberals again into power.

In the successful electoral campaign of 1880, Gladstone had maintained that Disraeli had carried the imperial idea too far. During their five-year tenure of office, consequently, the Liberals drew back the British outposts in the Transvaal. Afghanistan, and other points and turned their attention to domestic problems. Their greatest achievement at home was the extension of the suffrage to agricultural laborers. An act of 1884 lowered the qualifications for voting in the counties, and an act of 1885 created for the first time single-member districts which established approximately the principle of representation in proportion to population.

The growing strength of the home-rule movement forced the Liberal leaders to attempt a solution of the contentious Irish question. In the Parliament of 1874 a solid body of fifty-eight Irish members had refused to aline themselves with either of the two great British parties and had organized themselves as a Home Rule party. They soon found a leader of extraordinary ability in Charles Stewart Parnell. In 1879 the Irish leaders established a Land League, which successfully cut off from human fellowship both Irish landlords who evicted their tenants for arrears in rent and those who attempted to take the holding of the evicted tenant. Its agitation resulted in murders, the maiming of cattle, and much disorder of other kinds. From 1880 onward the new party made the Irish question dominant in British politics. Under the remarkable leadership of Parnell the Irish members threatened to destroy parliamentary life by their tactics of obstruction. Gladstone tried to appease the embittered Irish people by a drastic act, passed in 1881, which practically made Irish tenants joint proprietors with their landlords. It provided that rents should be fixed henceforth not by competition but by a land court, that tenants should have fixity of tenure so long as they paid their rents, and that they should have the right to sell their interests in their holdings. These concessions, however, failed to conciliate the Irish people.

When the Conservatives took office again in 1885 they presented to Parliament a measure that did much to solve the land question in Ireland. The new land policy applied on a large scale for the first time the principle of enabling the Irish tenant to become full owner of his holding. The government advanced to the landlord the full purchase price of the land and permitted the tenant to pay for his holding over a long period of time. So many Irish tenants took advantage of the opportunity to become owners of their own land that they exhausted the first governmental appropriation in a period of two years. Succeeding Parliaments, however, provided additional appropriations for this purpose. As a result of the new policy about one half of the land in Ireland had been transferred to Irish ownership by 1909.

The election of 1885 gave the Irish members practically control of the political situation. Though the Liberals held eighty-six more seats in the House of Commons than the Conservatives, the Home Rule party gained eighty-six of the one hundred and three Irish votes and obtained the balance of power in Parliament. Gladstone, whose mind had already been moving in the direction of home rule, thereupon declared himself in favor of self-government for Ireland and introduced a bill that provided for the establishment of an Irish parliament of two houses (with a responsible cabinet) empowered to legislate on all subjects except the crown, the army and navy, foreign and colonial affairs, trade and navigation, coinage, weights and measures, copyright, and the endowment or establishment of any religion. The introduction of this measure split the Liberal party. With the aid of the revolting Liberals the Conservatives defeated the Home Rule Bill and in the ensuing general election the country indicated its approval of their action.

During the greater part of the next two decades the Conservatives held power and again directed the attention of public opinion mainly to imperial and foreign problems. Their first term of office lasted six years. In 1887, on the occasion of the fiftieth anniversary of the accession of Queen Victoria, the Conservative government held a conference with representatives of the self-governing dominions, initiating by their action a policy that has done much to hold the empire together. In 1888 it steered through Parliament the County Councils Act. This measure transferred the administration of the counties from the centrally appointed justices of the peace to locally elected county councils. It constituted another step toward the transfer of political power from the British aristocracy to the British people.

During this period of Conservative predominance the Liberals were in office only three years. The elections of 1892 gave the Liberals and the Home Rule party a small majority. Gladstone formed his fourth ministry and promptly introduced a second bill providing home rule for Ireland. The new measure differed from the bill of 1886 in particular because it allowed Ireland to be represented in the imperial Parliament by eighty members. The bill passed the House of Commons but met defeat in the House of Lords. In 1894 Gladstone sponsored a Parish Councils Act, which gave the smallest local administrative unit self-government. After this achievement the famous Liberal leader resigned from office. Within a few months differences within the Liberal party caused his successor to give way in favor of the Conservatives.

4

THE NEW IMPERIALISM

During the eleven years of Conservative rule that followed, imperial affairs completely predominated over the domestic problems of the United Kingdom. The self-governing dominions became conscious of their maturity and the British cabinet initiated a number of venturesome enterprises.

For Canada the years following the establishment of unity were a period of material expansion and political stability. The Conservatives held power from 1878 to 1896 and then for fifteen years the Liberals continuously ruled the country. The Canadian people devoted their energies to development of the new federation. In 1885 they finished the Canadian Pacific Railway and the task of linking the provinces together. The completion of this transcontinental railroad made possible the development of the enormous expanse of fertile country between the Great Lakes and the Rocky Mountains. With the growth of material prosperity the Canadian people began to feel and act like a nation.

The history of New Zealand during these years is especially characterized by bold social experiments. From 1879 to 1895 the country suffered from stagnation and depression but thereafter it enjoyed a period of increasing population and growing prosperity. The years of social experimentation began in 1891 with the accession of the Liberals to power. Under the leadership of a remarkable politician, Richard Seddon, they passed legislation designed to prevent the formation of large estates and speculation in land, established an arbitration court and conciliation boards for the purpose of facilitating the settlement of industrial disputes, organized a system of old-age pensions, borrowed money freely for public works, and discouraged immigration, with the object of maintaining the existing high standard of living.

The Australian colonies experienced a rather peculiar development.

In Western Australia the discovery of gold led to a sudden inrush of immigrants and the establishment of responsible government. In the other colonies an unusual proportion of the population lived in four large cities and in the mining regions. This situation led to the early development of Labor parties, which played an important part in the politics of the Australian colonies. In 1900 the colonies finally united on a scheme of federation and took a place beside Canada as a self-governing dominion. In the formation of their union the Australians gave the central government only certain specific powers, made amendment of the constitution easy, and adopted the British parliamentary system.

In Africa the independence of the Transvaal had hardly been recognized by Gladstone in 1884 when the discovery of gold in this state began to revive the feeling of bitterness between the Boers and the British. Thousands of gold-diggers, shopkeepers, and professional men flocked into the Transvaal. Within ten years the new-comers owned a third of the land, and numbered more than half of the population. Fearful lest they should lose control of their country, the Boers, led by their prejudiced, stubborn President Paul Kruger, excluded practically all the incoming population from citizenship, burdened it with taxes, insisted on the use of Dutch in the schools, and attempted to divert the traffic of the Transvaal from Cape Colony to the Portuguese ports in Delagoa Bay. In self-defense many of the new-comers organized a Reform Union, which demanded equal political rights and the protection of Great Britain, the suzerain of the Transvaal.

Their appeal received a sympathetic hearing from Cecil Rhodes, the dominant figure in the politics of Cape Colony and one of the controlling personalities in the diamond-fields of Kimberley and the gold-mines of Johannesburg. At his urging the British had been gradually encircling the Transvaal for a decade. In 1885 he had persuaded the British government to proclaim a protectorate over Bechuanaland. In 1889 he organized the British South Africa Company, which was authorized to open up and colonize the region later known as Rhodesia. In 1890 he became Prime Minister of Cape Colony. He began to dream of uniting Cape Colony to Cairo and the obstinate Kruger stood in the way of the realization of his plans. Impatient at this opposition, he joined a conspiracy to overthrow his opponent that miscarried. The reckless attempt destroyed all hope of compromise between the two peoples. The British government took up the cause of the immigrants in the Transvaal and President Kruger, supported by the Boers of both the Transvaal and the Orange Free State, took a very stiff tone that made war inevitable.

Confident that he could drive the British out of South Africa, and unconscious of the vast resources of the British Empire, President

Kruger presented to the British authorities an ultimatum, in October, 1899, which precipitated the Boer War. The Boers invaded Natal and Cape Colony, laid siege to Mafeking, Kimberley, and Ladysmith, and defeated the British relieving forces. After these initial successes the latent strength of the British Empire began to tell. Reënforced by troops from Great Britain and her dominions, the British forces freed the beleaguered garrisons, pressed on into the Orange Free State and the Transvaal, and defeated all organized opposition. The Boers, however, kept up a troublesome guerrilla warfare until 1902. After their final surrender they became incorporated into the British Empire, but they received generous terms. Their defeat opened the way for the Union of South Africa.

5

AN ERA OF LIBERAL REFORMS

This neglect of domestic problems finally brought to a close the long period of Conservative ascendancy. A majority of the people of the British Isles came to feel that their vital interests were being sacrificed to imperialism. This feeling found expression in the general election of 1906. In this the Liberals gained a clear majority over all other parties, the Home Rule party won eighty-three seats in Parliament, and the new Labor party, fifty-one representatives. These three parties coöperated in the parliamentary struggles of the next eight years.

The Liberals came into power pledged to a program of reform. Their first important measure dealt with education. In contrast with an act of Parliament passed in 1902, which gave to voluntary schools the same aid as to public schools without placing them completely under public control, the new bill provided that schools supported by public taxes should be under public control and should not be permitted to enforce religious tests for teachers. The House of Lords, however, altered the bill so much by amendments that the House of Commons abandoned the measure. In the same session the House of Lords, composed of an overwhelming majority of Conservatives, rejected entirely a Plural Voting Bill designed to limit a man to a single vote and a Licensing Bill that, in the interest of temperance, would revoke for a period of fourteen years thirty thousand licenses for the sale of liquor and would compensate the holders of the revoked licenses from taxes levied on the liquor trade.

The Liberal ministry encountered less opposition to its Old Age Pension Bill. This revolutionary measure aimed to provide for the declining years of self-respecting persons who had never been in a position to accumulate any savings. It gave a pension to every person over seventy years of age who had an income of less than thirty-one pounds and ten shillings a year and who had been a British subject for twenty years and a resident of Great Britain for twelve years. The adoption of this measure constituted an abandonment of the principle of individualism.

In order to meet the demands on the treasury for old-age pensions and other social reforms, and for a larger navy, David Lloyd George, the Chancellor of the Exchequer, introduced a budget in 1909 that proposed new taxes designed to benefit the poor at the expense of the rich. It planned to prevent a deficit in the treasury by appropriating about three million pounds from the sum annually set aside for debt-reduction, increasing the duties on certain luxuries, especially liquor and tobacco, adding to the income and succession duties, and levying heavy rates on such monopolies as liquor licenses and on the increase in the value of unoccupied and uncultivated lands. The proposal to tax the unearned increment of land particularly aroused the fury of the Conservatives. They charged that the budget struck at the security of property and threatened to drive capital from the country. The Conservative majority in the House of Lords, therefore, rejected the new budget until the judgment of the country could be obtained.

The Liberals denounced the rejection of the budget of 1909 as a wanton breach of the settled practice of the constitution and appealed for the support of the country in a general election. They fought the political campaign on the issues of the budget, the abolition of the veto power of the House of Lords, and home rule for Ireland. They found themselves forced to commit themselves on this last issue in order to gain the support of the Irish Nationalists. The ensuing political campaign gave no party a majority and the Liberals, in consequence, became dependent on the support of the Irish Nationalists and the Labor party.

After securing the passage of the contested finance bill the Liberal coalition took up the question of the reform of the House of Lords. The three parties proposed to deprive the upper chamber entirely of power to control financial measures, and to permit it only to delay the adoption of other legislation desired by the House of Commons. In alarm the threatened House of Lords came forward with a resolution designed to improve the personnel of the upper chamber without impairing its powers. Just at this point in the struggle King Edward VII died. In order not to confront his untried successor, George V, with the problem, the leaders of the British political parties held a series of conferences in the hope of effecting a compromise, but they found their views irreconcilable. After the failure of these negotiations, the Liberals introduced a bill in the House of Commons that deprived the House of Lords of the right to veto a money bill, provided that a bill passed in three successive sessions of Parliament and during a period of more than two years should become a law in spite of the veto of the upper house, and reduced the life of a Parliament from seven to five years. When the House of Lords rejected this measure the Liberals appealed to the country for the second time within a year, this time on the sole issue of the reform of the House of Lords. This second election of 1910 left the political situation unchanged. Early in 1911, consequently, the Liberals and their political allies again passed in the House of Commons their bill for the reform of the House of Lords. When the upper chamber so amended it as practically to destroy it the Prime Minister announced that he had the promise of the King to create enough new lords to pass the bill in the House of Lords over the opposition of the Conservatives. Alarmed at the prospect of the revolution that would result from the creation of several hundred new peers, the House of Lords gave way and passed the bill.

With the upper chamber deprived of its power to obstruct their measures, the Liberals and their allies proceeded with their program of social and political legislation. In 1911 they forced through Parliament a National Insurance Act designed to provide insurance against unemployment and loss of health, to prevent sickness and to cure workers who were ill. Its provisions applied to all workers between the ages of sixteen and sixty-five with an annual income from property of less than twenty-six pounds. It derived the insurance funds from payments made by the employers, the workers, and the government. The unemployment provisions affected only the workers in the building and engineering trades. The Liberals also put through Parliament measures for the abolition of plural voting and for the disestablishment of the Church of England in Wales.

The most contentious item on the Liberal program was the Home Rule Bill. The Protestant minority in Ulster strongly opposed the idea of being subjected to a parliament dominated by Irish Roman Catholics, and the conservative Unionists of Great Britain sympathized with their fellow-religionists of Ireland and felt that the proposal to grant self-government to Ireland threatened the unity and safety of the empire. The Unionist majority in the House of Lords, consequently, rejected the Liberal Home Rule Bill three times and encouraged the Protestants of Ulster to push their opposition to the point of rebellion. The latter prepared for military resistance and signed a covenant pledging themselves not to recognize the authority of a home-rule parliament. The Catholics of southern Ireland, thereupon, began to arm in support of home rule. Just as the empire seemed on the point of civil war the World War broke out, and Parliament agreed not to attempt to enforce the Home Rule Act until after the close of the European struggle.

In the empire Liberalism found expression during these years in the Union of South Africa. After the close of the Boer War in 1902 the British authorities spent three years in the reconstruction of the two annexed republics. In 1906 the new Liberal cabinet took the bold step of establishing responsible government in the two Boer provinces. In the elections of the following year the Boers won a victory in Cape Colony as well as in the Transvaal and the Orange River Colony, but their victory did not revive the old antagonisms. On the contrary, an agitation began that resulted in the holding of a national convention of representatives of the four South African colonies, which drew up a plan of union. The plan won the approval of the four colonial and the imperial parliaments and in 1910 the Union of South Africa took its place beside the other self-governing dominions.

The Liberals did not meet with the same success in their attempts to satisfy public opinion in India. In 1905 the British authorities had divided the immense territory of Bengal into two provinces, in the interest of administrative efficiency. Their action produced an outburst of protest which expressed itself in a boycott of British goods, outrages, and assassinations. The Liberal government tried to meet this dangerous agitation in 1909 by introducing a substantial representative element into the Imperial Legislative Council, an elected Indian majority in the provincial legislative councils, and Indian representation in the councils of the Viceroy and the Secretary of State for India. But these concessions failed to satisfy the more eager Indian nationalists and the British government suffered from an incessant criticism in the legislative councils and in the press. For a time the visit of George V to India in 1911, to be crowned, eased the tension. In 1913, however, many of the Moslems joined the Hindus in opposition to British rule. By 1914 the opposition in India had become formidable.

After the Crimean War British and Continental history ceased to be even superficially similar. While the Continent suffered from wars and great political changes, the British people and their empire enjoyed, in the main, a peaceful development. In Great Britain interest shifted back and forth between domestic questions and imperial and foreign problems. At the opening of the period British complacency found expression and leadership in the jaunty Palmerston. For over twenty years after his death in 1865 Gladstone and Disraeli alternately stood at the head of the government, the former directing the attention of the British people to domestic problems and the latter emphasizing imperial and foreign questions. From 1886 to 1905 the Conservatives held power almost uninterruptedly, their policy culminating in the Boer War. In 1906 the Liberals came into power again, pledged to enact into law a vast program of social and political reforms. In the meantime Canada, New Zealand, Australia, and South Africa developed into mature self-governing nations able to take a place of equality beside Great Britain in the empire.

PART IV

INTERNATIONAL RELATIONS, 1871–1918

CHAPTER XXII

The voyage of Vasco da Gama in 1498 inaugurated a struggle between the European powers for colonies and commercial supremacy in Asia that has continued until the present day. Three centuries of conflict in southern and eastern Asia left the Portuguese in possession of a few scattered, decaying ports, the Spaniards in control of the Philippines, the Dutch with a valuable empire in the East Indies, the French with a few remnants of the territory that they once seemed on the verge of acquiring in India, and the British dominant in India and with almost a monopoly of trade in the Far East. At the same time exiles, settlers, and adventurers had been winning political control of the vast spaces of Siberia for the Russian Empire. With the industrialization of Europe in the nineteenth century the rivalry of the European powers for markets and for colonies grew keener and ambitious colonial administrators steadily extended the authority of their home governments in Asia. The tension between the European states became particularly great in the Middle East, the Indo-Chinese peninsula, and the Far East.

I

ANGLO-RUSSIAN RIVALRY IN THE MIDDLE EAST

After 1809 the British government had felt more or less fear of a Russian attack in the Middle East and had made special efforts to maintain friendly relations with the Sikhs of the Punjab, the Amirs of Sind in the Lower Indus Valley, and the wild mountain tribes of Afghanistan, the three independent native states controlling the roads into India through the dangerous northwestern frontier. In the thirties British alarm increased as the Russian outposts in Central Asia moved steadily southward and Russian agents began to establish friendly relations in Persia and Afghanistan. This fear of Russia caused the British authorities in India to make a succession of blunders. In 1838 they sent an expedition into Afghanistan that placed a rather futile exiled prince on the throne under the protection of a British army and the supervision of a British resident. Resentful at this policy, the fierce warriors of Afghanistan revolted and drove the British out of their country. In an effort to restore their prestige the British authorities attacked and annexed Sind. This action created unrest among the Sikhs and made necessary the annexation of the Punjab. These annexations brought the boundary of the British Empire to a natural frontier.

In the seventh decade of the nineteenth century the continued southward advance of Russia in Central Asia brought the Afghan question to the fore again. In 1868 the Russian government established its control over the Khanate of Bokhara and five years later over the Khanate of Khiva. These moves brought Russia to the very borders of Afghanistan and caused the Amir to turn to the British government for protection. Upon the refusal of the British to extend him aid he turned for support to the Russians. Struggling as they were against Russian influence in the Balkan peninsula, however, the British authorities soon came to feel that the situation in Central Asia was intolerable. In 1876, consequently, they established a British protectorate over the barren land of Baluchistan. Two years later, when the Amir received a Russian envoy with great honor but refused a British representative admission to his country, the British authorities declared war on Afghanistan. The conflict resulted in the negotiation of a treaty which left the Afghans their independence, gave their ruler a substantial annual subsidy and guaranteed his frontiers, and handed over to India control of the great mountain barrier on its northwestern frontier.

This agreement by no means allayed British suspicion of Russia. The interests of the two powers continued to clash in Central Asia. After 1898 Persia seemed to be falling under Russian influence and Great Britain began to be concerned about her position both in Persia and in the region surrounding the Persian Gulf. In that year the Persian government turned to Russia for a loan. Five years later it permitted the Russian government to organize a bank in order to advance its economic interests in Persia. In 1904 the news of the favorable reception accorded a Russian envoy in Tibet made the British government fearful of being outflanked on the north and led to the despatch of a remarkable British military expedition to that mysterious land. This tension in Persia, Tibet, and Afghanistan forms the background of the Anglo-Russian Entente of 1907.

2

THE ANGLO-FRENCH RIVALRY IN INDO-CHINA

In its expansion eastward from India the British finally came into conflict with the Kingdom of Burma, which had been extending its power on all sides since 1782. The Burmese treated with studied insolence British attempts to establish friendly relations, and avowed their intention of attacking Bengal. In 1823, accordingly, the British undertook a punitive campaign against Burma which, at the end of a campaign of three years, resulted in the cession to the British Empire of the two long coastal strips of Arakan and Tenasserim. In 1852 the complaints made by British traders of oppression and the interruption of trade caused a second war with Burma, which resulted in the cession of Lower Burma to the British Empire. In 1884 the arrogance of King Thebaw and fear lest Upper Burma should fall under French control caused a third British war with Burma that resulted in the annexation of the remainder of the Burmese Kingdom to the British Empire.

During these years of British expansion at the expense of Burma the French had been steadily gaining ground in the peninsula of Indo-China. In the days of the Second French Empire the persecution of native Christians and the murder of certain missionaries had given Napoleon III a pretext for the annexation of Cochin-China and the establishment of a protectorate over Cambodia. After the Franco-Prussian War of 1870 the efforts of a French citizen to open a trading route with southern China by way of the Red River led to French intervention in Tonking. His action involved the French in military conflicts with Annam and China, as both states laid claim to the province. The intervention of France in Tonking finally resulted in the defeat of China and the establishment of a French protectorate in Annam.

After 1885, the French and British watched each other in Indo-China with growing suspicion. In 1893 the two powers were brought to the verge of war by the contention of the French government that Siam had no title to any territory on the left bank of the Mekong River. After three years of negotiation the British and French established the Mekong River as the boundary line between their spheres of influence.

3

THE OPENING OF CHINA

At the opening of the nineteenth century the Chinese Empire and its civilization still exercised a widely recognized hegemony in the Far East. Its inhabitants had become highly civilized long before the peoples of Europe. At an early date they had invented the compass, gunpowder, porcelain, paper, and printing from movable blocks, and had become famous for their work in bronze, wood, lacquer, and silk. They had developed a social system that emphasized the family rather than the individual and bred a deep respect for the past and its ideas. They had evolved a political system that theoretically placed absolute power in the hands of an emperor but in practice left much to the control of the family and the local officials. They intrusted the administration of the country to an office-holding class selected on the basis of severe examinations in the literature and learning of China. From time to time their empire had extorted a recognition of its overlordship from Korea, Burma, and Indo-China. Their achievements and their isolation made the Chinese feel that they were a superior people.

This feeling caused the Chinese to treat in a contemptuous manner the insistent European traders coming to their ports in ever greater numbers. At first their feeling of contempt took a tolerant form. They permitted foreigners to trade in the southern Chinese ports and allowed Roman Catholic missionaries from Europe to carry on their work in China. The conduct of the European traders and missionaries, however, finally caused the Chinese to become intolerant. The Portuguese showed more interest in loot than in trade and waged a relentless war on the Moslem Arabs; the British offended the Chinese by their stiff manners; and the missionaries interfered with their ancestor-worship. In 1724, consequently, the Chinese government forbade further missionary activity in China and in 1757 it restricted foreign trade to the port of Canton. It also insisted on treating the representatives of European governments as the agents of dependent states.

Thenceforth European traders in China found themselves subjected to many exasperating restrictions. The Chinese government compelled them to leave their families at Macao, a Portuguese port across the bay from Canton, forced them to erect their factories outside the walls of Canton, refused to let them enter the city or wander in the neighboring country, and made them conduct their commercial transactions with the twelve or thirteen hong merchants who had the foreign traders at their mercy. Since it considered the tea, silks, and nankeen cloth of China indispensable to the European traders, the Chinese government frequently forbade all trade, to bring the foreign merchants to time.

For a long period the commerce of Europe with China was one-sided, the Europeans paying with specie for the Chinese commodities that they bought. In time the European traders developed in China a market for furs, rice, sandalwood, and cotton goods, but specie continued to hold an important place in the trade until the European merchants began the importation into China of opium from India. When the Chinese government tried to put a stop to this trade because of the harmful effects of opium-smoking, the European traders found the Chinese officials ready to connive at the smuggling of opium into China.

In 1838 the Chinese government appointed a special commissioner to check this illicit trade. After a brief study of the question he demanded that the foreign merchants should surrender the opium in their possession and give bond to abandon the trade in this commodity, and threatened a complete stoppage of commercial intercourse to enforce compliance with his demands. When the British superintendent of trade assumed responsibility for their property, the British merchants surrendered over twenty thousand chests of opium, but they refused to give the bond demanded of them. Thereupon the energetic Chinese commissioner surprised them by destroying the surrendered opium, stopped further commercial intercourse with them, and forbade the Chinese to furnish the European merchants with food, water, or service.

This vigorous action raised the whole question of Anglo-Chinese relations. The repeated efforts of the British government to establish satisfactory diplomatic relations had ended in failure. The Chinese government either ignored the communications of the British diplomatic representatives sent out to China or regarded them as petitions. The British traders and other foreigners mistrusted the Chinese courts and hesitated to hand European offenders over to the Chinese authorities for trial. In addition a number of hong merchants had become insolvent and owed the British traders considerable sums of money. Even if the opium question had not come up, the general situation would sooner or later have involved the British government in war with China.

While affairs were at this critical stage some British sailors killed a Chinaman in a riot. The special commissioner demanded their surrender. When the British superintendent of trade refused to comply with the demand, twenty-nine Chinese war-junks approached the British shipping and repeated the demand. When they refused to withdraw, two British war-ships opened fire and sank four of the junks. The British followed up this action by demanding satisfaction for the ill-treatment suffered by the superintendent of trade and other British subjects, indemnification for the confiscated opium, security for the future, and the cession of an island off the Chinese coast. When their demands were refused the British resorted to armed force. In 1841 a British squadron bombarded Canton and the Chinese ransomed the city for a large sum of money, and British troops captured a number of other ports along the coast of southern China. In 1842 the British forces continued to capture Chinese ports and the British fleet appeared in the vicinity of Nanking, the old capital of China.

These disasters compelled the Chinese to come to terms first with the British government and subsequently with the representatives of several other powers. These treaties made a beginning toward opening China to intercourse with the outside world. By the Treaty of Nanking the British government obtained the right to carry on trade with five Chinese ports; the cession of the island of Hongkong; indemnity for the destroyed opium, the threats against the lives of British subjects, and the British punitive expedition to China; compensation for the debts due British merchants; the abolition of the hong; a fair and regular tariff; and a recognition that the communications of the British government were not petitions. A supplementary treaty acknowledged in a rather vague way the principle of extraterritoriality. The French negotiators obtained the permission of the Chinese government for Roman Catholic missionaries to carry on their work. Upon learning of the religious differences among Europeans, the Chinese Emperor extended to Protestants the same rights that he had just conceded to the Roman Catholic missionaries.

These treaties neither satisfied the Europeans nor taught the Chinese the expected lesson. The higher Chinese officials at Peking seemed incapable of understanding the new situation and millions of their subjects knew nothing at all about the events of the war. The Chinese of the treaty ports resented the misconduct of unruly seamen, the losses suffered in the war, the treatment accorded the Chinese coolies, the continued smuggling of opium, and the evils of extraterritoriality. Foreigners complained of the high-handed treatment that they had received at the hands of the Chinese, the failure of the Chinese authorities to carry out the recently negotiated treaties, and their refusal to make further concessions.

In such a situation any incident might precipitate a new war. In 1856 the Chinese authorities arrested, tortured, and executed a French priest who had penetrated into the interior without the authorization of the Chinese government. As a result of the incident the French government determined to take action in defense of Roman Catholic missions in China and to join Great Britain, its recent ally in the Crimean War, in a demand for a revision of the unsatisfactory commercial treaties. The two governments agreed to demand reparation for the murder of the priest, satisfaction for the acts of hostility at Canton and elsewhere, and revision of the existing treaties, and to send a joint expedition to China to enforce these demands. Before they actually took action an incident occurred which the British government used to justify its policy of intervention in Chinese affairs. Late in 1856 Chinese officials, in an effort to arrest a notorious pirate, boarded a British vessel owned by a Chinese resident of Hongkong, hauled down the British flag, and took off twelve of the Chinese crew. The failure of the Chinese authorities to apologize for the insult to the British flag led to an open break between the British and the Chinese. The British captured the forts guarding Canton and bombarded the office of the local viceroy; this official ordered the extermination of the British villains and offered a reward for every British head brought to his office.

At the outset the British found themselves hampered in carrying out their agreement with the French by the necessity of diverting troops to quell the mutiny in India. In 1858, however, an Anglo-French force captured Canton. The two allies then shifted their attack to northern China and attempted to force their way up the Pei River to Tientsin and Peking. Their attack on the forts guarding the mouth of the river resulted in the negotiation of an agreement that conceded to the two powers the right to maintain ministers at Peking, to travel freely into the interior, to trade at certain specified ports on the Yangtse-Kiang River, the great central highway of China, to carry on trade at several additional ports on the coast, and that their citizens should be tried in European courts for crimes committed in China. The treaty also promised a large indemnity and the protection of native Christians. These concessions did not end the hostilities. After the capture of the forts at the mouth of the river the French and British troops forced their way to Tientsin and Peking and, as a punishment for the mistreatment of European hostages, destroyed the beautiful Summer Palace of the Emperor, an architectural monument built in the eighteenth century in accordance with plans drawn by Jesuit missionaries. This disaster led to the negotiation of the Treaty of Peking, which wrung from the defeated Chinese certain additional concessions.

By virtue of the most-favored-nation clause inserted in the various treaties signed by China the concessions extorted by the military and naval forces of France and Great Britain benefited all the Western states. The state that benefited most by the energetic action of the two powers in China was Russia, the enemy of France and Great Britain in the recent Crimean War. In 1858 the Russian government negotiated a treaty with China, which ceded the left bank of the Amur River to Russia, provided for the delimitation of a frontier, and opened up the Sungari and Ussuri Rivers to Russian merchants and travelers. Two years later Russia acquired the whole Manchurian coast from the Amur River to the frontier of Korea.

This second defeat did not change essentially the psychology of the officials of China. Though the Chinese government finally established a Foreign Office, in 1861 the imperial government refused to foreigners an imperial audience and failed to enforce the treaties with foreign powers. For most of the remaining years of the century, the strongly conservative Empress Dowager dominated the government as Regent first for her son and later for her nephew. The arrogance of the foreigners in China increased the general antagonism to outsiders, and with the penetration of missionaries into the interior anti-Christian riots began to take place.

The Chinese, however, found themselves unable to prevent the penetration of Western civilization into their country. In 1863 steam navigation began in China. In 1865 a college for the training of interpreters and the teaching of Western science was established. Seven years later a group of thirty Chinese boys was sent to the United States to be educated. In 1876 a beginning was made toward the construction of railroads, but out of deference to the popular opposition the government repurchased the railroad and tore up the rails. Two years afterwards a coal-mine was opened. In 1882 a telegraph-line was built between Shanghai and Tientsin. In 1887 permanent railway-construction really began in China. Three years later the Hanyang Iron Works began operations. Between 1860 and 1905 Chinese imports trebled and exports quadrupled. These new economic and social forces began to transform China slowly.

4

THE OPENING UP OF JAPAN

Until 1854 the Japanese government attempted to enforce the same policy of exclusion as did that of China. At first it had put no obstacle in the way of European traders and missionaries. Portuguese, Spanish, British, and Dutch merchants started profitable trading operations with the Japanese and by the end of the sixteenth century Roman Catholic missionaries had built some two hundred churches and made about seven hundred and fifty thousand converts in Japan. Finally, however, a fear that the missionaries were forerunners of political conquest caused a reaction against all foreign influences. Native Christians commenced to suffer from local persecutions. In 1587 the Japanese government ordered all missionaries to leave Japan. In 1612 it began to put into effect drastic measures against Christianity. In 1624 it issued orders for all Spaniards to leave the country. Twelve years later it ordered all foreigners out of Japan and forbade the Japanese to leave their own state under pain of death. For the next two hundred years the Japanese came into contact with the outside world only through a carefully restricted and regulated trade with the Dutch and the Chinese.

In the nineteenth century the aggressive representatives of Europe and America found the Japanese policy of exclusion increasingly irksome. They objected to the treatment accorded vessels and crews shipwrecked on the Japanese coast. American whaling-ships desired to obtain wood, water, and provisions. Traders desired to reopen commercial relations. After the opening up of California, steamships plying between the United States and China needed a coaling-station in Japan. This situation caused the United States government to send instructions to Commodore Matthew Perry, commander of the American naval forces in the Far East, to make an attempt to persuade Japan to give up its policy of exclusion.

In July, 1853, consequently, Perry sailed into the harbor of Yeddo with a naval squadron composed of two steam and two sailing vessels and handed the alarmed Japanese a letter for their Emperor from the President of the United States. At the urgent request of the Japanese authorities he then sailed away, giving the perplexed Japanese until the following year to formulate their answer to the American demands. The decision of the question, however, lay in the hands of the Shogun, an official who had gradually acquired all real authority in the state and had relegated the Emperor to an honorary position and a life of entire seclusion. The American demands placed the Shogun in a difficult position. Acceptance would put a weapon in the hands of those of the western clans of Japan which resented the elevation of the family of the Shogun to its position of great power. A refusal would expose Japan to the danger of a costly and perhaps disastrous war such as the Chinese had recently experienced. The Shogun and his advisers, therefore, finally decided to meet the American demands. They knew something of the West and its power, through the Dutch, and they feared the advance of the Russians. Upon the return of Perry, accordingly, they negotiated a treaty in which they promised to open two ports where Americans might obtain wood, water, and provisions, to treat shipwrecked men and goods well, to permit the opening of trade relations under Japanese regulations and through Japanese officials. During the next few months the British, Russians, and Dutch negotiated similar treaties.

The treaty wrested from Japan by Commodore Perry did not grant the traders of the United States the right to conduct general trade with the Japanese. Consequently the negotiation of such a treaty became the first objective of Townsend Harris, the able man sent out as first United States consul to Japan. In 1858 he succeeded in concluding a treaty that conceded to the United States the right to maintain a resident minister and to carry on general trade in the country. For a time the Shogun attempted vainly to gain the approval of the conservative Emperor for the new treaty. The news of the disasters that had overtaken China in the war with France and Great Britain caused the Shogun to decide to save his country from foreign intervention by signing the treaty on his own responsibility. The new agreement established regular diplomatic and consular arrangements between the United States and Japan, brought about the opening of four additional ports to general trade, and put into effect the principle of extraterritoriality. Within a short time most of the important powers of Europe negotiated similar treaties with Japan.

The patriotic action of the Shogun tended to bring the long-cherished resentment against his family to a head and to rally all the elements of opposition around the Emperor. As has been intimated, some of the western clans had always resented the rise of the family of the Shogun to a position of such great power in the state. The work of historical investigators had clearly shown that the Shogun had usurped authority that had once belonged to the Emperor. The revival of Shintoism, the national religion, had tended to revive the feeling of loyalty to the titular head of the state. After the Shogun defied conservative opinion by opening Japan to trade with the outside world, the Emperor put himself at the head of all the elements opposed to the Shogun.

The events of the next few years finally brought the Emperor and the conservative military clans of western Japan around to the same point of view that the Shogun had taken. In the seven years following the negotiation of the commercial treaty Japanese rioters killed twelve foreigners, attacked the British legation twice, and burned both the British and the American legations. These attacks resulted in naval demonstrations in which British, French, Dutch, and American warships took part; these revealed to the Emperor and to two of the most powerful of the western military clans their military and naval inferiority to the Western powers. In consequence they abandoned their antiforeign policy without giving up their opposition to the Shogun. The Emperor finally gave his approval to the commercial treaties negotiated after 1858, but the indemnities demanded by the aggrieved powers threw the finances of the Shogun into confusion.

In 1867 the power of the Shogun came to an end. Within a few months both the Shogun and the Emperor died. The successor of the old Shogun volunteered to surrender his administrative powers in order that Japan might present a united front to other states. A little later a palace revolution led to the complete abolition of the office. However, this transfer of authority to the Emperor did not hinder the progress of the opening of Japan to outside influences.

5

THE REORGANIZATION OF JAPAN

In the three decades following the abolition of the Shogunate Japan, led by a remarkable group of advisers around the young Emperor, underwent an amazing transformation. Convinced by their contact with the Western powers that Japan must adopt European institutions to protect itself from Western aggression, the Japanese leaders made sweeping reforms, which changed Japan from a feudal to a modern state. As a sign of the new era the Emperor transferred his residence from the scene of his former life of seclusion to Tokyo, and named the new period the era of enlightened government.

The new period opened with a remarkable sacrifice of their privileges by the heads of the feudal clans that had dominated the life of old Japan. In 1869 the chiefs of four of the great clans recognized the trend of the times and voluntarily surrendered their rights to the Emperor.

Within a few months two hundred and forty-one of the two hundred and seventy-six feudal lords of Japan had followed their example. In 1871 the Emperor decreed the abolition of feudalism. He assigned the former feudal lords a tenth of their previous revenues.

Contact with European and American naval forces quickly convinced the Japanese of the necessity of reorganizing their military and naval forces. Some of the feudal lords had introduced Western military tactics into their feudal levies even before the coming of Commodore Perry. A defeat of the forces of the Shogun at the hands of one of these clans caused that official to train some of his troops in the same way. After 1855 the Shogun and some of the feudal lords began to buy steam and sailing vessels in Europe and America. In 1871 Japan adopted the principle of universal conscription. In military matters the Japanese followed German traditions. In naval affairs they imitated British methods.

The machines and science of the West also quickly found their way into Japan. In 1870 the Japanese began the construction of the first two railroad-lines. By 1878 they felt able to carry on their own railroad construction, and by 1892 they had over two thousand miles of railway in operation. In 1869 they built the first telegraph-line in Japan. In 1871 they organized a postal service between Osaka and Yokohama and rapidly extended it to other parts of the empire. Within five years Japan joined the International Postal Union. As early as 1866 the Japanese government permitted young men to go abroad for study, and the Japanese commenced to purchase sailing and steam vessels for the purpose of engaging in commerce.

The Japanese government, likewise, quickly saw the need for educational reform. In 1871 it established a Department of Education. In the next year it declared that "all people, high or low, of both sexes, should receive education so that there should not be found one family in the whole empire, nor one member of a family, ignorant or illiterate." For the benefit of the higher schools it invited foreigners to take educational posts in Japan and it encouraged young Japanese to prepare themselves abroad. It rapidly organized elementary schools under the guidance of an American educator. It encouraged the translation of Western books and the writing of Japanese text-books. As a result of these measures the Japanese soon became one of the most literate peoples.

The development of schools prepared the way for participation of the Japanese in the work of governing. In 1877 the government provided in the cities and prefectures for elected assemblies empowered to determine the budget. Although their resolutions might be vetoed by the government, the power of the purse gave these assemblies an opportunity to bring pressure on the government. In 1881 an imperial decree promised the convening of a national assembly in 1890 and the govern-

ment immediately created a commission to study the problem of drawing up a new constitution. The final draft of its work showed that the
commission had been much influenced by German precedents. Within
a few years the government established a peerage with Western titles
in order to provide an upper house, and created a cabinet and a Privy
Council. In 1889 the government finally promulgated the new constitution. This document gave the Emperor a unique position in the government, provided for an upper legislative house composed of some
of the hereditary peers and other distinguished subjects, and established
a lower chamber elected by a very limited suffrage. The constitution,
however, did not destroy the extraconstitutional influence of the leaders
of the more influential feudal clans, popularly known as the Elder
Statesmen. In 1890 the government held the elections for the new
parliament.

As a result of these reforms the Japanese transformed themselves
from a weak Asiatic state into a strong modern power. The European
public, however, did not generally appreciate the significance of the
changes going on in Japan until the Chino-Japanese War of 1894–
1895.

6

THE CHINO-JAPANESE WAR OF 1894–1895

The struggle between China and Japan broke out over the question
of their respective rights in Korea. In this state the coming into power,
in 1863, of a weak boy as King inaugurated a contest for control of
the government and the opportunity to exploit the mass of the people.
The conservative faction, which desired to exclude all foreign influences,
looked for support to China, which had long claimed a sort of suzerainty
over Korea. The faction that believed in the necessity of opening up
the country looked to the Japanese for assistance. In 1876 the Japanese
government, in imitation of Perry, had extorted a commercial treaty
from the Korean government which asserted its complete independence.
The weakness of the Korean government opened the way for the intrigues of both the Chinese and the Japanese governments.

In 1893 the rise of a Korean society opposed to foreign influences
led to the military intervention of both China and Japan in Korea,
and precipitated the Chino-Japanese War. Upon the refusal of China
to withdraw her troops from the country the Japanese cleared the sea
by a naval action, sent more soldiers into Korea, secured possession
of the Korean capital and the person of the King, and finally drove
the Chinese forces out of northern Korea. After these victories one
Japanese army marched from Korea into Manchuria and another landed

near Port Arthur and shortly captured that important strategic point. When nothing stood in the way of the Japanese military forces moving on Peking, the capital of China, the surprised Chinese leaders decided to sue for peace.

In making peace, however, the victorious Japanese encountered unexpected opposition. In the Treaty of Shimonoseki the Japanese government extorted from the defeated Chinese government a recognition of the independence of Korea, the cession of Port Arthur and the whole Liaotung peninsula, the island of Formosa, and the Pescadores Archipelago, and a promise to pay an indemnity and to open four additional ports to trade. Before the agreement actually went into effect, however, three of the European powers intervened and prevented Japan from obtaining the expected results of her victory. The acquisition of Port Arthur would place Japan in the path of Russian expansion in the Far East. Russia, consequently, persuaded France, her ally, and Germany, which was anxious to play an important part in world politics, to join in a demand that Japan should give up the Liaotung peninsula in return for additional indemnity, on the ground that its possession by Japan would constitute a perpetual menace to the peace of the Far East. As it was not in a position to refuse the demand of the three powers, the Japanese government reluctantly gave up the Liaotung peninsula.

7

THE THREATENED PARTITION OF CHINA

The defeat of the Chinese by the Japanese revealed the helplessness of the great Chinese Empire, with its teeming population and its wealth of natural resources. The war showed that corrupt officials had robbed their government and provided it with inferior armaments and that southern China had little sympathy with northern China. These disclosures encouraged the European powers to take advantage of the weakness and disunion of China.

The first power to take energetic action was France. The French government desired a delimitation of the northern boundary of Tonking and a supplementary commercial treaty, and pointedly indicated to the Chinese government that it ought to show its gratitude for French intervention against the demands of Japan. As the Chino-Japanese War had left China in no position to resist the French demands, the Chinese authorities allowed three pieces of territory to pass into French possession, permitted the French to extend a railroad from their provinces in Indo-China into southern China, and conceded French engineers and manufacturers the right to be approached first in regard to the development of mines in the three southern provinces of Yunnan, Kwangsi, and Kwangtung.

Russia quickly followed the example of France. Posing as the savior of China from Japanese aggression, the Russian government persuaded the Chinese government in 1896 to sign a secret treaty of alliance. In this agreement the two powers promised to support each other against Japanese aggression. In order that Russian troops might reach the points threatened with a Japanese attack in the shortest possible time, China agreed to allow Russia to run the Trans-Siberian Railroad across Manchuria instead of around that province, a saving of three hundred and forty-three miles. The construction of this railroad opened Manchuria to economic and political penetration by Russia. In the fall of 1897 the Russian fleet unexpectedly took up winter quarters at Port Arthur and Russia demanded a lease of this strategic point. Confronted by this demand, the Chinese authorities found themselves compelled to lease this important harbor and adjacent territory on the Liaotung peninsula to Russia for twenty-five years, to permit the Russian government to fortify it, and to construct a railway to connect this port with the main line of the Trans-Siberian Railroad.

Even before Russia seized Port Arthur, Germany obtained important rights in the province of Shantung. For some time the German government had been looking for a naval base in the Far East. In November, 1897, the attack of a Chinese mob on a German mission station and its murder of two German missionaries opportunely gave the German government a pretext for making demands on China. A German squadron sailed into the harbor of Kiauchow and sailors and marines from the German fleet seized a fort. The German government then wrung from the helpless Chinese government a lease of two hundred square miles of territory around the harbor of Kiauchow for ninety-nine years and the right to construct railroads and exploit the mines in the province of Shantung.

The aggressions of France, Russia, and Germany gave an excuse for further encroachments on Chinese sovereignty. As soon as Russia leased Port Arthur, Great Britain, with the approval of Japan, occupied the neighboring naval base of Weihaiwei and demanded the whole peninsula opposite the island of Hongkong. In order not to be at a disadvantage, the French forced the Chinese government to lease to them the bay of Kwangchow. The success of the European powers in getting possession of these naval bases caused the world to begin to talk about the break-up of China.

To fortify themselves against such an event the European powers began to mark off regions for economic exploitation and possibly for political control as spheres of influence. Whenever it could be obtained each power secured from China a promise not to cede the region marked out for economic penetration. France obtained a promise from China not to cede the island of Hainan to any other power and to recognize the primacy of France in the three southern provinces of China adjoining French Indo-China. Great Britain secured a pledge from China not to cede the valley of the Yangtse-Kiang. Japan gained a similar promise concerning the province of Fukien. Germany had Shantung. Russia claimed the province of Chihli and all Chinese territory north of the Great Wall. As a next step each power tried to gain the recognition of other powers for its claims in China. This led to agreements between Great Britain and Germany, and between Great Britain and Russia.

Because it wished to preserve such equality of opportunity as had not already been destroyed, the United States opposed the policy followed by the European powers in China. In September, 1899, the American government ordered its accredited ministers to request from the governments of Great Britain, Germany, and Russia a declaration of their adherence to what came to be known as the open-door policy. It asked them not to interfere with any treaty port or vested interest within their spheres of influence, to levy only such duties as the Chinese tariff demanded, and to establish no discriminatory harbor dues or railroad-rates. Later in the same year the United States government made a similar request of the governments of Japan, Italy, and France. The action of the United States and the dangerous movement started in China by the aggressions of the European powers averted the threatened partition of China.

8

THE REACTION OF CHINA TO FOREIGN AGGRESSION

The humiliations suffered by the Chinese government between 1894 and 1899 made a deep impression on the more thoughtful Chinese and caused a division of government circles at Peking into two parties, a conservative, uninformed party from northern China, which favored an understanding with Russia, and a southern party, which stood for the adoption of a policy of reform similar to that so successfully followed by Japan. Through the influence of his tutor the reform party caught the ear of the young, weak Emperor and obtained from him a series of thirty-seven decrees designed to reform the corrupt and antiquated Chinese government and to modernize education, transportation, and the army. The policy of the reformers, however, gave rise to a rumor that they intended to imprison the Dowager Empress and to execute some of their opponents; one of the Chinese officials warned his superiors of their supposed danger. As a result of this warning the Dowager Empress assumed control of the government, seized and confined the young Emperor, rescinded the visionary reform measures, and drove into exile or punished the leaders of the reform party.

After this failure of the reformers the reactionary elements of China attempted to drive foreign influences out of the country by a popular rising, encouraged by the Chinese government, known as the Boxer movement. The superstitious peasants viewed with alarm the tunnels, cuts, and fills for the new railroads, which were disturbing the bones of their ancestors and contravening ancient beliefs, and held the foreigners, instead of their own corrupt officials, responsible for their failure to receive adequate compensation for the lands taken over by the new railway-lines. The Chinese people generally disliked the Christian missionaries and their converts because of their strange rites, their abandonment of traditional ways, their refusal to contribute to Chinese festivals, and the protection given them by the European powers. The people of northern China, the region of the worst foreign aggressions, felt most keenly the foreign encroachments on Chinese sovereignty. In the winter of 1899 and 1900 the appearance of famine conditions made the situation acute. Under the leadership of secret societies, organized ostensibly to promote boxing and gymnastics, Chinese mobs in the province of Shantung—the birthplace of the Chinese sage Confucius and the holy land of China—began to raid and to loot native villages. The participants in these attacks began to be spoken of as Boxers. The movement soon spread toward Peking, missionaries and other foreigners were soon being killed, and finally the Boxers cut off communication between Peking and the sea. This seemed to put the foreigners in the Chinese capital at the mercy of the Boxer movement.

The attempt of the European powers with a small force of soldiers, marines, and sailors, to relieve the threatened foreigners at Peking, precipitated open hostilities. The siege of the foreign legations and the Roman Catholic cathedral lasted for nearly two months, but owing to the influence of one faction around the imperial throne the Chinese government never employed all its resources against the besieged foreigners and Chinese converts. Meanwhile the European powers, Japan and the United States gathered an expeditionary force large enough to relieve the beleaguered foreign quarters of Peking. This body of troops finally reached the capital and rescued the besieged foreigners and the Chinese who were with them. After relieving Peking the members of the expeditionary force disgraced themselves by looting the city and caused great suffering among the Chinese by punitive expeditions sent into the surrounding territory.

The Boxer movement changed the whole situation in the Far East. The uprising gave the Russian government an opportunity to occupy all Manchuria, showed the other European governments the danger of their aggressive policy, and put an end to the talk of partitioning China south of the Great Wall. The disastrous outcome of the Boxer movement saddled China with a heavy indemnity and convinced even the most conservative elements in China of the necessity of making reforms. It did nothing, however, to improve the relations of Japan and Russia in Manchuria and Korea.

9

THE RUSSO-JAPANESE WAR

For a short time after the Chino-Japanese War the Japanese government dominated Korea. Within a few months, however, it lost this position through abetting the murder of the Queen of Korea, who had consistently opposed the Japanese policy of reforms, As a result of this attack the King fled for protection to the Russian consulate at the Korean capital, and Korea began to fall under the influence of Russia. A faction at the Russian court used the ascendancy of Russia in Korea to obtain timber and mining concessions. At the same time Russia took no steps toward evacuating Manchuria. The Japanese felt that this advance of Russia in the Far East threatened their vital interests.

Until 1902 the Japanese government did not feel strong enough to challenge the advance of Russia. In that year, however, Japan and Great Britain concluded an alliance for the protection of the interests of Japan in Korea and those of Great Britain in China. Assured of the support of the British government, the Japanese government stiffened its attitude toward Russia. It demanded of the Russian government a mutual engagement to respect the independence and integrity of the Chinese and Korean empires, reciprocal recognition of the rights of Russia in Manchuria and those of Japan in Korea, a limitation of the number of troops to be sent by the two powers into Korea in case of a crisis, and a promise on the part of Russia not to impede the expansion of the Korean Railway into southern Manchuria. When Russia failed to agree to these demands, Japan surprised the reckless advisers of the Tsar by declaring war.

The crisis found the two powers unequally prepared for a struggle. The advisers of the Tsar had never believed that Japan would resort to war and had made no preparation for a military conflict. The Russian people felt no interest in the struggle. The Russian government retained its first-class troops on the German frontier and found itself compelled to reënforce and equip the armies on the distant fighting front by means of the single-track Trans-Siberian Railroad, which was still uncompleted around Lake Baikal. The war revealed that the official class in Russia was shot through with ignorance, inefficiency, and corruption. The opening of the war found the Japanese people adequately prepared, and convinced that the policy of the Russian government threatened vital economic, political, and strategic interests of Japan.

This situation explains the swift victory of the Japanese in the ensuing war. Immediately after the opening of hostilities the Japanese fleet cleared the sea and Japanese troops occupied Korea and began the siege of Port Arthur. From these bases three armies advanced into Manchuria, inflicting two severe defeats on the military forces of Russia. After this tremendous effort both governments really desired peace. Port Arthur had fallen, the Russian people had risen in revolt and threatened the position of the ruling dynasty, and the Japanese had nearly exhausted their resources. At the suggestion of President Roosevelt representatives of the two powers met at Portsmouth, New Hampshire, and concluded a treaty of peace. As a result of the negotiations Japan secured recognition of her political, military, and economic interests in Korea, the evacuation of Manchuria by Russian troops, possession of Port Arthur and the Russian railroad in southern Manchuria, the cession of the southern half of the island of Sakhalin, and the payment of the expenses incurred in maintaining Russian prisoners of war. For the first time in modern history an Asiatic power had defeated a great European state.

10

THE REFORM IN CHINA

The showing made by Japan in the Russo-Japanese War convinced even the most conservative Chinese of the necessity of adopting a policy of reform. Taking Japan as a model, the Chinese government issued in rapid succession edicts for the reform of the administration, education, the army, and the constitution. The Chinese government substituted for the old classical examinations tests demanding a knowledge of Western learning, and made efforts to concentrate more authority in the hands of the central government. In 1907 a commission recommended the introduction of representative government. In the same year the government made provision for summoning in 1909 provincial assemblies elected by direct suffrage. A year later the government promised to set in operation in 1917 a constitution modeled after that of Japan and outlined a nine-year program of preparation for the constitution. In 1910 the government convened a National Assembly composed of persons appointed by the government and members elected by the provincial assemblies. In 1911 the reform policy of the established government in China was rudely interrupted by revolution.

The general situation favored the outbreak of a revolutionary movement. A severe famine, the worst in forty years, had devastated China and created great popular discontent. The policy of centralization ran counter to established practice and added to the dissatisfaction. The Boxer indemnity made taxes heavy. The more radical reformers suspected the sincerity of the government and held the old Manchu régime responsible for all the ills of China. The troops stood ready to mutiny and no one dared defend the old ruling class in China.

The revolutionary movement broke out in central China and quickly spread over the southern half of the empire. In northern China the Manchu dynasty placed practically dictatorial powers in the hands of Yuan Shi-kai, a Chinese official of great ability and prestige. In the south the revolutionists created a provisional government headed by Sun Yat-sen, the best known of the revolutionary leaders. Finding themselves unable to make further headway, the leaders of the two sections of the empire resorted to negotiations. These resulted in the acceptance of Yuan Shi-kai as head of the government by the leaders of southern China on condition that the Manchu rulers of China should abdicate. Their action made China a republic.

The new President found himself confronted by serious domestic and foreign problems. Russia and Japan had usurped authority in Manchuria. All the great powers possessed rights and privileges in China incompatible with her position as an independent state. The administrative machinery had to be reconstructed, the finances reorganized, and parliamentary institutions set in motion. China has not yet succeeded in finding a solution for these difficult questions.

The expansion of the European powers into Asia created three areas of tension and forced the Asiatic states out of their accustomed grooves. The advance of the British and the Russians gave rise to a delicate diplomatic situation in central Asia. The expansion of the British Empire at the expense of Burma and the establishment of the French in Indo-China brought France and Great Britain face to face. The impact of Western civilization in the Far East broke down the isolation of both Japan and China and produced intense rivalries between the imperialistic European powers. This rivalry in Asia helped to reveal to the European states the danger of their position and constituted one of the reasons for the formation of two European alliances.

CHAPTER XXIII

THE PARTITION OF AFRICA

For centuries after Europe began to expand overseas, Europeans regarded central and southern Africa merely as a source for the supply of negro slaves, gold, ivory, hides, wax, gum, and a few other commodities, as a point of call on the road to Asia, and as a field of missionary endeavor. Toward the end of the eighteenth century, however, Europe began to consider the African continent as a possible field for European colonization. The opponents of slavery and the slave-trade argued that Africa possessed extraordinary resources that could only be exploited after the suppression of the shameful trade in negro slaves, that most of the colonial products of America could just as well be raised in Africa, and that the consumption of European products in Africa would increase with the growth of its exports. At the same time the loss of some of their most valuable American colonies caused Great Britain and France to look for compensation toward the unclaimed portions of the African continent. They advocated the expansion of the old colonies and the founding of new ones, in the hope of increasing the production of cotton, indigo, rice, spices, coffee, tobacco, and sugarcane. Their attempts to realize their projects quickly proved the necessity of a preliminary exploration of the country.

I

THE EXPLORATION OF AFRICA

In 1788 a group of Englishmen interested in the colonization and exploration of Africa founded the African Association, which sent out Mungo Park in 1795 to explore the region from Gambia to the Upper Niger. His epoch-making expedition initiated a period of exploration that ended only in recent times. During the first three quarters of the nineteenth century British, French, German, and Portuguese explorers led expeditions through the interior of Africa which gave to the world for the first time a fairly accurate knowledge of the main features of the geography of the continent. In 1798 Francisco José de Lacerda, a Portuguese explorer, made a scientific expedition up the Zambezi River to Tete. Between 1802 and 1811 two half-caste Portuguese traversed Africa from Angola to Zambezi and made the first recorded journey across Africa. In the meantime Mungo Park succeeded in descending the Niger River to Bussa. In 1806 Cape Colony passed into the hands of Great Britain, an event that gave the British a foothold for further expansion in South Africa. In 1820 Mehemet Ali, ruler of Egypt, commenced the conquest of the Egyptian Sudan. Three years later three Englishmen reached Lake Chad. In the same decade two expeditions reached Timbuktu. In 1830 the French began the conquest of Algeria, a slow, painful task which was not completed until 1847. Simultaneously an English explorer discovered the mouth of the Niger River.

In 1840 a Scotchman, David Livingstone (1813–1873), who had been sent out to South Africa by the London Missionary Society, began work as a medical missionary in Bechuanaland. He soon became convinced that white missionaries should do the pioneer work of opening new territory, but leave to native agents the task of developing the new fields. He devoted the rest of his life to this work. In 1849, accompanied by two British sportsmen, he pushed northward across the Kalahari Desert and discovered Lake Ngami. Two years later he reached the Zambezi River. In 1853, while in search of a high healthy region for missionary posts, he started a journey that in two and a half years took him across the continent from east to west and back again. While descending the Zambezi River on the return trip he discovered the great Victoria Falls. This expedition brought him to the attention of the British public. He sent an account of his journey to the Royal Geographical Society and published his *Missionary Travels and Researches in South Africa,* a book written with a modesty and simplicity of style that captivated British readers. In 1857 he left the employ of the London Missionary Society and accepted a commission from the British government to act as consul in East Africa and to explore eastern and central Africa. He devoted the remaining fifteen years of his life to the task of opening up the region lying between the Zambezi River, the headwaters of the Nile, and the Upper Congo River, his movements being followed with anxious interest by the public in Europe and America. In 1873 he died in the heart of the continent that he had done so much to make known to white men. After his death his black companions bore his body to the African coast and his admiring countrymen interred it in Westminster Abbey, the national shrine for the famous British dead. During the thirty-three years that he spent in Africa he explored a third of the African continent, roused Europe and America against the evils of the slave-trade, and inspired an army of explorers and missionaries to study and civilize the regions that he had opened up.

Meanwhile other explorers had been making important contributions to the knowledge of Europeans concerning northern and central Africa. In 1858 Sir Richard Burton and John Speke visited Tanganyika and sighted Lake Victoria Nyanza. Four years afterwards Speke and James Grant followed the Nile River down to Egypt. In 1864 Sir Samuel Baker discovered Lake Albert Nyanza, another of the great sources of the Nile. In the years between 1860 and 1875 the German explorers Friedrich Rohlfs, Georg Schweinfurth, and Gustav Nachtigal traversed much of Morocco, the Sahara, and the Sudan.

In 1871 the public in Europe and America, long without news of Livingstone, had begun to fear for his safety. Convinced that the explorer still lived, the owner of the New York *Herald* decided to send in search of the vanished Livingstone his best reporter, Henry M. Stanley, an Englishman with a gift for vivid descriptive writing and well prepared for the task by a long series of adventurous travels in western America, Asia Minor, Transcaucasia, and Tibet. This mission launched Stanley on a dramatic career of African exploration. On his first journey in Africa he found Livingstone in the central part of the continent and provided him with much-needed supplies of food and medicine. In the years between 1874 and 1877 Stanley attacked some of the important geographical problems left unsolved by Livingstone. Crossing the continent from east to west, he descended the Congo and discovered for the first time its true course. This exploit attracted the attention of Leopold, King of Belgium, who finally induced Stanley to enter his employ.

2

THE SCRAMBLE FOR AFRICA

The leaders in the political and economic life of Europe utilized very slowly the work of the explorers of Africa. The abolition of the slave-trade destroyed the prosperity of most of the posts established by Europeans along the western coast of Africa. The climate, ignorance concerning the region, and a lack of capital prevented the success of the rosy plans for the establishment of plantations for the production of colonial products on an extensive scale. The colonies of freed negroes failed to prosper. The old trading-posts, occupied by a handful of administrators, small garrisons, and freed negroes, either fell into decay or grew very slowly as the demand in Europe for wax, ivory, gum, hides, and palm-oil increased. As late as 1875 Europeans had occupied only a small fraction of the African continent. Egypt, the Egyptian Sudan, Tunis, and Tripoli in northern Africa still remained nominally under the suzerainty of Turkey. In Morocco, Abyssinia, Zanzibar, and Liberia the native inhabitants maintained organized governments. The French possessed Algeria, a considerable colony in the valley of the

Senegal River, and small footholds at the mouth of the Casamance River, in French Guinea, on the Ivory Coast, at Gabun near the mouth of the Congo, and at Obrok on the coast of the Red Sea. The British had established commercial posts at Gambia, Sierra Leone, and Lagos (in the present colony of Nigeria), and agricultural settlements, occupied by a mixed population of Englishmen and Dutch Boers, in Cape Colony and the adjoining Natal. Other Boers, incensed at the abolition of slavery in the British colonies, had trekked across the veld with their families and their movable possessions and set up north of the Orange River the two sparsely settled little republics of the Orange Free State and the Transvaal. The Portuguese effectively occupied a few islands and other small areas on the eastern and western coasts of Africa. An Italian steamship company owned a coaling-station at Assab on the Red Sea, the nucleus of the later Italian colony of Eritrea. Negro peoples, with a primitive organization and civilization, occupied the rest of Africa.

The first European with prestige and ample resources to realize the practical significance of the work of the African explorers was Leopold II, the able King of the Belgians. In September, 1876, he brought together in the royal palace at Brussels a brilliant international assembly composed of geographers, explorers, and other unofficial representatives of the various countries of Europe who were interested in opening up Africa. In the speech of welcome to the conference he proposed a discussion of three questions: the bases of operation that should be acquired in Africa, the routes to be opened into the interior, and the creation of an international committee and national committees for the carrying out of these tasks. The deliberations of the conference resulted in the organization of an Association for the Repression of the Slave Trade and the Opening of Central Africa, with an executive committee headed by King Leopold himself, and with headquarters at Brussels. In spite of the apathy and the timidity of the Belgian people, the Belgian national committee, inspired to action by the enthusiasm and the resolution of the King, proved to be the most active of the national committees. It collected a considerable fund and sent out a Belgian officer with a commission to explore the great lake-region of central Africa.

In the London *Daily Telegraph* for October 17, 1877, however, appeared a telegram containing the startling news of the descent of the Congo by Stanley and of his arrival on the western coast of Africa after a journey of extraordinary hardships. The King of the Belgians divined at once the importance of the discovery of a populous region, capable of prosperity, and connected with the coast by a great navigable highway. Two representatives of the King met the explorer on his arrival at Marseilles and invited him to take service immediately with the international association. The English blood flowing in his veins, however prevented Stanley from accepting the offer of the Belgian sovereign immediately. Going to England, he tried for six months to interest the political, commercial, and banking leaders of the country of his birth in the empire that he had discovered in central Africa. Treated as a Don Quixote or an adventurer by the British public, he reluctantly entered the employ of Leopold II, who immediately organized to support him a new body, composed entirely of Belgian subjects, the Committee for the Study of the Upper Congo.

In 1879 the King of the Belgians sent Stanley back to the Congo at the head of a new expedition, with instructions to open up communications with the Upper Congo. In the next five years the explorer laid the foundations of the Congo Free State. He established a station at the head of navigation on the Lower Congo, built a road fifty-two miles in length through dense jungles around the cataracts that barred the way to the interior, transported piece by piece a number of steamers to the waters of the Upper Congo, made treaties with the native chieftains, and founded stations and made explorations above the cataracts of the Congo River. By this activity he gave Leopold II a solid basis for his claims.

The King of the Belgians, however, had no assurance that the European powers would give him a free hand in carrying out his private ventures in Africa. The explorations of Pierre de Brazza in behalf of France and the revival of old Portuguese claims threatened to nullify the work of Stanley. But by 1884, he had successfully warded off these dangers and given his enterprise an assured international status. He effected a satisfactory territorial compromise with the French government. He defeated the diplomatic campaign of Portugal to gain control of the region at the mouth of the Congo, by skilful manipulation of European public opinion and by enlisting German support. Through the good offices of an American representative he persuaded the government of the United States to give the International African Association official recognition. Within a few weeks most of the important European powers followed its example. As a result of this recognition Leopold II, with the approval of the Belgian parliament, assumed sovereignty of the new state, under the title of President of the Congo Free State, and concluded treaties with the neighboring colonial powers that gave him rule over an area of two million square miles that included some of the most fertile regions of central Africa.

The news of the remarkable journey of Stanley precipitated a veritable scramble for African territory by the European powers. The growing industries of England, France, Germany, and Belgium demanded a bounteous supply of raw materials and new outlets for their manufactured products. The abandonment of free trade in favor of a policy of protective tariffs by the Continental powers made the industrial states nervous over the question of markets. The acquisition of colonies promised to prevent further losses of population by emigration. Italy and Germany, belatedly entered into the ranks of the great powers, wished to take a position beside the great colonial states. France, still mindful of her former colonial empire, hoped to find compensation in Africa for her recent losses in Europe. The opening of the Suez Canal gave the lands bordering on the Mediterranean Sea a new importance. The Portuguese revived old claims to much of Africa. All hoped to find in the continent revealed by Stanley and earlier explorers the fulfilment of their dreams and ambitions.

3

THE EXTENSION OF FRENCH INFLUENCE IN AFRICA

France quickly followed the example of the King of the Belgians. Ever since the French conquest of Algeria (1830–1847) French statesmen had been considering the possibility of French expansion into Tunis. The presence of two such weak states as Tunis and Morocco on the borders of Algeria constituted a constant menace to that province. Border tribes from Morocco and Tunis repeatedly attacked French territory. If France did not occupy them, other European powers might at any time seize them or at least in case of war stir up the warlike tribesmen of Tunis and Morocco to attack Algeria. Until the Congress of Berlin in 1878 Great Britain blocked the French plans concerning the two states. The British government had no wish to see points of such strategic importance as Tangier and Bizerta fall into French hands. At that meeting of representatives of the powers, however, the political leaders of Great Britain changed their policy. The sharp clash of British and Russian interests made the British political leaders feel the need of diplomatic support. As a result, they voluntarily offered Tunis to the representatives of France as the French share of the spoils taken by the powers from the Turkish Empire, with the hearty approval of Bismarck. The German Chancellor hoped to divert the attention of the French people from thoughts of revenge for the loss of Alsace-Lorraine to the task of building up a colonial empire. Both Great Britain and Germany, too, looked forward with considerable satisfaction to seeing France adopt a policy that would set her at odds with Italy, the other great Mediterranean power.

In 1881 the French government felt that the time had come for action. Since the formation of the new Kingdom of Italy the Italians had been strengthening their political hold on Tunis. A considerable number of Italians had settled in the country and the Italian consul in

Tunis had met with much success in obtaining economic concessions for his countrymen. His acquisition of the railroad from Goletta to Tunis finally convinced the French ministers that they must act promptly. A providential sally of Tunisian tribesmen across the Algerian border offered France a pretext for intervention. Three divisions of French troops moved from Algeria into Tunis and the French fleet dropped anchor before Bizerta and landed eight thousand men. The Bey of Tunis found resistance impossible and signed the Treaty of Bardo, which established a French protectorate over Tunis. The occupation of Tunis by France humiliated and disappointed the Italian people and constituted one of the causes for their entrance into the Triple Alliance and their embarking on a colonial career in northeastern Africa.

In this same period France, through the efforts of Savorgnan de Brazza (1852–1905), a French naval officer of Italian origin, had been establishing a claim to the territory lying north of the Congo River. While stationed off the western coast of Africa he had become interested in exploring the Ogowe River, surmising that it might be the mouth of the Lualaba, a river of central Africa discovered by Livingstone. In 1875 he obtained permission to carry out his plans and explored the course of the Ogowe and the upper reaches of the Alima and the Ligonha, two rivers lying to the south of the Ogowe. Upon returning to France in 1878 Brazza learned of the descent of the Congo by Stanley and recognized that he himself had found two affluents of that stream. With the backing of the French government and the French national committee, created in 1876 as a result of the conference convened at Brussels by Leopold II, he returned to Gabun in 1880 and pushed the work of extending the territorial claims of France in the Congo region. In carrying on this work he seriously threatened for a time the success of Stanley. He founded Franceville on the Upper Ogowe, made treaties with the native chieftains, reached the Upper Congo and, before Stanley could arrive there, founded the post later called Brazzaville, connected the stations by a road, and started a flourishing trade with the natives. His work made possible the later French advances toward Lake Chad and the Nile.

At the same time the French had also been penetrating inland from their posts on the Senegal River. Until after the middle of the nineteenth century this colony consisted of a few scattered trading-posts. In 1855 it began a period of expansion. Under the leadership of General Louis Faidherbe it put an end to the raids of the Moors on the northern bank of the river on the negroes of the southern bank, established posts as far as the head of navigation on the Senegal River, and subdued the tribes living between the Senegal and the British colony of Gambia. The achievements of Stanley spurred the French on to new activity in West Africa. Between 1879 and 1883 they established a chain of fortified posts between the head of navigation of the Senegal River and the end of navigation on the Upper Niger and opened up an important trade-route into the interior. Their successes in this region suggested the linking of Algeria, the French Congo, and the West Coast colonies of Senegal, Cazanrance, French Guinea, the Ivory Coast, and Dahomey into one continuous empire.

The opening up of the Suez Canal in 1869 also called the attention of the European powers to northeastern Africa. The French suddenly remembered their long-neglected station at Obrok on the Red Sea. In 1882 the Italian government, smarting under its defeat in Tunis at the hands of France, formally annexed the Red Sea coaling-station of Assab, which had been acquired in 1862 by an Italian steamship company and purchased in 1879 by the Italian government. In the same year the British government began its long occupation of Egypt.

4

THE ESTABLISHMENT OF BRITISH INFLUENCE IN EGYPT AND NIGERIA

The state of the Egyptian finances made European intervention in Egypt inevitable. Between 1863 and 1876 the indebtedness of the country had mounted from about two and quarter million to over ninety-four million pounds. In 1876 this increase of indebtedness resulted in the establishment of an international control of Egyptian finances. In 1878 the European powers forced the Khedive to take representatives of Great Britain and France into the Egyptian ministry. In the following year, at the instigation of the powers, the Turkish Sultan compelled the ruler of Egypt to abdicate, as a punishment for his attempt to escape from foreign tutelage. This intervention of the European powers, however, stirred up a national movement against foreign interference which found much support in the Egyptian army and made a military officer, Arabi Pasha, the real ruler of the land. This situation threatened the security of the great mass of foreign investments in Egypt and the safety of the Suez Canal, the newly opened gateway to India and the Far East.

In 1882 an Egyptian mob at Alexandria murdered fifty Europeans and by their action precipitated a crisis. The incident convinced the British government that the rule of Arabi Pasha must be overthrown. When France and Italy refused to coöperate in Egypt, the British government decided to intervene alone. British troops seized control of the Suez Canal, marched into the Nile Valley, and defeated the Egyptian military forces. Their victory gave the British government control of Egypt. As a result of this victory the British authorities restored the Khedive as nominal ruler of Egypt, tried Arabi Pasha and banished

him from the country, and set to work at the task of restoring order
and prosperity.

Once in Egypt, the British government found it difficult to withdraw. It felt that it could not recall its troops until it had reconstructed
the administration in such a way as to insure the maintenance of peace,
order, and prosperity, the judicious development of self-government,
the fulfilment of the obligations of the Egyptian government toward
foreign powers, and the neutrality of the Suez Canal in time of war.
A considerable British military force remained in the country and a
British representative with the modest title of consul-general and diplomatic agent became the real ruler of Egypt. For the next twenty-three
years he applied himself to the task of reorganizing the Egyptian state.
He put the finances on a sound basis, created a well-disciplined army,
and organized an efficient police force. At the opening of the World
War the British government was still in Egypt.

In the vicinity of the Niger Valley British firms had long maintained posts for carrying on trade with the natives. Finding the competition of the various British, French, and German commercial concerns ruinous for all concerned, several of the British firms formed
themselves in 1879 into the United African Company, later known as
the National African Company. This action enabled the new firm to
command the market and regulate prices, explore the Lower and Middle Niger, and make agreements with the native chiefs. Because of
its desire for a settled government in the Niger region, in 1884 the
British government took the establishments of the company under British protection and laid the foundations for the colony of Nigeria.

5

GERMANY BECOMES A COLONIAL POWER

Although German historians, economists, political scientists, explorers, travelers, and missionaries had been talking about the acquisition
of colonies since the early years of the nineteenth century, the leaders
of German industry, commerce, and banking did not see any personal
advantage in the establishment of a colonial empire until about 1850.
After 1844 German firms became active on the East Coast of Africa.
After 1859 German trading-companies began establishing posts in the
regions later known as Togoland, Kamerun, and German Southwest
Africa, and at points on the eastern coast of Africa. After 1857 the
house of Godefroy and other German firms established trading-posts
at various points on the Pacific Ocean. In the years between 1879 and
1883 German exports to Africa increased 50 per cent and imports from
Africa at the port of Hamburg almost doubled. In the ten years from

1868 to 1878 the number of German ships trading with Samoa and the Tonga Islands nearly trebled. These firms quickly realized the advantage of an efficient consular service and a ubiquitous navy such as Great Britain maintained for the benefit of their English rivals, and consequently increasing numbers of Germans joined the German colonial party.

The advocates of a colonial empire made a deliberate attempt to arouse public opinion in favor of the acquisition of colonies. In 1882 they began to organize societies, and carried on their campaign of propaganda by organizing branches and by publishing books, pamphlets, brochures, and a journal, and by sending out lecturers. Between 1880 and 1882 forty books on colonization appeared in Germany. In these publications the advocates of a colonial empire painted alarming pictures of the progress of Great Britain and the danger of the absorption of German emigrants and capital by English-speaking countries, and emphasized the need of Germany for raw materials and for an outlet for her surplus products, her mission to spread her culture to inferior peoples, and the necessity for her to take a conspicuous part in the opening up of the non-European world. As a result of all this agitation articles on the colonial problem began to take a prominent place in German periodicals.

As a good politician Bismarck gradually yielded to the increasing pressure of the colonial party. By 1875 he began to make vigorous protests to other nations in behalf of German commercial interests. In 1879 he established a number of virtual German protectorates on the Pacific Ocean by treaties concluded with native chiefs. In 1880 he made an unsuccessful attempt to obtain a subsidy for the firm of Godefroy and Son, which was in financial difficulties. Learning from this experience that public opinion was not yet ready to sanction a colonial policy, the Chancellor continued to give secret encouragement to the colonial party. In 1881 he proposed the establishment of a steamship-line to the Far East. In 1884 he inaugurated a parliamentary struggle for a subsidy that would provide steamship connections between Germany and the principal Far Eastern ports. By 1884 he felt able to begin the actual work of establishing a colonial empire.

Germany owed its first African colony to the initiative of a Bremen tobacco merchant, Adolph Lüderitz. In 1882 he conceived the plan of making a settlement on the coast of southwestern Africa suitable for carrying on trade with the Boers of the Transvaal and the Orange Free State and the natives of the regions adjacent to the coast. He also hoped to establish plantations and ostrich-farms and to exploit the mineral wealth of the adjoining districts. The next year he sent a ship to southwestern Africa. Upon its arrival his representative purchased from a Hottentot chief for eighty pounds and two hundred old rifles a territory one hundred and fifty square miles in area situated on the bay of Angra Pequena. A little later Lüderitz purchased enough additional land to give him a territory nine hundred square miles in area. In 1884, after considerable negotiation with the British government Germany annexed the new settlement and set up official insignia at strategic points to indicate the establishment of German sovereignty from the Orange River to the southern boundary of the Portuguese colony of Angola.

In the same year Germany acquired two colonies on the Guinea Coast. In this region German merchants had long been active. They exchanged textiles, liquors, salt, arms, and cheap jewelry for ivory, palm-oil, gum, and dyewoods. In 1882 thirty-six ships arrived at the port of Hamburg from West Africa and ninety-six departed for this region. The port of Bremen carried on a much smaller body of trade with the Guinea Coast, but Germany, nevertheless, ranked next to Great Britain in the volume of its African trade. Hampered by the demands of the native chieftains and threatened with incorporation into the French or the British colonial empire, the German merchants pressed the German government to take their establishments under its protection. In response to their demands Bismarck despatched the famous German explorer Nachtigal to the western coast of Africa with instructions to conclude treaties with the native chieftains which would give the German government commercial and political rights in the unoccupied regions of the Guinea coast. In accordance with his instructions he concluded treaties that gave Germany a claim to Kamerun and Togoland.

6

THE PARTITION OF AFRICA

By 1884 the scramble for African territory had several times produced serious tension between the European powers and had convinced them of the advisability of making some effort to draw up the rules of the game. They therefore welcomed the proposal of the Portuguese government for a meeting of the powers to discuss African questions. The conference assembled at Berlin in December, 1884, and remained in session until January, 1885. Its deliberations resulted in a general act which established the principle of free trade in the basin of the Congo River and forbade trade in slaves in this region, declared the neutrality of the Congo Free State created by the efforts of Leopold II of Belgium, regulated the navigation of the Congo and the Niger, and drew up rules to govern the further occupation of African territory. The conference asserted that a state must notify the other powers in case of the occupation of new territory and the establishment of an organized government.

After the Conference of Berlin the struggle of the European powers for Africa continued. Each state pushed inward from its stations on the coast and cherished schemes for a great empire that would link up its scattered possessions. These plans brought into conflict the British and French in West Africa; the British, Portuguese, Boers, and Germans in South Africa; the British, French, and Italians in Northeast Africa; the French and British in Madagascar; the British and the Germans in East Africa; and the French and Germans in Morocco. These conflicts produced rivalries between the European powers which repeatedly brought the states of Europe to the verge of war and contributed toward the formation of the group of powers known as the Triple Entente and toward the loosening of the ties binding Italy to the central powers.

7

THE PARTITION OF EAST AFRICA

In contrast with the foundation of German Southwest Africa, Togoland, and Kamerun, the establishment of a German colony in East Africa was entirely the work of colonial enthusiasts. Disgusted with the policy of the Colonial Society, Doctor Karl Peters and a group of associates founded in 1884 a new Society for German Colonization and began to plan for the creation in East Africa of a German colony comparable to British India. Although they apparently received no encouragement from Bismarck, Peters and two companions secretly made their way late in 1884 to Zanzibar, pushed into its hinterland, and concluded a number of treaties with native chiefs which gave the society a claim to an area on the eastern coast of Africa about twice the size of Germany. In January, 1885, Peters returned home and pressed the German government to take under its protection the region claimed by the society. Although rather skeptical about the success of the project, Bismarck finally notified the powers that he had taken that part of East Africa under German protection.

Dr. Peters and his associates, however, did not succeed in realizing their dream of building up a great colonial empire stretching from Portuguese East Africa to Cape Guardafui. The British were also active on the East Coast. Early in 1884 H. H. Johnston, a British agent, obtained treaties from a number of native chiefs. Consequently, when Germany laid claim to German East Africa, the British government claimed the region later designated as British East Africa. Feeling the need of British good-will on account of the international political situation, Bismarck agreed in 1886 to make a line running northeastward from the coast to Lake Victoria the dividing line between the two colonies. The agents of the two countries then continued their rivalry in the region of Uganda, but the great Anglo-German settlement of 1890 assigned the contested area to Great Britain.

8

THE PARTITION OF NORTHEASTERN AFRICA

In northeastern Africa the British, French, and Italians struggled to establish colonial empires. After her reverse in Tunis Italy turned her attention to this region. In 1885 she commenced to expand the foothold that she had obtained in Eritrea and to reach out toward the healthful uplands of Abyssinia and the former Egyptian Sudan. In 1889 the Italian government extorted from King Menelik II, who was engaged in a desperate struggle for supremacy with his fellow-chieftains, a treaty ceding some territory to Italy and pretending to grant her a protectorate over the whole of Abyssinia. The next year, in order to hedge Abyssinia in on the south, Italy annexed Italian Somaliland. In the following year the British government recognized Abyssinia and a portion of the former Egyptian Sudan as lying within the Italian sphere of influence. In 1896, however, King Menelik, victorious over his rebellious tribesmen, felt strong enough to repudiate the treaty conceding Italy a protectorate over his country. In the ensuing struggle his tribesmen inflicted a disastrous defeat on the Italian military forces at Adowa, which put an end to Italian colonial expansion in northeastern Africa.

During these years Great Britain had been struggling with the problem of the Egyptian Sudan. In this region scattered garrisons of badly officered, undisciplined, sadly demoralized troops made a show of maintaining the authority of the Egyptian government. They did little to protect the native population from misrule or to suppress the slave-trade. In 1881, Mohammed Ahmed, who had acquired a great reputation among the Moslems for sanctity, placed himself at the head of an insurrection and proclaimed himself the Mahdi. He took advantage of the national movement in Egypt to defeat the Egyptian and British forces sent against him and to gain control of the Egyptian Sudan. Because of the financial situation in Egypt and the political situation in Great Britain, the British authorities advised the Egyptian government to abandon the Egyptian Sudan.

By 1896 the British authorities were ready to attempt the reconquest of the Egyptian Sudan. The Egyptian finances had been put in a satisfactory condition. The British public had been informed of the general situation in Egypt through such works as the *English in Egypt* of Sir Alfred Milner. In 1895 the British Conservatives, the imperial party, came into power. In that year, consequently, the British troops received orders to advance into the Egyptian Sudan, building a railroad as they went. In 1898 the battle of Omdurman practically destroyed the forces of the Khalifa, who had succeeded to the power of the Mahdi, and gave the Anglo-Egyptian military forces control of the Egyptian Sudan. This victory postponed indefinitely the withdrawal of the British from Egypt and opened the way for a clash between the British and French at Fashoda.

Meanwhile France had been establishing her rule over the vast area south of the Sahara Desert known as the Sudan, linking French Guinea, the Ivory Coast, and Dahomey with Senegal, and forestalling the expansion of the British colonies of Sierra Leone and Nigeria and the German colonies of Kamerun and Togoland. In 1885 the Sudan was still an unknown region, controlled by powerful native Moslem states and desolated by slave-raids. During the decade and a half following, adventurous Frenchmen explored the valleys of the Upper and Middle Niger, overthrew or brought under French protection the native states of the interior, and created an outlet for French products in the markets of Timbuktu and other hitherto half-fabulous cities. Other French missions blazed routes and established posts that connected French Guinea, the Ivory Coast, and Dahomey with the Sudan. These explorations prevented the British and German colonies on the Guinea Coast from expanding far into the interior.

While their compatriots were pushing southward from Algiers and eastward from Senegal, other Frenchmen were advancing northward from the French Congo toward Lake Chad and the Nile. In 1885 a few military posts manned by two or three French soldiers, a few scattered Roman Catholic mission stations, and some trading-posts held the region between Kamerun and the Congo Free State for France, and the Germans and the Belgians threatened to forestall the French efforts to advance into the interior. A succession of French missions, however, explored the territory between the Congo River and Lake Chad, negotiated treaties with the principal native chiefs, erected fortified posts, and established the claims of France to the region. Finally in 1898 a mission from the French Congo met the missions from Algiers and Senegal, put down the last important armed resistance, and took a great step toward the realization of the French dream of uniting her African colonies into a continuous empire.

From Lake Chad, France reached out toward the former Egyptian Sudan and French Somaliland. In 1896 the French government decided to establish a claim to the Egyptian Sudan and intrusted Captain Marchand with the execution of the mission. He left for the Nile Valley with a party of twenty-one Europeans and one hundred and fifty Senegalese sharpshooters. Early in January, 1898, the expedition reached the Nile River at Fashoda and raised the French flag.

The action of the French government in occupying the Egyptian Sudan created a serious diplomatic crisis with Great Britain. For two years an Anglo-Egyptian army had been methodically preparing to re-capture the territory abandoned since 1883 to the forces of the Mahdi and his successor. As soon as General Horatio Herbert Kitchener, the commander of the expedition, heard of the presence of the French on the Nile River at a point three hundred miles farther south, he hastened to Fashoda and demanded the withdrawal of the French troops. Upon the refusal of Marchand to withdraw without instructions from his government the two commanders referred the delicate question to the French and British governments for settlement. The British people displayed a determination to resort to war rather than to yield posses-sion of the Egyptian Sudan. Since it felt unequal to a military struggle with the British Empire, the French government finally recalled Cap-tain Marchand from Fashoda.

9

FRENCH RULE ESTABLISHED IN MADAGASCAR

The pretensions of France to Madagascar date from the days of Louis XIV. They encountered the open opposition of the British gov-ernment and of the Hovas, the dominant native people of the island. In 1885 the French government extorted from the Hovas a recogni-tion of the rights of France in the island, but the treaty remained prac-tically a dead letter. In 1895 the French government determined to make their treaty rights respected and to enforce a real recognition of the French protectorate. In 1896 they transformed Madagascar into a regular French colony.

10

THE POWERS COMPROMISE ON AFRICA

In the scramble for African territory each European power met with only partial success and found itself forced in the end to effect a series of compromises with its principal rivals. In 1890 Great Britain and Germany defined their respective spheres of influence in East, West, and Southwest Africa in such a way that Germany gave up her plans for a transafrican empire stretching from the East to the West Coast, and Great Britain abandoned her project of an all-red route from the Cape of Good Hope to Cairo. In an agreement concluded the same year Great Britain recognized the French protectorate over Madagascar and French influence in the Sahara and France conceded to Great Britain the region between the Lower Niger and Lake Chad. In the following year the Portuguese found themselves forced to permit the British to occupy Rhodesia and to give up the idea of connecting their possessions on the eastern and western coasts of Africa. In 1894 Germany recognized the Sudan as within the French sphere of influence. After the crisis precipitated by the French occupation of Fashoda, the French and British governments further delimited their possessions. The French gave up the project of connecting their colonies in North Africa, West Africa, and the Congo region with French Somaliland on the Red Sea, by conceding the valley of the Upper Nile to Great Britain, but gained recognition for the French claims to the territory connecting the French Congo with the French colonies in North and West Africa.

Toward the end of the eighteenth century Europe suddenly began to consider the long-neglected continent of Africa as a field for European expansion. The new interest in Africa gave rise to a period of exploration, which culminated in the momentous journey of Stanley across central Africa. The reports of this expedition rapidly convinced the business men and the political leaders of Europe of the value of the African continent and precipitated the European powers into a scramble for African territory. Each power gained footholds along the coast at various points and pushed inward in the hope of linking its scattered possessions into a great continuous empire. This rapid expansion of their colonial possessions in Africa produced a tension that more than once brought the powers of Europe to the verge of war. In the end each government found itself forced to abandon a portion of its imperial dreams and to seek protection and support for its colonial possessions by the formation of alliances and understandings with other European powers.

CHAPTER XXIV

The stirring events of the twelve years from 1859 to 1871 upset the balance of power in Europe and aroused the fears and suspicions of European governments and peoples. Prussia took the place of France as the leading state of Europe, but she dreaded the formation of an alliance of hostile powers. France and Austria-Hungary resented defeat at the hands of Prussia, and the French people felt themselves to be at the mercy of victorious Germany. In spite of the ties of blood and friendship uniting the ruling dynasties in Prussia and Russia, the majority of influential Russians disliked the new German Empire. Italy feared the intervention of the Roman Catholic states of Europe in behalf of the Pope. Austria-Hungary and Russia remained rivals in the Balkan peninsula. Victory and defeat, fears and ambitions, created a situation that started the European powers on a search for allies which continued until the principal states of Europe were organized into two armed camps.

I

THE LEAGUE OF THE THREE EMPERORS

On the conclusion of peace in 1871 Bismarck was especially anxious to reëstablish friendly relations with Austria-Hungary. After the victory of Königgrätz he had carefully refrained from humiliating Austria by annexing her territory or by allowing the victorious Prussian troops to enter Vienna. In the summer of 1871, accordingly, he had little difficulty in bringing about a personal meeting between Emperor William and Emperor Francis Joseph on Austrian soil. Later in the year the coming to power in the Austrian Foreign Office of the Magyar political leader, Count Julius Andrássy, an old friend of Bismarck, improved the relations of the two countries still more. Early in the following year the new Austrian Foreign Minister suggested to his sovereign that he should pay a return visit to the German Emperor. When the Tsar heard of the proposed visit he suggested the advisability of a meeting of the three eastern monarchs on German soil.

The interview of the three emperors resulted in the establishment of a close understanding among the three states represented at the conference and laid the basis for the later League of the Three Emperors. In 1873 the oral understanding of the preceding year was supplemented by two written agreements. A visit of Emperor William to St. Petersburg resulted in the signing of a secret convention in which Russia and Germany mutually promised the assistance of two hundred thousand men in case either was attacked by a third power. A few weeks later a visit of the Tsar to Emperor Francis Joseph resulted in the conclusion of an agreement by which Russia and Austria promised to consult one another on any question about which they might have divergent views, to come to an understanding with each other in case the aggression of a third power menaced the peace of Europe, and to conclude a special convention in case military action should become necessary. With the adhesion of the ruler of Prussia to the agreement the League of the Three Emperors came into being.

Bismarck at once assumed the leadership of the new league. He was the ablest of the three foreign ministers and represented the strongest of the three powers. As a result the German Chancellor dominated his colleagues. He used his position to hold France in check and to preserve the peace of Europe. Italy followed the lead of the three emperors; Great Britain clung to its traditional policy of splendid isolation; and France still felt too exhausted and too engrossed in domestic problems to threaten Germany.

The league had hardly been formed, however, when the course of events in Europe commenced to disturb the harmony between its members. In 1875 the French became convinced that Germany contemplated a preventive war against France. The Russian Foreign Minister circulated the rumor that Bismarck had sent a diplomatic agent to bribe Russia into giving Germany a free hand against France in return for freedom of action in the Balkan peninsula. Articles also appeared in the German newspapers which augmented the alarm of France and Great Britain. Whether Bismarck had any hand in inspiring the articles in the German press is uncertain, but he probably was quite willing to use them as a means of frightening France into giving up her plans for reorganization of the army. Under these circumstances the French government appealed to the Tsar and Queen Victoria to use their influence to prevent German aggression. After the Tsar had made it clear that Russia could not allow France to be crushed, the Russian Foreign Minister flattered his own vanity but angered Bismarck by pompously announcing from Berlin, "Now peace is assured." The incident made for cooler relations between Germany and Russia.

In the same year a revolt broke out in Herzegovina that started a train of events which finally resulted in the spread of the revolutionary movement to the adjoining Southern Slavs, a Russian declaration of war against Turkey in 1877, the Treaty of San Stefano, the Congress of Berlin, and the subsequent Treaty of Berlin. These events in the Balkan peninsula brought the old rivals, Russia and Austria-Hungary, face to face again. Russia desired to win back the portion of Bessarabia that she had lost as a result of the Crimean War, and was inclined to support the revolt of the Southern Slavs. Austria-Hungary had no wish to see the oppressed Christian peoples of the Balkan peninsula achieve independence and become political satellites of Russia. These conflicting points of view confronted Bismarck with the danger of a break-up of the League of the Three Emperors and the division of the European powers into Anglo-Austrian and Franco-Russian diplomatic groups. This would give Germany the thankless task of arbitrating between the two groups and expose her to the danger of having hostile powers on two fronts. Although Bismarck tried to play the rôle of an "honest broker" at the Congress of Berlin in 1878, Russia left the council-table with bitter feelings. The important gains obtained through the decisions of the congress looked slight besides those Russia would have acquired by the Treaty of San Stefano. In view of the support they had given Prussia in her wars with Denmark, Austria, and France, the Tsar and his people considered Bismarck guilty of the basest ingratitude for not energetically taking the part of Russia at the Congress of Berlin and began a violent campaign against the German Chancellor and the German Empire which put an end, for the time being, to the coöperation of the three conservative powers in the League of the Three Emperors.

2

THE FORMATION OF A DUAL ALLIANCE BY GERMANY AND AUSTRIA-HUNGARY

When they learned that the German representatives on the international commissions that had been appointed to delimit the new boundary-lines in the Balkan peninsula usually supported the Austrian contentions, the anger of the Tsar and the leaders of Russia overflowed. The Russian government increased its armaments and pushed its troops westward through Poland toward the German frontier. The Russian Minister of War worked openly for a French alliance. Prominent Russians made menacing statements. In the spring of 1879 Russian representatives sounded both Italy and France on the possibility of their coöperating with Russia in case of war. Later in the year the Tsar canceled at the last moment his plan for a visit to Berlin to attend the golden wedding of his uncle, Emperor William I, complained of the ingratitude of Germany, and warned the German government that it must alter its ways if the friendship of a hundred years was to continue.

This excitement of Russia and the news of the approaching resignation of his friend, Count Andrássy, the Austro-Hungarian Foreign Minister, convinced Bismarck of the necessity for seeking a defensive alliance with Austria-Hungary and averting the formation of a hostile league composed of Russia, France, and Austria-Hungary. Count Andrássy and his sovereign welcomed the suggestion but Emperor William refused to believe that there was danger of a Russian attack on Germany and only with the greatest reluctance gave his consent to the negotiation of the proposed alliance between Germany and Austria-Hungary. The German Chancellor would have liked to obtain an agreement in which the two states promised each other support in case of an attack by a third power, but Austria-Hungary declined to expose herself to the danger of an attack on her eastern frontier by Russia by promising to come to the assistance of Germany in case France should undertake a war of revenge. The secret alliance finally signed on October 7, 1879, consequently, contained the following provisions: Should Germany or Austria-Hungary be attacked by Russia, the other contracting power was bound to come to its assistance with its whole war strength; should one of the two parties to the treaty be attacked by another power, the other contracting state was bound to observe at least a benevolent neutrality; but should the attacking third power be supported by Russia, then both contracting powers were under obligation to assist each other in the war. The alliance was to continue for five years and was renewed from time to time until the outbreak of the World War. The agreement protected Germany against a French war of revenge and against a coalition of three hostile neighbors and gave Austria-Hungary a feeling of security against Russian Panslavism and Italian irredentism.

The conclusion of the Dual Alliance had a sobering effect on Russia. The attacks on Germany subsided and certain advisers of the Tsar broached to Bismarck the subject of an alliance between Russia and the German Empire. These advances, facilitated as they were by the accession of a new Tsar, Alexander III, finally resulted in 1881 in the negotiation of a very secret treaty that revived the League of the Three Emperors. In the new agreement the three contracting powers promised to observe a benevolent neutrality in case one of the contracting states became involved in war with a fourth power, to recognize the new position of Austria-Hungary in Bosnia and Herzegovina, to make no further modification of the situation in the Balkan peninsula without a common agreement, to make no exception in the principle of the closing of the Dardanelles and the Bosporus, and to recognize the right of Austria-Hungary to annex Bosnia and Herzegovina at any moment that she deemed fitting, and that of Bulgaria to incorporate Eastern Rumelia. The new treaty remained in force until 1887, when the revival of the rivalry of Russia and Austria-Hungary over the Balkans again broke up the League of the Three Emperors. Bismarck valued the new treaty because it tended to avert the danger of war between Russia and Austria-Hungary and to prevent the formation of an alliance between Russia and France. Russia prized the guarantee of protection against the attack of the British fleet in the Black Sea, the promise of German and Austro-Hungarian neutrality in case of war with Great Britain, and the approval of her plans in the Balkans. Austria-Hungary gained security against a Russian attack in case of a war with Italy, and the consent of Russia to the annexation of Bosnia and Herzegovina.

3

THE FORMATION OF THE TRIPLE ALLIANCE

The League of the Three Emperors had hardly been revived when Italy began to seek the alliance of Germany and Austria-Hungary. The success of France in acquiring Tunis in 1881 both alarmed and chagrined the Italian people. Wounded in their pride and held culpable for the national misfortune by their subjects, the King of Italy and his advisers sought to strengthen the position of both Italy and her ruling dynasty by obtaining an alliance with the central powers. At first Bismarck rejected the idea. He disliked the jackal foreign policy of Italy, as he called it, and he held the Italian army in small esteem. In the end he came to see the advantages of an alliance and referred the insistent Italian diplomats to Austria-Hungary. As the latter power had no wish to drive Italy into the arms of France or to expose the Austro-Hungarian Empire to the danger of a simultaneous attack by Italy and Russia, the Italian leaders finally obtained the alliance that they sought. In the treaty establishing the Triple Alliance, signed at Vienna on May 20, 1882, Italy, Germany, and Austria-Hungary mutually agreed to enter into no alliance or engagement directed against any one of the contracting states and to exchange ideas on political and economic questions of a general nature which might arise. In case Italy without direct provocation on her part should be attacked by France, the other two contracting powers pledged themselves to come to her assistance. If France should attack Germany without provocation, Italy promised to come to her aid. In case one, or two, of the allies, without direct provocation on their part, should be attacked by two or more non-signatory states, all the contracting powers would be bound to support the attacked state or states. If one of the members of the alliance should be attacked by only a single non-signatory state, the other two parties to the agreement bound themselves to be neutral. The treaty was to run for five years. The formation of the Triple Alliance made Austria-Hungary an ally of Italy instead of a potential enemy, gave the Kingdom of Italy the position and the prestige of a great power, freed Austria-Hungary from the danger of an attack by Italy in case of a war with Russia, and pledged Italy to come to the assistance of Germany against France.

The Triple Alliance was renewed four times and was in force at the outbreak of the World War. In 1887 the general situation enabled Italy to demand better terms. The Kingdom of Italy was far stronger than it had been five years earlier and Germany and Austria-Hungary stood in much greater need of its assistance. The war spirit seemed to be rising in France, and the course of events in Bulgaria had destroyed the good relations between Russia and Austria-Hungary so carefully maintained by Bismarck. As a result the Italian government extorted two important concessions from its allies. Italy and Austria-Hungary mutually promised to come to a previous agreement before taking any action tending to modify the situation in the Balkans, and Germany agreed to support Italy in northern Africa in case France threatened the position of the Italian state in the Mediterranean. In later renewals of the Triple Alliance these concessions were incorporated as articles of the treaty.

In 1883 Bismarck suggested to Austria-Hungary the advisability of adding Rumania to his "League of Peace." The suggestion met with the approval of both Austria-Hungary and Rumania and resulted in the negotiation of two agreements between the Rumanian government and the two central powers. In one of these treaties Rumania and Austria-Hungary promised each other support against aggression. In the other Germany undertook the same obligations toward Rumania and Austria-Hungary that they had just undertaken toward each other. Though Russia was not named, the two agreements were considered guarantees against an attack by her. In 1889 Italy adhered to the treaty between Austria-Hungary and Rumania. From time to time this quadruple agreement was renewed, with slight modifications.

4

THE DETACHMENT OF RUSSIA FROM THE CENTRAL POWERS

By the Dual Alliance, the Triple Alliance, the League of the Three Emperors, and the quadruple agreement with Rumania, Bismarck felt that he had made the position of Germany in Europe secure. The time for the second renewal of the League of the Three Emperors, however, came at a moment of severe tension between Russia and Austria-

Hungary. The annexation of Eastern Rumelia by Bulgaria in 1885 reopened the old feud between the two countries. The tension created between the two governments by this incident and subsequent events made impossible a renewal of the League of the Three Emperors in 1887. Russia was willing to consider a partition of the Balkan peninsula into two spheres of influence; Austria-Hungary aimed at the complete exclusion of Russian influence from the region. Both Bismarck and the Russian Foreign Minister, however, desired a maintenance of good relations between Russia and Germany. After long negotiations, consequently, they reached an understanding that they embodied in a Reinsurance Treaty. The two powers promised each other that if one of the parties to the contract should find itself at war with a third great power, the other would maintain a benevolent neutrality and would try to localize the conflict, but this provision was not to apply to a war against Austria-Hungary or France if it resulted from an attack by one of the contracting powers. Germany recognized the rights historically acquired by Russia in the Balkan peninsula, especially her preponderant and decisive influence in Bulgaria and Eastern Rumelia. The two powers also agreed to admit no modification of the territorial status quo in the peninsula without a previous agreement, to oppose every attempt to modify the existing situation there, and to prevent the use of the Dardanelles and the Bosporus for warlike operations. In an additional and very secret protocol Germany pledged herself to assist Russia to reëstablish a regular and legal government in Bulgaria, to refuse her consent to the restoration of Prince Alexander of Battenberg, and to maintain a benevolent neutrality if Russia should be compelled to defend the entrance to the Black Sea. The treaty was to run for three years and was not communicated to Austria-Hungary.

As the time for the renewal of the Reinsurance Treaty approached, Russia showed a readiness to prolong the duration of the agreement that the advisers of the young German Emperor, William II, did not share. Under the influence of the suspicious but powerful Holstein, an official of the German Foreign Office, the Emperor and the advisers who took the place of the dismissed Bismarck finally decided to drop the alliance with Russia, on the grounds that the agreement was contrary to the spirit, if not the letter, of the Triple Alliance, and that its deliberate or accidental publication might alienate Great Britain and Austria-Hungary, the chief rivals of Russia.

In all probability Germany would sooner or later have had to make the choice between Russia and Austria-Hungary. The growth of German industry, commerce, naval ambition, and colonies was starting the German Empire on the "new course" to Constantinople and Bagdad that would inevitably have antagonized Russia. German military leaders harbored a deep suspicion of Russia. The agreement effected between

Germany and Great Britain in 1890 caused Russia to suspect that those two governments were drawing together. The Panslavist movement was pushing Russia forward in the Balkan peninsula. Under these conditions Germany would soon have found it impossible to maintain her friendship with both Russia and Austria-Hungary.

5

THE FORMATION OF THE DUAL ALLIANCE BETWEEN FRANCE AND RUSSIA

Rebuffed by Germany, the Russian government finally turned for support to France. Until 1885 the responsible political leaders of the Third French Republic had followed a cautious foreign policy. Feeling too weak to assert herself, France had devoted her energies to the task of recuperation and the work of building up a great colonial empire. As the years passed, however, a growing number of Frenchmen came to feel that France should cease her policy of subservience to Germany and assert her own rights more vigorously. After 1886 they found a symbol for a time in the histrionic General Boulanger. After his fall they favored the conclusion of an alliance with Russia.

At the same time forces had been at work preparing Russia for such an alliance. A series of episodes steadily increased the irritation of Russia with Germany. The Tsar thoroughly believed the election of Ferdinand of Saxe-Coburg-Gotha as Prince of Bulgaria to be the result of a treacherous intrigue engineered by Bismarck, found himself unable to reconcile the assurances of the German Chancellor concerning the disinterestedness of Germany in the Balkan peninsula with the despatch of German officers to drill the Turkish army, and suspected that the treaty renewing the Triple Alliance in 1887 contained clauses hostile to the Russian plans in the Balkan peninsula. In that same year the Russian government had forbidden the acquisition or inheritance of landed property by foreigners in western Russia and their employment as managers of estates. This action led to a German newspaper campaign against Russian credit that caused a fall in the value of the Russian ruble and Russian securities. The Panslavist party in Russia had long been advocating a French alliance. Finally, in 1890 the German government had refused to renew the Reinsurance Treaty.

As a result of this movement of public opinion in both countries France and Russia had actually been drawing together for some time. In 1888 the Russian government found French bankers, who were shut off for the time being from investment in Italy by a commercial conflict, more than ready to lend money on attractive terms. In the following year the Russian government contracted two more loans. Simultaneously the French government allowed representatives of Russia to inspect the new French rifle and powder factories and to study the French system of mobilization, transport, and supply. Later the government of France agreed to manufacture a rifle similar to her own for the Russian army and to organize the manufacture of munitions in Russia. In 1890 the French government arrested a group of conspirators engaged in plotting against the Russian government. The French public also made the arrival of every notable from Russia the occasion for a popular demonstration.

In 1891 Russia published to the world its new policy toward France by the reception it accorded the French fleet on the occasion of its visit to Cronstadt, the first appearance of a French naval force in Russian waters since the Crimean War. Whether the reception was a spontaneous indication of the attitude of the Russian people toward France, a demonstration engineered by the Russian government, or the natural result of the removal of the customary restrictions on the public, it far surpassed the usual official greetings in its display of cordiality. The demonstration reached its climax at the moment when the Tsar, standing with head uncovered, ordered the Russian naval band to play the "Marseillaise," the French national anthem, hitherto forbidden in public places, and listened respectfully to its denunciation of tyrants.

The pageantry of the naval reception was promptly followed by the conclusion of a written accord. In this agreement the two governments promised to confer on every question of a nature to threaten peace and to concert measures if peace should be endangered, especially if one of the two powers should be menaced by aggression. This political agreement did not satisfy the political leaders of France. For more than two years they pressed the Russian government to supplement the political treaty with a military agreement. The Tsar feared that a military alliance might involve Russia in war with Germany over Alsace-Lorraine, a question in which she had no interest, and do nothing to further Russian ambitions concerning the opening of the Dardanelles and the Bosporus. So the military agreement drawn up by representatives of the two countries did not become a binding obligation between France and Russia until early in 1894.

The 1894 treaty stipulated the obligations of the two contracting states in case of an attack. It provided that Russia should attack Germany with all her forces in case France should be attacked by Germany or by Italy supported by Germany, that France should attack Germany with all her available military forces if Russia should be attacked by Germany or by Austria-Hungary supported by Germany, that France and Russia should mobilize immediately and simultaneously at the first news of the mobilization of the forces of the Triple Alliance, and that France should employ one million three hundred thousand men and

Russia seven to eight hundred thousand. Though the reception accorded by the French to the Russian squadron in 1893 when it repaid at Toulon the visit of the French fleet to Cronstadt two years earlier clearly indicated the establishment of the most cordial relations between the two states, the alliance was not officially acknowledged until 1895, a year after its conclusion.

Although the treaty gave great satisfaction to the French people, they paid a heavy price for the Russian alliance. They sent over four billion dollars in loans to Russia between the time of the conclusion of the alliance and the outbreak of the World War, an enormous sum which from the beginning they had little right to expect to recover. They obtained by the alliance no real support in the crises of Fashoda, Morocco, and the Balkan Wars, and they compelled Germany to reorganize her military plans in such a way as to make France bear the first shock of any future war. The added prestige and the psychological satisfaction derived by France from the conclusion of the alliance scarcely offset these disadvantages.

6

GREAT BRITAIN DECIDES TO ABANDON THE POLICY OF SPLENDID ISOLATION

At first Germany was not particularly disturbed over the negotiation of the Dual Alliance between France and Russia. The German government believed the forces of the Triple Alliance superior to those of the newly formed diplomatic group and confidently expected Great Britain to continue her policy of splendid isolation. A feeling of alarm appeared in Germany only after the British government showed signs of abandoning its traditional policy and after Italy displayed a tendency to forget her differences with France.

About the time of the conclusion of the Franco-Russian alliance, however, the political leaders of Great Britain began to feel the dangers to which the policy of isolation exposed the far-flung British empire. In the treaty concluded in 1894 Germany irritated the British government by handing over to France certain territories. In the same year Germany thwarted the agreement concluded by Great Britain with the Congo Free State, which would have made possible the realization of the dreams of Cecil Rhodes concerning an all-red route from Cape Colony to Egypt. After that date personal friction with his uncle, the Prince of Wales, and some political differences between the two states caused the German Emperor to abandon his annual visits to England. The British government finally came to the conclusion that the Turkish administration could not be reformed while Germany advocated the maintenance of the integrity of the Turkish Empire. Germany repeatedly irritated the British government and the British people by her policy in South Africa, particularly by the telegram despatched to President Kruger of the Transvaal on the occasion of the Jameson Raid. The rivalry of the European powers in the Far East and the clash with France over the occupation of Fashoda by French troops brought out even more unmistakably the dangers of the policy of splendid isolation. Finally, the outbreak of the Boer War revealed with crystal clearness the isolation of the British Empire. At last this series of events determined the British political leaders to seek the support of other powers.

7

THE NEGOTIATIONS WITH RUSSIA AND GERMANY

The responsible ministers of Great Britain first attempted to come to an understanding with the Russian government, a power whose interests conflicted with their own in the Near East, Central Asia, and the Far East. In 1898 they suggested to the spokesmen of Russia a division of Turkey and China into spheres of political influence without an actual partition of the territories of the two decaying empires. From the Russian government, however, they received little encouragement to proceed with their negotiations. Instead of seizing the opportunity to reduce the friction between the Russian and the British empires, the shifty, ambitious ministers of the Tsar increased the international tension by occupying Port Arthur.

Rebuffed by Russia, the British government sounded Germany on the question of an alliance. At a private dinner Joseph Chamberlain, the British Secretary of State for the Colonies, discussed with the German ambassador the possibility of a defensive alliance between the two countries. He urged the absence of any fundamental points of opposition between the two powers and offered to have the more innocuous portions of the treaty ratified by the British Parliament. If he had succeeded, the ambitious British minister would have won a great personal triumph. But his proposal encountered opposition from both his British colleagues and the German government. The occupants of the German Foreign Office feared that the British Parliament would never ratify a treaty and also that the conclusion of such an agreement might involve Germany in war on two fronts with Russia and France. The German Foreign Office therefore instructed its ambassador at London to come to an agreement on some of the outstanding colonial problems without concluding a definite alliance. A number of the colleagues of Chamberlain, on the other hand, preferred an agreement with France rather than one with Germany.

Because of these obstacles little came of the negotiations with Germany. The German Emperor tried to use them as a threat to force Russia to join with Germany in forming an alliance of the Continental powers. The British and German foreign offices signed a treaty in 1898 that provided for a division of the Portuguese colonies in Africa between them and another in 1900 that failed to allay their conflicting interests in China because of a dispute as to whether or not it applied to Manchuria. Several later attempts to revive the negotiations for a defensive alliance also ended in failure. The Boer War and the plans for the development of the German navy intensified the mutual ill-will of the peoples of the two countries and made impossible the conclusion of an alliance between Great Britain and Germany. The political leaders of Germany had no wish to pull chestnuts out of the fires caused by international conflicts for the British Empire and never dreamed that within the next few years the British government would negotiate agreements with Japan, France, and Russia that would result in the formation of a group of powers able to compete on equal terms with the states of the Triple Alliance.

8

ITALY BEGINS TO DRIFT AWAY FROM THE TRIPLE ALLIANCE

In the meantime Italy had begun to follow a policy which indicated that her partners in the Triple Alliance might not be able to count upon her in a crisis. Disappointment in her efforts to obtain a foothold in Tripoli through the support of the Triple Alliance, Italy began to turn to France. In 1896 she signed a convention that virtually recognized the French protectorate in Tunis, in return for certain political and commercial privileges. Two years later she concluded an agreement with France that brought to an end the ruinous tariff war that had raged for a decade between the two countries. In 1900 the two states negotiated a secret treaty that recognized the aspirations of Italy in Tripoli and those of France in Morocco. Outward signs of the reconciliation of the two powers then followed the conclusion of the secret bargain. The President of the French Republic bestowed the Grand Cross of the French Legion of Honor on the heir to the Italian throne, and the Italian fleet visited Toulon amid demonstrations of friendship which recalled the visit of the Russian fleet to the same port in 1891. Finally, in 1902 Italy and France exchanged notes which gave mutual assurance that neither power would attack the other in case of an attack on either state by one or more powers. In 1904 the President of the French Republic returned the visit of the King of Italy. In the accompanying festivities toasts hailed the new Franco-Italian friendship but ostentatiously omitted to mention the Triple Alliance. These agreements with France did not infringe the letter of the treaty of alliance with Germany and Austria-Hungary, but they gave an unmistakable indication that Italy could be counted on in any future crisis to follow only a policy dictated exclusively by Italian interests.

9

THE ANGLO-JAPANESE ALLIANCE

In 1902 the British government finally found an ally. Fear of Russia and consciousness of their diplomatic isolation drew Japan and Great Britain together. In the treaty of alliance concluded between them they recognized the independence of China and of Korea, promised to remain neutral in case either ally should become involved in war in defense of its special interests in the Far East, and agreed to assist each other in case either should be attacked by more than one power. The treaty assured Japan that she would not have to stand alone in case of attack by two powers and increased the strength of Great Britain in the Far East.

10

THE ANGLO-FRENCH ENTENTE OF 1904

Two years after the conclusion of the alliance with Japan the British government established an entente with its rival across the English Channel. In both Great Britain and France the political leaders gradually became convinced of the wisdom of establishing better relations between the two countries. The French began to feel that the rivalry with Great Britain stood in the way of their recovery of Alsace-Lorraine and the expansion of their colonial empire. In June, 1898, Théophile Delcassé, a man who shared this point of view, came to power in France. He seems to have made a compromise between the conflicting French and British interests the first object of his policy. While in office he settled a long-standing dispute with Great Britain over boundaries in the Niger Valley, withdrew the expedition of Major Marchand from Fashoda, and delimited the French and British spheres of influence in the valleys of the Upper Nile and the Upper Congo. For the moment public opinion and the ill-wind engendered between the two countries by the Boer War prevented him from going farther.

After their country had been rebuffed by Russia and Germany a number of British leaders, conscious of the dangerous position of the British Empire, began to work for the establishment of better relations with France. While president of the chamber of commerce at Paris Sir Thomas Barclay arranged for a meeting of the British chambers of commerce in Paris in 1900. The visit proved to be a decided success and was followed by a return visit of delegations from the French chambers of commerce and an exchange of visits by members of the two parliaments and their wives. Upon the death of Queen Victoria in 1901 and the retirement of Lord Salisbury from office, two men, who were more enthusiastic about a reconciliation with France, came into power— Edward VII and Lord Lansdowne. In 1903 the new British sovereign made a formal visit to France and did much by his speeches and by his tact to allay French hostility to Great Britain. Two months later the French President returned the royal visit and received many assurances of British good-will.

During this visit Delcassé, then French Minister of Foreign Affairs, commenced negotiations with the British Foreign Office which finally resulted, in 1904, in the conclusion of a treaty that settled all the points in dispute between the two countries. The negotiators found a basis for a bargain in Egypt and Morocco. In Egypt the British had found French diplomacy an obstacle to the carrying out of British policies. The French Foreign Office had never forgotten British assurances that the occupation of Egypt was simply for the purpose of restoring order, and through the machinery for international control of Egyptian finances it prevented the Egyptian government from using the surplus produced by British supervision of the country. For some time, on the other hand, the French government had regarded the incorporation of Morocco into its colonial empire as logical and highly desirable. Its acquisition would round out the French possessions on the south and the east, enable the French to put an end to the political disorders which continually caused trouble on the western frontier of Algeria, and offer a profitable field for commercial expansion and investment.

By 1904 the French had already made considerable progress toward obtaining control of Morocco. They had supplied a few military instructors to the Moroccan army. A French bank had made a small loan to relieve the financial stringency caused by the passion of the young Sultan for the bicycles, motor-cars, fireworks, cameras, and other attractions of European civilization. In 1900 France purchased the approval of Italy for her plans in Morocco by recognizing the Italian claims to the Turkish province of Tripoli. The conclusion of an agreement with Great Britain would be a logical step in the development of French policy in Morocco.

In the treaty finally signed by representatives of the two governments both powers made considerable concessions. France promised to make no further embarrassing inquiries about the British occupation of Egypt, to allow the British authorities to spend the surplus in the Egyptian treasury (as long as the payments on the Egyptian debt were met), and to erect no fortifications on the Moroccan coast opposite the fortress of Gibraltar. In return Great Britain pledged herself to offer no opposition to the French plans for Morocco and to make certain concessions with regard to the status of the Suez Canal in time of war. In the published treaty both powers solemnly declared their intention to make no change in the status of either Egypt or Morocco, but certain secret articles clearly revealed the purpose of the two governments to make reforms in Egypt and to partition Morocco between France and Spain. Later in the year Spain signed an agreement with France in which she accepted the proposed division of Moroccan territory.

With good-will displayed on both sides, the British and French governments had little difficulty in settling their differences in other colonial areas by similar compromises. In Newfoundland France gave up the right, conceded by the Treaty of Utrecht, of French fishermen to land on the so-called French Shore. In West Africa the British made concessions concerning the boundary between the colonies of Gambia and Senegambia, ceded the Los Islands commanding the capital of French Guinea, and modified the boundary of British Nigeria in such a way as to give the French access to the French territory on Lake Chad. The two countries established the boundaries of their respective spheres of influence in Siam. The British government abandoned its protest against the French tariff policy in Madagascar. For the New Hebrides the powers agreed to submit certain questions in dispute to a commission. There is little evidence that at the outset the British government planned to isolate Germany or to encourage France to count on anything more than diplomatic support in case of a dispute over Morocco.

II

THE MOROCCAN CRISIS

Having purchased the good-will of Italy and Great Britain by timely concessions, France continued her policy of peaceful penetration in Morocco. The French government began to press upon the Sultan the necessity of adopting reforms and with this end in view made the Moroccan government a considerable loan and forwarded to Fez, the capital of Morocco, a French mission. Upon its arrival the mission strongly urged the need for a reorganization of the police to restore order, the building of roads and telegraph-lines, and the establishment of a state bank. Before the negotiations had progressed very far, however, Germany intervened in the Moroccan question.

In its policy in regard to Morocco the French government had made the curious mistake of coming to no understanding with Germany, the power most to be feared. Its failure to do this aroused serious protests among certain elements in Germany and decided the German government to demonstrate to France that Germany could not be treated as a negligible quantity in the settlement of international questions. At the suggestion of the German Foreign Office the government of Germany executed a dramatic stroke. In March, 1905, the German Emperor landed from his imperial yacht at the Moroccan port of Tangier. In a series of bombastic speeches he emphasized the economic interests of Germany in Morocco and the independent status of the Sultan. The German Foreign Office followed up this spectacular action by complaining of the failure of France to inform Germany concerning the treaties negotiated with Italy, Great Britain, and Spain, and by suggesting the submission of the Morocco question to an international conference. Simultaneously German organs of public opinion began to drop threatening phrases which foreshadowed war.

The policy followed by the German government in regard to Morocco placed the responsible political leaders of France in a difficult situation. A continuance of the policy of Delcassé threatened to involve France in war with Germany. Submission to the demands of the German government might cause the loss of all the French gains in Morocco. A chauvinistic group of newspapers and public men urged the country to support Delcassé. Most of the responsible French leaders opposed the following of a policy that threatened to involve France in war with Germany. In consequence the French ministry accepted the resignation of the ambitious, bellicose, and imperialistic Minister of Foreign Affairs, came to an understanding with Germany, and agreed to the submission of the Moroccan problem to a conference of the European powers.

The resulting conference opened at Algeciras in January, 1906. In the preliminary negotiations Germany succeeded in gaining recognition for the principle that the Moroccan question concerned all the powers, but in the conference France received the support of most of the powers, including Italy, Russia, Spain, and Great Britain, and came off victor in most of the specific points considered by the representatives of the powers. The treaty ultimately concluded by the conference provided for the organization of a police force, instructed by French and Spanish officers and to be distributed among the eight ports, the appointment of a Swiss inspector-general for this body of troops, the organization of a state bank with capital advanced by the signatory powers, the protection of the public services against alienation, the admission of foreigners to the country, and the joint supervision of customs regulations by the agents of Morocco, France, and Spain.

The Moroccan policy of Germany, however, had the unforseen result of drawing Great Britain and France much closer together than either power had originally contemplated. During the crisis over Morocco, the French Foreign Office brought pressure on the British Foreign Office to take a step beyond the agreement of 1904. Sir Edward Grey, the British Secretary of State for Foreign Affairs, initiated—without the knowledge of most of his colleagues in the British ministry or of the British Parliament—a policy that morally committed the British government to give France military and naval support in case of war with Germany. He authorized the military and naval representatives of Great Britain to discuss with officers of the French army and navy the problems connected with the defense of France in case of war with Germany. In accordance with these discussions the British War Office reorganized the military forces of the British Empire in such a way as to make possible the placing of a British expeditionary force in France with the greatest possible rapidity. These conversations, which were continued down to the outbreak of the World War, caused France to assume that she could confidently rely on Great Britain for military and naval aid in case of war with Germany and encouraged the French government to speak more boldly in international crises.

12

THE ANGLO-RUSSIAN ENTENTE

The establishment of an entente with France naturally suggested the settling of the points in dispute between Great Britain and the power to which France was tied by bonds of friendship and alliance, by the conclusion of a similar agreement. Russia and Great Britain had come perilously close to war during the Russo-Japanese War as a result of the firing upon British fishermen in the North Sea by the Russian fleet on its way to the Far East. Their conflicting interests in Persia, Afghanistan, Tibet, and the Far East constantly threatened to embroil them. A mutual understanding would relieve both powers from the constant fear of war.

The idea of an Anglo-Russian Entente seems to have been mentioned first by King Edward VII to Alexander Isvolski while the latter held the comparatively unimportant post of Russian representative to Denmark. Flattered by the royal attention, he later took office as Russian Foreign Minister with the purpose of effecting a settlement with Great Britain. The treaty finally signed in August, 1907, settled the differences of Russia and Great Britain in the Middle East. The contracting parties recognized the territorial integrity of Tibet and agreed not to interfere with her internal affairs or to attempt to obtain special concessions there. In return for a British promise not to occupy or annex any of its territory Russia declared Afghanistan to be outside of her influence and agreed to deal with the Amir only through the British authorities. Though piously pretending to protect her integrity and independence, the two powers virtually divided Persia between them. They assigned a northern zone, comprising some of the most fertile and populous portions of the country, to Russia as a sphere of influence, gave a smaller strip of territory in Southern Persia to be controlled by Great Britain, and left a neutral region between them in which the two powers agreed that neither would seek concessions without the approval of the other. By these agreements Great Britain felt that she had safeguarded India from attack.

The negotiations for an Entente between Great Britain and Russia smoothed the way for the conclusion of agreements between France and Japan and between Japan and Russia. The first two powers agreed to respect the integrity and independence of China and to maintain economic equality in the Chinese Empire for all nations. Japan and Russia made agreements concerning fisheries, commerce, and the Manchurian railways that removed the tension surviving from the Russo-Japanese War.

The system of alliances begun by Bismarck to guarantee Germany against a hostile combination of powers gave rise to the organization of Europe into two great combinations of powers tied together by treaties and understandings. After the breakdown of the League of the Three Emperors, as a result of the crisis precipitated by the revolt of the Christian inhabitants of Herzegovina, Bismarck negotiated a Dual Alliance with Austria-Hungary. To this as a center gravitated Italy and Rumania, to form the group of powers known as the Triple Alliance. Until 1890 Bismarck kept Russia as an ally, first through a revival of the League of the Three Emperors and later by the Reinsurance Treaty. After the cutting of this tie by the German government Russia turned to France for support and finally concluded a Dual Alliance with that power. By the end of the century the political leaders of Great Britain had come to feel that their government must abandon the traditional British policy of "splendid isolation" and seek friends. This decision caused Great Britain to conclude a formal treaty of alliance with Japan in 1902 and to come to an understanding with France in 1904 and with Russia in 1907—the loosely tied group of powers, composed of Russia, France, and Great Britain, being known as the Triple Entente. Though this Entente, like the Triple Alliance, was formed for the purpose of guaranteeing peace, the ambitious members of the two groups already showed a tendency to use them for the furtherance of national and imperial aims.

CHAPTER XXV

THE GROWTH OF TENSION BETWEEN THE ALLIANCES

From the first, the powers of the Triple Alliance watched with anxiety France, Russia, and Great Britain, their potential enemies, compromise their ancient rivalries and form a second powerful diplomatic group in Europe. They realized their inferior naval, military, and economic strength and commenced to look with growing suspicion upon the activities of the members of the Triple Entente. As a result tension developed between the states of the two groups of powers in the Near East, over naval strength, in Morocco, and in the Balkans.

I

THE RIVALRY OF THE ALLIANCES IN THE NEAR EAST

Even before the conclusion of the ententes between Great Britain and France and Russia, the interests of Germany and the three powers belonging to the Triple Entente had begun to clash in the Near East. In 1889, the young William II had symbolized the interest of the new industrialized Germany in the economic opportunities offered by the Near East, by paying his first ceremonial visit to the hitherto isolated Sultan of Turkey. Within a few years the Germans became serious rivals of the British and the French in the Levant. German commercial travelers penetrated to every corner of the Turkish Empire; the Deutsche Bank founded a branch at Constantinople and German capitalists commenced to make loans in the Near East; and after the conclusion of a commercial treaty in 1890 German traders and artisans began to settle in the Turkish Empire. The advances of Germany were welcomed by the Sultan, Abdul Hamid. He seems to have felt that the Germans, unlike some of the other powers, aimed at nothing more than an opportunity to exploit the economic resources of his empire.

As a result of this encouragement the German government had continued to woo the Turkish authorities. At the time of the Armenian massacres and the difficulties in Crete, Germany gave evidences of her good-will toward Turkey which shocked public opinion in the rest of Europe. In 1896 the German Emperor presented the Sultan, the author of the terrible massacres, with a signed photograph of the German imperial family. Two years later William II made a second visit to the Turkish Empire, during which he skilfully ingratiated himself with Roman Catholics, Protestants, and Moslems. In a widely quoted speech delivered at Damascus he publicly assured Abdul Hamid and the three hundred million Moslems who reverenced him as their Khalifa of the friendship of the German Emperor for them.

This second visit of William paved the way for further economic concessions. In 1888, the year in which Constantinople became linked to central Europe by rail connections, a group of German financiers, in return for a loan, obtained a concession for ninety-nine years of the right to administer a railroad fifty-seven miles in length, extending inland from Haidar-Pasha, a port just across the Bosporus from the Turkish capital, and to continue the line on to Angora. After completing this railway in 1892 the German company received a concession that permitted it to build a branch to Koniah. In 1903 the Sultan authorized a more ambitious project, the construction of a line from Koniah to Bagdad via Adana and Mosul, with branches to various cities, the exploitation of all mineral deposits within twenty miles of the railroad, the development of ports at Bagdad and Basra, and the right to navigate the rivers of Asiatic Turkey in the service of the railroad.

The leaders of Germany felt the opposition that they encountered from the members of the Triple Entente to be significant. From the first Russia attempted to obstruct the Bagdad Railway project of Germany on various political, economic, and strategic grounds. After considerable hesitation the French government finally declared its opposition to the investment of French capital in the German undertaking and prevented the quotation of Bagdad Railway bonds on the Paris stock-exchange. In Great Britain public opinion felt that the German scheme would injure British interests of long standing in Mesopotamia and the Persian Gulf, increase German influence in the Turkish Empire at British expense, and threaten India, and this popular conviction caused the British government to obstruct the plans of the German financiers. It long refused to consent to the raising of the Turkish tariff from 8 to 11 per cent on the ground that the burden of the increase would fall on British traders. As a result of the British policy the Turkish government could not finance the bonds needed to continue the construction of the Bagdad Railway through the Taurus Mountains and the work of construction practically came to a standstill for several years.

For some years after 1905 Germany attempted in vain to secure the financial and political coöperation of France and Great Britain. Upon finding the British anxious to control the section of the proposed railway from Bagdad to the Persian Gulf as a "gate" for the protection of India, the German Emperor suggested in 1907 an agreement between Great Britain and Germany on this basis. However, the insistence of the British government that France and Russia should be parties to the agreement prevented the offer from coming to anything. The German government regarded the policy of the British government as evidence of the growing solidarity of the three powers of the Triple Entente.

2

THE ANGLO-GERMAN NAVAL RIVALRY

In the meantime the steady growth of the German navy began to alarm Great Britain. By the navy laws of 1898 and 1900 Germany suddenly laid the foundations for a strong navy. The leaders of Germany felt that the growing importance of her commerce and her colonies demanded the creation of a navy that would command respect. The British, on the other hand, considered the construction of a German navy a threat against British sea-power, the tie binding their far-flung empire together. The British government therefore took up what it regarded as a challenge from Germany. In 1903 it constructed a new first-class naval base and obtained the sanction of Parliament for the construction of four battle-ships annually. In the following year the British Admiralty commenced a drastic overhauling of the British navy. It denuded the China and the Mediterranean squadrons of battle-ships, abolished the North Pacific and the Atlantic squadrons, strengthened the Channel fleet, planned a new Atlantic fleet resting on Gibraltar as a base, and scrapped many obsolete vessels. In 1905 it laid the keel of a new type of battle-ship, the *Dreadnought,* the largest and most heavily armed vessel in the world.

The building of this war-ship had unexpected consequences. The new naval type doubled the cost of construction, made most of the existing vessels of both the British and the German navies practically obsolete, and enabled Germany to start construction of the new type of battle-ship on almost equal terms. Whereas the ratio between the two navies had been sixty-three to twenty-six, the ratio between the ships of the dreadnought type threatened to become by 1908 twelve to nine. Believing that because of conscription and lower costs of ship construction Germany could stand a race in naval armaments better than Great Britain, the German naval authorities pushed forward the construction of the new battle-ships. In 1906 a third German navy law authorized the construction of six large cruisers and the widening of the Kiel Canal to enable the new dreadnoughts to pass from the Baltic to the North Sea. Two years later the German naval authorities obtained approval of their proposal to reduce the period of replacement for naval vessels from twenty-five to twenty years and to construct, in the place of the discarded ships, the far more powerful vessels of the dreadnought type.

The rapid development of the German navy bred ill-will and suspicion in both Germany and Great Britain. The British felt that the new German navy was unnecessary for the protection and prosperity of Germany and a menace to the very foundation of the British Empire. Accordingly they repeatedly suggested to the leaders of Germany a limitation or at least a slowing up of German naval construction. The German authorities, on their part, suspected that the British were trying to arrest naval construction at a time when Great Britain was manifestly dominant on the seas and felt that it was incompatible with the dignity of Germany as a great power to limit her navy at the dictation of another state. The naval authorities of each country, consequently, became suspicious. Foolish speeches, provocative articles in the press, and wild rumors appeared in both countries and created genuine alarm.

Even honest efforts to allay the growing suspicion contributed toward the excitement in both countries. In 1908 the German Emperor addressed a private and personal letter on the naval situation to Lord Tweedmouth, the British First Lord of the Admiralty. Upon learning about this communication, the military correspondent of the London *Times* took the letter as an insidious attempt to influence a British minister in the interest of Germany just as the British naval estimates were before Parliament and published a brief letter in his newspaper. A sharp editorial in the same issue accused the German Emperor of trying to cut down British shipbuilding and steal a march on British naval supremacy. Later in the year an undated and anonymous interview with the German Emperor in another important English newspaper, the *Daily Telegraph,* again caused surprise and indignation in both countries, instead of promoting better relations. It incorrectly pictured the Emperor as a consistent friend of the British people during the Boer War in spite of the hostility of his own subjects and the failure of the British public to recognize his efforts in their behalf. The German people felt that their government had been revealed as guilty of playing a double game, of forwarding the war plans of Great Britain while professing friendship for the Boer people. The British readily believed the assertions of the Emperor concerning German hostility but doubted his declaration of his own undeviating good-will.

By 1908, therefore, the British public was in the grip of a veritable panic. In the autumn the British Admiralty heard that the German naval program was being accelerated. The British ministers met the supposed danger by obtaining the authorization of Parliament to build four and possibly eight capital ships for the British navy, but in order to put through their program they represented Germany as assured of having thirteen and possibly seventeen ships of the dreadnought class as compared to sixteen British vessels of the same type. The speeches of the British ministers benefited the British naval program but did irreparable damage to the relations between Germany and Great Britain. During the next three years the British government actually constructed eighteen ships of the dreadnought type, or those even more powerful, while Germany built only nine of the thirteen foretold by the alarmists. Suspicion and naval propaganda, however, had already done their work. In both Germany and Great Britain men began to speak openly of a war between the two countries as possible and even probable.

Thenceforth the British authorities prepared for a military conflict with Germany. They compiled a book containing instructions for the conduct of a war with the German Empire and printed or at least set up in type the necessary proclamations and orders in council, and constructed two additional naval bases. Thereafter the King never moved without carrying with him the papers required to set in motion the military and naval forces of the British Empire.

Simultaneously the idea that Great Britain was endeavoring to encircle the German Empire with a league of hostile powers found more and more believers among the German people. They watched with growing suspicion the interchange of visits and the interviews which followed the conclusion of the Anglo-Russian Entente. In May, 1908, the President of the French Republic visited England. During his visit the British Foreign Office tendered him a dinner attended only by Frenchmen and Englishmen and the Russian ambassador. Later in the year the British sovereign, accompanied by several important officials, visited the Tsar at Reval. These incidents seemed very significant to the already highly excited German public.

3

THE CONTINUED TENSION IN MOROCCO

During these years the situation in Morocco continued to be a source of anxiety to the European powers. For several years after the close of the Algeciras Conference Germany seemed inclined to regard the acquisition of Morocco by France as inevitable and to have the intention of withdrawing from the affair with as much dignity as possible. Under the influence of William II himself the German government took a conciliatory attitude toward France in 1908 in dealing with an unsuccessful attempt of the German consul at Casablanca to facilitate the escape of six deserters from the French Foreign Legion. Soon afterward it gave its approval to the agreement concluded by the French government with the successful claimant for the Moroccan throne. In 1909 the new German attitude resulted in the conclusion of an agreement designed to settle the Moroccan question. While professing to respect the integrity and independence of Morocco, France promised the Germans equality of economic opportunity in the country and Germany recognized the special political interests of France in the preservation of peace and order. For the moment the understanding gave great satisfaction in both countries and the financiers and industrialists of the nations began to negotiate for the joint exploitation of the opportunities for the opening of mines and the construction of railways and public works.

The agreement of 1909, however, did not settle the Moroccan question. The plans for the joint economic exploitation of Morocco by French and German interests encountered insurmountable opposition from firms with conflicting claims and from the governments of Spain and Great Britain, and conditions in Morocco gave the French a pretext for an extension of French influence in Morocco that threatened to transform the Moroccan state into a French protectorate. France felt that she could not modify her policy in Morocco without losing all the ground she had gained and throwing the country into anarchy, and Germany considered that the French action nullified both the decisions of the Algeciras Conference and the Franco-German agreement of 1909, and restored to the German government its freedom of action. The march of a French expeditionary force to Fez finally brought the situation to a crisis.

At first the official spokesmen of Germany maintained an ominous silence concerning the Morocco question. A part of the German press, however, commenced to demand either compensation for Germany or the partition of Morocco, and the French finally intimated in a cautious manner their willingness to talk of satisfying the demands of Germany. In order to get the best possible terms from France the German Foreign Office planned a brusk stroke. On the afternoon of July 1, 1911, the *Panther,* a German gunboat returning from South Africa, steamed into the Moroccan port of Agadir. Although considerably frightened by the action of Germany, the French refused to be bullied into ceding to Germany the whole of the French Congo.

To add to the embarrassment of Germany, the British government rallied to the support of France. For years the political leaders of Great Britain had feared the establishment of a German naval base on the Atlantic coast of Morocco. The "spring of the *Panther*" seemed to indicate the intention of the German government to seek compensation in western Morocco. Accordingly, three days after the *Panther* entered the harbor of Agadir, Sir Edward Grey, the British Secretary of State for Foreign Affairs, informed Germany that the British government would not recognize any new arrangement about which it had not been consulted. When France and Germany seemed unable to find a solution for the question of compensation and the silence of the German government as to its intentions appeared to indicate a purpose to stay at Agadir, the British Foreign Minister allowed his colleague in the cabinet, Lloyd George, the Chancellor of the Exchequer and a former pacifist, to announce to the world, in a speech made at the Mansion House, the determination of the British government to maintain at all hazards its prestige among the great powers of the world.

Although it caused an explosion of wrath in Germany, the announcement had a decisive influence on the international situation. Germany promptly allayed British fears concerning the establishment of a German naval base in western Morocco and greatly moderated the German demands on France. After four months of negotiations France and Germany finally reached an agreement. In this new compromise Germany virtually acknowledged that the French might establish their desired protectorate over Morocco. In return France ceded more than one hundred thousand square miles of the French Congo, a cession that gave the Germans two much-needed outlets to the Congo River for the export of the products of the German colony of Kamerun. In order to placate French public opinion Germany ceded to France in exchange a small valueless tract of Kamerun territory. The determination of the German Emperor and his pacific Chancellor, Von Bethmann-Hollweg, contributed greatly toward the reaching of an agreement by the two powers.

The Agadir crisis increased the existing friction between Germany and Great Britain but tightened the bonds between the French and British governments. Public opinion in Germany regarded the action of Great Britain with burning indignation and the British political leaders thenceforth suspected the motives of Germany more than ever. On the other hand France felt grateful for British diplomatic support and the British government permitted its military authorities to continue to hold conversations with the representatives of the French army. Its policy gave the French government every reason to feel that France could count on British military assistance in case of war.

4

THE TIGHTENING OF THE TRIPLE ENTENTE

The provocative policy of Germany in Morocco and elsewhere finally created a new spirit in France. It found its fullest expression in Raymond Poincaré, a French politician of ability, firmness, and determination. Poincaré and the group of political leaders who shared his views felt that France had yielded to German demands long enough. While they did not want war, they were ready to risk a military conflict in the next crisis rather than suffer a new humiliation. Under their influence the French government did much to tighten the bonds between the members of the Triple Entente and to commit the three powers to joint action in case of a diplomatic crisis.

With this purpose in view, Poincaré, first as head of the French ministry and later as President of France, gave much attention to cementing closer relations with Great Britain. The military authorities of France and Great Britain made more and more definite plans for British coöperation in case of war between France and Germany and the naval representatives of the two governments finally worked out a plan of coöperation which provided for the withdrawal of all units of the British navy to the English Channel and the concentration of the French fleet in the Mediterranean Sea. As this arrangement left the protection of the northern coast of France to the British fleet, the French finally persuaded the British cabinet to promise to consult with the French government in case of a crisis. By permitting the military discussions of officers of the two armies, by making the naval agreement, and by promising to consult with the French government in case of a crisis, the British ministers not only morally committed the British people to coöperate with France in time of war with Germany but they also encouraged the French and Russian governments to adopt bolder policies.

Simultaneously the French government was striving for greater solidarity with Russia. Owing to the late establishment of their naval staffs, the original agreements between France and Russia made no provision for naval coöperation between the two powers. By 1912, however, both governments recognized the desirability of common action and signed an agreement that provided for conferences at regular intervals between the naval staffs of the two countries and for the coöperation of their naval forces in all the eventualities contemplated by the original alliance between France and Russia. In 1912 and 1914 Poincaré also made official visits to Russia in order to promote the spirit of loyalty and confidence between the two governments. The new spirit in France and the secret assurances of Poincaré that France could count on the assistance of Great Britain in a crisis encouraged the Russian government to push forward plans in the Balkans that were certain to create a succession of crises in international relations.

5

THE GROWTH OF TENSION IN THE BALKANS

After 1908 Balkan questions gave rise to a steadily increasing tensilon between the already exacerbated European powers. Two years earlier two aggressive, ambitious adventurers assumed direction of foreign policy in Russia and in Austria-Hungary. Isvolski, the new Russian Minister of Foreign Affairs, aimed to modify the regulations concerning the Bosporus and the Dardanelles in such a way as to enable Russian war-ships to pass from the Black Sea into the Mediterranean without also permitting the naval vessels of other powers to use the Straits, and to win back in the Balkan peninsula the prestige lost by the defeat of Russia at the hands of Japan. Count Aloys von Aehrenthal, the Foreign Minister of Austria-Hungary, proposed to avert the threatened disruption of the Dual Monarchy by the Southern Slav agitation by annexing the "occupied" provinces of Bosnia and Herzegovina. The revolution engineered by the Young Turks in 1908 suddenly offered the two scheming ministers a favorable opportunity for a mutually advantageous bargain at the expense of Turkey. In an oral agreement concluded at the castle of Buchlau in Moravia, Isvolski and Aehrenthal seem to have agreed on the opening of the Straits by Russia and the annexation of the two "occupied" provinces by Austria-Hungary.

Upon the conclusion of this agreement the Austro-Hungary government acted promptly and announced the annexation of Bosnia and Herzegovina. Its action put Russia in an embarrassing situation. While Austria-Hungary immediately derived the promised benefits of the bargain, Isvolski bade fair to lose his share of the agreement. France and Great Britain refused their consent to the opening of the Straits. To add to his predicament, Serbia became highly indignant at the seizure of territory that she had earmarked for the Greater Serbia of her dreams, appealed for help to Russia as her protector, and prepared for war. As Russia was not in a position to wage a successful war, the embarrassed Russian Foreign Minister tried to extricate himself from his difficult situation by an unsuccessful effort to persuade the Austro-Hungarian government to submit the question of the annexation of Bosnia and Herzegovina to a conference of the European powers for revision. In the end Russia had to submit to the acquisition of the two provinces by the Dual Monarchy and Serbia had to promise to desist from her policy of protest against the annexations and to live on good terms henceforth with Austria-Hungary. The policy of Isvolski thus led to the humiliation of Russia and the embitterment of the Southern Slavs. Though she had really used her good offices in behalf of Russia, Germany had drawn upon herself the odium of having bullied the Russian government into submission.

In spite of this failure the political leaders of Russia did not abandon their efforts to open the Straits to Russian war-ships. In 1909 the Russian Foreign Office won the secret consent of Italy to the opening of the Dardanelles and the Bosporus for the exclusive benefit of Russia, in return for giving Italy a free hand in Tripoli, and the two powers agreed to coöperate in the Near East. In 1911 the Russian government thought the time ripe for gaining consent of the powers for its plans in the Balkans. Italy and Austria-Hungary had already given their approval of those plans. Germany, certain of the opposition of Great Britain, readily agreed to the Russian proposals. Out of deference for her British friend France gave a non-committal reply. The British government, however, would give its consent only on condition that the Straits were opened to all the powers.

6

THE BALKAN WARS

Although rebuffed in the question of the Straits, Russia did not abandon her activity in the Balkan peninsula, where the political situation invited her intervention. The annexation of Bosnia and Herzegovina and the seizure of power by the Young Turks had settled none of the fundamental problems of this troubled region. The Serbs still dreamed of and carried on an agitation for a Greater Serbia that would include the Southern Slav provinces of Austria-Hungary. The change of government at Constantinople did little to improve the position of the Christian populations of Turkey in Europe, and threatened to deprive them of valuable privileges in return for the rather doubtful opportunity to become Ottomans. The awakening of a Turkish nationalism suddenly endangered the plans of the Balkan states for expansion at the expense of the Turkish Empire. The Greeks still demanded the union of Crete with Greece. The Albanians, in revolt against the policy of Turkification, advanced claims in conflict with the ambitions of Serbia for an outlet to the Adriatic Sea.

With the assistance and encouragement of the Russian diplomatic representatives at Sofia and Belgrade, consequently, the Balkan states succeeded in putting aside their differences for the time being and coming to an agreement. In March, 1912, Serbia and Bulgaria concluded a secret treaty that mutually guaranteed their territories, pledged the two states to support each other in case any of the great powers should attack Balkan territory by force, provided for their joint action in case of disorder in Turkey, arranged for a division of Turkish territory, and made Russia the arbiter in case of any dispute. Two months later Greece and Bulgaria signed a defensive alliance. In August of the same year the three Balkan allies came to an understanding with Montenegro.

After the conclusion of these treaties the war spirit developed rapidly in the Balkan peninsula. Massacres of Christians in Novibazar and Macedonia stirred public opinion to fever heat. Popular mass-meetings in both Bulgaria and Turkey in Europe demanded autonomy for Thrace and Macedonia, and the four Balkan allies began to mobilize. On October 8, 1912, Montenegro declared war on Turkey and invaded the adjoining Turkish provinces. A few days later her three allies presented an ultimatum that made inevitable a general war between the four Balkan states and the Turkish Empire. In spite of the admonition of the great powers not to resort to arms and their warning to the Balkan powers that they would not be permitted to extend their boundaries, the Bulgarian army crossed the border of Thrace and advanced toward Adrianople, the Serbians pushed into adjoining Turkish provinces on the west, the south, and the east, and the Greeks started armies toward the valuable Ægean port of Saloniki and the city of Janina in southern Albania.

The military forces of Serbia, Greece, Bulgaria, and Montenegro surprised Europe by their rapid successes. The Bulgarians won great victories at Kirk Kilisseh and Lule Burgas, invested Adrianople, and halted their advance only at the strongly fortified Tchatalja lines before Constantinople. The Serbians occupied Uskup and Monastir, towns lying to the south once included in medieval Serbia, and the Adriatic port of Durazzo in northern Albania. The Greeks entered Saloniki, laid siege to Janina, and established their naval supremacy in the Ægean Sea. These victories brought about the conclusion of an armistice between Turkey and Serbia, Bulgaria and Montenegro, and the assembling of a peace conference at London of representatives of the five belligerent states under the surveillance of the diplomatic representatives of the great powers who were resident at the British capital.

The negotiations at London were rudely terminated, however, by a coup d'état at Constantinople engineered by a party determined to continue the war. In January, 1913, Enver Bey, a hero of the Turkish Revolution of 1908 and of the war in Tripoli in 1911, burst into the council-chamber, forced the Grand Vizier to resign, and shot the commander-in-chief of the Turkish army. The renewal of the conflict failed to improve the military situation for Turkey. The Greeks finally captured Janina and the Serbs and the Bulgarians took Adrianople. These victories forced the Turks to sue for a new armistice.

The great powers, however, were in no mood to give the victorious

Balkan allies a free hand in settling the future of the peninsula. Their success had alarmed Italy and Austria-Hungary. Italy had no desire to see either Serbia or Greece established on the Adriatic coast or to have her plans for obtaining control of the Albanian port of Avlona and building a railroad across the mountains to Saloniki thwarted. Austria-Hungary, for her part, watched with growing alarm the effect of the Serbian victories on her Southern Slav subjects, the closing of the door to Austro-Hungarian expansion toward Saloniki, and the appearance of the military forces of Serbia on the coast of northern Albania.

As a result of the influence of these two states, the great powers of Europe had decided as early as the peace conference at London on the establishment of Albania as an autonomous state. The peace treaty concluded in May, 1913, therefore provided for the delimitation of the frontiers of Albania by the great powers. The creation of the new state deprived Serbia of a large share of the territory assigned to her by the agreement made with Bulgaria before the outbreak of the Balkan Wars and left her still a landlocked country at the mercy of the tariff policies adopted by her neighbors. Serbia therefore asked for a revision of the earlier agreement and concluded a defensive and offensive alliance with Greece, a state drawn to her by common interests.

The tension over the division of the territory taken from Turkey finally resulted in a new Balkan War. In June, 1913, King Ferdinand of Bulgaria, without informing the civilian authorities of his action, treacherously ordered the Bulgarian troops in Macedonia to make a dash for Saloniki. The unexpected attack precipitated a short and disastrous conflict. To an accompaniment of hideous atrocities committed by both sides, the Greeks and the Serbians drove back the Bulgarian troops; the Rumanians, who had been demanding territorial compensation as the price of their neutrality since the opening of the Balkan Wars, advanced toward the Bulgarian capital; and the Turks reoccupied Adrianople. As a result of her defeat Bulgaria lost most of her anticipated territorial acquisitions, Rumania obtained a slice of Bulgarian territory inhabited by a quarter of a million people, and Turkey regained Adrianople. As a result of the Balkan Wars Greece acquired the greater part of Epirus, the port of Saloniki, southern Macedonia, Crete, and most of the Ægean islands, and increased her population 60 per cent; Serbia nearly doubled her area and increased her population by half; and Turkey lost five sixths of her territory and two thirds of her subjects in Europe.

7

THE CONTINUED TENSION IN THE BALKANS

The Treaty of Bucharest by no means restored tranquillity in Europe. In a way the Balkan Wars had been a defeat for Germany and Austria-Hungary as well as for Bulgaria and Turkey. Germany regarded the defeat of the German-trained Turkish armies as a blow to her prestige. Austria-Hungary watched with alarm the blocking of her plans for expansion toward Saloniki, the growth of Serbia in territory and ambition, the turning of the eyes of her own Southern Slav subjects more and more to the Serbian state for salvation, and the growth of hostility among the Rumanian people. Bulgaria and Turkey desired revenge for their defeat and their loss of territory. Russia emerged from the Balkan Wars with enhanced prestige and renewed determination to increase her influence in the peninsula. Each power regarded its rivals with suspicion and attempted to assure itself of the support of its allies. Fear of diplomatic isolation made each of the powers consent to policies on the part of its allies of which it disapproved. All the powers, consequently, developed nerves.

One result of the increased tension was a sudden renewal of preparations for war by several of the great powers. In 1912, after another failure to come to an understanding with Great Britain, Germany voted a new navy bill and made a considerable increase in her army. In 1913 a new German army law provided for a still larger increase in the size of her military forces. Before the plans for the new increase in the size of the German army were published, Poincaré and his associates had decided to present to the French parliament a bill extending the term of active training for French recruits from two to three years and the liability for service in the reserve from the age of forty-five to that of forty-eight, a measure designed to put France on a military equality with Germany. At the same time Russia made great efforts to train a larger proportion of her population for military service. By the spring of 1914 these military preparations had created an alarming state of uneasiness and suspicion.

The outcome of the Balkan Wars also gave the Young Turks another convincing proof of the necessity of Westernizing their state. In order to put Turkey in a position to meet another crisis they invited a number of distinguished foreigners to guide them in reorganizing the Turkish finances, judiciary, customs service, army, and navy. To help them in rehabilitating the army the Young Turks finally invited a group of forty-two German officers, headed by General Liman von Sanders. In order to be in a position to enforce his recommendations, however, the head of the new German military commission stipulated that he should have command of the First Turkish Army Corps, with headquarters at Constantinople.

The news of the German military mission to Turkey and of the proposal to put its head in actual command of the Turkish forces controlling the Straits greatly alarmed the Russian Foreign Office. Convinced by the outcome of the Balkan Wars of the likelihood of a speedy disruption of the Turkish Empire, the Russian authorities had been giving serious consideration again to the question of the Straits and the position of Russia in the Balkan peninsula. They had been making naval and military preparations for a seizure of the Straits in case a diplomatic crisis should arise, wooing the Rumanian people and their political leaders away from their alliance with the powers of the Triple Alliance, and encouraging Serbia in her preparations against Austria-Hungary. In order to carry through their plans they stood ready to risk a general European conflict by threatening the use of force to gain their objectives. They regarded the German military mission to Turkey, accordingly, as an attempt to increase the influence of the German Empire in Turkey and to thwart their plans concerning the Straits and the Balkan peninsula, a view shared by the French ambassador to Russia. As a result of the good-will displayed by Germany, however, a conflict between Russia and Germany was avoided. The incident is important mainly as showing the nervousness of the powers and the risks of provoking a general war that they were willing to take.

After the close of the Balkan Wars, Austria-Hungary, for her part, became more than ever concerned over the Southern Slav question. The victory of Serbia over Turkey and Bulgaria increased the self-confidence and the ambition of the Serbian nationalists and caused their Croat and Serbian kinsmen of the Dual Monarchy to look to them for leadership. The Narodna Odbrana, a secret society organized in Serbia at the time of the annexation of Bosnia and Herzegovina, continued its agitation in Serbia and the two annexed provinces. A more reckless element plotted the assassination of Austro-Hungarian officials. The Serbian government took a provocative tone toward Austria-Hungary. The leaders of the Dual Monarchy felt that the integrity of their state was imperiled, but they differed as to the policy Austria-Hungary should follow in regard to her Southern Slav subjects, and Serbia. The chief of the general staff and many of his associates advocated an attack on Serbia and a partition of her territory among the neighboring states; others proposed a reorganization of the Dual into a Triple Monarchy, with the Southern Slavs of Austria-Hungary as the third state, and advanced the idea of the incorporation of all the Southern Slavs into the Hapsburg state.

Out of this agitation in Serbia and Bosnia finally grew a plot that

brought the tense situation to a crisis. A group of young Bosnian revolutionists, eager to be considered as martyrs, to take revenge on
Austria-Hungary for its oppressive rule, and to do something to advance the cause of the Southern Slavs, determined to assassinate some
prominent official of the Dual Monarchy. Upon learning that the Archduke Francis Ferdinand, the heir to the Austro-Hungarian throne
and a man credited with plans for the reorganization of the Dual
Monarchy likely to thwart the formation of a Southern Slav state
around Serbia as a nucleus, was planning to pay an official visit to
Sarajevo, the Bosnian capital, and to command the troops stationed
in the provinces of Bosnia and Herzegovina during army maneuvers, the
conspirators marked him out for assassination. With the aid of Serbian
officers and officials belonging to two Serbian patriotic societies, the
Narodna Odbrana and the Black Hand, three of the conspirators pro-
cured bombs, weapons, and money, made their way across the Serbian
border to Sarajevo, and finally executed their plot. One of the three
principal conspirators threw a bomb at the carriage of the archduke
as it passed through the streets of the Bosnian capital and another fired
fatal shots at both Ferdinand and his morganatic wife.

The assassination of the heir to the Austro-Hungarian throne convinced Count Berchtold, the Foreign Minister of the Dual Monarchy,
that the crime must be used as an excuse for putting an end to the
Greater Serbia propaganda and the Russian intrigues in the Balkan
peninsula. The Greater Serbia and the Southern Slav movements responsible for the assassinations were steadily gathering adherents. Rumania could no longer be counted upon as an ally, and the agitation of the
Rumanian nationalists threatened to detach Transylvania from the monarchy. Russia was pushing forward her armaments and military railway
construction and was supposed to be organizing an alliance of Serbia,
Greece, and Rumania against Austria-Hungary. The new state of
Albania seemed on the point of dissolution. Italy could no longer be
relied upon in a crisis and Germany was critical of the policies of the
Austro-Hungarian government. If Austria-Hungary allowed the assassination of Francis Ferdinand to go unchallenged and unpunished her
prestige in the Balkans and in Europe would be gone forever.

Having made up his own mind, Berchtold had to assure himself of
the support of his associates and his allies. In order to win the support of Germany he drew up an ambiguous letter to be sent by Emperor Francis Joseph of Austria-Hungary to the German Emperor for
the purpose of convincing the German government of the responsibility
of Serbia for the crime and of winning its support for military action
by Austria-Hungary against Serbia. Shocked by the assassination of
his close personal friend, Emperor William II and his advisers seem
to have given Austro-Hungarian government a free hand in dealing

with Serbia and to have promised the loyal support of Germany. Count Berchtold had more difficulty, however, in gaining the consent of the Hungarian Prime Minister to the policy of taking some sort of action against Serbia. Thereupon he drafted in the greatest secrecy and on July 23 forwarded for presentation to Serbia and to the European powers an ultimatum, without receiving approval of his action from Emperor Francis Joseph or officially informing the allies of Austria-Hungary in the Triple Alliance in time for them to make an effective protest.

The demands upon Serbia were purposely made so severe that the Serbian government would never accede to them. After reciting at length the failure of Serbia to keep the promise she had made in 1909 to live as a good neighbor and the part played by Serbians in the recent crime, the ultimatum demanded a formal condemnation of the Serbian propaganda, the suppression of any publication inciting to hatred or contempt of Austria-Hungary, the dissolution of the Narodna Odbrana, the cessation of all propaganda against the Dual Monarchy in the schools, the punishment of those involved in the plot against Francis Ferdinand, and permission for the government of Austria-Hungary to collaborate in carrying out these demands. The note gave Serbia only forty-eight hours to formulate her reply.

The Serbian government had felt from the first that the terms of the Austro-Hungarian note were incompatible with its dignity and were presented to provoke a conflict. In framing their answer, consequently, the Serbian ministers aimed to win for their country the public opinion of Europe. They drew up a note more conciliatory in form than in substance which tended to place Austria-Hungary in the wrong. They denied that Serbia had at any time sought to change the political situation in Bosnia and Herzegovina and maintained that they could not be held responsible for agitation by private individuals. They promised to introduce a bill in the Serbian parliament designed to curb the press, to dissolve the Narodna Odbrana, to eliminate propaganda from the schools, to remove from military service all persons proved by a judicial inquiry to be guilty of acts directed against Austria-Hungary, to open an investigation of all persons implicated in the plot, to prevent the smuggling of arms and explosives across the frontier, to punish the border officials responsible for permitting the assassins to enter Bosnia, and to explain the remarks of Serbian officials. They maintained that they had arrested one Serbian officer immediately but had been unable to capture the other accused person. They refused to permit the government of Austria-Hungary to participate in the inquiry concerning the plot to be conducted by the Serbian government, but offered to refer the questions at issue to the International Tribunal of The Hague. So certain were they that Austria-

Hungary would not accept their reply that they mobilized the Serbian army three hours before handing their note to the diplomatic representative at Belgrade. As expected, the government of the Dual Monarchy rejected the Serbian note with unseemly haste and ordered the mobilization of its troops against Serbia and Montenegro the same night.

From the first the political leaders of Russia had felt vitally interested in the question. If they allowed Serbia to be humiliated or crushed by Austria-Hungary without protest, the influence and prestige of Russia in the Balkan peninsula would be destroyed and the Russian plans for opening the Straits would never be realized. Encouraged by the French government, which at the time was under the influence of Poincaré and his associates, the Russian leaders made it plain that they intended to take the side of Serbia in the crisis even at the risk of war. They ordered the putting into effect of various military measures "preparatory to war" and authorized the Russian Minister for Foreign Affairs to order a partial mobilization against Austria-Hungary as soon as the diplomatic situation demanded such action.

This attitude of Russia made the dispute between Serbia and the Dual Monarchy a European question. Her intervention in the question would be almost certain sooner or later to involve the other members of the two alliances in the war. As soon as the terms of the Austro-Hungarian note to Serbia became known, consequently, the foreign offices of Europe made genuine efforts to prevent the threatened war. In these attempts Sir Edward Grey, the British Secretary of State for Foreign Affairs, usually took the initiative. The various plans for the preservation of peace failed, however, because each power put the maintenance of the solidarity of its diplomatic group before the cause of peace. Until late in the negotiations Germany insisted on regarding the question as simply a dispute between Austria-Hungary and Serbia. Russia steadily asserted her vital interest in the matter. France and Great Britain refused to put pressure on their Russian ally. As a result the proposals of the powers for the preservation of peace met with no success.

As soon as the diplomats began to show their inability to find a solution for the problem, the military authorities began to assume control of the situation. In order to prevent the intervention of the European powers in the Serbian question the leaders of Austria-Hungary decided to declare war on Serbia on July 28, 1914. The action of the Dual Monarchy precipitated a struggle among the Russian political and military leaders between the advocates of partial and those of general mobilization. As soon as Austria-Hungary declared war on Serbia the leaders of Russia decided that the Russian army must mobilize on the Austro-Hungarian border. The military authorities, however, considered partial mobilization impossible for technical reasons and dangerous because it left the Russian forces on the Austro-Hungarian border open to an attack on the flank by Germany. They advocated, consequently, a Russian mobilization on both the German and the Austro-Hungarian borders. On July 29, 1914, the Tsar signed and then recalled an order for general mobilization. On the next day, however, he gave in to the pressure of the military authorities and ordered all the Russian forces to mobilize.

This action of Russia made war almost inevitable. France had repeatedly assured the Russian government of her intention to come to its aid in case of war. Upon receiving news of the Russian mobilization Austria-Hungary mobilized her forces on the Russian frontier and Germany proclaimed a "threatening danger of war" that set in motion various precautionary military measures. In case of war, however, German success would depend on the ability of Germany to mobilize speedily and deliver a powerful blow against France before the slower-moving Russians could attack. The German military authorities, in consequence, finally persuaded the civilian leaders of Germany to present, on August 1, 1914, ultimatums to the Russian and French governments. In reply the Russian government maintained its inability to suspend mobilization and the French spokesmen answered that France would consult her own interests. Germany, consequently, declared war on both Russia and France.

The formation of two diplomatic groups in Europe, the Triple Alliance and the Triple Entente, had unexpected results. Organized to insure the various states of Europe against the danger of isolation, their formation encouraged the member states to take greater risks and engage in more provocative policies. As a result of this situation tension arose between Germany and Great Britain over the strength of their respective navies, between France and Germany over Morocco, and between Russia and Austria-Hungary and Germany and Great Britain over the Balkan peninsula and the Near East. The tension finally reached a point where any incident might lead to war. Consequently the assassination of the heir to the Austro-Hungarian throne as a result of the Greater Serbia and Southern Slav agitation produced a situation that got beyond the control of the diplomacy of Europe. The Austro-Hungarian government held Serbia responsible for the agitation threatening the integrity of its empire. For the sake of her plans and her prestige in the Balkan peninsula Russia felt compelled to side with Serbia. From fear of breaking down the solidarity of the Triple Alliance and the Triple Entente, Germany supported Austria-Hungary, and France and Great Britain sided with Russia. All failed to make the maintenance of peace their first interest. Upon the failure of the diplomats to find a solution of the problem, the military leaders of the different states seized control of the situation. Under their influence one power after another mobilized. The demand of Germany that Russia and France should demobilize the troops which they had just called to the colors precipitated the World War.

CHAPTER XXVI

THE WORLD WAR, 1914–1918

The failure of European diplomacy to find a solution for the crisis produced by the demands of Austria-Hungary on Serbia plunged Europe into a great war. The military conflict lasted more than four years and finally involved most of the states of the world. Because of its broad scope the struggle has come to be known as the World War.

I

THE ATTACK ON BELGIUM

As soon as it was clear that mobilization would lead to war, Germany commenced to carry out her carefully worked out military plans. Counting upon a slow mobilization by Russia, the German military authorities planned to annihilate the French armies in a short campaign of a few weeks and then turn against the slowly gathering forces of Russia. The greater part of the German army, therefore, mobilized on the French frontier and left the task of defending the eastern border of Germany to a relatively small number of German troops and to the armies of Austria-Hungary. Because of her long and careful preparation for war Germany mobilized her troops more rapidly than France and took the offensive.

On account of the necessity of winning a decisive victory over France promptly, the German military authorities had long planned to disregard Belgian neutrality and march the greater part of their forces through Belgium in a surprise attack instead of attempting to attack the almost impregnable fortresses of eastern France. Early in the evening of August 2, 1914, accordingly, the German minister at Brussels handed the Belgian government a demand for permission to forestall an alleged French intention to make an attack through Belgium. In its note the German government offered to guarantee the rights and independence of Belgium, to evacuate her territory at the close of the war, to buy for cash all the necessities needed by the German troops, and to make compensation for all damages caused by the passage of the German forces. In case of a refusal of her demands, Germany threatened, she would treat Belgium as an enemy.

Although the Belgian government refused to sanction the proposed violation of its neutrality, the German military authorities immediately started three armies toward Lorraine, one in the direction of Luxemburg, and three across the Belgian frontier. Belgium could only delay for a little the invading German armies. The Belgian defense of Liége, however, held back the Germans for several days and gave the French and British governments more time to bring up their forces. After the fall of the last fort at Liége the three invading German armies easily drove the Belgian field-forces back toward Antwerp and pressed on toward France.

Until the presentation of the German ultimatum to Belgium the British attitude toward the conflict had been in doubt. Although they had given the French authorities reason to think that they could count on the support of the British military and naval forces in case of war, the leaders of Great Britain could not commit their country to take part in a great European conflict without being assured of the approval of the British Parliament and of British public opinion. The news of the German demands on Belgium and the resulting Belgian appeal to the British government stirred the emotions of the British people and assured the British government of popular approval of British participation in the war. On August 4, 1914, therefore, the British government forwarded to Berlin a demand for a withdrawal of the German ultimatum to Belgium and prepared to despatch an expeditionary force of one hundred and fifty thousand men to northern France and to throw the weight of its superior naval forces against Germany.

The entrance of Great Britain into the war had many important consequences. Germany found herself cut off from much of the rest of the world. The British navy kept the dreaded German fleet shut up in home waters, swept the seas clear of German cruisers and merchantmen, cut Germany off from her colonies and her markets and as a result slowly starved her population and her industries, and opened the resources of the world to the Entente powers. Their commanding position also gave France and Great Britain an opportunity to mold public opinion. Upon the outbreak of hostilities they cut the German cables, censored despatches, newspapers, and private correspondence, and as a consequence enlisted world public opinion to a large extent on the side of the Entente powers.

2

THE CAMPAIGN IN NORTHERN FRANCE

Surprised by the German plans for sweeping through Belgium and enveloping their exposed flank, the French military authorities attempted to take the offensive farther east. Operating from Belfort as a base, inadequate French forces made an unsuccessful dash into the lost province of Alsace. Other French armies attacked the Germans in Lorraine. These ill-considered attacks failed completely and employed troops that should have been held in reserve until the Germans disclosed their military plans.

The Germans almost succeeded in carrying out those plans. Overwhelmed by the German forces, the British and French armies strung out from Verdun to Mons found themselves forced to retreat with great rapidity one hundred and eighty miles toward Paris. In alarm, the French government moved to Bordeaux, many Parisians left Paris to escape the threatened siege, and the British expeditionary force transferred its base from the Channel ports to the Loire River. The Germans, however, had exhausted their troops by long forced marches and intermittent fighting without destroying the French and British forces opposing them. On September 5, 1914, the French and British forces, strengthened by reënforcements and the formation of new armies, suddenly struck back at the weary, advancing Germans along a front stretching from Paris to Verdun and compelled them to retreat to the heights above the Aisne River, a position some forty or fifty miles north of Paris. At this point the Germans intrenched themselves and brought the advance of the French and British forces to a standstill.

This first battle of the Marne gave the French people their first military hero of the war. The opening of the conflict found the armies of France under the command of General Joseph Joffre, a bluff, shrewd, kindly man of bourgeois stock and strong republican sentiments. After a noteworthy military career in the French colonies he had played an important part in the reorganization of the French army. In spite of his initial mistakes the French people continued to have faith in his courage and character. After the victory of the Marne they regarded him as the savior of France.

Having been brought to a standstill from a point north of Paris to the Swiss border, the Germans and the French and the British attempted to outflank each other at the western end of the long line of battle. Even though they failed to envelop the left wing of their opponents, the Germans might gain control of the French ports on the English Channel and use them as submarine bases against French and British shipping. Both sides, consequently, rapidly extended their lines. When their efforts to outflank the French and British failed, the Germans then made desperate but unsuccessful efforts to break through to the Channel ports.

3

THE OCCUPATION OF BELGIUM

Upon being thwarted in their efforts to reach the English Channel, the German military authorities turned their attention to the Belgian forces, which were operating from Antwerp as a base and menacing the lines of communication between Germany and the German armies in northern France. Repulsing the Belgian sorties, the German troops quickly crushed with heavy artillery the defenses of Antwerp and compelled the Belgian government and its military forces to evacuate the city. The Belgian army retreated southward along the coast and took over a small sector behind the Yser River beside the French and British forces. The fall of Antwerp put all but one small bit of Belgium into the hands of Germany.

The methods employed by the Germans in the territory overrun by their armies in Belgium and northern France, particularly in the first weeks of the war, did great damage to their cause. Fear of being attacked, a carefully formulated system of terrorism, and overindulgence in unfamiliar wines led to much destruction of life and property. They executed men, women, and children for alleged attacks on German soldiers and revived practices long considered obsolete by writers on international law. They seized prominent citizens as hostages and levied heavy fines on conquered cities under threat of their immediate destruction. In Belgium they deliberately destroyed several cities and wantonly looted many towns and villages. Before discipline was restored they had destroyed Louvain with its Gothic town hall, its historic church, and its famous university, and Main and Termonde with their similar treasures of architecture and painting. The Entente allies made skilful use of these excesses to prejudice neutral opinion against Germany.

In November, 1914, foodstuffs commenced to grow short in Belgium and northern France. To meet the situation relief committees sprang up everywhere and a Belgian National Relief Committee came into being. This organization found its efforts to import food from England complicated by the blockade maintained by the British government and appealed for help to an American, Herbert Hoover, who had just sprung into prominence through his work in repatriating some one hundred and fifty thousand Americans stranded in Europe as a result of the unusual conditions created by the outbreak of the war. Hoover and his associates organized the Commission for Relief in Belgium and arranged for the distribution of food and clothing in Belgium and northern France under the supervision of the embassies of Spain and the United States. They financed their extensive operations by appeals to world charity and the contributions of the governments of France, Great Britain, and eventually the United States. During the four years of the war the commission distributed about five million tons of food and clothing, valued at about one billion dollars. The relief work in Belgium and northern France made Hoover a world figure and tended to discredit Germany in the eyes of public opinion.

4

THE WAR ON THE EASTERN FRONT

Meanwhile Russia upset all the calculations of the German general staff by the speed with which she mobilized her military forces. Within two weeks after the declaration of war the Russians were ready to invade East Prussia and Galicia, operations necessary to relieve the pressure on the western front and to prepare the way for a forward movement on the eastern front. Two Russian armies invaded East Prussia. For a moment this province, the very hearthstone of the Junker class, seemed to be at their mercy, and fugitives from it began to pour into other parts of Germany. In the emergency the German government summoned from retirement General Paul von Hindenburg, an officer approaching seventy who knew the geography of the invaded region well, and associated with him as chief of staff General Erich Ludendorff, an officer of great ability who had attracted attention during the invasion of Belgium. The new German leaders made skilful use of the region of swamps and lakes—known as the Masurian Lakes —which separated the advancing Russian armies. Collecting and concentrating reënforcements by the splendid system of Prussian railways, the two officers struck powerful blows first at one and then at the other Russian army. Their strategy practically destroyed one incautious Russian army in the battle of Tannenberg and drove the other into Poland with a heavy loss in prisoners of war. The campaign in East Prussia deprived Russia of officers and materials of war that it could ill afford to lose, and made von Hindenburg the greatest German popular hero of the war. As a reward for his victory the German government made him a field-marshal and appointed him commander of all German military operations on the eastern front.

Simultaneously the Russians invaded Galicia. On a front of more than two hundred miles they inflicted defeat after defeat on the Austro-Hungarian forces opposing them. Early in September, 1914, they captured Lemberg, the capital of the province. Later in the month they invested the great fortress of Przemysl. In order to relieve the hard-pressed forces of the Dual Monarchy, German troops attacked Poland from Silesia. The struggle continued in Galicia throughout the winter. Finally in March, 1915, the Russians captured Przemysl.

5

THE WAR IN THE BALKANS AND THE NEAR EAST

During these months the armies of Austria-Hungary made little progress toward the achievement of the avowed purpose of the war, the punishment of Serbia. Although they subjected Belgrade, the Serbian capital, to an almost continuous bombardment after the outbreak of hostilities, the situation in Galicia prevented the Austro-Hungarian government from diverting sufficient forces for a serious invasion of Serbia. As a consequence the seasoned veterans of the Balkan Wars mobilized by Serbia succeeded in repelling a succession of attacks by the forces of Austria-Hungary in the closing months of 1914 and in the early part of 1915.

The German government meanwhile strove from the beginning of hostilities to draw Turkey into the war as an ally. At this time the Turkish government was under the control of a handful of Young Turks led by Enver Bey. In almost complete disregard of Turkish public opinion they decided at the end of October, 1914, to enter the war on the side of the central powers, and they immediately began to commit definite acts of aggression. They hoped to recover the lost provinces of the Turkish Empire and dreamed of calling the Moslem subjects of France and Great Britain in Africa and in India to a holy war against Christendom. Their entrance into the war endangered British control of Egypt, the Suez Canal, and the Persian Gulf and forced Russia to establish a new front in the Caucasus.

6

THE WAR IN AFRICA AND ON THE PACIFIC OCEAN

The war quickly spread from Europe to Africa and the Pacific Ocean. British, French, and colonial forces made preparations to seize the German colonies. Japanese military and naval forces captured the Marshall, Caroline, Pelew, and Ladrone islands in the north Pacific and Kiauchow, the German naval base in China. Long uneasy over the presence of German military and naval forces in Australasia, the British dominions of Australia and New Zealand eagerly grasped at the opportunity presented by the war to seize the German colonies in Kaiser Wilhelm Land in New Guinea, the Bismarck Archipelago, the Solomon Islands, and Samoa.

Before the end of the conflict, Germany lost all her colonies in Africa. Immediately after the outbreak of the war French and British forces from the Gold Coast and Dahomey easily captured Togoland. British and French troops from Nigeria and the French Congo encountered more opposition in the German colony of Kamerun, but within two months they had succeeded in overrunning all portions of the colony of any value to Germany. For a time the attitude of certain elements in South Africa delayed the conquest of German Southwest Africa. After quelling the revolt among the Boers Premier Louis Botha conquered the province with the military forces of the Union of South Africa. In German East Africa the German government possessed stronger defensive forces, and succeeded in maintaining control of the province until 1916. In that year British forces, commanded by General Jan Smuts, the chief lieutenant of General Botha in South Africa, with some assistance from Belgian and Portuguese troops, occupied all German East Africa. The resourceful German commander, however, maintained himself in Portuguese territory until the close of the war.

7

THE DEFEAT OF RUSSIA

By 1915 the German military authorities had come to the conclusion that Russia could be defeated more easily than France. In the campaign of 1914 the Russian troops had been successful only against the motley armies of Austria-Hungary. The strategic position and economic backwardness of Russia handicapped them in fighting Germany. They lacked everything but man-power for the defense of the nine-hundred-mile front stretching from the Baltic Sea to Rumania which they were attempting to maintain. The backward industries of Russia could not compete with the numerous and efficient factories of Germany in the production of rifles, artillery, munitions, and supplies; the location of Russia prevented the Russian military authorities from obtaining them through the Black Sea and Baltic Sea routes. A successful German attack in western Galicia might break the Russian line and cause a general Russian retreat from Galicia and Poland or even destroy the Russian armies entirely.

During the winter and spring of 1915, consequently, the German general staff secretly made preparations for an unprecedented attack on the eastern front. German scientists found substitutes for the essential products kept out of Germany by the British blockade. Throughout the winter the old men, the women, and the children of Germany toiled in the munition factories. In the spring the German military authorities withdrew from France every man and piece of artillery that could be spared and prepared to overwhelm the Russians on the eastern front. On May 1, 1915, the great attack began. The largest collection of artillery ever massed together suddenly burst forth in a murderous bombardment that completely obliterated the opposing forces and defenses. With their line broken on a wide front, the Russian armies from the Baltic Sea to Rumania began to fall back to prevent their being enveloped and destroyed. The Russian retreat continued throughout the summer. In the north a German army overran the Russian territory between East Prussia and Riga. In Galicia the steady German advance resulted in the fall of the recently captured fortresses, the abandonment of the passes into Hungary won by the Russians in the Carpathian Mountains, and in the end the evacuation of the whole province. In Poland the German pressure made Warsaw untenable and finally led to the withdrawal of the Russians to a line stretching from Riga to Rumania. The disastrous campaign inflicted on Russia tremendous losses in prisoners, officers, equipment, and supplies and accelerated the movements that finally caused the Russian Revolution of 1917.

8

THE EFFORTS OF FRANCE AND GREAT BRITAIN IN 1915

Public opinion in France and Great Britain looked forward to the campaign of 1915 with the greatest optimism. Russia was supposed to have unlimited man-power and Great Britain and the self-governing dominions of the British Empire were preparing new armies and gathering their resources. Public opinion expected in consequence a continuance of Russian success on the eastern front and confidently counted on the supposed superior resources of France and the British Empire to make themselves felt on the western front.

The year, however, was a great disappointment to France and Great Britain. Their successive offensives on the western front did little to change the general situation. Their isolated and uncoördinated attacks at most gained an observation-point, straightened or broadened a dangerous salient, or captured a few miles of territory blackened, pitted, and churned by exploding shells. The military authorities had not yet learned the futility and wastefulness of attacks made on a narrow sector with insufficient preparation. Although the gains did not justify the heavy losses in lives, the attacks did something to relieve the pressure on the retreating Russians on the eastern front.

In response to an appeal from Russia the British, with some assistance from the French, made a spectacular effort to force open the tortuous and narrow straits linking the Black Sea and the Ægean Sea.

In February, 1915, powerful French and British battle-ships made the dangerous attempt to try to silence the defending forts and batteries, clear the channel of mines and submarines, and force a passage through the Dardanelles, the Sea of Marmora, and the Bosporus. After some minor successes against the so-called outer forts, won through the sacrifice of five naval vessels, the British and French abandoned the naval attack and made preparations to capture the forts defending the Dardanelles by an attack made from the rear by British, Australian, and French colonial troops. Landing at several points on the western and southern edges of the Gallipoli peninsula, the expeditionary force strove for months to defeat the defending Turkish forces and capture the forts and batteries barring the passage through the Straits. Months after the failure of the expedition was patent to every one, the British and French withdrew their troops and sent them to the new Saloniki front to operate against the Bulgarians.

Somewhat later the defeat and capture of a small military force in Mesopotamia did further damage to British prestige in the Near East and throughout Asia. Strategic considerations induced a small body of troops guarding British interests in the region of the Persian Gulf to push northward up the valleys of the Tigris and Euphrates rivers. Their success in this operation prompted the military authorities at the head of the expedition to make a reckless and disastrous dash for the glamorous city of Bagdad. Upon being repulsed the expedition retreated to Kut-al-Amara, where it was besieged for five months and finally, in April, 1916, forced to surrender.

9

THE INTERVENTION OF BULGARIA

In the meantime the defeat of Russia and the repulse of the efforts of the British and French to force their way through the Straits had exercised a determining influence on the delicate diplomatic and military situation in the Balkans. Ever since the Balkan Wars Ferdinand of Bulgaria and his people had felt aggrieved at the loss of their expected territorial gains. After the outbreak of the World War both sides began to bid for Bulgarian support. The central powers, however, were in position to offer more than the Entente Allies. While France, Russia, and Great Britain hesitated to ask Serbia, Greece, and Rumania to make territorial concessions to Bulgaria, the central powers made generous promises of coveted Serbian and even of a small strip of Turkish territory. In July, 1915, consequently, King Ferdinand of Bulgaria secretly concluded a treaty with Germany.

The decision of the Bulgarian government to enter the war on the side of the central powers had serious consequences for Serbia. In October, 1915, she suddenly found herself attacked on three sides by German, Bulgarian, and Austro-Hungarian armies. Weakened by the ravages of war and disease and deserted in the emergency by her ally, Greece, Serbia found herself unable to defend her territory. With the greatest difficulty the Serbian military forces eluded capture and made their way across the mountains of northern Albania to the protection of Entente naval forces in the Adriatic Sea. The victorious attacking armies occupied Serbia and Montenegro and opened a route from Berlin to Turkey. After months of recuperation and rehabilitation the remnants of the Serbian troops took their places on the Saloniki front with the composite army that had been created too late to save Serbia.

10

THE ENTRANCE OF ITALY INTO THE WAR

The only encouraging event of the year 1915 for the Entente Allies was the entrance of Italy into the war on their side. From the beginning of the diplomatic crisis the traditions and interests of Italy pointed to a policy of neutrality. At the opening of the conflict, consequently, the Italian government declared the struggle a war of aggression against Serbia and refused to come to the aid of its allies, Germany and Austria-Hungary. As the war continued, sentiment in favor of the entrance of Italy on the side of the Entente powers developed rapidly. A growing number of Italians felt that their government should seize the opportunity offered by the conflict to obtain at least a part of unredeemed Italy. In response to this pressure the Italian government took the position that the occupation of Serbia upset the political balance in the Balkan peninsula, and demanded compensation. As a result of the pressure exerted by Germany the government of Austria-Hungary made a grudging offer to cede certain territory at the close of the war. The Entente powers, in contrast, offered a far more generous share of Austro-Hungarian territory. In the secret Treaty of London, signed April 26, 1915, they promised the Italian government the Trentino, Southern Tyrol up to the Brenner Pass, Trieste, Istria to the Quarnero, the province of Dalmatia, most of the islands of the Adriatic Sea, twelve islands in the Ægean Sea, a fair share in the event of the partition of Turkey, a share in any war indemnity, compensation in Africa for any enlargement of the colonial possessions of France and Great Britain at the expense of Germany, and a financial loan in return for Italian assistance in the war. On May 23, 1915, accordingly, Italy declared war on Austria-Hungary.

To the great disappointment of the Entente powers, however, the entrance of Italy seemed to have very little effect on the course of the war. Her armies began offensive operations in regions that offered many natural obstacles to an advance. Along much of the northern frontier the Italian troops had to advance in a maze of foothills and mountains that ultimately rose to snow-covered crests. Toward Trieste they had to fight their way across a barren tableland of limestone that was honeycombed with defensive works. Because of these obstacles, a comparatively small Austro-Hungarian defensive force succeeded in holding large masses of Italian troops in check.

II

THE CAMPAIGN OF 1916

In 1916 the Germans shifted their attention again to the western front. They hoped by an early attack to forestall the plan of the Entente powers to exert a steady pressure with their superior resources on all fronts, and possibly bring the war to a close before the rapidly dwindling German reserves were exhausted. The military authorities chose as the point for their attack the great French fortress of Verdun. They anticipated that its capture would impress on France the hopelessness of continuing the struggle and lead to her withdrawal from the war. During the winter, therefore, they secretly concentrated a great number of men and masses of artillery on the western front. On February 21, 1916, they began a bombardment that poured one hundred thousand shells per hour for twelve and a half hours into the ill-prepared French lines defending the city. At first the German forces made considerable progress and threatened to capture Verdun. In the end, however, the French succeeded in bringing the German advance to a standstill. After several months of fighting, marked by terrible losses on both sides, the French regained practically all the ground that they had lost.

In order to relieve the pressure on Verdun the British and French prepared carefully for an attack on the German lines on the Somme. As a result of the response of the people in Great Britain and her dominions to its appeals the British government was at last ready to play an important part in the fighting on the western front. After a formidable bombardment, consequently, the British and French troops began a slow, steady advance that did not stop until the setting in of bad weather in the autumn. The principal result of the military operations around Verdun and on the Somme was a great depletion of the man-power of the combatant powers.

In the meantime the Austrians had been executing an attack on the Italian front. Concentrating four hundred thousand men in the Trentino, they struck in the direction of the Venetian plain with the aim of effecting the retreat or the capture of a large section of the Italian army by the seizure of one or both of the two lines of railroad forming the main lines of communication with the Isonzo front. By June, 1916, only one more mountain separated them from the Venetian plain. At that point, however, the Italian forces succeeded in checking the Austro-Hungarian advance and in recapturing most of the lost ground. Before the campaign of 1916 closed, the Italians captured the fortress of Gorizia on the Isonzo front, an important step toward the conquest of the port of Trieste.

The Austro-Hungarian advance on the Italian front was brought to a standstill as much by events on the Russian front as by the efforts of the Italian troops. After their defeat in the campaign of 1915 the Russians made desperate efforts to reorganize their fighting forces. They drew on their vast reserves of man-power, increased their facilities for the production of war material, built a new railroad from St. Petersburg to Archangel, and improved the Trans-Siberian Railway, thus making possible the importation of a larger amount of war material from Japan, France, Great Britain, and America. In March, 1916, the Russian military authorities launched a great offensive on the eastern front, with the purpose of relieving the pressure on Verdun. Their attack met unexpected success on the Austro-Hungarian front. They advanced one hundred kilometers on a wide sector and captured six hundred pieces of artillery and four hundred thousand prisoners.

The success of the Russian attack encouraged the Rumanians to enter the conflict with the object of annexing Transylvania and adjoining districts of Austria-Hungary to the Kingdom of Rumania. During the first two years of the war King Charles had succeeded in holding his people neutral. After the accession of his nephew Ferdinand they could no longer be restrained from entering the war. In August, 1916, Rumania declared war against the central powers and prepared to invade the province of Transylvania. At first the Rumanian troops made rapid progress in the invasion, but their fortune soon changed. In spite of the demands made on their resources by the western and eastern fronts, the German military authorities sent reënforcements and one of their best generals to the assistance of Austria-Hungary. One army of the central powers defeated the Rumanians invading Transylvania, while another army, composed of Germans and Bulgarians, advanced from the south into the Dobruja. The two armies then combined and finally captured Bucharest. These successes put under German control the Dobruja, Walachia, and southern Moldavia, with their valuable resources.

After this victory the leaders of Germany felt that they could propose peace negotiations without loss of prestige. They estimated that they would probably never be in a better position to negotiate. They held on every front broad stretches of enemy territory with which to bargain and in case they were rebuffed they could throw on their opponents the odium of refusing to come to terms. In December, 1916, therefore, they proposed negotiations for peace to the governments of France, Great Britain, Russia, Japan, Serbia, and Rumania. Through fear of destroying German morale by their leniency, however, they offered the Entente powers no definite terms. But the opponents of Germany refused to enter a peace conference without knowing the terms she stood ready to offer. The German government attempted to use the refusal of the Entente powers to negotiate to influence the neutral powers and to stiffen German resistance.

12

THE UNITED STATES INTERVENES IN THE WORLD WAR

For a long time the vast majority of the inhabitants of the United States had no thought of being drawn into the conflict raging in Europe. At the outbreak of the war President Woodrow Wilson had declared their country neutral and asked them to be neutral even in thought. Before long, however, the American people began to discover that they could not hold themselves entirely aloof from the struggle. Great Britain used her naval superiority to prevent the importation of war material by the central powers. She seized and searched neutral vessels and gradually extended her definition of contraband. Her policy interfered greatly with American trade and caused a growing annoyance. Germany, however, aroused even greater irritation in the United States by the measures she adopted in retaliation for the cutting off of foodstuffs and much-needed war material and in the hope of restricting the military effort of Great Britain on the Continent. In February, 1915, Germany declared the waters around the British Isles a war zone and announced her intention to use submarines to sink all vessels found in these waters except recognizable neutrals. In pursuance of this policy a German submarine sank without warning the British liner *Lusitania,* and caused the loss of some twelve hundred lives, over one hundred of them being American citizens. The deed evoked great popular indignation in the United States and threatened to cause the entrance of that country into the war. In order to avert American intervention the German government first ordered its submarine commanders to cease attacking liners and finally, in May, 1916, it definitely promised to abandon the practice of sinking merchant-ships without warning or without rescuing their crews.

The German promises improved the relations of the United States and Germany only temporarily. By 1917 the German military leaders came to the conclusion that they could only compel the Entente powers to conclude peace by resuming unrestricted submarine warfare. After the failure of their peace proposals, therefore, the civilian leaders of Germany gave in to the pressure of the German military authorities. On the last day of January, 1917, they announced that after that date all sea-traffic in certain specified waters adjoining Great Britain, France, and Italy, and in the eastern Mediterranean would be prevented by all weapons. They conceded to the United States, however, the right to send one passenger-steamer a week to Great Britain provided it carefully observed a number of rules. They calculated that the resumption of unrestricted submarine warfare would bring the war to a close before the United States could make its latent strength felt in the struggle.

The policy followed by Germany gradually created a war spirit in the United States. From the first the majority of American citizens drew their information mainly from French and British sources of information. They read with growing indignation of the violation of Belgian neutrality, the alleged inhumanity of the German administrators and soldiers in the occupied districts of Belgium and northern France, the destruction of private property and of historic and artistic monuments, the supposed atrocities of the German troops, the execution of the English nurse, Edith Cavell, the slaughter of women and children in air raids, and the clumsy attempts of German agents to hinder the manufacture of war material in the United States by strikes, sabotage, and the blowing up of plants. As a result a growing number of Americans, particularly in the northeastern section of the United States, became convinced that the Entente Allies were fighting in defense of civilization and that their country should enter the war against Germany. The German leaders' handling of the submarine question finally convinced the other sections of the United States of the necessity of American intervention in the war. A great power was not likely to brook affronts to which a weaker state might submit.

The resumption of unrestricted submarine warfare soon produced a crisis. During February, 1917, a number of ships were torpedoed with the loss of additional American lives. The British government also intercepted a diplomatic note which revealed that Germany had tried to stir up the Mexican government to attack the United States. President Wilson, consequently, declared that the recent course of the German government constituted nothing short of war against the United States and advised a declaration of war. On April 6, 1917, the Congress of the United States formally declared war on Germany.

The American people entered the conflict ill prepared to make their vast resources felt. The entrance of the United States into the struggle, however, immediately revived the flagging spirits of the French and

British peoples. The American government also promptly despatched a naval contingent to Europe to aid the British fleet against the serious submarine menace. Before the end of April it enacted the first of a series of war-finance measures that provided funds both for American war expenditures and for loans to the powers associated with the United States in the war. In June it sent General John J. Pershing and a staff of officers to France to make preparations for the military coöperation of the United States on the western front. In July the President appointed Herbert Hoover Food Controller. In the following month the Congress passed food-control and shipping acts. It also made ambitious plans for increasing American shipments of food and war materials, for the rapid construction of new ships to replace those sunk by German submarines, and for raising and equipping a great army. With the small trained military force at its disposal it could not take an important part in the fighting on the western front before the summer of 1918.

13

THE WESTERN, ITALIAN, BALKAN, AND NEAR EAST FRONTS IN 1917

On the western front the steady attrition of both armies continued, unmarked by any notable successes. To shorten and straighten their line, disarrange the military plans of the French and British for a great offensive, and put themselves in a more defensible position, the Germans abandoned at the opening of the campaign of 1917 about a thousand square miles of French territory and retired to a new system of trenches. In April the British met with considerable success in an attack in the vicinity of Arras. While this operation was in progress the French made a costly experiment with new methods. Yielding to the clamor of certain groups that had become impatient with the slow man-wasting tactics of the victor of the first battle of the Marne, the French government replaced Joffre with General Robert Nivelle, hero of the French counter-offensive at Verdun. The new commander foresaw the end of trench fighting and victory within two days by the adoption of new methods. The results were disappointing. Although they met with considerable success in their attacks, the French suffered very heavy casualties that dangerously impaired the morale of both soldiers and civilians in the Entente countries. In France a number of divisions openly mutinied and prominent civilians plainly hinted at the desirability of negotiations with Germany. In Great Britain Lord Lansdowne, one of the most prominent of the Conservative leaders, made himself the spokesman of the advocates of peace negotiations. In Italy the national morale was at an even lower ebb. For the rest of the year, consequently, the Entente powers devoted their attention mainly to reëstablishing the fighting spirit both at the front and behind the lines and carried out no large-scale military operations. A symbol of the new morale in France was the rise of Clemenceau to political power.

On the Italian front the German military authorities decided that they must do something to reëstablish discipline among the badly demoralized Austro-Hungarian troops. They therefore made preparations for a surprise attack by a newly formed army, composed of German and Austro-Hungarian contingents, at a point in the Julian Alps where a successful offensive might enable them to cut off the Italian forces operating on the Isonzo front. They happened to strike one of the weakest links in the Italian line of defense. Italy had entered the war with public opinion sharply divided over the question of Italian participation in the struggle. As the conflict progressed propaganda, alarming rumors, and war-weariness led to riots and strikes behind the lines and discouragement and the breaking down of discipline in the Italian armies. In order to quell the disturbances at Turin, one of the chief munition centers, the government had recently canceled the exemption of many workers from military service and sent them to the sector that the central powers planned to attack. As a result of this situation the German and Austro-Hungarian forces broke through the treason-ridden Italian troops near Caporetto and captured one hundred thousand prisoners and seven hundred pieces of artillery before the Italians succeeded in extricating themselves from their precarious position and bringing the exhausted forces of the central powers to a standstill along the line of the Piave River. This military disaster caused the abandonment of all the Italian gains in the direction of Trieste and the loss of great quantities of war material, immense numbers of effective troops, and a wide stretch of Italian territory.

On the Balkan front the motley Entente army, composed of British, French, Italian, and Serbian troops, had been held practically immobile for a year and a half by the attitude of Greece. In order to improve the military situation in this region the Entente powers took drastic action. They seized the Greek navy, blockaded the Greek coast, compelled the Greek government to transfer most of its troops to the Peloponnesus, took possession of the Isthmus of Corinth and strategic points in Thessaly, and finally forced the pro-German King Constantine to abdicate and the Crown Prince to renounce his rights of succession. These invasions of Greek sovereignty freed the Entente forces on the Saloniki front from the menace of an attack.

These defeats of the Entente powers in Europe were only in part offset by British successes in Mesopotamia and Palestine. In order to retrieve the disaster that had overtaken the small British force at Kut-al-Amara in the preceding year, the British government sent reënforcements from India and Great Britain to the head of the Persian Gulf and made preparations to advance up the Tigris Valley. In March, 1917, the reorganized British forces captured Bagdad. This military operation gave them possession of one of the magic cities of Asia and did much to restore British prestige.

In Palestine also a British forward movement met with success. In 1916 the Sherif of Mecca had proclaimed the independence from the Turkish empire of the Arab Kingdom of the Hedjaz and had promptly received the recognition of the Entente powers. In bringing this action about T. E. Lawrence, a young Oxford graduate who had learned Arabic while engaged in archæological excavations in Syria and Mesopotamia, had played a romantic and indispensable part. With the aid of their new Arab allies the British began an advance toward Palestine. By the end of the year the British and their allies had captured Jerusalem. The capture of Bagdad and Jerusalem gave striking proof of the crumbling of Turkish resistance.

14

RUSSIA AND RUMANIA WITHDRAW FROM THE WAR

In Russia the year 1917 brought unlooked-for developments. On the eve of the war the Russian people had been on the verge of another revolutionary movement. For a few months after the outbreak of the conflict the Russian nation seemed to rally again around its ruler and his government. A more intelligent sovereign might have seized the offered opportunity to unite the throne and its subjects once more. By its conduct of the war, however, the Russian government only widened the breach between the Tsar and his people. The war required terrible sacrifices from the Russian people. As defeat followed defeat the dissatisfaction grew. Led in many instances by incompetent officers and lacking the most essential equipment and supplies, the Russian troops suffered indescribable agonies in the campaigns in Poland and in the snowy passes of the Carpathian Mountains. In all they lost four million men by death, capture, and wounds, for a cause that they hardly understood. The Tsar and the Tsarina, both mystics in religion, retained at court as their trusted counselor Grigoni Rasputin, a reputed monk of coarse manners and evil reputation. The reactionary officials seemed bent on the maintenance of the autocracy even at the price of defeat and gave the Russian people no opportunity to advise or coöperate with the government in the conduct of the war. High officials were accused of disloyalty. The inadequate, inefficiently managed transportation system broke down under the strain of the war and caused a shortage of food in the cities. The prices of commodities rose steadily and at times coal and other necessities became unobtainable. Industries came to a standstill because of a lack of fuel and raw materials. In 1916 and 1917 a winter of exceptional severity added to the distress.

In March, 1917, this situation finally produced a revolution. Eighty thousand or more starving workmen of Petrograd—the former St. Petersburg—struck work and joined the masses demonstrating in the streets. The revolutionary elements in the population at once tried to turn the menacing situation to their own advantage. The attempt of the government to crush the spirit of the working-men and to disperse the middle-class Liberals of the Duma by the use of force miscarried. In contrast to their behavior in 1905, many of the soldiers, conscious of their own grievances, refused to fire on the crowds; part of the army declared for the Duma, and the leaders of that body disregarded the order proroguing that body and took into their own hands the task of reëstablishing public order and the authority of the state. At the same time representatives of soldiers and the factory workers organized a council or committee known as a soviet. After some desultory fighting attended by comparatively little loss of life, the capital fell under the control of the revolutionists. The leaders of the Duma thereupon organized a provisional government that included one representative of the soviet. Upon learning of the uprising the Tsar attempted to reach the capital. When the working-men stopped his train by pulling up the tracks he tried to despatch troops to quell the revolutionary movement. After the greater part of this army had gone over to the side of the revolutionists the reluctant Tsar decided to concede the responsible ministry that the president of the Duma had urged upon him several days before. But his decision came too late to save the dynasty. By this time public opinion demanded his abdication. Powerless and broken in spirit, Nicholas II abdicated, merely requesting that the crown should go directly to his brother and that he should be permitted to retire to his estates. But his brother cautiously announced that he would accept the throne only with the approval of a constituent assembly elected by universal suffrage. This decision made Russia a republic for the time being.

The provisional government at once set to work at its well-nigh impossible task. The able men composing it aimed at the establishment of democratic government and a successful prosecution of the war. They pardoned all political offenders and permitted some eighty thousand political exiles to return to Russia. They guaranteed speedy trial to accused persons, made arbitrary arrests illegal, abolished capital punishment, allowed the workers to organize labor-unions and to strike, proclaimed freedom of speech, of the press, and of religion, freed the Jews from their restrictions, restored constitutional government in Finland, and promised the Poles their independence.

Unfortunately for their permanent success, they neither represented a majority of the Russian people nor enjoyed their full confidence. With the exception of Aleksandr Kerenski, a Social Revolutionary and a member of the soviet in Petrograd, the ministers of the provisional government belonged to the Octobrist and the Social Democratic parties and aimed at a vigorous prosecution of the war and the establishment of parliamentary institutions. The workers, peasants, and soldiers were all war-weary and had little sympathy with the imperialistic aims of the government. The peasants desired the seizure and division of the great estates without compensation for the owners. The workers wanted the capitalists expelled and the workers put in charge of the factories. In imitation of Petrograd, consequently, the workers, peasants, and soldiers organized soviets in the army, the rural communes, and cities. In April, 1917, representatives of these local soviets held a congress that demanded of the provisional government the abandonment of imperialism, acceptance of the principle of self-determination, and the conclusion of peace without annexations or indemnities. In May, 1917, the pressure of the soviets led to the withdrawal of some of the abler men from the provisional government and their replacement by members of the Social Revolutionary and Menshevik parties. Finally, when the situation seemed to be getting entirely beyond the control of the moderate Russian parties, the provisional government made way for a non-partizan national government, headed by Kerenski, which included only two members of the original cabinet.

Kerenski, however, soon found the task of carrying on the government beyond his powers. Under the remarkable leadership of Nikolay Lenin, long the acknowledged chief of the party, the Bolshevik wing of the Social Democratic party carried on a campaign that ended in the overthrow of the government of Kerenski. The March revolution found Lenin living in exile in Zurich, Switzerland. Hurrying back to Russia, he began a campaign against the provisional government. He exploited every difficulty of the government and every desire and prejudice of the Russian people. He proposed the immediate conclusion of peace, confiscation of landed estates for the benefit of the peasants, seizure and operation of the factories by the workers, national control of production and distribution, substitution of the soviets for the provisional government, and the exclusion of the propertied classes from political rights. He also attempted to incite the soldiers and the civilians to revolt. The campaign of the Bolsheviks met with success. Discipline disappeared in the army, desertions increased, and the mass of the troops threatened to leave the trenches. In consequence, during the summer, the army suffered defeat after defeat. The discontent with the provisional government grew steadily, and the Bolsheviks increased in number and captured a majority of the soviets.

By November 6, 1917, the Bolsheviks felt ready to seize control of Russia. During the night they occupied public buildings, railway stations, telegraph and telephone offices, bridges, power-plants, and the Bank of Russia. On the following day they proclaimed the overthrow of the provisional government, asked for the support of the army, and arrested and imprisoned all the members of the provisional government except Kerenski. The next day the All-Russian Congress of Soviets approved of the revolution and established a new provisional government headed by Lenin and Leon Trotski. Once in control of the capital, the Bolsheviks acted with vigor. They promptly repressed all resistance, held out to the peasants the prospect of an immediate division of the landed estates, proposed an armistice on all fronts, and dissolved the Duma when it showed some signs of independence.

The Bolsheviks at once took steps to bring the war to an end. Though the Entente powers ignored their peace proposals, the Germans eagerly seized the opportunity to negotiate. On December 3, 1917, Russia signed an agreement for a cessation of hostilities with all the central powers. Seven days later the peace conference opened at Brest Litovsk. The Bolsheviks spun out the negotiations as long as possible in an effort to incite the German people to revolt against their government. The negotiations temporarily broke down over the question of the future of the occupied Russian territory. In the crisis the Bolsheviks took the unique step of withdrawing from the war without signing a treaty of peace. A new German advance, however, forced the Bolshevik leaders to capitulate and make a formal peace agreement. In the Treaty of Brest Litovsk, signed on March 3, 1918, Russia agreed to give up its claims to Poland, Courland, and Lithuania, to evacuate Livonia, Estonia, Finland, and the Aland Islands, to withdraw from the Ukraine and recognize the treaty negotiated by the central powers with the newly organized Ukrainian People's Republic, to surrender Ardahan, Kars, and Batum to Turkey, and to cease its propaganda in the territory of the central powers.

The withdrawal of Russia from the war left Rumania at the mercy of the central powers. In order to save as much as possible from the disaster the Rumanian government signed on May 7, 1918, the Treaty of Bucharest, by which it ceded pieces of Rumanian territory to Hungary and Bulgaria and permitted the Germans to occupy the province of Walachia until the end of the war. The treaty gave the central powers access to the much-needed oil and grain of Rumania.

15

THE ENTENTE POWERS ANNOUNCE THEIR WAR AIMS

Before the campaign of 1918 opened the Entente powers made two formal statements of war aims that exercised a profound influence on the course of the war. On January 5, 1918, Premier David Lloyd George of Great Britain stated the ideas of the British government before the British trade-unions. Three days later President Wilson announced in behalf of the United States his famous Fourteen Points, which ultimately served as a basis for the peace negotiations with Germany and put a note of idealism into the last phases of the war. The American president asked for open covenants openly arrived at; absolute freedom of navigation upon the seas, outside territorial waters; the removal of economic barriers and the establishment of an equality of trade conditions among all nations; the reduction of national armaments to the lowest point consistent with domestic safety; a free and impartial adjustment of colonial claims based equally upon the interests of the populations concerned and the equitable claims of the government whose title is to be determined; the evacuation of all Russian territory and the settlement of all questions affecting Russia in such a way as to give her an opportunity for the independent determination of her own political development and national policy; the evacuation and restoration of Belgium without any limit to her sovereignty; the evacuation and restoration to France of Alsace-Lorraine; a readjustment of Italian frontiers along clearly recognized lines of nationality; the freest opportunity for the autonomous development of the peoples of Austria-Hungary; the evacuation and restoration of Rumania, Serbia, and Montenegro and a free and secure access to the sea for Serbia; secure sovereignty for the Turkish portions of the Ottoman Empire and security and autonomous development for the other nationalities under Turkish rule; the erection of an independent Polish state with a free and secure access to the sea; and the formation of a general association of nations.

16

THE FINAL EFFORT OF GERMANY

The German government was not yet ready to accept these terms. The withdrawal of Russia from the war released many German troops and gave Germany for the time being a numerical superiority on the western front. The German military leaders thought that they saw a chance to end the war on favorable terms before the slowly gathering forces of the United States were ready to throw their weight into the conflict. In February, 1918, they explained their plan to a secret session of the Reichstag and obtained its approval.

On March 21, 1918, the German military leaders suddenly launched a tremendous attack, with greatly superior forces, in the direction of Paris at the point where the British and French armies joined. Employing with great success new methods of attack, they overwhelmed the defending British forces and advanced a distance of thirty-five miles before being brought to a standstill. The attack came so near to breaking through that the Entente governments and the United States appointed General Ferdinand Foch commander-in-chief of the Allied armies on the western front. In April, 1918, the Germans struck in the direction of the vital Channel ports and drove the British back fifteen to twenty miles before they were stopped. The two attacks cost the Germans over half a million casualties. At the end of May the Germans struck a third terrific blow between Soissons and Rheims, in the hope of reaching Paris by way of the Marne Valley. Though they drove the French back some thirty miles, they again failed to break through. In June they attacked again with the object of straightening their front between the two great salients that threatened Paris but they succeeded in pushing their lines forward only about six miles. On July 14, 1918, the Germans launched a last great offensive planned to capture the city of Rheims, break through the French front, and permit the Germans to sweep down the Marne Valley to Paris.

By the middle of July, however, the military situation had materially changed. The German offensive had been made at the cost of enormous losses. The forces of their opponents, on the contrary, were being steadily augmented by the arrival of fresh troops from the United States. Warned of the impending attack on Rheims by the reconnoitering of his aviators and the interrogation of prisoners of war, General Foch prepared to counter-attack as soon as the first fury of the German offensive movement had spent itself. On July 18, 1918, French and American troops attacked the flank of one of the great German salients between Soissons and Château-Thierry and forced the Germans to withdraw a second time from the Marne to the Aisne. This success encouraged General Foch to launch offensives along the whole western front that drove the German forces back along the whole line and forced them in November to conclude an armistice. On August 13, 1918, the German military authorities admitted their defeat and advised their government to begin peace negotiations. Throughout August and the first weeks in September the forces of the Entente powers and the United States continued their advance. By September 8 the military leaders of Germany found themselves back at the point from which they had started their series of great drives, and they informed the civilian authorities that they must have peace as soon as possible. Before the end of the month the newly organized American army showed its strength by taking the St.-Mihiel salient in eastern France. Farther north the British and French troops broke the so-called Hindenburg line. On September 28 General Ludendorff informed the German Emperor that all was lost. Two days later William II announced that the German people should henceforth coöperate more effectively in deciding the fate of the fatherland. In fulfilment of this promise the Emperor intrusted control of the empire to a coalition cabinet that included two Socialists. The first act of the new government was an appeal to President Wilson for a cessation of hostilities and an announcement of its readiness to negotiate peace on the basis of the Fourteen Points.

17

THE COLLAPSE OF THE CENTRAL POWERS

Even before the new German government made this appeal the central powers had begun to collapse. On September 15, 1918, the composite Entente army on the Saloniki front had begun its long-delayed advance. In the battle of the Vardar it defeated the war-weary Bulgarians. With its troops routed and driven back into their own territory, the Bulgarian government sued for an armistice. On September 30, 1918, Bulgaria withdrew from the war. Her withdrawal from the conflict opened the way for an attack on Turkey and threw on Austria-Hungary the burden of maintaining the Balkan front. By the end of October, in consequence, the hard-pressed Turks also asked for an armistice and withdrew from the war, and the Entente forces drove the military forces of Austria-Hungary back to the Danube and occupied Serbia. Both Bulgaria and Turkey surrendered unconditionally.

Meanwhile Austria-Hungary too had been rapidly going to pieces under the shock of defeat. For a time after the outbreak of the war the government repressed all popular agitation and the subjects of the Dual Monarchy displayed an appearance of loyalty to it. As defeat followed defeat, however, the peoples of the empire revived their national ambitions. The defeat of Russia allayed the fears of the Poles and stimulated a demand for a revival of Poland. The entrance of Rumania into the war made every Rumanian subject of the Hapsburgs a "potential rebel." On July 20, 1917, representatives of Serbia and of the Serbs, Croats, and Slovenes of the Dual Monarchy met at Corfu and reached an agreement that laid the foundation for the organization of a Southern Slav state. Later, representatives of the Southern Slavs and the Italians reached an understanding, but failed to settle the all-important question of the future frontier of the two peoples. Deserters and prisoners of war formed Polish, Czechoslovak, and Southern Slav legions, which took a place beside the Entente forces in France and Russia. The monarchy found itself forced to make concessions to the Magyars and the subject peoples of Austria. By the first of November, 1918, the Dual Monarchy had broken into national fragments. Under these conditions military resistance crumbled. Italian offensives in the Trentino and on the Piave routed the demoralized forces of Austria-Hungary and forced the Austro-Hungarian government to sign an armistice on November 3, 1918. Before it was concluded, however, the Dual Monarchy had ceased to exist.

In the meantime the forces of the United States and the Entente powers had continued to advance on the western front. During October they practically cleared France and regained control of the Belgian coast. Under pressure of the military situation the new German government carried on throughout the month negotiations with President Wilson for an armistice. After receiving assurances concerning the democratizing of Germany and her willingness to evacuate enemy territory without destruction of property and to cease submarine attacks, the President directed the German government to apply to the commander-in-chief of the armies of the United States and the Entente powers.

On November 8, 1918, General Foch gave the representatives of the German government his terms. He demanded the evacuation of France, Belgium, Luxemburg, and Alsace-Lorraine within two weeks and of all territory on the left bank of the Rhine within one month, the surrender of the bridge-heads across the Rhine at Mainz, Coblenz, and Cologne, the establishment of a neutral zone ten kilometers wide on the right bank of the Rhine, annulment of the treaties concluded with Russia and Rumania, the withdrawal of all German troops from Russia, Rumania, and Turkey, the handing over of a specified number of locomotives, railway cars, motor-lorries, submarines, battle-ships, and aircraft, the immediate repatriation, without reciprocity, of prisoners, and a continuance of the blockade. The acceptance of these terms by the German government brought the World War to a close at eleven o'clock on the morning of November 11, 1918.

PART V

RECONSTRUCTION AND EXPERIMENTATION

CHAPTER XXVII

INTERNATIONAL RELATIONS SINCE 1918

The terms of the armistice concluded by the belligerent powers on the western front made a renewal of the World War impossible and suddenly turned the thoughts of Europe from war to peace. The leaders of the victorious powers found an enormous number of confusing problems confronting them. The war had brought the populations of whole countries to the verge of starvation and threatened to decimate with disease and famine those surviving the military struggle. The economic machinery of Europe had been adjusted to the task of carrying on the war. Empires had been destroyed and new states with ill-defined boundaries had made their appearance. All of Europe and much of the rest of the world had to be started again on the road to peace. The unexpected close of the war found the leaders and peoples of Europe singularly unprepared to cope with the problem of restoring peace. They had devoted all their energies for more than four years to the waging of the military conflict and had thought little about the problems of peace. The passions, cupidity, and fears aroused by the armed conflict ill prepared them to approach the delicate task in a judicial frame of mind. While President Wilson had voiced a noble idealism in his speeches and state papers, the other leaders of the victorious powers came to the Peace Conference at Paris bound by old fears and by secret commitments.

I

THE PEACE CONFERENCE AT PARIS

As a compliment to France the Peace Conference met at Paris. On January 12, 1919, two representatives from each of the four powers, France, Italy, Great Britain, and the United States, met informally and made plans for the convening and organizing of the conference. They decided that the thirty-two powers which had broken off diplomatic relations with Germany should be represented in plenary sessions by plenipotentiaries varying in number from one to five, but they reserved real control of the work of the conference for a Council of Ten, consisting of two representatives from each of the five most powerful of the victorious powers—France, Italy, Japan, Great Britain, and the United States—and constituting in a sense a continuation of the Supreme Inter-Allied War Council. This decision excluded the defeated powers from the preliminary conference and threw the burden of formulating the terms of the peace treaty on the principal representatives of the five powers and on the scarcely noted members of a large number of committees and commissions created to prepare data and give advice on specific problems.

The three dominant personalities of the conference, by reason of their official positions and their personal qualities, were President Wilson of the United States, Premier Lloyd George of Great Britain, and Premier Clemenceau of France. The head of the delegation from the United States had risen to his high office from the background of a Presbyterian parsonage and the university lecture-room. As governor of New Jersey he had attracted the attention of the liberal elements in the United States and had won the Democratic nomination for the Presidency. As a result of the divisions existing at the time in the Republican party he had been elected President. In this office he had gradually made himself the spokesman of the idealism and the hopes of a world outraged and suffering from the most terrible of all wars. In January, 1918, he had summarized them in a striking manner in his Fourteen Points.

President Wilson and those who sympathized with him had to contend with statesmen who regarded the ideas of the American President as impractical, and had committed themselves during the World War to agreements based on principles in complete contrast with the Fourteen Points. Chief among these was the Premier of France, Clemenceau. He had begun his political life as an opponent of the régime of Napoleon III. Under the Third Republic he had developed into a cynical, sarcastic, courageous opponent of the governments in power. During the World War he had become the symbol of the French determination to win the military conflict and had become Premier of his country. He brought to the Peace Conference the bitter memories of three fourths of a century and a resolute purpose to insure the security of France by well-tried methods.

The duel between idealism and realism found the chief British representative playing a characteristic part. A son of the people, he had forced his way by sheer ability to a succession of important cabinet positions in Liberal governments and finally to the headship of a war cabinet supported by a coalition of British parties. With a reputation for Liberalism, he had given hostages to the reactionary elements among the British people by his promises in the electoral campaign of December, 1918, to hang the Kaiser and to make Germany pay "until the pips squeaked." He brought to the tasks of the conference a nimble brain, a mind none too well informed on Continental affairs, a remarkable sensitiveness to personalities and to shifts in public opinion, a thorough comprehension of British interests, and a genuine desire to find a just and workable peace.

On January 18, 1919, the Peace Conference formally began its work. The first plenary session elected Clemenceau as president and approved of the arrangements made in the preliminary conferences of the representatives of the principal Allied and Associated powers. After this opening session the Council of Ten and the experts of the committees and commissions appointed by it set to work at the task of reconstructing the world. In addition to the principal task of drawing up the various treaties of peace, the Council of Ten found itself confronted by the problems of supervising the work of the armistice commission, controlling the defeated and the newly established states of Europe, and starting the economic life of the European world again. The Council of Ten began to hear the arguments of the innumerable delegations demanding the consideration of the Peace Conference. On February 8, 1919, it set up a Supreme Economic Council, which became for a time the most important institution in Europe through its relief work in famine-stricken areas, its supervision of public finance and the various blockades maintained by the victorious powers, its reëstablishment of communications, and its allocation of shipping and raw materials. After a few weeks the leaders of the Peace Conference came to the conclusion that the procedure of the Council of Ten was too cumbersome and time-consuming and they organized a more informal Council of Four, composed of the principal representatives of Italy, France, Great Britain, and the United States, a body which made all the important decisions of the Peace Conference.

One of the first questions taken up by the Peace Conference was the proposed League of Nations. Before the World War various societies had been organized in Europe and America to work for the cause of peace. This struggle gave a great impetus to the movement to organize the peoples of the world against war. By the time that the Peace Conference convened there was a general demand for some sort of a league of nations, but a division of opinion as to whether the constitution of the league should be incorporated in the treaty of peace or set forth in a separate document. The second plenary session of the Peace Conference voted to make the Covenant of the League of Nations an integral part of the treaty of peace and intrusted the work of drafting the document to a commission headed by President Wilson. On April 28, 1919, the Covenant drawn up by this body was definitely approved by the Peace Conference.

One of the most difficult problems handled by the conference was the question of insuring the security of France, with a population of only thirty-nine million, against attack by Germany, a state with sixty-five million inhabitants. The solution proposed by the French was the establishment of the Rhine as the western frontier of Germany and the organization of the German territory on the left bank of that river into a neutral autonomous state. Premier Lloyd George and President Wilson, however, opposed the creation of another and larger Alsace-Lorraine. The dispute was finally compromised. Clemenceau gave up his demand for the creation of a separate state on the left bank of the Rhine, and obtained in return the occupation of this territory by an inter-Allied military force for a period of fifteen years as a guarantee of the execution of the terms of the treaty of peace, the demilitarization of all German territory west of a line fifty kilometers east of the Rhine, and the promise of treaties guaranteeing the assistance of Great Britain and the United States in case of an unprovoked attack by Germany.

As a further security against aggression, the victorious powers provided for the destruction of the German military machine, which had brought victory to Prussia in 1864, 1866, and 1870 and had dominated Europe since the founding of the German Empire, and for the limitation of the size of the German navy, which the British people had feared so much. The Peace Conference decided to abolish the great general staff and the Prussian system of universal military service, and compelled Germany to establish a professional army recruited by voluntary enlistment for a minimum term of twelve years. The Peace Conference likewise forbade the use of submarines and poison-gases, ordered the surrender of much military equipment and munitions and the destruction of certain fortresses, and established commissions of control to supervise the execution of the military clauses of the treaty.

The representatives of the victorious powers sought to weaken Germany further by seizure of her territory, the infliction of war indemnities, and the loss of commercial rights. They gave Belgium two small bits of German territory and the neutral district of Moresnet, and loosed Luxemburg from the German customs union. They attempted to solve the dispute between Denmark and Germany over Schleswig by allowing the inhabitants of the province to determine their future political status by a plebiscite. The voting resulted in the cession of Northern Schleswig to Denmark. The resurrection of Poland and Lithuania as independent states also forced the members of the Peace Conference to consider the whole problem of the eastern boundary of Germany. They deprived Germany of Memel, a small district at the extreme eastern end of East Prussia inhabited by a mixed population of Germans and Lithuanians, with the intention of handing it over to Lithuania after its status had been definitely determined.

The claims of Poland created a number of difficult problems. The

Poles had been led to expect that they would obtain access to the sea and possession of all districts indisputably Polish in population. The attempt to meet their claims created two problems, the Polish Corridor and the question of the future of Upper Silesia. The port of Danzig and the valley of the Lower Vistula in the province of West Prussia constituted the natural outlet for the commerce of Poland. Though the district had a large Polish population, its cession would cut the German province of East Prussia off from the rest of Germany and place the German inhabitants of Danzig and other districts under Polish rule. The situation in consequence was almost insoluble. The Peace Conference attempted to solve the problem by giving most of West Prussia to Poland, making Danzig an independent city under the supervision of a high commissioner appointed by the League of Nations, and giving Germany railroad, telegraph, and telephone rights across the Polish Corridor. Upper Silesia proved, if anything, to be a more complicated problem than the Polish Corridor. The province contained a large population of Poles and important mines of coal, lead, and zinc. The Poles claimed it on national, the Germans on economic and historic, grounds. The Peace Conference finally arranged for the holding of a plebiscite in the region to furnish data for making a decision of the question. The voting only complicated the problem. In spite of the Polish majority in Upper Silesia, the inhabitants of the region voted in favor of Germany. But the results of the plebiscite in no way lessened the insistence of the Poles in urging their claims. After working months at the problem the Peace Conference turned the question over to the League of Nations for solution. That body finally adopted a compromise which divided the province between Germany and Poland on the basis of a report made by neutral experts, but provided for reciprocal rights of trade and freedom of movement for the citizens of both states in the region for a limited period, in order to work as little economic injury to the province as possible.

The Peace Conference also deprived Germany of her colonies. Nominally, at least, they remained by the terms of the treaty of peace under the supervision of the League of Nations in order to insure the native populations good government, give other nations fair commercial rights, and partially meet the rising demand for international control of colonies. The colonial possessions of Germany consequently passed under the control of the victorious powers, under the name of mandates. Great Britain and France divided Togoland unequally between them. The Union of South Africa took control of German Southwest Africa. Great Britain acquired most of German East Africa and at last completed her long-dreamed-of all-red route from the Cape to Cairo. Australia assumed supervision over New Guinea and the adjacent islands, New Zealand that over German Samoa. Japan obtained control of the German islands in the Pacific Ocean north of the equator and the rights of Germany in the province of Shantung. Most people felt that these should have gone back to China, the original owner, but Japan insisted that her position in Shantung be recognized. The Japanese government finally promised, however, to negotiate with China over the return of the province.

During the negotiations for an armistice Germany also agreed to make compensation for all damage done in the Allied countries to the civilian population and their property. As soon as Germany was disarmed, however, the British and French delegates to the Peace Conference began to argue in favor of saddling Germany with the cost of the war. After this point of view had been vigorously combated by President Wilson as inconsistent with the promises made by the Allies to Germany, a heated controversy arose among the delegates to the Peace Conference over the definition of damages. They finally agreed that reparation should be made to include compensation for injuries caused by acts of war or mistreatment, payments made to prisoners of war and their families, forced labor, fines and levies in occupied areas, damage to property, pensions paid to disabled soldiers and to widows and orphans, separation allowances to wives and children, and the war debt of Belgium.

After the meaning of damages had at last been defined the debate shifted to the amount of the reparation payments and the method of paying them. France and to a less extent Great Britain felt that Germany should pay as much as possible. The American delegation contended for the establishment of a fixed and reasonable sum. As a result of these differences of opinion the Peace Conference could not reach a final decision concerning the payment of reparation. It merely demanded the payment of $5,000,000,000 in gold or its equivalent and the delivery of certain quantities of commodities by May, 1921, and left the determination of the total amount of reparation ultimately to be required to be determined by a Reparation Commission.

As compensation for the needless wrecking of French coal-mines by the German army of occupation, the representatives of France to the Peace Conference asked for the Saar Basin, a highly industrialized district about seven hundred square miles in area inhabited by six hundred and fifty thousand persons. Its coal-deposits more than equaled those of France and constituted over one fifth of those of the German Empire. As both the British and American delegations opposed the French demands, the Peace Conference compromised by handing over the government of the region to a commission under the control of the League of Nations, ceding its coal-mines to France, and placing its territory within the French customs union. At the end of fifteen years all persons resident in the district at the date of the signature of the treaty were promised an opportunity to determine the future political status of the Saar Basin.

The war propaganda made almost inevitable the inclusion of punitive clauses in the treaty of peace. As finally drawn up, consequently, the peace treaty affirmed the guilt of Germany in causing the World War, charged the German Emperor with a supreme offense against international morality and the sanctity of treaties, and provided for the surrender and trial of all German violators of the laws and customs of war. Though only slightly enforced, these clauses aroused intense exasperation as soon as they became known in Germany.

The treaty of peace with Germany, like those concluded with its various allies, included sections dealing with almost innumerable highly technical but exceedingly important problems. It disposed of all German rights and interests in China, Siam, Liberia, Morocco, and Egypt, provided for inter-Allied commissions of control, regulated the repatriation of prisoners of war and interned civilians and the care of war graves, arranged many financial problems, took measures to prevent discrimination in commercial relations and in the treatment of shipping and nationals, provided for the payment of debts by Germany, made provision for the transfer of property, rights, and interests, and legislated concerning aërial navigation, ports, waterways, and railroads. The whole treaty was drafted with the double purpose of reëstablishing peace and preventing a renewal of the war by Germany.

On May 7, 1919, the Treaty of Versailles was ready to be presented to the representatives of the new German Republic. The ceremony took place in the same Hall of Mirrors in which Bismarck had proclaimed the establishment of the German Empire. The German government was given three weeks in which to make a reply. On May 29 the German representatives presented their observations on the treaty. After making a few slight concessions, the Peace Conference demanded that Germany should declare her willingness to sign and threatened in case of her refusal to terminate the armistice and resume hostilities. One German cabinet declared the treaty unacceptable but another finally assumed the unpleasant responsibility of signing a document that deprived Germany of an area greater than Belgium and the Netherlands, reduced her population by seven million, and took away from her coal and other mineral deposits vital to German prosperity.

2

THE CONCLUSION OF TREATIES OF PEACE WITH AUSTRIA, HUNGARY,
BULGARIA AND TURKEY

In dealing with the rest of Central Europe the Peace Conference was forced, to use the apt phrase of another writer, to act as executor of the Hapsburg monarchy. Before the close of the war Austria-Hungary had fallen apart into her constituent national fragments. Austria and Hungary, the two partners in the Dual Monarchy, had lost most of their territory to Czechoslovakia, Poland, Rumania, Yugoslavia, and Italy. No one of the heirs of Austria-Hungary, however, had as yet received legal title to her claims. The Peace Conference assumed the task of passing judgment on the pretensions of the new, grasping, inchoate states of central Europe.

Before the conclusion of the Treaty of Versailles with Germany the question of the future of Fiume and the eastern coast of the Adriatic Sea had nearly disrupted the Peace Conference. Before entering the war Italy had won from her prospective allies a promise of the two ports of Trieste and Pola and a part of the province of Dalmatia. At the Peace Conference the Italian government broadened its demands in such a way as to include the port of Fiume and other territory of strategic and economic importance beyond the boundary-line proposed in the Treaty of London concluded in 1915 between Italy and the Entente powers. The Yugoslavs opposed the Italian demands on the grounds of the nationality of an overwhelming majority of the inhabitants of the region and the need of their newly created state for an outlet to the sea. President Wilson supported the claims of the Yugoslavs. His action caused the Italian delegation to withdraw for a time from the Peace Conference. The Peace Conference finally found itself compelled to leave the thorny question to be settled by direct negotiations between Italy and Yugoslavia. The two states did not reach a final agreement for several years. In November, 1920, their representatives signed the Treaty of Rapallo, which recognized Fiume as a free, independent state and gave Yugoslavia all of the Dalmatian coast except the town of Zara. Two years later the two states agreed to divide Fiume between them. They assigned the city proper to Italy and an adjacent suburb with port facilities to Yugoslavia.

While the Peace Conference was waiting for the reply of Germany to the Treaty of Versailles, the representatives of the Allied powers and the United States presented the Treaty of St.-Germain to Austria (June 2, 1919). This document deprived Austria of all her subject peoples and some of her German population as well. It gave up to Italy Southern Tyrol (with some two hundred and fifty thousand German-speaking inhabitants), Trieste, Istria, and two islands off the coast of Dalmatia. It surrendered to Czechoslovakia part of Lower Austria, most of Austrian Silesia, a portion of Teschen, Moravia, and Bohemia. It handed over to Poland Galicia and the rest of Teschen, and to Rumania the province of Bukovina. These provisions of the treaty separated twenty-three and a half million of the former subjects of Austria from her rule and left her a struggling republic with a population of only about six and a half million inhabitants. The Treaty of St.-Germain also forced Austria to assume reparation payments to be fully determined before May 1, 1921, by the Reparation Commission, to safeguard the racial, religious, and linguistic rights of minorities, and to give Czechoslovakia commercial access to the Adriatic Sea. The treaty also limited the Austrian army to thirty thousand men, abolished compulsory military service, and confiscated the former imperial navy with the exception of certain cruisers and auxiliary vessels. It likewise forbade the proposed union of Austria with Germany except with the express consent of the Council of the League of Nations. On September 10, 1919, the representatives of Austria finally signed the Treaty of St.-Germain.

At about the same time that Austria received the Treaty of St.-Germain the Peace Conference presented Bulgaria with the Treaty of Neuilly. This document compelled the Bulgarian government to cede to Greece all of western Thrace held by it, a cession which cut Bulgaria off from direct access to the Ægean Sea, to surrender certain mountain passes to Yugoslavia in order to protect the Nish-Saloniki railroad, to limit its military forces to twenty thousand men and to abolish compulsory military service, to give up most of its navy, and to obligate itself to pay two billion and a quarter francs in reparation within a period of thirty-seven years. On November 27, 1919, the representatives of Bulgaria signed the treaty that reduced their state to a minor rôle even in the Balkan peninsula.

The conclusion of peace with Hungary was delayed until June 4, 1920, by civil war and by foreign intervention. In March, 1919, the moderate government which had replaced the fallen monarchy gave way to a Communist régime headed by Béla Kun. In August of that same year Rumanian troops advanced into Hungary, overthrew the Communist government, and treated the country as conquered territory. The Treaty of Trianon finally signed by a coalition government awarded Croatia, Slavonia, and part of the Banat of Temesvar to Yugoslavia, gave Transylvania, part of the Hungarian plain, and the rest of the Banat of Temesvar to Rumania, ceded northern Hungary, including the area inhabited by the Slovaks and by about half a million Ruthenians, to Czechoslovakia, handed over western Hungary to Austria, and left the fate of the port of Fiume to be decided by direct negotiation between Italy and Yugoslavia. These cessions reduced the area of Hungary from one hundred and twenty-five thousand to thirty-five thousand square miles and her population from twenty million to eight million. The remaining clauses of the Treaty of Trianon closely resembled those of the treaty imposed upon Austria. They limited Hungary to an army of thirty-five thousand men and abolished compulsory military service, forced her to surrender practically all the naval forces of

Austria-Hungary, and compelled her to pay to the Allied powers an amount of reparation to be determined by the Reparation Commission.

In making a treaty with Turkey the Peace Conference encountered unforeseen opposition. At the time of the conclusion of the armistice Turkey and her empire seemed to be at the mercy of their enemies. The Peace Conference, consequently, put off the completion of a settlement with Turkey until after treaties had been concluded with her allies in the war. From the beginning the separation of Syria, Palestine, Mesopotamia, and Arabia from the empire had been taken for granted. During the conference the Greek government gained the assent of the Big Four, as the representatives of the four principal Allied powers were called, to the idea of the occupation of Smyrna and eastern Thrace by the Greeks in the name of nationality. For a time there was talk of the United States government's accepting an Armenian mandate in Turkey. The Treaty of Sèvres, consequently, was not ready to be presented to the representatives of Turkey until April 24, 1920. By the terms of this document Turkey surrendered sovereignty over all her non-Turkish provinces. It recognized the independence of the Kingdom of the Hedjaz in Arabia, provided for the organization of Syria as a French mandate and Palestine and Mesopotamia as British mandates, intrusted the administration of Smyrna and its hinterland to Greece for five years, ceded the Dodecanese and Rhodes to Italy and the other Greek islands in the Ægean and most of eastern Thrace to Greece, agreed to recognize an Armenian state with boundaries to be drawn by President Wilson, to give the Kurds autonomy or, if a plebiscite so decided, independence, and to allow the Straits and adjoining territory to be internationalized. These terms would have made Turkey a small state confined to Asia Minor.

Although the Sultan and his advisers felt compelled to sign this humiliating treaty on August 10, 1920, the Turkish nation rejected it. Under the skilful leadership of Mustapha Kemal, an experienced army officer, a congress of Turkish notables met at Sivas. This body denounced the cession of territories inhabited mainly by Turks and formulated and signed the National Pact, which became the creed of the Turkish national movement. In this document the Turkish nationalists agreed to the cession of the Arab provinces and the opening of the Straits to international commerce but demanded the retention by Turkey of all territory containing an Ottoman majority, the holding of a plebiscite in western Thrace, provision for the security of Constantinople, and, by implication, the abolition of the capitulations. When, at the dictation of the Allied powers, the Sultan dissolved the Turkish parliament and denounced the Turkish nationalists, they held a grand national assembly at Angora, established a government headed by Mustapha Kemal, and organized armies which began to threaten the British across the Straits from Constantinople, the French in Cilicia, and the Greeks in the region of Smyrna. In this crisis the Greeks, with the approval of the Allied powers, began military operations in Asia Minor that carried them at one time within two hundred miles of Angora, but which finally ended in failure.

By this time the Allied powers realized that the Treaty of Sèvres would have to be modified. France, exhausted by the World War, somewhat jealous of her British ally, and turned against Greece because of her acceptance again of King Constantine, adopted an independent policy and reached a compromise with the Turkish nationalists. By the terms of a treaty concluded on October 20, 1921, France abandoned her claims to Cilicia and modified the northern boundary of Syria in return for certain economic concessions. Thus divided among themselves, the Allies thereupon offered radical modifications of the Treaty of Sèvres, which the Turkish nationalists, confident of their ultimate victory, refused to accept. Italy then announced the signing of a treaty in which the Turkish national government at Angora promised to examine favorably Italian applications for mines, railways, and public works in Asia Minor. In August and September, 1922, the Turkish national forces decisively defeated the Greeks and drove them out of Asia Minor. As a result of this victory the Allied powers invited Greece and Turkey to a peace conference. The long-drawn-out negotiations that followed finally resulted, on July 24, 1923, in the signing of the Treaty of Lausanne. By the terms of this document Turkey extended her boundaries in Europe to the Maritza River and at one point even a little beyond, obtained the frontier previously established by the separate agreement with France, made arrangements for the future settlement of the northern boundary of Mesopotamia, which in the meantime had become the British mandate of Iraq, and retained certain islands surrendered by the Treaty of Sèvres. On the other hand the Treaty of Lausanne renounced all the rights and titles of Turkey over Libya, Egypt, and the Sudan, and recognized the annexation of Cyprus by Great Britain and the independence of Iraq, Arabia, Syria, and Palestine. In a sense the signing of this treaty finally brought the World War to an end.

3

THE LEAGUE OF NATIONS

The most notable achievement of the Peace Conference was the organization of the League of Nations. Owing to the insistence of President Wilson and to the state of public opinion in Europe, the Covenant of the League of Nations constituted the first part of each of the treaties of peace. The Peace Conference invited the thirty-two states (including India and four of the self-governing British dominions) that had broken off diplomatic relations with Germany, and thirteen neutral states, to become members of the proposed league. For a time the new organization excluded the defeated central powers and certain neutral states like Russia and Mexico which had not yet received diplomatic recognition. They might become members of the League of Nations by a two thirds vote of the assembly. States might withdraw from the organization provided they gave two years' notice of their intention to do so and had fulfilled all their international obligations. The seat of the new league was to be established at Geneva.

The Covenant provided that the action of the League of Nations should be effected through the instrumentality of an Assembly, a Council, and a Permanent Secretariat. The Assembly was to consist of representatives of states belonging to the league, to meet at stated intervals and from time to time as the occasion might require, and to deal at its meetings with any matter within the sphere of action of the league or affecting the peace of the world. In its meetings each member state was to have only one vote and not more than three representatives. The Council was to consist of representatives of the five principal Allied and Associated powers—France, Italy, Japan, Great Britain, and the United States—together with representatives of four other member states to be selected from time to time by the Assembly. With the approval of a majority of the Assembly the Council might name additional permanent and elected members. It was required to invite states belonging to the league to send representatives to sit on the Council during the consideration of matters specially affecting their interests. Each member state represented in the Council was to have one vote. Except where otherwise provided decisions at any meeting of the Assembly or of the Council were to require the agreement of all members of the League represented. The Permanent Secretariat was to be established at the seat of the league and was to comprise a secretary-general and such secretaries and staff as might be required. Its expenses were to be borne by the members of the league in accordance with the apportionment of the expenses of the International Bureau of the Universal Postal Union.

The League of Nations was established for the purpose of promoting international coöperation and achieving international peace and security. In the Covenant, consequently, the signatory powers recognized the necessity of reducing national armaments and provided for the establishment of a permanent commission to advise the Council concerning the formulation and execution of plans for the limitation of armaments. The members of the league also agreed to submit any question likely to lead to a diplomatic rupture either to arbitration or to inquiry by the Council and in no case to resort to war until three months after the award of the arbitrators or the report of the Council. They further pledged themselves to carry out in good faith any award and not to go to war against a member of the league that complied with it. Any member state of the league that resorted to war in disregard of its covenants was to be deemed to have committed an act of war against all other members of the league. The states joining the League of Nations therefore pledged themselves to sever all trade and financial relations with such a power, to prohibit all intercourse between themselves and the nationals of the covenant-breaking state, and to prevent all financial, commercial, and personal intercourse with its nationals. In the event of such a case the Council of the league was to recommend to the several governments what military, naval, and aërial forces member states should contribute to the armed forces of the league. The states belonging to the organization also bound themselves to register with the Secretariat all treaties and international engagements, to endeavor to secure and maintain fair and humane conditions of labor for men, women, and children, to insure the just treatment of the native inhabitants of territories under their control, to intrust the league with general supervision of the trade in arms and ammunition, to secure freedom of transit and communication, and to take steps for the prevention and control of disease. The Covenant placed under the direction of the league all existing international bureaus and commissions for the regulation of matters of international interest. The Covenant itself might be amended by a unanimous vote of the Council and a majority vote of the Assembly.

Since its organization the League of Nations has undergone certain changes. The Senate of the United States unexpectedly failed to ratify the Covenant and its action greatly impaired the effectiveness of the new body. Brazil has ceased to belong and Argentina has withdrawn from active participation. In spite of these reverses, the total number of states belonging to the league has risen from forty-two to fifty-five. The Council has become an executive organ, directing the permanent tasks and special organizations of the league. The number of its permanent members has risen to five and of its elected members to nine. The Assembly has become an organization which enables the governments of the world to obtain an annual review of the international situation, and determines the general lines of policy of the League of Nations.

In handling international problems the league has shown notable fluctuations in effectiveness. It has not yet achieved any reduction in armaments. It made a success of the task of reconstructing the finances of Austria and Hungary. It successfully supervised the withdrawal from Turkey of a million and a half Greek refugees and a much smaller number of Bulgarians, and their settlement in Greece and Bulgaria. It has administered the Saar Basin and the city of Danzig, and done something at least to protect minorities numbering in the neighborhood of thirty million persons. In settling disputes between states its success has been affected by the difficulty of some of the problems and the nature of the political situation. It settled a dispute between Sweden and Finland over the Aland Islands, failed to effect a settlement of the conflict between Poland and Lithuania over Vilna, stopped a Yugoslav invasion of Albania, handled with success an incident which threatened to cause a diplomatic break between Greece and Bulgaria, but, on the whole, rather failed in its efforts to adjust a dispute between Italy and Greece and one between Great Britain and Turkey. The commissions and committees of the League of Nations have done an immense amount of work in improving health conditions, regulating the traffic in drugs, and suppressing the white-slave traffic. The league also made a success of its efforts to organize a Permanent Court of International Justice.

One of the principal organs of the League of Nations set up by the Peace Conference was the International Labor Organization. It consists of two essential bodies, the General Conference and the International Labor Office. The General Conference meets at least once a year. It is composed of four representatives from each of the fifty-five member states, two representing the government, one the employers, and one the workers. Its chief task is the discussion and drafting of international conventions designed to improve the conditions of the workers. The International Labor Office at Geneva seeks to obtain ratification by the states of international conventions drawn up by the General Conference, collects and distributes information on all subjects relating to the international adjustment of conditions of industrial life and labor, conducts special investigations upon order of the General Conference, and edits a periodical. The International Labor Organization has wielded an important influence in improving working conditions throughout the world.

4

THE PERMANENT COURT OF INTERNATIONAL JUSTICE

In December, 1920, the governments belonging to the League of Nations carried out the article of the Covenant providing for the formulation by the Council of plans for the organization of a Permanent Court of International Justice. The statute finally drafted by a committee, headed by Elihu Root of the United States, arranged for the election by the Council and the Assembly of the League of Nations, from a list presented for their consideration by the Permanent Court of

Arbitration at The Hague, of eleven judges and four deputy judges for terms of nine years, and for the holding of annual sessions by the new court. In coming to a decision the judges are expected to make use of international conventions and customs, general principles of law recognized by civilized nations, judicial decisions, and the teachings of the most highly qualified publicists. By an optional clause states can recognize decisions of the court as compulsory. The new court is to give advisory opinions upon the written request of the Assembly or the Council of the League of Nations. In June, 1922, the Permanent Court of International Justice opened for work.

5

REPARATION AND SECURITY

In spite of these international institutions, the restoration of peacetime conditions was long prevented by the two problems of reparation and security. In April, 1920, representatives of Great Britain, France, Belgium, Italy, and Japan began work on the problem of computing the liability of Germany and the other enemy countries for damages and of deciding the share of each of the Allied states in the proposed reparation payments. The views of the Allied powers and of Germany proved to be far apart. In January, 1921, at a conference held at Paris, the representatives of the victorious Allies tentatively agreed to ask Germany for forty-two annual payments beginning at two milliard gold marks a year and rising at the end of eight years to six milliard gold marks. Germany, in contrast, angered the Allied powers by the meager sums that she offered to pay and by the conditions which she attempted to attach to the payments. In April, 1921, the Reparation Commission announced its decision that Germany should be asked to pay one hundred and thirty-two milliard marks in annuities of five hundred million gold marks plus 26 per cent of German exports. Upon the basis of this report the London Conference issued an ultimatum to Germany, and in consequence in September, 1921, the German government actually paid the first milliard gold marks due. Almost immediately, however, difficulties began to arise in regard to subsequent reparation payments. In December, 1921, the government of Germany notified the Reparation Commission that it could not make the next payment in full. After holding a number of conferences the Allied powers eventually granted Germany a moratorium.

At this point differences began to arise among the Allies regarding the policy to be pursued toward Germany. The British government had gradually become more interested in the reëstablishment of normal business conditions in Germany, its best market before the World War, than in exacting reparation in money and in kind that injured British trade. The French, on the other hand, had spent large sums on the reconstruction of the devastated areas in anticipation of future reparation payments and felt that Germany had made no real effort to meet her treaty obligations. The French government, therefore, would consider reducing the amount demanded of Germany only in case its own debts to its Allies and to the United States were remitted, and began preparations to weaken Germany and at the same time force her to pay reparation by seizing the Ruhr district, a highly industrialized region adjoining the German territories already occupied by the troops of the Allied powers and the United States. Through French influence the Reparation Commission declared Germany in default and the French and Belgian governments organized a mission of mining and smelting engineers and of French and Belgian troops to exploit the Ruhr district. At midday on January 11, 1923, the mission entered Essen with the object of supervising the activity of the coal syndicate. In the face of this appeal to force the German government made a legal protest and adopted a policy of passive resistance. At the command of their government the German mine-owners, miners, and transportation employees refused to deliver coal to France. They counted confidently on the French government's bankrupting itself by an unsuccessful effort to operate the industries of the region. The French retaliated by expelling German officials, requisitioning automobiles and other vehicles, imprisoning individuals for incitement to passive resistance, and seizing raw materials and machinery in the factories. In carrying out the orders of the French government incidents arose which resulted in the killing and wounding of many persons.

For a time it looked as if the French occupation of the Ruhr district would prove a complete failure. By April, the French mission had made little headway in obtaining coal, and the inhabitants of the Rhineland had shown little indication of a desire to break away from the rest of Germany. In the end, however, Germany proved unequal to the strain of financing the policy of passive resistance. The German government found it increasingly difficult to maintain the unemployed workers of the Ruhr district, as it was necessary to send larger and larger sums into the area for the support of those thrown out of work by its policy. The stoppage of industry in the Ruhr region gradually affected the demand for the commodities of other parts of Germany and reduced their ability to support the policy of passive resistance. In order to meet the demands on the treasury the German government resorted to an inflation policy that completely deranged the currency. The situation finally caused great social unrest. In the face of these conditions the German government was compelled, in September, 1923, to give up the policy of passive resistance without receiving any promise of consideration for its difficulties from the French government.

The surrender of Germany brought forward again the question of the total amount of reparation to be demanded of the German government and the method by which it should be paid. As a result of a suggestion made in a public speech by Mr. Hughes, the Secretary of State of the United States, two committees of experts, representing France, Belgium, Italy, Great Britain, and the United States, were appointed by the Reparation Commission. One—popularly known as the Dawes Committee, from the name of its American chairman—was formed to make proposals for stabilizing the currency and balancing the budget. The other and less important committee was to consider means of estimating the amount of German capital exported and the means of bringing it back into the country. In making its report the Dawes Committee treated the problem as an economic rather than a political question. It recommended the freeing of the economic forces of Germany from outside control, the establishment of a Reichsbank to issue notes on a gold basis, to fix the official rate of discount, to act as banker for the government, and to hold on deposit reparation payments, and the adoption of a definite plan of reparation payments for a term of years. The committee proposed a schedule of payments which started at a thousand million gold marks and rose after the lapse of five years to twenty-five hundred million gold marks. As security for the payment of reparation it recommended taxes and railway and industrial debentures. The whole German system of railways was to be removed from government control and used as a guarantee for the issuing of bonds and in addition was to be subject to a transport-tax. Certain designated revenues were also to be set aside for reparation payments and certain industrial debentures were to be issued for a similar purpose. The proposed scheme was to operate under the supervision of a director and a reparation commission with drastic powers. In August, 1924, the governments concerned finally adopted the report of the Dawes Committee and took steps to put its recommendations into immediate operation.

During the struggle over the reparation question the European powers had also been searching in vain for security. Much of the harshness of the French government toward Germany arose from its fear that financial relief of Germany would increase the insecurity of France. In 1924, during the period when Ramsay MacDonald and Édouard Herriot headed the British and French governments and gave a more conciliatory turn to international relations, the powers belonging to the League of Nations attempted to find a solution of the problem in the Geneva Protocol, a scheme intended to secure international peace by pledging each state to submit its legal disputes with other states to the Permanent

Court of International Justice or to some form of arbitration, and to go to war only in self-defense or for the punishment of a state which refused to settle a dispute peacefully. The plan encountered, however, the opposition of the British Conservatives after they came into power. After the acceptance of the Dawes Plan had cleared the international atmosphere to a considerable extent, the German government brought forward suggestions that finally ripened in 1925 into the Locarno Pact. In the principal treaty concluded at the little Swiss town of Locarno, Germany, Belgium, France, Italy, and Great Britain mutually guaranteed the inviolability of the frontiers between Germany and her two neighbors, France and Belgium, and undertook never to wage war against each other except in legitimate defense or to fulfil their obligations as members of the League of Nations, to settle disputes by pacific means, and to come to the aid of France, Belgium, or Germany in case of a breach of the agreement. In other treaties Germany and her four neighbors, France, Belgium, Poland, and Czechoslovakia, agreed to arbitrate their disputes, and France and her two allies, Poland and Czechoslovakia, pledged their mutual support.

The conclusion of this agreement marked the opening of a new period in international relations. At Locarno the representatives of Germany were received by the representatives of the other powers of Europe on terms of cordial equality. After a hard struggle the German parliament agreed to the ratification of the Locarno agreements and to the application of Germany for admission to the League of Nations. After a prolonged fight, marked by the efforts of several states to gain permanent seats in the Council, Germany was admitted to the League of Nations by the unanimous vote of the Assembly, and received a permanent place in the Council. With the entrance of Germany, the League of Nations ceased to be an organization entirely dominated by the victorious powers. The conclusion of the Locarno Pact reassured the French government sufficiently to cause it to begin the evacuation of the Rhineland. France valued the Locarno agreements for the security they offered, Germany for the promise of justice that they held out.

Although Germany made the payments stipulated in the Dawes Plan promptly and in full each year, the governments of Europe soon began to feel the need of a complete and final settlement of the question of reparation. In 1928 the six most interested powers, Germany, Belgium, Italy, France, Japan, and Great Britain, finally agreed upon the constitution of a new committee of experts to consider the two problems of reparation and the evacuation of the Rhineland. In June, 1929, the committee brought in its report, known as the Young Plan, again because of the American chairman of the committee. This document established a relationship between the reparation payments of Germany and the war debts of her creditors, and called for somewhat smaller annual payments by Germany than the Dawes Plan had stipulated. The new payments were to continue for fifty-nine years. After September 1, 1929, Germany was to be relieved of responsibility for the costs of the military occupation of the Rhineland. After the committee of experts had completed its work its report had to be adopted by the six governments. That work came near to being wrecked because of the protest of the British government at the share of the reparation payments assigned to it. After the report had been modified in the interest of Great Britain, however, it was finally adopted, and the question of the evacuation of the Rhineland was arranged at a conference of representatives of the six powers held at The Hague. On November 1, 1929, the Young Plan went into operation, and in 1930 the last French soldier left German soil. The settlement of these two questions may be said to have restored approximately normal political conditions in western Europe.

In 1931, however, the economic strength of Germany proved unequal to the strain of meeting the reparation payments called for by the Young Plan. The world-wide economic depression struck Germany with especial severity. In the emergency President von Hindenburg appealed to President Hoover for aid. In response to this almost unprecedented appeal President Hoover proposed a moratorium on all war debts for a year. The proposal led to a series of conferences which finally resulted in the adoption of measures designed to rescue Germany from its financial difficulties. The German government was relieved for a year from making reparation payments and the time for the meeting of a large number of short-term notes was extended. These measures, however, did not settle the problem of the repayment of private debts.

Since 1918 the attention of the European powers has been largely taken up with problems arising out of the World War. At the Peace Conference at Paris two conflicting ideals struggled for the mastery. The treaties of peace, in consequence, represented a compromise between new ideals of international justice and old ideas concerning the punishment of the defeated powers and the compensation and security of the victors. The idealism of the world expressed itself in the clauses providing for the establishment of a League of Nations and a Permanent Court of International Justice and for the recognition of the rights of nations and peoples. Tradition found expression in the clauses concerning the payment of reparation and the military occupation of the Rhineland. Since the close of the Peace Conference, the League of Nations and the Permanent Court of International Justice have functioned with moderate success; the problems of reparation and security have embittered the relations of the governments of Europe. The Dawes Plan, the Locarno Pact, the Young Plan, the evacuation of the Rhineland, the admission of Germany to the Council of the League of Nations, and the moratorium suggested by President Hoover have all contributed, however, toward an amelioration of international relations.

CHAPTER XXVIII

After the conclusion of the armistice terminating the World War each European state found itself confronted both with new conditions created by that conflict and with the old chronic problems. In each country the situation had distinctive features. Great Britain found herself face to face with such domestic problems as the reëstablishment of her old economic position and the Irish question; France found herself confronted by the problems of reconstruction and the reintegration of Alsace-Lorraine; and Italy took up all the old social, economic, religious, and political problems, which had been greatly aggravated by the war and by the outcome of the Peace Conference.

I

GREAT BRITAIN

The World War greatly changed the political situation in Great Britain. In the years immediately preceding 1914 a Liberal cabinet, headed by Lord Asquith, had been kept in power by the support extended to it by the Irish Nationalists and the members of the new Labor party. In 1915 it made way for a coalition ministry composed of Conservatives, Liberals, and Labor members. In the following year Lloyd George forced Asquith, the titular head of his party, out of office and took his place as chief of the war cabinet. During the closing years of the war the Liberal party broke into two hostile factions headed by Asquith and Lloyd George. At the close of the World War Lloyd George shrewdly attempted to prolong the life of the coalition ministry and his own tenure of office by holding a parliamentary election before the enthusiasm and good-will engendered by victory waned.

The World War, however, had made a further democratization of Great Britain inevitable. After asking the whole nation to sacrifice life and property in the military conflict the government felt that something must be done to meet the insistent demand for the right of suffrage made by the classes still excluded from political life. In 1918, Parliament had passed a law which doubled the number of voters. It conferred the suffrage on practically all British men and on all women thirty years of age who had the right to vote in local elections or were the wives of men entitled to such a vote. It also redistributed the seats in Parliament in such a way as to make the single-member constituencies more equal in size, and greatly reduced plural voting. The admission of such a large body of new voters to the suffrage made the proposed election one of the most incalculable in the history of British politics.

The electoral campaign resulted in the return of Lloyd George to power, but plainly indicated the political changes wrought by the World War. The coalition gained an overwhelming victory but control of its policies shifted almost completely to the Conservatives. The independent wing of the Liberal party, headed by Asquith, became an unimportant minority. The Labor party greatly increased its representation in Parliament and became the official opposition. The Irish people voted for the Sinn Fein candidates instead of the Irish Nationalists. The election thus made the coalition responsible for finding a solution for the problems confronting Great Britain.

The World War also greatly changed the economic situation of Great Britain. It transformed her industrial establishments into plants designed to further the prosecution of the military conflict, and destroyed the old demand for British goods. Although a brief period of prosperity followed the conclusion of the armistice, British industry soon found that the maintenance of the blockade of hostile countries interfered with exports, that the war had impoverished some of its most important former foreign markets, that its products had to compete with commodities manufactured by countries with a depreciated currency, that many new tariff barriers hindered the free flow of British goods, and that new competitors had developed. These conditions soon caused an economic depression marked by a decline in foreign trade, a decrease in the demand for shipping, the closing of factories, industrial unrest, and unemployment. The British people scarcely felt compensated for these conditions by the acquisition of new mandates and new resources.

The unemployment problem has troubled each succeeding British government. For in spite of exporting less than before the war, the population increased, women in mounting numbers were demanding work, rising taxes and waning incomes drove many members of the leisure class into gainful occupations, and the British soldiers and sailors demanded a rapid demobilization. By the middle of 1921 the unemployed numbered more than two million persons. The coalition government sought without success to solve the problem by increasing the amount of the unemployment-insurance payments, by encouraging emigration from Great Britain to the British dominions, and by adopting the protective-tariff measure known as the Safeguarding of Industries Act.

At the same time that it was vainly attempting to solve the unemployment problem the coalition government was harassed by the situation in Ireland. As has been noted, the outbreak of the World War caused the British government to postpone the inauguration of the Home Rule Bill adopted by Parliament in 1914. The delay in setting up the promised home-rule government worked to the disadvantage of the moderate Irish Nationalist party and favored the growth of the far more radical Sinn Fein party. In the election of 1918, as has already been explained, this party was victorious. It obtained seventy-three seats, while the Irish Nationalists captured only six. The leaders of the victorious party immediately interpreted the election as a demand for the establishment of an Irish Republic. They consequently refused to take their seats in the British Parliament, organized an Irish parliamentary body known as the Dail Eireann, elected representatives to the Peace Conference, chose a President, and established a ministry. For several months after they took this action a state of war existed between the British government and the Irish Republic. In many parts of Ireland legal government broke down and the Irish people recognized only the authority of the Sinn Fein party.

In 1920 the British government attempted to solve the Irish question by the enactment of a new Home Rule Bill. This piece of legislation provided for the establishment of a parliament for the six counties in Ulster and of another parliament for the rest of the island. It placed such services as the army, the navy, foreign relations, customs, and the excise under the control of the British Parliament, gave the two proposed sections of Ireland a greatly reduced representation in the British House of Commons, and called for the organization of a council, composed of members nominated by the two Irish parliaments and designed to promote the coöperation of the two Irish governments. Northeastern Ireland at once organized the new political machinery, but the Sinn Fein leaders ignored the new legislation.

In 1921, therefore, the British government made another offer to the Sinn Fein party. The prolonged negotiations that followed finally resulted in the establishment of the Irish Free State. The treaties drawn up by the representatives of the British government and the Irish leaders gave the new state approximately the same constitutional status in the British Empire as the self-governing dominions. The negotiations, however, split the Sinn Fein party into two factions. A majority in the Dail Eireann voted for the ratification of the treaty, established a provisional government, and set to work at the task of drafting a constitution. A minority attempted by a system of terrorism to prevent the operation of the new government and to influence the elections. Its efforts proved of no avail. A majority of the newly electedly Irish parliament favored acceptance of the treaty negotiated with the British government, and the Irish authorities used vigorous measures to suppress their opponents. They thereupon established a democratic government, obtained the admission of the Irish Free State to the League of Nations, sent diplomatic representatives to Washington and other capitals, and settled the boundary-line between the two political divisions of Ireland. With the transformation of the extremists into a constitutional opposition in 1927, the Irish problem seemed to be solved.

By 1922 the coalition government of Great Britain could no longer be held together. In that year the leaders of the Conservative party announced their intention to withdraw from the coalition. Upon the publication of this announcement Lloyd George resigned and a Conservative ministry took office, which dissolved Parliament. The ensuing elections resulted in the return of the Conservatives to power, the decline of the Liberals, and the continuance of the Labor party as the strongest group in the opposition. Had the Conservative leaders been satisfied to follow a moderate policy, they might have remained in power for an indefinite period. Instead of following this course of action, however, they suddenly decided to advocate the policy of a protective tariff as a solution for the economic problem harassing the British people. The new policy threatened the British free-trade tradition of three quarters of a century and aroused the determined opposition of both the reunited Liberals and the Labor party. In the electoral campaign the two opposition parties had little difficulty in convincing the country that a protective tariff would not cure the economic depression and the resulting unemployment. The Conservatives consequently lost their majority in Parliament, while the Labor party gained forty-eight additional seats. As a result of these developments the Conservatives resigned from power and a Labor government took office in January, 1924, for the first time in the history of Great Britain. It was headed by Ramsay MacDonald, and supported by the Liberals.

Although the leaders of the new government were avowed Socialists, they were not in a position to attempt any radical changes. As they did not control a majority of the votes in the House of Commons, they could only stay in office with the support of either the Liberals or the Conservatives. The new Prime Minister promised to walk and not to jump toward his ultimate goal. He made the immediate objectives of government the establishment of peace and the fostering of the well-being of the nation. The Labor government gained the confidence and respect of the country by the manner in which it handled an epidemic of strikes. It abolished most of the protective duties established by the Conservatives and eased the burden of some of the indirect taxes. It did little to solve the serious problems of housing and unemployment. Its greatest successes came in the field of foreign relations. Premier MacDonald restored cordial relations between the British and the French government, recognized the Russian government, and advocated the acceptance of the Dawes Plan for Germany. His Russian policy, however aroused so much opposition that he felt compelled to dissolve Parliament and seek the approval of the electorate. The elections resulted in the return of the Conservative party to power. Many British voters feared the establishment of a Socialist state and many British workmen felt disappointed at the failure of the Labor party to remedy the unemployment situation. As a result of the election the Conservatives again gained a clear majority in the House of Commons, the Labor party lost nearly one fourth of the seats which it had held in the previous Parliament, and the Liberals became an almost negligible party.

The Conservatives remained in office five years. During their term of office the dissatisfaction among the British coal-miners reached a climax. After the close of the World War the British owners of coal-mines found that they could not recapture their former markets. The development of water-power on the Continent, the increased use of oil and foreign coal as fuel, and the delivery of German coal in Italy and France as a part of the reparation payments all decreased the demand for British coal and lowered its price. Many of the British mine-owners found themselves compelled to reduce wages and increase the number of working hours in order to prevent the operation of their mines at a loss. Finally in 1926, after protracted negotiations between the owners and the representatives of the miners, the Trades Union Congress called a strike in certain vital industries such as the transportation lines and the printing-trade. In popular opinion the country faced the prospect of a general strike. The acute crisis lasted only nine days. The government appealed for volunteers and the general response of the British people enabled the country to continue the operation of the essential services. The government finally persuaded the Trades Union Congress to call off the strike. After a struggle that lasted more than seven months, the return of many miners to work, the exhaustion of its funds, and the approach of winter caused the Miners Union to surrender and to accept a longer working day and lower wages. The Conservatives took advantage of the situation to pass legislation which made a general strike illegal, forbade picketing, prevented unions from disciplining their members for refusing to participate in an illegal strike, abolished the exemption of labor-unions from legal action, and permitted them to make political levies on their members only in case they received specific permission.

During their term of office the Conservatives completed the work of giving the suffrage to all adults. The legislation of 1918 concerning the franchise denied many younger women the vote, for fear of transferring political power from the men to the women. In 1928 the Conservatives fulfilled their earlier campaign pledge by giving the suffrage to all women twenty-one years of age, on equal terms with men.

In foreign affairs the Conservatives continued, in the main, the policy of conciliation begun by Premier MacDonald. They coöperated in the negotiation of the Locarno Pact, but reversed the Russian policy of the preceding Labor government. They discovered the close relations of the Russian authorities and the Communist party in Great Britain and their subsidizing of the British miners during the great coal-strike. They suspected the headquarters of the Russian trading agency in Great Britain of being responsible for the disappearance of certain secret documents from the British War Office, and held the Russian government answerable for the falling off of British trade with China. The British government, consequently, severed all relations with Russia.

In 1929 the Conservatives had to submit their administration of the government to the British electorate for approval. In the campaign their opponents made their failure to solve the problems of unemployment and the revival of British trade the principal issues and proposed enticing plans for their solution. The Conservatives asked for their approval by the electorate as the defenders of the constitution and society against the menace of socialism and as the party calculated to lead the country toward practical policies. In the election the Labor party gained one hundred and twenty-five seats and became the largest political party in Parliament but failed to obtain a clear majority in the House of Commons. For the next two years it conducted the government only with the aid of the Liberals. The government showed no inclination to pass radical measures. Dissension divided the ranks of its supporters and its failure to find remedies for the domestic ills of the country cost it much of its popularity. In August, 1931, it found itself confronted by a situation which forced the Labor cabinet to resign from office. The financial difficulties in Austria and Germany arising out of the world economic crisis reacted unfavorably upon the financial situation in Great Britain. Since it was well known that British banks had much money tied up in the hard-pressed countries of central Europe, apprehension began to be felt by foreign creditors for the safety of their funds on deposit in London and the British gold-reserve began to be rapidly reduced. A parliamentary report concerning the unsatisfactory state of the British budget and the likelihood of a treasury deficit added to the alarm. The situation demanded that the budget should be put on a sound basis immediately. A part of the Labor cabinet, however, refused to approve the adoption of a policy which called for a reduction of the payments to the unemployed. Faced by this situation, the Labor government resigned.

The emergency was the occasion for one of the most dramatic events in the history of British politics. The King invited Ramsay MacDonald, the head of the former Labor cabinet and one of the founders of the Labor party, to form a coalition government. From a strong sense of duty and patriotism he accepted the invitation, at the risk of ending his political career, and organized a small emergency cabinet consisting of four members of the Labor party, four Conservatives, and two Liberals. The great majority of his party disapproved of his action and read him and his three associates out of the organization. The coalition cabinet proposed to balance the budget by drastic economies and new taxation. Feeling the need, however, of greater assurance of popular support, they decided to hold a new parliamentary election, which cut the representation of the Labor party in half and gave the coalition an overwhelming majority.

2

FRANCE

France emerged from the World War both enriched and impoverished. The armistice restored to her Alsace-Lorraine with its resources of iron, coal, oil and potash, and its blast-furnaces, steel plants, and textile mills. The Treaty of Versailles gave her as mandates portions both of the former German colonies and of the Turkish empire. The occupation of important French industrial regions by German armies for a period of more than four years had stimulated the development of industries and mineral resources in other parts of France. These gains made France the second largest country in Europe and put her in a much stronger economic position than before. They were offset, however, by certain losses. The World War reduced the population of France by more than two million persons, a most serious decline in a country where the birth-rate scarcely exceeded the death-rate. It likewise cut manufacturing in half, increased the public debt enormously, diminished exports to a quarter of their former volume, and destroyed the stability and much of the purchasing power of the currency.

The most striking effect of the World War, as far as France was concerned, was the material damage wrought in her northern provinces. The first rush of the German armies carried them almost to the gates of Paris. During the remaining years of the conflict the surging military forces successively advanced and retreated over great areas of French territory, soldiers of both armies dug vast networks of trenches along a front five hundred miles in length, and thousands of pieces of artillery rained destructive shells on public buildings, cities and villages, and woods, fields and meadows. Before their final retreat the German military authorities systematically destroyed factories, coal-mines, bridges, stations, and railroads with the double aim of preventing the advance of the French and British armies and of crippling the economic power of the French people. In this way the World War drove some two million persons from their homes and their cattle and stock from the fields, destroyed some three hundred thousand dwellings and wrecked as many more, ruined about twenty thousand industrial establishments, tore up twenty-four hundred kilometers of railroad, and left the ground furrowed with a maze of trenches, filled with dangerous unexploded shells, and encumbered with hundreds of thousands of tons of debris.

After brief but unforgettable demonstrations over the return of peace, therefore, the French people directed their attention to the pressing problem of material reconstruction. Contrary to precedent, the French government, early in the conflict, had promised the inhabitants of the devastated regions that it would assume the burden of compensating them for their losses during the war and had taken some preliminary steps toward fulfilling its pledge. In April, 1919, the government adopted a comprehensive plan for making reparation for war damages. By its terms the complainant was entitled to compensation for his actual loss. In case he used the money for the reconstruction of his property he was promised an amount necessary to restore his property to its original condition. The carrying out of the plan of the French government entailed exasperating delays. Nearly three million claims for losses were filed with the government. While cantonal commissions slowly sifted this mass of papers, the inhabitants of the devastated regions, living in crowded temporary quarters and in desperate need of capital, chafed over their dilatoriness. Five years after the close of the World War, however, the task was approximately completed. The fields had been cleared and leveled, towns and villages had been rebuilt, roads had been repaired, and factories and railroads had been reconstructed.

In reconstructing the devastated regions and indemnifying the inhabitants for their losses, the French government expended an enormous sum. At first it confidently expected that Germany would ultimately pay the bill. It therefore resorted to loans as a temporary expedient and, relying on reparation payments for the reimbursement of its creditors, created a special budget for reconstruction, separate from the ordinary budget. This situation caused the French government to direct its attention largely to the problem of reparation and explains many of the strange turns of French politics in the years following the close of the World War. Their need of reparation payments accounts for the absorption of both the French government and the French people in the course of the Peace Conference, the fear of France in regard to setting a definite amount for Germany to pay, the seeming harshness of the French attitude toward Germany, the failure of an advocate of moderate and conciliatory policies like Aristide Briand to remain at the head of the French government, and the coming into power of an unyielding nationalist like Poincaré.

Nevertheless, a reaction finally set in against the policies of the extreme nationalists. Their measures failed to wring from Germany the expected reparation payments. The purchasing power of the franc continued to fall, the French debt mounted steadily, and taxes constantly grew heavier. In 1924, consequently, after the occupation of the Ruhr district had failed to extort the expected reparation payments from Germany, the National Bloc supporting Poincaré lost more than a hundred seats in the parliamentary elections and a political combination organized by Briand and composed of parties of the Left came into office. During the eighteen months that it was in power this bloc forced out of office not only Premier Poincaré, but also President Alexandre Millerand—because of his unusual display of partizanship in the conduct of the Presidency—revived the French anticlerical traditions, collaborated more closely in foreign affairs with Great Britain, and took a more conciliatory attitude toward Germany.

The religious policy of this political group during its tenure of power brought to a head the discontent in Alsace-Lorraine. At first the two provinces had seemed to welcome their restoration to French rule. After the enthusiasm of the first tumultuous demonstrations waned, however, the inhabitants of the regained territories began to find the transition from German to French administration trying. They lost the measure of autonomy finally conceded to them by the German government and found themselves divided into departments and subjected to the highly centralized government of France. As long as the National Bloc remained in power the French government left the old religious and educational arrangements undisturbed, but as soon as the parties of the Left came into office they attempted to complete the incorporation of the two provinces into France. They introduced secular schools, required the teaching of the French language in educational institutions, and ignored almost completely the local rights of Alsace-Lorraine. The policy of the government aroused a great deal of opposition in the two provinces. The Roman Catholic school-children united in a great strike and the disaffected among the adult population started an autonomist movement. In spite of these protests the French government established common schools for the instruction in the academic branches of children of all confessions, insisted on the teaching of the French language, and forced the two provinces to adapt themselves to the French political system. It permitted, however, the separation of children of the different faiths for religious instruction.

By 1925 the financial situation had become the most serious problem confronting the French government. The World War had increased the French debt enormously. After the close of that conflict, as we have seen, the French government had relied on Germany's paying the cost of reconstruction and had made no effort to balance the budget. Instead of increasing taxation it had resorted to inflation of the currency and had sold bonds and short-term notes. By 1925 the economic situation had become alarming. The franc had steadily declined in purchasing power, the French people showed an increasing unwillingness to make further loans to the government, prices were rising rapidly, the real income of French bondholders had fallen persistently, and the floating debt was beginning to come due. Because of their unwillingness to resort to radical remedial measures the financial situation caused the fall of a succession of French cabinets. The political leaders of France finally met the grave crisis by organizing a National cabinet, headed by Poincaré, which included six former premiers. The new government took drastic measures. Abandoning its policy of relying on Germany to balance the French budget, it introduced new measures of taxation to increase the revenues of the state and made administrative reforms that reduced expenditures. As a result of this action the government balanced the budget for the first time since the opening of the World War, the franc rose in value until it reached about one fifth of its pre-war worth, where it was stabilized, and the public regained confidence in the government sufficiently to lend money on better terms. With the cessation of the work of reconstruction and an increase in the German reparation payments as a result of the Dawes Plan, the economic life of France again became approximately normal. In 1928, Poincaré resigned from office on account of ill-health and Briand again became the dominant political figure in France. Under his leadership France directed her attention largely to the problems of security and international peace.

3

ITALY

The Italian people came out of the World War with great social and national expectations. The victorious combatants, particularly those members of the middle class who had risen to the rank of officer in the army, counted confidently on finding lucrative employment and on retaining the social position which they had temporarily enjoyed during the war. Even prior to the World War Italian nationalism had been growing in strength. The attack on Tripoli in 1911 had been a symptom of the new spirit astir in the Italian peninsula. The entrance of Italy into the World War had been another indication of the same thing. After the dramatic defeat of the Austro-Hungarian armies in the closing days of that conflict, the whole Italian people looked forward with confidence to the fulfilment by the Peace Conference of the promises made to the Italian government by France and Great Britain at the time it entered the war. The more ardent nationalists, as we have seen, sought not only to acquire the territories promised to their government in the Treaty of London—the Trentino, Southern Tyrol, Trieste, and northern Dalmatia—but the city of Fiume, southern Dalmatia, a foothold in Albania, the Dodecanese Islands, and a base and an economic sphere in Asia Minor.

To these ardent nationalists peace proved disappointing. The military struggle left Italy in a worse economic situation than that of any of the other victorious powers. Fearful of demoralizing industry and arousing the hostility of the capitalists and the workers, the government hesitated to reduce expenditures and was spending approximately three times as much as it received. The public services were crowded with useless employees. Many returned soldiers could find no work. Prices were rising faster than wages. The Socialists quickly seized the opportunity proffered to them. Taking advantage of the relaxation of the war régime, they consciously emulated their Russian comrades and fomented a revolutionary agitation. Strikes and riots broke out in every trade. In the election of 1919 the Socialists doubled their representation in the parliament. In local elections they captured control of many of the municipalities of northern Italy. In the autumn of 1920 these tendencies came to a climax in a series of economic disturbances. In September the metal-workers seized control of factories in various parts of northern Italy and attempted to operate them. About the same time the peasants in Sicily and other provinces tried to expropriate the large estates. After reaching this high pitch the movement began to subside. The workers found themselves unable to operate the factories, the majority of the Socialists began to listen to more moderate counsels, and the government made timely concessions.

At the same time a majority of the Italian people felt chagrined and humiliated over foreign affairs. The Peace Conference refused to concede the extreme territorial claims of the Italian nationalists, and left the question of the future of Fiume and Dalmatia to direct negotiations between Italy and Yugoslavia. In 1920 the governments of the two countries established a joint boundary-line, recognized the independence of Fiume, and gave Yugoslavia control of all Dalmatia except Zara, a town which was to have autonomy under the suzerainty of Italy. The Italian government then proceeded to expel from Fiume the picturesque D'Annunzio and his nationalist followers, who had defied the Peace Conference and occupied the city. In the same year the attacks of Albanian bands on Italian outposts and garrisons caused the Italian government to withdraw its troops from Albania and to recognize the freedom of all her soil except the island of Saseno, a position from which the government of Italy hoped to dominate the port of Avlona and the Strait of Otranto. The treaties concluded with the Turkish government, furthermore, handed control of the Dodecanese Islands and the port of Smyrna in Asia Minor to Greece, and the Turkish nationalist movement forced the Italian government to withdraw from Adalia.

The odium for the domestic disorder and the course of foreign affairs fell on the Italian parliamentary system. The multiplicity of parties made necessary the formation of coalitions which found difficulty in uniting on clear policies and feared to resort to radical measures. The returned officers resented the insults of the Socialists and other elements in Italian society that had opposed the entry of Italy into the World War. The capitalists and industrialists felt alarmed for their property. The nationalists blamed the government for its weakness and its surrender of Italian interests. Many felt that the time was ripe for new methods.

Certain elements among the Italian people attempted to take the situation into their own hands. Groups of ex-soldiers, intellectuals, nationalists, sons of wealthy men, and students tried to break up the strikes fomented by the Socialists and to intimidate their opponents by the administration of castor-oil, beatings, and even assassination. At first these groups were independent of each other. The one at Milan was organized by Benito Mussolini. Before the World War he had risen to a position of some prominence in the Socialist party by his work as an agitator and an editor. After the entrance of Italy into that struggle he had seen service for a time in the army. After the organization of these groups of self-constituted preservers of order he gradually captured control of the movement and organized those participating in it into a political party. From the followers of D'Annunzio they adopted war-cries and many symbols, such as the black shirt and the Roman salute. In the elections of 1919 the Fascisti, as they were called, met with no success, but two years later they obtained thirty-five seats in the parliament. Though their membership had risen to approximately four hundred thousand by 1922, the old political leaders of Italy hardly took them seriously.

The situation, however, changed rapidly. In October, 1922, Mussolini convened a congress of the party at Naples for the purpose of making the movement appear national in scope and impressing southern Italy. Forty thousand members of the party attended. Their leader demanded that the government should settle the internal and external problems of Italy or resign. When the government paid little heed to their threats, the Fascists seized control of prefectures, police headquarters, and railroad and telegraph lines in many localities and, assembling at Civitavecchia, a place a little north of Rome, they marched on the city. The ministry wished to declare martial law, but at the suggestion of certain Conservatives the King refused to sign the decree and invited Mussolini to take office as Prime Minister at the head of a coalition cabinet, which at first included only three other Fascists.

The new cabinet immediately asked for full powers until the end of 1923, in order to enable it to carry through its program. It proposed a reduction of expenditures, reform of the civil service, a new system of taxation, and a firmer tone in foreign affairs. Threatened with its assumption of the necessary powers in any case, the Italian parliament authorized the ministry to carry out its program. The cabinet thereupon weeded out many old and incapable officials, revised appointments made since 1915, abolished many abuses, effected drastic economies of various sorts, reorganized taxation, and attempted to encourage economic activity.

At the same time Mussolini and his associates in the Fascist party took steps to gain complete control of the machinery of government. They gradually placed members of their party in office as prefects and police officials and in public departments, and eliminated the Socialists, Communists, and members of other parties that had been in control of the government. In the summer of 1923 they introduced a bill designed to remedy the situation created by the multiplicity of parties, which had hitherto prevented the parliament from functioning effectively. It provided that the party obtaining a plurality of votes in the whole nation should be given two thirds of all the seats in each constituency regardless of the local vote, the remaining third of the seats in the parliament being distributed among the other parties according to their electoral strength. After some hesitation the Italian parliament accepted the proposed bill and by this action practically terminated its own existence. In the ensuing elections, held in April, 1924, the Italian people seemed to ratify the policies of the new government. The Fascist party picked its candidates with great care and in many places took measures designed to insure their election. The electoral results surprised even the Fascists, for they obtained nearly two thirds of the popular vote.

In spite of this overwhelming victory, however, the Fascists still had a good many opponents in the parliament. These attacked the lawlessness of the Fascists and condemned their measures as unconstitutional. In May, Giacomo Matteotti, a Socialist deputy who had threatened to expose the Fascist party, suddenly disappeared. Later the public discovered that he had been spirited away by a group of Fascists with a shady past, and finally found his burial-place. The opponents of the Fascist party attempted to use the incident to upset the government. Drawing on their knowledge of Roman history, they withdrew from the Chamber of Deputies to the Aventine Hill. The Fascist régime suddenly lost much of its popularity. The press attacked the Facists bitterly and many of them deserted their party. Mussolini, however, handled the situation with great skill. He took steps to remedy the conditions responsible for the assassination of Matteotti, treated the remaining members of the Chamber of Deputies as a parliament, waited until dissensions broke the unity of the opposition, and then refused to allow the seceding deputies to take their places in the Chamber of Deputies again.

After they had successfuly met this crisis Mussolini and his associates set to work to make Italy a Fascist state. They applied the press law passed the previous year and bought or suppressed the opposition news-papers. They struck at the power of the Freemasons by ordering all as-sociations to communicate their statutes and membership lists, and for-bade civil servants to join the organization. They enacted legislation authorizing the government to deprive opponents living abroad of citizen-ship and even of property. With the purpose of centralizing political power, they placed Rome under the control of an appointed governor and an advisory council, and finally put all communes under the administration of appointed podestàs. Considering uninterrupted production essential for such a poor state as Italy, they enacted legislation that made strikes and lockouts illegal, intrusted labor tribunals with jurisdiction over labor disputes, and made the Fascist organizations the legal representatives of the employers and their employees. In 1928 the government radically mod-ified the existing electoral system. It passed a law which empowered thir-teen national confederations of employers and employees to send to the grand council of the Fascist party a list of eight hundred names to be considered for membership in the Chamber of Deputies. From this list and other names the council was to choose a list of four hundred candi-dates to be submitted to the voters for their approval. In the same year they made the Fascist party a legal and inseparable part of the state by intrusting it with important constitutional functions.

The greatest achievement of the Fascist party has been the apparent settlement of the Roman question. As early as 1926 Mussolini expressed a desire to find a solution for the vexed problem of the relations of the papacy and the Italian state. After protracted negotiations the representa-tives of the Italian government and the Pope concluded a political treaty, a concordat, and a financial agreement. The political treaty constituted the territory left under the control of the Pope in 1870 as a tiny inde-pendent state, and placed at its disposal such public services as telegraph, telephone, wireless, broadcasting, and postal facilities. The concordat recognized the marriages of Roman Catholics as a sacrament to be regu-lated by the laws of the Church and made religious instruction compul-sory for their children in the elementary and secondary schools. The financial agreement indemnified the Pope for the loss of territory suf-fered by the papacy in 1870.

In each of the three states, Great Britain, France, and Italy, the post-war problems have taken a somewhat different form and the current of events has followed a distinct course. In Great Britain the most striking events have been the solution of the age-old Irish problem and the rise of the Labor party to a position of great political power. In France the successive governments have struggled especially with the problems of balancing the budget and assuring the security of the country. In Italy the economic depression and irritation over the outcome of the Peace

Conference gave an opportunity for the rise of the Fascist party to political power. Since coming into office it has obtained complete control of the state and has apparently settled the vexed question of the relations of the papacy and the Italian government.

CHAPTER XXIX

THE GERMAN REPUBLIC

The German people did not long give unanimous support to the war policy of the imperial government. Even in August, 1914, several Social Democrats in their party caucus opposed the policy of voting in favor of the war credits requested by the authorities of the empire. In December of that year Karl Liebknecht actually defied party discipline and voted against the extension of further war credits to the government. In the following year a score of Social Democrats followed his example and an equal number abstained from voting. The question finally split the Social Democratic party into the Majority Socialists, who continued to support the war policy of the government, and the Independent Socialists, who opposed it. On the extreme left wing developed the Sparticists, a radical group headed by Karl Liebknecht and Rosa Luxemburg, which took its name from the *Spartacus Letters* which began to appear on the occasion of the fifty-seventh birthday of the Emperor. In these letters Karl Liebknecht and his associates denounced the war and summoned the German people to prevent its prosecution. After the failure of the German peace offer in 1916 and of the subsequent intervention of the Pope in behalf of a cessation of hostilities, the Majority Socialists and the Roman Catholic Center party joined the opposition to the government and began to work together in the parliament for the termination of the war.

The opponents of the imperial government found fertile ground in which to sow their propaganda. Defeat, decimation, and deprivation gradually destroyed the morale of the German people. The blockade maintained by the Entente powers eventually brought millions of Germans to a condition approaching starvation. In the last two years of the World War, in consequence, the death-rate, particularly among the old and the young, rose steadily. Many articles of food disappeared entirely from German tables. Bread, butter, milk, sugar, meat, eggs, and potatoes were carefully rationed. In 1916 the potato-crop failed and the German people attempted to substitute coarse fodder turnips for potatoes. The government system of distributing food frequently broke down entirely. The rich obtained illegally most of the necessaries and some of the luxuries of life, while the mass of the

448

people in the cities suffered from chronic hunger and discomfort. At the same time the troops grew weary of the mud, vermin, and inadequate living-quarters of the trenches, the arrogance of the officers, and the frightful casualties which seemed to bring peace no nearer. In January, 1918, these conditions caused a half-million workers to strike. The government retaliated by drafting many of the striking workers into the army, where they did much to increase the spirit of discontent.

After 1917 outside forces contributed toward the undermining of the position of the imperial government. As soon as they had gained control of the political machinery in Russia the Bolshevists sent emissaries, well supplied with money, into Germany to carry on a campaign of revolutionary propaganda. After the signing of the Treaty of Brest Litovsk, the Russian embassy at Berlin attempted to incite a revolutionary movement in Germany by the distribution of arms, money, and Communist literature. After the entrance of the United States into the World War the speeches and the state papers of President Wilson penetrated into Germany and set many Germans thinking about the political organization and the foreign policy of their country.

I

THE GERMAN REVOLUTION

As a result of these conditions, the military defeat of the German army on the western front in the summer and the fall of 1918 precipitated a revolution. The greater part of the German people held the heads of the imperial government responsible for the disasters that had overtaken Germany, and the Center party, the National Liberals, and the Majority Socialists began to work together for the establishment of parliamentary and democratic institutions. In an effort to save himself the Emperor invited Prince Max of Baden, a man long considered a Liberal, to become Chancellor of the empire. In October the new Chancellor formed a coalition ministry, which included two Majority Socialists, and took steps which promised to democratize the governments of the empire, Prussia, and Alsace-Lorraine. These concessions, however, came too late. The German people had already begun to demand the abdication of the Emperor. On October 23 the leader of the Independent Socialists voiced this demand on the floor of the Reichstag. Two days later the influential middle-class *Frankfurter Zeitung* advocated the abdication of both the Emperor and the Crown Prince as a means of satisfying the demands of President Wilson. On the evening of October 29 the Emperor fled in alarm from Berlin to the headquarters of the German army at Spa.

The German government, however, had already unwittingly provoked a revolutionary movement. For some time the morale of the German battle-fleet had been deteriorating. The sailors came from regions where Socialism was strong. They resented the attitude of their officers, suffered at times for want of food, and grew weary of their monotonous task. The entry of the United States into the war and the German defeat on the western front completed the disintegrating process. On October 28, 1918, the Admiralty brought the discontent to a head by ordering the fleet to steam out of the harbor of Wilhelmshaven for the purpose of facilitating the retreat through Belgium of the German forces on the western front. Feeling that they were about to be recklessly sacrificed to prevent the surrender of the German navy, the sailors of the battle-fleet mutinied and refused to permit the ships to proceed. When the government arrested some of the leaders of the mutineers and dispersed the fleet the sailors of the squadron sent to Kiel decided, in a meeting held ashore, to effect the release of their comrades, refused to return on board their ships, and armed themselves. On November 5 the revolutionary movement spread from the sailors to the Socialist shipyard workers, and the government found itself compelled to yield to the principal demands of the revolutionists. From Kiel the revolution spread to the cities, towns, and naval stations along the German coast. Everywhere the revolutionists organized councils of workers and sailors, disarmed naval and military officers, drove imperial officials from their posts, and held popular demonstrations.

Meanwhile the revolt had also broken out in Bavaria. On November 3 the veteran Independent Socialist leader, Kurt Eisner, had called a meeting to protest against the prolongation of the war. At its close the crowd actually effected the release of those who earlier in the year had been arrested for striking. Other great demonstrations followed. On November 7 a hundred thousand persons assembled in a great outdoor meeting and demanded the abdication of the Emperor. The garrison soon joined the revolt and the revolutionary leaders organized councils of peasants, workmen, and soldiers, and proclaimed the establishment of a people's state in Bavaria. The royal family fled from the city, and a few days later the King formally abdicated.

The events in Bavaria gave the signal for a general revolt against the imperial government. On November 8 most of the cities of southern and central Germany rose, and the demand for the abdication of the Emperor became general. The old governments found themselves powerless to stay the revolution. At Berlin the Independent Socialists had for some time been planning an uprising. On the night of November 8 the city seemed to be on the eve of a serious revolt. Armed revolutionists had entered the city, arms had been distributed by the Independent Socialists, and a majority of the workmen of Berlin were prepared for a rising. Forces of the government patrolled the streets of the city and held strategic points. On the following morning a general strike broke out spontaneously in the factories, and a little later the garrison began to mutiny and to elect soldiers' councils. For several days the Chancellor had been attempting to convince the Emperor at army headquarters of the seriousness of the situation and of the necessity of his abdicating. William II, however, supposed that he could still depend on the army and remained deaf to the pleas and arguments of his minister. At last Prince Max of Baden took the serious step of announcing without authorization the abdication of the Emperor. He hoped by this action to preserve peace and the monarchical principle. The announcement came too late. Pressed on by the course of events, the leaders of the Majority Socialists informed the Chancellor that they must be intrusted with the government in order to save Germany. On November 9, accordingly, the Chancellor handed over political power to the Majority Socialists, who proclaimed a "people's government." Meanwhile the Emperor had finally realized his desperate situation and had fled to Holland for safety. After his departure the other princes of Germany soon found their positions untenable, and abdicated.

2

THE STRUGGLE FOR POWER

The revolution placed the control of the political machinery of Germany, for the time being, in the hands of the Majority Socialists. Recognizing the necessity for the Socialists' presenting a united front against the upper and middle classes of Germany, the Independent Socialists demanded a place in the government and the acceptance of their political program. On November 10, 1918, the Majority Socialists accepted their demands and the two parties organized a cabinet of six commissioners, three from each Socialist group, which was at once recognized by the army, the bureaucracy, the principal federal states, and the overwhelming majority of the German people.

From the first the Socialists found themselves hopelessly divided. The Majority Socialists advocated the reëstablishment of order, the organization of a strong democratic government in Germany by a constitutional assembly elected by universal suffrage, the setting in motion again of the economic machinery of the country, and the conclusion of a just peace. They felt that the socialization of Germany must be postponed. The Independent Socialists also realized that the socialization of the country must be realized progressively, but they wished to intrust the execution of their program to the care of the workers' and soldiers' councils. They feared that the convening of a National Constitutional Convention would transfer political power to the upper and middle classes. The Spartacists scorned the Majority and the Independent Socialists as practical politicians and opportunists, and adopted the program of the Russian Bolshevists.

The fate of the provisional government depended on the attitude of the workers' and soldiers' councils which had sprung up spontaneously all over Germany during the revolution. The first general congress of these councils met on December 16, 1918. It proved to be a relatively conservative body. It rejected the demand of the Spartacists for the disarming of the army leaders and the arming of the revolutionary working classes, and refused to give full voting privileges to their leaders, Karl Liebknecht and Rosa Luxemburg. On the third day the congress took the decisive step of voting to convene a national assembly, transferred its legislative and executive power to the provisional government, and merely gave a central executive council supervision over the imperial and Prussian cabinets. The embittered Independent Socialists then made the mistake of leaving the hall. Their action enabled the Majority Socialists to gain complete control of the central council.

After their failure to have their way with the congress of soldiers' and workers' councils the Spartacists prepared to prevent the assembling of the proposed National Constitutional Convention. They regarded it as an obsolete inheritance from former middle-class revolutions which promised nothing to the proletariat of Germany. On December 30, 1918, they opened a convention of the party, which determined to establish a dictatorship of the proletariat at the risk of civil war and formulated a program designed to pave the way for the organization of a Communist régime. The armed struggle that resulted from this decision began on January 5, 1919, with the seizure of the principal newspaper offices, the Brandenburg Gate, the government printing-offices, several barracks, the railway-stations, and other public buildings. During the day many government troops surrendered their arms or declared their neutrality. Only the lack of military leadership prevented the Spartacists from gaining control of Berlin. The government, however, finally defeated the revolutionary movement. Under the direct leadership of Gustav Noske, it collected loyal troops and gradually recaptured the ground which it had lost. By January 15 the entire city was again under its control. The government forces marred their victory by callously assassinating Karl Liebknecht and Rosa Luxemburg, the principal instigators of the civil war.

After the suppression of the Communist revolt the government decided to hold the elections for the proposed national assembly on January 19, 1919. The old parties of pre-war days either disappeared or adopted new names and new policies. The German Nationalist party, composed of Pan-Germans, militarists, most of the members of the Junker class, and other reactionary elements, took the place of the former Conservative party and championed the monarchical principle and private ownership of property. The representatives of big business, led by Gustav Stresemann, organized the German People's party and adopted a program that condemned class rule, strikes, Socialism, Communism, and anarchy. The former Roman Catholic Center party became for the time being the Christian People's party. It advocated a democratic régime but opposed the establishment of a Socialist state. The left wing of the old National Liberal party and the former Progressive party united to form the German Democratic party and formulated a democratic and semisocialistic platform. The Social Democrats made no change in their name and urged the achievement of a socialized state by parliamentary methods. The Independent Socialists prepared to wage a bitter campaign against the Majority Socialists because of their alleged treason to Socialism. The Communists, to use the name which the Spartacists finally assumed, refused to take part in an electoral campaign. The elections favored the moderate parties. The Majority Socialists gained one hundred and sixty-five, the Christian People's party eighty-eight, and the German Democratic party seventy-five seats, while the German Nationalists won only forty-two, the Independent Socialists twenty-two, and the German People's party twenty-one seats. As a result of the elections the Majority Socialists gave up control of the government and joined with the Center and the Democratic parties in forming a cabinet known as the Weimar coalition.

3

THE NATIONAL ASSEMBLY

The provisional government decided to convene the newly elected National Constitutional Convention at Weimar instead of Berlin because of the cultural traditions of the former city and its removal from the monarchical past of Germany and from the recent scenes of civil war. The first acts of the assembled constitutional body were the election of Friedrich Ebert, leader of the Majority Socialists and head of the provisional government, as President of the German Republic, and the adoption of a temporary constitution. After months of work and discussion, on July 31, 1919, the National Constitutional Assembly finally adopted a permanent constitution for the German Republic.

The new constitution declared Germany to be a republic with all political power derived from the people, and required all of the eighteen

German states composing the German commonwealth to have a republican form of government. It reduced the rights and privileges of the states, and increased the power of the central government. It vested executive power in a President elected for a term of seven years by the vote of the whole German people. It provided that the President should exercise his wide powers through a Chancellor and a cabinet responsible for all the executive acts of the government. It entrusted legislative authority to a National Assembly and a National Council. The delegates to the National Assembly were to be elected for a term of four years by the universal, equal, direct, and secret suffrage of the men and women of Germany over twenty years of age. The National Council represents the German States. In this body each state has at least one vote, the larger states one vote for every million inhabitants. No state may have more than two fifths of the votes in the upper house. In Prussia half of the representatives are at the disposal of the provincial administrations and half are members of the Prussian cabinet. The other states are represented in the National Council only by members of their cabinets. The new constitution made the National Assembly the predominant power in legislation. The National Council may object to laws passed by the National Assembly and cause their return to that body, but a two thirds vote of the lower house obligates the President to promulgate the measure as a law or to refer it to the people. In case two thirds of its membership are in attendance the National Assembly may amend the constitution by a vote of two thirds of the members present, but the National Council may compel the submission of an amendment to the vote of the people. The constitution also provided for the referendum and the initiative. The President, one third of the National Assembly, or one twentieth of the qualified voters may compel the submission of legislative proposals for popular approval, and one tenth of the voters may compel by petition the reference of a measure to a popular vote.

Although not constituting a majority of the National Constitutional Assembly, both the Socialists and the Center party left their impress on the new constitution. The document makes it the duty of the government of the commonwealth to acquire the ownership of railways and waterways. It provides for the representation of wage-earners and salaried employees in factory, district, and national workers' councils for the purpose of looking after their social and economic interests, and for the meeting of the district and national workers' councils with representatives of employers and other interested classes of people in district and national economic councils empowered to consider proposed economic legislation. The constitution also provides for the establishment of private schools under state supervision, and for making religious instruction a part of the regular school curriculum. It leaves the participation of the pupils in the religious instruction to the decision of their parents. On August 11, 1919, the German government promulgated the new constitution.

4

THE FIGHT FOR THE MAINTENANCE OF THE REPUBLIC

The Weimar constitution was a compromise that gave satisfaction only to the moderate elements of Germany. The German government, consequently, has had to fight to maintain the republic against the Communists on the one hand and the Monarchists on the other. For some time the situation in Germany favored the growth of the Communist party. The Allied blockade was still in force, food was scarce, industry was at a standstill, many demobilized soldiers could find nothing to do, the currency had begun to depreciate, rumors of drastic peace terms commenced to circulate in Germany, and the German people suffered from the depression and weariness of the war years. During 1919, in consequence, the Communist agitation gave rise to riots, strikes, and uprisings, which harassed and threatened the stability of the republican government. Under the leadership of Noske, however, the government succeeded in suppressing the armed risings of the Communists. Since the summer of 1919 the latter have confined their demonstrations to parades, the singing of songs, and the flaunting of banners. They have grown to be a considerable parliamentary group, the party at one time holding sixty-two seats in the National Assembly, but they have lost much of their driving force. Their movement, however, has helped to strengthen the Monarchists.

After the suppression of the Communists the Conservative extremists began to organize for the overthrow of the republic. The publication of the humiliating terms of the Treaty of Versailles and the reduction of the size of the German army furnished new recruits for the movement. In March, 1920, the reactionaries openly revolted against the legal government. On the morning of March 13, General Baron von Lüttwitz, one of the military commanders, seized control of Berlin with the aid of marines and about eight thousand soldiers of an irregular Army of the Baltic that had refused to disband, and proclaimed Dr. Wolfgang Kapp, a former East Prussian official, Chancellor. Although the legal government was forced to flee in haste to Dresden and on to Stuttgart, the so-called *Putsch* proved a complete failure. Many of the Monarchists, the greater part of the army, and the propertied classes failed to rally round the leaders of the revolt, and a general strike called by the legal government stopped the gas, water, and electrical services, the railroads, and the street-cars, and paralyzed the normal life of the country. Under the pressure of the working classes the revolutionary movement collapsed.

The Monarchist agitation, however, continued to harass the German Republic. The legend arose that the ills of Germany grew out of the defeat of the German army, which was asserted to have been stabbed in the back by the republican revolutionary movement. The Monarchists also began a campaign of assassination. In 1921 they assassinated Matthias Erzberger, the brilliant leader of the Center party, the chief German delegate in drawing up the armistice, and a signer of the Treaty of Versailles. In 1922 they murdered Dr. Walther Rathenau, the most prominent Jew in Germany and one of the ablest men in the republic. They planned to kill other prominent persons, including the President of Germany. In 1920 the elections revealed the growth of the opposition to the republic. The Majority Socialists lost fifty seats, the Center party, twenty-one, and the Democrats, thirty. The Nationalists increased their representation by twenty-four, and the German People's party, by forty-one. As a result of the election the Weimar cabinet was reorganized so as to include members of the German People's party. The Majority Socialists supported the new ministry but did not form a part of it. Since that date the economic difficulties of Germany have favored the growth of the more conservative parties. The German Nationalists have become the second strongest party in the state, and the National Socialists, led by Adolf Hitler, have grown rapidly in strength. In 1927, however, the German Nationalists were forced to recognize the republic as the only form of government admissible under existing conditions in Germany.

For a time a change in the Presidency caused grave concern to the friends of the Republic. In 1925 the death of President Ebert made necessary the selection of a new head of the state. In the first elections seven candidates divided the popular vote. As none of them had received the requisite majority, the German parties formed two political coalitions for the second election stipulated by the constitution. The Center, Democratic, and Social Democratic parties put forward as their candidate the leader of the Center party. The German Nationalist and the German People's parties unexpectedly united on the popular hero, General von Hindenburg. His name carried the election. His success has had the unexpected effect of strengthening the republic. He took the oath of loyalty to the constitution without qualification and has done much to win the less reactionary elements among the Monarchists for the republic. By his character and conduct he has made himself the moral leader of the new Germany.

Notwithstanding these developments, the moderate parties have continued to remain in control of the machinery of government. In this work the Center party and the Majority Socialists have taken a decisive part, the Center party by its unwavering loyalty to the republic, and the Majority Socialists by their tacit support of a succession of moderate ministries in which they did not participate. In 1923 the Independent Socialists ceased to be a separate party. The greater part of its members reunited with the Majority Socialists to form the United Social Democratic party. The extremists gravitated to the Communist party.

5

THE FALL OF THE MARK

The German government also has had to contend with serious financial problems. In 1919 the value of German currency began to decline. The republic inherited from the imperial régime an inflated medium of exchange. After the conclusion of the armistice the policy of inflation was continued. Faced by the need of paying extensive unemployment doles, purchasing food and raw materials, and making reparation payments, the German government shrank from the obvious remedy of increasing the taxation of war profiteers and other persons of wealth, and printed more marks. By June, 1919, as a consequence, the mark had declined from five to the dollar to sixty. By November, 1922, it had sunk to seven thousand to the dollar. For a time Germany experienced a false prosperity based in part on her ability to undersell foreign competitors, and in part on her need for goods of all sorts. The ultimate effect of the decline of the mark, however, was disastrous. People delayed the payment of taxes for months to get the full benefit of the decline, and upset the government budget still further. Business men hastened to transform their German money into goods or to exchange it for foreign currency before it lost its purchasing power. The cost of living rose rapidly, and wages lagged far behind prices. The situation benefited shrewd industrialists but impoverished the middle classes and weakened the resistance of the workers. Taking advantage of the cheap labor, easy loans, and rapidly falling currency, the more far-seeing made safe investments, enlarged and modernized their plants, and paid off their indebtedness. The middle classes and the trade-unions lost their savings and accumulated funds.

When in 1923 the situation became so bad that the merchants and the farmers refused to sell their commodities, the government at last took remedial measures. In November it intrusted a new currency commissioner with the task of stabilizing the old mark and introducing a new rentenmark. As a first step he stopped the printing of the old marks and issued the new currency, supposedly based on a mortgage of all the wealth of Germany. The government meanwhile took steps to balance the budget. It began to calculate taxes on a gold basis, improved its method of collecting them, decreased the number of government employees, cut salaries, and stopped the payment of reparation. Though the new policy entailed much hardship, it ultimately restored an orderly economic life in the country.

6

THE ECONOMIC RECOVERY OF GERMANY

After the stabilization of the currency Germany began to recover her former economic position. The World War had not been fought on German soil, and the mines, factories, and railroads of Germany had in no way been harmed. The fall of the mark did nothing to diminish the real wealth of the country, transferred much property to Germans through the sale abroad of worthless currency and securities, and enabled German industrialists to expand and modernize their plants. The adoption of the Dawes Plan furnished Germany the needed international credit to stimulate her into economic activity. Under its influence Germany began to utilize her water-power to replace her lost coal-deposits, to improve her methods of steel-manufacture, to put her rolling-stock in condition again, and to regain her former position in shipping. After 1929, however, the world-wide economic crisis bore with especial severity upon the German government and its citizens.

Since the close of the World War Germany has devoted her energies largely to the task of establishing the republic. The military defeat of the monarchy gave rise to a republican movement that overthrew the former rulers of Germany, and led to the establishment of democratic governments in the empire and in the states of Germany. The new republic, however, has had to overcome many obstacles. The advocates of the immediate socialization of Germany attempted in vain to prevent the holding of a National Constitutional Convention. After adopting the most democratic constitution in Europe the new republic had to contend with the determined opposition of the Communists and of the Monarchists, the heritage of social and economic ills left by the war and defeat, the problem of reparation payments, and the fall of the mark. In the years that have intervened since the war the moderate parties have succeeded in retaining control of the machinery of government, the Communists have lost something of their initial vigor, and the Monarchists have in part become reconciled to the republic, the reparation burden has been adjusted to fit the capacity of Germany to pay, and the economic revival has begun. Since 1929, however, Germany has suffered even more than other countries from the world-wide economic depression.

CHAPTER XXX

The revolution of November, 1917, as we have seen, gave a pre-carious hold on a part of the former Russian Empire to the Bolshevists, a party committed to a revolutionary social, economic, and religious program. Before it lay the task of establishing itself firmly in power and of inaugurating its plans for Russian society. After concluding the Treaty of Brest Litovsk with Germany on March 3, 1918, accordingly, the Bolshevist leaders turned their attention to the problem of gaining control of the Russian Empire and its peoples.

I

THE BOLSHEVISTS GAIN CONTROL OF RUSSIA

The Bolshevists quickly alienated the peasants of Russia. They neutralized the effect of the decree of November 8, 1918, nationalizing the large estates for the benefit of the dissatisfied peasantry, by the measures which they took to insure the Russian workers in the cities a sufficient supply of food. They sent into the villages under their control armed bands commissioned to seize food supplies. The threatened peasants tried to hide or to destroy their grain and in some instances they took up arms in self-defense. The Bolshevist authorities neutral-ized the opposition of the peasantry, however, by setting the richer and poorer peasants at odds. Dividing them into classes, the Bolshevists organized the peasants without cattle or grain into committees of the poor empowered to see that the richer peasants did not hide their grain and cattle. The resulting social strife practically destroyed, for the time being, the political influence of the peasants.

The Bolshevists soon found their authority restricted and opposed by the former allies of Russia, the Czechoslovak troops on the Russian front, and the other Russian political parties. After the signing of the Treaty of Brest Litovsk, the United States, France, and Great Britain sent troops to Murmansk and Archangel to prevent the military sup-plies there, which had been forwarded to these ports to aid in the prose-cution of the war, from falling into the hands of Germany. Under the protection of these foreign forces a provisional government hostile to the Bolshevist régime was organized in northern Russia. The inhabitants of the region, however, failed to rally to its support and many soldiers in the small army organized by the provisional government deserted to the side of the enemy. Upon the withdrawal of the Allied military forces in September, 1919, the provisional government collapsed and the Bolshevists occupied northern Russia.

In western Russia the Finns, Estonians, Letts, Lithuanians, and Poles had seized the opportunity offered by the Russian Revolution to demand their independence. In the Treaty of Brest Litovsk the Bolshevists had been forced by Germany to recognize the independence of Finland, Estonia, Latvia, Lithuania, and Poland. In Estonia, General Nikolay Yudenich, with British aid, collected an army, and attempted to set up a provisional government in northwestern Russia. In October, 1919, his troops advanced to a point within sight of Petrograd, only to be driven back. Thereupon Estonia quarreled with General Yudenich and made peace with the Bolshevists.

For a time the Bolshevists lost control of Siberia and of Russia east of the Volga and Kama rivers. While Russia was still a participant in the World War, a military force numbering forty-three thousand troops had been organized from Czech and Slovak prisoners of war for service on the Russian front. After the withdrawal of Russia from the conflict the Czechoslovak National Council at Paris asked for permission to transfer these troops to France, and in March, 1918, it concluded an agreement with the Bolshevist government for their transportation by way of the Trans-Siberian Railroad. After the trains bearing the Czechoslovak troops were strung out from eastern Russia to Manchuria, the German government apparently protested against the agreement as an infringement of the Treaty of Brest Litovsk, and the local soviets became fearful lest the Czechoslovak troops should join the counter-revolution, and tried to disarm them. Thereupon the Czechoslovak forces seized control of the Trans-Siberian Railroad and all the principal cities between the Volga River and Vladivostok. At the same time soldiers of Japan and the United States occupied Vladivostok with the avowed objects of preventing the seizure of the military supplies accumulated there, protecting the Czechoslovak troops against the attacks of Austrian and German prisoners, and supporting any Russian attempt to establish self-government and a new fighting front. Under the protection of the Czechoslovak troops a group of members of the prorogued Duma organized a provisional government at Omsk, which formed an army that held for a time a line of positions along the Volga and Kama rivers in eastern Russia. In November, 1919, however, the military men became impatient with the Socialists and Social Revolutionaries in the provisional government, seized political power in Siberia, selected Admiral Kolchak as dictator, and threw into prison all persons who resisted his rule. The new leader lacked the appeal and the moral authority of the overthrown government; the peasants, soldiers, and town laborers became hostile; the war began to go against him; and in the end his power crumbled. A semi-Bolshevist revolutionary committee obtained control of affairs in the rear of the army of Admiral Kolchak, cut him off from his troops, and arrested, tried, and finally, in February, 1920, executed him. The military forces of the Bolshevists, however, did not gain complete control of the region east of Lake Baikal in Siberia until after the withdrawal of the Japanese troops in 1922.

In southern Russia the Bolshevists soon found themselves confronted by both a revolutionary and a counter-revolutionary movement. In January, 1918, the Ukraine proclaimed itself an independent republic. From the first it was under the domination of representatives of the central powers. After the withdrawal of the German army the new republic fell for a time under the control of a Socialist chieftain. At the same time elsewhere in southern Russia, Cossacks, former officers of the imperial army, cadets, and university students organized a military force, led by General Anton Denikin, which gained control for a time of a considerable area. After the close of the World War this army received aid in the form of arms and supplies from the British and actual military assistance from the French. Aided by widespread peasant uprisings, it at one time made a serious advance on Moscow, but was finally repulsed.

In an effort to save himself from defeat, General Baron Ferdinand Wrangel, the new commander of the anti-Bolshevist forces in southern Russia, made overtures to Poland. At first the Poles met with considerable success in their campaign against the Bolshevists, and took Kiev, the capital of the Ukraine. Later the Bolshevist military forces drove them back to the outskirts of Warsaw and forced them to appeal to France and Great Britain for help. With the aid received from these sources the Poles in turn made a successful counter-attack. Finally in October, 1920, the Poles and the Bolshevists made peace. Realizing that he could not withstand the Bolshevists with the military forces under his command, General Wrangel evacuated southern Russia.

The civil war and foreign intervention transformed Russia into a military power again. For a time after the disintegration of the imperial armies the Bolshevists depended on regiments of Communist workmen hastily organized into a rather undisciplined Red Army. The civil war and foreign intervention made necessary the formation of a more effective military force. In June, 1918, consequently, the Bolshevist authorities reëstablished conscription. Many former imperial officers returned to the army because of either patriotism or lack of other means of earning a living. The intervention of Poland in the civil war caused a revival of national feeling in Russia and rallied many persons opposed to the Bolshevist régime to the side of the government. As a result of these developments a well-equipped, well-trained army was finally developed in Russia under the leadership of Trotski, as Commissar of War.

The civil war and foreign intervention also gave rise to a reign of terror in Russia. In order to purge the country of enemies of the revolution the Bolshevists developed an organization popularly known as the Cheka, which was empowered to arrest, try, and shoot all persons considered dangerous. After an attempt on the life of Lenin in August, 1918, this body instituted a reign of terror which resulted in the arrest and imprisonment of thousands of persons. It resorted to the methods of the Tsarist police and to the use of spies. It arrested persons on suspicion and then either gave them their freedom or, without explanation, stood them before a firing-squad. It seized the relatives of suspected persons as hostages and often executed them. Among its victims were the Tsar and his family. After the abdication of the Tsar the members of the imperial family had twice been moved for greater safety and the government finally transferred them to Ekaterinburg. During the excitement incident to the advance of the army of Kolchak, the local soviet seems to have ordered their execution.

2

THE GOVERNMENT OF BOLSHEVIST RUSSIA

The revolution of November, 1917, professed to place political power in Russia in the hands of the soviets, the committees composed of representatives of different parties that had sprung up spontaneously at the time of the March Revolution in the armies, the towns, and the rural villages. This made the All-Russian Congress of Soviets nominally the highest political authority in the state. Immediately after the November Revolution the second Congress of Soviets recognized the authority of the provisional government set up by Lenin and his Bolshevist associates, known as the Council of the People's Commissars. On July 10, 1918, the fifth Congress of Soviets finally adopted the constitution of the Russian Socialist Federative Soviet Republic.

This document nominally put political power in the hands of the Russian workers. It admitted to the franchise productive workers, and the housekeepers of soldiers, sailors, and productive workers, who had reached the age of eighteen. These provisions deprived of the vote persons who employed hired labor for their own profit, individuals who had an income from a source other than their own labor, private merchants and brokers, monks and the clergy of all denominations, employees and agents of the former Tsarist police and secret service, members of the former reigning family, and criminals, lunatics, and persons under guardianship. These restrictions excluded from the suffrage the aristocracy and the middle classes, or a number estimated to be about 8 per cent of the total population. In the main the active citizens were organized by the provisions of the constitution into vocational rather than regional groups, the peasants, the soldiers, and the workers in a particular industry or factory voting together. They vote, however, by show of hands, a method which permits intimidation of the voters.

The constitution created a hierarchy of soviets, congresses, and executive committees. The active voters were to elect rural and urban soviets for the conduct of local government. Representation in the bodies above the village and the city soviets was to be indirect. The peasants were to send representatives directly or indirectly to district, county, regional, and provincial congresses of soviets, the urban workers only to the regional and provincial congresses. The district and county congresses were thus to represent the peasants alone, the regional and provincial congresses were to contain representatives of both the peasants and the urban workers. A disproportionate weight, however, was given to the votes of the individual urban workers.

The constitution nominally intrusted control of the central government to the All-Russian Congress of Soviets, a body composed of representatives chosen by the urban soviets and by the provincial soviets. But while the urban delegates each represented twenty-five thousand voters, the provincial delegates each represented one hundred and twenty-five thousand inhabitants. This arrangement gave the individual urban worker not only a double vote but a disproportionate amount of influence. The All-Russian Congress of Soviets is a large and cumbersome body. Between sessions it delegates its authority to the Central Executive Committee. This body in turn really intrusts the management of the Russian Socialist Federative Soviet Republic to the Council of People's Commissars, a sort of cabinet. Since the constitution makes no distinction between administrative and legislative functions, this body both makes and executes the laws.

This governmental machinery is controlled by the Bolshevists, known since the revolution as the Communist party. This militant organization is composed of a carefully selected body of workers, which is ready to make great sacrifices for the Communist cause and is bound together by a strong, centralized discipline. From time to time the party weeds out the members undesirable because of disloyalty, loose conduct in private life, slackness in zeal, corruption, criticism of the party, or association with suspected persons. This policy of careful selection makes the members of the party the shock-troops of the revolution. They are organized in the first place into local "cells" in villages, factories, and so on. These organizations send representatives to an annual congress which elects the executive machinery of the party. This includes a central committee of about sixty members, a political bureau of nine members which directs the policy of the party, and a control commission to purify the party. Until his death in 1924, Lenin, its founder, actually dominated the whole organization. After his death a short, sharp struggle resulted in the rise of Joseph Stalin to power.

After the close of the period of civil war and foreign intervention, the Communist masters of Russia felt that the time had come for the creation of additional political machinery. After the collapse in 1919 of the counter-revolutionary movement in southern Russia, the Bolshevists overran the Ukraine and established a Ukrainian Socialist Soviet Republic. About the same time they organized a White Russian Republic in order to win the sympathy of White Russia. By the close of 1922 they had aided in one way or another in the creation of four other Socialist soviet republics with institutions similar to those developed in the Russian Socialist Federative Soviet Republic. The tenth All-Russian Congress of Soviets, accordingly, declared in favor of a Union of Socialist Soviet Republics and appointed delegates to collaborate with representatives of the six allied republics in the drafting of a treaty of federation. On July 6, 1923, the new treaty went into effect. It created a Union Congress of Soviets, similar to the All-Russian Congress of Soviets, a Union Central Executive Committee, a bicameral body composed of about four hundred representatives of the signatory republics and one hundred and thirty representatives of the numerous ethnic groups within the union, and a Union Council of Commissars consisting of a president, a vice-president, the chairman of the Supreme Economic Council, and commissars for foreign affairs, war and marine, foreign trade, ways and communications, posts and telegraphs, workers' and peasants' inspection, labor, food, and finance. The treaty gives these governmental organs practically a monopoly of political power except within the sphere of local government.

The Soviet régime makes no pretense of guaranteeing individual rights. It distinguishes in many ways between workers and non-workers. It favors the workers in the distribution of food, in voting, in the courts, and in the schools. It offers no protection against the invasion of the home. It does not establish freedom of the press, of assembly, or of conscience.

3

THE COMMUNIST ECONOMIC POLICY

The Communist party came into power committed to the economic ideas of Karl Marx. It stood, consequently, for the prevention of the exploitation of the workers by the capitalists and the landlords, and for the nationalization of all the means of production, trade, transportation, banking, and insurance. Immediately after the revolution of November, 1917, accordingly, the Communist leaders proclaimed the nationalization of the land and "workers' control" of industrial production and distribution.

The Decree of Land was promulgated at a time when an anarchical seizure of lands was already well under way. By the spring of 1918 the pillage and redistribution of estates, communal land, and peasant holdings was completed. The land within each county was parceled out on a numerical basis. As the counties varied greatly in respect to size, population, and amount of arable land, the new allotments varied greatly in area. The Decree of Land abolished private property and vested its control in the village community. Thenceforth the government regarded the peasant as a workman operating public land, seized his produce at will to feed the urban workers, and left him only enough grain to supply the needs of his family and the seed for the next sowing. As a result the peasant no longer had any desire to raise more crops than he needed for his own use and in consequence the cultivated area declined between 1916 and 1921 from eighty-six million to fifty-four million dessiatines (approximately 232,200,000, acres and 145,800,000 acres), the number of horses dropped from thirty-one million to twenty-four million, and the number of cattle from fifty million to less than thirty-seven million. In 1920 and 1921 a drought struck impoverished Russia and produced a terrible famine. In 1921 the harvest failed throughout all southern Russia. By the following year the situation threatened thirty-five million people with starvation, reduced fifteen million more to a state of semistarvation, and caused the death of from five million to nine million. The loss of life would have been greater except for the work of various relief agencies, and particularly that of Mr. Hoover, who organized and administered the American Relief Administration. This organization expended over sixty-one million dollars, furnished over seven hundred thousand tons of commodities, and fed at the time of greatest need over ten million men, women, and children daily.

The seizure of industry by the government had almost as unfortunate results as the confiscation of the land and its produce. The Communist leaders planned a gradual and systematic nationalization of large-scale industry and its concentration into trusts. The Russian people forestalled them by a haphazard seizure of the control of industry. In 1920, therefore, the government nationalized all industrial establishments employing more than five laborers and using mechanical power, and placed those below this limit under government control. A Supreme Economic Council took over the task of supplying industry with fuel, machinery, and raw materials, and the workers with food and other articles of consumption. Under the new economic system trade, banks, and money became unnecessary. The seizure of the factories produced industrial chaos. The workers lacked the training and the education necessary to conduct the factories and no longer had the old incentives for putting forth their best efforts. In spite of the introduction in 1918 of the principle of forced labor, production fell off alarmingly. In 1920, Russian industries produced only 13.2 per cent as much as in 1913.

The failure of the industrial workers to produce manufactured goods and of the peasants to raise food created widespread dissatisfaction, which expressed itself in risings of the sailors and the peasants and convinced the Communist leaders of the necessity of adopting a new economic policy to increase production. They promised to take henceforth only a definite proportion of the product of the labor of the peasants in the form of a tax and to permit them to dispose of the rest as they should see fit. They denationalized all industries employing less than fifteen workers, and somewhat later those giving work to twenty or less workers. They ceased to supply tools and raw materials to the factories, and attempted to attract foreign capital by economic concessions. In July, 1921, they decreed freedom of trade within Russia. They also introduced a stabilized currency. As a result of the new economic policy industry and agriculture reached their pre-war level by 1927.

The Communists, however, did not return completely to a capitalist economy. The new economic policy was characterized by an excessive governmental control. The state retained a monopoly of foreign trade, and did not reintroduce the right of ownership of small individual farms. After 1921 it attempted to guide and control the economic activities of the peasantry through coöperatives under its own control. These organizations operate farms, creameries, flour-mills, and rural activities. Through them the state attempts to equalize the differences between peasant households and to prevent the development of rich peasants.

4

THE RELIGIOUS POLICY OF THE COMMUNISTS

The Communists came into power avowed opponents of all religions. They considered religion as merely an "opiate of the people." They at once nationalized all lands and buildings belonging to the Eastern Orthodox Church and its monastic institutions, and forbade all ecclesiastical and religious associations to possess property. They turned over the buildings actually needed for purposes of worship to associations of twenty or more persons, but transformed many of the structures into schools, club-rooms, and museums. They stopped the payment of state subsidies to the Eastern Orthodox Church and compelled it to depend on voluntary contributions. They forbade public religious processions, abandoned the old Russian calendar in favor of the one in use in western Europe, and deprived the former state church of control of marriage, divorce, the registration of births and deaths, cemeteries, and schools. They put no restrictions on church attendance except for members of the Communist party.

The Communists have not succeeded, as yet, in extirpating religion in Russia. In spite of the attitude of the government the Eastern Orthodox Church has continued to christen, instruct, and bury the majority of the Russian peasants, and has remained the center of the village life in the rural districts. The revolution gave Protestant churches greater freedom than they had ever enjoyed, and the Baptists, the Methodists, and the Lutherans took advantage of the situation to extend their work. By 1929, according to the estimates of the Communists, the Protestant churches had made twenty million converts. Their activity stimulated the Eastern Orthodox Church to engage in a program of social-welfare work. This success of the various churches in Russia caused the government considerable alarm. In later decrees it attempted to restrict their social and educational work and to prevent the propagation of their religious views.

5

THE COMMUNISTS AND EDUCATION

Until 1905 popular education spread very slowly in imperial Russia. After the creation of the Duma it made rapid progress until the World War and the Revolution of 1917 checked its progress. The plans of the Duma called for the introduction of universal education by 1922. After the close of the civil war the Communists turned their attention to the problem. They look to the schools for the trained experts needed to take the places left vacant as a result of the persecution of the aristocracy and the middle classes, and for the new generation of loyal adherents to the Communist ideals. Their program also calls for universal education. At first the bankruptcy of the state, the civil war, foreign intervention, famine, and economic disorganization prevented much progress toward its realization. After the introduction of the new economic policy the educational plans of the Communists began to make progress. Russia became a vast laboratory of educational experimentation. By 1926 elementary education had again reached the level of 1914 and secondary, vocational, professional, and higher education showed a great growth in numbers. Much has been done for the backward nationalities of the Union of Socialist Soviet Republics. As yet, however, the elementary schools of Russia can accommodate only about three quarters of the children of school age. The plans of the Communist party call for the wiping out of illiteracy by 1933.

6

THE FOREIGN POLICY OF THE COMMUNISTS

For a time after their seizure of power in Russia the Communists had high hopes of bringing about the overthrow of all capitalist governments. They looked upon Russia at first as merely a base of operations. During the final months of the World War they zealously spread Communist propaganda among the war prisoners in Russia. After the close of this conflict they organized the Third International for the purpose of organizing and spreading Communism. In Europe they succeeded in establishing for brief periods Communist governments in Hungary and Bavaria, and in forming the more radical members of the Socialist and Labor parties of Europe into separate Communist parties. In Asia they sought to win the sympathy of its peoples by the surrender of the privileges, capitulations, extraterritorial rights, and concessions extorted from them by the Tsarist régime. They denounced the Anglo-Russian agreements of 1907 which divided Persia into spheres of influence, recognized the sovereignty of Afghanistan, and professed to surrender the special privileges won by Russia in China. After their victory over the opposing forces in eastern Siberia, however, they began to reëstablish Russia in its old position in Mongolia and in Manchuria. In the end their Communistic propaganda met with comparative failure. Asia lacked the industrial and intellectual classes that would naturally furnish recruits for Communism. In India and among the Moslems of other Asiatic countries religion proved an effective barrier against the spread of their doctrine. In China, however, the Communists won the support of considerable numbers among the intellectual and laboring classes.

The adoption of the new economic policy compelled the Russian government to change its foreign policy. Although it did not abandon entirely its propaganda against capitalist governments, the predominant immediate objective of the Communist leaders became the opening of trade relations with Europe as a means of hastening the economic revival of Russia. This change in Russian policy met with a favorable reception at the hands of the governments of Europe. The European political leaders believed the economic restoration of the Continent to be impossible without the coöperation of Russia. They needed her raw materials and her markets for manufactured products. Beginning in 1921, accordingly, the Communist leaders of Russia began to secure trade agreements with a number of the European states. In 1922 they obtained from Germany recognition of their government and the relinquishment of all German claims for debts and damages. Two years later, as a result of the coming into office of the Labor party in Great Britain and the radical party in France, Russia secured political recognition from a number of other states. In 1927 Great Britain again broke off diplomatic relations with Russia, only to resume them once more two years later.

7

RUSSIA UNDER THE SUCCESSORS OF LENIN

In January, 1924, death cut short the practical dictatorship exercised in Russia by Lenin. Although his words continued to be a sort of Bible for Russian Communists, his tomb became a Communist shrine, and Petrograd became Leningrad, his death raised the question of a successor. At first a triumvirate, composed of Communists of long standing, replaced Lenin. It had to contend with factions within the Communist party which threatened its unity. Deposed from power, Trotski, the most brilliant collaborator of Lenin, headed an opposition of the Left which accused the triumvirate of disloyalty to the ideals of pure Communism. Another faction wished the adoption of a policy that would swing Russia still further to the Right. From the intense debates engendered by these conflicts, Stalin, a member of the triumvirate and a man of firm will and excellent organizing ability, emerged as dictator of the Communist party. He used his power to silence or to banish his opponents.

Under his leadership the Soviet Union adopted in 1928 a Five Year Plan designed to enable Russia within a period of five years to supply her domestic needs and have a surplus for export. Stalin and his Communist associates hope to more than double the Russian output of iron ore, and to increase the production of coal from forty million six hundred thousand to seventy-five million tons, of steel from four million eight hundred thousand to nearly eleven million metric tons, and of petroleum from less than eighty-eight million to one hundred and ninety million barrels. They intend to raise the amount of electric power generated from six billion five hundred million to twenty-two billion kilowatt hours. They aim to increase the production of grain about a third. This program called for the construction of huge factories for the manufacture of automobiles, tractors, and agricultural machinery. The Communist leaders estimated that the execution of the gigantic plan would cost about thirty-two billion three hundred million dollars. They hoped to obtain this sum from the proceeds of industry, increases in exports, added taxation, particularly of the richer peasants, and the issue of paper money.

The Five Year Plan also aimed to increase the number of Soviet and collective farms. In 1928–1929 the Union of Socialist Soviet Republics was operating fifty-five gigantic farms covering an area of more than six million acres. In the following year the Communist leaders planned to increase the number of farms to one hundred and twenty and their area to fourteen million acres. They planned a still greater expansion of the collective farms. In 1928–1929 there were thirty thousand of these farms, each comprising the former farms of one thousand to five thousand peasants and operated with the aid of modern agricultural machinery. By the end of 1929 the Russian authorities hoped to quadruple their area. Within two or three years they hoped to complete the collectivization of Russian agriculture. In practice, however, they have found themselves unable to obtain the amount of machinery necessary to carry out their agricultural plans.

8

THE RUSSIAN BORDERLANDS

The World War gave a number of peoples formerly subject to the Russian Empire an opportunity to gain their freedom. One of the subject peoples to take advantage of the situation was the Finns. Upon the overthrow of the Tsar they declared their independence, asserting that the fall of this ruler severed the merely personal tie uniting Finland with Russia. Within a few weeks after taking this action they obtained recognition from Soviet Russia, Sweden, France, Germany, Norway, and Denmark. For a time, however, they suffered from civil war and foreign intervention. A radical wing of the Finnish Social Democrats attempted to introduce the soviet form of government and received assistance from Russia in the form of arms, munitions, and soldiers. Early in 1918 they gained control of all southern Finland. The middle and upper classes thereupon took up arms and, aided by German troops, defeated the Communist forces. After the close of the World War a reaction against Teutonic influences set in and the Finns established a republic with a President, a responsible ministry, and a diet of two hundred members. In 1920 the Finnish government came to terms with Soviet Russia. The Russian government ceded to Finland a strip of territory which gave the Finns an ice-free port on the Arctic Ocean. Finland attempted without success to obtain the cession of eastern Karelia. Later in the same year she was admitted to the League of Nations. As at present constituted the new state contains a population of three million people, who have attained a high average level of culture.

South of the Gulf of Finland live the Estonians and the Letts. In the Middle Ages the Germans established themselves in this region as the ruling class. In the eighteenth century it fell under the control of the Russian Empire. With the progress of education both the Estonians and the Letts became bitterly hostile to both their German landlords and their Slavic rulers. After the revolution of March, 1917, the Russian provisional government recognized the desire of the Estonians for self-government and conceded them a considerable degree of autonomy. After the Russian Revolution of 1917, the Estonian National Council proclaimed the political independence of Estonia. This action provoked a Russian invasion of the country and a bitter civil war. In February, 1918, the Germans drove the Russians out of Estonia. Upon the withdrawal of the Germans at the close of the World War the Russians invaded the region again, but after two months of severe fighting the Soviet government signed an armistice with the Estonian authorities. In 1920 Russia concluded a treaty with the new state that recognized its independence but conceded Russia free transit to its Baltic ports. The World War and subsequent movements thus created a new state of a little over a million inhabitants.

The Letts went through a somewhat similar experience. After 1915 the Germans occupied most of the region inhabited by the Letts and attempted to bring them under their permanent rule. At the end of the World War the Letts seized the opportunity offered them to proclaim their independence. For a time an invasion of the Russians and the intrigues of the Baltic barons threatened the new state. In 1920, however, it obtained a recognition of its independence from Russia, and adopted a democratic constitution. Since its establishment Latvia has carried through a thoroughgoing expropriation of the large estates of the German landlords for the benefit of the Lett peasants. In order to allay the danger of Russian plotting, Latvia accorded Russia the same transit privileges to its Baltic ports as Estonia had given. In 1923 Latvia and Estonia sought to strengthen their position further by the conclusion of a defensive alliance.

To the south of the Letts were to be found the Lithuanians. Long merged with the Poles, they gradually awoke to a consciousness of their separate nationality. By 1905 they were demanding autonomy within the Russian Empire. During the World War they began to ask for independence. In February, 1918, they proclaimed their freedom, and in July of the same year a German prince accepted the Lithuanian crown. After the close of the World War the new state had to contend with both the Russians and the Poles. In 1920 it concluded a favorable treaty of peace with Russia. With the Poles, however, the Lithuanians waged a long and bitter fight for the possession of Vilna, the ancient capital of Lithuania. In 1923 they imitated the brusk policy of the Poles in regard to Vilna and seized the city of Memel in defiance of the Allied powers.

The World War destroyed the old régime in Russia and broke up the former Russian Empire. In the greater part of its territories the Russian Communists attempted to set up a state based on the ideas of Karl Marx. At first they had to contend with civil war, foreign intervention, drought, famine, the hostility of the peasants, and the mismanagement of industry by the workers. They saved their régime only by a temporary abandonment of their theories. The resulting change in their situation enabled them to carry out their program in Russia and to conduct an extensive propaganda abroad. They have been forced to let the Baltic borderlands have their independence, but they have succeeded in recapturing much of the other ground lost during the World War.

CHAPTER XXXI

Since the days of the French Revolution the fear of a dissolution of their empire had haunted the political leaders of the Hapsburg Monarchy. Until 1859 they had attempted to avert the impending disaster by a rigid maintenance of absolute government. In 1867, after experimenting with two other forms of organization, they had tried to hold the peoples of the empire together by the establishment of a Dual Monarchy. In the years between the adoption of this form of organization and the opening of the World War this solution of the problem had proved increasingly unsatisfactory. Under the stress of the military conflict, defeat, and propaganda Austria-Hungary went to pieces completely.

I

THE EFFORTS OF THE SUBJECT PEOPLES TO USE THE WORLD WAR TO GAIN THEIR INDEPENDENCE

At first the subject peoples of Austria-Hungary made no open protest against the war policy of the Dual Monarchy. The majority of the populations of the two states hardly understood the significance of the outbreak of the struggle and the reservists responded to the summons to military service. The government tolerated no dissent. The whole monarchy felt the weight of its repressive policy and suspected areas suffered especially severe treatment. In every Serbian village of Bosnia, Slavonia, and the Voyvodina the military authorities feared treason and hanged without ceremony to the nearest tree every priest of the Eastern Orthodox Church upon whom they could lay their hands. They forced many politicians, intellectuals, and members of the clergy to flee from the country. The government watched with almost equal suspicion the inhabitants of Bohemia and the regions adjoining Russia. It arrested and imprisoned leading Czech politicians, prosecuted newspapers, and attempted to suppress Czech books and schools.

From the beginning, however, certain far-sighted leaders of the subject peoples realized the opportunity offered them by the World War. The Czechs found such a leader in Thomas Masaryk. In the years before the World War he had made an international reputation for himself as a scholar, a university lecturer, a politician, and a fearless opponent of the Austro-Hungarian government and its policies. As early as December, 1914, realizing the necessity of organizing the colonies of Czechs and Slovaks living abroad and of presenting their case to the leaders of the Entente governments, he left Bohemia and started on Entente soil a campaign of propaganda and organization. With the aid of able assistants like Edvard Beneš and Štěpanek and with the help of money advanced for the most part by Czechs and Slovaks living in the United States, he kept in touch by various means with some of the political leaders in Bohemia, established journals for the dissemination of propaganda, lectured at foreign universities, issued, with the secret approval of the Czech leaders at home, a declaration of Czech independence, founded a Czechoslovak National Council at Paris, established offices for the diffusion of information at other capitals, and finally organized Czechoslovak military units on the French and Russian fronts.

A group of Southern Slav leaders in Austria-Hungary attempted to carry on a similar campaign in behalf of the Croats and Serbs of the Dual Monarchy. At first they sought to win the support of the Italian government. But the secret Treaty of London, concluded in 1915 between Italy and the Entente powers, soon forced them to transfer their headquarters to France and Great Britain. In May, 1915, they established a Yugoslav Committee to direct their campaign of propaganda. In the summer of 1917 they negotiated with the exiled Serbian government and with representatives of all the Serbian political parties the Declaration of Corfu, which prepared the way for the organization of a Yugoslav state.

The opening of the World War found the Polish leaders divided. As a result of the favors received at the hands of the Austrian government in Galicia, a considerable portion of the Polish people at first favored the central powers and applauded the Austro-Hungarian troops on their way to fight Russia. These Poles organized a Polish National Committee at Cracow, which aimed at the union of Galicia and Congress Poland as a third member of the Dual Monarchy. Thousands of Polish students, intellectuals, and workers volunteered for service in the Polish Legion organized by the political refugee Józef Pilsudski, to fight against Russia. The plans of the Polish National Committee, however, encountered insuperable obstacles. Both the Magyars and the Germans opposed a trialist solution of the Austro-Hungarian problem. The most that the political leaders of the two dominant peoples of the monarchy would offer was greater self-government for Galicia and autonomy for a Congress Poland closely connected with Germany and Austria-Hungary in which the German authorities really would retain all administrative power. In addition the legionaries of Pilsudski received a very cool reception at the hands of their fellow-nationals when they marched into Russian Poland. Then in order to obtain food from the Ukrainians the leaders of Austria-Hungary abandoned the Poles and offered to organize the Ruthenians of eastern Galicia and Bukovina into an Austrian crownland. After her breakdown Russia ceased to be a danger to the plans of the Austrian Poles, and Germany and Austria-Hungary became the principal obstacles to the resurrection of Poland. Pilsudski thereupon refused to allow his little army to leave Polish territory, turned against the central powers, resigned his command, and sought to establish relations with the Entente governments. When the troops of Pilsudski refused to take an oath of allegiance to the governments of Germany and Austria-Hungary the military authorities caused his arrest and imprisonment at Magdeburg and the internment of his military force.

In the meantime a Polish committee with headquarters at Warsaw had denied the right of the Crakow committee to speak for the whole Polish nation, and the famous pianist Paderewski had organized a general committee in France, Great Britain, and the United States, to assist Polish victims of the war. The Warsaw committee protested its loyalty to the Tsar and attempted to form a Polish Legion. Paderewski collected enormous sums of money and organized a powerful movement in the United States in behalf of the Poles. He united the four million Poles of all factions, founded a school for the training of Polish officers, secured from the Canadian government a military camp where more than twenty-two thousand Polish recruits were trained, and finally obtained permission to organize a Polish Legion in France.

At first the exiled leaders of the subject peoples of Austria-Hungary seemed to make little progress toward gaining the recognition of the Entente powers or toward stirring their countrymen at home to action. The plans of the Southern Slavs conflicted with the promises made to Italy, and the Entente leaders had no thought at first of compassing the break-up of Austria-Hungary. On the contrary, they entertained hopes of inducing the leaders of the Dual Monarchy to conclude a separate peace. As the war continued, however, the situation changed. The hope of negotiating a separate treaty of peace with Austria-Hungary gradually faded; the Polish, Yugoslav, and Czechoslovak agitation began to gain ground in the Entente countries and in the United States; the Polish, Yugoslav, and Czechoslovak legions, particularly the Czechoslovak troops in Russia, promised to be of real service in winning the war. Professor Masaryk succeeded in impressing his views concerning the necessity of breaking up Austria-Hungary on President Wilson and other leaders of the Allied and Associated powers. In the Fourteen Points of January 8, 1918, accordingly, President Wilson asked to have assured and safeguarded the place of the peoples of Austria-Hungary among the nations and their opportunity of autonomous development, and for the erection of an independent Polish state. In August, 1918, the principal states fighting against Austria-Hungary sealed her fate by according recognition to the Czechs as members of an allied and belligerent state. Because of their promises to Italy they never made the same concession to the claims of the Southern Slavs. In the last months of the World War the Allied and Associated powers did all they could to shake the loyalty of the subject peoples of Austria-Hungary. Entente agents convened at Rome a Congress of the Oppressed Nationalities which included Italians, Yugoslavs, Czechoslovaks, and Rumanians, and organized, from prisoners and refugees, Czech, Rumanian, and Yugoslav legions which fought opposite their countrymen in the Alps. Entente airplanes scattered over the Austro-Hungarian trenches and towns tons of propaganda inciting the Czechs, Poles, Croats, Rumanians, and Magyars to lay down their arms. Phonographs in the Entente lines played the national songs of the Austro-Hungarian soldiers in order to make them homesick, and Entente agents enticed them to desert.

Alarmed for the unity of the Dual Monarchy, Emperor Charles, the young, well-meaning successor of Francis Joseph, attempted after his accession to regain the loyalty of his subject peoples by concessions. In 1917 the speech from the throne made vague promises of reorganizing the monarchy in such a manner as to permit the free development of the subject nationalities. A little later the Austrian authorities released from prison some of the leaders of the Czech national movement, and toyed with the proposal to crown Emperor Charles in Prague. They attempted unsuccessfully to solve the Bohemian problem by organizing the province into twelve administrative districts that separated the Czechs and the Germans, for the most part, in the work of local government. A plan to create a Southern Slav state within the limits of Austro-Hungary shattered on the immemorial opposition of the Magyars to the dismemberment of Hungary.

2

AUSTRIA SINCE 1918

By October 21, 1918, the disintegration of the Dual Monarchy had progressed so far that an assembly composed of all the German members of the lower house of the Austrian parliament constituted themselves into a Provisional National Assembly, and declared the German territories formerly under the rule of the Hapsburgs an independent state to be known as Austria. On October 30 this body assumed supreme authority in all the former Austrian territories that it claimed to be predominantly German. On Novermber 12 the revolutionary movement that broke out in Vienna forced the Provisional National Assembly to declare Austria a republic and a component part of the new German Republic. Ten days later the new Austrian Republic laid claim to the hereditary lands of the old Austrian Empire except for the districts inhabited by Italians and Southern Slavs. By this action it came into conflict with the Czechs over the predominantly German districts in Bohemia and Moravia. The new state retained the provincial organization established by the Austrian constitution of February, 1861. The Peace Conference, however, refused to concede the claims of the new Austrian Republic to the German districts of Bohemia and Moravia and forbade it to unite with the new German Republic.

The newly established state soon found itself in a serious economic plight. Austria-Hungary had been to an unusual degree a self-sufficing economic unit. She produced most of the food consumed by her population and the greater part of the raw materials used by her industries. Her annual export and import trade per person amounted only to about fifteen dollars. Her economic as well as her political capital was Vienna. This city served to a large extent as the banking center of the Dual Monarchy, owned a large share of its industries, and carried on a large intermediary business between western and eastern Europe. The disintegration of Austria-Hungary as a result of the World War broke up this self-contained economic unit, and left Vienna, a city of nearly two million inhabitants, as the capital of a little state with an area of only thirty-two thousand three hundred and fifty-two square miles and a population of about six and a half million. The Austrian Republic suddenly found herself unable to feed her citizens, poor in raw materials, and deprived of her former markets. The situation soon became desperate. The people of Vienna found themselves unable to procure the bare necessities of life. Burdened by relief payments and the maintenance of a staff of employees far beyond its requirements, the state kept going only by inflating the currency and obtaining temporary relief from the Allied and Associated powers. Day by day the medium of exchange fell in value, taxation ceased to yield appreciable amounts for the support of the government, and the industries struggled in vain against the unfavorable economic conditions.

The economic situation made difficult the permanent political reorganization of the new republic. The elections placed in power a National Constitutional Assembly in which none of the three parties, the Social Democrats, the Christian Socialists, or the Pan-Germans, obtained a majority. The Social Democrats found their principal support among the workers in Vienna and other industrial districts, part of the official class, and the lower middle class. The adherents of the Christian Socialists included all the agricultural classes, and the upper classes of Vienna and the provincial towns. The central political problem became in consequence the relation of Vienna and the historic provinces to the state. The party situation compelled a compromise. The constitution adopted in October, 1920, declared Austria to be a democratic republic, composed of seven provinces and the city of Vienna, and provided for a President chosen for a term of four years by the two houses of the parliament assembled for a joint session, an Assembly elected for a term of four years by popular vote, and a First Chamber with advisory powers chosen by the provincial diets in proportion to their population. The constitution adopted in 1929 increased the number of provinces to nine and provided for the election of the President by popular vote.

By 1922 the economic situation was so desperate that the Austrian authorities appealed to Europe for help. As a result of this appeal the Assembly of the League of Nations decided to undertake the financial reconstruction of Austria. The plan finally adopted provided for a new declaration of her independence and sovereignty by Austria, a moratorium for reparation payments for twenty years, the raising of a loan guaranteed by foreign governments, budget reform, and a reorganization of the national bank. The plan was to be executed under the supervision of a high commissioner. As a result of the aid of the League of Nations the economic situation of Austria has improved considerably. The expenses of the state have been reduced by the pensioning of one hundred thousand employees and the cutting down of the salaries of others employed by the state; Vienna has recovered much of its former position in banking and commerce; and Austria has freed herself finally from outside control.

Since her financial reconstruction Austria has wrestled with the problems of economic recovery, the rivalry of the Social Democrats and the Christian Socialists, and relations with neighboring states. The Social Democrats have tended to lose ground in elections and have organized military forces for self-defense. The upper and middle classes have replied by forming armed bodies of their own. At times the two rival military organizations have threatened the peace of the state. The question of union with Germany has continued to agitate Austrian and European politics. As a preparatory step toward the ultimate amalgamation of Austria and Germany, the two governments have harmonized many conditions in the two countries. Until the Austrian and Italian governments reached an agreement in 1930, the treatment accorded by Italy to the Germans of Southern Tyrol seriously disturbed the relations of Italy and Austria.

3

CZECHOSLOVAKIA

Other fragments of the disintegrated Austrian Empire were incorporated into Czechoslovakia, Poland, Italy, and Yugoslavia. The organization of a government for the new Czechoslovak state required considerable time. On October 14, 1918, the National Council which had so skilfully guided the affairs of the Czechs and the Slovaks during the trying days of the war announced to the Allied and Associated governments the establishment, on September 26, 1918, of an interim Czechoslovak government at Paris. The new government was promptly recognized by France, Italy, Great Britain, and the United States. On October 26, 1918, the political leaders of the Czechs in Bohemia and Moravia arrived in Geneva for an exchange of views with the representatives of the Czech National Council at Paris, and for the formulation of plans for the organization of the future government of the proposed Czechoslovak state. The conference merged the Czech movement at home with the Czech movement abroad, assured the Allied and Associated powers that the Czechs and Slovaks of the Dual Monarchy supported the government established at Paris, and gave the new Czechoslovak state a republican form of government. On October 28, 1918, the situation in Prague caused the Czech National Committee to proclaim the independence of the Czechoslovak state and to take in hand the administration of the territories claimed by the Czechs. Two days later the Slovak National Council declared in favor of Czechoslovak unity. On November 13, 1918, after conferences between the Czech authorities at Paris and at Prague, the Czech National Committee issued an interim constitution. The next day a Czechoslovak National Assembly, composed of two hundred and forty-nine Czechs and forty Slovaks (but no Germans), unanimously elected Masaryk as first President of the Czechoslovak Republic, and organized a government made up of the chief figures in the wartime movement for independence. Not until early in 1920 did the National Assembly adopt a permanent constitution. This document provided for a President elected for a term of seven years by the two legislative chambers meeting in joint session, a Chamber of Deputies of three hundred members elected for a term of six years, and a Senate of one hundred and fifty members chosen for a term of eight years.

The Czechoslovak movement for national independence united into one political entity the three former Austrian provinces of Bohemia, Moravia, and Austrian Silesia, and Slovakia in the northern part of the former Kingdom of Hungary. The union of these territories created a state with a population composed of six million Czechs, more than two million Slovaks, about two and a half million Germans, and nearly a half-million Ruthenians. The Germans had for centuries been the dominant people in the Kingdom of Bohemia and resented their sudden subjection to the Czechs. Both peoples had long been in touch with the cultural influences emanating from France and Germany and had developed a complex and progressive industrial and commercial society in

Bohemia and Moravia. The Slovaks and Ruthenians occupied a sparsely settled pastoral and agricultural region and clung to many old customs and primitive methods. The new government faced the difficult task of welding these diverse elements into a nation.

Czechoslovakia has been the most successful of the succession states. The new state has been fortunate in having as President a man with the personal prestige of Professor Masaryk. Since the establishment of the republic its foreign policy has been conducted with great skill and energy by Edvard Beneš, the collaborator with Masaryk in the struggle for independence. Although the relations with Hungary remain tense because of the inclusion of many Magyars in Czechoslovakia, working arrangements have been concluded with most of the neighboring states. At the same time the delicate domestic situation has been handled with considerable tact. The Ruthenians have been given autonomy; the recalcitrant Germans of Bohemia and Moravia have been persuaded to participate in the political life of the state. The new government also adopted measures to revive the economic life of the country. It immediately took steps for the establishment of an independent currency and in 1922 succeeded in stabilizing it. Favored by a stable medium of exchange, commercial agreements with most of the neighboring states, mineral wealth, and industrial skill, Czechoslovakia has succeeded in obtaining an enviable economic position.

4

HUNGARY

The World War had much the same effect on Hungary that it had on Austria. As the conflict progressed without bringing victory to the central powers, the opposition to the policy of the Hungarian government grew stronger and stronger in Hungary. In October, 1918, the obvious hopelessness of the military situation brought the discontent to a head. On October 25 the middle-class radicals, led by Count Michael Károlyi, organized a National Council, and announced a program calling for the dissolution of the parliament, the adoption of universal suffrage, and the conclusion of a speedy peace. Popular demonstrations forced King Charles to abandon his own plans for Hungary and to appoint Károlyi head of the government. In November 13, King Charles renounced participation in the conduct of state affairs, and three days later the National Council proclaimed the Hungarian People's Republic.

The new government hoped to save Hungary from the consequences of defeat by winning the good-will of the Entente powers. It ordered the Hungarian troops home and disarmed them upon their arrival in Hungary. In the Magyar districts outside of Budapest, however, representatives of the soldiers, students, workers, and peasants organized councils on the Russian model. In the rest of Hungary, the subject peoples—the Slovaks, Croats, Serbs, and Rumanians—organized national councils which took over the administration of the border districts, and raised weak military forces which occupied the regions claimed by the Czechoslovaks, Rumania, and the Southern Slavs. Efforts to induce the subject peoples of Hungary to accept a reorganization of the kingdom into cantons, a plan based on Swiss precedents, failed completely. On November 8, 1918, General Franchet d'Esperey, commander of the Entente forces on the Saloniki front, compelled Károlyi to accept the loss of the territories claimed by Yugoslavia, Rumania, and Czechoslovakia. In the following March the Entente Allies extended the new Rumanian frontier farther west, and occupied a large part of Hungary in order to suppress disorder.

The failure of the pacifist policy of Károlyi and the prospect of economic disaster threw the Magyar districts of Hungary for a time into the hands of the Communists. On November 19, Béla Kun, a former insurance agent, arrived in Hungary by using a forged passport after having spent a period of captivity in Russia. He came for the purpose of organizing a revolutionary movement on the Russian model among the proletariat of Hungary. He found a sympathetic hearing among the disillusioned masses upon whom the government of Károlyi had no hold. Hoping to take advantage of the anarchical situation to establish their own power, the Socialists formed an alliance with Béla Kun. On March 21, 1919, Károlyi resigned from office and the Socialist party of Hungary, as Béla Kun and his allies styled themselves, took over the government. The new rulers of Hungary organized an army, disarmed the middle classes, formed an alliance with Russia, and proceeded to introduce Communism. They confiscated all the mines and business establishments, declared trade a state monopoly, expropriated all the banks, looted rich residences and depots of supplies, seized leading middle-class politicians as hostages, stopped the circulation of all middle-class newspapers, appropriated church property, waged war on ecclesiastical symbols, threw church dignitaries into prison, and attacked the institution of the family and many moral customs of the Magyar people. The introduction of Communism soon embittered all classes except the industrial workers. Purchases and sales stopped after a few weeks; the factories shut down for want of raw material; the peasants refused to supply the towns with food. Many opposed the Communist régime because of the prominent part played in it by Jews. During most of the time that they were in power Béla Kun and his associates waged almost continuous warfare with Rumania, Yugoslavia, and Czechoslovakia.

The occupation of Hungary by Rumanian troops at the instigation of a counter-revolutionary government set up by a group of Conservative Magyars cut short the Communist régime. On August 1, 1919, Béla Kun and his associates fled from the country. Three days later Rumanian troops appeared in the suburbs of Budapest. On August 5 they began to pillage Hungary. During their occupation of Hungary they requisitioned supplies freely, and at the time of their withdrawal in November, 1919, they carried away live stock, railway equipment, and industrial machinery. They took property estimated to be worth nearly twenty-nine million dollars. Belatedly the Entente powers sent four generals to Budapest to protect the Magyars against injustice.

After the withdrawal of the Rumanians, the opponents of the Communist régime took control of Hungary. Under the leadership of Admiral Horthy, they set about the task of reëstablishing order in the country. Early in 1920 they held elections, on the basis of universal suffrage, for a new National Assembly which put the conservative elements among the Magyars in power. In March, 1920, the new legislative body restored the old Hungarian constitution, dissolved the connection between Hungary and Austria, proclaimed Hungary a kingdom without naming a sovereign, and appointed Admiral Horthy Regent. In the meantime the adherents of the new masters of Hungary had been taking vengeance on those responsible for the Communist régime. Bands led by ex-officers of the army executed without judicial authority over three hundred persons.

The Conservatives assumed power over a state which had been impoverished by the war and its aftermath and had been suddenly reduced to the rank of a small power. They have encountered many difficulties in their efforts to restore order and prosperity. In 1921 King Charles twice returned to the country and attempted to reëstablish himself on the throne. The incorporation of many Magyars into the newly organized states has tended to make the relations between Hungary and the neighboring states unsatisfactory. In self-defense Czechoslovakia, Rumania, and Yugoslavia formed an alliance in 1921, known as the Little Entente, drove thirty thousand Magyars, mostly officials, back into Hungary to be supported by the already overburdened treasury, imposed frontier restrictions that hampered her economic recovery, and threatened on several occasions to occupy Hungarian territory. The Conservative leaders of the country resisted the transfer of Burgenland to Austria and finally effected an agreement with the Austrian government which saved a portion of the province to Hungary. In the end the Hungarian government found itself forced to call on the League of Nations for help in reconstructing the finances of the country. It quelled the agitation among the peasants by making additional land available for their use. It tightened the grip of the Conservatives on the machinery of government by restoring the upper house of the parliament and abolishing the secret ballot everywhere except in the cities. In September, 1922, Hungary gained admission to the League of Nations. In recent years she has improved her relations with some of the neighboring powers, notably with Italy. Hungary still remains, however, one of the conservative and resentful states of Europe.

5

RUMANIA

Another of the heirs of dismembered Austria-Hungary was Rumania. In 1916 this state had entered the World War on the side of the Entente powers as a result of being promised the Banat, Transylvania, and the Hungarian plain as far as the Tisza River, and Bukovina as far as the Prut River. Until 1918 the policy of intervention brought only disaster to the Rumanian people. After its defeat at the hands of the central powers the Rumanian government found itself forced to re-cede the southern half of the Dobruja to Bulgaria, to submit to the occupation of the northern half of the province by the central powers, to allow adjustments to be made in the Rumanian frontier in favor of Hungary, and to suffer the inflation of its currency, the disorganization of its finances, the exportation of its live stock, the cutting down of its forests, the dismantling of its factories, and the reduction of its population to famine conditions. The only favorable turn of events for Rumania during this period was the annexation of Bessarabia after the withdrawal of Russia from the World War.

The defeat of the central powers changed the situation completely. On October 27, 1918, the Rumanians of Transylvania announced their intention to cut loose from Hungary by establishing a National Council. On December 1 a convention convened by this body proclaimed the union of Transylvania with the Kingdom of Rumania but promised to respect the rights and liberties of the other peoples of the province. On January 21, 1919, the Saxon inhabitants of the province gave their adherence to the proclamation. The Entente Allies, however, did not determine the new western boundary of Rumania until 1920. They finally gave Rumania only about two thirds of the Banat. In Bukovina the last Austrian government attempted to hand political power over to the Ruthenians. On October 27, 1918, however, representatives of the Rumanian inhabitants of the province met at Czernowitz and proclaimed a Constituent Assembly, which voted in favor of the union of Bukovina, with its historic boundaries, to Rumania and appealed to the Rumanian government for military assistance. On November 11, 1918, Rumanian military forces occupied the province. On November 27, 1918, the National Council that had been organized in Bessarabia after the Bolshevist revolution in Russia decided in favor of unconditional union of the province with Rumania. In 1920 these changes received the approval of the Entente powers. These acquisitions considerably more than doubled the area and the population of the Kingdom of Rumania.

With the Communists in permanent control of Russia and temporarily in power in Hungary, the Rumanian Conservatives in control of the political machinery did not dare to ignore completely the insistent demand for the breaking up of the large estates and for the distribution of their lands to the peasants. In a land law of 1920 they provided for the total expropriation of the estates of absentee landlords, foreigners, and entailed properties, and the partial confiscation of other large holdings. This measure resulted in the seizure of estates of more than five hundred hectares in area in the older provinces of the kingdom and of those of more than one hundred hectares in area in the annexed provinces of Bessarabia, Transylvania, and Bukovina. The peasants who were benefited by the legislation were to pay, over a period of forty-five years, 65 per cent and the state 35 per cent of the cost of the land distributed to them. Though over sixteen thousand estates were expropriated, the execution of this measure still left nearly half a million peasants landless.

Territorial expansion and political developments made necessary radical changes in the fundamental laws of Rumania. The new constitution adopted in 1923 gave the King a suspensive veto; provided for the organization of a legislative council to formulate legislative and administrative measures for the parliament, of a Senate composed of life, ex-officio, and elected members, and a Chamber of Deputies chosen by universal suffrage; created an administration modeled after that of France and designed to weld the separate provinces into a unified kingdom; and declared the subsoil and the forests nationalized.

The enlarged state has had to struggle with many perplexing problems. On account of its annexation of territory at their expense it has felt threatened by Hungary, by Bulgaria, and especially by Russia. It has attempted to guard against attack by these powers by the conclusion of agreements with Poland, Czechoslovakia, and Yugoslavia. It has felt menaced by Communism and has carried on a determined struggle against the adherents of that political faith. It has been harassed by outbursts of anti-Semitism among the students. The death of King Ferdinand in 1927 made the question of the succession an acute problem. Though he had renounced the throne before the death of his father, the eldest son of the late King and his partizans gave unmistakable evidence of their desire to bring about his elevation to the throne of Rumania, and in 1930 the National Peasants party finally brought about the return of Prince Charles to the country and made him King in place of his young son.

6

YUGOSLAVIA

In August, 1918, the Southern Slav movement for independence gave rise to the organization of a National Yugoslav Council. In October of that year this body appointed a Central Executive Committee commissioned to establish an independent Southern Slav state composed of the Serbs, Croats, and Slovenes. At the end of October the Croatian diet declared all relations between Croatia and Hungary severed. Early in November, 1918, representatives of the National Yugoslav Council, the Serbian government, and the Yugoslav Committee of London met at Geneva and proclaimed a common ministry for a united state of the Serbs, Croats, and Slovenes, but announced the temporary retention of the existing administrative systems. At the end of November the National Yugoslav Council voted for union with Serbia and Montenegro and recognized Crown Prince Alexander of Serbia as Regent. In December, 1918, this body organized in coöperation with the Serbian parliament a representative body that was to act as a legislative body for Yugoslavia until the convening of a Constitutional Assembly.

Though the boundaries of the new state were not definitely established at all points until the negotiation of the agreement with Italy in 1924, this action of the Southern Slavs created the Kingdom officially named the Serb, Croat, and Slovene State and popularly known as Yugoslavia, a country composed of provinces and peoples of diverse origin. It united in one state the former kingdoms of Serbia and Montenegro, the former Austrian provinces of Dalmatia (with the exception of the town of Zara and the two islands of Lagosta and Pelagosa), and Slovenia, made up of Southern Styria, the greater part of Carniola, and a few communes of Carinthia, the former Hungarian province of Croatia-Slavonia (without Fiume) and a part of the Voyvodina, and the two provinces of Bosnia and Herzegovina, formerly under the joint control of the two halves of the Dual Monarchy. The union of these territories brought under the rule of the new state some nine million Serbs and Croats, over one million Slovenes, more than half a million Germans, a quarter of a million Rumanians, and a mixture of other peoples. The Serbs, constituting about a third of the population of Yugoslavia, were mainly peasants, were communicants of the Eastern Orthodox Church, and possessed organized political machinery in the Serbian government. The Roman Catholic Croats numbered nearly a quarter of the total population. Both the Croats and the Slovenes surpass the Serbs of Serbia and Montenegro in respect to culture and economic development. After the death of his father Prince Alexander became King.

While the frontier dispute with Italy was still pending the new Yugoslav government hesitated to hold new elections and governed the country with the aid of the improvised legislative body composed of members of the old Serbian parliament and delegates from the former provinces of Austria-Hungary who owed their positions largely to their membership in the numerous revolutionary committees that sprang up in October, 1918. Upon the resumption of political life in 1920, a keen struggle developed in the Constitutional Assembly between the Radicals, who stood for a centralized state and the domination of the Serbs, and a new Democratic party, composed of opposition groups in Serbia, the old Serbo-Croat coalition of Croatia-Slavonia, and the Slovene Liberals, which favored a federal constitution. At the time of the adoption of the constitution in 1921 the Radicals won by the narrow margin of thirteen votes, and the Croat delegates withdrew from the convention and refused to participate in the political life of Yugoslavia during the next four years. As a result of the existence of minor parties neither of the two large parties has been able to obtain a majority in the parliament for more than a brief period. The elections in Bosnia, Croatia, and Slovenia have consistently shown a majority in favor of the establishment of autonomous governments in those provinces and in consequence each succeeding ministry has had only a precarious hold on office. In 1928 a Serb partizan killed outright two Croat opponents and seriously wounded the leader of the Croat national movement. Thereupon the Croats again refused to participate in the government and went so far in their opposition as to establish their own parliament in Zágráb. In 1929 King Alexander attempted to solve the deadlock by a coup d'état. He pledged himself to a program calling for unity, decentralization, and improved administration, and promised to introduce a new democratic, parliamentary régime. In reality the dictatorship has tried to crush the separatist movement by the suppression of discussion and agitation, the abolition of the old historic administrative divisions, and the arrest and trial of the leaders of the opposition.

7

POLAND

One of the most startling results of the World War was the political resurrection of Poland. During the military conflict the three powers that had divided Poland found themselves compelled to bid for the support of the Polish people. On August 14, 1914, Russia began the wooing of the Poles by issuing a proclamation that promised to unite the three parts of Poland into an autonomous state. This offer won the support of a Polish National Committee at Warsaw and certain elements in Galicia. After the defeat of the armies of the Dual Monarchy in 1916 the governments of Germany and Austria-Hungary issued a proclamation which held out the hope of the reëstablishment of Russian Poland as a hereditary constitutional monarchy closely attached to the central powers, and Emperor Francis Joseph promised Galicia a greater degree of autonomy. On March 30, 1917, after the first revolution, the revolutionary government in Russia recognized the right of Poland to self-determination and promised the creation of a new Polish state. This action left the Entente governments at last free to declare in favor of the freedom of Poland. In October, 1917, the two central powers set up a Polish Regency, composed of three members and intrusted with only limited power. In the Treaty of Brest Litovsk of 1918 the Bolshevist leaders of Russia renounced all claims to Poland. In the same year, however, the government of Austria-Hungary completely alienated the Polish people by ceding to the Ukraine the province of Chelm and by promising to form eastern Galicia and Bukovina into a separate crownland. As soon as these facts became known, the representatives of the Poles in the Austrian parliament went over to the side of the opposition, the Polish cabinet at Warsaw resigned, and a remnant of the legion organized by Pilsudski, commanded by General Haller, refused to fight longer for the central powers and fought its way to the coast in order to join the Polish army in France organized by the Polish National Committee at Paris, headed by Roman Dmowski.

The defeat of the central powers in 1918 gave the Poles an opportunity to gain their independence. On October 6, 1918, after the defeat of the central powers was apparent, the Polish Regency set up at Warsaw by the central powers issued a manifesto to the Polish nation declaring its intention to form a representative national government and to summon a diet. On October 15 it invited the Polish representatives in the Austrian Reichsrat, who had declared in favor of a free united Poland, to Warsaw to take a part in forming the new Polish government. On November 3 the cabinet established by it proclaimed the organization of the Polish Republic. Upon the release of Pilsudski from his German prison on November 10 the Regency appointed him commander of the Polish army and he proclaimed himself head of the national government. In December, 1918, Paderewski returned to Poland, reached an understanding with Pilsudski, and for a moment reunited the Poles by assuming the premiership.

The leaders of the resurrected state found everything in chaos. Austrian and Russian Poland had been devastated by the war. All the factories lacked raw material and many of them had been dismantled. Fields had been laid waste, the stock for the most part had been driven off, and thousands of houses had been wrecked or burned. Famine and disease threatened to decimate the population. The boundaries of the new state were undetermined. Political parties were numerous but without political experience. The elements for the establishment of an orderly government were lacking. Influences from Russia kept the Polish people perturbed. Historic memories of past glories and of oppression kindled dangerous hates and ambitions.

The new government first turned its attention to a vigorous assertion of the territorial claims of Poland. It laid claim not only to all the provinces that had once belonged to Poland but also to all that could be asked for on economic or national grounds. Paderewski left for Paris to present the views of the Polish government to the Peace Conference, and Pilsudski, using the Polish Legion assembled in France as a nucleus, organized an army that finally numbered eight hundred thousand troops and carried on diplomatic or military struggles with Germany over Upper Silesia, West Prussia, and Danzig, with Czechoslovakia over Teschen, with the Ukraine over eastern Galicia, with Russia over the extension of the boundaries of Poland eastward, and with Lithuania over Vilna. Definite decisions concerning the Polish claims were reached only gradually. The frontier on the side of Germany, except for the case of Upper Silesia, was decided by the Treaty of Versailles. On November 20, 1919, after considerable fighting had taken place in the disputed area, the Peace Conference assigned eastern Galicia to Poland for a period of twenty-five years on condition that the province should enjoy local autonomy. At the end of that period the League of Nations was to determine the future of the province. In October, 1921, a decision of the League of Nations settled the quarrel over Upper Silesia. A resolution by the Council of Ambassadors, representing the Allied powers, finally adjusted the contests for possession of Teschen and Vilna. This body divided Teschen between Poland and Czechoslovakia and gave Vilna entirely to the Poles. In 1921, after a serious military struggle had taken place, the Treaty of Riga established the boundary of Poland on the side of Russia. In 1923 the Council of Ambassadors and the United States recognized the new frontiers. These extensions of the Polish boundaries created a state with a population of thirty million, but brought a large non-Polish minority, constituting about 31 per cent of the population, into Poland.

The new republic did not take up the task of drafting a permanent constitution until 1921. The document finally adopted provided for a President, elected for a term of seven years by the houses of the parliament sitting as a National Assembly, for a responsible ministry, and for a Senate and a Diet elected by universal suffrage on a system of proportional representation. In 1926, Marshal Pilsudski, for ten years the most prominent man in Poland, engineered a coup d'état and introduced radical changes in the government. Disgusted with the parliament and concerned at the proposal to subordinate the commander of the army to that body, he introduced changes that greatly strengthened the executive while leaving the outward structure of the parliament and the electoral system intact.

The domestic history of Poland has been marked by constant alarms and excursions. There have been many complaints of Polish oppression of the Jews and other minorities, especially the Germans. Efforts to increase the landholdings of the peasants have failed. In 1923 the country came to the verge of financial collapse and saved itself only by vigorous measures. The government has been embroiled with most of the neighboring states and in consequence has been greatly concerned over the problem of security.

The World War broke up or partially dismembered four empires— Austria-Hungary, Turkey, Russia, and Germany. From their ruins emerged an Austria and a Hungary greatly reduced in area and population, the new states of Czechoslovakia and Yugoslavia, a Rumania doubled in size and in number of inhabitants, and a resurrected Poland. Each of these succession states has faced such problems as the setting up of new political machinery or the adapting of an old administrative organization to new conditions, the establishing of new boundaries, and the making of working arrangements with suspicious and aggressive neighboring states. In addition each state has struggled with a group of distinctive domestic problems arising out of local conditions. The peoples of eastern and central Europe, in consequence, have neither completed the work of political and social reconstruction nor finished the experiment of breaking up Austria-Hungary and some of the neighboring empires into a group of small states.

SOME LISTS OF USEFUL BOOKS IN WESTERN EUROPEAN LANGUAGES

The author has included in this bibliography works likely to be found in any first-class American library. He hopes that it will prove useful to graduate students, librarians, teachers of history, and serious general readers.

GENERAL WORKS, 1815–1871

ALBIN, P., *Les grands traités politiques* (Paris, 1912).

ANDREWS, C. M., *The Development of Modern Europe*, 2 vols. (London, 1896–98).

ASHLEY, P. W. L., *Europe from Waterloo to Sarajevo* (New York, 1926).

BEAZLEY, C. R., *Nineteenth Century Europe and Britain* (London, 1922).

BOURGEOIS, E., *Manuel historique de politique étrangère*, 3 vols. (Paris, 1906).

BROWNING, O., *A History of the Modern World*, 2 vols. (London, 1916).

BULLE, C., *Geschichte des zweiten Kaiserreiches und des Königreiches Italien* (Berlin, 1890).

The Cambridge Modern History, Vols. X, XI, and XII (New York, 1907, 1909, 1910).

CARTELLIERI, A., *Geschichte der neueren Revolutionen* (Leipzig, 1921).

DEBIDOUR, A., *Histoire diplomatique de l'Europe, 1814–1878*, 2 vols. (Paris, 1919–20).

DRIAULT, E., and MONOD, G., *Évolution du monde moderne* (Paris, 1911).

——————, *Histoire contemporaine, 1815–1917* (Paris, 1917).

DYER, H. T., *Modern Europe*, Vol. 5. (London, 1877).

FEYEL, P., *Histoire politique du XIXe siècle*, 2 vols. (Paris, 1913–14).

FLATHE, T., *Das Zeitalter der Restauration und Revolution, 1815–1851* (Berlin, 1883).

——————, *Restoration and Revolution* (Philadelphia, 1905).

——————, *The Reconstruction of Europe* (New York, 1905).

FUETER, E., *World History, 1815–1920* (New York, 1922).

——————, *Weltgeschichte der letzten hundert Jahre, 1815–1920* (Zurich, 1921).

FYFFE, C. A., *A History of Modern Europe, 1792–1878*, 3 vols. (New York, 1881–90) ; 1 vol. (New York, 1896).

HALL, W. P., and BELLER, E. A., *Historical Readings in Nineteenth Century Thought* (New York, 1928).

HAWKESWORTH, C. E. M., *The Last Century in Europe, 1814–1910* (London and New York, 1913).

HAYES, C. J. H., *A Political and Social History of Modern Europe*, Vol. 2 (New York, 1924, 1926, 1928, and 1929).

HAZEN, C. D., *A History of Europe since 1815* (New York, 1910), 2 vols. (New York, 1923).
————, *Modern Europe* (New York, 1924).
HEARNSHAW, F. J. C., *An Outline Sketch of the Political History of Europe in the Nineteenth Century* (London, 1919).
————, *Main Currents of European History, 1815–1915* (London, 1917).
HERBERT, S., *Modern Europe, 1789–1914* (London, 1916).
HERTSLET, L., *Map of Europe by Treaty (1815–75)*, 3 vols. (London, 1875–91).
JANE, L. C., *From Metternich to Bismarck, 1815–1878* (New York, 1910).
JEFFERY, R. W., *The New Europe, 1789–1889* (Boston, 1911).
JUDSON, H. P., *Europe in the Nineteenth Century* (Meadville, Penna., 1894).
KIRKPATRICK, F. A., *Lectures on the History of the Nineteenth Century* (Cambridge, 1902).
LAVISSE, E., and RAMBAUD, A., *Histoire générale du IVe siècle à nos jours*, Vols. X–XII (Paris, 1893–1901).
LIPSON, E., *Europe in the Nineteenth Century* (London, 1916).
MARRIOTT, SIR J. A. R., *The Remaking of Modern Europe, 1789–1878* (London, 1914).
MOWAT, R. B., *A History of European Diplomacy, 1815–1914* (London, 1923).
MÜLLER, W., *A Political History of Recent Times, 1816–1875* (New York, 1882).
OGG, F. A., *Economic Development of Modern Europe* (New York, 1926).
PHILLIPS, W. A., *Modern Europe, 1815–1899* (London, 1908).
POSTGATE, R. W., *Revolution from 1789–1906* (London, 1920).
RAULICH, I., *Manuale di storia contemporanea d'Europa* (Turin, 1909).
ROBINSON, J. H., and BEARD, C. A., *The Development of Modern Europe*, Vol. 2 (Boston, 1930).
————, *Readings in the History of Modern Europe*, Vol. 2 (Boston, 1909).
ROSE, J. H., *A Century of Continental History, 1780–1880* (London, 1911).
SCOTT, J. F., and BALTZLY, A., *Readings in European History since 1814* (New York, 1930).
SEIGNOBOS, C., *Histoire politique de l'Europe contemporaine (1814–1914)*, (Paris, 1924–26).
————, *A Political History of Europe since 1814* (New York, 1900).
SHAPIRO, J. S., *A History of Modern and Contemporary Europe* (Boston, 1931).
STERN, A., *Geschichte Europas seit den Verträgen von 1815 bis zur Frankfurter Frieden von 1871*, 7 vols. (Berlin, 1894–1924).
————, *Die französische Revolution, Napoleon und die Restauration 1789–1848* (Berlin, 1929).
TURNER, E. R., *Europe since 1789* (Garden City, N. Y., 1928).
WEILL, G., *L'éveil des nationalités et le mouvement libéral (1815–1848)* (Paris, 1930).
ZURLINDEN, S., *Der Weltkrieg*, 6 vols. (Zürich, 1917, 1918–   ).

HISTORIES OF COUNTRIES AND REGIONS

Austria-Hungary:

BIBL, V., *Der Zerfall Oesterreichs,* 2 vols. (Vienna, 1922–24).
BRETHOLZ, B., *Geschichte Böhmens und Mährens,* 4 vols. in 2 (Reichenberg, 1921).
CHARMATZ, R., *Geschichte der auswärtigen Politik Oesterreiches im neunzehnten Jahrhundert,* 2 vols. (Leipzig, 1912–14).
COXE, W., *History of the House of Austria,* Vol. IV (London, 1854–64).
KRONES, F., *Geschichte der Neuzeit Oesterreichs* (Berlin, 1879).
LEGER, L., *History of Austria-Hungary* (New York, 1889).
SPRINGER, A. H., *Geschichte Oesterreichs seit dem Wiener Frieden,* 2 vols. (Leipzig, 1863–65).
WHITMAN, W. S., *Austria* (New York, 1906).

ECKART, F., *Introduction à l'histoire hongroise* (Paris, 1928).
SZEKFÜ, J., *Der Staat Ungarn* (Berlin, 1918).
TELEKI, P., *The Evolution of Hungary and Its Place in European History* (New York, 1923).
VÁMBÉRY, A., *The Story of Hungary* (New York, 1886).

The Balkans:

ANCEL, J., *Manuel historique de la question d'orient (1792–1925)* (Paris, 1926).
DRIAULT, E., *La question d'orient depuis ses origines jusqu'à nos jours* (Paris, 1905).
FORBES, N., TOYNBEE, A. J., MITRANY, D., and HOGARTH, D. G., *The Balkans* (Oxford, 1915).
JORGA, N., *Histoire des états balcaniques à l'époque moderne* (Bucharest, 1914).
—————, *Histoire des états balcaniques jusqu'à 1924* (Paris, 1925).
LA JONQUIÈRE, A., VICOMTE DE, *Histoire de l'empire ottoman* (Paris, 1914).
MARRIOTT, SIR J. A. R., *The Eastern Question* (Oxford, 1924).
MILLER, W., *The Balkans* (New York, 1908).
—————, *The Ottoman Empire and Its Successors, 1815–1913* (Cambridge, 1913).
—————, *The Ottoman Empire and Its Successors, 1815–1921* (Cambridge, 1921).
SCHEVILL, F., *The History of the Balkan Peninsula* (New York, 1922).
SETON-WATSON, R. W., *The Rise of Nationality in the Balkans* (London, 1917).

BOUSQUET, G. H., *Histoire du peuple bulgare* (Paris, 1909).
BUCHAN, J., ed., *Bulgaria and Romania* (Boston, 1924).
SAMUELSON, J., *Bulgaria Past and Present* (London, 1888).
SONGEON, G., *Histoire de la Bulgarie depuis les origines jusqu'à nos jours (485–1913)* (Paris, 1913).

BARTHOLDY, K. M., *Geschichte Griechenlands,* 2 vols. (Leipzig, 1870, 1884).
DRIAULT, E., *La renaissance de l'hellénisme* (Paris, 1920).
FINLAY, G., *History of Greece,* Vols. V–VII (Oxford, 1877).
HERTZBERG, G. F., *Geschichte Griechenlands,* Vol. IV (Gotha, 1879).
MILLER, W., *History of the Greek People, 1821–1923* (New York, 1923).
SERGEANT, L., *New Greece* (London, 1878).

BUCHAN, J., ed., *Roumania* (Boston, 1924).
JORGA, N., *History of Rumania* (London, 1926).
XÉNOPOL, A. D., *Histoire des roumains* (Paris, 1896).

BUCHAN, J., ed., *Yugoslavia* (Boston, 1913).
COQUELLE, P., *Le royaume de Serbie* (Paris, 1894).
GOPČEVIČ, S., *Russland und Serbien von 1804 bis 1915* (Munich, 1916).
LAZAROVICH-HREBELIANOVICH, PRINCE and PRINCESS, *The Serbian People,* 2 vols. (New York, 1910).
RACHITCH, V. V., *Le royaume de Serbie* (Paris, 1901).
RANKE, L. VON, *A History of Servia* (London, 1847).
SAINTE-RENÉ-TALLANDIER, R. G. E., *La Serbie au XIXe siècle* (Paris, 1875).
TEMPERLEY, H. W. V., *History of Serbia* (London, 1917).
WARING, L., *Serbia* (New York, 1917).
YAKSCHITCH, G., *L'Europe et la résurrection de la Serbie, 1804–1834* (Paris, 1907).

Belgium:

BOULGER, D. C., *The History of Belgium, 1815–1865* (London, 1913).
CAMMAERTS, E., *Belgium* (London, 1921).
CHARRIAUT, H., *La Belgique moderne* (Paris, 1910).
DEWITT, A., *Histoire de la Belgique contemporaine, 1830–1914* (Brussels, 1928-   ).
ENSOR, R. C. K., *Belgium* (London, 1915).
VAN DER ESSEN, L., *A Short History of Belgium* (Chicago, 1916).
GRIFFIS, W. E., *Belgium* (Boston, 1912).
VAN DER LINDEN, H., *Belgium, the Making of a Nation* (Oxford, 1920).
MAC DONNELL, J. DE C., *Belgium* (London, 1915).
OMOND, G. W. T., *The Kingdom of Belgium and the Grand Duchy of Luxembourg* (Boston, 1923).
REED, T. H., *Government and Politics of Belgium* (Yonkers, 1924).

Great Britain and the British Empire:

ANDREWS, C. M., *A History of England* (Boston, 1903).
ARNOLD, B. W., *England's Progress, 1793–1921* (Boston, 1922).
BRIGHT, J. F., *A History of England,* Vols. III–V (London, 1877–1904).
BRINKMANN, C., *Englische Geschichte, 1815–1914* (Berlin, 1924).
BRODERICK, G. C., and FOTHERINGHAM, J. K., *The History of England from*

Addington's Administration to the Close of William IV's Reign (*1801–1837*) (London, 1906).
Cambridge History of British Foreign Policy, 1783–1919, 3 vols. (Cambridge, 1922–23).
CANA, F. R., *South Africa from the Great Trek to the Union* (London, 1909).
CECIL, A., *British Foreign Secretaries, 1807–1916* (London, 1927).
CHEYNEY, E. P., *A Short History of England* (Boston, 1904).
————, *An Introduction to the Industrial and Social History of England.* (New York, 1930).
————, *Modern English Reform* (Philadelphia, 1931).
CLAPHAM, J. H., *An Economic History of Modern Britain, the Early Railway Age, 1820–1850* (Cambridge, 1926).
CROSS, A. L., *A History of England and Greater Britain* (New York, 1914).
————, *A Shorter History of England and Greater Britain* (New York, 1929).
DIETZ, F. C., *A Political and Social History of England* (New York, 1927).
EGERTON, H. E., *A Short History of British Colonial Policy* (London, 1920).
FAERBRIDGE, D., *A History of South Africa* (London, 1918).
FAY, C. R., *Great Britain from Adam Smith to the Present Day* (New York, 1928).
FLETCHER, C. R. L., *An Introductory History of England* (New York, 1910).
GARDINER, S. R. *A Student's History of England* (London, 1929).
HALÉVY, E., *Histoire du peuple anglais au XIXe siècle,* 3 vols. (Paris, 1912–23).
HULME, E. M., *A History of the British People* (New York, 1924).
INNES, A. D., *A History of England and the British Empire,* 4 vols. (New York, 1913–15).
JOSE, A. W., *The Growth of Empire* (London, 1910).
KEITH, A. B., *Selected Speeches and Documents on British Colonial Policy, 1763–1917,* 2 vols. (London, 1918).
————, *Speeches and Documents on Indian Policy, 1750–1921,* 2 vols. (London, 1922).
LARSON, L. M., *History of England and the British Commonwealth* (New York, 1924).
LOW, S., and SANDERS, L. C., *The History of England during the Reign of Queen Victoria* (*1837–1901*) (London, 1907).
LUNT, W. E., *A History of England* (New York, 1928).
MC CARTHY, J., *The Story of the People of England in the Nineteenth Century,* 2 vols. (New York, 1899).
MARRIOTT, SIR J. A. R., *England since Waterloo* (New York, 1922).
MARTINEAU, H., *History of the Peace,* 4 vols. (London, 1877–78).
MAXWELL, SIR H. E., *A Century of Empire, 1801–1900* (London, 1909–11).
MOLESWORTH, W. N., *The History of England from the Year 1830 to 1874,* 3 vols. (London, 1874).
MOWAT, R. B., *A History of Great Britain* (Oxford, 1922).
MUIR, R., *A Short History of the British Commonwealth,* 2 vols. (London, 1920–22).
PAUL, H., *History of Modern England,* 5 vols. (New York, 1904–06).

POLLARD, A. F., *The History of England* (New York, 1912).

POWELL, F. Y., and TOUT, T. F., *History of England* (London, 1910).

PRENTOUT, H., *Histoire d'Angleterre* (Paris, 1920).

RANSOME, C., *A Short History of England* (London, 1891, 1897).

RAYNER, R. M., *Nineteenth Century England* (London, 1927).

ROBINSON, C. E., *A History of British Progress from the Early Ages to the Present Time* (New York, 1928).

ROBINSON, H., *History of Great Britain* (Boston, 1927).

——————, *The Development of the British Empire* (Boston, 1922).

SWEET, A. H., *History of England* (New York, 1931).

THEAL, G. M., *South Africa,* 5 vols. (New York, 1899).

TOUT, T. F., *An Advanced History of Great Britain* (New York, 1919).

TREVELYAN, G. M., *British History in the Nineteenth Century (1782–1901)* (London, 1924).

VAUCHER, P., *Le monde anglo-saxon au XIX siècle* (Paris, 1926).

WALPOLE, S., *History of England from the Conclusion of the Great War in 1815,* 5 vols. (London, 1879–86).

WILLIAMSON, J. A., *The Evolution of England* (Oxford, 1931).

——————, *A Short History of British Expansion* (London, 1922).

WINGFIELD-STRATFORD, E. C., *The History of British Civilization* (London, 1928).

WOODWARD, W. H., *A Short History of the Expansion of the British Empire, 1500–1930* (Cambridge, 1931).

France:

ANDERSON, F. M., *The Constitutions and Other Select Documents Illustrative of the History of France, 1789–1907* (Minneapolis, 1908).

BAINVILLE, J., *Histoire de France* (Paris, 1924).

——————, *Histoire de trois générations, 1815–1918* (Paris, 1918).

BARDOUX, A., *La bourgeoisie française, 1789–1848* (Paris, 1893).

BERRY, W. G., *France since Waterloo* (London, 1908).

BORDIER, H., *Histoire de France pour tous* (Paris, 1900).

BOURGEOIS, E., *Modern France,* 2 vols. (Cambridge, 1919).

BUCHAN, J., ed., *France* (Boston, 1923).

CAHEN, L., *Histoire de l'Europe et particulièrement de la France, 1789–1848* (Paris, 1929).

CHAMPION, E., *Vue générale de l'histoire de France* (Paris, 1908).

COUBERTIN, P. DE, *France since 1814* (New York, 1900).

DAVIS, W. S., *A History of France* (New York, 1919).

DEBIDOUR, A., *L'église et l'état en France de 1789 à 1870* (Paris, 1898).

DICKINSON, G. L., *Revolution and Reaction in Modern France* (London, 1892).

DUGUIT, L., and MONNIER, H., *Les constitutions et les principales lois politiques de la France depuis 1789* (Paris, 1925).

DURUY, V., *Histoire de France,* 2 vols. (Paris, 1886).

——————, *A History of France* (New York, 1920).

DUVERGIER DE HAURANNE, P., *Histoire du gouvernement parlementaire en France——1814–1848,* 10 vols. (Paris, 1857–71).

ELTON, G., *The Revolutionary Idea in France* (New York, 1923).
GUIGNEBERT, C. A. H., *A Short History of the French People*, 2 vols. (New York, 1930).
HANOTAUX, G., *Histoire de la nation française*, 15 vols. (Paris, 1920–29).
HARDY, G., *Histoire de la colonisation française* (Paris, 1928).
HASSALL, A., *The French People* (New York, 1912).
Histoire de France illustrée, Vol. II (Paris, n.d.).
HUDDLESTON, S., *France* (New York, 1927).
HUDSON, W. H., *France* (New York, 1917).
JAURÈS, J., *Histoire socialiste*, Vols. VII–XII (Paris, 1901–08).
LATIMER, E. W., *France in the Nineteenth Century* (Chicago, 1892).
LAVISSE, E., *Histoire de France contemporaine*, Vols. IV–IX (Paris, 1920–22).
LEBON, A., *Cent ans d'histoire intérieure 1789–1895* (Paris, 1898).
——————, *Modern France, 1789–1915* (New York, 1916).
MALET, A., *Histoire de France* (Paris, 1928).
MARSHALL, H. E., *A History of France* (New York, 1912).
MORETON-MACDONALD, J., *A History of France*, 3 vols. (London, 1915).
MUEL, L., *Gouvernements, ministères, et constitutions de la France depuis 1789* (Paris, 1895).
PELLISON, M., *Les orateurs politiques de la France de 1830 à nos jours* (Paris, 1898).
RENARD, G. F., *Les étapes de la société française au XIXe siècle* (Paris, 1913).
SEDGWICK, H. D., *France* (London, 1930).
SÉE, H., *Esquisse d'une histoire économique et sociale de la France* (Paris, 1929).
SOLTAU, R. H., *French Political Thought in the Nineteenth Century* (New Haven, 1931).
TILLEY, A. A., *Modern France* (Cambridge, 1922).
WEILL, G., *La France sous la monarchie constitutionelle (1814–1848)* (Paris, 1912).
——————, *Histoire du parti républicain en France de 1814 à 1870* (Paris, 1900).
——————, *L'Alsace française de 1789 à 1870* (Paris, 1916).

Germany:

BARING-GOULD, S., *The Story of Germany* (New York, 1889).
BIEDERMANN, K., *1815–1840: Fünf und zwanzig Jahre deutscher Geschichte*, 2 vols. (Breslau, 1890).
——————, *1840–1870: Dreissig Jahre deutscher Geschichte*, 2 vols. (Breslau, 1896).
BONNEFON, C., *Histoire d'Allemagne* (Paris, 1925).
BRANDI, K., *Deutsche Geschichte* (Berlin, 1919).
CLASS, H., *Deutsche Geschichte* (Leipzig, 1914).
Deutsche Geschichtsquellen des neunzehnten Jahrhunderts, 2 vols. (Leipzig, 1922–23).

Das Deutsche Jahrhundert, 2 vols. (Berlin, 1901).

DEVENTER, M. L., *Cinquante années de l'histoire fédérale de l'Allemagne* (Brussels, 1870).

FLATHE, T., *Deutsche Reden*, 2 vols. (Leipzig, 1893–94).

GEBHARDT, B., *Handbuch der deutschen Geschichte*, 6th ed., 3 vols. (Stuttgart, 1922–23).

Germany in the Nineteenth Century (Manchester, 1915).

GOLTZ, C., FREIHERR VON DER, *Kriegsgeschichte Deutschlands im neunzehnten Jahrhundert*, 2 vols. (Berlin, 1910–14).

GOOCH, G. P., *Germany* (New York, 1925).

HÄUSSER, L., *Deutsche Geschichte vom Tode Friedrichs des Grossen bis zur Gründung des Deutschen Bundes*, 4 vols. (Berlin, 1869).

HENDERSON, E. F., *A Short History of Germany*, Vol. II (New York, 1916).

HEYCK, E., *Deutsche Geschichte*, Vol. III (Bielefeld, 1906).

HINTZE, O., *Die Hohenzollern und ihr Werk* (Berlin, 1916).

HOFMANN, A. VON, *Politische Geschichte der Deutschen*, Vol. V (Stuttgart, 1928).

JÄGER, O., *Deutsche Geschichte*, Vol. II (Munich, 1910).

JASTROW, I., *Geschichte der deutschen Einheitstraumes und seiner Erfüllung* (Berlin, 1891).

KÄMMEL, O., *Der Werdegang des deutschen Volkes*, Vols. III–IV (Berlin, 1920–23).

KAUFMANN, G., *Geschichte Deutschlands im neunzehnten Jahrhundert* (Berlin, 1912).

LAMPRECHT, K. G., *Deutsche Geschichte*, Vols. IX–XI (Berlin, 1894–1909).

LICHTENBERGER, H., *Das Moderne Deutschland und seine Entwickelung* (Dresden, 1908).

——————, *Germany and Its Evolution in Modern Times* (London, 1913).

MÜLLER, D., *Geschichte des deutschen Volkes* (Berlin, 1919).

MÜLLER, W., *Political History of Recent Times, 1816–1875* (New York, 1882).

PHILLIPS, W. A., *A Short History of Germany and Her Colonies* (London, 1914).

PINNOW, H., *Deutsche Geschichte* (Berlin, 1929).

PRIEST, G. M., *Germany since 1740* (New York, 1915).

SALOMON, L., *Deutschlands Leben und Streben im neunzehnten Jahrhundert* (Stuttgart, 1893).

SCHÄFER, D., *Deutsche Geschichte*, Vol. II (Jena, 1910).

SCHEVILL, F., *The Making of Modern Germany* (Chicago, 1916).

SCHNIZER, O., *Deutsche Geschichte fürs deutsche Volk* (Stuttgart, 1929).

STURMHOEFEL, K., *Geschichte des deutschen Volkes*, Vol. II (Leipzig, 1926).

TREITSCHKE, H. G. VON, *Deutsche Geschichte im neunzehnten Jahrhundert* (Leipzig, 1886–89).

——————, *History of Germany in the Nineteenth Century*, 7 vols. (New York, 1915–19).

WARD, A. W., *Germany, 1815–90*, 3 vols. (Cambridge, 1916–18).

WUESSING, F., *Geschichte des deutschen Volkes* (Berlin, 1921).

WUSTMANN, R., *Deutsche Geschichte im Grundriss,* Vol. II (Leipzig, 1907).
ZWIEDINECK-SÜDENHORST, H. VON, *Deutsche Geschichte,* 3 vols. (Stuttgart, 1897–1905).
ZINK, T., *Deutsche Geschichte,* Vol. II (Kaiserlautern, 1907).

MARRIOTT, SIR J. A. R., and ROBERTSON, C. G., *The Evolution of Prussia* (Oxford, 1915).
PRUTZ, H., *Preussische Geschichte,* Vol. IV (Stuttgart, 1902).
SCHMOLLER, G., *Preussische Verfassungs-, Verwaltungs-, und Finanzgeschichte* (Berlin, 1921).

Italy:

BERTOLINI, F., *Storia generale d'Italia,* Vol. IV (Milan, 1897).
BUCHAN, J., ed., *Italy* (Boston, 1923).
CAPPELLETTI, L., *Storia d'Italia,* Vol. II (Genoa, 1902).
CROZALS, J. DE, *L'unité italienne (1815–1870)* (Paris, 1898).
FARINI, L., *The Roman State from 1815–1850,* 4 vols. (London, 1851–54).
FERRARI, A., *La preparazione intellettuale del risorgimento italiano (1748–1789)* (Milan, 1923).
FORESTER, C. S., *Victor Emmanuel II and the Union of Italy* (New York, 1927).
GIFFORD, A., *Italy, Her People and Their Story* (Boston, 1905).
HARTMANN, L. M., *Hundert Jahre italienischer Geschichte, 1815–1915* (Munich, 1916).
HOFMANN, A. VON, *Das Land Italien and seine Geschichte* (Stuttgart, 1921).
KING, B., *A History of Italian Unity,* 2 vols. (London, 1924).
MARTINENGO-CESARESCO, E., *Italian Characters in the Epoch of Unification* (London, 1901).
MARTINENGO-CESARESCO, E., *The Liberation of Italy, 1815–1870* (London, 1895).
ORSI, P., *Cavour and the Making of Modern Italy, 1810–1861* (London, 1914).
——————, *Modern Italy, 1748–1922* (London, 1923).
PROFESSIONE, A., *Storia d'Italia e della civiltà e società italiana,* Vol. II (Rome, 1909).
RAULICH, I., *Manuale di storia contemporanea d'Europa e specialmente d'Italia dal 1750 ai nostri giorni* (Turin, 1909).
REUCHLIN, H., *Geschichte Italiens,* 4 vols. (Leipzig, 1859–73).
SEDGWICK, H. D., *A Short History of Italy* (Boston, 1905).
SOLMI, A., *Il risorgimento italiano* (Milan, 1919).
——————, *The Making of Modern Italy* (London, 1925).
STILLMAN, W. J., *The Union of Italy* (Cambridge, 1899).
THAYER, W. R., *The Dawn of Italian Independence,* 2 vols. (Boston, 1892).
TREVELYAN, J. P., *A Short History of the Italian People* (New York, 1920).

The Kingdom of the Netherlands:

BLOK, P. J., *Geschiedenis van het Nederlandsche Volk,* Vol. VII (Gröningen, 1907).

——————, *History of the People of the Netherlands,* Vol. V (New York, 1912).
EDMUNDSON, G., *History of Holland* (Cambridge, 1922).

Norway:

GJERSET, K., *History of the Norwegian People* (New York, 1915).

Poland:

DYBOSKI, R., *Outlines of Polish History* (London, 1925).
FELDMANN, W., *Geschichte der politischen Ideen in Polen* (Munich, 1917).
GRAPPIN, H., *Histoire de la Pologne des origines à 1922* (Paris, 1922).
HANISCH, E., *Die Geschichte Polens* (Leipzig, 1923).
KONOPCZYNSKI, W., *A Brief Outline of Polish History* (Geneva, 1919).
LAUBERT, M., *Die Preussische Polenpolitik von 1772–1914* (Berlin, 1920).
LEWINSKI-CORWIN, E. H., *The Political History of Poland* (New York, 1917).
MARTIAL, R., *La Pologne jadis et de nos jours* (Paris, 1928).
MORFILL, W. R., *Poland* (New York, 1903).
PHILLIPS, W. A., *Poland* (New York, 1915).
PRIVAT, E., *L'Europe et l'odyssée de la Pologne au XIXe siècle* (Lausanne, 1918).
WHITTON, F. E., *A History of Poland* (London, 1917).

Russia:

BARING, M., *The Russian People* (London, 1911).
BEAZLEY, R., FORBES, N., and BIRKETT, G. A., *Russia from the Varangians to the Bolsheviks* (Oxford, 1918).
CRÉHANGE, G., *Histoire de la Russie* (Paris, 1896).
DAUDET, E., *Soixante années du règne des Romanoffs Nicolas I et Alexandre II* (Paris, 1919).
EPHIMENTO, A., *A Short History of Russia* (London, 1920).
HEWITT, N., *The Rulers of Russia* (London, 1924).
HODGETTS, E. A. B., *The Court of Russia in the Nineteenth Century,* 2 vols. (London, 1908).
KLEINSCHMIDT, A., *Drei Jahrhunderte russischer Geschichte (1598–1898)* (Berlin, 1898).
KORNILOV, A., *A Modern Russian History,* 2 vols. (New York, 1917).
MAKEEF, N., and O'HARA, V., *Russia* (New York, 1925).
MAVOR, J., *An Economic History of Russia,* rev. ed., Vol. II (New York, 1925).
MORFILL, W. R., *Russia* (New York, 1908).
MUNRO, H., *The Rise of the Russian Empire* (London, 1900).
PANTENIUS, T. H., *Geschichte Russlands* (Leipzig, 1917).
PARES, B., *A History of Russia* (New York, 1928).
PLATONOV, S. F., *History of Russia* (New York, 1925).
POKROWSKI, M., *Geschichte Russlands von seiner Entstehung bis neuesten Zeit* (Leipzig, 1928).

QUADFLIEG, F., *Russische Expansionspolitik von 1774 bis 1914* (Berlin, 1914).
RAMBAUD, A., *Histoire de Russie* (Paris, 1914).
————, *History of Russia*, 3 vols. (Boston, 1880–82).
SKRINE, F. H. B., *The Expansion of Russia, 1815–1900* (Cambridge, 1904).
STÄHLIN, K., *Geschichte Russlands von den Anfängen bis zur Gegenwart* (Stuttgart, 1923).
UEBERSBERGER, H., *Russlands Orientpolitik in den letzten zwei Jahrhunderten* (Stuttgart, 1913).
VERNADSKY, G., *A History of Russia* (New Haven, 1929).
WALLACE, D. M., KROPOTKIN, PRINCE, MIJATOVICH, C., and BOURCHIER, J. D., *A Short History of Russia and the Balkan States* (London, 1914).

Spain:

AGUADO, S., *Manual de historia de España* (Bilbao, 1927–28).
ALTAMIRA, R., *Historia de la civilizacion española* (Barcelona, 1928).
BALLESTER, R., *Histoire de l'Espagne* (Paris, 1928).
CHAPMAN, C., *A History of Spain* (New York, 1918).
CLARKE, B., *Modern Spain, 1815–1898,* (New York, 1907).
HUME, M. A. S., *Modern Spain* (London, 1923).
————, *The Spanish People* (New York, 1909).
IBAÑEZ, BLASCO, *Historia de la revolución española, 1808–1874* (Barcelona, 1890).
MADARIAGA, S. DE, *Spain* (New York, 1930).
PI Y MARGÀLL, F., *Historia de España en el siglo XIX* (Barcelona, 1910).
SEDGWICK, H. D., *Spain* (Boston, 1926).

Sweden:

STOMBERG, A. A., *History of Sweden* (New York, in press).

Switzerland:

DÄNDLIKER, K., *A Short History of Switzerland* (London, 1899).
GAGLIARDI, E., *Geschichte der Schweiz*, Vols. II–III (Zurich, 1920–27).
HUG, L., *Switzerland* (New York, 1890).
MC CRACKAN, W. D., *The Rise of the Swiss Republic* (Boston, 1892).
MARTIN, W., *Histoire de la Suisse* (Paris, 1926).
OECHSLI, W., *History of Switzerland, 1499–1914* (Cambridge, 1922).

CHAPTER I

EUROPE AT THE OPENING OF THE NINETEENTH CENTURY

Excellent bibliographies for the Ancien Régime, the French Revolution, and the Napoleonic period can be found in BOURNE, H. E., *The Revolutionary Period in Europe, 1763–1815,* and in GOTTSCHALK, L. R., *The Era of the French Revolution (1715–1815).*

PART I

CHAPTER II

THE REACTION OF EUROPE AGAINST THE FRENCH REVOLUTION AND THE RULE
OF NAPOLEON

The National Risings against Napoleon:

BIGELOW, P., *History of the German Struggle for Liberty*, 2 vols. (New
York, 1896).
FORD, G. S., *Stein and the Era of Reform in Prussia, 1807–1815* (Princeton,
1922).
HARTUNG, F., *Deutschlands Zusammenbruch und Erhebung im Zeitalter der
französischen Revolution, 1792–1815* (Bielefeld, 1922).
HÄUSSER, L., *Deutsche Geschichte vom Tode Friedrichs des Grossen bis
zur Gründung des deutschen Bundes*, Vol. IV (Berlin, 1869).
LANGSAM, W. C., *The Napoleonic Wars and German Nationalism in Austria*
(New York, 1930).
MEINECKE, F., *Das Zeitalter der deutschen Erhebung, 1795–1815* (Bielefeld,
1906).
ONCKEN, W., *Zeitalter der Revolution, des Kaiserreiches, und der Be-
freiungskriege* (Berlin, 1886).
SYBEL, H. VON, *Erhebung Europas gegen Napoleon I* (Boston, 1893).
ULMANN, H., *Geschichte der Befreiungskriege*, 2 vols. (Munich, 1914, 1915).

Congress of Vienna:

FOURNIER, A., *Die Geheimpolizei auf dem Wiener Kongress* (Vienna, 1913).
HAZEN, C. D., THAYER, W. R., and LORD, R. H., *Three Peace Congresses of
the Nineteenth Century* (Cambridge, 1917).
KLÜBER, J., *Acten des Wiener Congresses*, 8 vols. (Erlangen, 1815–18).
LA GARDE-CHAMBONAS, COUNT DE, *Anecdotal Recollections of the Congress
of Vienna* (London, 1902).
————————, *Fêtes et souvenirs du congrès de Vienne*, 2 vols. (Paris, 1840).
WEBSTER, C. K., *The Congress of Vienna, 1814–1815* (New York, 1919).
————————, *British Diplomacy, 1813–1815* (London, 1921).
WEIL, M. H., *Les dessous du Congrès de Vienne*, 2 vols. (Paris, 1917).

Leaders of the Congress of Vienna:

BERNHARDI, T. VON, *Geschichte Russlands und der europäischen Politik in
den Jahren 1814 bis 1831*, 4 vols. (Leipzig, 1863–77).
CZARTORYSKI, A. J., *Alexandre Ier et le prince Czartoryski, 1811–1823*
(Paris, 1865).
Le gouverneur d'un prince (Lausanne, 1902).
RAIN, P., *Un tsar idéologue, Alexandre Ier (1777–1825)* (Paris, 1913).
RAPPAPORT, A. S., *The Curse of the Romanoffs* (New York, 1907).
WALIZEWSKI, K., *Le règne d'Alexandre Ier* (Paris, 1923).

CASTLEREAGH, R. S., VISCOUNT, *Memoirs and Correspondence of Viscount Castlereagh*, 12 vols. (London, 1848–53).
HASSAL, A., *Viscount Castlereagh* (New York, 1908).
WEBSTER, C. K., *The Foreign Policy of Castlereagh, 1812–1815* (New York, 1931).

GENTZ, F. VON, *Tagebücher*, 4 vols. in 2 (Leipzig, 1873–74).
WITTICHEN, F. C., *Briefe an und von Friederich von Gentz*, 3 vols. in 4 (Munich, 1909–13).

CRESSON, W. P., *Diplomatic Portraits* (New York, 1923).
DEMELITSCH, F. VON, *Metternich und seine auswärtige Politik* (Stuttgart, 1898).
MALLESON, G. B., *Metternich* (Philadelphia, 1888).
MAZADE-PERCIN, C., *Un chancelier d'ancien régime* (Paris, 1889).
METTERNICH, PRINCE VON, *Aus Metternich's nachgelassenen Papieren*, 8 vols. (Vienna, 1880–84).
————, *Mémoires*, 8 vols. (Paris, 1881–1908).
————, *Memoirs*, 3 vols. (New York, 1881–82); 4 vols. (London, 1880).
SANDEMAN, G. A. C., *Metternich* (London, 1911).
SRBIK, H. VON, *Metternich, der Staatsmann und der Mensch*, 2 vols. (Munich, 1925).
WOODWARD, E. L., *Three Studies in European Conservatism* (London, 1929).

BLENNERHASSET, LADY, *Talleyrand* (Berlin, 1894, London, 1894).
LACOMBE, B. DE, *La vie privée de Talleyrand* (1910).
LACOUR-GAYET, G., *Talleyrand, 1754–1838*, 2 vols. (Paris, 1928, 1930).
MCCABE, J., *Talleyrand* (London, 1906).
PALLAIN, M. G., ed., *Correspondence inédite du prince Talleyrand et du roi Louis XVIII pendant le Congrès de Vienne* (Paris, 1881).
————, *The Correspondence of Prince Talleyrand and King Louis XVIII during the Congress of Vienna* (New York, 1881).

FORTESCUE, J. W., *Wellington* (New York, 1925).
HOOPER, G., *Wellington* (London, 1889).
TALLEYRAND, PRINCE DE, *Mémoires*, 5 vols. (Paris, 1891–92).
WELLINGTON, DUKE OF, *The Dispatches of Field Marshall, Duke of Wellington*, 12 vols. (London, 1837–38).
————, *Despatches, Correspondence, and Memoranda of Field Marshal Arthur, Duke of Wellington*, 8 vols. (London, 1867–80).

First and Second Restorations in France:

ARTZ, F. B., *France under the Bourbon Restoration, 1814–1930* (Cambridge, 1931).
BEAU DE LOMÉNIE, E., *La carrière politique de Chateaubriand de 1814 à 1830*, 2 vols. (Paris, 1929).
CROUSAZ-CRETET, L. DE, *Le duc de Richelieu en Russie et en France, 1766–1822* (Paris, 1897).
DAUDET, E., *Louis XVIII et Decazes* (Paris, 1899).
DUPUIS, C., *Le ministère de Talleyrand en 1814*, 2 vols. in 1 (Paris, 1919–20).

DUVERGIER DE HAURANNE, P., *Histoire du gouvernement parlementaire en France, 1814–1848*, 10 vols. (Paris, 1857–71).
FORSSELL, N., *Fouché, the Man Napoleon Feared* (New York, 1928).
HALL, J., *The Bourbon Restoration* (Boston, 1909).
HOUSSAYE, H., *1814* (Paris, 1918).
————, *1815*, 3 vols. (Paris, 1918–21).
LANZAC DE LABORIE, L., *Les passions politiques sous la restauration* (Paris, 1900).
LUCAS-DUBRETON, J., *Louis XVIII* (New York, 1927).
————, *The Restoration and the July Monarchy* (New York, 1929).
MADELIN, L., *Fouché, 1759–1820*, 2 vols. (Paris, 1903).
PINGAUD, L., *L'empereur Alexandre et la seconde restauration* (Paris, 1900).
POLOVTSOFF, A., *Correspondance diplomatique des ambassadeurs et ministres en France et de France en Russie avec leur gouvernements de 1814 à 1830*, 2 vols. (St. Petersburg, 1902–07).
POZZO DI BORGO, COUNT DI, *Correspondance diplomatique du comte Pozzo di Borgo et du comte de Nesselrode*, 2 vols. (Paris, 1890–97).
RAIN, P., *L'Europe et la restauration des Bourbons* (Paris, 1908).
SIMON, P., *L'élaboration de la charte constitutionelle de 1814* (Paris, 1906).
SOREL, A., *L'Europe et la révolution française*, Vol. VIII (Paris, 1904).
THIERS, A., *Le consulat et l'empire*, Vol. XX (Paris, 1862).
VAULABELLE, A. T., *Histoire de deux restaurations*, 10 vols. (Paris, 1874).
VIEL-CASTEL, L. DE, *Histoire de la restauration*, 20 vols. (Paris, 1860–80).

CHAPTER III
THE FIRST REVOLUTIONARY MOVEMENTS OF THE NINETEENTH CENTURY

BECKER, J., *Historia de las relaciones exteriores de España*, Vol. I (Madrid, 1924).
BIGNON, L. P. E., BARON, *Du Congrès de Troppau* (Paris, 1821).
CHATEAUBRIAND, F. R., VISCOUNT DE, *Le Congrès de Vérone*, 2 vols. (Paris, 1838).
CRESSON, W. P., *The Holy Alliance* (New York, 1922).
GEOFFROY DE GRANDMAISON, C. A., *L'expédition française d'Espagne en 1823* (Paris, 1928).
JOHNSTON, R. M., *The Napoleonic Empire in Southern Italy and the Rise of Secret Societies*, Vol. II (New York, 1904).
PHILLIPS, W. A., *Confederation of Europe* (London, 1920).
VILLA-URRUTIA, MARQUIS DE, *Fernando VII rey constitucional* (Madrid, 1922).
WEBSTER, C. K., *The Foreign Policy of Castlereagh, 1815–22* (London, 1925).

CHAPTER IV
THE INDUSTRIAL AND AGRICULTURAL REVOLUTIONS, 1760–1850

The English Industrial Revolution:

ASHTON, T. S., *Iron and Steel in the Industrial Revolution* (Manchester, 1924).

BAINES, SIR E., *History of the Cotton Manufacturing in Great Britain* (London, 1835).
BOWDEN, W., *Industrial Society in England toward the End of the Eighteenth Century* (New York, 1925).
BUER, M. C., *Health, Wealth, and Population in the Early Days of the Industrial Revolution (1760–1815)* (London, 1926).
BYRN, E. W., *The Progress of Invention in the Nineteenth Century* (New York, 1900).
CANTRILL, T. C., *Coal Mining* (New York, 1914).
CHAPMAN, S. J., *Lancashire Cotton Industry* (Manchester, 1904).
CLAPHAM, J. H., *The Woollen and Worsted Industries* (London, 1907).
CLEVELAND-STEVENS, E. C., *English Railways* (New York, 1915).
COOKE-TAYLOR, R. W., *The Modern Factory System* (London, 1891).
CUNNINGHAM, W., *The Growth of English Industry and Commerce in Modern Times,* 3 vols. (Cambridge, 1892).
DANIELS, G. W., *The Early English Cotton Industry* (Manchester, 1920).
DUNLOP, O. J., and DENMAN, R. D., *English Apprenticeship and Child Labour* (London, 1912).
ENGELS, F., *Condition of the Working Class in England in 1844* (London, 1892).
FRENCH, G. J., *Life and Times of Samuel Crompton* (Manchester, 1860).
GASKELL, P., *Manufacturing Population of England* (London, 1833).
GIBBINS, H. DE B., *Industry in England* (London, 1920).
GILBERT, J., *The Railways of England* (London, 1839).
GRINLING, C. H., *History of the Great Northern Railway* (London, 1898).
GUEST, R., *History of the Cotton Manufacture with a Disapproval of the Sir Richard Arkwright's Claim to His Inventions* (Manchester, 1823).
HAMILTON, H., *The English Brass and Copper Industries to 1800* (New York, 1926).
HAMMOND, J. L. and B., *The Rise of Modern Industry* (New York, 1926).
————, *The Town Labourer, 1760–1832* (New York, 1917).
————, *The Skilled Labourer, 1760–1832* (New York, 1920).
————, *The Village Labourer, 1760–1832* (New York, 1913).
HEATON, H., *Yorkshire Woollen and Worsted Industries* (Oxford, 1920).
HOBSON, J. A., *Evolution of Modern Capitalism* (London, 1928).
JACKMAN, W. T., *The Development of Transportation in Modern England,* 2 vols. (New York, 1916).
JEAFFRESON, J. C., *Life of Robert Stephenson* (London, 1866).
KIRKALDY, A. W., *British Shipping* (New York, 1914).
————, and EVANS, A. D., *The History of Transport* (London, 1915).
KNOWLES, L. C. A., *The Industrial and Commercial Revolutions in Great Britain during the Nineteenth Century* (New York, 1922).
LEVI, L., *History of British Commerce, 1763–1870* (London, 1872).
LIPSON, E., *History of the Woollen and Worsted Industries* (London, 1921).
LLOYD, G. I. H., *The Cutlery Trades* (London, 1913).
LORD, J., *Capital and Steam Power* (London, 1923).
MANTOUX, P., *La révolution industrielle au XVIIIe siècle* (Paris, 1906).
MEREDITH, H. O., *Outlines of the Economic History of England* (London, 1908).

MOFFIT, L. W., *England on the Eve of the Industrial Revolution* (London, 1925).

MUIRHEAD, J., *The Origin and Progress of the Mechanical Inventions of James Watt,* 3 vols. (London, 1854).

PERRIS, G. H., *The Industrial History of Modern England* (New York, 1914).

PINCHBECK, I., *Women Workers and the Industrial Revolution* (New York, 1930).

PRATT, E. A., *A History of Inland Transport and Communication in England* (London, 1912).

PREBBLE, G. H., *A Chronological History of the Origin and Development of Steam Navigation* (Philadelphia, 1883).

REES, J. F., *Social and Industrial History of England, 1815–1918* (London, 1920).

SLATER, G., *The Making of Modern England* (Boston, 1915).

SMART, W., *Economic Annals of the Nineteenth Century,* 2 vols. (London, 1910–17).

SMILES, S., *Iron Workers and Tool Makers* (Boston, 1864).

————, *Lives of the Engineers,* 4 vols. (London, 1862–68).

————, *George and Robert Stephenson* (New York, 1868).

STEEL, W., *The History of the London and Northwestern Railway* (London, 1914).

THURSTON, R. H., *History of the Growth of the Steam Engine* (New York, 1884).

TOYNBEE, A., *Lectures on the Industrial Revolution* (London, 1912).

UNWIN, G., HULME, A., and TAYLOR, G., *Samuel Oldknow and the Arkwrights* (New York, 1924).

URE, A., *The Philosophy of Manufactures* (London, 1835).

USHER, A. P., *An Introduction to the Industrial History of England* (Boston, 1920).

————, *A History of Mechanical Inventions* (New York, 1929).

WADSWORTH, A. P., and MANN, J. DEL., *The Cotton Trade and Industrial Lancashire, 1600–1780* (Manchester, 1931).

WARNER, G. T., *Landmarks in English Industrial History* (London, 1911).

WILLIAMS, F. S., *The Midland Railway, Its Rise and Progress* (London, 1876).

WOOD, H. T., *Industrial England in the Middle of the Eighteenth Century* (London, 1910).

The Industrial Revolution on the Continent:

BALLOT, C., *Introduction du machinisme dans l'industrie française* (Paris, 1923).

BECK, L., *Die Geschichte des Eisens in technischer und kulturgeschichtlicher Beziehung,* 5 vols. (Brunswick, 1884–1903).

BEIL, J. A., *Stand und Ergebnisse der Europäischer Eisenbahnen bis zu dem Jahr 1846* (Vienna, 1846).

BIRNIE, A., *An Economic History of Europe, 1760–1930* (New York, 1930).

BOURGIN, G., *Les patrons, les ouvrières et l'état* (Paris, 1912).

BOURGOING, P. C. A., *Tableau de l'état actuel et des progrès probables des chemins de fer de l'Allemagne et du continent européen* (Paris, 1842).

CILLEULS, A. DE., *Histoire et régime de la grande industrie en France aux XVIIe et XVIIIe siècles* (Paris, 1898).

CLAPHAM, J. H., *The Economic Development of France and Germany, 1815–1914* (Cambridge, 1921).

DEVYS, J., *Les chemins de fer de l'état belge* (Paris, 1910).

ERNEST-CHARLES, J., *Les chemins de fer en France pendant la règne de Louis Philippe* (Paris, 1896).

GIBBINS, H. DE B., *Economic and Industrial Progress of the Century* (Toronto, 1903).

GRIPPON-LAMOTTE, L., *Histoire du réseau des chemins de fer français* (Paris, 1904).

KNIGHT, M. M., BARNES, H. E., and FLÜGEL, F., *Economic History of Europe in Modern Times* (Boston, 1928).

LAVELEYE, A. F. L. DE, *Histoire des vingt-cinq premières années des chemins de fer belges* (Brussels, 1862).

LE CHATELIER, L., *Chemins de fer d'Allemagne* (Paris, 1845).

LEVAINVILLE, J., *L'industrie du fer en France* (Paris, 1922).

LEVASSEUR, E., *Histoire des classes ouvrières et de l'industrie en France de 1789 à 1870*, 2 vols. (Paris, 1903–04).

LEVY, R., *Histoire économique de l'industrie cotonnière en Alsace* (Paris, 1912).

MARTIN, G., *La grande industrie en France sous le règne de Louis XV* (Paris, 1901).

MASCHER, H. A., *Das deutsche Gewerbewesen* (Potsdam, 1866).

MAYER, A., *Geschichte und Geographie der deutschen Eisenbahnen*, 2 vols. (Berlin, 1891).

MAYER, T., *Deutsche Wirtschaftsgeschichte der Neuzeit* (Leipzig, 1928).

MEHRENS, B., *Die Entstehung und Entwickelung der grossen französischen Kreditinstitute* (Stuttgart, 1911).

NICOLAI, E., *Les chemins de fer de l'état en Belgique, 1834–1884* (1885).

PICARD, A. M., *Les chemins de fer français,* Vol. I (Paris, 1884).

POHLE, L., *Das deutsche Wirtschaftsleben seit Beginn des neunzehnten Jahrhunderts* (Leipzig, 1930).

REDEN, F. W. O. L. VON, *Die Eisenbahnen Frankreichs* (Berlin, 1846).

REUSSE, H., *Die deutschen Eisenbahnen* (Cassel, 1844).

SARTORIUS VON WALTERHAUSEN, A., *Deutsche Wirtschaftsgeschichte 1815–1914* (Jena, 1920).

SÉE, H., *L'évolution commerciale et industrielle de la France sous l'ancien régime* (Paris, 1925).

—————, *La vie économique et les classes sociales en France au XVIIIe siècle* (Paris, 1924).

—————, *Economic and Social Conditions in France during the Eighteenth Century* (New York, 1927).

The English Agricultural Revolution:

BLAND, A. E., BROWN, P. A., and TAWNEY, R. H., *English Economic History, Select Documents* (New York, 1914).

CURTLER, W. H. R., *The Enclosure and Redistribution of Our Land* (Oxford, 1920).
FORDHAM, M., *A Short History of English Rural Life* (London, 1916).
GARNIER, R. M., *Annals of the British Peasantry* (London, 1895).
————, *History of the English Landed Gentry* (London, 1893).
GONNER, E. C. K., *Common Land and Enclosure* (London, 1912).
HASBACH, W., *History of the English Agricultural Labourer* (London, 1908).
JOHNSON, A. H., *The Disappearance of the Small Landowner* (Oxford, 1909).
LECKY, W. E. H., *History of England in the Eighteenth Century,* Vol. VII (London, 1887).
PROTHERO, R. E., *English Farming Past and Present* (London, 1927).
SLATER, G., *The English Peasantry and the Enclosure of the Common Fields* (London, 1907).
YOUNG, A., *Tour through the North,* 4 vols. (London, 1770).
————, *Tour in the Southern Counties,* 4 vols. (London, 1769).
————, *The Farmer's Tour through the East of England,* 4 vols. (London, 1771).

The Agricultural Revolution on the Continent:

GOLTZ, T. VON DER, *Geschichte der deutschen Landwirtschaft,* 2 vols. (Stuttgart, 1902–03).
GRAS, N. S. B., *A History of Agriculture in Europe and America* (New York, 1925).
LAVERGNE, L. G. DE, *Économie rurale de la France depuis 1789* (Paris, 1877).
SÉE, H., *Esquisse d'une histoire du régime agraire en Europe aux XVIII et XIX siècles* (Paris, 1921).
SOMBART, W., *Die deutsche Volkswirtschaft im neunzehnten Jahrhundert* (Berlin, 1903).
WEULERESSE, G., *Le mouvement physiocratique en France,* 2 vols. (Paris, 1910).
YOUNG, A., *Travels in France during the Years 1787, 1788, and 1789* (Dublin, 1793).

CHAPTER V

FIRST DEFEATS OF CONSERVATIVE EUROPE

Break-up of the Concert of Europe:

BAGOT, J. F., *George Canning and His Friends,* 2 vols. (London, 1909).
EGERTON, H. E., *British Foreign Policy in Europe* (London, 1917).
HILL, F. H., *George Canning,* (New York, 1887).
PHILLIPS, W. A., *Confederation of Europe* (New York, 1914).
TEMPERLEY, H. W. V., *Life of Canning* (London, 1905).
————, *Foreign Policy of Canning, 1822–1827* (London, 1925).
WEBSTER, C. K., *The Foreign Policy of Castlereagh (1815–1822)* (London, 1925).

Defeat of the Conservative Powers in South America:

CRESSON, W. P., *Diplomatic Portraits* (New York, 1923).
DUNNING, W. A., *The British Empire and the United States* (New York, 1914).
FORD, W. C., *John Quincy Adams, His Connection with the Monroe Doctrine* (Cambridge, 1902).
HART, A. B., *The Monroe Doctrine* (London, 1916).
LATANÉ, J. H., *The United States and Latin America* (Garden City, N. Y., 1920).
LAWSON, L. A., *The Relation of British Policy to the Declaration of the Monroe Doctrine* (New York, 1922).
PERKINS, D., *The Monroe Doctrine, 1823–1826* (Cambridge, 1927).
REDDAWAY, W. F., *The Monroe Doctrine* (Cambridge, 1898).
ROBERTSON, W. S., *History of the Latin-American Nations* (New York, 1922).

The Greek Revolt:

CHESNEY, F. R., *The Russo-Turkish Campaigns of 1828 and 1829* (London, 1854).
CRAWLEY, C. W., *The Question of Greek Independence* (Cambridge, 1931).
DIETRICH, K., *Deutsche Philhellenen in Griechenland, 1821–1822* (Hamburg, 1929).
MOLDEN, E., *Die Orientpolitik des Fürsten Metternich, 1829–1833* (Vienna, 1913).
PANTSCHOFF, M., *Kaiser Alexander I und der Aufstand Ypsilantis* (Leipzig, 1891).
PHILLIPS, W. A., *The War of Greek Independence* (New York, 1897).
POUQUEVILLE, F. C. H. L., *Histoire de la régénération de la Grèce* (Paris, 1824).

The Revolution of 1830 in France:

BLANC, L., *Vor fünfzig Jahren, Geschichte der Juli-revolution* (Leipzig, 1880).
CABET, E., *Révolution de 1830* (Paris, 1832).
GUICHEN, VICOMTE DE, *La révolution de juillet et l'Europe* (Paris, 1916).

The Reform Movement in Great Britain:

BUTLER, J. R. M., *The Passing of the Great Reform Bill* (New York, 1914).
DICKINSON, G. L., *The Development of Parliament in the Nineteenth Century* (London, 1895).
DUNLOP, R., *Daniel O'Connell* (New York, 1900).
GWYNN, D. R., *Daniel O'Connell* (New York, 1929).
LECKY, W. E. H., *Leaders of Public Opinion in Ireland* (New York, 1903).
PORRITT, E., *The Unreformed House of Commons*, 2 vols. (Cambridge, 1902, 1909).
SEYMOUR, C., *Electoral Reform in England and Wales* (New Haven, 1915).

TREVELYAN, G. M., *Lord Grey of the Reform Bill* (New York, 1920).
VEITCH, G. S., *The Genesis of Parliamentary Reform* (1913).
WARD, B., *The Dawn of Catholic Revival in England, 1781–1803*, 2 vols. (London, 1909).
—————, *The Eve of Catholic Emancipation, 1803–29*, 3 vols. (London, 1911–1912).

CHAPTER VI

AGITATION AND REPRESSION IN FRANCE, ITALY AND GREAT BRITAIN, 1830–1848

The Political System of Louis Philippe, 1830–1848:

BARDOUX, A., *Guizot* (Paris, 1894).
BLANC, L., *Histoire de dix ans (1830–1840)*, 5 vols. (Paris, 1877).
—————, *The History of Ten Years, 1830–40*, 2 vols. (London, 1844–45).
CALMON, M. A., *Histoire parlementaire des finances de la monarchie de juillet*, 4 vols. (Paris, 1895–99).
CRÉTINEAU-JOLY, *Histoire de Louis Philippe et d'Orléanisme*, 2 vols. (Paris, 1867).
Essays from the London Times (New York, 1852).
FESTY, O., *Le mouvement ouvrier au début de la monarchie de juillet (1830–1834)* (Paris, 1908).
GOLLIET, M., *Louis Blanc, sa doctrine, son action* (Paris, 1903).
GUIZOT, F. P. G., *Mémoires pour servir à l'histoire de mon temps*, 8 vols. (Paris, 1858–67).
HALL, J., *England and the Orleans Monarchy* (London, 1912).
HAMEL, E., *Histoire du règne de Louis Philippe*, 2 vols. (Paris, 1889–90).
HAUSSONVILLE, COUNT D', *Histoire de la politique extérieure du gouvernement français (1830–1848)*, 2 vols. (Paris, 1850).
HILLEBRAND, K., *Geschichte Frankreich von der Thronbesteigung Louis Philippe's bis zum Fall Napoleons III*, 2 vols. (Berlin, 1877–79).
KELLER, P., *Louis Blanc und die Revolution von 1848* (Zurich, 1926).
LAITY, A., *Relation historique des évènements du 30 octobre 1836: le prince Napoléon à Strasbourg* (Paris, 1838).
LOUIS NAPOLEON, *Des idées napoliennes* (Paris, 1860).
NOUVION, V. DE, *Histoire du règne de Louis Philippe*, 4 vols. (Paris, 1857–61).
PELLISON, M., *Les orateurs de la France de 1830 à nos jours* (Paris, 1898).
REGNAULT, E., *L'histoire de huit ans (1840–1848)*, 3 vols. (Paris, 1851).
RITTIEZ, *Histoire du règne de Louis Philippe*, 3 vols. (Paris, 1855–58).
ROBIN, C., *Louis Blanc, sa vie, ses œuvres* (Paris, 1851).
SIMPSON, F. A., *The Rise of Louis Napoleon* (New York, 1909).
TCHERNOFF, J., *Louis Blanc* (Paris, 1904).
—————, *Le parti républicain sous la monarchie de juillet* (Paris, 1901).
THUREAU-DANGIN, P. M. P., *Histoire de monarchie de juillet*, 7 vols. (Paris, 1897–1906).
WARSCHAUER, O., *Geschichte des Socializmus und Communizmus* (Berlin, 1896).

WEILL, G., *Histoire du catholicisme libéral en France, 1828–1908* (Paris, 1909).
——————, *Un précurseur du socialisme: Saint-Simon et son œuvre* (Paris, 1894).
WOODWARD, E. L., *Three Studies in European Conservatism* (London, 1920).

Agitation and Repression in Italy, 1830–1848:

HOLLAND, R. S., *Builders of United Italy* (New York, 1908).
KING, B., *Joseph Mazzini* (London, 1903).
MARRIOTT, SIR J. A. R., *The Makers of Modern Italy* (London, 1889).
VIDAL, C., *Charles Albert et le risorgimento italien, 1831–1848* (Paris, 1928).
——————, *Mazzini et les tentatives révolutionaires de la jeune Italie dans les états sardes (1833–1834)* (Paris, 1928).

Great Britain, 1832–1854:

ASCHROTT, P. F., *The English Poor Law System Past and Present* (London, 1902).
BARNES, D. G., *A History of the English Corn Laws from 1660–1846* (New York, 1930).
BELL, K. N., and MORRELL, W. P., *Select Documents on British Colonial Policy, 1830–1860* (Oxford, 1928).
BEER, M., *A History of British Socialism*, 2 vols. (London, 1919, 1920).
BUXTON, S., *Finance and Politics* (London, 1888).
CHRISTIE, O. F., *The Transition from Aristocracy, 1832–1867* (London, 1929).
COLE, G. D. H., *Robert Owen* (London, 1925).
——————, *A Short History of the British Working Class Movement, 1789–1848* (London, 1927).
CORY, G. E., *The Rise of South Africa* (London, 1910).
DEHÉRAIN, H., *L'expansion des Boers au XIX siècle* (Paris, 1905).
DOLLEANS, E., *Le chartisme* (Paris, 1912).
EDGERTON, H. E., *British Foreign Policy in Europe* (Oxford, 1917).
——————, *Short History of British Colonial Policy* (London, 1915).
FOWLE, T. W., *The Poor Law* (London, 1881).
GAMMAGE, R. G., *History of Chartism* (London, 1854, 1894).
GRETTON, R. H., *Commercial Politics (1837–1856)* (London, 1914).
HAMMOND, J. L., and B., *The Age of the Chartists* (London and New York, 1930).
HOBSON, J. A., *Richard Cobden, the International Man* (New York, 1919).
HODDER, E., *Life and Work of the Seventh Earl of Shaftesbury* (London, 1893).
HOVELL, M., *The Chartist Movement* (Manchester, 1918).
HUTCHINS, B. L., and HARRISON, A., *A History of Factory Legislation* (London, 1903).
LEONARD, E. M., *Early History of English Poor Law Relief* (Cambridge, 1900).
LEYDS, W. J., *The First Annexation of the Transvaal* (London, 1906).
LOVETT, W., and COLLINS, J., *Chartism* (London, 1841).

Mc Carthy, J., *The Epoch of Reform, 1830–1850* (New York, 1882).

Morley, J., *Richard Cobden*, 2 vols. (Boston, 1881).

Munro, W. B., *Government of European Cities* (New York, 1909).

Neff, W. E., *Victorian Working Women* (New York, 1929).

Nichols, Sir G., and Mackay, T., *A History of the English Poor Law* (London, 1898).

O'Brien, G., *The Economic History of Ireland from the Union to the Famine* (New York, 1921).

Odgers, W. B., *Local Government* (London, 1907).

Parker, C. S., *Sir Robert Peel*, 3 vols. (London, 1891–99).

Peel, Sir R., *Memoirs*, 2 vols. (London, 1856).

Podmore, F., *Robert Owen* (London, 1924).

Redlich, J., *Local Government in England* (London, 1903).

Reed, S. J., *Life and Letters of the First Earl of Durham*, 2 vols. (London, 1906).

Rosenblatt, B. F., *Social and Economic Aspects of the Chartist Movement* (London, 1916).

Siegfried, A., *Edward Gibbon Wakefield et sa doctrine de la colonisation systématique* (Paris, 1904).

Slosson, P. W., *Decline of the Chartist Movement* (New York, 1916).

Thurfield, J. R., *Peel* (London, 1891).

Trevelyan, G. M., *John Bright* (New York, 1913).

————, *Lord Grey of the Reform Bill* (London, 1920).

Wakefield, E. G., *A View of the Art of Colonization* (London, 1849).

Walpole, S., *Life of Lord John Russell*, 2 vols. (London, 1889).

Webb, S. and B., *English Local Government, 1688–1835*, 3 vols. (London and New York, 1906–08).

————, *History of Trade Unionism* (New York, 1902).

West, J., *History of the Chartist Movement* (London, 1920).

CHAPTER VII

AGITATION AND REPRESSION IN CENTRAL AND EASTERN EUROPE, 1830–1848

Balleydier, A., *Histoire de l'empereur Nicolas*, 2 vols. (Paris, 1857).

Bauer, B., *Der Aufstand und Fall des deutschen Radicalismus vom Jahre 1842*, 3 vols. in 1 (Berlin, 1850).

Bauer, E., *Geschichte der constitutionellen und revolutionären Bewegungen in südlichen Deutschland in den Jahren 1831–1834*, 3 vols. (Charlottenburg, 1845).

Bibescu, G., *Roumanie d'Andrinople à Balta-Liman (1829–1849)*, 2 vols. (Paris, 1893–94).

Bibl, V., *Der Zerfall Oesterreiches*, Vol. I (Vienna, 1922).

Filitti, J. C., *Les principautés roumaines sous l'occupation russe (1828–1834)* (Bucharest, 1904).

Headley, P. C., *The Life of Louis Kossuth* (Auburn, N. Y., 1852).

Korf, M. A., *L'avènement au trône de l'empereur Nicolas I* (Paris, 1857).

Kulenkampff, L., *Der erste preussische Landtag 1847* (Berlin, 1912).

Legge, J. G., *Rhyme and Revolution in Germany* (London, 1918).

PYPIN, A., *Die geistigen Bewegungen in Russland in der ersten Hälfte des XIX Jahrhunderts* (Berlin, 1894).
SCHIEMANN, T., *Geschichte Russlands unter Kaiser Nikolaus I*, 4 vols. (Berlin, 1904–08).
WISCHNITZER, M., *Die Universität Göttingen und die Entwickelung der liberalen Ideen in Russland im ersten Viertel des neunzehnten Jahrhunderts* (Berlin, 1907).

CHAPTER VIII

THE REVOLUTIONS OF 1848

The Revolution in France:

CAHEN, G., *L. Blanc et la commission du Luxembourg* (Paris, 1897).
CHEETHAM, F., *Louis Napoleon and the Genesis of the Second Empire* (London, 1908).
CRÉMIEUX, A., *La révolution de février* (Paris, 1912).
CURTIS, E. N., *The French Assembly of 1848 and American Constitutional Doctrine* (New York, 1918).
DESJOYEAUX, C. N., *La fusion monarchique, 1848–1873* (Paris, 1913).
GARNIER-PAGE, L. A., *Histoire de la révolution de 1848*, 8 vols. (Paris, 1861–62).
GIRARDIN, E., ed., *Le droit du travail au Luxembourg et à l'assemblée nationale*, 2 vols. (Paris, 1849).
LA GORCE, P. DE, *Histoire de la seconde république française*, 2 vols. (Paris, 1914).
LAMARTINE, A. DE, *History of the French Revolution of 1848* (Paris, 1875).
LEBEY, A., *Louis-Napoléon Bonaparte et la révolution de 1848* (Paris, 1907).
L'HÉRITIER, L. F., *Geschichte der französischen Revolution von 1848 und der zweiten Republik* (Stuttgart, n.d.).
MARRIOTT, SIR J. A. R., *The French Revolution of 1848 in Its Economic Aspect*, 2 vols. (Oxford, 1913).
MARX, K., *Die Klassenkämpfe in Frankreich 1848 bis 1850* (Berlin, 1895).
————, *La lutte des classes en France (1848–1850)* (Paris, 1900).
QUENTIN-BAUCHART, P., *Lamartine et la politique étrangère de la révolution de février* (Paris, 1907).
RENARD, G., *La république de 1848* (Paris, 1907).
VERMOREL, A. J. M., *Les hommes de 1848* (Paris, 1869).
WHITEHOUSE, H. R., *Life of Lamartine* (Boston, 1918).

The Revolution in Germany:

BASSERMANN, F. D., *Denkwürdigkeiten . . . 1811–1855* (Frankfort, 1926).
BECKER, B., *Die Reaktion in Deutschland gegen die Revolution von 1848* (Brunswick, 1873).
BIEDERMANN, K., *Erinnerungen aus der Paulskirsche* (Leipzig, 1849).
BLOS, W., *Die deutsche Revolution* (Stuttgart, 1893).
BLUM, H., *Die deutsche Revolution, 1848–1849* (Florence, 1898).
BÖRNERS, P., *Erinnerungen eines Revolutionärs*, 2 vols. (Leipzig, 1920).
BRANDENBURG, E., *Die deutsche Revolution, 1848* (Leipzig, 1919).

BRUNNER, L., *Politische Bewegungen in Nürnberg, 1848–1849* (Heidelberg, 1907).

GNEIST, R., *Berliner Zustände* (Berlin, 1849).

HARNACK, A. VON, *Friederich Daniel Bassermann und die deutsche Revolution von 1848–49* (Munich, 1920).

HARTMANN, M., *Revolutionäre Erinnerungen* (Leipzig, 1919).

LÜDERS, G., *Die demokratische Bewegung in Berlin im Oktober 1848* (Berlin, 1909).

MARX, K., *Revolution and Counter Revolution in Germany in 1848* (London, 1896).

MATTER, P., *Bismarck et son temps,* Vol. 1 (Paris, 1905).

MEINECKE, F., *Radowitz und die deutsche Revolution* (Berlin, 1913).

REICHENSPERGER, P., *Erlebnisse eines alten Parlamentäriers im Revolutionsjahre 1848* (Berlin, 1882).

SCHURZ, C., *Reminiscences,* Vol. I (New York, 1907).

VALENTIN, V., *Die erste deutsche Nationalversammlung* (Munich, 1918).

————, *Frankfurt am Main und die Revolution von 1848–49* (Stuttgart, 1908).

WERNER, A., *Die politischen Bewegungen in Mecklinburg und der ausserordentliche Landtag im Frühjahr 1848* (Berlin, 1907).

The Revolution in Austria:

AUERBACH, B., *Tagebuch aus Wien* (Breslau, 1849).

BACH, M., *Geschichte der Wiener Revolution im Jahre 1848* (Vienna, 1898).

BALLEYDIER, A., *Histoire des révolutions de l'empire d'Autriche années 1848 et 1849,* 2 vols. (Paris, 1853–54).

HELFERT, J. A. VON, *Geschichte der österreichischen Revolution,* 2 vols. (Freiburg, 1907–09).

————, *Geschichte Oesterreichs vom Ausgange des Wiener October–Aufstandes 1848,* 4 vols. in 6 (Leipzig, 1869–86).

HÜBNER, J. A., *Une année de ma vie, 1848–1849* (Paris, 1891).

IRANYI, D., *Histoire politique de la révolution de Hongrie, 1847–1849,* 2 vols. (Paris, 1859–60).

KOLOWRAT-KAKOWSKY, L. VON, *Meine Erinnerungen aus den Jahren 1848 und 1849* (Vienna, 1905).

MAURICE, C. E., *The Revolutionary Movements of 1848 in Italy, Austria-Hungary, and Germany* (New York, 1887).

RESCHAUER, H., *Das Jahr 1848,* 2 vols. (Vienna, 1872).

The Revolution in Italy:

JOHNSTON, R. M., *The Roman Theocracy and the Republic, 1846–1849* (London, 1901).

MARTIN, H., *Daniel Manin* (Paris, 1859).

ORIOLES, P. G. D', *La rivoluzione siciliana del 1848* (Genoa, 1928).

TREVELYAN, G. M., *Manin and the Venetian Revolution of 1848* (London, 1923).

CHAPTER IX

THE DEFEAT OF THE REVOLUTIONS OF 1848 BY THE CONSERVATIVE
FORCES OF EUROPE

Conquest of the Revolutionary Movements:

Affairs of Hungary, 1849–50 (Washington, 1910).
ANGELI, M. VON, *Wien nach 1848* (Vienna, 1905).
BALLEYDIER, A., *Histoire de la guerre de Hongrie en 1848–1849* (Paris, 1853).
BECKER, B., *Die Reaktion in Deutschland gegen die Revolution von 1848* (Brunswick, 1873).
BECKER, J. P., and C. E., *Geschichte der süddeutschen Mai-revolution des Jahres 1849* (Geneva, 1849).
BERGSTRÄSSER, L., *Das frankfurter Parlament in Briefen und Tagebüchern* (Frankfort, 1929).
BRASS, A., *Der Freiheitskampf in Baden und in der Pfalz im Jahre 1849* (St. Gall, 1849).
GAZLEY, J. G., *American Opinion of German Unification, 1848–71* (New York, 1926).
GÖRGEI, A., *My Life and Acts in Hungary in the Years 1848 and 1849* (New York, 1852).
HAYM, R., *Die Deutsche Nationalversammlung* (Berlin, 1848–50).
KLAPKA, GYÖRGY, *Der Nationalkrieg in Ungarn und Siebenburgen in den Jahren 1848 und 1849,* 2 vols. (Leipzig, 1851).
MARCHAN, R., *Les tchèques et les allemands en 1848* (Prague, 1898).
MAY, A. J., *Contemporary American Opinion of the Mid-Century Revolutions in Central Europe* (Philadelphia, 1927).
S., E. O., *Hungary and Its Revolutions from the Earliest Period to the Nineteenth Century with a Memoir of Louis Kossuth* (London, 1854).
SPROXTON, C., *Palmerston and the Hungarian Revolution* (Cambridge, 1919).
TREVELYAN, G. M., *Garibaldi's Defence of the Roman Republic* (London, 1907).
WENDEL, H. C. M., *The Evolution of Industrial Freedom in Prussia, 1845–1849* (New York, 1921).

Karl Marx and the Socialist Movement:

BEER, M., *The Life and Teaching of K. Marx* (London, 1921).
KIRKUP, T., *A History of Socialism* (London, 1892).
LAIDLER, H. W., *A History of Socialist Thought* (New York, 1927).
MARKHAM, S., *A History of Socialism* (London, 1930).
MARX, K., *Das Kapital,* 3 vols. in 4 (Leipzig, 1867–94).
——————, *Capital* (New York, 1929).
——————, *Friedrich Engels: historisch-kritische Gesamtausgabe* (Frankfort, 1927–31).
——————, and ENGELS, F., *The Communist Manifesto* (New York, 1930).

MARX, K., *Der Briefwechsel zwischen Friederich Engels und Karl Marx, 1844 bis 1883,* 4 vols. (Stuttgart, 1921).
MAYER, G., *Friederich Engels, eine Biographie* (Berlin, 1920).
MEHRING, F., *Karl Marx* (Leipzig, 1923).
RIAZANOV, D., *Karl Marx and Friedrich Engels* (New York, 1927).
————, *Karl Marx-Friedrich Engels; historisch-kritische Gesamtausgabe* (Frankfort, 1927–31).
RÜHLE, O., *Karl Marx* (New York, 1929).
SPARGO, J., *Karl Marx* (New York, 1910).
TAYLOR, G. R. S., *Leaders of Socialism* (New York, 1910).

PART II

CHAPTER X

THE NEAR EAST, 1829–1870

BAMBERGER, F., *Geschichte der orientalischen Angelegenheit in Zeitraum des Pariser und des Berliner Friedens* (Berlin, 1892).
BAPST, G., *Le maréchal Canrobert,* Vol. II (Paris, 1910–14).
BAZANCOURT, C. L., *L'expédition de Crimée,* 2 vols. (Paris, 1856).
BEER, A., *Die orientalische Politik Oesterreichs seit 1774* (Prague, 1883).
BRÉHIER, L., *L'Égypt de 1798 à 1900* (Paris, 1900).
CABROL, J. F. H. B., *Le maréchal de Saint-Arnaud en Crimée* (Paris, 1895).
CADALVENE, E. DE, *Histoire de la guerre de Méhémed Ali* (Paris, 1837).
CALTHORPE, S. J. G., *Letters from Headquarters* (London, 1858).
CAMERON, D. A., *Egypt in the Nineteenth Century* (London, 1898).
CULBERG, A., *La politique du roi Oscar I pendant la guerre de Crimée* (Stockholm, 1912).
Diplomatic Study of the Crimean War (1852–1856), 2 vols. (London, 1882).
DODWELL, H., *The Founder of Modern Egypt* (London, 1931).
DOUGLAS, SIR G. B. S., *The Panmure Papers,* 2 vols. (London, 1908).
DRIAULT, E., *La formation de l'empire de Mohammed-Aly de l'Arabie au Soudan, 1814–1823* (Paris, 1928).
DU CASSE, A., BARON, *La Crimée et Sébastopol de 1853 à 1856* (Paris, 1892).
————, *Précis historique des opérations militaires en orient de mars 1854 à septembre 1855* (Paris, 1856).
EAST, W. G., *The Union of Moldavia and Wallachia, 1859* (New York, 1929).
FRIEDJUNG, H., *Der Krimkrieg und die österreichische Politik* (Stuttgart, 1907).
GEFFCKEN, F. H., *Zur Geschichte des orientalischen Krieges 1853–1856* (Berlin, 1881).
HAMLEY, E. B., *The War in the Crimea* (London, 1894).
HASENCLEVER, A., *Geschichte Aegyptens im neunzehten Jahrhundert, 1798–1914* (Halle, 1917).
————, *Die orientalische Frage in den Jahren 1838–1841* (Leipzig, 1914).
HOLLAND, T. E., *The European Concert in the Eastern Question* (Oxford, 1885).
KINGLAKE, A. W., *The Invasion of the Crimea,* 6 vols. (London, 1874–88).

LANE-POOLE, S., *Life of Stratford Canning*, 2 vols. (London, 1868).
MARRIOTT, SIR J. A. R., *The Eastern Question* (Oxford, 1917).
MENGIN, F., *Histoire de l'Égypte sous le gouvernement de Mohammed-Aly*, 2 vols. (Paris, 1823).
MONICAULT, G. DE, *La question d'orient* (Paris, 1898).
NAPIER, SIR C., *The War in Syria*, 2 vols. (London, 1842).
NIEL, A., *Siège de Sébastopol* (Paris, 1858).
PHILIPSON C., and BUXTON, N., *The Question of the Bosphorus and the Dardanelles* (London, 1917).
RIKER, T. W., *The Making of Roumania* (New York, 1932).
RODKEY, F. S., *The Turko-Egyptian Question in the Relations of England, France, and Russia, 1832–1841* (Urbana, 1924).
ROUSSET, C. F. M., *Histoire de la guerre de Crimée*, 2 vols. (Paris, 1877).
RUSSELL, W. H., *Complete History of the Russian War* (New York, 1856).
SABRY, M., *L'empire égyptien sous Mohamed-Ali et la question d'orient, 1811–1849* (Paris, 1930).
THOMAS, G. F. M., *La guerre d'orient de 1854 à 1855* (Paris, 1901).
WAMBAUGH, S., *A Monograph on Plebiscites* (New York, 1920).
YOUNG, G., *Egypt* (New York, 1927).

CHAPTER XI

THE TRIUMPH OF NATIONALITY IN ITALY

AZEGLIO, M. D', *Recollections of Massimo d'Azeglio*, 2 vols. (London, 1868).
BERTI, D., *Il conte di Cavour avanti il 1848* (Rome, 1886).
BOURGIN, G., *La formation de l'unité italienne* (Paris, 1929).
Il carteggio Cavour-Nigra dal 1858 al 1861, 5 vols. (Bologna, 1926).
CAVOUR, COUNT DI, *Gli scritti del conte di Cavour*, 2 vols. (Bologna, 1892).
————————, *Nouvelles lettres inédites* (Turin, 1889).
CHIALA, L., *Lettere di C. Cavour*, 7 vols. (Turin, 1883–87).
DUMAS, A., *On Board the Emma* (New York, 1929).
HANCOCK, W. K., *Ricasoli and the Risorgimento in Tuscany* (London, 1926).
LUZIO, A., *Garibaldi, Cavour, Verdi* (Turin, 1924).
MATTER, P., *Cavour et l'unité italienne* (Paris, 1922).
MAZZINI, G., *Scritti editi ed inediti*, 58 vols. (Imola, 1906–31).
NIGRA, COMTE DE, *Le Comte de Cavour et la Comtesse de Circourt* (Turin, 1894).
O'CLERY, P. K., *The Making of Italy (1856–1870)* (London, 1892).
PANZINI, A., *Il 1859* (Milan, 1926).
TREVELYAN, G. M., *Garibaldi and the Thousand* (New York, 1912).
————————, *Garibaldi and the Making of Italy* (New York, 1912).
WHYTE, A. J., *The Early Life and Letters of Cavour* (London, 1925).
————————, *The Political Life and Letters of Cavour, 1848–1861* (Oxford, 1931).

CHAPTER XII

LOUIS NAPOLEON AND THE GROWTH OF FRENCH PRESTIGE

ARNAUD, R., *La deuxième république et le second empire* (Paris, 1929).

BOURGEOIS, E., and CLERMONT, E., *Rome et Napoléon III* (Paris, 1907).

BULLE, K., *Geschichte des zweiten Kaiserreiches und des Königreiches Italien* (Berlin, 1890).

CALMAN, A. R., *Dedru-Rollin and the Second French Republic* (New York, 1922).

Court Life of the Second French Empire, 1852–1870 (New York, 1908).

COWLEY, H. R. C. W., EARL OF, *The Paris Embassy during the Second Empire* (London, 1928).

DELORD, T., *Histoire du second empire,* 6 vols. (Paris, 1869–75).

EGERTON, H. E., *British Foreign Policy in Europe* (Oxford, 1917).

EVANS, T. W., *Memoirs of Dr. Thomas W. Evans* (New York, 1906).

FISHER, H. A. L., *Bonapartism* (Oxford, 1908).

GRIPPON-LAMOTTE, L., *Histoire du réseau des chemins de fer français* (Paris, 1904).

GUEDALLA, P., *The Second Empire* (London, 1922).

HÜBNER, *Neun Jahre der Erinnerungen eines österreichischen Botschafters in Paris unter dem zweiten Kaiserreich 1851–1859,* 2 vols. (Berlin, 1904).

JERROLD, B., *Life of Napoleon III,* 4 vols. (London, 1874–82).

KERRY, H. W. E. P-F., EARL OF, *The Secret of the Coup d'État* (London, 1924).

LA GORCE, P. DE, *Histoire de la seconde république française,* 2 vols. (Paris, 1887, 1914).

————, *Histoire du second empire,* 7 vols. (Paris, 1896–1905).

NAPOLEON III, *La politique impériale exposée par les discours et proclamations de l'empereur Napoléon III* (Paris, 1865).

OLLIVIER, E., *L'empire libéral,* 2 vols. (Paris, 1894).

SIMPSON, F. A., *Louis Napoleon and the Recovery of France, 1848–1856* (London, 1923).

TCHERNOFF, J., *Le parti républicain au coup d'état et sous l'empire* (Paris, 1906).

WALLACE, SIR R., *An Englishman in Paris,* 2 vols. (London, 1892); 1 vol. (London, 1893).

CHAPTER XIII

THE DECLINE OF FRENCH PRESTIGE AND THE LIBERALIZATION OF THE EMPIRE

ANGEBERG, *Recueil des traités, conventions . . . et pièces diplomatiques concernant la guerre franco-allemande,* 5 vols. (Paris, 1873).

BAPST, G., *Le maréchal Canrobert,* 6 vols. (Paris, 1898–1914).

BENEDETTI, V., COUNT, *Ma mission en Prusse* (Paris, 1871).

BERTON, H., *L'évolution constitutionnelle du second empire* (Paris, 1900).

BISMARCK, PRINCE OTTO VON, *Bismarck's Letters to His Wife from the Seat of War, 1870–1871* (New York, 1903).

CHUQUET, A., *La guerre 1870–71* (Paris, 1895).

Der deutsch-französische Krieg 1870–1881 (Berlin, 1872–81).

EDLESTON, R. H., *Napoleon III and Italy,* 3 vols. in 1 (Darlington, Eng., 1922).

ERNOUF, A. A., *Histoire des chemins de fers français pendant la guerre franco-prussienne* (Paris, 1874).

FESTER, R., *Briefe, Aktenstücke und Regesten zur Geschichte der Hohenzollern Thronkandidatur in Spanien*, 2 vols. (Leipzig, 1913).

GRANIER, H., *Die Einmarschkämpfe der deutschen Armeen in August 1870* (Berlin, 1896).

GUEDALLA, P., *The Second Empire* (London, 1922).

KÖPPEN, G., *Der deutsch-französische Krieg, 1870 und 1871* (Milwaukee, 1890).

LORD, R. H., *The Origins of the War of 1870* (Cambridge, 1924).

Ministère des Affaires Étrangères, *Les origines diplomatiques de la guerre de 1870–1871*, 26 vols. (Paris, 1910–29).

MOLTKE, H. VON, *Geschichte des deutsch-französischen Krieges* (Berlin, 1891).

—————, *The Franco-German War of 1870–71* (New York, 1892).

OLLIVIER, E., The Franco-Prussian War and Its Hidden Causes (Boston, 1912).

ONCKEN, H., *Die Rheinpolitik Kaiser Napoleons III*, 2 vols. (Stuttgart, 1926).

—————, *Napoleon III and the Rhine* (New York, 1928).

PICARD, E., *1870*, 5 vols. (Paris, 1907–11).

RAYMOND, D. N., *British Policy and Opinion during the Franco-Prussian War* (New York, 1921).

WACHTER, A., *La guerre franco-allemande de 1870–71*, 2 vols. (Paris, 1895).

WELSCHINGER, H., *La guerre de 1870*, 2 vols. (Paris, 1911).

CHAPTER XIV

THE FORMATION OF THE GERMAN EMPIRE

BISMARCK, PRINCE OTTO VON, *Bismarck, the Man and the Statesman*, 2 vols. (New York, 1899).

—————, *Bismarck, the Man and the Statesman*, 3 vols. (Leipzig, 1899).

—————, *Gedanken und Erinnerungen*, 2 vols. (Stuttgart, 1898) ; 3 vols., (Stuttgart, 1919).

—————, *New Chapters of Bismarck's Autobiography* (London, 1920).

—————, *The Kaiser vs. Bismarck* (New York, 1921).

—————, *Die politischen Reden des Fürsten Bismarck*, 14 vols. (Stuttgart, 1892–1905).

—————, *Die politischen Berichte des Fürsten Bismarck aus Petersburg und Paris*, 2 vols. (Berlin, 1920).

—————, *Bismarcks Briefwechsel mit dem Minister Freiherrn von Schleinitz, 1858–1861* (Stuttgart, 1905).

—————, *The Love Letters of Bismarck* (New York, 1901).

—————, *Die gesammelte Werke*, 13 vols. (Berlin, 1924–30).

Bismarck in Private Life, by a Fellow-Student (New York, 1890).

BRANDENBURG, E., *Die Reichsgründung*, 2 vols. (Leipzig, 1916).

—————, *Briefe und Aktenstücke zur Geschichte der Gründung des deutschen Reiches (1870–1871)*, 2 vols. (Leipzig, 1911).

—————, *Untersuchungen und Aktenstücke zur Geschichte der Reichsgründung* (Leipzig, 1916).

BUSCH, M., *Bismarck: Some Secret Pages of His History* (New York, 1898).

DENIS, E., *La fondation de l'empire allemande, 1852–1871* (Paris, 1906).
Die deutschen Kriege von 1864, 1866, 1870–71 in wohlfeiler Bearbeitung nach den grossen Generalstabswerken, 3 vols. (Berlin, 1889).
DOEBERL, V. M., *Bayern und die bismarckische Reichsgründung* (Munich, 1925).
FORBES, A., *William of Germany* (London, 1888).
FRIEDJUNG, H., *Oesterreich von 1848 bis 1860,* 2 vols. (Stuttgart, 1908).
———, *Der Kampf um die Vorherrschaft in Deutschland* (1897).
HAHN, L., *Fürst Bismarck,* 5 vols. (Berlin, 1878–91).
HEADLAM, J. W., *Bismarck and the Foundation of the German Empire* (New York, 1901).
HEYCK, E., *Bismarck* (Bielefeld, 1898).
HOFF, W., *Die deutsche Krisis des Jahres 1866* (Melsungen, 1896).
KAINDL, R. F., *Oesterreich, Preussen, Deutschland* (Vienna, 1926).
KLEIN-HATTINGEN, O., *Geschichte des deutschen Liberalismus,* 2 vols. (Berlin, 1911–12).
KLÜFFEL, K., *Geschichte der deutschen Einheitsbestrebungen* (Berlin, 1872).
LACOUR-GAYET, G., *Bismarck* (Paris, 1918).
LENZ, M., *Geschichte Bismarcks* (Leipzig, 1902).
LORENZ, O., *Kaiser Wilhelm und die Begründung des Reichs, 1866–1871* (Jena, 1902).
LOWE, C., *Prince Bismarck,* 2 vols. (London, 1885).
MALET, SIR A., *The Overthrow of the Germanic Confederation by Prussia in 1866* (London, 1870).
MALLESON, G. B., *The Refounding of the German Empire, 1848–1914* (London, 1914).
———, *The Refounding of the German Empire, 1848–1871* (London, 1904).
MANTEUFFEL, O. VON, *Preussens auswärtige Politik 1850–1858,* 3 vols. (Berlin, 1902).
MARCKS, E., *Bismarck,* Vol. I (Stuttgart, 1909).
———, *Kaiser Wilhelm I* (Leipzig, 1899).
MATHIAS, A., *Bismarck* (Munich, 1918).
MATTER, P., *Bismarck et son temps,* 3 vols. (Paris, 1908–14).
MAURENBRECHER, W., *Gründung des deutschen Reiches, 1859–1871* (Leipzig, 1892).
MAYER, G., *Bismarck und Lassalle* (Berlin, 1928).
MEYER, A. O., *Bismarck's Kampf mit Oesterreich (1851–1859)* (Berlin, 1927).
ONCKEN, H., *Grossherzog Friedrich I von Baden und die deutsche Politik von 1854–1871,* 2 vols. (Berlin, 1927).
ONCKEN, W., *Das Zeitalter des Kaisers Wilhelm,* 2 vols. (Berlin, 1890–92).
PFISTER, A., *Kaiser Wilhelm I und seine Zeit* (Leipzig, 1906).
POSCHINGER, H. VON, *Preussen im Bundestag 1851 bis 1859* (Leipzig, 1882–84).
———, *Preussens auswärtige Politik 1850 bis 1858,* 3 vols. (Berlin, 1902).
RAPP, A., *Grossdeutsch und Kleindeutsch* (Munich, 1922).

RITTER, G., *Die preussische Konservativen und Bismarcks deutsche Politik, 1858–1876* (Heidelberg, 1913).

SMITH, M., *Bismarck and German Unity* (New York, 1923).

SPAHN, M., *Bismarck* (Strassburg, 1915).

STEARNS, F. P., *The Life of Prince Otto von Bismarck* (Philadelphia, 1899).

Stenographische Berichte über die Verhandlungen des Reichstages des Norddeutschen Bundes 1867–1870, 14 vols. in 13 (Berlin, 1867–70).

STIEBRITZ, A., *Der eiserne Kanzler* (Leipzig, 1915).

SYBEL, H. VON, *Die Begründung des deutschen Reiches durch Wilhelm I*, 7 vols. (Munich, 1890–94).

————, *The Founding of the German Empire*, 7 vols. (New York, 1890–98).

WERTHHEIMER, E. VON, *Bismarck im Politischen Kampf* (Berlin, 1930).

WIEGLER, P., *Wilhelm der Erste* (Hellerau bei Dresden, 1927).

WOLF, G., *Bismarck's Lehrjahre* (Leipzig, 1907).

ZIEKURSCH, J., *Politische Geschichte des neuen deutschen Kaiserreiches*, Vol. I (Frankfort, 1925).

PART III

GENERAL WORKS, 1871–1918

Many of the books listed under General Works, 1815–1871, also cover the period after 1871.

ANDREWS, C. M., *Contemporary Europe, Asia and Africa* (Philadelphia, 1905).

COOKE, W. H., and STICKNEY, E. P., *Readings in European International Relations since 1879* (New York, 1931).

DAVIS, W. S., *The Roots of the War* (New York, 1923).

————, *Armed Peace* (London, 1919).

DONNER, H., *Die Vorgeschichte des Weltkrieges* (Berlin, 1927).

EGELHAAF, G., *Geschichte der neuesten Zeit*, 2 vols. (Stuttgart, 1920).

GOOCH, G. P., *History of Modern Europe, 1878–1919* (New York, 1923).

HAUSER, H., *Histoire diplomatique de l'Europe* (1871–1914), 2 vols. (Paris, 1929).

HAZEN, C. D., *Fifty Years of Europe, 1870–1919* (New York, 1919).

HELMOLT, H. F., *Ein Vierteljahrhundert Weltgeschichte 1894–1919* (Charlottenburg, 1919).

HOLT, L. H., and CHILTON, A. W., *The History of Europe from 1862 to 1914* (New York, 1917).

MARRIOTT, SIR J. A. R., *Europe and Beyond, 1870–1920* (London, 1921).

MOWAT, R. B., *European History, 1878–1923* (London, 1924).

————, *The Concert of Europe* (London, 1930).

ROSE, J. H., *The Development of the European Nations, 1870–1921* (New York, 1922).

————, *The Development of the European Nations, 1870–1900*, 2 vols. (New York, 1905).

SLOSSON, P. W., *Twentieth Century Europe* (Boston, 1927).

TURNER, E. R., *Europe since 1870* (New York, 1927).

CHAPTER XV

THE THIRD FRENCH REPUBLIC, 1870–1914

AJALBERT, J., *Quelques dessous de procès de Rennes* (Paris, 1901).

BARTHÉLEMY, J., *Le gouvernement de la France* (Paris, 1924).

BERNARD, J., *Le procès de Rennes, 1899* (Paris, 1900).

CORNÉLY, J. J., *Notes sur l'affaire Dreyfus* (Paris, n.d.).

COUBERTIN, P., *L'évolution française sous la troisième république* (Paris, 1896).

DEBIDOUR, A., *L'église catholique et l'état de 1870 à 1906,* 2 vols. (Paris, 1906).

DENIS, S., *Histoire contemporaine,* 4 vols. (Paris, 1902).

DESCHANEL, P. E. L., *Gambetta* (Paris, 1920).

DUBREUIL, R., *L'affaire Dreyfus devant la cour de cassation* (Paris, 1899).

Enquête parlementaire sur l'insurrection du 18 Mars 1871 (Paris, 1872).

ERNEST-CHARLES, J., *Practiciens politiques (1870–1899)* (Paris, 1899).

FAVRE, J., *Gouvernement de la défense nationale,* 3 vols. (Paris, 1871–75).

FERRY, J., *Lettres de Jules Ferry, 1846–1893* (Paris, 1914).

FLOURENS, G., *Paris livré* (Paris, 1871).

GHEUSI, P. B., *Gambetta par Gambetta* (Paris, 1909).

GOLDSCHMIDT, H., *Bismarck und die Friedensunterhändler 1871* (Berlin, 1929).

GOODNOW, F. J., *Comparative Administrative Law,* 2 vols. (New York, 1892).

GUÉRARD, A. L., *French Civilization in the Nineteenth Century* (London, 1914).

GURIAN, W., *Die politischen und sozialen Ideen des französischen Katholizmus, 1789–1914* (Gladbach, 1929).

GUYOT, Y., *La revision du procès Dreyfus* (Paris, 1898).

HAIME, E., *Affaire Dreyfus* (Paris, 1898).

HALÉVY, D., *Le courrier de M. Thiers* (Paris, 1921).

HANOTAUX, G., *Histoire de la France contemporaine,* 4 vols. (Westminster, 1903).

Histoire de France contemporaine de 1871 à 1913 (Paris, 1916).

HUBERT, L. L., *Ce qu'il faut connaître; des grandes journées parlementaires de la IIIe république* (Paris, 1928).

JAURÈS, J. L., *Les preuves* (Paris, 1898).

LA CROISERIE, A. DE, *La réforme du régime parlementaire* (Paris, 1889).

LAWTON, F., *The Third French Republic* (London, 1909).

LAZARE, B., *Une erreur judiciare* (Paris, 1897).

LISSAGARAY, P., *Histoire de la commune de 1871* (Brussels, 1876, 1896).

LOWELL, A. L., *Governments and Parties of Continental Europe* (Boston, 1897).

——————, *The Governments of France, Italy, and Germany* (Cambridge, 1914).

MAILLARD, F., *Histoire des journaux publiés à Paris pendant le siège et sous la commune* (Paris, 1871).

——————, *Les publications de la rue pendant la siège et la commune* (Paris, 1874).

MARX, K., *La commune de Paris* (Paris, 1901).
MASON, E. S., *The Paris Commune* (New York, 1930).
MATER, A., *La politique religeuse de la république française* (Paris, 1909).
——————, *Les textes de la politique française en matière ecclésiastique, 1905–08* (Paris, 1909).
MENDÈS, C., *Les soixante-treize journées de la commune* (Paris, 1871).
MUEL, L., *Précis historique des assemblies parlementaires jusqu'en 1895* (Paris, 1895).
POINCARÉ, R., *How France Is Governed* (London, 1914).
PRESSENSÉ, F. DE, *Un héros; le colonel Picquart* (Paris, 1898).
RAMBAUD, A., *J. Ferry* (Paris, 1903).
RECOULY, R., *La troisième république* (Paris, 1927).
REINACH, J., *La vie politique de Léon Gambetta* (Paris, 1918).
——————, *Histoire de l'affaire Dreyfus*, 7 vols. (Paris, 1901–11).
RÉMUSAT, P. DE, *Thiers* (Paris, 1889).
SAIT, E. M., *Government and Politics of France* (New York, 1920).
SCHEFER, C., *D'une guerre à l'autre (1871–1914)* (Paris, 1920).
SIMON, J., *Souvenirs du 4 septembre*, 2 vols. (Paris, 1876).
——————, *The Government of M. Thiers from 8th Feb., 1871 to 24 May, 1873*, 2 vols. (London, 1879).
SOLTAU, R. H., *French Parties and Politics* (London, 1922).
TESTE, L., *Les monarchistes sous la troisième république* (Paris, 1891).
THIERS, A., *Discours parlementaires de M. Thiers*, 16 vols. (Paris, 1879–89).
VOGEL, K., *Die dritte französische Republik bis 1895* (Stuttgart, 1895).

CHAPTER XVI

THE NEW GERMAN EMPIRE, 1871–1914

AULNEAU, J., *Les aspirations autonomistes en Europe* (Paris, 1913).
BACHEM, K., *Vorgeschichte, Geschichte und Politik der deutschen Zentrumspartei*, 7 vols. (Cologne, 1927).
BARKER, J. E., *The Foundations of Germany* (New York, 1919).
BAZIN, G., *L'Allemagne catholique au XIX siècle* (Paris, 1896).
BECKER, B., *Geschichte der Arbeiteragitation Ferdinand Lassalles* (Brunswick, 1875).
BERGSTRÄSSER, L., *Der politische Katholizmus*, 2 vols. (Munich, 1921–23).
——————, *Geschichte der politischen Parteien in Deutschland* (Mannheim, 1928).
BERNSTEIN, E., *Ferdinand Lassalle as a Social Reformer* (London, 1893).
——————, *Evolutionary Socialism* (London, 1909).
—————— and KAUTSKY, K., *Die Geschichte des Sozialismus* (Stuttgart, 1895).
BLONDEL, G., *L'essor industriel et commerciel du peuple allemand* (Paris, 1898).
BLUM, H., *Das deutsche Reich zur Zeit Bismarcks* (Leipzig, 1893).
BORNHAK, K., *Deutsche Geschichte unter Kaiser Wilhelm II* (Leipzig, 1922).
BRANDES, G., *Ferdinand Lassalle* (Berlin, 1877).
BRAUER, A. VON, MARCKS, E., and MÜLLER, K. A. VON, *Erinnerungen an Bismarck* (Stuttgart, 1915).

BROCKHAUS, E., *Stunden mit Bismarck, 1871–1878* (Leipzig, 1929).
BRUCH, H., *Die Kulturkampfbewegung in Deutschland, 1872 bis 1900* (Mainz, 1901).
BÜLOW, PRINCE VON, *Imperial Germany* (New York, 1917).
————, *Denkwürdigkeiten*, 4 vols. (Berlin, 1930–31).
————, *Memoirs of Prince von Bülow*, Vol. I (Boston, 1931).
BUSCH, M., *Bismarck und sein Werk* (Leipzig, 1898).
————, *Tagebuchblätter*, 2 vols. (Leipzig, 1899).
CALMANN, H. M., *Die Finanzpolitik der deutschen Sozialdemokratie, 1867–1914* (Munich, 1922).
CERF, B., *Alsace-Lorraine since 1870* (New York, 1919).
DAVIS, A. N., *The Kaiser as I Know Him* (New York, 1918).
DAWSON, W. H., *German Socialism and Ferdinand Lassalle* (London, 1891).
————, *Bismarck and State Socialism* (London, 1890).
————, *The Evolution of Modern Germany* (London and New York, 1908).
————, *The German Empire, 1867–1914*, 2 vols. (London, 1919).
EPPSTEIN, G., BARON VON, *Fürst Bismarcks Entlassung* (Berlin, 1920).
ESCHENBURG, T., *Das Kaiserreich am Scheideweg* (Berlin, 1929).
EYCK, E., *Die Monarchie Wilhelms II nach seinen Briefen, seinen Randbemerkungen, und den Zeugnissen seiner Freunde* (Berlin, 1924).
FASOLT, F., *Die sieben grössten deutschen Elektrizitätsgesellschaften* (Dresden, 1904).
FIFE, R. H., *The German Empire between Two Wars* (New York, 1916).
FLANDRIN, E., *Institutions politiques de l'Europe contemporaine*, Vol. II (Paris, 1901–02).
GAUSS, C., *The German Emperor as Shown in His Public Utterances* (New York, 1915).
GOODNOW, F. J., *Comparative Administrative Law*, 2 vols. (New York, 1897).
GOYAU, G., *Bismarck et l'église*, 4 vols. (Paris, 1913–22).
HALLER, J., *Die Aera Bülow* (Stuttgart, 1922).
HAMMANN, O., *Der neue Kurs* (Berlin, 1918).
HARMS, PAUL, *Vier Jahrzehnte Reichspolitik, 1878–1918* (Leipzig, 1924).
HARTUNG, F., *Deutsche Geschichte vom Frankfurter Frieden bis zum Vertrag von Versailles, 1871–1919* (Bonn, 1924).
HAUSER, H., *Germany's Commercial Grip on the World* (New York, 1918).
HEFFTER, H., *Die Kreuzzeitungspartei und die Kartellpolitik Bismarcks* (Leipzig, 1927).
HOFMANN, H., *Fürst Bismarck, 1890–1898*, 2 vols. (Stuttgart, 1914).
HOHENLOHE-SCHILLINGFURST, PRINCE CHLODWIG ZU, *Denkwürdigkeiten*, 2 vols. (Stuttgart, 1907).
————, *Memoirs*, 2 vols. (London, 1907).
HOHLFELD, J., *Geschichte des deutschen Reiches, 1871–1924* (Leipzig, 1924).
————, *Deutsche Reichsgeschichte in Dokumenten, 1849–1926*, 2 vols. (Berlin, 1927).
HOWARD, B. E., *The German Empire* (New York, 1906).
HOWARD, E. D., *The Cause and Extent of the Recent Industrial Progress of Germany* (Boston, 1907).

Howe, F. C., *Socialized Germany* (New York, 1917).

Hubener, E., *Die deutsche Wirtschaftskrisis von 1873* (Berlin, 1895).

Jessem, F. C. von, *Manuel historique de la question du Slesvig* (Copenhagen, 1906).

Jeudels, O., *Das Verhältniss der deutschen Grossbanken zur Industrie* (Leipzig, 1905).

Kissling, J. B., *Geschichte des Kulturkampfes im deutschen Reiche*, 3 vols. (Freiburg, 1911–16).

Klein-Hattingen, O., *Bismarck und seine Welt*, 2 vols. in 3 (Berlin, 1902–04).

——————, *Geschichte des deutschen Liberalismus*, 2 vols. (Berlin, 1911).

Krüger, F. K., *Government and Politics of the German Empire* (Yonkers, 1915).

Lamprecht, K. G., *Deutsche Geschichte der jüngsten Vergangenheit und Gegenwart*, 3 vols. (Berlin, 1912–13).

Lassalle, F., *Gesammelte Reden und Schriften*, 3 vols. (Berlin, 1892–93).

Lavisse, E., *Trois empereurs de l'Allemagne* (Paris, 1888).

Lotz, W., *Verkehrsentwickelung in Deutschland 1800–1900* (Leipzig, 1920).

Lowell, A. L., *Governments and Parties in Continental Europe*, 2 vols. (Boston, 1897).

——————, *The Governments of France, Italy, and Germany* (Cambridge, 1914).

Markham, S., *A History of Socialism* (London, 1930).

Martin, W., *La crise politique de l'Allemagne contemporaine* (Paris, 1913).

Mayer, G., *Bismarck und Lassalle* (Berlin, 1928).

Mehring, F., *Geschichte der deutschen Sozialdemokratie*, 4 vols. (Stuttgart, 1903).

Meinecke, F., *Preussen und Deutschland im 19 und 20 Jahrhundert* (Munich, 1918).

Mommsen, W., *Bismarcks Sturz und die Parteien* (Stuttgart, 1924).

Niemann, A., *Wanderungen mit Kaiser Wilhelm II* (Leipzig, 1924).

Nowak, K. F., *Kaiser and Chancellor* (New York, 1930).

——————, *Das dritte deutsche Kaiserreich* (Berlin, 1929).

O'Farrel, H. H., *The Franco-German War Indemnity and Its Economic Results* (London, 1913).

Oncken, W., *Zeitalter des Kaisers Wilhelm II*, 2 vols. (Berlin, 1890–92).

Perris, H., *Germany and the German Emperor* (New York, 1912).

Philippson, M., *Das Leben Kaiser Friedrichs III* (Wiesbaden, 1900).

Pingaud, A., *Le développement économique de l'Allemagne contemporaine (1871–1914)* (Paris, 1916).

Platzhoff, W., *Bismarck und die nordschleswigsche Frage, 1864–1879* (Berlin, 1925).

Ponsonby, F., *Letters of the Empress Frederick* (London, 1929).

Poschinger, H., *Fürst Bismarck und die Diplomaten, 1852–1890* (Hamburg, 1900).

——————, *Fürst Bismarck und die Parlamentärier*, 3 vols. (Breslau, 1894–95).

——————, *Kaiser Friedrich*, 3 vols. (Berlin, 1898–1900).

526   BIBLIOGRAPHY

——————, *Bismarck Portfeuille* (Stuttgart, 1898–1900).

RICHTER, E., *Im alten Reichstag*, 2 vols. (Berlin, 1894–96).

RIESSER, F., *Zur Entwickelungsgeschichte der deutschen Grossbanken* (Jena, 1910).

ROBERTSON, C. G., *Bismarck* (New York, 1919).

ROBOLSKY, H., *Der deutsche Reichstag* (Berlin, 1897).

ROËLL, P. VON, and EPSTEIN, G., *Bismarcks Staatsrecht* (Berlin, 1903).

SCHMIDT-PAULI, E. VON, *Der Kaiser* (Berlin, 1928).

SCHIROKAUER, A., *Lassalle* (New York, 1932).

SCHMOLLER, G., *Zwanzig Jahre deutscher Politik (1897–1917)* (Munich, 1920).

SCHRÖDER, W., *Handbuch der sozialdemokratischen Parteitage von 1863 bis 1909* (Munich, 1910).

SHAW, S., *William of Germany* (London, 1913).

VERMEIL, E., *L'empire allemand, 1871–1900* (Paris, 1900).

WAHL, A. E. A., *Deutsche Geschichte von der Reichsgründung bis zum Ausbruch des Weltkrieges (1871–1914)*, Vols. 1–2 (Stuttgart, 1926, 1929).

WARSCHAUER, O., *Geschichte des Socialismus und neuern Kommunismus* (Leipzig, 1892–96).

WETTERLE, E., *Les coulisses du Reichstag* (Paris, 1918).

——————, *Behind the Scenes in the Reichstag* (London, 1918).

WILHELM II, *The Kaiser's Memoirs* (New York, 1922).

——————, *Kaiserreden* (Leipzig, 1902).

——————, *The Kaiser's Speeches* (New York, 1903).

ZECHLIN, E., *Staatstreichpläne Bismarcks und Wilhelms II, 1890–1894* (Stuttgart, 1929).

ZEDLITZ-TRÜTZSCHLER, COUNT R., *Zwölf Jahre am deutschen Kaiserhof* (Stuttgart, 1923).

——————, *Twelve Years at the Imperial German Court* (New York, 1924).

ZIEKURSCH, J., *Politische Geschichte des neuen deutschen Kaiserreiches*, Vols. II–III (Frankfurt, a. M., 1925, 1930).

CHAPTER XVII

THE AUSTRIAN PROBLEM, 1860–1914

AUERBACH, B., *Les races et les nationalités en Autriche-Hongrie* (Paris, 1898).

BAGGER, E., *Francis Joseph, Emperor of Austria-King of Hungary* (New York, 1928).

BENEŠ, E., *Le problème autrichien et la question tchèque* (Paris, 1908).

BERTHE, A. DE, *La Hongrie moderne, 1849–1901* (Paris, 1901).

BIBL, V., *Der Zerfall Oesterreiches*, Vol. II (Vienna, 1924).

CAPEK, T., *The Slovaks of Hungary* (New York, 1906).

CHARMATZ, R., *Oesterreichs innere Geschichte von 1848 bis 1895*, 2 vols. (Leipzig, 1918).

——————, *Oesterreichs äussere und innere Politik von 1895 bis 1914* (Leipzig, 1918).

DRAGE, G., *Austria-Hungary* (London, 1909).

ERNST, O., *Franz Joseph in Seinen Briefen* (Vienna, 1924).

——————, *Franz Joseph as Revealed by His Letters* (London, 1927).

FRANZ JOSEPH I, *Briefe Kaisers Franz Joseph I an seine Mutter, 1838–1872*, (Munich, 1930).

GAYDA, V., *Modern Austria* (London, 1915).

GONNARD, R., *La Hongrie au XXe siècle* (Paris, 1908).

HEVESY, A. DE, *L'agonie d'un empire* (Paris, 1923).

——————, *Nationalities in Hungary* (London, 1919).

HUBER, A., *Oesterreichische Reichsgeschichte* (Vienna, 1901).

KETTERL, E., *The Emperor Francis Joseph* (London, 1929).

KLEINWÄCHTER, F. F. G., *Der Untergang der oesterreichisch-ungarischen Monarchie* (Leipzig, 1920).

KOHUT, A., *Kaiser Franz Joseph I als König von Ungarn* (Berlin, 1916).

LOWELL, A. L., *Governments and Parties of Continental Europe*, 2 vols. (Boston, 1897).

MAHAFFY, R. P., *Francis Joseph I* (London, 1915).

MARGUTTI, A., BARON VON, *The Emperor Francis Joseph and His Times* (London, 1921).

PALATSKY, F., *L'idée de l'état autrichien* (Prague, 1907).

REDLICH, J., *Emperor Francis Joseph of Austria* (New York, 1928).

——————, *Das Oesterreichische Staats- und Reichsproblem*, 3 vols. (Leipzig, 1920–26).

RUMBOLD, SIR H., *Francis Joseph and His Times* (New York, 1909).

SAMASSA, P., *Der Völkerstreit im Habsburgerstaat* (Leipzig, 1910).

SETON-WATSON, R. W., *Corruption and Reform in Hungary* (London, 1911).

——————, *The Southern Slav Question* (London, 1911).

——————, *German, Slav, and Magyar* (London, 1916).

SOSNOKY, T., *Die Politik im Habsburgerreiche*, 2 vols. in 1 (Berlin, 1912–13).

SRB, A., *Histoire politique de la nation tchèque*, 2 vols. (Prague, 1899).

STEED, H. W., *The Habsburg Monarchy* (London, 1914).

TSCHUPPIK, K., *Franz Joseph I* (Hellerau bei Dresden, 1928).

——————, *Francis Joseph I* (New York, 1930).

VOINOVITCH, COUNT L., *Dalmatia and the Jugoslav Movement* (New York, 1920).

WERTHEIMER, E. VON, *Graf Julius Andrassy*, 3 vols. (Stuttgart, 1910–13).

CHAPTER XVIII

ITALY, 1861–1914

CASE, L. M., *Franco-Italian Relations, 1860–1865* (Philadelphia, 1832).

CROCE, B., *Storia d'Italia dal 1871 al 1915* (Bari, 1928).

KING, B., and OAKEY, T., *Italy To-Day* (London, 1909).

LAPWORTH, C., *Tripoli and Young Italy* (London, 1912).

LEMONON, E., *L'Italie économique et sociale (1861–1912)* (Paris, 1913).

LOWELL, A. L., *Governments and Parties of Continental Europe*, 2 vols. (Boston, 1897).

——————, *The Governments of France, Italy, and Germany* (Cambridge, 1914).

PINGAUD, A., *L'Italie depuis 1870* (Paris, 1915).

ROBERTSON, A., *Victor Emmanuel III* (New York, 1925).
UNDERWOOD, F. M., *United Italy* (London, 1912).
WALLACE, W. K., *Greater Italy* (New York, 1917).

CHAPTER XIX
RUSSIA, 1856–1914

ALEXINSKY, G., *Russia and Europe* (London, 1917).
DUBNOW, S. M., *History of the Jews in Russia,* 3 vols. (Philadelphia, 1916, 1918, 1920).
FLOURENS, E. L., *Alexandre III* (Paris, 1894).
HEDENSTRÖM, A. VON, *Geschichte Russlands vom 1878 bis 1918* (Stuttgart, 1924).
HÖTZSCH, O., *Russland* (Berlin, 1917).
KOVALEVSKI, M. M., *Russian Political Institutions* (Chicago, 1902).
KROPOTKIN, PRINCE P. A., *Memoirs of a Revolutionist* (Boston, 1899).
MARC, P., *Au seuil du 17 octobre 1905* (Leipzig, 1914).
MILYUKOV, P., *Russia and Its Crisis* (Chicago, 1905).
NEVINSON, H. W., *The Dawn in Russia* (London, 1906).
NICHOLAS II, *Das Tagebuch des letzten Zaren von 1890 bis zum Fall* (Berlin, 1923).
OLGIN, M. J., *The Soul of the Russian Revolution* (New York, 1917).
POBYEDONOSTSEV, P. K., *Reflections of a Russian Statesman* (London, 1898).
PALÉOLOGUE, G. M., *Le roman tragique de l'empereur Alexandre II* (Paris, 1923).
PARES, B., *Russia and Reform* (New York, 1907).
PERRIS, G. H., *Russia in Revolution* (London, 1905).
ROSEN, BARON, *Forty Years of Diplomacy,* Vol. II (New York, 1922).
SKRINE, F. H. B., *The Expansion of Russia* (Cambridge, 1915).
STEPNIAK, S., *Underground Russia* (New York, 1883).
WITTE, COUNT S. I., *The Memoirs of Count Witte* (London, 1921).

CHAPTER XX
THE BALKAN STATES, 1870–1909

ANCEL, J., *Manuel historique de la question d'orient (1792–1923)* (Paris, 1923).
————————, *L'unité de la politique bulgare, 1870–1919* (Paris, 1919).
BAMBERG, F., *Geschichte der orientalischen Angelegenheiten im Zeitraume des Pariser und des Berliner Friedens* (Berlin, 1892).
BLOWITZ, H. S., *My Memoirs* (London, 1903).
CAHUET, A., *La question d'orient dans l'histoire contemporaine (1821–1905)* (Paris, 1905).
CHAUMIER, A., *La Bulgarie* (Paris, 1909).
CHOUBLIER, M., *La question d'orient depuis le traité de Berlin* (Paris, 1899).
CORTI, E. C., *Alexander von Battenberg* (Vienna, 1920).
DENIS, F., *La Grande Serbie* (Paris, 1919).
DRANDAR, A. G., *Les évènements politiques en Bulgarie* (Brussels, 1896).
DRIAULT, E., *La question d'orient* (Paris, 1905).

HUHN, A. E. VON, *The Kidnapping of Prince Alexander of Battenberg* (London, 1887).
KOCH, A., *Prince Alexander of Battenberg* (London, 1887).
LANDEMONT, COUNT DE, *L'Europe et la politique orientale, 1878–1912* (Paris, 1912).
LARMEROUX, J., *La politique extérieure de l'Autriche-Hongrie, 1875–1914* (Paris, 1918).
MACDONALD, J., *Czar Ferdinand and His People* (London, 1913).
MANDL, L., *Die Habsburger und die serbische Frage* (Vienna, 1918).
MILLER, W., *The Balkans* (London, 1908).
MURRAY, W. S., *The Making of the Balkan States* (New York, 1910).
PANARETOFF, S., *Near Eastern Affairs and Conditions* (New York, 1922).
SETON-WATSON, R. W., *The Rise of Nationality in the Balkans* (London, 1917).
SLIVENSKY, I., *La Bulgarie depuis le traité de Berlin et la paix dans les Balkans* (Paris, 1927).
STEAD, A., *Servia by the Servians* (London, 1909).
STEVENSON, F. S., *A History of Montenegro* (London, 1912).
TYLER, M. W., *The European Powers and the Near East, 1875–1908* (Minneapolis, 1925).

CHAPTER XXI

THE BRITISH EMPIRE, 1856–1914

ADAMS, E. D., *Great Britain and the American Civil War*, 2 vols. (New York, 1925).
ALDEN, P., *Democratic England* (New York, 1912).
ASQUITH, H. H., EARL OF OXFORD and, *Fifty Years of British Parliament*, 2 vols. (Boston, 1926).
BALFOUR, A., *Aspects of Home Rule* (London, 1912).
BARKER, E., *Ireland in the Last Fifty Years* (Oxford, 1919).
BENSON, A. C., and ESHER, VISCOUNT, ed. *Letters of Queen Victoria, 1837–1861*, 3 vols. (London, 1907).
BOURINOT, J. G., *Canada* (Cambridge, 1900).
BUCKLE, G. E., *Letters of Queen Victoria*, Second Series (London, 1926).
BURDETT, O., *Gladstone* (London, 1927).
The Cambridge History of India (New York, 1922–29).
CECIL, LADY G., *Life of Robert Marquis of Salisbury* (New York, 1921).
CHURCHILL, W., *Lord Randolph Churchill*, 2 vols. (London, 1906).
COX, H., *Whig and Tory Administrations, 1855–1868* (London, 1868).
————, *History of the Reform Bills of 1866 and 1867* (London, 1868).
DICEY, A. V., *England's Case against Home Rule* (London, 1887).
DOYLE, A. C., *Great Boer War* (London, 1903).
EVERSLEY, LORD, *Gladstone and Ireland* (London, 1912).
FARRER, J. A., *England under Edward VII* (London, 1922).
FITZMAURICE, E., *Life of Earl Granville*, 2 vols. (London, 1905–06).
FORREST, G. W., *A History of the Indian Mutiny*, 3 vols. (Edinburgh, 1904–12).

FRAZER, R. W., *British India* (New York, 1897).

GILLESPIE, F. E., *Labor and Politics in England, 1850–1867* (Durham, 1927).

GLADSTONE, HERBERT, VISCOUNT, *After Thirty Years* (London, 1928).

GORST, H. E., *The Fourth Party* (London, 1906).

GREEN, F. E., *History of the English Agricultural Labourer, 1870–1920* (London, 1920).

GRETTON, R. H., *Imperialism and Mr. Gladstone (1876–1887)* (London, 1923).

——————, *History of England, 1880–1910*, 2 vols. (Boston, 1913).

GUEDALLA, P., *Palmerston* (New York, 1927).

HALÉVY, E., *Histoire du peuple anglais au XIXe siècle: Épilogue (1895–1914)*, Vol. I (Paris, 1926).

HALL, W. P., *Mr. Gladstone* (New York, 1931).

——————, *Empire to Commonwealth* (New York, 1928).

HAYES, C. J. H., *British Social Politics* (Boston, 1913).

HOLE, H. M., *The Making of Rhodesia* (London, 1916).

HOLMES, T. R., *History of the Indian Mutiny* (London, 1913).

HOSKINS, H. L., *British Routes to India* (New York, 1928).

The Indian War of Independence (London, 1909).

JEYES, S. H., *Mr. Chamberlain* (New York, 1903).

KAYE, SIR J. W., *A History of the Sepoy War in India,* 3 vols. (London, 1896).

KEBBEL, T. E., *Lord Beaconsfield and Other Tory Memoirs* (New York, 1907).

KEITH, A. B., *Responsible Government in the Dominions,* 3 vols. (Oxford, 1912).

KNAPLUND, P., *Gladstone and Britain's Imperial Policy* (New York, 1927).

KNOWLES, L. C. A., *The Economic Development of the British Overseas Empire* (London, 1924).

LANG, A., *Life, Letters, and Diaries of Sir Stafford Northcote,* 2 vols. (London, 1890).

LEE, S., *Queen Victoria, a Biography* (New York, 1903).

——————, *King Edward VII* (New York, 1925).

LEYDS, W. J., *The Transvaal Surrounded* (London, 1919).

MC CARTHY, J., *History of Our Own Times,* 5 vols. (New York, 1881–1905).

MACDONAGH, M., *Home Rule Movement* (Dublin, 1920).

MALMESBURY, J. H., EARL OF, *Memoirs of an Ex-Minister,* 3 vols. (Leipzig, 1885).

MAUROIS, M., *Disraeli* (London, 1927).

MEECH, T. C., *This Generation,* 2 vols. (New York, 1927–28).

MONYPENNY, W. F., and BUCKLY, G. E., *Life of Benjamin Disraeli, Earl of Beaconsfield,* 6 vols. (New York, 1910).

MORLEY, J. VISCOUNT, *Life of W. E. Gladstone,* 3 vols. (New York, 1903).

——————, *Recollections,* 2 vols. (New York, 1917).

MORRIS, J. E., *Great Britain and Ireland, 1845–1910* (London, 1914).

NEWTON, A. P., *Select Documents relating to the Unification of South Africa,* 2 vols. (London, 1924).

O'BRIEN, R. B., *Life of Charles Stuart Parnell,* 3 vols. (London, 1899).

O'CONNOR, T. P., *Lord Beaconsfield* (London, 1884).

PARK, J. H., *The English Reform Bill of 1867* (New York, 1920).

PARKER, C. S., *Life and Letters of Sir James Graham*, 2 vols. (London, 1907).

PAUL-DUBOIS, L., *Contemporary Ireland* (London, 1908).

RAYMOND, E. T., *Life of Arthur James Balfour* (Boston, 1920).

——————, *Mr. Lloyd George* (New York, 1922).

SPENDER, H., *General Botha* (Boston, 1916).

SPENDER, J. A., *Life of Sir Henry Campbell-Bannerman*, 2 vols. (London, 1923).

STRACHEY, L., *Queen Victoria* (New York, 1921).

TROTTER, L. J., *History of British India under Queen Victoria*, 2 vols. (London, 1886).

TURNER, E. R., *Ireland and England* (New York, 1919).

WITTKE, C., *A History of Canada* (New York, 1928).

PART IV
CHAPTER XXII
INTERNATIONAL PENETRATION AND RIVALRY IN ASIA

ASAKAWA, K., *The Russo-Japanese Conflict* (Boston, 1904).

BAIN, H. F., *Ores and Industry in the Far East* (New York, 1927).

BAU, M. J., *The Foreign Relations of China* (New York, 1921).

——————, *The Open Door Doctrine in Relation to China* (New York, 1923).

BELL, SIR C., *Tibet, Past and Present* (New York, 1924).

BING, LI UNG, *Outlines of Chinese History* (Shanghai, 1914).

BOULGER, D. C., *Central Asian Questions* (London, 1885).

——————, *England and Russia in Central Asia*, 2 vols. (London, 1879).

BURLEIGH, B., *The Empire of the East* (London, 1905).

CANDLER, E., *The Unveiling of Lhasa* (London, 1905).

CHENG, SIH-GUNG, *Modern China* (Oxford, 1919).

CHIROL, V., *The Middle Eastern Question* (New York, 1903).

CLEMENT, E. W., *A Short History of Japan* (Chicago, 1915).

CLYDE, P. H., *International Rivalries in Manchuria* (1689–1922).

CORDIER, H., *L'expédition de Chine, 1857–58* (Paris, 1905).

——————, *L'expédition de Chine de 1860* (Paris, 1906).

——————, *Histoire des relations de la Chine avec les puissances occidentales, 1860–1900*, 3 vols. (Paris, 1901–02).

——————, *Histoire générale de la Chine*, Vol. IV (Paris, 1920).

CURZON OF KEDLESTON, G. N., MARQUIS, *Russia in Central Asia* (London, 1889).

DENNETT, T., *Americans in Eastern Asia* (New York, 1922).

——————, *Roosevelt and the Russo-Japanese War* (Garden City, N. Y., 1925).

DENNIS, A. L. P., *The Anglo-Japanese Alliance* (Berkeley, California, 1923).

DOUGLAS, R. K., *China* (New York, 1899).

——————, *Europe and the Far East* (New York, 1928).

DRIAULT, E., *La question d'extrême-orient* (Paris, 1908).

DUBOSC, A., *L'évolution de la Chine (1911–1921)* (Paris, 1921).

DYER, H., *Japan in World Politics* (London, 1909).

FARJENEL, F., *Through the Chinese Revolution* (London, 1915).
FOSTER, J. W., *American Diplomacy in the Orient* (Boston, 1903).
FRANKE, O., *Die Grossmächte in Ostasien von 1894 bis 1914* (Brunswick, 1923).
GIBBONS, H. A., *The New Map of Asia* (New York, 1919).
GODSHALL, W. L., *The International Aspects of the Shantung Question* (Philadelphia, 1923).
GOWEN, H. H., *Asia* (Boston, 1926).
————————, *An Outline History of Japan* (New York, 1927).
————————, and HALL, J. W., *An Outline History of China* (New York, 1927).
HARRIS, N. D., *Europe and the East* (Boston, 1926).
HOLCOMBE, A. N., *The Chinese Revolution* (Cambridge, 1930).
HOLDICH, COL. SIR T., *The Indian Borderland, 1880–1900* (London, 1909).
HORNBECK, S. K., *Contemporary Politics in the Far East* (New York, 1916).
HSIEH, PAO CHAO, *The Government of China* (Baltimore, 1925).
HSÜ, SHUHSI, *China and Her Political Entity* (New York, 1926).
JONES, F. C., *Extra-territoriality in Japan* (New Haven, 1931).
KEETON, G. W., *The Development of Extra-territoriality in China,* 2 vols. (London, 1928).
KENT, P. H., *The Passing of the Manchus* (London, 1912).
KING-HALL, S., *Western Civilization and the Far East* (New York, 1924).
KITAZAWA, N., *The Government of Japan* (Princeton, 1929).
KUROPATKIN, A., *The Russian Army and the Japanese War,* 2 vols. (London, 1909).
LA MAZELIÈRE, A. R., MARQUIS DE, *Le Japon, histoire et civilisation,* Vols. IV–V (Paris, 1907–10).
LANDON, P., *Lhasa,* 2 vols. (London, 1905).
LATOURETTE, K. S., *The Development of China* (Boston, 1920).
————————, *The Development of Japan* (New York, 1920).
————————, *A History of Christian Missions in China* (New York, 1929).
LAVOLLÉE, C., *France et Chine* (Paris, 1900).
LINEBARGER, P., *Sun Yat Sen and the Chinese Republic* (New York, 1925).
LIONEL, J., *The War in the Far East, 1904–1905* (London, 1905).
LONGFORD, J. H., *The Evolution of New Japan* (Cambridge, 1913).
————————, *The Story of Korea* (New York, 1911).
LYONS, G., *Afghanistan: The Buffer State* (London, 1910).
MACMURRAY, J. V. A., *Treaties and Agreements with and concerning China, 1894–1919,* 2 vols. (New York, 1919).
MCNAIR, H. F., *Modern Chinese History, Selected Readings* (Shanghai, 1923).
MALLESON, G. B., *The Russo-Afghan Question and the Invasion of India* (London, 1885).
MOON, P. T., *Imperialism and World Politics* (New York, 1926).
MORSE, H. B., *The Trade and Administration of China* (New York, 1913).
————————, *The International Relations of the Chinese Empire,* 3 vols. (London, 1910–18).
MURDOCH, J., *A History of Japan,* Vol. III (London, 1926).
MURRAY, D., *Japan* (New York, 1906).

The Official History of the Russo-Japanese War, 5 vols. (London, 1908–10).

OKUMA, COUNT S., *Fifty Years of New Japan* (New York, 1909).

ORCHARD, J. E., *Japan's Economic Position* (New York, 1930).

OVERLACH, T. W., *Foreign Financial Control in China* (New York, 1919).

PORTER, R. P., *Japan, The Rise of a Modern Power* (Oxford, 1918).

RAVENSTEIN, E. G., *The Russians on the Amur* (London, 1861).

REINSCH, P., *World Politics at the End of the Nineteenth Century* (New York, 1900).

ROTTACH, E., *La Chine en révolution* (Paris, 1914).

ROUIRE, DR., *La rivalité anglo-russe au XIXe siècle en Asie* (Paris, 1908).

Russland in Asien, 11 vols. (Leipzig, 1889–1911).

SOOTHILL, W. E., *China and the West* (Oxford, 1925).

STEIGER, G. N., BEYER, H. O., and BENITEZ, C., *A History of the Orient* (New York, 1926).

TANG, LEANG-LI, *The Inner History of the Chinese Revolution* (London, 1930).

TREAT, P. J., *Japan and the United States, 1853–1921* (Boston, 1921).

————, *The Far East* (New York, 1928).

UYEHARA, G. E., *The Political Development of Japan, 1867–1909* (London, 1910).

VÁMBÉRY, A., *Central Asia and the Anglo-Russian Frontier Question* (London, 1874).

VINACKE, H. M., *Modern Constitutional Development in China* (Princeton, 1920).

————, *A History of the Far East in Modern Times* (New York, 1928).

WEIGH, KEN SHEN, *Russo-Chinese Diplomacy* (Shanghai, 1928).

WILLIAMS, E. T., *China, Yesterday and Today* (New York, 1923).

WILLOUGHBY, W. W., *Foreign Rights and Interests in China*, 2 vols. (Baltimore, 1927).

WRIGHT, G. F., *Asiatic Russia*, 2 vols. (New York, 1902).

YOUNG, C. W., *The International Legal Status of the Kwangtung Leased Territory* (Baltimore, 1931).

YOUNGHUSBAND, SIR F., *India and Thibet* (London, 1910).

CHAPTER XXIII

THE PARTITION OF AFRICA

Africa and Its Exploration as Told by Its Explorers, 2 vols. (London, 1891).

BLUNT, W. S., *Secret History of the English Occupation of Egypt* (London, 1922).

BROWN, R., *The Story of Africa and Its Explorers*, 4 vols. (London, 1892–95).

BRUNET, L., *L'œuvre de la France à Madagascar* (Paris, 1903).

BRYCE, J., *Impressions of South Africa* (New York, 1899).

CHIROL, V., *The Egyptian Problem* (London, 1921).

COLVIN, SIR A., *The Making of Modern Egypt* (London, 1906).

CROMER, LORD, *Modern Egypt*, 2 vols. (New York, 1916).

DARCY, J., *France et Angleterre* (Paris, 1904).

DARMSTÄDTER, P., *Geschichte der Aufteilung und Kolonization Afrikas,* 2 vols. (Berlin, 1913–20).

DAUZAT, A., *L'expansion italienne* (Paris, 1914).

DAYE, P., *L'empire colonial belge* (Bruxelles, 1923).

DICEY, E., *The Story of the Khedivate* (London, 1902).

ELIOT, C., *The East African Protectorate* (London, 1905).

ELLIS, A. B., *A History of the Gold Coast of West Africa* (London, 1893).

FROELICHER, J. E., *Trois colonisateurs* (Paris, 1903).

GAFFAREL, P. L. J., *Histoire de l'expansion coloniale de la France* (Marseilles, 1905).

—————, *Les colonies françaises* (Paris, 1899).

GIBBONS, H. A., *The New Map of Africa* (*1900–1916*) (New York, 1918).

HAGEN, M. VON, *Bismarcks Kolonialpolitik* (Stuttgart, 1923).

HANOTAUX, G., *Histoire des colonies françaises et de l'expansion de la France dans le monde,* Vols. I–III (Paris, 1929, 1930, 1931).

HANSEN, M. L., *German Schemes of Colonization before 1860* (Northampton, 1924).

HARRIS, N. D., *Europe and Africa* (Boston, 1927).

—————, *Intervention and Colonization in Africa* (Boston, 1914).

HERTSLET, SIR E., *The Map of Africa by Treaty,* 3 vols. (London, 1909).

HOSKINS, H. L., *European Imperialism in Africa* (New York, 1930).

JOHNSTON, SIR H. H., *The Opening Up of Africa* (New York, 1911).

—————, *History of the Colonization of Africa* (Cambridge, 1913).

KEITH, A. B., *West Africa* (Oxford, 1913).

—————, *The Belgian Congo and the Berlin Act* (Oxford, 1919).

KELLER, A. G., *Colonization* (New York, 1908).

KELTIE, J. S., *Partition of Africa* (London, 1895).

KINGLEY, M., *The Story of West Africa* (London, 1899).

LEGENDRE, P., *Notre épopée coloniale* (Paris, 1900).

LEROY-BEAULIEU, P., *De la colonisation chez les peuples modernes,* 2 vols. (Paris, 1902).

LEWIN, P. E., *The Germans and Africa* (New York, 1915).

LICHTERVELDE, COUNT L. DE, *Leopold of the Belgians* (New York, 1929).

LIVINGSTONE, D., *Missionary Travels and Researches in South Africa* (New York, 1858).

—————, *The Last Journals of David Livingstone in Central Africa* (New York, 1875).

LUCAS, SIR C., *The Partition and Colonization of Africa* (Oxford, 1922).

MARTIN, E. C., *The British West African Settlements, 1750–1821* (London, 1927).

MILNER, A., VISCOUNT, *England in Egypt* (London, 1892).

MONDAINI, G., *Manuale di storia e legislazione coloniale del regno d'Italia* (Rome, 1927).

MOREL, E. D., *Red Rubber* (London, 1907).

NEWMAN, MAJ. E. W. P., *Great Britain in Egypt* (London, 1928).

ROBERTS, S. H., *History of French Colonial Policy* (*1870–1925*), 2 vols. (London, 1929).

ROUARD DE CARD, E., *Les territoires africains et les conventions franco-anglaises* (Paris, 1901).

ROUARD DE CARD, E., *Les traités de protectorat conclus par la France en Afrique, 1870–1895* (Paris, 1897).

ROYLE, C., *The Egyptian Campaigns* (London, 1900).

SANDERSON, E., *Great Britain in Modern Africa* (London, 1907).

SCHEFER, C., *L'Algérie et l'évolution de la colonisation française* (Paris, 1928).

STANLEY, H. M., *The Congo and the Founding of Its Free State*, 2 vols. (New York, 1885).

————, *Through the Dark Continent*, 2 vols. (New York, 1878).

STUHLMACHER, W., *Bismarcks Kolonialpolitik* (Halle, 1927).

TOWNSEND, M. E., *The Rise and Fall of Germany's Colonial Empire, 1884–1918* (New York, 1930).

TRAILL, H. D., *England, Egypt, and the Sudan* (Westminster, 1900).

VALENTIN, V., *Kolonialgeschichte der Neuzeit* (Tübingen, 1915).

WEIGALL, A. E. R., *Egypt from 1798 to 1914* (New York, 1915).

WOOLF, L., *Empire and Commerce in Africa* (New York, 1920).

YOUNG, G., *Egypt* (New York, 1927).

ZIMMERMANN, A., *Die europäischen Kolonien*, 5 vols. (Berlin, 1896–1903).

————, *Geschichte der deutschen Kolonialpolitik* (Berlin, 1914).

CHAPTER XXIV

GROWTH OF TWO GREAT EUROPEAN ALLIANCES

ASQUITH, H. H., EARL OF OXFORD and, *The Genesis of the War* (London, 1923).

BAERNREITHER, J. M., *Fragments of a Political Diary* (New York, 1930).

BAKELESS, J., *The Economic Causes of Modern War* (New York, 1921).

BARNES, H. E., *The Genesis of the World War* (New York, 1926).

BARTHOLDY, A. M., and THIMME, F., ed., *Die auswärtige Politik des deutschen Reiches, 1871–1914*, 4 vols. (Berlin, 1928).

BAUSMAN, F., *Let France Explain* (London, 1922).

BECKER, W., *Fürst Bülow und England, 1897–1909* (Greifswald, 1929).

BERNSTEIN, H., *The Willy-Nicky Correspondence* (New York, 1918).

BILLOT, A., *La France et l'Italie*, 2 vols. (Paris, 1905).

BISSOLATI, L., *La politica estera dell' Italia dal 1897 al 1920* (Milan, 1923).

BORNHAK, K., *Die Kriegsschuld* (Berlin, 1929).

BOURGEOIS, E., and PAGE, G., *Les origines et les responsabilités de la grande guerre* (Paris, 1922).

BRANDENBURG, E., *Von Bismarck zum Weltkriege* (Berlin, 1924).

————, *From Bismarck to the World War* (London, 1927).

British Documents on the Origins of the War, 1898–1914, 11 vols. (London, 1926–   ).

Briefwechsel des Botschafters General Hans Lothar von Schweinitz (Berlin, 1928).

BRUNEL, G. E. A., *Les incidents franco-allemands de 1871 à 1914* (Paris, 1917).

BÜLOW, PRINCE VON, *Deutsche Politik* (Berlin, 1917).

————, *Denkwürdigkeiten*, 4 vols. (Berlin, 1930–31).

Bülow, Prince von, *Letters* (London, 1930).

Carroll, E. M., *French Public Opinion and Foreign Affairs, 1870–1914* (New York, 1931).

Chang, C., *The Anglo-Japanese Alliance* (Baltimore, 1931).

Cyon, E. de, *Histoire de l'entente franco-russe, 1886–1894* (Paris, 1895).

Demartial, G., *La guerre de 1914* (Paris, 1922).

Despagnet, F. C. R., *La diplomatie de la troisième république et le droit des gens* (Paris, 1904).

Dickinson, G. L., *The International Anarchy, 1904–1914* (New York, 1926).

Die deutsche Nationalversammlung, Beilagen . . . über die öffentliche Verhandlungen des (ersten) Untersuchungsausschusses (Berlin, 1920–21).

Donner, H., *Die Vorgeschichte des Weltkrieges* (Berlin, 1927).

Dugdale, E. T. S., ed., *German Diplomatic Documents, 1871–1914,* 4 vols. (London, 1928–30).

Dupin, G., *Conférence sur les responsabilités de la guerre* (Paris, 1925).

Du Taillis, J., *Le nouveau Maroc* (Paris, 1923).

Eckardstein, H., baron von, *Lebenserinnerungen und politische Denkwürdigkeiten,* 2 vols. (Leipzig, 1919).

——————, *Ten Years at the Court of St. James, 1895–1905* (London, 1921).

Ewart, J. S., *The Roots and Causes of the Wars, 1914–1918,* 2 vols. (New York, 1925).

Fabre-Luce, A., *La victoire* (Paris, 1924).

——————, *The Limitations of Victory* (New York, 1926).

Falkenstein, H. T. von, *Bismarck und die Kriegsgefahr des Jahres 1887* (Berlin, 1924).

Fay, S. B., *The Origins of the World War,* 2 vols. (New York, 1928).

Feis, H., *Europe, the World's Banker, 1870–1914* (New Haven, 1930).

Friedjung, H., *Das Zeitalter des Imperialismus, 1884–1914,* 3 vols. (Berlin, 1919, 1920).

Fuller, J. V., *Bismarck's Diplomacy at Its Zenith* (Cambridge, 1922).

Gallavresi, G., *Italia e Austria (1859–1914)* (Milan, 1922).

Giffen, M. B., *Fashoda, the Incident and Its Diplomatic Setting* (Chicago, 1930).

Gooch, G. P., *Franco-German Relations, 1871–1914* (London, 1923).

——————, *Recent Revelations of European Diplomacy* (London, 1923, 1928, 1929, 1930).

Gorianov, S., *Le Bosphore et les Dardanelles* (Paris, 1910).

Grey of Fallodon, E., Viscount, *Twenty-five Years (1892–1916),* 2 vols. (New York, 1925).

Die grosse Politik der europäischen Kabinette, 1871–1914, 40 vols. in 54 (Berlin, 1922–27).

Hale, O. J., *Germany and the Diplomatic Revolution* (Philadelphia, 1931).

Hammann, O., *Zur Vorgeschichte des Weltkrieges* (Berlin, 1918).

——————, *Der missverstandene Bismarck* (Berlin, 1921).

——————, *Deutsche Weltpolitik, 1890–1912* (Berlin, 1925).

——————, *Der neue Kurs* (Berlin, 1918).

——————, *The World Policy of Germany, 1890–1912* (London, 1927).

HANOTAUX, G., *Fachoda* (Paris, 1909).

HERZFELD, H., *Die deutsch-französische Kriegsgefahr von 1875* (Berlin, 1922).

HIPPEAU, E. G., *Histoire diplomatique de la troisième république (1870–1889)* (Paris, 1889).

HÖIJER, O., *Le comte d'Aerenthal et la politique de violence* (Paris, 1922).

HÖNIGER, R., *Russlands Vorbereitung zum Weltkrieg* (Berlin, 1919).

HOYOS, A., *Der deutsch-englische Gegensatz und sein Einfluss auf die Balkanpolitik Oesterreich-Ungarns* (Berlin, 1922).

KANTOROWICZ, H. V., *Der Geist der englischen Politik und das Gespenst der Einkreisung Deutschlands* (Berlin, 1929).

KAUTSKY, K., MONTGELAS, M., and SCHÜCKING, W., *Die deutschen Dokumente zum Kriegsausbruch*, 4 vols. (Berlin, 1919).

————, *Outbreak of the World War* (New York, 1924).

KORFF, BARON S. A., *Russia's Foreign Relations during the Last Half Century* (New York, 1922).

LANGER, W. L., *The Franco-Russian Alliance, 1890–1894* (Cambridge, 1929).

————, *European Alliances and Alignments, 1871–1890* (New York, 1931).

LARMEROUX, J., *La politique extérieure de l'Autriche-Hongrie, 1875–1914*, 2 vols. (Paris, 1918).

LENZ, M., *Deutschland im Kreis der Grossmächte, 1871–1914* (Berlin, 1925).

LUTZ, H., *Lord Grey and the World War* (New York, 1928).

MARGUERITE, V., *Les criminels* (Paris, 1925).

MEINECKE, F., *Geschichte des deutsch-englischen Bündnisproblems, 1890–1901* (Munich, 1927).

MEYENDORFF, BARON A., *Correspondance diplomatique de M. de Staal (1884–1900)*, 2 vols. (Paris, 1929).

MICHON, G., *The Franco-Russian Alliance, 1891–1917* (New York, 1929).

MINISTÈRE DES AFFAIRES ÉTRANGÈRES, *Documents diplomatiques français (1871–1914)* (Paris, 1929–).

MORHARDT, M., *Les preuves* (Paris, 1924).

MOWAT, R. B., *Contemporary Europe and Overseas, 1898–1920* (New York, 1931).

NOACK, U., *Bismarcks Friedenspolitik und das Problem des deutschen Machtverfalls* (Leipzig, 1928).

OSTWALD, P., *Von Versailles 1871 bis Versailles 1920* (Berlin, 1922).

PLEHN, H., *Bismarcks auswärtige Politik nach der Reichsgründung* (Munich, 1920).

POINCARÉ, R., *Les origines de la guerre* (Paris, 1921).

————, *The Origins of the War* (London, 1922).

————, *Au service de la France*, 4 vols. (Paris, 1926–27).

————, *The Memoirs of Raymond Poincaré* (New York, 1926).

La politique extérieure de l'Allemagne, 1870–1914, Vols. I–XIV (Paris, 1927–   ).

PRIBRAM, A. F., *Die politischen Geheimverträge Oesterreich-Ungarns, 1879–1914*, 2 vols. (Vienna, 1920).

————, *The Secret Treaties of Austria-Hungary, 1879–1914*, 2 vols. (Cambridge, 1922–23).

PRIBRAM, A. F., *England and the International Policy of the European Powers* (New York, 1932).

RAAB, G., *Der deutsch-russische Rüchversicherungsvertrag* (Wetzlar, 1923).

RACHFAL, F., *Deutschland und die Weltpolitik, 1871–1914* (Stuttgart, 1923).

REVENTLOW, E., COUNT ZU, *Deutschlands auswärtige Politik, 1888–1914* (Berlin, 1918).

ROCHES, F., *Manuel des origines de la guerre* (Paris, 1919).

ROHRBACH, P., *Deutschland unter den Weltvölkern* (Stuttgart, 1921).

ROTHFELS, H., *Bismarcks englische Bündnisspolitik* (Stuttgart, 1924).

SASS, J., *Die deutschen Weissbücher zur auswärtigen Politik, 1870–1914* (Berlin, 1928).

SCHEFER, C., *D'une guerre à l'autre* (Paris, 1920).

SCHMITT, B. E., *England and Germany, 1740–1914* (Princeton, 1916).

SCHWERTFEGER, B., *Die diplomatischen Akten des auswärtigen Amtes, 1871–1914*, 2 vols. (Berlin, 1923).

SEYMOUR, C., *The Diplomatic Background of the War, 1870–1914* (New Haven, 1916).

SIMPSON, J., ed., *The Saburov Memoirs, or, Bismarck versus Russia* (New York, 1929).

SOSNOSKY, T. VON, *Die Balkanpolitik Oesterreich-Ungarns seit 1866* (Stuttgart, 1913–14).

SPICKERNAGEL, W., *Fürst Bulow* (Hamburg, 1921).

STIEVE, F., *L'Allemagne et la politique européenne, 1890–1914* (Paris, 1929).

STUART, G. H., *French Foreign Policy from Fashoda to Serajevo (1898–1914)* (New York, 1921).

TARDIEU, A., *La conférence d'Algésiras* (Paris, 1907).

TIRPITZ, ADM. A. P. F. VON, *Erinnerungen* (Leipzig, 1919).

———, *My Memoirs*, 2 vols. (New York, 1919).

———, *Politische Dokumente*, 2 vols. (Stuttgart, 1924).

VALENTIN, V., *Deutschlands Aussenpolitik* (Berlin, 1921).

———, *Bismarcks Aussenpolitik von 1871–1890* (Berlin, 1922).

VERMEIL, E., *Les origines de la guerre et la politique extérieure de l'Allemagne au début du XXe siècle* (Paris, 1926).

WIENEFELD, R. H., *Franco-German Relations, 1878–1885* (Baltimore, 1929).

WILHELM, CROWN PRINCE, *Ich Suche die Wahrheit* (Stuttgart, 1925).

WILHELM II, *Briefe Wilhelms II an den Zaren, 1894–1914* (Berlin, 1920).

———, *Letters from the Kaiser to the Czar* (New York, 1920).

WILSON, H. W., *The War Guilt* (London, 1928).

CHAPTER XXV

THE GROWTH OF TENSION BETWEEN THE ALLIANCES

ALBIN, P., *Le coup d'Agadir* (Paris, 1912).

ASHMEAD-BARTLETT, E., *With the Turks in Thrace* (New York, 1913).

BAERNREITHER, J. M., *Fragments of a Political Diary* (London, 1930).

BARBAGALLO, C., *Come si scatenò la guerra mondiale* (Milan, 1923).

BARBY, H., *Les victoires serbes* (Paris, 1913).

BERTIE, LORD, *The Diary of Lord Bertie of Thame, 1914–1918*, 2 vols. (New York, 1925).

BEYENS, BARON, *Deux années à Berlin, 1912–1914* (Paris, 1931).
——————, *Germany before the War* (London, 1916).
BOGIČEVIČ, M., *Die auswärtige Politik Serbiens, 1903–1914,* 3 vols. (Berlin, 1928–31).
——————, *Kriegsursachen* (Zürich, 1919).
BUCHANAN, SIR G., *My Mission to Russia and Other Diplomatic Memories,* 2 vols. (London, 1923).
BUXTON, N. E., *With the Bulgarian Staff* (London, 1913).
Carnegie Endowment for International Peace, *Enquête dans les Balkans* (Paris, 1914).
——————, *Outbreak of the World War* (New York, 1924).
CHEKREZI, C. A., *Albania, Past and Present* (New York, 1919).
CHLUMECKY, L. VON, *Erzherzog Franz Ferdinands Wirken und Wollen* (Berlin, 1929).
CHURCHILL, W. S., *The World Crisis, 1911–1914,* 2 vols. (London, 1923).
CONSTANTINE I, *A King's Private Letters* (London, 1923).
DEMARTIAL, G., *L'évangile du Quai d'Orsay* (Paris, 1926).
Diplomatische Aktenstücke zur Vorgeschichte des Krieges, 1914, 3 vols. (Vienna, 1919).
DIRR, P., *Bayerische Dokumente zum Kriegsausbruch und zum Versailler Schuldspruch* (Munich, 1925).
DOBROROLSKI, S., *Die Mobilmachung der Russischen Armee, 1914* (Berlin, 1922).
DUMAINE, A., *La dernière ambassade de France en Autriche* (Paris, 1921).
DUPIN, G., *Considérations sur les responsabilités de la guerre* (Paris, 1925).
DURHAM, M. E., *Twenty Years of the Balkan Tangle* (London, 1920).
——————, *The Serajevo Crime* (London, 1925).
——————, *The Struggle for Scutari* (London, 1914).
EARLE, E. M., *Turkey, the Great Powers, and the Bagdad Railway* (New York, 1924).
EGGLING, B. VON, *Der russische Mobilmachung und der Kriegsausbruch* (Oldenburg, 1919).
FISCHER, E., *Die kritischen 39 Tage von Sarajevo bis zum Weltbrand* (Berlin, 1928).
FRANTZ, G., *Russlands Eintritt in den Weltkrieg* (Berlin, 1924).
GAUVAIN, A., *L'Europe au jour le jour,* Vols. I–VI (Paris, 1917–23).
GIBBONS, H. A., *The New Map of Europe (1911–1914)* (New York, 1914).
GOOS, R., *Das Wiener Kabinet und die Entstehung des Weltkrieges* (Vienna, 1919).
GOUTTENOIRE DE TOURY, F., *Poincaré a-t-il voulu la guerre?* (Paris, 1921).
GUESHOFF, I. E., *L'alliance balkanique* (Paris, 1915).
——————, *The Balkan League* (London, 1915).
——————, *Le genèse de la guerre mondiale* (Berne, 1919).
HALDANE, R. B., VISCOUNT, *Before the War* (London, 1920).
HANOTAUX, G., *La politique de l'équilibre, 1907–1911* (Paris, 1914).
——————, *La guerre des Balkans et l'Europe, 1912–1913* (Paris, 1914).
HEADLAM, J. W., *The History of Twelve Days, July 24 to Aug. 4th, 1914* (London, 1915).
HOCHWAECHTER, G., *Mit den Türken in der Front* (Berlin, 1913).

HOIJER, O., *Le comte d'Aehrenthal et la politique de violence* (Paris, 1922).
HÖTZENDORF, C. VON, *Aus meiner Dienstzeit, 1906–1918,* 4 vols. (Vienna, 1922–23).
JÄCKH, E., *Deutschland im Orient nach dem Balkankrieg* (Munich, 1913).
JAGOW, G. VON, *Ursachen und Ausbruch des Weltkrieges* (Berlin, 1919).
JOVANOVIČ, L., *The Murder of Serajevo* (Belgrade, 1924).
JUDET, E., *George Louis* (Paris, 1925).
KANNER, H., *Kaiserliche Katastrophenpolitik* (Vienna, 1922).
KAUTSKY, K., *Wie der Weltkrieg entstand* (Berlin, 1919).
————, *The Guilt of William Hohenzollern* (London, 1920).
LEGER, L. P. M., *Serbes, croates et bulgares* (Paris, 1913).
LICHNOWSKY, K. M., *Meine Londoner Mission, 1912–1914* (New York, 1918).
————, *My Mission to London, 1912–1914* (Toronto, 1918).
————, *Heading for the Abyss* (New York, 1928).
LOREBURN, EARL, *How the War Came* (London, 1919).
LUTZ, H., *Die europäische Politik in der Julikrisis, 1914* (Berlin, 1930).
MARCHAND, R., ed., *Un livre noir,* 3 vols. in 4 (Paris, 1922–23).
MEYER, A., *Der Balkankrieg 1912/13* (Berlin, 1913–14).
MINISTÈRE DES AFFAIRES ÉTRANGÈRES, *Les affaires balkaniques,* 3 vols. (Paris, 1922).
MOLDEN, B., *Alois Graf Aehrenthal* (Stuttgart, 1917).
MONGELAS, M., *Leitfaden zur Kriegsschuldfrage* (Berlin, 1929).
————, *The Case for the Central Powers* (New York, 1925).
————, *British Foreign Policy under Sir Edward Grey* (New York, 1928).
MORLEY, J., VISCOUNT, *Memorandum on Resignation* (London, 1928).
MUKTAR PASCHA, M., *Meine Führung im Balkankriege 1912* (Berlin, 1913).
NIKOLAIDES, K., *Griechenlands Anteil an den Balkankriegen 1912/1913* (Vienna, 1914).
NOCK, A. J., *The Myth of a Guilty Nation* (New York, 1922).
Official German Documents Relating to the World War, 2 vols. (New York, 1923).
Oesterreich-Ungarns Aussenpolitik, 1908–1914, 9 vols. (Vienna, 1930).
Pharos, der Prozess gegen die Attentäter von Sarajewo (Berlin, 1918).
PHILIPSON, C., and BUXTON, N., *The Question of the Bosphorus and the Dardanelles* (London, 1917).
POURTALES, J., COUNT VON, *Am Scheidewege zwischen Krieg und Frieden* (Charlottenburg, 1919).
PRIBRAM, A. F., *Austrian Foreign Policy, 1908–1918* (London, 1923).
PRICE, M. P., *The Diplomatic History of the War* (New York, 1914, 1915).
RANKIN, R., *The Inner History of the Balkan War* (London, 1914).
REINACH, J., *Histoire de douze jours* (Paris, 1917).
RENOUVIN, P., *Les origines immédiates de la guerre, 24 juin–4 août, 1914* (Paris, 1925).
————, *The Immediate Origins of the War* (New Haven, 1928).
Report of the International Commission to Inquire into the Causes and Conduct of the Balkan Wars (Washington, 1914).
REVENTLOW, E., *Politische Vorgeschichte des grossen Krieges* (Berlin, 1919).
ROMBERG, G. VON, ed., *Falsifications of the Russian Orange Book* (New York, 1923).

ROMBERG, G. VON, ed., *Die Fälschungen des russischen Orangebuches* (1922).
SANDERS, GEN. L. VON, *Fünf Jahre Türkei* (Berlin, 1920).
————, *Five Years in Turkey* (Baltimore, 1927).
SAZONOV, S., *Fateful Years (1909–1916)* (New York, 1928).
SCHILLING, BARON, *How the War Began in 1914* (London, 1925).
SCHMITT, B. E., *The Coming of the War, 1914,* 2 vols. (New York, 1930).
SCHNEE, H., *Weltpolitik vor und nach dem Kriege* (Leipzig, 1924).
SCHÖN, W. E., BARON VON, *Erlebtes* (Stuttgart, 1921).
————, *The Memoirs of an Ambassador* (London, 1922).
SCHURMAN, J. G., *The Balkan Wars, 1912–1913* (Princeton, 1914).
SCHWERFEGER, B., *Zur europäischen Politik,* 6 vols. (Berlin, 1925).
SCOTT, J. B., *Diplomatic Documents Relating to the Outbreak of the European War,* 2 vols. (New York, 1916).
SCOTT, J. F., *Five Weeks* (New York, 1927).
SETON-WATSON, R. W., *Sarajevo* (London, 1925).
SEYMOUR, C., *The Intimate Papers of Colonel House,* 4 vols. (Boston, 1926–28).
SIEBERT, B. VON, ed., *Diplomatische Aktenstücke zur Geschichte der Ententepolitik der Vorkriegsjahre* (Berlin, 1921).
———— and SCHREINER, G. A., *Entente Diplomacy and the World (1909–1914)* (New York, 1921).
STANOJEVIČ, S., *Die Ermordung des Erzherzogs Franz Ferdinand* (Frankfort, 1923).
STICKNEY, E. P., *Southern Albania or Northern Epirus in European International Affairs, 1912–1913* (Stanford, 1923).
STIEVE, F., ed., *Der diplomatische Schriftwechsel Iswolskis, 1911–1924,* 5 vols. (Berlin, 1924).
————, *Isvolski und der Weltkrieg* (Berlin, 1924).
————, *Isvolsky and the World War* (New York, 1925).
SUCHOMLINOW, W. A., *Erinnerungen* (Berlin, 1924).
SZILASSY, J. VON, *Der Untergang der Donau-Monarchie* (Berlin, 1922).
TARDIEU, A., *Le mystère d'Agadir* (Paris, 1912).
TRAPPMAN, A. H., *The Greeks Triumphant* (London, 1915).
WEGERER, A. VON, *Die Widerlegung der Versailler Kriegsschuldthese* (Berlin, 1918).
————, *A Refutation of the Versailles War Guilt Thesis* (New York, 1930).
WERTHEIMER, O. VON, *Graf Stefan Tisza: Briefe, 1914–1918* (Berlin, 1928).
WILSON, LT. COL. A. T., *The Persian Gulf* (Oxford, 1928).
YOUNG, G., *Nationalism and War in the Near East* (Oxford, 1915).

CHAPTER XXVI
THE WORLD WAR, 1914–1918

ABBOTT, G. F., *Greece and the Allies, 1914–22* (London, 1922).
ARTHUR, SIR G., *Life of Lord Kitchener,* 3 vols. (New York, 1920).
AULARD, F. V. A., *1914–1918; histoire politique de la grande guerre* (Paris, 1924).
AYRES, L. P., *The War with Germany, a Statistical Summary* (Washington, 1923).

BAKER, R. S., *Woodrow Wilson, Life and Letters*, 2 vols. (Garden City, N. Y., 1927).

———— and DODD, W. E., *The Public Papers of Woodrow Wilson*, 6 vols. in 3 (New York, 1925–27).

BASSETT, J. S., *Our War with Germany* (New York, 1919).

BETHMANN-HOLLWEG, T. VON, *Kriegsreden* (Berlin, 1919).

————, *Betrachtungen zum Weltkriege*, 2 vols. (Berlin, 1919–22).

————, *Reflections on the World War* (London, 1920).

BERNHARDI, GEN. F. VON, *Deutschlands Heldenkampf* (Munich, 1922).

BERTIE, LORD, *The Diary of Lord Bertie of Thame, 1914–1918*, 2 vols. (New York, 1924).

BOGART, E. L., *Direct and Indirect Cost of the Great War* (New York, 1919).

BRIDGE, F. M., *A Short History of the Great World War* (London, 1920).

BRIDGE, MAJ. W. C., *How the War Began in 1914, Being the Diary of the Russian Foreign Office* (London, 1925).

BRUSSILOV, A. A., *A Soldier's Note-Book, 1914–1918* (London, 1930).

BUCHAN, J., *A History of the Great War*, 4 vols. (Boston, 1922).

BURNET, MAJ. C., *Foch Talks* (London, 1929).

BÜLOW, B. W. VON, *Die Krisis* (Berlin, 1922).

BÜLOW, PRINCE VON, *Denkwürdigkeiten*, 4 vols. (Berlin, 1930–31).

CALLWELL, MAJ. GEN. C. E., *Field Marshall Sir Henry Wilson, His Life and Diaries*, 2 vols. (New York, 1927).

CADORNA, GEN. L., *La guerra alla fronte italiana*, 2 vols. (Milan, 1921).

CAPELLO, GEN. L., *Note di guerra*, 2 vols. (Milan, 1920, 1921).

CAREY, G. V., *An Outline History of the Great War* (New York, 1929).

CHARTERIS, BRIG. GEN. J., *Field Marshall Earl Haig* (London and New York, 1929).

CHESTER, S. B., *Life of Venizelos* (New York, 1921).

CHURCHILL, W. S., *The World Crisis*, 3 vols. (New York, 1923–27).

————, *The Unknown War; the Eastern Front* (New York, 1931).

COCKS, F., *The Secret Treaties and Understandings* (London, 1918).

Commission d'Enquête, *Guerre 1914–1918 en Belgique*, 6 vols. (Brussels, 1921–1923).

CORBETT, J. S., *Naval Operations*, 5 vols. in 8 (London, 1920–31).

CROWE, J. H. V., *General Smuts' Campaign in East Africa* (London, 1918).

CZERNIN, O., *Im Weltkriege* (Berlin, 1919).

————, *In the World War* (London, 1919).

DANE, E., *British Campaigns in the Nearer East*, 2 vols. (London, 1919).

————, *British Campaigns in Africa and the Pacific, 1914–1918* (London, 1919).

DAUZET, P., *Gloria; histoire illustrée de la guerre, 1914–1918* (Paris, 1919).

DICKINSON, G. L., *Documents and Statements Relating to Peace Proposals and War Aims, 1916–1918* (New York, 1919).

Economic and Social History of the World War (a series in many volumes edited by J. T. Shotwell).

FALKENHAYN, GEN. E. VON, *Die oberste Heeresleitung, 1914–1916, in ihren wichtigsten Entschliessungen* (Berlin, 1920).

————, *General Headquarters and Its Critical Decisions* (London, 1919).

FAYLE, C. E., *Seaborne Trade*, 2 vols. (London, 1920, 1923).

FOSS, M., *Der See- und Kolonialkrieg* (Halle, 1919).

FRENCH, VISCOUNT, *1914* (Boston, 1919).

FROTHINGHAM, T. G., *A Guide to the Military History of the World War, 1914–1918* (Boston, 1921).

——————, *The American Reënforcement in the World War* (New York, 1927).

——————, *The Naval History of the World War*, 3 vols. (Cambridge, 1924–26).

GALLIÉNI, GEN., *Mémoires du général Galliéni* (Paris, 1920).

GAY, G. I., and FISCHER, H. H., *Public Relations of the Commission for Relief in Belgium*, 2 vols. (Stanford University, 1929).

GIBSON, C. R., *War Inventions and How They Were Invented* (London, 1918).

GOLDER, F. A., *Documents of Russian History, 1914–1917* (New York, 1927).

GUICHARD, L., *Histoire du blocus naval, 1914–1918* (Paris, 1929).

HAMILTON, SIR I., *Gallipoli Diary*, 2 vols. (New York, 1920).

HANOTAUX, G., *Le maréchal Foch* (Paris, 1929).

HAYES, C. J. H., *A Brief History of the Great War* (New York, 1926).

HELFERICH, K., *Der Weltkrieg*, 3 vols. (Berlin, 1919).

HENDRICK, B. J., *The Life and Letters of Walter Hines Page*, 3 vols. (Garden City, N. Y., 1922–25).

HINDENBURG, P. VON, *Aus meinen Leben* (Leipzig, 1920).

——————, *Out of My Life* (New York, 1920).

History of the Great War, Vols. I–V (London, 1922–   ).

HURD, A. S., *The Merchant Navy*, Vols. I–III (London, 1921–   ).

——————, *The British Fleet in the Great War* (London, 1918).

JELLICOE, VISCOUNT, *The Grand Fleet, 1914–1916* (New York, 1919).

JOHNSON, D. W., *Battlefields of the World War* (New York, 1921).

KANNENGIESSER, H., *The Campaign in Gallipoli* (London, 1928).

KNOX, SIR A. W., *With the Russian Army* (London, 1921).

KLUCK, GEN. A. VON, *The March on Paris and the Battle of the Marne* (London, 1920).

LASSWELL, H., *Propaganda Technique in the World War* (New York, 1928).

LAWRENCE, T. E., *Revolt in the Desert* (New York, 1927).

LECOMTE, C. C., *Georges Clemenceau, the Tiger of France* (New York, 1919).

HART, B. H., *Reputations Ten Years After* (Boston, 1928).

LETTOW-VORBECK, P. E. VON, *Meine Erinnerungen aus Ostafrika* (Leipzig, 1920).

——————, *My Reminiscences of East Africa* (London, 1920).

LUCAS, SIR C., *The Empire at War*, 5 vols. (New York, 1921–26).

LUDENDORFF, E. VON, *Meine Kriegserinnerungen, 1914–1918* (Berlin, 1919).

——————, *Ludendorff's Own Story*, 2 vols. (New York, 1919).

——————, *Urkunden der obersten Heeresleitung* (Berlin, 1920).

——————, *The General Staff and Its Problems*, 2 vols. (New York, 1920).

MANTEY, E. V., ed., *Der Krieg zur See, 1914–1918*, 5 vols. (Berlin, 1920, 1921, 1922).

MASSEY, W. T., *How Jerusalem Was Won* (London, 1919).

————————, *Allenby's Final Triumph* (London, 1920).

MC MASTER, J. B., *The United States in the World War*, 2 vols. (New York, 1919–20).

MC PHERSON, W. L., *The Strategy of the Great War* (New York, 1919).

MALLETERRE, P. M. G., *Les campagnes de 1915* (Paris, 1918).

MARTIN, W., *Statesmen of the World War in Retrospect, 1918–1928* (New York, 1928).

MORGENTHAU, H., *Ambassador Morgenthau's Story* (New York, 1919).

NEGULESCO, G., *Rumania's Sacrifice* (New York, 1918).

NEUMANN, G. P., *The German Air Force in the Great War* (London, NEVINSON, H. W., *The Dardanelles Campaign* (London, 1918).

1920).

NEWBOLT, H., *A Naval History of the War, 1914–1918* (London, 1920).

New York Times Current History, 19 vols. (New York, 1914–19).

ODDONE, A., *Storia della guerra d'Italia (1915–1918)* (Brescia, 1926).

PAGE, T. N., *Italy and the World War* (New York, 1920).

PALAT, GEN., *La grande guerre sur le front occidental*, 14 vols. (Paris, 1917–29).

PALÉOLOGUE, M., *La Russie des tsars pendant la grande guerre*, 3 vols. (Paris, 1922).

PALMER, F., *Our Greatest Battle* (New York, 1919).

PERSHING, GEN. J. J., *My Experiences in the World War*, 2 vols. (New York, 1931).

PÉTAIN, MARSHALL H. P., *La bataille de Verdun* (Paris, 1929).

PHOCAS-COSMETATOS, S. P. P., *The Tragedy of Greece* (London, 1928).

POLLARD, A. F., *Short History of the Great War* (New York, 1920).

POLONSKY, J., *Documents diplomatiques secrets russes 1914–1917* (Paris, 1928).

PULESTON, W. D., *The Dardanelles Expedition* (Annapolis, 1927).

RALEIGH, SIR W., *The War in the Air*, Vol. I (Oxford, 1922).

RECOULY, R., *Foch, the Winner of the War* (New York, 1920).

————————, *M. Jonnart en Grèce et l'abdication de Constantin* (Paris, 1918).

REPINGTON, LT. COL. C. A., *The First World War*, 2 vols. (Boston, 1920).

RIVOYRE, LT. DE, *Histoire de la guerre navale, 1914–1918* (Paris, 1921).

ROBERTSON, SIR W. R., *Soldiers and Statesmen, 1914–1918* (London, 1926).

RUPPRECHT, CROWN PRINCE of Bavaria, *Mein Kriegstagebuch*, 3 vols. (Munich, 1928).

SANDERS, GEN. L. VON, *Fünf Jahre Türkei* (Berlin, 1920).

————————, *Five Years in Turkey* (Baltimore, 1928).

SCHEER, R., *Deutschlands Hochseeflotte im Weltkrieg* (Berlin, 1920).

————————, *Germany's High Seas Fleet in the World War* (New York, 1920).

SCHNEE, H., *Deutsch-Ostafrika im Weltkriege* (Leipzig, 1919).

SCHWENKE, A., *Die Tragödie von Verdun 1916* (Oldenburg, 1929).

SCHNITLER, COL. G., *La guerre mondiale (1914–1918)* (Paris, 1929).

SEYMOUR, C., *The Intimate Papers of Colonel House,* 4 vols. (Boston, 1926–28).

——————, *Woodrow Wilson and the World War* (New Haven, 1921).

SIMONDS, F. H., *History of the World War,* 5 vols. (Garden City, N. Y., 1917–20).

SIMS, ADM. W. S., *The American Navy in the War* (1920).

——————, *The Victory at Sea* (Garden City, 1920).

STUART, SIR C., *Secrets of Crewe House* (London, 1920).

THOMAS, L., *Raiders of the Deep* (New York, 1929).

THOMAZI, A., *La marine française dans la grande guerre, 1914–1918,* 3 vols. (Paris, 1925–1927).

TIRPITZ, ADM. A. VON, *My Memoirs,* 2 vols. (New York, 1919).

TOWNSHEND, SIR C., *My Campaign in Mesopotamia* (London, 1920).

TREVELYAN, G. M., *Scenes from Italy's War* (Boston, 1919).

TURNER, C. C., *The Struggle in the Air, 1914–1918* (New York, 1919).

VILLARI, L., *The Macedonian Campaign* (London, 1922).

VAN EVERY, D., *The A.E.F. in Battle* (New York, 1928).

WAVELL, COL. A. P., *The Palestine Campaigns* (London, 1928).

WESTER-WEMYSS, LORD R. E., *The Navy in the Dardanelles Campaign* (London, 1924).

WHEELER, W. R., *China and the World War* (New York, 1919).

WHITLOCK, B., *Belgium: A Personal Narrative,* 2 vols. (New York, 1919).

WOOD, H. C., *The Cradle of the War* (Boston, 1918).

PART V

GENERAL WORKS ON THE PERIOD AFTER 1918

AUBERT, L., *The Reconstruction of Europe* (New Haven, 1925).

BAGGER, E. S., *Eminent Europeans* (New York, 1922).

BEARD, C. A., *Cross Currents in Europe To-Day* (Boston, 1922).

BOWMAN, I., *The New World* (Yonkers, 1928).

BUELL, R. L., *Europe: A History of Ten Years* (New York, 1928).

GIBBONS, H. A., *Europe since 1918* (New York, 1923).

GRAHAM, M. W., *The New Governments of Central Europe* (New York, 1924).

——————, *New Governments of Eastern Europe* (New York, 1927).

GUEST, L. H., *The Struggle for Power in Europe, 1917–1921* (London, 1921).

HUDDLESTON, S., *Those Europeans* (New York, 1924).

LAIDLER, H. W., *A History of Socialist Thought* (New York, 1927).

McBAIN, H. L., and ROGERS, L., *The New Constitutions of Europe* (New York, 1923).

MACARTNEY, M. H. H., *Five Years of European Chaos* (London, 1923).

MC LAUGHLIN, M. C., *Newest Europe* (London, 1931).

MARKHAM, S., *A History of Socialism* (London, 1930).

MOWAT, R. B., *A History of European Diplomacy, 1914–1925* (New York, 1927).

MUNRO, W. B., *The Governments of Europe* (New York, 1931).

SFORZA, COUNT C., *Diplomatic Europe since the Treaty of Versailles* (New Haven, 1928).

SLOSSON, P. W., *Twentieth Century Europe* (Boston, 1927).
These Eventful Years, 2 vols. (New York, 1924).
TOYNBEE, A. J., *The World after the Peace Conference* (London, 1925).
————, *Survey of International Affairs, 1920/23–1929,* 12 vols.
(London, 1925–31).

CHAPTER XXVII

INTERNATIONAL RELATIONS SINCE 1918

The Peace Conference at Paris:

ANTONELLI, E., *L'Afrique et la paix de Versailles* (Paris, 1921).
BAKER, R. S., *What Wilson Did at Paris* (Garden City, N. Y., 1920).
————, *Woodrow Wilson and World Settlement,* 3 vols. (New York, 1922).
BARUCH, B. M., *The Making of the Reparation and Economic Sections of the Treaty* (New York, 1920).
BEER, G. L., *African Questions at the Peace Conference* (New York, 1923).
BOWMAN, I., *The New World* (Yonkers, 1928).
BROCKDORF-RANTZAU, A. K. C. COUNT VON, *Dokumente* (Charlottenburg, 1920).
CARNEGIE ENDOWMENT FOR INTERNATIONAL PEACE, *The Treaties of Peace, 1919–1923,* 2 vols. (New York, 1924).
CHURCHILL, W. S., *The Aftermath* (New York, 1929).
DEWALL, W. VON, *Der Kampf um den Frieden* (Frankfort, 1929).
DILLON, E. J., *The Inside Story of the Peace Conference* (New York, 1920).
DONALD, SIR R., *The Tragedy of Trianon* (London, 1928).
EBRAY, A., *A Frenchman Looks at the Peace* (London, 1927).
EDWARDS, J. H., *David Lloyd George* (New York, 1929).
GRAUX, L., *Histoire des violations du traité de paix,* 4 vols. (Paris, 1921–27).
HASKINS C. H., and LORD, R. H., *Some Problems of the Peace Conference* (Cambridge, 1920).
HOUSE, E. M., and SEYMOUR, C., *What Really Happened at Paris* (New York, 1921).
HUDDLESTON, S., *Peace Making at Paris* (London, 1919).
HUNGARIAN PEACE DELEGATION, *The Hungarian Peace Negotiations,* 4 vols. (1921).
HYNDMAN, H. M., *Clemenceau* (New York, 1919).
KEYNES, J., *Economic Consequences of the Peace* (New York, 1920).
KRAUS, H., *Chronik der Friedensverhandlungen* (Berlin, 1920).
LANSING, R., *The Big Four and Others of the Peace Conference* (Boston, 1921).
————, *The Peace Negotiations, a Personal Narrative* (Boston, 1921).
MALLET, SIR C. E., *Mr. Lloyd George* (London, 1930).
MARTET, J., *G. Clemenceau* (London, 1930).
MILLER, D. H., *The Drafting of the Covenant,* 2 vols. (New York, 1928).
————, *My Diary at the Conference of Paris,* 21 vols. (New York, 1928).
SCOTT, A. P., *An Introduction to the Peace Treaties* (Chicago, 1920).

TARDIEU, A., *The Truth about the Treaty* (Indianapolis, 1921).
TEMPERLEY, H. W. V., *A History of the Peace Conference at Paris,* 6 vols. (London, 1920–24).
WILLE, C. A., *Der Versailler Vertrag und die Sanktionen* (Berlin, 1925).

The League of Nations:

BAKER, P. J. N., *The League of Nations at Work* (London, 1926).
BARNES, G. N., *History of the International Labour Office* (London, 1926).
BASSETT, J. S., *The League of Nations* (New York, 1928).
BRADFIELD, B., *A Little Book of the League of Nations, 1920–1927* (Geneva, 1927).
JOHNSTON, G. A., *International Social Progress* (London, 1924.)
LEAGUE OF NATIONS, *Ten Years of World Coöperation* (London, 1930).
OLIVER, E. M., *The World's Industrial Parliament* (London, 1925).
POTTER, P. B., *An Introduction to the Study of International Organization* (New York, 1928).
QUIGLEY, H. S., *From Versailles to Locarno* (Minneapolis, 1927).

The Permanent Court of International Justice (World Court):

BUSTAMENTE Y SIRVEN, A. S. DE, *The World Court* (New York, 1925).
FACHIRI, A. P., *The Permanent Court of International Justice* (London, 1925).
FRANQUEVILLE, B. DE, *L'œuvre de la cour permanente de justice internationale,* 2 vols. (Paris, 1928).
HUDSON, M. O., *The Permanent Court of International Justice* (Cambridge, 1925).
——————, *The Work of the Permanent Court of International Justice during Four Years* (Boston, 1926).
LEAGUE OF NATIONS, *The Permanent Court of International Justice* (Geneva, 1930).
——————, *Statute of the Court* (Leyden, 1926).
LINDSEY, E., *The International Court* (New York, 1931).
WHEELER-BENNETT, J. W., *Information on the Permanent Court of International Justice* (London, 1925).

Reparations:

ABERNON, VISCOUNT D', *Diary of an Ambassador,* 2 vols. (Garden City, N. Y., 1928–30).
ALEXANDER, F., *From Paris to Locarno, and After* (London, 1928).
AULD, G. P., *The Dawes Plan and the New Economics* (Garden City, N. Y., 1928).
BERGMANN, K., *The History of Reparations* (Boston, 1927).
CALMETTE, G., *Recueil de documents sur l'histoire de la question des réparations* (Paris, 1924).
DAWES, R. C., *The Dawes Plan in the Making* (Indianapolis, 1925).
GLASGOW, G., *From Dawes to Locarno* (New York, 1926).
GREER, G., *The Ruhr-Lorraine Industrial Problem* (New York, 1925).

LICHTENBERGER, H., *The Ruhr Conflict* (Washington, 1923).
LONG, R. E. C., *The Mythology of Reparations* (London, 1928).
MOULTON, H. G., *The Reparation Plan* (New York, 1924).
————— and PASVOLSKY, L., *World War Debt Settlements* (New York, 1926).
RHEINHOLD, P. P., *The Economic, Financial, and Political State of Germany since the War* (London, 1928).
WORLD PEACE FOUNDATION, *The Dawes Report* (Boston, 1923).
SCHACHT, H., *The End of Reparations* (New York, 1931).
SERING, M., *Germany under the Dawes Plan* (London, 1929).

The Problem of Security:

BAKER, P. J. N., *Disarmament* (London, 1926).
—————, *The Geneva Protocol for the Pacific Settlement of International Disputes* (London, 1925).
CARNEGIE ENDOWMENT FOR INTERNATIONAL PEACE, *Locarno Treaties* (New York, 1926).
RAUCHBERG, H., *Die Verträge von Locarno* (Prague, 1926).
WHEELER-BENNETT, J. W., *Information on Reduction of Armaments* (London, 1925).
—————, and LANGERMANN, F. E., *The Problem of Security* (London, 1926).
WILLIAMS, B. S., *State Security and the League of Nations* (Baltimore, 1927).

CHAPTER XXVIII

RECONSTRUCTION AND EXPERIMENTATION IN GREAT BRITAIN, FRANCE, AND
ITALY

Great Britain:

GWYNN, D. K., *The Irish Free State, 1922–1927* (London, 1928).
HAMILTON, M. A., *J. Ramsay Macdonald* (New York, 1929).
HENRY, R. M., *The Evolution of Sinn Fein* (New York, 1920).
LUBIN, I., and EVERETT, H., *The British Coal Dilemma* (New York, 1927).
MURRAY R. H., and LAW, H., *Ireland* (Boston, 1924).
PHILLIPS, W. A., *The Revolution in Ireland, 1906–1923* (London and New York, 1926).
PLACHY, F., *Britain's Economic Plight* (Boston, 1926).
SIEGFRIED, A., *Post-War Britain* (New York, 1925).
—————, *England's Crisis* (New York, 1931).
TILTMAN, H. H., *J. Ramsay Macdonald, Labor's Man of Destiny* (New York, 1929).
WILLERT, SIR A., *Aspects of British Foreign Policy* (London, 1928).

France:

BUELL, R. L., *Contemporary French Politics* (New York, 1920).
DULLES, E. L., *The French Franc, 1914–1928* (New York, 1929).
HAIG, R. M., *Public Finances of Post-War France* (New York, 1929).

HUDDLESTON, S., *France* (London, 1926).

————, *Poincaré* (Boston, 1924).

MACDONALD, W., *Reconstruction in France* (New York, 1922).

MOON, P. T., *Foreign Policies of Post-War France* (New York, 1929).

MOULTON, H. G., and LEWIS, C., *The French Debt Problem* (New York, 1925).

OGBURN, W. F., and JAFFÉ, W., *The Economic Development of Post-War France* (New York, 1929).

PEEL, G., *The Financial Crisis of France* (London, 1926).

ROGERS, J. H., *The Process of Inflation in France, 1914–1927* (1929).

SAPOSS, D. J., *The Labor Movement in Post-War France* (New York, 1931).

SOLTAU, R. H., *French Parties and Politics* (London, 1922).

THÈRY, E., *Conséquences économiques de la guerre pour la France* (Paris, 1922).

Italy:

BARNES, J. S., *The Universal Aspects of Fascism* (London, 1927).

BECKERATH, E. VON, *Wesen und Werden des fascisten Staates* (Berlin, 1927).

BOLITHO, W., *Italy under Mussolini* (New York, 1926).

BORDEAUX, V. J., *Benito Mussolini—the Man* (New York, 1927).

GAY, H. N., *Strenuous Italy* (Boston, 1927).

GIOLITTI, G., *Mémoires de ma vie* (Paris, 1923).

HERRON, G. D., *The Revival of Italy* (London, 1922).

HULLINGER, E. W., *The New Fascist State* (New York, 1928).

La legislazione fascista, 1922–1928 (Rome, 1929).

LEMONON, E., *L'Italie d'après guerre, 1914–1921* (Paris, 1922).

MC GUIRE, C. E., *Italy's International Economic Position* (New York, 1926).

MUSSOLINI, B., *My Diary* (Boston, 1925).

PARSONS, W., *The Pope and Italy* (New York, 1929).

PENNACHIO, A., *The Corporative State* (New York, 1927).

SCHNEIDER, H. W., and CLOUGH, S. B., *Making Fascists* (Chicago, 1929).

————, *Making the Fascist State* (New York, 1928).

CHAPTER XXIX

THE GERMAN REPUBLIC

ANGEL, J. W., *The Recovery of Germany* (New Haven, 1929).

AHNERT, K., *Die Entwickelung der deutschen Revolution und das Kriegsende in der Zeit vom 1 Oktober bis 30 November 1918* (Nuremberg, 1918).

BARTH, E., *Aus der Werkstatt der deutschen Revolution* (Berlin, 1919).

BERNSTEIN, E., *Die deutsche Revolution* (Berlin, 1921).

BEVAN, E. R., *German Social Democracy during the War* (London, 1918).

BOUTON, S. M., *And the Kaiser Abdicates* (New Haven, 1931).

BLOSS, W., *Von der Monarchie zum Volkstaat*, 2 vols. (Stuttgart, 1922–23).

BLÜCHER VON WAHLSTATT, E. M., *An English Wife in Berlin* (London, 1920).

BREITHAUPT, W., *Volksvergiftung* (Berlin, 1925).

BROWN, P., *Germany in Dissolution* (London, 1920).

BRUNET, R., *The New German Constitution* (New York, 1922).

BUCHNER, E., *Revolutionsdokumente* (Berlin, 1921).

COAR, J. F., *The Old and New Germany* (New York, 1924).

DANIELS, H. G., *The Rise of the German Republic* (New York, 1928).

DANTON, G. H., *Germany Ten Years After* (Boston, 1928).

DAWSON, SIR P., *Germany's Industrial Revival* (London, 1926).

DRAHN, E., *Unterirdische Literatur im revolutionären Deutschland während des Weltkrieges* (Berlin, 1920).

FISKE, O. H., ed., *Germany's Constitutions of 1871 and 1919* (Cincinnati, 1928).

GOOCH, G. P., *Germany* (New York, 1927).

GUILLEBAUD, C. W., *The Works Council* (Cambridge, 1928).

HARMS, B., ed., *Strukturwandlugen der Deutschen Volkswirschaft,* 2 vols. (Berlin, 1929).

HORKENBACH, C., *Das deutsche Reich von 1918 bis 1930* (Berlin, 1930).

International Conciliation, *Manifesto of Spartacus Group* (April, 1919, No. 137).

JÄCKH, E., *The New Germany* (London, 1927).

KOCH-WESER, E., *Deutschlands Aussenpolitik in der Nachkriegzeit, 1919–1929* (Berlin, 1929).

KRAUS, H., *Germany in Transition* (Chicago, 1924).

LUEHR, E., *The New German Republic* (New York, 1929).

LUTZ, R. H., *The German Revolution, 1918–1919* (Stanford University, 1922).

MATTERN, J., *Bavaria and the Reich* (Baltimore, 1923).

MATTHAEI, L. E., *Germany in Revolution* (New York, 1920).

MAXIMILIAN OF BADEN, PRINCE, *Erinnerungen und Dokumente* (Stuttgart, 1928).

—————, *The Memoirs of Prince Max of Baden,* 2 vols. (London and New York, 1928).

MEAKIN, W., *The New Industrial Revolution* (New York, 1929).

MORGAN, J. H., *The Present State of Germany* (Boston, 1923).

MÜLLER, H., *Die November-Revolution* (Berlin, 1928).

—————, *Der Bürgerkrieg in Deutschland* (Berlin, 1925).

MÜLLER, R., *Vom Kaiserreich zur Republik,* 2 vols. (Vienna, 1924–25).

NOSKE, G., *Von Kiel bis Kapp* (Berlin, 1920).

OPPENHEIMER, H., *The Constitution of the German Republic* (London, 1923).

OLDEN, R., *Stresemann* (New York, 1930).

PERNOT, M., *L'Allemagne aujourd'hui* (Paris, 1927).

PRICE, M. P., *Germany in Transition* (London, 1922).

QUIGLEY H., and CLARK, R. J., *Republican Germany* (New York, 1928).

REINHOLD, P. P., *The Economic, Financial, and Political State of Germany since the War* (London, 1928).

RHEINBABEN, R., *Stresemann, the Man and the Statesman* (New York, 1929).

ROSENBERG, A., *Die Entstehung der deutschen Republik, 1871–1918* (Berlin, 1928).

SCHACHT, H., *The Stabilization of the Mark* (Stuttgart, 1928).

SCHEIDEMANN, P., *Memoiren eines Sozialdemokraten,* 2 vols. (Dresden, 1928).

—————, *The Making of New Germany*, 2 vols. (New York, 1929).

SCHULZE, A., *Das neue deutsche Reich* (Dresden, 1927).

SERING, M., *Germany under the Dawes Plan* (London, 1929).

STROEBEL, H., *The German Revolution and After* (London, 1923).

—————, *Socialization in Theory and Practice* (London, 1922).

STÜMKE, B., *Die Entstehung der deutschen Republik* (Frankfort, 1923).

Die Ursachen des deutschen Zusammenbruchs im Jahre 1918, vols. I–II (New York, 1928–   ).

WETERSTETTEN, R., *The Biography of President von Hindenburg* (New York, 1930).

YOUNG, G., *The New Germany* (London, 1920).

CHAPTER XXX

RUSSIA AND HER BORDERLANDS

Russia:

ALEKSINSKI, G., *Du tsarisme au communisme* (Paris, 1923).

American Trade Union Delegation, *Soviet Russia in the Second Decade* (New York, 1928).

ANET, C., *La révolution russe,* 4 vols. (Paris, 1918–19).

ARNOT, R. P., *Soviet Russia and Her Neighbors* (New York, 1927).

BATSELL, W. R., *Soviet Rule in Russia* (New York, 1929).

BLANC, E. T., *The Coöperative Movement in Russia* (New York, 1924).

BRAILSFORD, H. N., *How the Soviets Work* (New York, 1927).

British Trade Union Delegation, *Russia* (London, 1925).

BRYANT, L., *Mirrors of Moscow* (New York, 1923).

BUCHANAN, SIR G., *My Mission to Russia,* vol. II (Boston, 1923).

BURY, H., *Russia from Within* (London, 1927).

CANTACUZÈNE, PRINCESS J., *Revolutionary Days* (Boston, 1919).

—————, *Russian People* (New York, 1920).

CHAMBERLAIN, W. H., *Soviet Russia* (Boston, 1930).

COOKE, R. J., *Religion in Russia under the Soviets* (New York, 1924).

DENIKIN, A. J., *The Russian Turmoil* (London, 1922).

DENNIS, A. L. P., *The Foreign Policies of Soviet Russia* (New York, 1924).

DOBB, M., and STEVENS, H. C., *Russian Economic Development since the Revolution* (New York, 1928).

DUNN, R. W., *Soviet Trade Unions* (New York, 1928).

EASTMAN, M., *Since Lenin Died* (New York, 1925).

FISHER, H. H., *The Famine in Soviet Russia, 1919–1923* (New York, 1927).

FISHER, L., *The Soviets in World Affairs,* 2 vols. (London, 1930).

FLORINSKI, M. T., *The End of the Russian Empire* (New Haven, 1931).

FRANCIS, D. R., *Russia from the American Embassy* (New York, 1921).

FÜLÖP-MILLER, R., *Rasputin* (Garden City, N. Y., 1928).

—————, *The Mind and Face of Bolshevism* (New York, 1929).

GILLIARD, P., *La tragique destin de Nicolas II et sa famille* (Paris, 1922).

GOLDER, F. A., *Documents of Russian History, 1914–1917* (New York, 1927).

————— and HUTCHINSON, L., *On the Trail of the Russian Famine* (Stanford University, 1927).

GOURKO, B., *War and Revolution in Russia, 1914–17* (New York, 1919).

GRONSKY P. P., and ASTROV, N. J., *The War and the Russian Government* (New Haven, 1929).

HARPER, S. N., *Making Bolshevists* (Chicago, 1931).

——, *Civic Training in Soviet Russia* (Chicago, 1929).

HEWITT, N., *The Rulers of Russia* (London, 1924).

HINDUS, M. G., *Humanity Uprooted* (New York, 1929).

——, *The Russian Peasant and the Revolution* (New York, 1920).

HOOVER, C. B., *The Economic Life of Soviet Russia* (New York, 1931).

HULLINGER, E. W., *The Reforging of Russia* (New York, 1925).

KARLGREN, A., *Bolshevist Russia* (New York, 1927)

KATZENELLENBAUM, S. S., *Russian Currency and Banking, 1914–1924* (London, 1925).

KERENSKY, A. F., *The Catastrophe* (New York, 1927).

KNOX, SIR A. W. F., *With the Russian Army, 1914–1917,* 2 vols. (London, 1921).

KOMAROFF-KURLOFF, *Das Ende des russischen Kaisertums* (Berlin, 1920).

KORFF, S. A., *Autocracy and Revolution in Russia* (New York, 1923).

LAWTON, L., *The Russian Revolution, 1917–1926* (London, 1927).

LEGRAS, J., *Mémoires de Russie* (Paris, 1921).

LEE, I., *Present Day Russia* (New York, 1928).

LENIN, N., *Preparing for Revolt* (London, 1929).

——, *The Revolution of 1917,* 2 vols. (New York, 1927).

LEVINE, I. D., *The Man Lenin* (New York, 1924).

——, *Stalin* (New York, 1931).

Lettres des grand-ducs à Nicolas II (Paris, 1926).

LEVY, R., *Trotsky* (Paris, 1920).

Livre rouge; recueil des documents diplomatiques relatifs aux relations entre la Russie et la Pologne, 1918–1920 (Moscow, 1920).

MAKEEF, N., and O'HARA, V., *Russia* (New York, 1925)

MARCU, V., *Lenin, Thirty Years of Russia* (New York, 1928).

MARYE, G. T., *Nearing the End in Imperial Russia* (Philadelphia, 1929).

MAVOR, J., *The Russian Revolution* (New York, 1928).

MILIUKOV, P. N., *Russia Today and Tomorrow* (New York, 1922).

MIRSKY, D. S., *Lenin* (Boston, 1931).

NICHOLAS II, *The Letters of the Tsar to the Tsaritsa* (London, 1929).

NOLDE, B. E., *L'ancien régime et la revolution russe* (Paris, 1928).

PALÉOLOGUE, G. M., *La Russie des tsars pendant la grande guerre,* 3 vols. (Paris, 1921–22).

——, *An Ambassador's Memoirs,* 3 vols. (New York, 1923–25).

PETRUNKEVITCH, A., HARPER, S. N., GOLDER, F. A., and KERNER, R. J., *The Russian Revolution; The Jugoslav Movement* (Cambridge, 1918).

PRICE, M. P., *My Reminiscences of the Russian Revolution* (London, 1921).

RODZIANKO, M. V., *The Reign of Rasputin: An Empire's Collapse* (New York, 1927).

SAROLEA, C., *Impressions of Soviet Russia* (London, 1924).

SIMANOUITSCH, A., *Rasputin, der allmächtige Bauer* (Berlin, 1928).

SMILG-BENARIO, M., *Der Zusammenbruch der Zarenmonarchie* (Zurich, 1928).

The Soviet Union and Peace (New York, 1929).
SPINKA, M., *The Church and the Russian Revolution* (New York, 1927).
SKHOMLINOV, V. A., *Erinnerungen* (Berlin, 1924).
TROTSKY, L., *The History of the Russian Revolution* (London, 1919).
——————, *The Real Situation in Russia* (New York, 1928).
VERNADSKY, G., *Lenin, Red Dictator* (New Haven, 1931).
——————, *A History of Russia* (New Haven, 1930).
VULLIAMY, C. E., *The Letters of the Tsar to the Tsaritsa, 1914-1917* (New York, 1929).
YARMOLINSKY, A., *The Jews and Other Minor Nationalities under the Soviets* (New York, 1929).
ZIMAND, S., *State Capitalism in Russia* (New York, 1926).

The Baltic States:

BIHLMANS, A., *Latvia in the Making* (Riga, 1928).
BUCHAN, J., ed., *The Baltic and Caucasian States* (Boston, 1923).
BUTLER, R., *The Eastern Europe* (New York, 1919).
CROZAT, C., *Les constitutions de Pologne, de Dantzig, d'Esthonie et de Finland* (Toulouse, 1925).
CZEKEY, S. VON, *Die Verfassungsentwickelung Estlands, 1918-1928* (1928).
FOX, F., *Finland Today* (London, 1927).
Great Britain, Foreign Office, *Finland* (London, 1920).
——————, *Courland, Livonia, and Esthonia* (London, 1920).
HARRISON, E., *Lithuania, Past and Present* (London, 1922).
HURWICZ, E., *Der Neue Osten* (Berlin, 1927).
La Lettonie (Riga, 1922).
ÖHQUIST, J., *Finnland* (Leipzig, 1919).
PELLISSIER, J., *Les principaux artisans de la renaissance nationale lituanienne* (Lausanne, 1918).
RUHL, A. B., *New Masters of the Baltic* (New York, 1921).
RUTENBERG, G., *Die baltischen Staaten und das Völkerrecht* (Riga, 1928).
RUTTER, O., *The New Baltic States and Their Future* (London, 1925).
SÖDERHJELM, H., *The Red Insurrection in Finland, 1918* (London, 1920).
STOROST, W., *La Lituanie dans le passé et dans le présent* (Geneva, 1918).
WALTERS, M., *Lettland* (Rome, 1923).

CHAPTER XXXI

THE SUCCESSION STATES

Austria:

ANDRASSY, COUNT J., *Diplomatie und Weltkrieg* (Berlin, 1920).
——————, *Diplomacy and the World War* (London, 1921).
AUERBACH, B., *L'Autriche et la Hongrie pendant la guerre* (Paris, 1925).

BAUER, O., *Die oesterreichische Revolution* (Vienna, 1923).
————, *The Austrian Revolution* (London, 1925).
BURIAN VON RAJECZ, S., *Drei Jahre aus der Zeit meiner Amtsfuhrung im Kriege* (Berlin, 1923).
————, *Austria in Dissolution* (London, 1925).
CRANE, J. O., *The Little Entente* (New York, 1930).
CZERNIN, COUNT O., *Im Weltkriege* (Berlin, 1919).
————, *In the World War* (New York, 1919).
GOPČEVIČ, S., *Oesterreichs Untergang* (Berlin, 1920).
HEVESY, A. DE, *L'agonie d'un empire, l'Autriche-Hongrie* (Paris, 1923).
JASZI, O., *The Dissolution of the Habsburg Monarchy* (Chicago, 1929).
KARL I, *Aus Kaiser Karls Nachlass* (Berlin, 1925).
KERCHNAWE, H., ed., *Der Zusammenbruch der oesterreichisch-ungarischen Wehrmacht im Herbst 1918* (Munich, 1921).
KLEINWÄCHTER, F. F. G., *Der Untergang der oesterreichisch-ungarischen Monarchie* (Leipzig, 1920).
MACARTNEY, C. A., *The Social Revolution in Austria* (Cambridge, 1926).
MOUSSET, A., *La petite entente* (Paris, 1923).
NOWAK, K. F., *Der Sturz der Mittelmächte* (Munich, 1921).
————, *The Collapse of Central Europe* (London, 1924).
PASVOLSKY, L., *Economic Nationalism of the Danubian States* (New York, 1928).
REDLICH, J., *Oesterreichische Regierung und Verwaltung im Weltkriege* (Vienna, 1925).
————, *Austrian War Government* (New Haven, 1929).
SZILASSY, BARON J. VON, *Der Untergang der Donau-Monarchie* (Berlin, 1921).
WERKMANN, BARON C. VON, *The Tragedy of Charles of Habsburg* (London, 1924).
WINDISCHGRAETZ, PRINCE L., *My Memoirs* (Boston, 1921).

Czechoslovakia:

BENEŠ, E., *Souvenirs de guerre et de révolution* (Paris, 1929).
————, *My War Memories* (Boston, 1928).
BOROVICKA, J., *Ten Years of Czechoslovak Politics* (Prague, 1929).
CAPEK, T., JR., *Origins of the Czechoslovak State* (New York, 1926).
CHMELAR, J., *Political Parties in Czechoslovakia* (Prague, 1926).
CISAR, J., and POKORNY, F., *The Czechoslovak Republic* (London, 1922).
Declaration of Independence of the Czechoslovak Nation (New York, 1918).
DĚDEČEK, V., *La Tchecoslovaquie et les tchecoslovaques* (Paris, 1919).
EISMANN, L., *La Tchecoslovaquie* (Paris, 1921).
HERBEN, J., *T. G. Masaryk* (Prague, 1923).
HOETZL, J., and JOACHIM, V., eds., *The Constitution of the Czechoslovak Republic* (Prague, 1920).
INTERNATIONAL CONCILIATION, *The Constitution of the Czechoslovak Republic* (New York, October, 1922).
MASARYK, T. G., *The Making of a State* (London, 1927).
NOSEK, V., *Independent Bohemia* (London, 1918).

Opočensky, J., *The Collapse of the Austro-Hungarian Monarchy and the Rise of the Czechoslovak State* (Prague, 1928).
Papoušek, J., *The Czechoslovak Nation's Struggle for Independence* (Prague, 1928).
Seton-Watson, R. W., *The New Slovakia* (Prague, 1924).
Textor, L. E., *Land Reform in Czechoslovakia* (London, 1923).

Hungary:

Apponyi, Count A., *Justice for Hungary* (London, 1928).
Ashmead-Bartlett, E., *The Tragedy of Central Europe* (London, 1923).
Birinyi, L. K., *The Tragedy of Hungary* (Cleveland, 1924).
Donald, Sir R., *The Tragedy of Trianon* (London, 1928).
Herczeg, G., *Bela Kun* (Berlin, 1928).
Jaszi, O., *Revolution and Counter-revolution in Hungary* (London, 1924).
Karolyi, M., *Fighting the World* (London, 1924).
Street, C. J. C., *Hungary and Democracy* (London, 1923).

Poland:

Boncza, S. J., *The Founder of Polish Independence, Joseph Pilsudski* (London, 1921).
Bujak, F., *Poland's Economic Development* (London, 1926).
Dyboski, R., *Poland Old and New* (London, 1925).
Fisher, H. H., *America and the New Poland* (New York, 1928).
Korostovets, V. K., *The Rebirth of Poland* (London, 1928).
Landau, R., *Pilsudski and Poland* (New York, 1929).
Pilsudski, J., *Joseph Pilsudski, the Memories of a Polish Revolutionary and Soldier* (London, 1931).
Winter, N. O., *The New Poland* (Boston, 1923).

Rumania:

Basilescu, N., *La Roumanie dans la guerre et dans la paix* (Paris, 1919).
Buchan, J., ed., *Bulgaria and Roumania* (Boston, 1924).
Cabot, J. M., *The Racial Conflict in Transylvania* (Boston, 1926).
Clark, C. U., *Greater Rumania* (New York, 1922).
——————, *Bessarabia, Russia, and Rumania on the Black Sea* (New York, 1927).
Cornish, L. C., *Transylvania in 1922* (Boston, 1923).
Deak, F., *The Hungarian-Rumanian Land Dispute* (New York, 1928).
Dragomir, S., *The Ethnical Minorities in Transylvania* (Geneva, 1927).
Evans, I. L., *The Agrarian Revolution in Roumania* (Cambridge, 1924).
Gillard, M., *La Roumanie nouvelle* (Paris, 1922).
Romenhöller, C. G., *La grande Roumanie* (The Hague, 1926).
Roumania Ten Years After (Boston, 1928).
Stahel de Capitani, H., *Rumanien* (Zurich, 1925).
Szasz, S., *The Minorities in Roumanian Transylvania* (London, 1927).

Jugoslavia:

ANCEL, J., *Peuples et nations des Balkans* (Paris, 1926).

ARMSTRONG, H. F., *The New Balkans* (New York, 1926).

BAERLEIN, H. P. B., *The Birth of Jugoslavia,* 2 vols. (London, 1922).

BEARD, C. A., and RADIN, G., *The Balkan Pivot: Yugoslavia* (New York, 1929).

BUCHAN, J., ed., *Yugoslavia* (London, 1923).

EVELPIDI, C., *Les états balkaniques* (Paris, 1930).

JOVANOVIČ, N., *Étude sur la constitution du royaume des serbes, croates et slovènes du juin 1921, avec texte official intégral* (Paris, 1924).

KERNER, R. J., *The Jugoslav Movement* (Cambridge, 1918).

LONČAREVIČ, D. A., *Jugoslaviens Entstehung* (Zurich, 1929).

MOUSSET, A., *Le royaume des serbes, croates, et slovènes* (Paris, 1926).

SPELLANZON, C., *La questione d'oriente* (Milan, 1926).

TAYSEN, F. VON, *Das jugoslawische Problem* (Berlin, 1927).

WENDEL, H., *Der Kampf der Südslawen um Freiheit und Einheit* (Frankfort, 1925).

INDEX

Mustapha Kemal, 422

Naples, intervention of Austria in, 42
Napoleon, reaction of Europe against, 19; first abdication, 22; defeat at Leipzig, 23; return from Elba, 30; defeat at Waterloo, 30; second abdication, 30
Napoleon III, meets Cavour at Plombières, 157; opens peace negotiations, 159; delicate position in Central Italy of, 160; negotiates treaty, 161; consents to intervention of Sardinia in Central Italy, 163; domestic policies of, 169; efforts to win the army, 170; courts the Church, 170; measures in behalf of the working classes, 170; early diplomatic and military successes, 171; takes up Rumanian question, 172; intervention in Italy, 172; adopts free trade, 172; concessions to his political opponents, 174; later foreign policy of, 176; Polish policy of, 176; policy toward Schleswig-Holstein, 176; policy toward Italy, 177; policy toward the United States, 177; Mexican policy of, 177; asks for Grand Duchy of Luxemburg, 179; reoccupation of Rome by, 179; further concessions to domestic discontent, 180; capture of, 183
Napoleonic Imperialism, 13
Napoleonic régime, disadvantages of, 16; movement in Austria against, 20; reaction of Great Britain to, 35
Narodna Odbrana, 381, 382
Nassau, annexation of, 195
National Assembly, election of, 203; first measures of, 204
National Liberal Party, formation of, 196
National Workshops, 115
Nationalism, progress in the Balkans of, 105; awakening of, among Bulgarians, 107
Naval rivalry, Anglo-German, 370
Near East, crisis in, 141; rivalry of alliances in, 368
Neo-Guelphs, 85
Netherlands, popular revolt against French rule in, 23

New Course, 233
New Lanarck, 89
New Zealand, 92, 300, 306
Niazi Bey, 292
Nicholas I, accession of, 109; policy after 1831, 110; problem of serfdom, 111; aids in suppressing revolution in Hungary, 130; death of, 147; return to watchwords of, 271
Nicholas II, promises of, 276; abdication of, 404
Nigeria, establishment of British influence in, 341
Nihilism, appearance of, in Russia, 269
North German Confederation, organization of, 196; expansion of, 199
Northern France, campaign in, 388
Northern Schleswig, cession to Denmark, 416

O'Connel, Daniel, agitation of, 77; movement for repeal of the union, 90
October Diploma, 239
Opium War, 319
Orange, House of, restored to political power, 23
Organization of Labor, 82
Orleanists, unite with moderate Republicans, 208
Ottoman Empire, reform movement in, 143
Owen, Robert, 88

Pacific, World War in the, 392
Paderewski, 475
Palacky, František, 127, 242
Palmerston, Lord, 297
Panther, spring of, 373
Papacy, breaking of relations with, 216; reestablishment of diplomatic relations with, 225
Papal Guarantees, Law of, 256
Paris, Count of, 208
Paris, defense of, 203; siege of, 203; surrender of, 203; capture of, 206; Peace Conference at, 413
Parmentier, Antoine-Auguste, 61
Parnell, Charles Stewart, 304
Party of Order, formation of, 116; break of Louis Napoleon with, 166
Peace Conference at Paris, leading personalities of, 414; opening of, 415; votes to establish a League of Na-